THE GOLFER
to
Wales

By
John Pinner

© Travel Publishing Ltd.

Published by:

Travel Publishing Ltd
7a Apollo House, Calleva Park
Aldermaston, Berks, RG7 8TN

ISBN 1-902-00759-X

© Travel Publishing Ltd

First Published: 2001

Golfers Guides:

East Anglia	Ireland
Wales	West Country

Hidden Inns Series:

Central & Southern Scotland	Heart of England
Southeast England	South of England
Wales	Welsh Borders
West Country	Yorkshire

Regional Titles in the Hidden Places Series:

Cambridgeshire & Lincs	Chilterns
Cornwall	Derbyshire
Devon	Dorset, Hants & Isle of Wight
East Anglia	Gloucestershire & Wiltshire
Heart of England	Hereford, Worcs & Shropshire
Highlands & Islands	Kent
Lake District & Cumbria	Lancashire and Cheshire
Lincolnshire & Notts	Northumberland & Durham
Somerset	Sussex
Thames Valley	Yorkshire

National Titles in the Hidden Places Series:

England	Ireland
Scotland	Wales

Printing by: Scotprint, Haddington

Maps by: © MAPS IN MINUTES ™ 2001 © Crown Copyright, Ordnance Survey 2001

Editor: John Pinner

Cover Design: Lines & Words, Aldermaston

Cover Photographs: Coldra Wood Course, Celtic Manor, Monmouthshire; Bull Bay Hotel, Isle of Anglesey; The Hand Hotel, Clwyd; The Cedars, Powys

Foreword

There are an increasing number of golfers from this country and overseas who are very happy to play away from their home courses to experience the many different types of terrain (and weather!) available in the British Isles. In fact in the U.K. each year well over 3 million trips, involving varying lengths of overnight stay, are made to play at least one game of golf. Golf and travel therefore are inextricably linked and this was a prime driving force behind the *Golfers Guide* series that will eventually cover the whole of the U.K. and Ireland and which was launched with the publication of the much acclaimed *Golfers Guide to Ireland* last year.

The Golfers Guide to Wales is very much a comprehensive guide to playing 18-hole golf but it also offers the golfer an insight into the magnificent scenery and many places of interest in the Principality. And, importantly, it provides the golfing visitor with details of over 200 places to stay, eat and drink all of which have been linked to the nearest golf clubs whom we would like to thank for providing information and photographs. It is therefore the ideal guide for planning every aspect of a golfing trip to Wales.

It has been a pleasure to have worked on the book with such a well-respected and experienced golf writer as John Pinner whose knowledge of golf in Wales is unsurpassed. In his introduction John refers to the perception of Wales as "the poor relation of British golf". When you read about, and hopefully play, such courses as the idyllic *Monmouthshire GC* surrounded by the seven hills of Abergavenny and with views of the Black Mountains or the the magnificent links course of *Royal St Davids GC* lying in the great shadow of Harlech castle, you cannot fail to regard Wales as a country blessed with a wealth of excellent golf courses. Add to this the dramatic landscapes of Wales – rugged mountains, wild moorlands, deep valleys, craggy coastlines and enchanting forests - *and* the rich cultural heritage full of myths and legends, we are sure that you will wish to return to Wales time and time again as both a golfer and tourist!

We hope you enjoy reading and using *The Golfers Guide to Wales*. We are always interested to receive readers' comments on the contents of the book, on the golf courses covered (or not covered) and of course on the places to stay, eat and drink. This will help us refine and improve the future editions. Equally, if you wish to explore further the golfing opportunities or wide variety of countryside and many places of interest throughout the British Isles you may wish to read one of our other guides details of which can be found to the rear of this guide or on our website www.travelpublishing.co.uk

Enjoy your golf!

Travel Publishing

Location Map of Wales

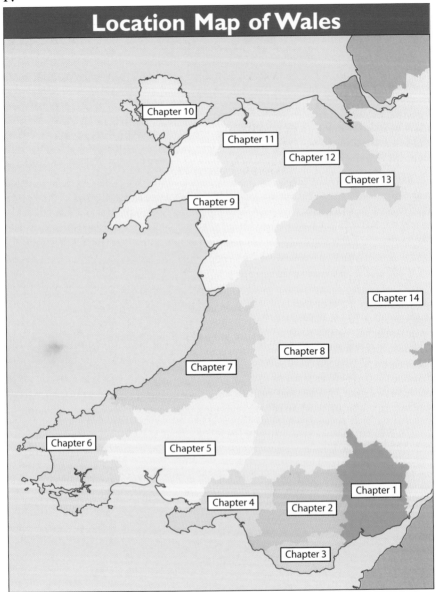

Contents

SECTION I: GOLF COURSE INFORMATION

SECTION II: ACCOMMODATION, FOOD AND DRINK

How to Use

The Golfers Guide to Wales has been specifically designed as an easy-to-use guide so there is no need for complicated instructions. However the reader may find the following guidelines helpful in planning the perfect golfing holiday.

CHOOSING WHERE TO PLAY GOLF IN WALES

The golfing information for each county may be found as "chapters" in Section I of the guide. Use the **Contents Page** to find the area of your choice. Each "chapter" contains a review of golf in the county, useful information for players on each golf club and detailed reviews of selected courses. Use this information to decide where to play. Whether you are individuals or a society we do recommend that you contact the Golf Club in advance to avoid disappointment. The telephone number, fax number and e-mail address (where available) may be found under each golf club listing.

GOLFING ITINERARIES

If you wish to experience the varied terrains (links, parkland or heathland) on offer in Wales without travelling long distances during your golfing holiday you should refer to the list of recommended golfing itineraries prepared by John Pinner. This can be found on the next page.

CHOOSING WHERE TO STAY, EAT AND DRINK

When you have decided on the golf courses you wish to play simply refer to the list of places to stay, eat and drink found after each golf course. Use the **red reference number** beside each listed entry to find more information (including a photograph) on the places of your choice in Section II of the guide. The telephone number, fax number and e-mail address (where available) are listed for each place should you wish to make a booking

INTERNATIONAL CALLING

Please note that callers from outside the United Kingdom should first dial the country code (00 44) followed by the number shown in the guide with the leading zero dropped.

LOCAL CURRENCY

All prices quoted in the guide are in **Pounds Sterling.**

Golfing Itineraries

In selecting these various itineraries I have in some cases included certain courses more than once. This is because some courses are easily reachable to courses in other itineraries in the county, neighbouring counties and the English border counties. For example: St Mellons is close to a number of the Newport (Monmouthshire) courses as well as the Cardiff (South Glamorgan) courses. In counties such as Monmouthshire, for example, where I cannot include links (none exist) and only one heathland course, I have offered variety by including a few interesting mountain venues and courses with water. (Where an asterisk is shown next to a course this denotes a course in a neighbouring county or an English border county).

MONMOUTHSHIRE (GWENT)

- St Pierre, Shirenewton, Dewstow, Llanwern, Celtic Manor
- The Newport, Celtic Manor, Tredegar Park, Woodlake Park, St Mellons*
- Rolls of Monmouth, Monmouth, Raglan Parc, Monmouthshire, Wernddu, Celtic Manor, Belmont*, Burghill Valley*, Ross-on-Wye*
- Woodlake Park, Alice Springs, Greenmeadow, Pontypool, Monmouthshire, West Monmouthshire, Bryn Meadows*
- West Monmouthshire, Monmouthshire, Tredegar and Rhymney, Pontypool, Bryn Meadows*

POWYS

- Cradoc, Builth Wells, Llandrindod Wells, Welshpool, Belmont*, Monmouthshire*
- Llandrindod Wells, Welshpool, Ludlow*

WEST GLAMORGAN

- Clyne, Langland Bay, Fairwood Park, Pennard, Morriston, Gower
- Neath, Glynneath, Swansea Bay, Langland Bay, Pontardawe
- Clyne, Neath, Morriston, Earlswood, Swansea Bay, Maesteg*
- Neath, Glynneath, Aberdare*, Mountain Ash*, Morlais Castle*

MID GLAMORGAN

- Aberdare, Bargoed, Bryn Meadows, Mountain Ash, Morlais Castle, Mountain Lakes
- Rhondda, Pontypridd, Southerndown, Pyle & Kenfig, Royal Porthcawl
- Creigau, Pontypridd, Mountain Lakes, Vale of Glamorgan*

SOUTH GLAMORGAN

- St Mellons, Cardiff, Whitchurch, Peterstone, Llanishen, Radyr, Newport*
- Vale of Glamorgan, St Mary's Hotel & GC, Wenvoe Castle, Brynhill, Southerndown*
- Glamorganshire, Dinas Powis, Wenvoe Castle, Southerndown*

CARDIGANSHIRE (CERIDIGION)

- Aberystwyth, Borth & Ynylas, Cardigan, Penrhos, Aberdovey*

CARMARTHENSHIRE. (DYFED)

- Ashburnham, Carmarthen, Glynhir

PEMBROKESHIRE

- Tenby, South Pembrokeshire, Trefloyne, Haverfordwest, Milford Haven

GWYNEDD

- Aberdovey, Royal St David's, Porthmadog, Criccieth, Pwllheli
- Abersoch, Nefyn & District, Caernarfon, St Deinol, Royal St David's
- Royal St David's, Porthmadog, Caernarfon, St Deinol, Conwy (Caernarvonshire)*

ISLE OF ANGLESEY (YNYS MON)

- Anglesey, Holyhead, Bull Bay, St Deniol*, Conwy*

CONWY (GWYNEDD)

- Conwy (Caernarvonshire), North Wales, Llandudno(Maesdu), Rhos-on-Sea
- Abergele & Pensarn, Rhos-on-Sea, Prestatyn*, Rhuddlan*

DENBIGHSHIRE (CLWYD)

- Prestatyn, Rhuddlan, Denbigh, Holywell*
- Denbigh,Vale of Llangollen, Chirk*, Wrexham*

FLINTSHIRE

- Holywell, Mold, Hawarden, Mold, Northop Country Park, Prestatyn*
- Northop Country Park, Old Padeswood, Padeswood & Buckley, Wrexham, Vale of Llangollen*
- Wrexham, Chirk, Vale of Llangollen*, Llanymynech*

John Pinner

We do hope you enjoy playing at these golf clubs but please do not hesitate to send us your own recommendations on the ideal combination of courses to play. We look forward to hearing from you!

Travel Publishing

Authors Introduction

In writing this Golfer's Guide to Wales I have taken the liberty of listing (where appropriate) the Welsh counties by the more recognizable names of past years. Being a South Walian I know from experience that many golfers in the South of the Principality woudn't know their Ceredigion from their Clwyd, but ask them to drive to Cardiganshire or the Denbighshire/ Flintshire counties, which are now officially named by the two former names, and they would not even have to consult a road map - so familiar are they with the latter. The same goes for the people from the northern area of Wales. They are more familiar with the name of Monmouthshire in the south than they are with Gwent. I have also taken into consideration that many visitors may be carrying copies of the Golfer's Handbook (the golfer's bible), which list the Welsh clubs under exactly the same county names that I have used. You may find on your travels through the Principality that many Welsh people also still prefer to proudly call the county they were born or brought up in by its original name (people, for instance, from Cardiganshire have long been called "Cardis" and are proud of their nickname, and many adverts of hotels, guest houses and golf clubs, to name a few, still prefer the old county name to be used in their address. Somewhat confusing, I agree, but I am certain you will not now lose your way when visiting the wonderful country of Wales.

Although written for the golfing visitor the Golfer's Guide to Wales is more than just simply a book which lists golf courses and suitable places in which to stay, eat and drink. In listing each county individually, I am able to also add a few pages giving information on what each county has to offer by way of historical interest, the make up and history of the towns and certain villages well worth visiting for their beauty or local colour or where you can hear the Welsh language being spoken, the seaside resorts with their award winning beaches, the best areas of outstanding coastline to visit and walk and the magnificent rural countryside with its pleasant hills, valleys and dramatic mountain ranges to explore. All in all, a holiday travel guide in miniature inside a guidebook for golfers. Intentionally done, this is because we recognize the fact that many holiday golfers often bring along other members of their families, or friends, who are non-golfers and also have to be entertained. In doing this, it provides a Golfer's Guide, which is different to others and well worth the purchase price.

With regards to the golf, I have long felt that Wales is the poor relation of British golf and needs to be more broadly publicised. There are many truly outstanding golf courses to be discovered inside the proud Principality, many of which are hidden gems - even to Welshmen in other areas of Wales. Yes, we have done rather well in keeping our best courses to ourselves over the years, but with the possibility that Wales could at last be named to host the 2009 Ryder Cup, maybe it's time to let our pedigree courses out of the proverbial bag. Enjoy your visit to Wales.

John Pinner

MONMOUTHSHIRE (GWENT)

The first county to welcome golfing visitors to Wales who choose to enter the proud Principality by road and by way of crossing either of the two impressive bridges which span the mighty Severn Estuary-the historic natural border which separates South Wales and the West of England-will be that of Monmouthshire (also known as Gwent).

To get a quick taste of what this pleasant county has to offer, it is best to cross the bridge which carries the M48 across the River Severn and also the River Wye. After paying the fee (currently £4.20 for cars, much extra for large vans, lorries and buses) at the toll gate-yes, you have to pay for the privilege of entering Wales by this route but we do, however, allow you to leave free of charge after, of course, reducing your bank balance somewhat!-take the first exit over the bridge and follow the signs to the historic town of Chepstow.

Famous for its racecourse, Chepstow can also boast many fine inns and eating places, a fine shopping centre and many places of interest, which includes the mediaeval gateway to the town and the superb Norman cas-tle where the regicide, Henry Marten, was confined for twenty years after the Resto-ration period. Indeed, there are many castles and historic sights worth visiting in the county if you can somehow manage to tear yourself away from the attraction of the many and varied golf courses on offer, including the nearby Shirenewton course on the outskirts of the pleas-ant Shirenewton village.

Chepstow Castle

Just a short drive from Chepstow alongside the A48 to Newport lies the Marriot St Pierre golf complex, made famous as a result of being host to a number of Euro-pean Tour events as well as a couple of international team tournaments. St Pierre, however, was already famous long before golf arrived. Indeed, King Harold is recorded as having a hunting lodge alongside this ancient deer park before his demise in 1066, which means the place has an historic association going back almost a 1000 years.

It was while doing research on St Pierre, many years ago, that I discovered an ancestor of mine, William Pinner, a captain in the Royalist army, who was garrisoned in the St Pierre mansion during the Civil War before being imprisoned in Chepstow Castle along with 120 other Royalist soldiers after the Roundheads captured the fortress. Another remarkable piece of history, which is not generally known, is that after the original family name of St Pierre disappeared through death and marriage and the powerful Welsh family of Tredegar carne into the heritage, the Crown Jewels came to be deposited at St Pierre. It so happened because King Henry V, desperate for funds to raise an army to fight in France and which brought about the Battle of Agincourt, borrowed money from a member of the Tredegar clan, Sir David, who fought in France under Henry IV and V, and was Governer of Calais. As security the Crown Jewels were shipped to St Pierre and secreted in its tower, being redeemed by Henry VI in 1457. By coincidence this was the same year that James II of Scotland issued an edict that football and golf be banned because their popularity interfered with archery practice-the first ever mention of the existence of the Royal and Ancient game.

Other than proof that Urien St. Pierre was buried in the quaint little church at St Pierre (the coffin lid is still preserved) in 1295, no other records can be traced of the St Pierre family or the original mansion. The descendant of the Tredegar family accepted the name William Lewis of St. Pierre, and he and his son George were mainly responsible for much of the present house built in 1500. The Lewis family owned and lived at St Pierre for five centuries, with Charles Lewis being the last of the line in 1893. After which the whole estate was broken up in the 1920's.

Further along the A48 at Caerwent, visitors to the well appointed Dewstow Golf Club will be surprised to be confronted near the entrance by a fine example of a huge and colourful Red Indian totem pole, expertly carved by an enthusistic local. Quite near the village of Caerwent are the remains of what was once the famous Roman city, Venta Silurum, while at nearby Caldicot is another ancient castle to view.

Continue towards Newport until the A48 meets the huge Coldra roundabout and where it links with the M4 and other routes, and you cannot fail to see the imposing Celtic Manor 400-bedroom hotel building which dominates the skyline and also forms part of the spectacular and most expensive jewel in the crown of Welsh golf resorts. Created by electronics billionaire, Terry Matthews, the richest man from Wales and among the top-listed richest people in Britain, this resort is truly magnificent and will surely take your breath away. Make sure you don't miss it.

Wye Valley

With many other fine hotels also dotted round the Coldra road exits, this is an ideal place to make your base as you will find all the courses in the county easily accessible and within a radius of less than 20 miles.

Newport is the largest town in this county which, although famous for its rugby and possessing a fine example of a transporter brldge, is also the town where the Chartist riots in South Wales were finally quelled with much bloodshed. It is the birthplace of the poet tramp W. H. Davies, who wrote, among other fine nature poems, the well known poem *"Leisure"*; which begins with: *"What is this life if full of care, we have no time to stand and stare"*. Today Newports' main attraction is its wide range of shops but there are however, a number of courses, including Celtic Manor, bordering Newport. The most well known is Newport G. C. at Rogerstone. Founded in 1903, the club has hosted many amateur championships and also the Welsh Professional Championship in 1951. Many many decades ago a young man named Hailsey was offered employment as a green-keeper for six months to "get the course in shipshape order". He was obviously good at his job as he stayed on for forty years, before calling it a day at the age of seventy-three with a sizeable pension from the grateful club. Other courses in the area are Tredegar Park, Llanwern and the Parc Golf Academy.

Before leaving the Newport area I recommend a visit to the old Roman town of Caerleon. Just a driver and a five-iron shot from Celtic Manor, this was once one of the most famous towns in Britain. Once known by the Latin name *Isca Silurum*, it was the capital town and headquarters of the Roman Legions which inhabited Wales. Remains of the ampitheatre can still be seen and the fine museum of Roman antiquaries is well worth a visit. Also in Caerleon is a Donald Steel designed 9-hole course should you fancy a quick round before leaving the area.

The other famous historic town in Monmouthshire is the county town of Monmouth, which is noted as the birthplace of Henry V and the honorable C. S. Rolls of Rolls Royce fame. This delightful market town also boasts a fine example of a medieval gateway and an old school where many famous personalties have been educated, including Guy Gibson who led the devastating 'Dambusters' bomber squadron attack on the Rhur Valley during World War Two.

Take the old road from Chepstow to Monmouth, which takes you along the banks of the River Wye and through Tintern with its famous Cistercian Abbey, founded by Walter de Clare in 1131 and immortalized by Wordsworth in his ode on Tintern. If you have time to stop and stare don't miss this route, which you will find unforgettable and one of the most attractive areas in the whole of Britain. Close to Monmouth is a golf club of the same name. Once a small nine-holer, it is now a tough test of eighteen holes with a pleasant new clubhouse. Some four miles at the other end of the town lies the majestic Rolls of Monmouth course. When Tony Jacklin made a visit during the 1980's he remarked: *"Why have you kept it a secret? It's a truly magnificent place!"*

Driving from Monmouth, in the direction of Abergavenny, one cannot help being excited by the sight of the approaching Black Mountains and the imposing Brecon Beacons beyond. Nevertheless, take a breather at the village of Raglan (yes, there is a fine full-sized golf course nearby) to visit the castle. A beautiful example of Norman architecture, Raglan Castle was the last stronghold to fall to the Cromwellian armies, but not before Charles I escaped to seek refuge at the Kings Arms at Monmouth (now a Wetherspoons hostelry)!

Abergavenny is renowned as the Gateway of Wales and is situated close to where the River Usk (famous, along with the Wye, for it's salmon fish-

Tintern Abbey

ing) flows into the county from Powys. It is a busy market town where crowds flock every Tuesday and Friday from the Welsh valleys and the bordering English counties to roam the market stalls.

To the east, alongside the Usk and below the foot of the Blorenge mountain, lies the century-old Monmouthshire Golf Club, while to the west of the town can be found the Wernddu Golf Club, one of the youngest courses in the county. Food connoisseurs will be delighted that at Llanvetherine, close to Abergavenny, the celebrated Walnut Tree Inn can be found. Listed as one of the top eating places in Europe, it has a long waiting list for reservations, but excellent bar snacks are readily available.

Leaving this stunning area, one would do well to head for Blaenavon, which lies atop the Blorenge, to take a peep into the lost world of the cruel ninteenth century coal and iron industries that ravaged the beautiful countryside and inspired the late Alexander Cordell to write the *"Rape of the Fair Country"* trilogy. Preserved in tune and the only one of it's kind, is the Big Pit museum, which attracts thousands of visitors deep into the bowels of the earth. Lower down the valley is the town of Pontypool, famous for it's international rugby front row and home of the now defunct Japanware industry. Well worth a visit is the mountain-top based golf course, which offers a panoramic view of the distant Bristol Channel. Before finally leaving magnificent Monmouthshire, a trip to the ancient and charming town of Usk is a must; not only for it's many fine eating places, old inns and an interesting folk museum, but also the excellent golf courses on either side of the Usk river-Woodlake Park at Glascoed and Alice Springs at Chainbridge. Any last minute shopping is best done at the bustling new town of Cwmbran. However, before reluctantly packing the clubs away you may be tempted to test your skills at Pontnewyyd Golf Club, which holds claim as the oldest nine hole course in Wales, the Greenmeadows course at Croesyceiliog (how's that for a real tounge-twister)or the par-three course at Llanyrafon.

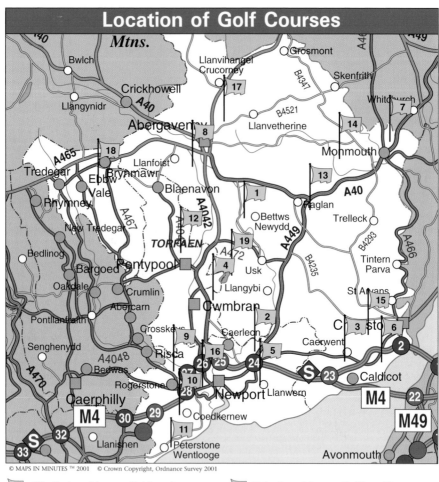

Location of Golf Courses

© MAPS IN MINUTES ™ 2001   © Crown Copyright, Ordnance Survey 2001

1	Alice Springs, Monmouthshire 5	11	Peterstone, Monmouthshire 19
2	Celtic Manor, Monmouthshire 6	12	Pontypool, Monmouthshire 21
3	Dewstow, Monmouthshire 8	13	Raglan Parc, Monmouthshire 22
4	Greenmeadow, Monmouthshire 9	14	Rolls of Monmouth, Monmouthshire 23
5	Llanwern, Monmouthshire 11	15	Shirenewton, Monmouthshire 25
6	Marriott St Pierre, Monmouthshire 11	16	Tredegar Park, Monmouthshire 26
7	Monmouth, Monmouthshire 14	17	Wernddu , Monmouthshire 27
8	Monmouthshire, Monmouthshire 15	18	West Monmouthshire, Monmouthshire 29
9	Newport, The, Monmouthshire 17	19	Woodlake Park, Monmouthshire 30
10	Parc, Monmouthshire 18		

Alice Springs

Court Wyndermere, Bettws Newydd, Usk,
Monmouthshire NP5 1JY

Tel: 01873 880244 Fax: 01873 880838

Sec/Manager:	Keith Morgan
Professional:	Paul Williams
Directions:	4½ miles N of Usk. From Usk take B4598 (Llanvihangel). Entrance is on the right hand side after 4 miles just before the bridge over the River Usk.
Visitors:	Welcome: Contact Club in advance
Societies:	Welcome: Contact Club in advance
Facilities:	Putting Green, Chipping Green, Club Hire, Trolley Hire, Buggy Hire, Bar, Restaurant, Driving Range

Usk

Date Founded:	1986
Type of Course:	Parkland
No of Holes:	18
Length:	5934 yds (5477 mtrs)
Par:	70
SSS:	70
Green Fees:	Weekdays: £15 per day; Weekends/Bank Holidays: £17 per day

Monnow

Date Founded:	2000
Type of Course:	Parkland
No of Holes:	18
Length:	5544 yds (5117 mtrs)
Par:	69
SSS:	69
Green Fees:	Weekdays: £15 per day; Weekends/Bank Holidays: £17 per day

Accommodation, Food and Drink

Reference numbers below refer to detailed
information provided in section 2

Accommodation

The Belmont Inn, Abergavenny,
Monmouthshire NP7 5HH
Tel: 01873 850074
A warm and welcoming pub on the A40 a short walk from the town centre. Large, comfortable bar, home-cooked food, two rooms for B&B.   106

Brooklands Farm, Raglan,
Monmouthshire NP1 2EN
Tel: 01291 690782
e-mail: brooklandsfarm@raglanfsbusiness.co.uk
Large property on a working dairy farm with four letting rooms. Excellent breakfasts and dinner by arrangement. TV lounge and garden.   102

The Crown Hotel, Varteg, Nr. Pontypool,
Monmouthshire NP4 8UG
Tel: 01495 774312
Good atmosphere and good fun in a cheerful pub-hotel with B&B accommodation and evening meals with notice.

J D Llewellyn, Cwrt-y-Gaer, Wolvesnewton,
Chepstow, Monmouthshire NP16 6PR
Tel: 01291 650700
Superbly equipped self-catering accommodation in three separate flats, including a cottage designed for disabled guests. Quiet, scenic surroundings.

The Star Inn, Llanfihangel Tor-y-Mynydd,
Llansoy, Monmouthshire NP15 1DT
Tel: 01291 650256
A lovely out-of-the-way inn with two splendidly appointed letting bedrooms and a varied menu served in the non-smoking restaurant.

Ty Shon Jacob Farm, Coch-y-North Lane,
Tranch, Nr. Pontypool,
Monmouthshire NP4 6BP
Tel/Fax: 01495 757536
e-mail: tyshonfarm@aol.com
Peace, quiet and great views on a 36-acre farm 1,250 feet above sea level. Three twin bedrooms for B&B: dinner by arrangement.

The Wenallt, Gilwern, Nr. Abergavenny,
Gwent NP7 0HP
Tel: 01873 830694
e-mail: thewenallt@talk21.com
A 16th century Welsh longhouse in a superb hillside setting in the Brecon Beacons National Park. Large, comfortable bedrooms: three-course dinners.   107

Food and Drink

The Belmont Inn, Abergavenny,
Monmouthshire NP7 5HH
Tel: 01873 850074
A warm and welcoming pub on the A40 a short walk from the town centre. Large, comfortable bar, home-cooked food, two rooms for B&B.   106

The Crown Hotel, Varteg, Nr. Pontypool,
Monmouthshire NP4 8UG

Tel: 01495 774312

Good atmosphere and good fun in a cheerful pub-hotel with B&B accommodation and evening meals with notice.

The Ship Inn, High Street, Raglan, Monmouthshire NP15 2DY

Tel: 01291 690635

Family-run 16th century village inn with cosy bars, log fires, real ales and food lunchtime and evening. Darts and pool.

The Star Inn, Llanfihangel Tor-y-Mynydd, Llansoy, Monmouthshire NP15 1DT

Tel: 01291 650256

A lovely out-of-the-way inn with two splendidly appointed letting bedrooms and a varied menu served in the non-smoking restaurant.

Celtic Manor Hotel & Country Club

Coldra Woods, Newport NP18 1HQ

Tel: **01633 413000** Fax: **01633 410272**

It was surely an act of fate that saw Canadian-based Welsh billionaire Terry Matthews taking a nostlalgic sideways glance at the Lydia Beynon maternity hospital when driving along the M4 motorway during a rare business trip to Newport at the beginning of the 1980's. Surprised to see it in a derelict state and realising it stood in a prime position close to a major road junction of the motorway, linking

South Wales to London, the Midlands and the West country, his keen business brain went into overdrive. To cut a long story short, the mercurial Welshman with the midas touch quickly purchased the attractive old stone building and, as time went by, he added a further 1,400 acres of surrounding countryside to create a golf hotel and leisure resort which is equal to anything similar worldwide.

The resort now offers a 400 room, 32 suite luxury hotel, 40 function rooms, 1500 delegate convention centre, 4 top class restaurants, 3 championship golf courses and 2 truly outstanding health clubs and spa. For golfers there is also a top quality clubhouse, which is arguably the larg-

est in Europe. It offers a magnificent highbeamed, firelit lounge, two bars and an excellent dining terrace with panoramic views overlooking the Roman Road 18th green and the Severn Estuary, extensive banqueting facilities and luxurious oak-panelled locker rooms. This suberb clubhouse also houses the Dylan Health and Fitness Club, which alone attracts many visitors.

As if that is not enough for the discerning golfer after treading the fairways, nearby there is also the equally impressive Ian Woosnam Golf Academy, which features a 24-bay two-tier, floodlit driving range, a practise range, short range play areas, a well stocked golf shop and three teaching bays equipped with the A star video swing analysis coaching system.

The most well known and demanding of the three courses is the resort's par-72 *Wentwood Hills*. Designed by Robert Trent Jones Jnr and described by Seve Ballesteros as *"A fantastic course in a fabulous location"*, it has already seen The Wales Open European Tour event and the biennial PGA Cup matchplay event between the leading club pro-

fessionals of Great Britain & Ireland and the USA staged there. A testing course with lots of water, including the River Usk, it fairly bristles with spectacular and tough holes demanding your full concentration.

The easier but still troublesome par-69 *Roman Road* course, designed by the legendary Trent Jones Snr, has also quickly gained distinction by being voted best inland course in Wales by a panel of experts on behalf of *Golf Monthly*. Quite undulating and with every hole offering a good challenge, this equally exciting layout needs your full attention if you wish to return a decent scorecard.

The *Coldra Woods* course, a PGA short course championship venue - the par is 59 - has been described by many top tournament professionals as second only to the celebrated short course at Augusta, which lies close to the hugely famous Augusta National course, where the US Masters event is staged every April. Coldra Woods is truly a rather delightful sort of fun place to test your skills. However, despite its low par rating, don't be fooled into thinking it a "piece of cake". Indeed with its steeply rolling fairways and difficult terrain I advise you to take a buggy. It really is a rollercoaster type of experience, and equally exhilarating!

At the time of writing Terry Matthews was awaiting to hear if his bid to bring the Ryder Carp to Wales for the first time ever with the venue being Celtic Manor, had been successful. If not he reckons to keep on putting in a bid until it finally does. If fate has anything to do with it he must surely succeed in doing so!

Sec/Manager:	Chris Baron
Professional:	Scott Patience
Directions:	NE outskirts of Newport near M4. From M4 junction 24 take A48 (Newport Centre). After 400 yds turn right into Hotel entrance and follow right

through to golf club.

Visitors:	Welcome: Contact Club in advance
Societies:	Welcome: Contact Club in advance
Facilities:	Putting Green, Chipping Green, Club Hire, Trolley Hire, Buggy Hire, Bar, Restaurant, Driving Range

Coldra Woods

Date Founded:	1995
Type of Course:	Parkland
No of Holes:	18
Length:	4200 yds (3876 mtrs)
Par:	59
SSS:	61
Green Fees:	Weekdays: £16 per day; Weekends/Bank Holidays: £16 per day

Roman Road

Date Founded:	1995
Type of Course:	Parkland
No of Holes:	18
Length:	6900 yds (6369 mtrs)
Par:	69
SSS:	73
Green Fees:	Weekdays: £37 per day; Weekends/Bank Holidays: £37 per day

Wentwood Hills

Date Founded:	1999
Type of Course:	Parkland
No of Holes:	18
Length:	7400 yds (6830 mtrs)
Par:	72
SSS:	73
Green Fees:	Weekdays: £55 per day; Weekends/Bank Holidays: £55 per day

Accommodation, Food and Drink

Reference numbers below refer to detailed information provided in section 2

Accommodation

Clawdd Coch Guest House, Pendoylan, Vale of Glamorgan CF71 7UP

Tel: 01446 760645
Versatile B&B facilities in a 17th century house with
five beautifully appointed bedrooms. Golfing breaks a
speciality.   115

Great House, Isca Road, Old Village, Caerleon, South Wales NP18 1QG

Tel: 01633 420216
e-mail: price.greathouse@tesco.net
website: www.visitgreathouse.co.uk
Three lovely letting bedrooms - two twins and a
single - in a Grade 2, 16th century building of
character with gardens overlooking the River Usk.

The Milton Hotel, Llanwern, Newport, Gwent NP16 6DU

Tel: 01633 412432
Home-cooked food, real ales and self-catering
accommodation in a former hunting lodge an easy
drive from exit 24 of the M4.   110

The Priory Hotel & Restaurant, Caerleon, South Wales NP18 1AG

Tel: 01633 421241 Fax: 01633 421271
A historic hotel of exceptional quality and character,
set in its own secluded grounds in the Roman town of
Caerleon.   112

Food and Drink

The Greyhound Inn, Christchurch, Newport, South Wales NP18 1JJ

Tel: 01633 420306 Fax: 01633 430588
A handsome late 19th century gabled inn with a
proper village atmosphere, real ales and very good
food. Friendly and inviting.   109

The Milton Hotel, Llanwern, Newport, Gwent NP16 6DU

Tel: 01633 412432
Home-cooked food, real ales and self-catering
accommodation in a former hunting lodge an easy
drive from exit 24 of the M4.   110

The Priory Hotel & Restaurant, Caerleon, South Wales NP18 1AG

Tel: 01633 421241 Fax: 01633 421271
A historic hotel of exceptional quality and character,
set in its own secluded grounds in the Roman town of
Caerleon.   112

St Julian Inn, Newport, South Wales NP18 1QA

Tel: 01633 243548 Fax: 01633 243562
A welcoming old inn with the road on one side and
the River Usk on the other. Bar-style menu, award-
winning real ales.   108

Dewstow Golf Club

Dewstow, Caerwent, Newport,
Monmouthshire NP6 4AH

Tel: **01291 430444** Fax: **01291 425816**

Dewstow Golf Club, with it's two splendid eighteen-hole courses (the Valley and the Park), is a
wonderful example of how, with special care and
attention to detail, rough and bumpy farmland
can be created into a top class, thriving golf complex within just over a decade of planning
permission being granted. Situated just five miles
west of the oldest of the two Severn Bridges (M48),
and off the A48 at Caerwent, you will discover
on arrival that the Valley Course is the premier
course by virtue of it being the oldest established
of the two. Nevertheless, the excellent Park Course
is an equally challenging test of one's scoring ability. A special feature on this course is a huge and
magnificent wooden effigy of a Roman centurion,
which commemorates the time when Caerwent
was an important Roman stronghold.

This effigy, along with the equally impressive
Indian totem pole near the entrance of the club
was carved by a local member.

Lengthwise the two courses are similar-the Valley being 6123 yards (par 72) and the Park slightly
longer at 6147 yards. Both have a number of water features, troublesome trees and dog-legs to
negotiate, and some nasty short holes to overcome.

Dewstow also has a sizeable driving range to
add to the visitor's entertainment, while the splendidly appointed clubhouse has the added
attraction of an excellent award winning restaurant to persuade the discerning visitor to prolong
a stay.

Sec/Manager:	John Harris
Professional:	Jonathan Skuse
Directions:	8 miles E of Newport, close to M48. From M4 junction 24 take A48 (Chepstow). After 7 miles in Caerwent turn right into Dewstow Rd. Entrance is after ½ mile on right hand side.
Visitors:	Welcome: Excluding Thursday am. Contact Club in advance

Societies:	Welcome: By arrangement. Contact Club in advance
Facilities:	Putting Green, Club Hire, Trolley Hire, Bar, Restaurant, Practice Ground

Valley

Date Founded:	1988
Type of Course:	Parkland
No of Holes:	18
Length:	6100 yds (5630 mtrs)
Par:	72
SSS:	69
Green Fees:	Weekdays: £16 per day; Weekends/Bank Holidays: £19 per day

Park

Date Founded:	1992
Type of Course:	Parkland
No of Holes:	18
Length:	6200 yds (5723 mtrs)
Par:	69
SSS:	69
Green Fees:	Weekdays: £16 per day; Weekends/Bank Holidays: £19 per day

Accommodation, Food and Drink

Reference numbers below refer to detailed information provided in section 2

Accommodation

The Crown at Whitebrook, Whitebrook, Nr. Monmouth, Monmouthshire NP25 4TX

Tel: 01600 860254 Fax: 01600 860607
e-mail: crown@whitebrook.demon.co.uk
website: www.crownatwhitebrook.co.uk

A superb restaurant and hotel in a lovely secluded Wye Valley setting. The food is outstanding, the bedrooms well equipped and full of character.   101

J D Llewellyn, Cwrt-y-Gaer, Wolvesnewton, Chepstow, Monmouthshire NP16 6PR

Tel: 01291 650700

Superbly equipped self-catering accommodation in three separate flats, including a cottage designed for disabled guests. Quiet, scenic surroundings.

The Milton Hotel, Llanwern, Newport, Gwent NP16 6DU

Tel: 01633 412432

Home-cooked food, real ales and self-catering accommodation in a former hunting lodge an easy drive from exit 24 of the M4.   110

The Star Inn, Llanfihangel Tor-y-Mynydd, Llansoy, Monmouthshire NP15 1DT

Tel: 01291 650256

A lovely out-of-the-way inn with two splendidly appointed letting bedrooms and a varied menu served in the non-smoking restaurant.

Food and Drink

The Boat Inn, Chepstow, Monmouthshire NP16 5HH

Tel: 01291 628192 Fax: 01291 628193
e-mail: boat@inn.net

An ancient hostelry in a delightful setting with a beer garden on the river bank. Bar, family area and restaurant open for dinner daily.   113

The Crown at Whitebrook, Whitebrook, Nr. Monmouth, Monmouthshire NP25 4TX

Tel: 01600 860254 Fax: 01600 860607
e-mail: crown@whitebrook.demon.co.uk
website: www.crownatwhitebrook.co.uk

A superb restaurant and hotel in a lovely secluded Wye Valley setting. The food is outstanding, the bedrooms well equipped and full of character.   101

The Milton Hotel, Llanwern, Newport, Gwent NP16 6DU

Tel: 01633 412432

Home-cooked food, real ales and self-catering accommodation in a former hunting lodge an easy drive from exit 24 of the M4.   110

The New Inn, Pwllmeyric, Chepstow, Monmouthshire NP16 6LF

Tel: 01291 622670

A handsome roadside inn dating from 1745, serving high-quality food in a friendly, relaxed atmosphere. Large car park.   111

The Star Inn, Llanfihangel Tor-y-Mynydd, Llansoy, Monmouthshire NP15 1DT

Tel: 01291 650256

A lovely out-of-the-way inn with two splendidly appointed letting bedrooms and a varied menu served in the non-smoking restaurant.

Greenmeadow Golf Club

Treherbert Road, Croesyceilog, Cwmbran NP44 2BZ

Tel: 01633 862626 Fax: 01633 868430

Sec/Manager:	Peter Richardson
Professional:	Peter Stebbings
Directions:	2 miles NE of Cwmbran centre. From M4 junction 26 join the A4051 (Cwmbran). After 1 mile turn right onto the A4042

(Pontypool). After 3 miles turn right at roundabout at end of dual carriageway into Treherbert Rd. Entrance after ¼ mile on left hand side.

Date Founded:	1979
Type of Course:	Parkland
No of Holes:	18
Length:	6078 yds (5610 mtrs)
Par:	70
SSS:	68
Green Fees:	Weekdays: £17.00; Weekends/ Bank Holidays: £19.00
Visitors:	Welcome: Contact Club by telephone in advance. Unable to play at certain times at weekend's
Societies:	Welcome: Contact Club by telephone in advance.
Facilities:	Putting Green, Driving Range, Trolley Hire, Buggy Hire, Bar, Restaurant

Accommodation, Food and Drink

Reference numbers below refer to detailed information provided in section 2

Accommodation

The Crown Hotel, Varteg, Nr. Pontypool, Monmouthshire NP4 8UG

Tel: 01495 774312

Good atmosphere and good fun in a cheerful pub-hotel with B&B accommodation and evening meals with notice.

Great House, Isca Road, Old Village, Caerleon, South Wales NP18 1QG

Tel: 01633 420216
e-mail: price.greathouse@tesco.net
website: www.visitgreathouse.co.uk

Three lovely letting bedrooms - two twins and a single - in a Grade 2, 16th century building of character with gardens overlooking the River Usk.

Mill Farm, Cwmafon, Nr. Pontypool, South Wales NP4 8XJ

Tel/Fax: 01495 774588

Old-world charm aplenty in a 15th century farmhouse that offers complete tranquillity, antique-furnished bedrooms and breakfast until noon.   104

The Priory Hotel & Restaurant, Caerleon, South Wales NP18 1AG

Tel: 01633 421241 Fax: 01633 421271

A historic hotel of exceptional quality and character, set in its own secluded grounds in the Roman town of Caerleon.   112

Ty Shon Jacob Farm, Coch-y-North Lane, Tranch, Nr. Pontypool, Monmouthshire NP4 6BP

Tel/Fax: 01495 757536
e-mail: tyshonfarm@aol.com

Peace, quiet and great views on a 36-acre farm 1,250 feet above sea level. Three twin bedrooms for B&B: dinner by arrangement.

Food and Drink

The Crown Hotel, Varteg, Nr. Pontypool, Monmouthshire NP4 8UG

Tel: 01495 774312

Good atmosphere and good fun in a cheerful pub-hotel with B&B accommodation and evening meals with notice.

The Greyhound Inn, Christchurch, Newport, South Wales NP18 1JJ

Tel: 01633 420306 Fax: 01633 430588

A handsome late 19th century gabled inn with a proper village atmosphere, real ales and very good food. Friendly and inviting.   109

The Priory Hotel & Restaurant, Caerleon, South Wales NP18 1AG

Tel: 01633 421241 Fax: 01633 421271

A historic hotel of exceptional quality and character, set in its own secluded grounds in the Roman town of Caerleon. 112

**St Julian Inn, Newport,
South Wales NP18 1QA**

Tel: 01633 243548 Fax: 01633 243562

A welcoming old inn with the road on one side and the River Usk on the other. Bar-style menu, award-winning real ales. 108

Llanwern Golf Club

Tennyson Avenue, Llanwern,
Newport NP18 2DW

Tel: 01633 412029 Fax: 01633 412029

Sec/Manager:	Mike Penny
Professional:	Stephen Price
Directions:	3 miles E of Newport Centre. From M4 junction 24 take the A455 (Liswerry, Newport). After ¾ mile turn left into Cot Hill and lead into Station Rd. Entrance 1 mile from A455 at the end of Station Rd.
Date Founded:	1928
Type of Course:	Parkland
No of Holes:	18
Length:	6177 yds (5701 mtrs)
Par:	70
SSS:	69
Green Fees:	Weekdays: £20; Weekends/ Bank Holidays:£25
Visitors:	Welcome: Contact Club by telephone in advance
Societies:	Welcome: Contact Club by telephone in advance
Facilities:	Putting Green, Chipping Green, Practice Field, Bar, Restaurant

Accommodation, Food and Drink

Reference numbers below refer to detailed information provided in section 2

Accommodation

**Great House, Isca Road, Old Village, Caerleon,
South Wales NP18 1QG**

Tel: 01633 420216
e-mail: price.greathouse@tesco.net
website: www.visitgreathouse.co.uk

Three lovely letting bedrooms - two twins and a single - in a Grade 2, 16th century building of character with gardens overlooking the River Usk.

**J D Llewellyn, Cwrt-y-Gaer, Wolvesnewton,
Chepstow, Monmouthshire NP16 6PR**

Tel: 01291 650700

Superbly equipped self-catering accommodation in three separate flats, including a cottage designed for disabled guests. Quiet, scenic surroundings.

**The Milton Hotel, Llanwern, Newport,
Gwent NP16 6DU**

Tel: 01633 412432

Home-cooked food, real ales and self-catering accommodation in a former hunting lodge an easy drive from exit 24 of the M4. 110

**The Priory Hotel & Restaurant, Caerleon,
South Wales NP18 1AG**

Tel: 01633 421241 Fax: 01633 421271

A historic hotel of exceptional quality and character, set in its own secluded grounds in the Roman town of Caerleon. 112

Food and Drink

**The Greyhound Inn, Christchurch, Newport,
South Wales NP18 1JJ**

Tel: 01633 420306 Fax: 01633 430588

A handsome late 19th century gabled inn with a proper village atmosphere, real ales and very good food. Friendly and inviting. 109

**The Milton Hotel, Llanwern, Newport,
Gwent NP16 6DU**

Tel: 01633 412432

Home-cooked food, real ales and self-catering accommodation in a former hunting lodge an easy drive from exit 24 of the M4. 110

**The Priory Hotel & Restaurant, Caerleon,
South Wales NP18 1AG**

Tel: 01633 421241 Fax: 01633 421271

A historic hotel of exceptional quality and character, set in its own secluded grounds in the Roman town of Caerleon. 112

St Julian Inn, Newport, South Wales NP18 1QA

Tel: 01633 243548 Fax: 01633 243562

A welcoming old inn with the road on one side and the River Usk on the other. Bar-style menu, award-winning real ales. 108

Marriot St Pierre Country Club

St Pierre Park, Chepstow NP16 6YA

Tel: 01291 625261 Fax: 01291 629975

Like the Dewstow Club, the Marriots St. Pierre golf complex lies close to the original Severn Bridge and alongside the A48 in the direction of Newport. The history of St. Pierre can be traced

back to over a thousand years, but it is only from 1962 that it has found fame in the the numerous history books dedicated to the game of golf. When Bill Graham purchased the magnificent St Pierre Estate during the beginning of the aptly-named "Swinging Sixties", little did the traders of Chepstow realise that the ambitious local businessman and entrepreneur was doing them a service which would be of enormous benefit in later years when thousands of vistors flocked to the area to watch their golfing idols. Indeed, in no time at all Graham created a golfing complex of the highest standards which quickly gained international repute.

Old age has meant that Bill Graham has moved on into pleasant retirement on the Isle of Man, but not before he saw his beloved creation being put well and truly on the world golfing map with the staging and television coverage of the Dunlop Masters over many years. This was immediately followed by the Silk Cut Masters, which proved to be the major breakthrough in the career of Ian Woosnam when he triumphantly lifted the title in 1983. Then along came the Japanese electronics company, Epson, with the Epson Matchplay Championship followed by the Epson Stokeplay tournament, which continued until 1991. Women golfers also witnessed the staging of top class events on St. Pierre's Old Course, namely the: Curtis Cup, The Solhiem Cup and the Bulmers Woodpecker strokeplay event and many top amatuer tournaments.

A feature of the Old Course is its centuries old Oak and Chestnut trees with their enormous girths and dating back to over 500 years. Every hole here offers an interesting challenge, with the signature hole being the famous par-3 finishing

hole where you have to carry the picturesque and ancient boating lake.

St Pierre's other eighteen-hole course-the Mathern Course-which lies to the rear of the impressive hotel and leisure buildings, gives the impression of being a rather easy challenge because of its flatness. Nevertheless, there are many hidden ditches and streams awaiting to catch the unwary golfer.

Sec/Manager:	Terry Cleary
Professional:	Craig Dun
Directions:	2 miles SW of Chepstow centre. From M48 junction 2 take the A466 (Chepstow). At the first roundabout on the outskirts of Chepstow take the A48 (Crick, Newport). Entrance after 1¾ miles just after going under the M48.
Visitors:	Welcome: Contact Club by telephone in advance.
Societies:	Welcome: Contact Club by telephone in advance.
Facilities:	Putting Green, Chipping Green, Club Hire, Trolley Hire, Buggy Hire, Bar, Restaurant, Driving Range, Caddy Service, Private Rooms

Old

Date Founded:	1962
Type of Course:	Parkland
No of Holes:	18
Length:	6818 yds (6293 mtrs)
Par:	71
SSS:	74
Green Fees:	Weekdays: £50 (Summer) £30 (Winter); Weekends/Bank Holidays: Contact Club for fee.

Mathern

Date Founded:	1975
Type of Course:	Parkland
No of Holes:	18
Length:	5732 yds (5291 mtrs)
Par:	68
SSS:	68
Green Fees:	Weekdays: £35 (Summer) £25 (Winter); Weekends/Bank Holidays: Contact Club for fee

Accommodation, Food and Drink

Reference numbers below refer to detailed information provided in section 2

Accommodation

The Crown at Whitebrook, Whitebrook, Nr. Monmouth, Monmouthshire NP25 4TX

Tel: 01600 860254 Fax: 01600 860607
e-mail: crown@whitebrook.demon.co.uk
website: www.crownatwhitebrook.co.uk
A superb restaurant and hotel in a lovely secluded Wye Valley setting. The food is outstanding, the bedrooms well equipped and full of character. 101

Forest House Hotel, Cinderhill, Coleford, Gloucestershire GL16 8HQ

Tel: 01594 832424
Situated in the ancient woodlands of the Forest of Dean, with eight well appointed en suite rooms. Comfortable lounge and a dining room serving a la carte with fine wines. 225

Great House, Isca Road, Old Village, Caerleon, South Wales NP18 1QG

Tel: 01633 420216
e-mail: price.greathouse@tesco.net
website: www.visitgreathouse.co.uk
Three lovely letting bedrooms - two twins and a single - in a Grade 2, 16th century building of character with gardens overlooking the River Usk.

Llanishen House, Llanishen, Chepstow, Monmouthshire NP16 6QS

Tel: 01600 860700 Fax: 01600 860700
Bed & Breakfast accommodation in a private suite in the former stables of a country house in 7 acres of lovely secluded grounds.

Mill End House, Newland, Coleford, Gloucestershire GL16 8NF

Tel: 01594 832128   e-mail: apriljohnt@aol.com
An 18th century house with lovely gardens and splendid views. Three en suite bedrooms, excellent breakfasts. Two miles west of Coleford, signposted from the town square. Four golf courses within 15 minutes.

Mill Farm, Cwmafon, Nr. Pontypool, South Wales NP4 8XJ

Tel/Fax: 01495 774588
Old-world charm aplenty in a 15th century farmhouse that offers complete tranquillity, antique-furnished bedrooms and breakfast until noon. 104

Poolway House Hotel, Gloucester Road, Coleford, Gloucestershire GL16 8BN

Tel: 01594 833937
e-mail: poolway@btinternet.com
16th century country house with seven comfortable en suite rooms, good home cooking and a well-chosen wine list. Pleasant garden setting.

The Priory Hotel & Restaurant, Caerleon, South Wales NP18 1AG

Tel: 01633 421241 Fax: 01633 421271
A historic hotel of exceptional quality and character, set in its own secluded grounds in the Roman town of Caerleon. 112

Food and Drink

The Crown at Whitebrook, Whitebrook, Nr. Monmouth, Monmouthshire NP25 4TX

Tel: 01600 860254 Fax: 01600 860607
e-mail: crown@whitebrook.demon.co.uk
website: www.crownatwhitebrook.co.uk
A superb restaurant and hotel in a lovely secluded Wye Valley setting. The food is outstanding, the bedrooms well equipped and full of character. 101

Forest House Hotel, Cinderhill, Coleford, Gloucestershire GL16 8HQ

Tel: 01594 832424
Situated in the ancient woodlands of the Forest of Dean, with eight well appointed en suite rooms. Comfortable lounge and a dining room serving a la carte with fine wines. 225

The Greyhound Inn, Christchurch, Newport, South Wales NP18 1JJ

Tel: 01633 420306 Fax: 01633 430588
A handsome late 19th century gabled inn with a proper village atmosphere, real ales and very good food. Friendly and inviting. 109

The New Inn, Pwllmeyric, Chepstow, Monmouthshire NP16 6LF

Tel: 01291 622670
A handsome roadside inn dating from 1745, serving high-quality food in a friendly, relaxed atmosphere. Large car park. 111

The Priory Hotel & Restaurant, Caerleon, South Wales NP18 1AG

Tel: 01633 421241 Fax: 01633 421271

A historic hotel of exceptional quality and character, set in its own secluded grounds in the Roman town of Caerleon. 112

St Julian Inn, Newport, South Wales NP18 1QA

Tel: 01633 243548 Fax: 01633 243562

A welcoming old inn with the road on one side and the River Usk on the other. Bar-style menu, award-winning real ales. 108

Monmouth Golf Club

Leasebrook Lane, Monmouth NP5 3SN

Tel: 01600 712212 Fax: 01600 772399

Sec/Manager:	Liz Edwards
Professional:	Brian Girling
Directions:	1 mile NE of Monmouth centre. From centre take Dixton Rd (A466 Ross on Wye) and enter slip road to the A40. Entrance is at the end of slip road on left hand side.
Date Founded:	1896
Type of Course:	Parkland
No of Holes:	18
Length:	5698 yds (5259 mtrs)
Par:	69
SSS:	69
Green Fees:	Weekdays: £16; Weekends/ Bank Holidays:£20
Visitors:	Welcome: Contact Club by telephone in advance. Unable to play on Sunday Morning.
Societies:	Welcome: Contact Club by telephone in advance.
Facilities:	Putting Green, Practice Area, Club Hire, Trolley Hire, Buggy Hire, Bar, Restaurant

Accommodation, Food and Drink

Reference numbers below refer to detailed information provided in section 2

Accommodation

The Crown at Whitebrook, Whitebrook, Nr. Monmouth, Monmouthshire NP25 4TX

Tel: 01600 860254 Fax: 01600 860607
e-mail: crown@whitebrook.demon.co.uk
website: www.crownatwhitebrook.co.uk

A superb restaurant and hotel in a lovely secluded Wye Valley setting. The food is outstanding, the bedrooms well equipped and full of character. 101

Forest House Hotel, Cinderhill, Coleford, Gloucestershire GL16 8HQ

Tel: 01594 832424

Situated in the ancient woodlands of the Forest of Dean, with eight well appointed en suite rooms. Comfortable lounge and a dining room serving a la carte with fine wines. 225

Llanishen House, Llanishen, Chepstow, Monmouthshire NP16 6QS

Tel: 01600 860700 Fax: 01600 860700

Bed & Breakfast accommodation in a private suite in the former stables of a country house in 7 acres of lovely secluded grounds.

Mill End House, Newland, Coleford, Gloucestershire GL16 8NF

Tel: 01594 832128 e-mail: apriljohnt@aol.com

An 18th century house with lovely gardens and splendid views. Three en suite bedrooms, excellent breakfasts. Two miles west of Coleford, signposted from the town square. Four golf courses within 15 minutes.

Poolway House Hotel, Gloucester Road, Coleford, Gloucestershire GL16 8BN

Tel: 01594 833937
e-mail: poolway@btinternet.com

16th century country house with seven comfortable en suite rooms, good home cooking and a well-chosen wine list. Pleasant garden setting.

Food and Drink

The Boat Inn, Chepstow, Monmouthshire NP16 5HH

Tel: 01291 628192 Fax: 01291 628193
e-mail: boat@inn.net

An ancient hostelry in a delightful setting with a beer garden on the river bank. Bar, family area and restaurant open for dinner daily. 113

The Crown at Whitebrook, Whitebrook, Nr. Monmouth, Monmouthshire NP25 4TX

Tel: 01600 860254 Fax: 01600 860607
e-mail: crown@whitebrook.demon.co.uk
website: www.crownatwhitebrook.co.uk

A superb restaurant and hotel in a lovely secluded Wye Valley setting. The food is outstanding, the bedrooms well equipped and full of character. 101

Forest House Hotel, Cinderhill, Coleford, Gloucestershire GL16 8HQ

Tel: 01594 832424

Situated in the ancient woodlands of the Forest of Dean, with eight well appointed en suite rooms. Comfortable lounge and a dining room serving a la carte with fine wines. 225

The Fountain Inn, Orcup Hill, Herefordshire HR2 8EP

Tel: 01981 540304

A friendly country pub in a hilltop setting south of Hereford. Splendid home cooking, excellent wine list, real ales.   217

The New Harp Inn, Hoarwithy, Nr. Hereford, Herefordshire HR2 6QH

Tel: 01432 840213

Seventeenth century pub near the River Wye serving good bar snacks and full meals. Three letting bedrooms, large gardens.   215

Monmouthshire Golf Club

Gypsy Lane, Llanfoist, Abergavenny NP7 9HE
Tel: 01873 852606 Fax: 01873 852606

Lying two miles southwest of Abergavenny near the small village of Llanfoist, the Monmouthshire Golf Club sits proudly at the foot of the imposing Blorenge Mountain basking in the knowledge that it is the oldest constituted club in the historic county of Monmouthshire and one of the oldest clubs in Wales (the nine-hole course at Pontnewydd still remains listed as being founded in 1875, but sadly there is no written evidence to support such a claim). Golf however was not the first sport to be enjoyed on this pleasant parkland site. Indeed, it was the sport of kings (horseracing) which took pride of place here for many years and the National Hunt Chase took place here in 1872 before moving to its permanent home at Cheltenham. Proudly hanging in in the comfortable clubhouse are a number of old prints depicting the races held here, and also a priceless golf cartoon showing the dreaded sixth tee as it was before the riverside trees grew there; presented to the club by the famous Fleet Street cartoonist Jon (Jones), who resided at nearby Raglan and where his remains lie buried following his death in 1992.

Founded in 1892 and designed by James Braid, the club only came into being when someone laid a bet with Mr. C. F. David as to whether a golf

club would succeed or prove a white elephant. Determined to win, David gathered together a more than mighty band of enthusiasts, including Lord Llangattock, the Marquess of Abergavenny , and that most formidable golfing MP, Arthur. Balfour who was the first British prime minister to be addicted to golf. In no time at all the members were housed in the "Old Kennel" clubhouse"which, although dating back some 600 years, still remains as the clubhouse (albeit with a few alterations).

On the whole quite flat (which is rare in Wales as all our flat bits were quickly snapped up for rugby pitches), the course is unusual inasmuch that it provides three par-5's in a row from the

sixth to the eighth hole, and also six par-3's. The most difficult of these is the 234 yards 16th, where you drive from an elevated tee and over the corner of a pond, with trees guarding the rollercoaster green. This is indisputably the club's signature hole.

An idyllic place this, what with the surrounding seven hills of Abegavenny and the Black Mountains beyond creating a veritable sun trap whenever the sun decides to put its hat on. Don't miss it.

Sec/Manager: R Bradley
Professional: B Edwards
Directions: 1 mile S of Abergavenny. From centre take Merthyr Rd (A4143 Llanfoist) past Safeway Superstore, bear left at Llanfoist onto B4269. Entrance after 1 mile on left hand side.
Date Founded: 1892
Type of Course: Parkland
No of Holes: 18
Length: 5806 yds (5359 mtrs)
Par: 70
SSS: 69
Green Fees: Weekdays:£25; Weekends/Bank

Holidays:£30

Visitors:	Welcome: Contact Club by telephone in advance. Unable to play at weekends.
Societies:	Welcome: Contact Club in advance. Unable to play at certain times.
Facilities:	Putting Green, Chipping Green, Practice Area, Club Hire, Trolley Hire, Bar, Restaurant

Accommodation, Food and Drink

Reference numbers below refer to detailed information provided in section 2

Accommodation

The Belmont Inn, Abergavenny, Monmouthshire NP7 5HH

Tel: 01873 850074

A warm and welcoming pub on the A40 a short walk from the town centre. Large, comfortable bar, home-cooked food, two rooms for B&B.   106

The Bulls Head Hotel, 86 The Street, Brecon, Powys LD3 7LS

Tel: 01874 622044 Fax: 01874 625321

Good-value overnight accommodation (2 rooms sleeping up to 6), pub grub and a great selection of real ales. Town-centre location.

The County House, 100 The Street, Brecon, Powys LD3 7LS

Tel: 01874 625844
e-mail: countyhouse@ukworld.net

Licensed accommodation in a fine Georgian house. Three excellent en suite bedrooms: sitting room, dining room. B&B with dinner option.

Llandetty Hall Farm, Talybont-on-Usk, Powys LD3 7YR

Tel: 01874 676415

A Grade ll listed farmhouse in the Brecon Beacons National Park, offering non-smoking B&B accommodation in three spacious bedrooms.   145

Mill Farm, Cwmafon, Nr. Pontypool, South Wales NP4 8XJ

Tel/Fax: 01495 774588

Old-world charm aplenty in a 15th century farmhouse that offers complete tranquillity, antique-furnished bedrooms and breakfast until noon.   104

The Old Ford Inn, Llanhamlach, Nr. Brecon, Powys LD3 7YB

Tel/Fax: 01874 665220
e-mail: enquiries@theoldfordinn.co.uk
website: www.theoldfordinn.co.uk

A fine old country inn offering wonderful views, a warm ambience, excellent food and drink and very comfortable B&B accommodation.   147

The Wenallt, Gilwern, Nr. Abergavenny, Gwent NP7 0HP

Tel: 01873 830694
e-mail: thewenallt@talk21.com

A 16th century Welsh longhouse in a superb hillside setting in the Brecon Beacons National Park. Large, comfortable bedrooms: three-course dinners.   107

Werngochlyn Farm, Llantilio Pertholey, Nr. Abergavenny, Monmouthshire NP7 8BH

Tel: 01873 857357
website: www.cottageguide.co.uk/werngochlyn

Four well-appointed self-catering cottages on a working farm three miles from Abergavenny. Indoor swimming pool, games room, children's activity area, riding school, lots of friendly animals. Also B&B available in the farmhouse.

The White Swan, Llanfrynach, Brecon, Powys LD3 7BZ

Tel: 01874 665276
website: www.the-white-swan.com

An excellent pub-restaurant in a row of smart black-and-white cottages. Sister establishment offering luxurious self-catering accommodation nearby.   150

Ye Olde Crown Inn, Pant-y-Gelli, Monmouthshire NP7 7HR

Tel/Fax: 01873 853314
e-mail: yeoldcrown@aol.com

An attractive and very popular 15th century inn on a hillside north of Abergavenny. Real ales, very good food and excellent overnight accommodation.   103

Food and Drink

The Axe & Cleaver, Much Birch, Nr. Hereford, Herefordshire HR2 8HU

Tel/Fax: 01981 540203

An attractive black and white pub on the A49 south of Hereford, with lovely gardens and a great reputation for the quality of its food and drink.   223

The Belmont Inn, Abergavenny, Monmouthshire NP7 5HH

Tel: 01873 850074

A warm and welcoming pub on the A40 a short walk from the town centre. Large, comfortable bar, home-cooked food, two rooms for B&B.   106

The Bulls Head Hotel, 86 The Street, Brecon, Powys LD3 7LS

Tel: 01874 622044 Fax: 01874 625321

Good-value overnight accommodation (2 rooms sleeping up to 6), pub grub and a great selection of real ales. Town-centre location.

The Lancaster Arms, Pandy, Nr. Abergavenny, Monmouthshire NP7 8DW

Tel: 01873 890699

1840s cottage converted into a pub, with a cosy interior, good real ales and home-cooked food. Five miles north of Abergavenny.   105

The Old Ford Inn, Llanhamlach, Nr. Brecon, Powys LD3 7YB

Tel/Fax: 01874 665220
e-mail: enquiries@theoldfordinn.co.uk
website: www.theoldfordinn.co.uk
A fine old country inn offering wonderful views, a warm ambience, excellent food and drink and very comfortable B&B accommodation. 147

The Prince Llewellyn Inn, Cilmery, Brecon, Powys LD2 3NU

Tel: 01982 552694
A friendly inn four miles west of Builth Wells on the A483, with a lovely garden, comfortable bars, good beer and an excellent restaurant.

The Ship Inn, High Street, Raglan, Monmouthshire NP15 2DY

Tel: 01291 690635
Family-run 16th century village inn with cosy bars, log fires, real ales and food lunchtime and evening. Darts and pool.

The White Swan, Llanfrynach, Brecon, Powys LD3 7BZ

Tel: 01874 665276
website: www.the-white-swan.com
An excellent pub-restaurant in a row of smart black-and-white cottages. Sister establishment offering luxurious self-catering accommodation nearby. 150

Ye Olde Crown Inn, Pant-y-Gelli, Monmouthshire NP7 7HR

Tel/Fax: 01873 853314
e-mail: yeoldcrown@aol.com
An attractive and very popular 15th century inn on a hillside north of Abergavenny. Real ales, very good food and excellent overnight accommodation. 103

The Newport Golf Club

Great Oak, Rogerstone, Newport NP1 9FX

Tel: 01633 892643 Fax: 01633 896676

Newport Golf Club, situated 3 miles west of Newport and close to the village of Rogerstone, is one

of the older Monmouthshire clubs, having been laid down in 1903. It came into existence when golf at Ladyhill, to the east of Newport, came to an abrupt halt when the local authority decided it was needed for a housing estate. A number of members broke away to create Newport Golf Club at Great Oak Farm, whilst the remainder started up at Tredegar Park which, incidently, moved quite recently to its present site also in Rogerstone- its third move in 75-years!.

Newport has long held a reputation as one of the best inland courses in the Principality and has come a long way since member John Hunt decided to draw 500 gold sovereigns from the bank to persuade the somewhat stubborn farmer to sell his farm to the golf starved group. He obviously took a great liking to the pile of gold!

Over the years the club has hosted many important tournaments, including the Welsh Professional Championship, the Women's Home Internationals and The Welsh Ladies' Amateur Stokeplay Championship. It is also the home of the Great Oak amateur event, a prestigious men's tournament which is staged every July and counts towards the Welsh Golfing Union's Order of Merit table.

Fairly undulatling but without any steep climbing, the course stretches to 6460 yards, par72, and is laid out around Llwyni Wood, which gives a number of holes their character; the most daunting being the 11th where one has to hit an accurate tee-shot to avoid the narrow avenue of trees which stand guard along the full length of this excellent par-4 hole. Club professional at this memorable course, is the likeable Paul Mayo, the former Welsh Professional champion, Dunhill Cup and European Tour player, whose promising tournament career sadly ended when he suffered a serious back injury whilst taking his clubs out of the boot of his car at the beginning of the 1990's. Such was his immense talent his amateur record makes impressive reading: Amateur Champion, Walker Cup player, Welsh Amateur Champion, British Youths Champion, Welsh Boys Champion and the leading amateur in the 1987 Open.

Sec/Manager:	John Dinsdale
Professional:	Paul Mayo
Directions:	3 miles NW of Newport centre. From M4 junction 27 take the B4591 (Rogerstone, Risca). After the second roundabout (1½ miles) turn right into Pontymason Lane. Entrance is after ¼ mile on right hand side.
Date Founded:	1903
Type of Course:	Parkland
No of Holes:	18
Length:	6460 yds (5963 mtrs)
Par:	72
SSS:	71
Green Fees:	Weekdays:£30 per day; Weekends/Bank Holidays: Unable to play
Visitors:	Welcome: Excluding Weekends & Tuesdays. Contact Club in advance
Societies:	Welcome: Excluding weekends & Tuesdays. Contact Club in advance
Facilities:	Putting Green, Chipping Green, Practice Area, Club Hire, Trolley Hire, Buggy Hire, Bar, Restaurant

Accommodation, Food and Drink

Reference numbers below refer to detailed information provided in section 2

Accommodation

Great House, Isca Road, Old Village, Caerleon, South Wales NP18 1QG

Tel: 01633 420216
e-mail: price.greathouse@tesco.net
website: www.visitgreathouse.co.uk
Three lovely letting bedrooms - two twins and a single - in a Grade 2, 16th century building of character with gardens overlooking the River Usk.

The Milton Hotel, Llanwern, Newport, Gwent NP16 6DU

Tel: 01633 412432
Home-cooked food, real ales and self-catering accommodation in a former hunting lodge an easy drive from exit 24 of the M4.   110

The Priory Hotel & Restaurant, Caerleon, South Wales NP18 1AG

Tel: 01633 421241 Fax: 01633 421271
A historic hotel of exceptional quality and character, set in its own secluded grounds in the Roman town of Caerleon.   112

The White Horse Inn, Davis Row, Pentwyn, Nr. Fochriw, Bargoed, Mid-Glamorgan CF81 9NP

Tel: 01685 841215
Popular inn open seven days a week for breakfast, lunch and dinner. Super home-made pies and lots more. Two B&B rooms planned.

Food and Drink

The Greyhound Inn, Christchurch, Newport, South Wales NP18 1JJ

Tel: 01633 420306 Fax: 01633 430588
A handsome late 19th century gabled inn with a proper village atmosphere, real ales and very good food. Friendly and inviting.   109

The Milton Hotel, Llanwern, Newport, Gwent NP16 6DU

Tel: 01633 412432
Home-cooked food, real ales and self-catering accommodation in a former hunting lodge an easy drive from exit 24 of the M4.   110

The Priory Hotel & Restaurant, Caerleon, South Wales NP18 1AG

Tel: 01633 421241 Fax: 01633 421271
A historic hotel of exceptional quality and character, set in its own secluded grounds in the Roman town of Caerleon.   112

St Julian Inn, Newport, South Wales NP18 1QA

Tel: 01633 243548 Fax: 01633 243562
A welcoming old inn with the road on one side and the River Usk on the other. Bar-style menu, award-winning real ales.   108

The White Horse Inn, Davis Row, Pentwyn, Nr. Fochriw, Bargoed, Mid-Glamorgan CF81 9NP

Tel: 01685 841215
Popular inn open seven days a week for breakfast, lunch and dinner. Super home-made pies and lots more. Two B&B rooms planned.

Parc Golf Club

Church Lane, Coedkernew, Newport NP1 9TU

Tel: **01633 680933** Fax: **01633 681011**

Sec/Manager:	Mike Cleary
Professional:	Darren Griffiths
Directions:	4 miles SW of Newport centre. From centre take the A48 (St Mellons, Llanrumney). After reaching roundabout at M4 go 1 mile to next roundabout on A48 and turn left. After ¼ mile turn right at roundabout into Church Lane. Entrance after ¼ mile on right hand side.

Date Founded: 1988

Type of Course: Parkland

No of Holes: 18

Length: 5600 yds (5169 mtrs)

Par: 70

SSS: 68

Green Fees: Weekdays: £13 per day;
Weekends/Bank Holidays: £16 per day

Visitors: Welcome: Contact Club in advance

Societies: Welcome: Unable to play at weekends. Contact by phone or in writing

Facilities: Putting Green, Chipping Green, Driving Range, Trolley Hire, Buggy Hire, Bar, Restaurant

Accommodation, Food and Drink

Reference numbers below refer to detailed information provided in section 2

Accommodation

Great House, Isca Road, Old Village, Caerleon, South Wales NP18 1QG

Tel: 01633 420216
e-mail: price.greathouse@tesco.net
website: www.visitgreathouse.co.uk

Three lovely letting bedrooms - two twins and a single - in a Grade 2, 16th century building of character with gardens overlooking the River Usk.

The Milton Hotel, Llanwern, Newport, Gwent NP16 6DU

Tel: 01633 412432

Home-cooked food, real ales and self-catering accommodation in a former hunting lodge an easy drive from exit 24 of the M4. 110

The Priory Hotel & Restaurant, Caerleon, South Wales NP18 1AG

Tel: 01633 421241 Fax: 01633 421271

A historic hotel of exceptional quality and character, set in its own secluded grounds in the Roman town of Caerleon. 112

The White Horse Inn, Davis Row, Pentwyn, Nr. Fochriw, Bargoed, Mid-Glamorgan CF81 9NP

Tel: 01685 841215

Popular inn open seven days a week for breakfast, lunch and dinner. Super home-made pies and lots more. Two B&B rooms planned.

Food and Drink

The Greyhound Inn, Christchurch, Newport, South Wales NP18 1JJ

Tel: 01633 420306 Fax: 01633 430588

A handsome late 19th century gabled inn with a proper village atmosphere, real ales and very good food. Friendly and inviting. 109

The Milton Hotel, Llanwern, Newport, Gwent NP16 6DU

Tel: 01633 412432

Home-cooked food, real ales and self-catering accommodation in a former hunting lodge an easy drive from exit 24 of the M4. 110

The Priory Hotel & Restaurant, Caerleon, South Wales NP18 1AG

Tel: 01633 421241 Fax: 01633 421271

A historic hotel of exceptional quality and character, set in its own secluded grounds in the Roman town of Caerleon. 112

St Julian Inn, Newport, South Wales NP18 1QA

Tel: 01633 243548 Fax: 01633 243562

A welcoming old inn with the road on one side and the River Usk on the other. Bar-style menu, award-winning real ales. 108

The White Horse Inn, Davis Row, Pentwyn, Nr. Fochriw, Bargoed, Mid-Glamorgan CF81 9NP

Tel: 01685 841215

Popular inn open seven days a week for breakfast, lunch and dinner. Super home-made pies and lots more. Two B&B rooms planned.

Peterstone Golf Club

Peterstone, Wentloog, Cardiff CF3 8TN

Tel: 01633 680009 Fax: 01633 680563

Peterstone Lakes Golf Club and Hotel, which under new management has seen much extra development, now includes the Fairways restaurant and the Crystal Suite. Both are licensed for civil weddings. There are also conference rooms, while the 18-hole Bob Sandow-designed parkland course is also open to visitors through the whole of the year-weekends included.

Sec/Manager:	Peter Miller
Professional:	Darren Clark
Directions:	7 miles NE of Cardiff City Centre. From M4 junction 28 take the A48 (Cardiff) and after 2½ miles turn left at Castleton into Marshfield Rd, shortly after the Travel Inn. Entrance after 2 miles by the T-junction with the B4239. From the City Centre proceed via Roath and the B4239 (Peterstone Wentloog).
Date Founded:	1990
Type of Course:	Links, Parkland
No of Holes:	18
Length:	6552 yds (6048 mtrs)
Par:	72
SSS:	72
Green Fees:	Contact Club for current rates.
Visitors:	Welcome: No restrictions. Contact Club in advance.
Societies:	Welcome: Some Restrictions. Contact club in advance.
Facilities:	Putting Green, Chipping Green, Driving Range, Trolley Hire, Buggy Hire, Bar, Restaurant, Private Rooms

Accommodation, Food and Drink

Reference numbers below refer to detailed information provided in section 2

Accommodation

Great House, Isca Road, Old Village, Caerleon, South Wales NP18 1QG
Tel: 01633 420216

e-mail: price.greathouse@tesco.net
website: www.visitgreathouse.co.uk
Three lovely letting bedrooms - two twins and a single - in a Grade 2, 16th century building of character with gardens overlooking the River Usk.

The Milton Hotel, Llanwern, Newport, Gwent NP16 6DU
Tel: 01633 412432
Home-cooked food, real ales and self-catering accommodation in a former hunting lodge an easy drive from exit 24 of the M4.   110

The Priory Hotel & Restaurant, Caerleon, South Wales NP18 1AG
Tel: 01633 421241 Fax: 01633 421271
A historic hotel of exceptional quality and character, set in its own secluded grounds in the Roman town of Caerleon.   112

The White Horse Inn, Davis Row, Pentwyn, Nr. Fochriw, Bargoed, Mid-Glamorgan CF81 9NP
Tel: 01685 841215
Popular inn open seven days a week for breakfast, lunch and dinner. Super home-made pies and lots more. Two B&B rooms planned.

Food and Drink

The Greyhound Inn, Christchurch, Newport, South Wales NP18 1JJ
Tel: 01633 420306 Fax: 01633 430588
A handsome late 19th century gabled inn with a proper village atmosphere, real ales and very good food. Friendly and inviting.   109

The Milton Hotel, Llanwern, Newport, Gwent NP16 6DU
Tel: 01633 412432
Home-cooked food, real ales and self-catering accommodation in a former hunting lodge an easy drive from exit 24 of the M4.   110

The Priory Hotel & Restaurant, Caerleon, South Wales NP18 1AG
Tel: 01633 421241 Fax: 01633 421271
A historic hotel of exceptional quality and character, set in its own secluded grounds in the Roman town of Caerleon.   112

St Julian Inn, Newport, South Wales NP18 1QA
Tel: 01633 243548 Fax: 01633 243562
A welcoming old inn with the road on one side and the River Usk on the other. Bar-style menu, award-winning real ales.   108

The White Horse Inn, Davis Row, Pentwyn, Nr. Fochriw, Bargoed, Mid-Glamorgan CF81 9NP
Tel: 01685 841215
Popular inn open seven days a week for breakfast, lunch and dinner. Super home-made pies and lots more. Two B&B rooms planned.

Pontypool Golf Club

Lasgarn Lane, Trevethin, Pontypool,
Torfen NP4 8TR

Tel: 01495 763655

Sec/Manager: Peter Jones

Professional: Jim Howard

Directions: 2 miles N of Pontypool. From
A4042 running through
Pontypool take the A472
(Crumlin). After ¾ mile turn
right onto A4043 (Blaenavon).
Proceed 1 mile and turn right
at Esso Service Station into
Hospital Rd, then first right
Church Lane, fourth left
Church Av and eighth right
into Lasgarn Lane. Entrance
after ¼ mile.

Date Founded: 1903

Type of Course: Undulating Heathland

No of Holes: 18

Length: 5963 yds (5504 mtrs)

Par: 69

SSS: 69

Green Fees: Weekdays: £20 per day;
Weekends/Bank Holidays: £34
per day

Visitors: Welcome: Contact Club in
advance

Societies: Welcome: Excluding weekends.
Contact Club in advance

Facilities: Putting Green, Practice

Ground, Trolley Hire, Buggy
Hire, Bar, Restaurant

Accommodation, Food and Drink

Reference numbers below refer to detailed
information provided in section 2

Accommodation

**The Belmont Inn, Abergavenny,
Monmouthshire NP7 5HH**

Tel: 01873 850074

A warm and welcoming pub on the A40 a short walk
from the town centre. Large, comfortable bar, home-
cooked food, two rooms for B&B.   106

**The Crown Hotel, Varteg, Nr. Pontypool,
Monmouthshire NP4 8UG**

Tel: 01495 774312

Good atmosphere and good fun in a cheerful pub-
hotel with B&B accommodation and evening meals
with notice.

**Mill Farm, Cwmafon, Nr. Pontypool,
South Wales NP4 8XJ**

Tel/Fax: 01495 774588

Old-world charm aplenty in a 15th century
farmhouse that offers complete tranquillity, antique-
furnished bedrooms and breakfast until noon.   104

**Ty Shon Jacob Farm, Coch-y-North Lane,
Tranch, Nr. Pontypool, Monmouthshire NP4 6BP**

Tel/Fax: 01495 757536
e-mail: tyshonfarm@aol.com

Peace, quiet and great views on a 36-acre farm 1,250
feet above sea level. Three twin bedrooms for B&B:
dinner by arrangement.

**Ye Olde Crown Inn, Pant-y-Gelli,
Monmouthshire NP7 7HR**

Tel/Fax: 01873 853314
e-mail: yeoldcrown@aol.com

An attractive and very popular 15th century inn on a
hillside north of Abergavenny. Real ales, very good
food and excellent overnight accommodation.   103

Food and Drink

**The Belmont Inn, Abergavenny,
Monmouthshire NP7 5HH**

Tel: 01873 850074

A warm and welcoming pub on the A40 a short walk
from the town centre. Large, comfortable bar, home-
cooked food, two rooms for B&B.   106

**The Crown Hotel, Varteg, Nr. Pontypool,
Monmouthshire NP4 8UG**

Tel: 01495 774312

Good atmosphere and good fun in a cheerful pub-
hotel with B&B accommodation and evening meals
with notice.

Ye Olde Crown Inn, Pant-y-Gelli, Monmouthshire NP7 7HR

Tel/Fax: 01873 853314
e-mail: yeoldcrown@aol.com
An attractive and very popular 15th century inn on a hillside north of Abergavenny. Real ales, very good food and excellent overnight accommodation.   103

Raglan Parc Golf Club

Parc Lodge, Raglan NP5 2ER

Tel: 01291 690077 Fax: 01291 690075

Sec/Manager:	Simon Clay
Professional:	Gareth Gage
Directions:	½ mile SE of Raglan centre. From centre take Monmouth Rd towards junction with A449 (east), after 300 yds turn right into Station Rd, bear right at the end. Entrance is straight ahead.
Date Founded:	1994
Type of Course:	Parkland
No of Holes:	18
Length:	6604 yds (6096 mtrs)
Par:	73
SSS:	72
Green Fees:	Weekdays: £15 per day; Weekends/Bank Holidays: £20 per day
Visitors:	Welcome: Contact Club in advance
Societies:	Welcome: Excluding weekends subject to availability. Contact Club in advance
Facilities:	Putting Green, Practice Ground, Trolley Hire, Buggy Hire, Bar, Restaurant

Accommodation, Food and Drink

Reference numbers below refer to detailed information provided in section 2

Accommodation

Brooklands Farm, Raglan, Monmouthshire NP1 2EN

Tel: 01291 690782
e-mail: brooklandsfarm@raglanfsbusiness.co.uk
Large property on a working dairy farm with four letting rooms. Excellent breakfasts and dinner by arrangement. TV lounge and garden.   102

The Crown at Whitebrook, Whitebrook, Nr. Monmouth, Monmouthshire NP25 4TX

Tel: 01600 860254 Fax: 01600 860607
e-mail: crown@whitebrook.demon.co.uk
website: www.crownatwhitebrook.co.uk
A superb restaurant and hotel in a lovely secluded Wye Valley setting. The food is outstanding, the bedrooms well equipped and full of character.   101

J D Llewellyn, Cwrt-y-Gaer, Wolvesnewton, Chepstow, Monmouthshire NP16 6PR

Tel: 01291 650700
Superbly equipped self-catering accommodation in three separate flats, including a cottage designed for disabled guests. Quiet, scenic surroundings.

Llanishen House, Llanishen, Chepstow, Monmouthshire NP16 6QS

Tel: 01600 860700 Fax: 01600 860700
Bed & Breakfast accommodation in a private suite in the former stables of a country house in 7 acres of lovely secluded grounds.

The Star Inn, Llanfihangel Tor-y-Mynydd, Llansoy, Monmouthshire NP15 1DT

Tel: 01291 650256
A lovely out-of-the-way inn with two splendidly appointed letting bedrooms and a varied menu served in the non-smoking restaurant.

Food and Drink

The Boat Inn, Chepstow, Monmouthshire NP16 5HH

Tel: 01291 628192 Fax: 01291 628193
e-mail: boat@inn.net
An ancient hostelry in a delightful setting with a beer garden on the river bank. Bar, family area and restaurant open for dinner daily.   113

The Crown at Whitebrook, Whitebrook, Nr. Monmouth, Monmouthshire NP25 4TX

Tel: 01600 860254 Fax: 01600 860607
e-mail: crown@whitebrook.demon.co.uk
website: www.crownatwhitebrook.co.uk
A superb restaurant and hotel in a lovely secluded Wye Valley setting. The food is outstanding, the bedrooms well equipped and full of character.   101

The New Inn, Pwllmeyric, Chepstow, Monmouthshire NP16 6LF

Tel: 01291 622670
A handsome roadside inn dating from 1745, serving high-quality food in a friendly, relaxed atmosphere. Large car park.   111

The Ship Inn, High Street, Raglan, Monmouthshire NP15 2DY

Tel: 01291 690635
Family-run 16th century village inn with cosy bars, log fires, real ales and food lunchtime and evening. Darts and pool.

The Star Inn, Llanfihangel Tor-y-Mynydd, Llansoy, Monmouthshire NP15 1DT
Tel: 01291 650256
A lovely out-of-the-way inn with two splendidly appointed letting bedrooms and a varied menu served in the non-smoking restaurant.

The Rolls of Monmouth Golf Club

The Hendre, Monmouth NP25 5HG
Tel: 01600 715353 Fax: 01600 713115

Fellow Welshman, golf writer and good friend, Peter Corrigan, once wrote: *"Exploring Wales in search of new golfing experiences is like stumbling upon a row of Rembrandts in the attic"*. A beautifully constructed sentence describing perfectly what joys lie in wait for golfers visiting the Principality-Any better sentence is still waiting to be written about the many golfing masterpieces to be found in the valleys, mountains and coastline of Wales. One such masterpiece is a course built on land with royal connections. Situated just four miles west of Monmouth is the majestic Rolls of Monmouth, so-called because it lies serenly in the Home Park of the Hendre Estate, which was once the home of the Honourable Charles Stewart Rolls of Rolls Royce fame. Indeed, motoring enthusiasts will, no doubt, be interested to know that the building which houses the comfortable clubhouse is the actual workshop where the first of the famous Rolls Royce engines was developed.

The connection with royalty came about when, in 1900, the Duke and Duchess of York, the future King George V and Queen Mary, made a seven-day visit to The Hendre, when they were driven from London by none other than C S Rolls. The room in which the royal pair stayed during their visit was the west wing of the magnificent Jacobean-style mansion, which is now a listed building. This historic room now looks over the green of the signature hole - the par-3 18th - and is called the King's Room. To mark their visit, the royal couple planted two fine sycamore trees on the fringe of the aboretum. The trees now lie close to the fourth green and the border of the third fairway. These two holes are named, appropriately, the *Duke of York* and the *Duchess of York*.

Visitors to the Rolls of Monmouth are amazed to discover that the course only dates back to 1982, the reason being that the old estate is awash with a splendid array of mature bushes and trees. A herd of deer lives on the estate, but mainly keep inside the dense forest which borders much of the area.

Having been a founder member, I had the privilege of introducing Greg Norman to the course. Being a lover of classical cars and also top class golf courses, he instantly fell in love with the place and ended up becoming its tournament professional for a number of years. I also took Nick Faldo there, and he, like Tony Jacklin, remarked: *"Why are you keeping this magnificent course a close secret?"*

A championship length course with an abundance of outstanding holes , I once described it as : *"The Gleneagles of the South"*. Roy White, formally of the Daily Telegraph, also once remarked to me : *" I found myself having to keep stopping to listen to the wonderful silence ! A truly majestic and magical place to play golf"*

Sec/Manager: S.J Orton

Professional: None

Directions: 3½ miles W of Monmouth centre. From the centre take Monnow St (south) and turn right at the Riverside Hotel onto the B4233 (Rockfield, Llantilio Crossenny). After 4 miles turn left at cross roads (Dingestow). Entrance is after ¼ mile on left hand side.

Date Founded: 1982

Type of Course: Parkland

No of Holes: 18

Length: 6283 yds (5799 mtrs)

Par: 72

SSS: 71

Green Fees: Weekdays: £34 per day;
Weekends/Bank Holidays: £38
per day

Visitors: Welcome: Unable to play on
Sunday mornings. Contact
Club in advance

Societies: Welcome: Contact Club in
advance

Facilities: Putting Green, Club Hire,
Trolley Hire, Buggy Hire, Bar,
Restaurant

Accommodation, Food and Drink

Reference numbers below refer to detailed
information provided in section 2

Accommodation

**Brooklands Farm, Raglan,
Monmouthshire NP1 2EN**

Tel: 01291 690782
e-mail: brooklandsfarm@raglanfsbusiness.co.uk

Large property on a working dairy farm with four
letting rooms. Excellent breakfasts and dinner by
arrangement. TV lounge and garden.   102

**The Crown at Whitebrook, Whitebrook,
Nr. Monmouth, Monmouthshire NP25 4TX**

Tel: 01600 860254 Fax: 01600 860607
e-mail: crown@whitebrook.demon.co.uk
website: www.crownatwhitebrook.co.uk

A superb restaurant and hotel in a lovely secluded
Wye Valley setting. The food is outstanding, the
bedrooms well equipped and full of character.   101

**Forest House Hotel, Cinderhill, Coleford,
Gloucestershire GL16 8HQ**

Tel: 01594 832424

Situated in the ancient woodlands of the Forest of
Dean, with eight well appointed en suite rooms.
Comfortable lounge and a dining room serving a la
carte with fine wines.   225

**Llanishen House, Llanishen, Chepstow,
Monmouthshire NP16 6QS**

Tel: 01600 860700 Fax: 01600 860700

Bed & Breakfast accommodation in a private suite in
the former stables of a country house in 7 acres of
lovely secluded grounds.

**Mill End House, Newland, Coleford,
Gloucestershire GL16 8NF**

Tel: 01594 832128   e-mail: apriljohnt@aol.com

An 18th century house with lovely gardens and
splendid views. Three en suite bedrooms, excellent
breakfasts. Two miles west of Coleford, signposted
from the town square. Four golf courses within 15
minutes.

**Poolway House Hotel, Gloucester Road,
Coleford, Gloucestershire GL16 8BN**

Tel: 01594 833937
e-mail: poolway@btinternet.com

16th century country house with seven comfortable
en suite rooms, good home cooking and a well-
chosen wine list. Pleasant garden setting.

**Werngochlyn Farm, Llantilio Pertholey,
Nr. Abergavenny, Monmouthshire NP7 8BH**

Tel: 01873 857357
website: www.cottageguide.co.uk/werngochlyn

Four well-appointed self-catering cottages on a
working farm three miles from Abergavenny. Indoor
swimming pool, games room, children's activity area,
riding school, lots of friendly animals. Also B&B
available in the farmhouse.

Food and Drink

**The Axe & Cleaver, Much Birch, Nr. Hereford,
Herefordshire HR2 8HU**

Tel/Fax: 01981 540203

An attractive black and white pub on the A49 south
of Hereford, with lovely gardens and a great
reputation for the quality of its food and drink.   223

**The Boat Inn, Chepstow,
Monmouthshire NP16 5HH**

Tel: 01291 628192 Fax: 01291 628193
e-mail: boat@inn.net

An ancient hostelry in a delightful setting with a beer
garden on the river bank. Bar, family area and
restaurant open for dinner daily.   113

The Comet Inn, Madley, Herefordshire HR2 9NJ

Tel: 01981 250600 e-mail: cometinn@madley

Large white-painted pub with a traditional ambience
and lovely gardens. Bar meals, à la carte, real ales.
Four miles from Hereford off the B4352 Hay road. 220

**The Crown at Whitebrook, Whitebrook,
Nr. Monmouth, Monmouthshire NP25 4TX**

Tel: 01600 860254 Fax: 01600 860607
e-mail: crown@whitebrook.demon.co.uk
website: www.crownatwhitebrook.co.uk

A superb restaurant and hotel in a lovely secluded
Wye Valley setting. The food is outstanding, the
bedrooms well equipped and full of character.   101

**Forest House Hotel, Cinderhill, Coleford,
Gloucestershire GL16 8HQ**

Tel: 01594 832424

Situated in the ancient woodlands of the Forest of
Dean, with eight well appointed en suite rooms.
Comfortable lounge and a dining room serving a la
carte with fine wines.   225

The Fountain Inn, Orcup Hill, Herefordshire HR2 8EP

Tel: 01981 540304

A friendly country pub in a hilltop setting south of Hereford. Splendid home cooking, excellent wine list, real ales. **217**

The Lancaster Arms, Pandy, Nr. Abergavenny, Monmouthshire NP7 8DW

Tel: 01873 890699

1840s cottage converted into a pub, with a cosy interior, good real ales and home-cooked food. Five miles north of Abergavenny. **105**

The New Harp Inn, Hoarwithy, Nr. Hereford, Herefordshire HR2 6QH

Tel: 01432 840213

Seventeenth century pub near the River Wye serving good bar snacks and full meals. Three letting bedrooms, large gardens. **215**

Shirenewton Golf Club

Shirenewton, Chepstow NP6 6RL

Tel: **01291 641642** Fax: **01291 641472**

Sec/Manager:	Christine Leather
Professional:	Lee Pagett
Directions:	3 miles W of Chepstow centre. From the A466 (St Lawrence Rd) at Chepstow northern outskirts, turn west onto the B4235 (Mynydd-Bach). At Mynydd-Bach turn left into Spout Hill, first right into Earlswood Rd and second left into Crick Rd. Entrance is after ¼ mile on right hand side.
Date Founded:	1995
Type of Course:	Parkland
No of Holes:	18
Length:	6607 yds (6098 mtrs)
Par:	72
SSS:	72
Green Fees:	Weekdays: Summer £15 per day. Winter £12 per day; Weekends/Bank Holidays: Summer £18 per day. Winter £15 per day
Visitors:	Welcome: Contact Club in advance
Societies:	Welcome: By arrangement. Contact Club in advance
Facilities:	Putting Green, Chipping Green, Club Hire, Trolley Hire, Buggy Hire, Bar, Restaurant, Private Rooms

Accommodation, Food and Drink

Reference numbers below refer to detailed information provided in section 2

Accommodation

The Crown at Whitebrook, Whitebrook, Nr. Monmouth, Monmouthshire NP25 4TX

Tel: 01600 860254 Fax: 01600 860607
e-mail: crown@whitebrook.demon.co.uk
website: www.crownatwhitebrook.co.uk

A superb restaurant and hotel in a lovely secluded Wye Valley setting. The food is outstanding, the bedrooms well equipped and full of character. **101**

J D Llewellyn, Cwrt-y-Gaer, Wolvesnewton, Chepstow, Monmouthshire NP16 6PR

Tel: 01291 650700

Superbly equipped self-catering accommodation in three separate flats, including a cottage designed for disabled guests. Quiet, scenic surroundings.

Llanishen House, Llanishen, Chepstow, Monmouthshire NP16 6QS

Tel: 01600 860700 Fax: 01600 860700

Bed & Breakfast accommodation in a private suite in the former stables of a country house in 7 acres of lovely secluded grounds.

The Milton Hotel, Llanwern, Newport, Gwent NP16 6DU

Tel: 01633 412432

Home-cooked food, real ales and self-catering accommodation in a former hunting lodge an easy drive from exit 24 of the M4. **110**

The Star Inn, Llanfihangel Tor-y-Mynydd, Llansoy, Monmouthshire NP15 1DT

Tel: 01291 650256

A lovely out-of-the-way inn with two splendidly appointed letting bedrooms and a varied menu served in the non-smoking restaurant.

Food and Drink

The Boat Inn, Chepstow, Monmouthshire NP16 5HH

Tel: 01291 628192 Fax: 01291 628193
e-mail: boat@inn.net

An ancient hostelry in a delightful setting with a beer garden on the river bank. Bar, family area and restaurant open for dinner daily. **113**

The Crown at Whitebrook, Whitebrook, Nr. Monmouth, Monmouthshire NP25 4TX

Tel: 01600 860254 Fax: 01600 860607
e-mail: crown@whitebrook.demon.co.uk
website: www.crownatwhitebrook.co.uk

A superb restaurant and hotel in a lovely secluded

Wye Valley setting. The food is outstanding, the bedrooms well equipped and full of character. 101

The Milton Hotel, Llanwern, Newport, Gwent NP16 6DU
Tel: 01633 412432
Home-cooked food, real ales and self-catering accommodation in a former hunting lodge an easy drive from exit 24 of the M4. 110

The New Inn, Pwllmeyric, Chepstow, Monmouthshire NP16 6LF
Tel: 01291 622670
A handsome roadside inn dating from 1745, serving high-quality food in a friendly, relaxed atmosphere. Large car park. 111

The Star Inn, Llanfihangel Tor-y-Mynydd, Llansoy, Monmouthshire NP15 1DT
Tel: 01291 650256
A lovely out-of-the-way inn with two splendidly appointed letting bedrooms and a varied menu served in the non-smoking restaurant.

Tredegar Park Golf Club

Parc-y-Brain Road, Rogerstone, Newport NP10 9TG

Tel: 01633 895219 Fax: 01633 897152

Sec/Manager:	Tony Trickett
Professional:	Mervin Morgan
Directions:	3½ miles NW of Newport centre. From M4 junction 27 take the B4591 (Rogerstone, Risca). After ½ mile take second right into Cefn Walk then left into Cwm Lane,. Go over the canal and take first right. Entrance after 400 yds.
Date Founded:	1999
Type of Course:	Parkland
No of Holes:	18

Length:	6248 yds (5767 mtrs)
Par:	72
SSS:	70
Green Fees:	Weekdays: £15 per day; Weekends/Bank Holidays: Unable to play
Visitors:	Welcome: Excluding weekends. Contact Club in advance
Societies:	Welcome: Excluding weekends. Contact Club in advance
Facilities:	Putting Green, Practice Area, Trolley Hire, Buggy Hire, Bar, Restaurant

Accommodation, Food and Drink

Reference numbers below refer to detailed information provided in section 2

Accommodation

Great House, Isca Road, Old Village, Caerleon, South Wales NP18 1QG
Tel: 01633 420216
e-mail: price.greathouse@tesco.net
website: www.visitgreathouse.co.uk
Three lovely letting bedrooms - two twins and a single - in a Grade 2, 16th century building of character with gardens overlooking the River Usk.

J D Llewellyn, Cwrt-y-Gaer, Wolvesnewton, Chepstow, Monmouthshire NP16 6PR
Tel: 01291 650700
Superbly equipped self-catering accommodation in three separate flats, including a cottage designed for disabled guests. Quiet, scenic surroundings.

The Milton Hotel, Llanwern, Newport, Gwent NP16 6DU
Tel: 01633 412432
Home-cooked food, real ales and self-catering accommodation in a former hunting lodge an easy drive from exit 24 of the M4. 110

The Priory Hotel & Restaurant, Caerleon, South Wales NP18 1AG
Tel: 01633 421241 Fax: 01633 421271
A historic hotel of exceptional quality and character, set in its own secluded grounds in the Roman town of Caerleon. 112

The White Horse Inn, Davis Row, Pentwyn, Nr. Fochriw, Bargoed, Mid-Glamorgan CF81 9NP
Tel: 01685 841215
Popular inn open seven days a week for breakfast, lunch and dinner. Super home-made pies and lots more. Two B&B rooms planned.

Food and Drink

The Greyhound Inn, Christchurch, Newport, South Wales NP18 1JJ

Tel: 01633 420306 Fax: 01633 430588

A handsome late 19th century gabled inn with a proper village atmosphere, real ales and very good food. Friendly and inviting.   109

The Milton Hotel, Llanwern, Newport, Gwent NP16 6DU

Tel: 01633 412432

Home-cooked food, real ales and self-catering accommodation in a former hunting lodge an easy drive from exit 24 of the M4.   110

The Priory Hotel & Restaurant, Caerleon, South Wales NP18 1AG

Tel: 01633 421241 Fax: 01633 421271

A historic hotel of exceptional quality and character, set in its own secluded grounds in the Roman town of Caerleon.   112

St Julian Inn, Newport, South Wales NP18 1QA

Tel: 01633 243548 Fax: 01633 243562

A welcoming old inn with the road on one side and the River Usk on the other. Bar-style menu, award-winning real ales.   108

The White Horse Inn, Davis Row, Pentwyn, Nr. Fochriw, Bargoed, Mid-Glamorgan CF81 9NP

Tel: 01685 841215

Popular inn open seven days a week for breakfast, lunch and dinner. Super home-made pies and lots more. Two B&B rooms planned.

Wernddu Golf Club

Old Ross Road, Abergavenny NP7 8NG

Tel: 01873 856223 Fax: 01873 856223

Sec/Manager:	Lyn Turvy
Professional:	Allan Ashmead
Directions:	1½ miles from Abergavenny centre. From centre take Hereford Rd ((B4521). After crossing the A465 (Hereford to Merthyr Tydfil road) take the first right off Old Ross Rd. Entrance is signed.
Date Founded:	1993
Type of Course:	Parkland
No of Holes:	18
Length:	5413 yds (4996 mtrs)
Par:	68
SSS:	67
Green Fees:	Weekdays: £15 per day; Weekends/Bank Holidays: £15 per day
Visitors:	Welcome: Contact Club in advance
Societies:	Welcome: Contact Club in advance
Facilities:	Putting Green, Chipping Green, Driving Range, Club Hire, Trolley Hire, Bar, Restaurant

Accommodation, Food and Drink

Reference numbers below refer to detailed information provided in section 2

Accommodation

The Belmont Inn, Abergavenny, Monmouthshire NP7 5HH

Tel: 01873 850074

A warm and welcoming pub on the A40 a short walk from the town centre. Large, comfortable bar, home-cooked food, two rooms for B&B.   106

The Bulls Head Hotel, 86 The Street, Brecon, Powys LD3 7LS

Tel: 01874 622044 Fax: 01874 625321

Good-value overnight accommodation (2 rooms sleeping up to 6), pub grub and a great selection of real ales. Town-centre location.

The County House, 100 The Street, Brecon, Powys LD3 7LS

Tel: 01874 625844

e-mail: countyhouse@ukworld.net

Licensed accommodation in a fine Georgian house. Three excellent en suite bedrooms: sitting room, dining room. B&B with dinner option.

The Crown Hotel, Varteg, Nr. Pontypool, Monmouthshire NP4 8UG

Tel: 01495 774312

Good atmosphere and good fun in a cheerful pub-hotel with B&B accommodation and evening meals with notice.

Llandetty Hall Farm, Talybont-on-Usk, Powys LD3 7YR

Tel: 01874 676415

A Grade ll listed farmhouse in the Brecon Beacons National Park, offering non-smoking B&B accommo-dation in three spacious bedrooms.   145

Mill Farm, Cwmafon, Nr. Pontypool, South Wales NP4 8XJ

Tel/Fax: 01495 774588

Old-world charm aplenty in a 15th century farmhouse that offers complete tranquillity, antique-furnished bedrooms and breakfast until noon.   104

The Old Ford Inn, Llanhamlach, Nr. Brecon, Powys LD3 7YB

Tel/Fax: 01874 665220

e-mail: enquiries@theoldfordinn.co.uk

website: www.theoldfordinn.co.uk

A fine old country inn offering wonderful views, a

warm ambience, excellent food and drink and very
comfortable B&B accommodation. 147

Seland Newydd, Pwllgloyw, Nr. Brecon, Powys LD3 9PY

Tel: 01874 690282
website: www.selandnewydd.co.uk
Real ales, excellent wines, fine food and comfortable
new en suite bedrooms in a country inn halfway
between Builth Wells and Cradoc. 146

The Wenallt, Gilwern, Nr. Abergavenny, Gwent NP7 0HP

Tel: 01873 830694
e-mail: thewenallt@talk21.com
A 16th century Welsh longhouse in a superb hillside
setting in the Brecon Beacons National Park. Large,
comfortable bedrooms: three-course dinners. 107

Werngochlyn Farm, Llantilio Pertholey, Nr. Abergavenny, Monmouthshire NP7 8BH

Tel: 01873 857357
website: www.cottageguide.co.uk/werngochlyn
Four well-appointed self-catering cottages on a
working farm three miles from Abergavenny. Indoor
swimming pool, games room, children's activity area,
riding school, lots of friendly animals. Also B&B
available in the farmhouse.

The White Swan, Llanfrynach, Brecon, Powys LD3 7BZ

Tel: 01874 665276
website: www.the-white-swan.com
An excellent pub-restaurant in a row of smart black-
and-white cottages. Sister establishment offering
luxurious self-catering accommodation nearby. 150

Ye Olde Crown Inn, Pant-y-Gelli, Monmouthshire NP7 7HR

Tel/Fax: 01873 853314
e-mail: yeoldcrown@aol.com
An attractive and very popular 15th century inn on a
hillside north of Abergavenny. Real ales, very good
food and excellent overnight accommodation. 103

Food and Drink

The Axe & Cleaver, Much Birch, Nr. Hereford, Herefordshire HR2 8HU

Tel/Fax: 01981 540203
An attractive black and white pub on the A49 south
of Hereford, with lovely gardens and a great
reputation for the quality of its food and drink. 223

The Belmont Inn, Abergavenny, Monmouthshire NP7 5HH

Tel: 01873 850074
A warm and welcoming pub on the A40 a short walk
from the town centre. Large, comfortable bar, home-
cooked food, two rooms for B&B. 106

The Bulls Head Hotel, 86 The Street, Brecon, Powys LD3 7LS

Tel: 01874 622044 Fax: 01874 625321

Good-value overnight accommodation (2 rooms
sleeping up to 6), pub grub and a great selection of
real ales. Town-centre location.

The Crown Hotel, Varteg, Nr. Pontypool, Monmouthshire NP4 8UG

Tel: 01495 774312
Good atmosphere and good fun in a cheerful pub-
hotel with B&B accommodation and evening meals
with notice.

The Lancaster Arms, Pandy, Nr. Abergavenny, Monmouthshire NP7 8DW

Tel: 01873 890699
1840s cottage converted into a pub, with a cosy
interior, good real ales and home-cooked food. Five
miles north of Abergavenny. 105

The Old Ford Inn, Llanhamlach, Nr. Brecon, Powys LD3 7YB

Tel/Fax: 01874 665220
e-mail: enquiries@theoldfordinn.co.uk
website: www.theoldfordinn.co.uk
A fine old country inn offering wonderful views, a
warm ambience, excellent food and drink and very
comfortable B&B accommodation. 147

The Prince Llewellyn Inn, Cilmery, Brecon, Powys LD2 3NU

Tel: 01982 552694
A friendly inn four miles west of Builth Wells on the
A483, with a lovely garden, comfortable bars, good
beer and an excellent restaurant.

Seland Newydd, Pwllgloyw, Nr. Brecon, Powys LD3 9PY

Tel: 01874 690282
website: www.selandnewydd.co.uk
Real ales, excellent wines, fine food and comfortable
new en suite bedrooms in a country inn halfway
between Builth Wells and Cradoc. 146

The Ship Inn, High Street, Raglan, Monmouthshire NP15 2DY

Tel: 01291 690635
Family-run 16th century village inn with cosy bars,
log fires, real ales and food lunchtime and evening.
Darts and pool.

The White Swan, Llanfrynach, Brecon, Powys LD3 7BZ

Tel: 01874 665276
website: www.the-white-swan.com
An excellent pub-restaurant in a row of smart black-
and-white cottages. Sister establishment offering
luxurious self-catering accommodation nearby. 150

Ye Olde Crown Inn, Pant-y-Gelli, Monmouthshire NP7 7HR

Tel/Fax: 01873 853314
e-mail: yeoldcrown@aol.com
An attractive and very popular 15th century inn on a
hillside north of Abergavenny. Real ales, very good
food and excellent overnight accommodation. 103

West Monmouthshire Golf Club

Golf Road, Pond Road, Nantyglo NP3 4QT

Tel: 01495 310233 Fax: 01495 311361

Sec/Manager:	Tony Flower
Professional:	None
Directions:	7½ miles SW of Abergavenny. From A40 at southern outskirts of Abergavenny take the A465 (Brynmawr). After 7 miles turn left onto the A467 (Blaina). At the second roundabout, after ½ mile take third exit Pond Rd. Entrance after ¾ mile.
Date Founded:	1906
Type of Course:	Heathland
No of Holes:	18
Length:	6300 yds (5815 mtrs)
Par:	72
SSS:	69
Green Fees:	Weekdays: £10 per day; Weekends/Bank Holidays: £15 per day
Visitors:	Welcome: Unable to play at weekends. Contact Club in advance
Societies:	Welcome: Unable to play at weekends. Contact Club in advance
Facilities:	Putting Green, Trolley Hire, Buggy Hire, Bar, Restaurant

Accommodation, Food and Drink

Reference numbers below refer to detailed information provided in section 2

Accommodation

The Belmont Inn, Abergavenny, Monmouthshire NP7 5HH

Tel: 01873 850074

A warm and welcoming pub on the A40 a short walk from the town centre. Large, comfortable bar, home-cooked food, two rooms for B&B. 106

The Bulls Head Hotel, 86 The Street, Brecon, Powys LD3 7LS

Tel: 01874 622044 Fax: 01874 625321

Good-value overnight accommodation (2 rooms sleeping up to 6), pub grub and a great selection of real ales. Town-centre location.

The County House, 100 The Street, Brecon, Powys LD3 7LS

Tel: 01874 625844
e-mail: countyhouse@ukworld.net

Licensed accommodation in a fine Georgian house. Three excellent en suite bedrooms: sitting room, dining room. B&B with dinner option.

The Crown Hotel, Varteg, Nr. Pontypool, Monmouthshire NP4 8UG

Tel: 01495 774312

Good atmosphere and good fun in a cheerful pub-hotel with B&B accommodation and evening meals with notice.

Llandetty Hall Farm, Talybont-on-Usk, Powys LD3 7YR

Tel: 01874 676415

A Grade ll listed farmhouse in the Brecon Beacons National Park, offering non-smoking B&B accommodation in three spacious bedrooms. 145

Mill Farm, Cwmafon, Nr. Pontypool, South Wales NP4 8XJ

Tel/Fax: 01495 774588

Old-world charm aplenty in a 15th century farmhouse that offers complete tranquillity, antique-furnished bedrooms and breakfast until noon. 104

The Old Ford Inn, Llanhamlach, Nr. Brecon, Powys LD3 7YB

Tel/Fax: 01874 665220
e-mail: enquiries@theoldfordinn.co.uk
website: www.theoldfordinn.co.uk

A fine old country inn offering wonderful views, a warm ambience, excellent food and drink and very comfortable B&B accommodation. 147

The Wenallt, Gilwern, Nr. Abergavenny, Gwent NP7 0HP

Tel: 01873 830694
e-mail: thewenallt@talk21.com

A 16th century Welsh longhouse in a superb hillside setting in the Brecon Beacons National Park. Large, comfortable bedrooms: three-course dinners. 107

Werngochlyn Farm, Llantilio Pertholey, Nr. Abergavenny, Monmouthshire NP7 8BH

Tel: 01873 857357
website: www.cottageguide.co.uk/werngochlyn

Four well-appointed self-catering cottages on a working farm three miles from Abergavenny. Indoor swimming pool, games room, children's activity area, riding school, lots of friendly animals. Also B&B available in the farmhouse.

The White Swan, Llanfrynach, Brecon, Powys LD3 7BZ

Tel: 01874 665276
website: www.the-white-swan.com

An excellent pub-restaurant in a row of smart black-and-white cottages. Sister establishment offering luxurious self-catering accommodation nearby. 150

**Ye Olde Crown Inn, Pant-y-Gelli,
Monmouthshire NP7 7HR**

Tel/Fax: 01873 853314
e-mail: yeoldcrown@aol.com
An attractive and very popular 15th century inn on a hillside north of Abergavenny. Real ales, very good food and excellent overnight accommodation. 103

Food and Drink

**The Axe & Cleaver, Much Birch, Nr. Hereford,
Herefordshire HR2 8HU**

Tel/Fax: 01981 540203
An attractive black and white pub on the A49 south of Hereford, with lovely gardens and a great reputation for the quality of its food and drink. 223

**The Belmont Inn, Abergavenny,
Monmouthshire NP7 5HH**

Tel: 01873 850074
A warm and welcoming pub on the A40 a short walk from the town centre. Large, comfortable bar, home-cooked food, two rooms for B&B. 106

**The Bulls Head Hotel, 86 The Street, Brecon,
Powys LD3 7LS**

Tel: 01874 622044 Fax: 01874 625321
Good-value overnight accommodation (2 rooms sleeping up to 6), pub grub and a great selection of real ales. Town-centre location.

**The Crown Hotel, Varteg, Nr. Pontypool,
Monmouthshire NP4 8UG**

Tel: 01495 774312
Good atmosphere and good fun in a cheerful pub-hotel with B&B accommodation and evening meals with notice.

**The Lancaster Arms, Pandy, Nr. Abergavenny,
Monmouthshire NP7 8DW**

Tel: 01873 890699
1840s cottage converted into a pub, with a cosy interior, good real ales and home-cooked food. Five miles north of Abergavenny. 105

**The Old Ford Inn, Llanhamlach, Nr. Brecon,
Powys LD3 7YB**

Tel/Fax: 01874 665220
e-mail: enquiries@theoldfordinn.co.uk
website: www.theoldfordinn.co.uk
A fine old country inn offering wonderful views, a warm ambience, excellent food and drink and very comfortable B&B accommodation. 147

**The Prince Llewellyn Inn, Cilmery, Brecon,
Powys LD2 3NU**

Tel: 01982 552694
A friendly inn four miles west of Builth Wells on the A483, with a lovely garden, comfortable bars, good beer and an excellent restaurant.

**The Ship Inn, High Street, Raglan,
Monmouthshire NP15 2DY**

Tel: 01291 690635

Family-run 16th century village inn with cosy bars, log fires, real ales and food lunchtime and evening. Darts and pool.

**The White Swan, Llanfrynach, Brecon,
Powys LD3 7BZ**

Tel: 01874 665276
website: www.the-white-swan.com
An excellent pub-restaurant in a row of smart black-and-white cottages. Sister establishment offering luxurious self-catering accommodation nearby. 150

**Ye Olde Crown Inn, Pant-y-Gelli,
Monmouthshire NP7 7HR**

Tel/Fax: 01873 853314
e-mail: yeoldcrown@aol.com
An attractive and very popular 15th century inn on a hillside north of Abergavenny. Real ales, very good food and excellent overnight accommodation. 103

Woodlake Park Golf Club

Glascoed, Usk NP4 0TE
Tel: 01291 673933 Fax: 01291 673811

Woodlake Park is a relatively young course (opened in 1993) but, nevertheless, is a fine place to visit because it has grown into maturity very quickly, which is a credit to the owners, the Wood family, who designed and developed the course with a little help from David Feherty, the former European Tour and Ryder Cup player. A feature of the course is the magnificent 434 acre Llandegfedd reservoir which borders the western edge of the course and which has turned the place into a photographer's dream. A rolling undulating course it also offers many fine views of the lower Usk valley and breathtaking vistas of the Black Mountains and the distant Brecon Beacons. Indeed, like the Rolls of Monmouth, it is set in an area of natural outstanding beauty making it a delightful place to visit. The pleasant clubhouse overlooks the reservoir and boasts a large suntrapped patio. Attached to the clubhouse can be found an excellent indoor practice area for one to warm up before taking on the challenging championship course, which has a par of 71 and SSS of 72.

An advantage to visititors during the winter months is the fact the superb greens are constructed to a specification which allows them to be playable in the winter. After a fairly comfortable start the course comes into its own with the impressive and difficult third hole, a par-5 which stretches to 537 yards of utter frustration if you lose your concentration while admiring the wonderful scenery.

Sec/Manager:	Mr. Wood
Professional:	A. Pritchard
Directions:	2 miles W of Usk centre. From centre take Bridge St (A472, Monkswood). After 2¾ miles turn left to Glascoed and go through village. Turn left into Glascoed Lane from Wem Lane. Entrance after ¾ mile on right hand side.
Date Founded:	1993
Type of Course:	Undulating Parkland
No of Holes:	18
Length:	6400 yds (5907 mtrs)
Par:	71
SSS:	72
Green Fees:	Weekdays: Summer £20 per day. Winter £15 per day; Weekends/Bank Holidays: Summer £15 per day. Winter £20 per day
Visitors:	Welcome: By arrangement. Contact Club in advance
Societies:	Welcome: By arrangement. Contact Club in advance
Facilities:	Putting Green, Chipping Green, Trolley Hire, Buggy Hire, Bar, Restaurant

Accommodation, Food and Drink

Reference numbers below refer to detailed information provided in section 2

Accommodation

The Belmont Inn, Abergavenny, Monmouthshire NP7 5HH

Tel: 01873 850074

A warm and welcoming pub on the A40 a short walk from the town centre. Large, comfortable bar, home-cooked food, two rooms for B&B.   106

Brooklands Farm, Raglan, Monmouthshire NP1 2EN

Tel: 01291 690782
e-mail: brooklandsfarm@raglanfsbusiness.co.uk

Large property on a working dairy farm with four letting rooms. Excellent breakfasts and dinner by arrangement. TV lounge and garden.   102

The Crown Hotel, Varteg, Nr. Pontypool, Monmouthshire NP4 8UG

Tel: 01495 774312

Good atmosphere and good fun in a cheerful pub-hotel with B&B accommodation and evening meals with notice.

J D Llewellyn, Cwrt-y-Gaer, Wolvesnewton, Chepstow, Monmouthshire NP16 6PR

Tel: 01291 650700

Superbly equipped self-catering accommodation in three separate flats, including a cottage designed for disabled guests. Quiet, scenic surroundings.

The Star Inn, Llanfihangel Tor-y-Mynydd, Llansoy, Monmouthshire NP15 1DT

Tel: 01291 650256

A lovely out-of-the-way inn with two splendidly appointed letting bedrooms and a varied menu served in the non-smoking restaurant.

Ty Shon Jacob Farm, Coch-y-North Lane, Tranch, Nr. Pontypool, Monmouthshire NP4 6BP

Tel/Fax: 01495 757536
e-mail: tyshonfarm@aol.com

Peace, quiet and great views on a 36-acre farm 1,250 feet above sea level. Three twin bedrooms for B&B: dinner by arrangement.

The Wenallt, Gilwern, Nr. Abergavenny, Gwent NP7 0HP

Tel: 01873 830694
e-mail: thewenallt@talk21.com

A 16th century Welsh longhouse in a superb hillside setting in the Brecon Beacons National Park. Large, comfortable bedrooms: three-course dinners.   107

Food and Drink

The Belmont Inn, Abergavenny, Monmouthshire NP7 5HH

Tel: 01873 850074

A warm and welcoming pub on the A40 a short walk from the town centre. Large, comfortable bar, home-cooked food, two rooms for B&B.   106

The Crown Hotel, Varteg, Nr. Pontypool, Monmouthshire NP4 8UG

Tel: 01495 774312

A good atmosphere and good fun in a cheerful pub-hotel with B&B accommodation and evening meals with notice.

The Ship Inn, High Street, Raglan, Monmouthshire NP15 2DY

Tel: 01291 690635

Family-run 16th century village inn with cosy bars, log fires, real ales and food lunchtime and evening. Darts and pool.

The Star Inn, Llanfihangel Tor-y-Mynydd, Llansoy, Monmouthshire NP15 1DT

Tel: 01291 650256

A lovely out-of-the-way inn with two splendidly appointed letting bedrooms and a varied menu served in the non-smoking restaurant.

MID GLAMORGAN

Like the extreme northern area of neighbouring Monmouthshire, the pattern of life in the north of Mid Glamorgan has seen a profound change over the last few decades. The boom days of towns like Ebbw Vale, Merthyr Tydfil, Tredegar, Aberdare, Cwm and many others, which had seen many thousands of people arriving in hordes to swell the population of the once barren moorland area and to seek out a good living, is now almost a distant memory. The booms days of this area, like much of South Wales, was kindled by the wars between Britain and the new French republic during the latter part of the 18th century and the early 19th century. Coal, iron ore and limestone were all discovered in this area; the coal fired the mighty furnaces that turned the iron ore into cannon balls and the guns that fired them. The demands of Wellington's great armies and Nelson's navy were so great that the iron and coal barons rapidly expanded their factories and mines and also built many more close to the source of the important mineral deposits-the result being similar to that of the Klondike gold rush.

Hamlets quickly grew into villages, and villages into large towns almost overnight as the news of "jobs for everyone" spread. The result being that the very heart of this spectacular and beautiful area of Glamorganshire and Monmouthshire was torn to shreds and the greenery of the countryside besmirched by smoke from the furnaces and the black, clinging grime of the ugly coaltips. Historical novelist Alexander Cordell summed it up perfectly when he named the title of his first book about the harsh life and exploitation of the workers of those early days "The Rape of the Fair Country", which he penned whilst living in the Old Vicarage at the pleasant village of Llanellen, in Monmouthshire. Cordell went on to write many more novels about the savagery of the working conditions imposed by the greedy masters of industry and the inevitable riots that the proud people of the Welsh valleys were forced to make to stop the suffering. The books all became bestsellers and still remain in print years after the great author's death.

In time life got better for the workers, and two world wars meant much prosperity in the area from the giant steelworks in the Ebbw Vale area and the continuing richness of the coalfields with

Caerphilly Castle

its seemingly never-ending "Black Diamonds". Over the last few decades, however, the coalmines have completely disappeared (except for the mining museums) and the mighty steelworks are now on their knees just waiting for the knockout punch from the foreign consortiums who are taking their vast profits and moving elsewhere into Europe. As a result the proud old working towns have declined over the years, but are now fighting back with new light industries being attracted to those areas in decline.

Today the villages and towns are having a spring-clean as the "new money" arrives and the revitalisation programme gradually takes effect. The crowds are returning to the old valley towns-albeit rather slowly-and the devastated countryside is speedily returning to its glory days of spectacular and outstanding natural beauty. The famous A465"Heads of the Valleys" roadway from Abergavenny to Swansea is now a joy to travel along-despite being only three lanes at the present moment-because of the magnificent and unspoilt vistas now reappearing after centuries of industrial abuse. From this mighty roadway all the industrial valleys of South Wales can be entered. The Mid Glamorgan valley towns of Hengoed, Merthyr Tydfil, Bargoed, Aberdare, Mountain Ash and the towns of the famous Rhondda Valleys can all be easily reached from each specific roundabout. From the direction of Abergavenny and after passing the first of these roundabouts, which leads to Brynmawr and the valley towns of Monmouthshire, the next one leads to Ebbw Vale, also in Monmouthshire. Famous for its rugby team and steelmaking, the old town was also chosen to host the Garden Festival of Wales in 1991, which proved a huge success as thousands of visitors from all over the world flocked to witness the magnificent spectacle. Luxury houses now adorn the site and also a spe-

Cyfarthfa Castle

cial modern shopping centre, where many bargains can be found. The town itself, like all the valley towns, still bears a few industrial scars, but this adds to the atmosphere, as does the fantastically friendly valley people-typical of all Welsh valley folk.

Further along the roadway lies the exit lane for Merthyr Tydfil. Before the Industrial Revolution of South Wales it was merely an insignificant village, but with the arrival of the ironmasters it quickly grew into what was then the largest town in Wales. As the years went by it became a downtrodden sort of town, but an injection of government money has revived its fortunes. As well as a new civic centre, there are also newly-built shops and a thriving trading estate. But it was the Chartist Riots of 1831 that put Merthyr Tydfil well and truly on the map. The uprising proved so fierce that it took severe military force to quell the angry rioters. Cyfarthfa Castle, the neo-gothic home of the powerful Crawshay family, the mighty ironmasters who had complete control of the town along with their rich fellow business compatriots, the Guest family of Dowlais and the powerful Homfray family. The castle, which was built directly opposite the Crawshay's over-powering Cyfarthfa ironworks, now serves as an interesting museum of the industrial era. Despite what many history books will tell you, Merthyr Tydfil was the birthplace of the world's Railway Age. Contrary to popular belief, it was here that the Cornish inventor Richard Trevithick invented and ran the world's first steam engine. Pulling a line of trucks full of excited passengers from Merthyr to Abercynon in 1804, it amazingly beat Stephenson's Rocket by 20 years.

Another interesting piece of Merthyr's historical past is a row of workers cottages known as Chapel Row. Here at house number 4 was born the composer Dr Joseph Parry, who wrote the beautiful and haunting Welsh melody "Myfanwy". In 1900 Merthyr also laid another claim to fame when they elected Kier Hardie to become their MP, thus making them the first town in Britain to elect a Socialist into Parliament. Close to Merthyr lies Aberfan, where a coal tip turned to slurry after heavy rainfalls in 1966 and slid down on to the local school, burying many children and some teachers in a disaster that could and should have been averted. The tip was flattened later, but the graves of those who tragically lost their lives remain on a hillside close by.

The abundance of coal and iron during the 19th century saw many other towns like Merthyr grow and flourish in the many valleys connected to the A469, and should be visited if one wants savour the atmosphere of those days. There are so many such places, but space is too limited for me to describe them all, nevertheless, Aberdare, which lies at the head of the now beautiful Cynon Valley deserves a mention as it is on par with Merthyr as a once important town. Surrounded by towering mountainsides with much awesome beauty after a mighty makeover, Aberdare sits comfortably in an expansive vale, which gives the bustling old town a feeling of airiness. Like Pontypool in Monmouthshire, Aberdare boasts a large and lovely Park, complete with a fine boating lake, woodland and large grassed areas. The Dale Valley Country Park at the west of the town, offers many attractions inside its 480 acres, including fishing, walking, a Valley Inheritance Centre and an Industrial Trail, to name but a few. From Aberdare one can also enter the famous Rhondda Valleys southwards to Pontypridd by taking the A4233 road westwards out of Aberdare. This takes you past many of the towns downtrodden by the heavy industry, but the mountainsides that created the valleys now bear little evidence of the huge coalfields. Indeed, some spectacular scenery can now be enjoyed as one drives from the north to the borders of the southlands of Mid Glamorgan.

Pontypridd (pronounced Pontypreed) lies at the foot of the Rhondda valleys and at the junction of the rivers Rhondda and Taff. Within easy reach of all the valleys, Pontypridd now prospers from the fact that crowds flock there to shop at the new shopping precinct and huge market. On market days the town is bursting to overflowing in the same way as the Monmouthshire market town of Abergavenny. Famous for its rugby team, Pontypridd also has a good mountainside golf course, as does a number of the Rhondda towns. Tom Jones, the big-earning pop star, is said to be from Pontypridd, but is actually from the nearby town of Treforest. Two other well-known singers, Stuart Burrows and the late Sir Geraint Evans, were actually born in the same street at Cilfynydd on the outskirts of Pontypridd. Surely there must be something good in the air of the region for three world-renowned singers to originate from the Pontypridd area!

Leaving Pontypridd southwards on the A470 you drive to Caerphilly, which is famous for its fine cheese and a castle famous for not only being the second largest to Windsor Castle in Britain but also because of one of its mighty towers, which leans at a greater angle than the Tower at Pisa in Italy. This magnificent fortress has a huge moat and, despite the attempts by Cromwell's soldiers to destroy it-hence the leaning tower-it still remains in good order and well worth a visit. A pleasant town, Caerphilly also has a good 18-hole golf course at its outskirts and named after the town, and also a recently constructed 9-hole course known as Virginia Park Golf Club. A mere drive of 7 miles over the 888 feet Caerphilly Mountain is the great capital city of Cardiff (see South Glamorgan). On the way there lies the village of Tongwynlais with its rather attractive fairy-tale style of castle known as Castell Coch. Magnificently constructed, the castle is perched among woods close to the M4 motorway, just asking to be visited. Lying at the foot of the castle is a very good Par-3 golf course, which is in a beautiful setting and well worth a short visit after viewing the castle. Further beyond the castle golfers are spoilt for choice at Mountain Lakes Golf Club, which also has in its grounds the attractive Castell Heights 9-hole course. Both designed by Bob Sandow, they are catered for by a single enormous clubhouse. Mountain Lakes, set in amongst spectacular rolling woodland, offers a mighty challenge to every class of golfer. Also just off the A470 from Pontypridd, but in the opposite direction to Caerphilly, is the small town of Llantrisant set on a ridge above the beautiful Vale of Glamorgan. The town still celebrates the fact that it sent 100 crack Welsh archers to fight at the Battle of Crecy. Two other notable facts are that it is the home of the Royal Mint and also where cremation became established as a legal act. The rather eccentric Dr William Price, a radical, heir to the Druids, a Chartist supporter and a pioneer of the Permissive society, lived with a young girl at Llantrisant, who bore him a son when he was eighty-three (he begot several children while in his eighties). The son died at an early age, and he set about burning the body on a hilltop. Arrested by the police for unlawful behaviour, he proved successful in his defence during the trial in 1884, and cremation became established as a legal

Castell Coch

right. A statue to the eccentric Dr Price stands in the centre of the town. A small town but an interesting one is Llantrisant, which also offers official walking areas in the forest on the outskirts of the town and an excellent 18-hole golf course.

At the western end of the Vale of Glamorgan can be found the old market town of Bridgend. Another rugby stronghold, the town is fortunate inasmuch that a Royal Ordinance factory and a Ford Motor Company factory are sited there. This is a busy, bustling place with the added attraction of being close to the coastal resorts of Mid Glamorgan. Close to Bridgend and off the Sarn junction of the M4 motorway is the huge Blaen Gawr Country Park. Within easy reach of the town (2 miles south) is the small and attractive village of Merthyr Mawr. Famous for its charming thatched cottages, there are also some of the highest sand dunes in Europe quite close to the village. This is the delightful coastal area of Mid Glamorgan and a complete contrast to the old industrial regions in the north of the county. The main town here and the major seaside resort of South Wales is Porthcawl. Throughout the centuries it remained the popular holiday resort of the South Wales mining community, who came in their thousands during the miners holiday weeks in the summer-attracted by the fine beaches, huge caravan sites, comfortable guest houses and the huge funfair at Coney Beach. Alas, with the closure of the mines the town is less busy and the atmosphere and cheery character (like Blackpool) of the resort has changed. However, the beaches at Rest Bay, Sandy Bay and Trecco Bay still remain popular with the more casual holiday-maker. The keen golfers of South Wales love visiting the area, because of the three top quality courses here at Royal Porthcawl, Southerndown and Pyle and Kenkig. Many good coastal and clifftop walks along with pleasant picnic sites, also means the coastline of Mid Glamorgan offers something of interest to every visitor.

Location of Golf Courses

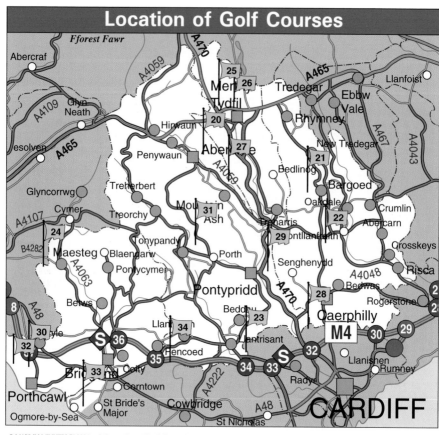

© MAPS IN MINUTES ™ 2001   © Crown Copyright, Ordnance Survey 2001

Aberdare Golf Club

Abernant, Aberdare, Mid Glamorgan CF44 0RY

Tel: 01685 872797 Fax: 01685 872797

Founded by the local gentry and up-and-coming businessmen of Aberdare in 1921, the pleasant parkland course of Aberdare Golf Club has long been a favourite of golfers from the many valley towns in easy reach of this Cynon Valley based club. I have many pleasant memories of playing this delightful 18-hole course during their Open Weekend tournaments, and was surprised to find that many golfers from the Birmingham and Midlands region had somehow discovered the Aberdare club and were quite happy to set out from home as early as 5am to enjoy the course and the wonderful views of the Welsh countryside. Situated high above the old mining and ironworks town of Aberdare, it is perhaps better to describe the course as mountainside with many parkland features rather than simply parkland, as it often is. Nevertheless, there are no exhausting climbs to endure because whoever designed the lay-out (no-one's quite sure who it was) did an extremely good job of placing the holes lengthways across the mountainside in the shape of a narrow type of loop starting at the front of the clubhouse and finishing at the rear of it, if my memory serves me correctly.

There are a number of blind holes at Aberdare and a few cleverly placed trees to negotiate, plus a number of good par-three holes to add to the challenge of this course. At 5,875 yards the course is short by modern day standards, but the sss of 69 is not easy to achieve.

What is not generally known about the Aberdare club is that this is the place where that great Welsh golfer Dai Rees, the former and successful Ryder Cup captain, really got to grips with the game when he was aged 13 and his father, also named Dai, took the job as professional at the Aberdare club. As can be expected, there are lots of good stories to be heard about Dai junior from the older members who spent their boyhood days at school and on the course with the great man. One such story relates how Dai and his friends learned to play golf on two holes they had shaped on the coal tips of the local colliery, and there they stayed until darkness fell. In Dai Rees' early days the clubhouse was merely a wooden shack of a place, where Dai and his parents lived. As time went by two old army huts were purchased for £100 to replace the shack. Who would have realised then that "the young nipper", as Rees was called, would become a famous golfer and would one day return as guest of honour with his mother and sister to open the splendid new brick-built clubhouse, which happened in 1967. A man with a famous name can still be found at Aberdare Golf Club. His name is A. Palmer, the club professional, who, although a fine golfer, is not the original!

The town of Aberdare has long been known as "Queen of the Valleys". A name that could also be used to describe Aberdare Golf Club.

Sec/Manager:	Tony Mears
Professional:	A. Palmer
Directions:	½ mile NE of Aberdare. From center cross the A4059 and take Abernant Rd. After ½ mile turn right into Forge Place. Entrance is at the end.
Date Founded:	1921
Type of Course:	Parkland
No of Holes:	18
Length:	5875 yds (5423 mtrs)
Par:	69
SSS:	69
Green Fees:	Weekdays: Summer £16 per day, Winter £14 per day; Weekends/Bank Holidays: Summer £20 per day, Winter £18 per day
Visitors:	Welcome: Contact Club in advance
Societies:	Welcome: Contact Club in advance
Facilities:	Putting Green, Trolley Hire, Bar, Restaurant

Accommodation, Food and Drink

Reference numbers below refer to detailed information provided in section 2

Accommodation

The Bulls Head Hotel, 86 The Street, Brecon, Powys LD3 7LS

Tel: 01874 622044 Fax: 01874 625321

Good-value overnight accommodation (2 rooms

sleeping up to 6), pub grub and a great selection of real ales. Town-centre location.

Drws Nesaf, Abergwrelych House, Pontwalby, Glynneath SA11 5LN

Tel: 01639 720035

A charming mid-Victorian cottage in beautiful walking country. Self-catering accommodation comprises sitting room/diner, kitchen, 2 bedrooms, shower room, patio.

The Tai'r Bull Inn, Libanus, Nr. Brecon, Powys LD3 8EL

Tel: 01874 625849

A very well-kept roadside inn offering good food, B&B accommodation and superb views of the Brecon Beacons.   148

Ty Andrew Guest House, 33 Seymour Street, Aberdare, Mid-Glamorgan CF44 7BL

Tel: 01685 876603

Bed & Breakfast guest house with rooms (some en suite) ranging from singles to a family room. Drying facilities available.

The White Swan, Llanfrynach, Brecon, Powys LD3 7BZ

Tel: 01874 665276

website: www.the-white-swan.com

An excellent pub-restaurant in a row of smart black-and-white cottages. Sister establishment offering luxurious self-catering accommodation nearby.   150

Food and Drink

The Bulls Head Hotel, 86 The Street, Brecon, Powys LD3 7LS

Tel: 01874 622044 Fax: 01874 625321

Good-value overnight accommodation (2 rooms sleeping up to 6), pub grub and a great selection of real ales. Town-centre location.

The Tai'r Bull Inn, Libanus, Nr. Brecon, Powys LD3 8EL

Tel: 01874 625849

A very well-kept roadside inn offering good food, B&B accommodation and superb views of the Brecon Beacons.   148

The Wheatsheaf, Wheat Street, Brecon, Powys LD3 7DG

Tel: 01874 611109

A town-centre pub with a long, spacious bar. Pool table. Good bar food, good beer, young crowd.

The White Swan, Llanfrynach, Brecon, Powys LD3 7BZ

Tel: 01874 665276

website: www.the-white-swan.com

An excellent pub-restaurant in a row of smart black-and-white cottages. Sister establishment offering luxurious self-catering accommodation nearby.   150

Bargoed Golf Club

Heolddu, Bargoed CF81 9GF

Tel: 01443 830143

Sec/Manager:	Geoff Williams
Professional:	Clive Coombes
Directions:	14 miles N of Cardiff. From M4 junction 32 take A470 (Pontypridd). Ater 4 miles turn right onto A468 then A469 Bargoed. At start of Bargoed turn left into Western Drive and after 1 mile lead into Hoelldu Crescent. Entrance is on the left hand side after 200 yds .
Date Founded:	1923
Type of Course:	Mountainous
No of Holes:	18
Length:	6049 yds (5583 mtrs)
Par:	70
SSS:	70
Green Fees:	Weekdays: £18 per day; Weekends/Bank Holidays: Only with member
Visitors:	Welcome: Unable to play at weekends. Contact Club in advance
Societies:	Welcome: Unable to play at weekends. Contact Club in advance
Facilities:	Chipping Green, Trolley Hire, Bar, Restaurant

Accommodation, Food and Drink

Reference numbers below refer to detailed information provided in section 2

Accommodation

The Crown Hotel, Varteg, Nr. Pontypool, Monmouthshire NP4 8UG

Tel: 01495 774312

Good atmosphere and good fun in a cheerful pub-hotel with B&B accommodation and evening meals with notice.

Ty Andrew Guest House, 33 Seymour Street, Aberdare, Mid-Glamorgan CF44 7BL

Tel: 01685 876603

Bed & Breakfast guest house with rooms (some en suite) ranging from singles to a family room. Drying facilities available.

Ty Shon Jacob Farm, Coch-y-North Lane, Tranch, Nr. Pontypool, Monmouthshire NP4 6BP

Tel/Fax: 01495 757536

e-mail: tyshonfarm@aol.com

Peace, quiet and great views on a 36-acre farm 1,250 feet above sea level. Three twin bedrooms for B&B: dinner by arrangement.

The White Horse Inn, Davis Row, Pentwyn, Nr. Fochriw, Bargoed, Mid-Glamorgan CF81 9NP

Tel: 01685 841215

Popular inn open seven days a week for breakfast, lunch and dinner. Super home-made pies and lots more. Two B&B rooms planned.

Food and Drink

The Belmont Inn, Abergavenny, Monmouthshire NP7 5HH

Tel: 01873 850074

A warm and welcoming pub on the A40 a short walk from the town centre. Large, comfortable bar, home-cooked food, two rooms for B&B.   106

The Crown Hotel, Varteg, Nr. Pontypool, Monmouthshire NP4 8UG

Tel: 01495 774312

Good atmosphere and good fun in a cheerful pub-hotel with B&B accommodation and evening meals with notice.

The White Horse Inn, Davis Row, Pentwyn, Nr. Fochriw, Bargoed, Mid-Glamorgan CF81 9NP

Tel: 01685 841215

Popular inn open seven days a week for breakfast, lunch and dinner. Super home-made pies and lots more. Two B&B rooms planned.

Bryn Meadows Golf Hotel

The Bryn, Hengoed, Mid Glamorgan CF8 7SM

Tel: 01495 225590 Fax: 01495 224103

Bryn Meadows Golf and Country Club is one of the great success stories of the valley clubs. Sadly, it is also one of the great tragic stories of Welsh golf. It all began in 1973 when local builder and golf nut, Bryn Mayo, decided it was time to fulfil a dream of building his own golf club. Along with two business associates he negotiated and quickly purchased some rough meadow and farmland on the outskirts of his hometown of Blackwood, in Monmouthshire, but which actually lay over the border and close to the Mid Glamorgan town of Hengoed. Included in the purchase was an old stone farmhouse which Bryan Mayo expertly turned into a rather attractive clubhouse by retaining all the external and internal stone features. Also designing the course with E. Jefferies, one of

his new found partners, they and their third co-partner waited with bated breath as the course developed to discover if and how many golfers and would-be golfers the club would attract as members. To their immense relief the membership grew in double quick time as large as Pinocchio's nose. All went along quite smoothly until 1979. Bryan Mayo had a habit of licking his golf ball before putting out; he was playing in a society match at Glamorganshire Golf Club, where they had sprayed weed killer onto the greens that morning. Bryan had lost his spleen following a car accident some years earlier. Therefore, the toxic weed killer caused a reaction, which his body could not fight and he fell into a coma. To cut a long and tragic story short, the end result was that both his legs were amputated above the knee. While still in hospital both his partners explained it was better to sell the golf club. Still not knowing if he was going to survive, he made the decision to buy them out. With great courage he survived countless operations, learned to walk on false legs, continued to play golf and reduced his handicap from 9 to 7!

His determination came from reading Douglas Bader's biography Reach for the Sky, and he afterwards helped to raise money for the Douglas Bader Foundation by putting on a special Pro-Celebrity tournament on an annual basis at his club. He also founded the British Amputee Golf Open, which raised many thousands of pounds for amputee charities. For all his efforts he was awarded the MBE some years ago. With much encouragement from his wife, Fay, their two sons and a dedicated staff, he built his club into something special. Bryn Meadows now boasts an excellent 20-bedroomed hotel, an impressive leisure centre, a large function room, conference rooms and an excellent restaurant, which makes it the finest golf and hotel complex in Mid Glamorgan. Sadly, Bryan Mayo passed away a few short years ago when in his mid-50s, after picking up a virus when on a golfing holiday in Florida, where he owned a property. This time the loss of his spleen proved to be fatal. A good friend to myself and many others, he is sadly missed, but as an example of how to triumph over adversity he will be long remembered by those in similar circumstances whom he helped.

The hotel holds the Wales Tourist Board's top Five Crowns category, and like the rest of the impressive complex is run personally by the Mayo family, so be assured you will receive a warm welcome. Set in the heart of the Rhymney Valley and offering wonderful views from every hole, the course offers an excellent challenge with the fourth being the signature hole. With a carry of 165 yards over a lake and from an elevated tee, it offers a stern challenge. A tough par 72, but all the amputees who have played here love the course. So why not you? When pulling into the huge car park, look out for the clock above the entrance. It's something special. After the inaugural British Amputee Open it was decided by the amputees to make a collection in order to erect this clock in appreciation of Bryan Mayo's efforts. The then club captain jokingly stated that this would cost an arm and a leg! This resulted in the hands of the clock, quite appropriately, being in the shape of an arm and a leg, therefore unique in this type of clock in telling the time without any hands!

Sec/Manager:	Mr Mayo
Professional:	Bruce Hunter
Directions:	12 miles N of Cardiff City Centre. From M4 junction 32 take the A470 (Pontypridd), after 2½ miles turn right onto the A468, then A469 (Hengoed). At Hengoed turn right into Main Rd (A472, Newbridge). After 1¼ miles turn right at roundabout. Entrance on right hand side after 300 yds.
Date Founded:	1973
Type of Course:	Parkland
No of Holes:	18
Length:	6156 yds (5625 mtrs)
Par:	72
SSS:	70
Green Fees:	Weekdays: £17.50; Weekends/Bank Holidays: £22.50
Visitors:	Welcome: Contact Club in advance
Societies:	Welcome: Contact Club in advance
Facilities:	Putting Green, Practice Area, Club Hire, Trolley Hire, Buggy Hire, Bar, Restaurant, Private Rooms

Accommodation, Food and Drink

Reference numbers below refer to detailed information provided in section 2

Accommodation

The Crown Hotel, Varteg, Nr. Pontypool, Monmouthshire NP4 8UG
Tel: 01495 774312
Good atmosphere and good fun in a cheerful pub-hotel with B&B accommodation and evening meals with notice.

Ty Andrew Guest House, 33 Seymour Street, Aberdare, Mid-Glamorgan CF44 7BL
Tel: 01685 876603
Bed & Breakfast guest house with rooms (some en suite) ranging from singles to a family room. Drying facilities available.

Ty Shon Jacob Farm, Coch-y-North Lane, Tranch, Nr. Pontypool, Monmouthshire NP4 6BP
Tel/Fax: 01495 757536
e-mail: tyshonfarm@aol.com
Peace, quiet and great views on a 36-acre farm 1,250 feet above sea level. Three twin bedrooms for B&B: dinner by arrangement.

The White Horse Inn, Davis Row, Pentwyn, Nr. Fochriw, Bargoed, Mid-Glamorgan CF81 9NP
Tel: 01685 841215
Popular inn open seven days a week for breakfast, lunch and dinner. Super home-made pies and lots more. Two B&B rooms planned.

Food and Drink

The Crown Hotel, Varteg, Nr. Pontypool, Monmouthshire NP4 8UG
Tel: 01495 774312
Good atmosphere and good fun in a cheerful pub-hotel with B&B accommodation and evening meals with notice.

St Julian Inn, Newport, South Wales NP18 1QA
Tel: 01633 243548 Fax: 01633 243562
A welcoming old inn with the road on one side and the River Usk on the other. Bar-style menu, award-winning real ales. 108

The White Horse Inn, Davis Row, Pentwyn, Nr. Fochriw, Bargoed, Mid-Glamorgan CF81 9NP
Tel: 01685 841215
Popular inn open seven days a week for breakfast, lunch and dinner. Super home-made pies and lots more. Two B&B rooms planned.

Creigiau Golf Club

Creigiau, Cardiff CF4 8NN
Tel: 02920 890263 Fax: 02920 890706

Four miles north-west of Cardiff in the direction of Llantrisant lies the Creigiau Golf Club. Yet another parkland course and an 18-hole layout, the holes stretch away from the spacious clubhouse along a narrow section of land and then opens out into good parkland. The inward nine has a tough finish with narrow fairways to negotiate and much rough and trees to avoid over the final few holes.

Sec/Manager:	A Greedy
Professional:	Ian Luntz
Directions:	8 miles NW of Cardiff City Centre. From M4 junction 34 take the A4119 (Llantrisant) and after ¾ mile turn right at traffic lights onto A4119 Groesfaen &Cardiff). After 1 mile turn left into Tynant Rd then at T-junction turn left into Heol Creigiau. Entrance after 200 yds on left hand side.
Date Founded:	1921
Type of Course:	Parkland and Heathland
No of Holes:	18
Length:	6200 yds (5723 mtrs)
Par:	72
SSS:	69
Green Fees:	Weekdays: £30; Weekends/ Bank Holidays: £30
Visitors:	Welcome: Contact Club by telephone in advance.
Societies:	Welcome: Contact Club in advance, unable to play on Monday, Tuesday, Thursday and Weekends.
Facilities:	Putting Green, Chipping Green, Driving Range, Trolley Hire, Caddy Service, Bar, Restaurant

Accommodation, Food and Drink

Reference numbers below refer to detailed information provided in section 2

Accommodation

**Clawdd Coch Guest House, Pendoylan,
Vale of Glamorgan CF71 7UP**

Tel: 01446 760645

Versatile B&B facilities in a 17th century house with five beautifully appointed bedrooms. Golfing breaks a speciality.   115

**Crossways House, Cowbridge,
Vale of Glamorgan CF71 7LJ**

Tel: 01446 773171 Fax: 01446 771707

e-mail: enquiries@crosswayshouse.co.uk
website: www.crosswayshouse.co.uk

Three B&B bedrooms and a self-catering flat in a lovely country mansion set in 6 acres ¾ mile west of Cowbridge (B4270).

**Fairways Hotel, Porthcawl,
South Glamorgan CF36 3LS**

Tel: 01656 782085 Fax: 01656 785351
e-mail: fairwayshotel@aol.com
website: www.bridgend.gov.uk

Twenty-five en suite bedrooms in a smartly refurbished family-run hotel near the seafront. Restaurant, lounge bar, residents' lounge.   114

St Julian Inn, Newport, South Wales NP18 1QA

Tel: 01633 243548 Fax: 01633 243562

A welcoming old inn with the road on one side and the River Usk on the other. Bar-style menu, award-winning real ales.   108

**The White Horse Inn, Davis Row, Pentwyn,
Nr. Fochriw, Bargoed, Mid-Glamorgan CF81 9NP**

Tel: 01685 841215

Popular inn open seven days a week for breakfast, lunch and dinner. Super home-made pies and lots more. Two B&B rooms planned.

**Windmill Cottages, Llansannor, Cowbridge,
Vale of Glamorgan CF71 7TF**

Tel/Fax: 01446 772470
e-mail: rosser@globalnet.co.uk

Quality self-catering accommodation in 19th century barn conversions adjacent to a working farm. Lovely rural setting five minutes from Cowbridge.   116

Food and Drink

**Fairways Hotel, Porthcawl,
South Glamorgan CF36 3LS**

Tel: 01656 782085 Fax: 01656 785351
e-mail: fairwayshotel@aol.com
website: www.bridgend.gov.uk

Twenty-five en suite bedrooms in a smartly refurbished family-run hotel near the seafront. Restaurant, lounge bar, residents' lounge.   114

**The White Horse Inn, Davis Row, Pentwyn,
Nr. Fochriw, Bargoed, Mid-Glamorgan CF81 9NP**

Tel: 01685 841215

Popular inn open seven days a week for breakfast, lunch and dinner. Super home-made pies and lots more. Two B&B rooms planned.

Maesteg Golf Club

Mount Pleasant, Neath Road,
Maesteg CF34 9PR

Tel: 01636 732037 Fax: 01656 734106

Sec/Manager:	Keith Lewis
Professional:	Chris Riley

Directions: 9 miles NW of Bridgend. From M4 junction 36 take the A4063 (Maesteg). After 6 miles in Maesteg turn left onto the B4282 (Bryn). Entrance on left hand side after ¾ mile.

Date Founded: 1912

Type of Course: Mountainous

No of Holes: 18

Length: 5939 yds (5426 mtrs)

Par: 70

SSS: 69

Green Fees: Weekdays: £17; Weekends/ Bank Holidays: £20

Visitors: Welcome: Contact Club in advance

Societies: Welcome: Contact Club in advance

Facilities: Putting Green, Trolley Hire, Buggy Hire, Bar, Restaurant

Accommodation, Food and Drink

Reference numbers below refer to detailed information provided in section 2

Accommodation

Drws Nesaf, Abergwrelych House, Pontwalby, Glynneath SA11 5LN

Tel: 01639 720035
A charming mid-Victorian cottage in beautiful walking country. Self-catering accommodation comprises sitting room/diner, kitchen, 2 bedrooms, shower room, patio.

Fairways Hotel, Porthcawl, South Glamorgan CF36 3LS

Tel: 01656 782085 Fax: 01656 785351
e-mail: fairwayshotel@aol.com
website: www.bridgend.gov.uk
Twenty-five en suite bedrooms in a smartly refurbished family-run hotel near the seafront. Restaurant, lounge bar, residents' lounge.   114

Hurst Dene Guest House, Uplands, Swansea SA2 0LJ

Tel/Fax: 01792 280920
website: www.hurstdene.co.uk
Ten bedrooms for Bed & Breakfast in a large Victorian terraced house. Also self-catering units. In a Swansea suburb near the sea.   124

Ty'n-y-Caeau, Margam Village, Port Talbot, West Glamorgan SA13 2NW

Tel: 01639 883897 Fax: 01639 895570
e-mail: gaen@tynycaeau.freeserve.co.uk
A large country house with superb gardens and comfortable en suite double or family rooms. Self catering also available.

Food and Drink

CJ's Wine Bar & Restaurant, Oystermouth, Swansea SA3 4DN

Tel: 01792 361246 Fax: 01792 419849
Cosy, friendly wine bar-café-restaurant in a row of shops close to the seafront. Varied menu with steaks and grill specialities and a vast cocktail list.   122

Fairways Hotel, Porthcawl, South Glamorgan CF36 3LS

Tel: 01656 782085 Fax: 01656 785351
e-mail: fairwayshotel@aol.com
website: www.bridgend.gov.uk
Twenty-five en suite bedrooms in a smartly refurbished family-run hotel near the seafront. Restaurant, lounge bar, residents' lounge.   114

The Mardy Hotel, 117 High Street, Gorseinon, Swansea SA4 2BT

Tel: 01792 892616
Snacks, burgers, scampi and steaks on the menu, with roasts on Sunday. Darts, pool, live entertainment three nights a week.

Merthyr Tydfil Golf Club

Cilsanws Mountain, Cefn Coed, Merthyr Tydfil CF48 2NU

Tel: 01685 723308

Sec/Manager: Viv Place

Professional: None

Directions: 1½ miles NW of Merthyr Tydfil. From centre take High St (A4054) north. After 1½ miles turn right into Cilsanws Lane. Entrance signed.

Date Founded: 1908

Type of Course: Mountainous

No of Holes: 18

Length: 5622 yds (5189 mtrs)

Par: 69

SSS: 69

Green Fees: Weekdays: £10 per day; Weekends/Bank Holidays: £15 per day

Visitors: Welcome: Excluding Saturday. Contact Club in advance

Societies: Welcome: Excluding Saturday afternoon and some Sundays. Contact Club in advance

Facilities: Putting Green, Buggy Hire, Bar, Restaurant

Accommodation, Food and Drink

Reference numbers below refer to detailed information provided in section 2

Accommodation

The Bulls Head Hotel, 86 The Street, Brecon, Powys LD3 7LS

Tel: 01874 622044 Fax: 01874 625321

Good-value overnight accommodation (2 rooms sleeping up to 6), pub grub and a great selection of real ales. Town-centre location.

Drws Nesaf, Abergwrelych House, Pontwalby, Glynneath SA11 5LN

Tel: 01639 720035

A charming mid-Victorian cottage in beautiful walking country. Self-catering accommodation comprises sitting room/diner, kitchen, 2 bedrooms, shower room, patio.

The Tai'r Bull Inn, Libanus, Nr. Brecon, Powys LD3 8EL

Tel: 01874 625849

A very well-kept roadside inn offering good food, B&B accommodation and superb views of the Brecon Beacons. 148

Ty Andrew Guest House, 33 Seymour Street, Aberdare, Mid-Glamorgan CF44 7BL

Tel: 01685 876603

Bed & Breakfast guest house with rooms (some en suite) ranging from singles to a family room. Drying facilities available.

The White Swan, Llanfrynach, Brecon, Powys LD3 7BZ

Tel: 01874 665276
website: www.the-white-swan.com

An excellent pub-restaurant in a row of smart black-and-white cottages. Sister establishment offering luxurious self-catering accommodation nearby. 150

Food and Drink

The Bulls Head Hotel, 86 The Street, Brecon, Powys LD3 7LS

Tel: 01874 622044 Fax: 01874 625321

Good-value overnight accommodation (2 rooms sleeping up to 6), pub grub and a great selection of real ales. Town-centre location.

The Tai'r Bull Inn, Libanus, Nr. Brecon, Powys LD3 8EL

Tel: 01874 625849

A very well-kept roadside inn offering good food, B&B accommodation and superb views of the Brecon Beacons. 148

The Wheatsheaf, Wheat Street, Brecon, Powys LD3 7DG

Tel: 01874 611109

A town-centre pub with a long, spacious bar. Pool table. Good bar food, good beer, young crowd.

The White Swan, Llanfrynach, Brecon, Powys LD3 7BZ

Tel: 01874 665276
website: www.the-white-swan.com

An excellent pub-restaurant in a row of smart black-and-white cottages. Sister establishment offering luxurious self-catering accommodation nearby. 150

Morlais Castle

Pant, Dowlais, Merthyr Tydfil CF48 2UY
Tel: 01685 722822 Fax: 01685 388700

Sec/Manager:	Myrig Price
Professional:	Huw Jarrett
Directions:	2¼ miles NE of Merthyr Tydfil. From M4 junction 32 take the A470 (Pontypridd, Merthyr Tydfil). After 16 miles turn right onto the A4060, proceed 4 miles, turn left onto the A465 (Heads of the Valleys road). After 1 mile turn right into Pant Rd. Entrance after 1¼ miles.
Date Founded:	1900
Type of Course:	Moorland
No of Holes:	18
Length:	6320 yds (5775 mtrs)
Par:	71
SSS:	71
Green Fees:	Weekdays: £16; Weekends/Bank Holidays: £20
Visitors:	Welcome: Contact Club in advance, weekends by prior arrangement
Societies:	Welcome: Contact Club in advance
Facilities:	Putting Green, Chipping Green, Club Hire, Trolley Hire, Buggy Hire, Bar, Restaurant

Accommodation, Food and Drink

Reference numbers below refer to detailed
information provided in section 2

Accommodation

The Bulls Head Hotel, 86 The Street, Brecon, Powys LD3 7LS

Tel: 01874 622044 Fax: 01874 625321

Good-value overnight accommodation (2 rooms
sleeping up to 6), pub grub and a great selection of
real ales. Town-centre location.

Drws Nesaf, Abergwrelych House, Pontwalby, Glynneath SA11 5LN

Tel: 01639 720035

A charming mid-Victorian cottage in beautiful
walking country. Self-catering accommodation
comprises sitting room/diner, kitchen, 2 bedrooms,
shower room, patio.

The Tai'r Bull Inn, Libanus, Nr. Brecon, Powys LD3 8EL

Tel: 01874 625849

A very well-kept roadside inn offering good food, B&B
accommodation and superb views of the Brecon
Beacons.   148

Ty Andrew Guest House, 33 Seymour Street, Aberdare, Mid-Glamorgan CF44 7BL

Tel: 01685 876603

Bed & Breakfast guest house with rooms (some en
suite) ranging from singles to a family room. Drying
facilities available.

The White Swan, Llanfrynach, Brecon, Powys LD3 7BZ

Tel: 01874 665276

website: www.the-white-swan.com

An excellent pub-restaurant in a row of smart black-
and-white cottages. Sister establishment offering
luxurious self-catering accommodation nearby.   150

Food and Drink

The Bulls Head Hotel, 86 The Street, Brecon, Powys LD3 7LS

Tel: 01874 622044 Fax: 01874 625321

Good-value overnight accommodation (2 rooms
sleeping up to 6), pub grub and a great selection of
real ales. Town-centre location.

The Tai'r Bull Inn, Libanus, Nr. Brecon, Powys LD3 8EL

Tel: 01874 625849

A very well-kept roadside inn offering good food, B&B
accommodation and superb views of the Brecon
Beacons.   148

The Wheatsheaf, Wheat Street, Brecon, Powys LD3 7DG

Tel: 01874 611109

A town-centre pub with a long, spacious bar. Pool
table. Good bar food, good beer, young crowd.

The White Swan, Llanfrynach, Brecon, Powys LD3 7BZ

Tel: 01874 665276

website: www.the-white-swan.com

An excellent pub-restaurant in a row of smart black-
and-white cottages. Sister establishment offering
luxurious self-catering accommodation nearby.   150

Mountain Ash Golf Club

Cefnpennar, Mountain Ash CF45 4DT

Tel: 01443 479459 Fax: 01443 479459

Sec/Manager:	Mr. Mathews
Professional:	Marcus Wills
Directions:	1 mile N of Mountain Ash. Take A4059 Pontypridd to Aberdare road. At roundabout by Cwmbach Station just north of Mountain Ash, turn right, signed Cwmbach, into Bro Deg. Follow round and join Cefnpennar Rd. Follow this road for ¾ mile and entrance is on right hand side.
Date Founded:	1908
Type of Course:	Moorland
No of Holes:	18
Length:	5553 yds (5125 mtrs)
Par:	69
SSS:	67
Green Fees:	Weekdays: £15 per day; Weekends/Bank Holidays: £18 per day
Visitors:	Welcome: Contact Club in advance
Societies:	Welcome: Unable to play Friday, Saturday and Sunday. Contact Club in writing or by phone

Facilities: Putting Green, Trolley Hire, Bar, Restaurant

Accommodation, Food and Drink

Reference numbers below refer to detailed information provided in section 2

Accommodation

The Bulls Head Hotel, 86 The Street, Brecon, Powys LD3 7LS

Tel: 01874 622044 Fax: 01874 625321

Good-value overnight accommodation (2 rooms sleeping up to 6), pub grub and a great selection of real ales. Town-centre location.

Drws Nesaf, Abergwrelych House, Pontwalby, Glynneath SA11 5LN

Tel: 01639 720035

A charming mid-Victorian cottage in beautiful walking country. Self-catering accommodation comprises sitting room/diner, kitchen, 2 bedrooms, shower room, patio.

The Tai'r Bull Inn, Libanus, Nr. Brecon, Powys LD3 8EL

Tel: 01874 625849

A very well-kept roadside inn offering good food, B&B accommodation and superb views of the Brecon Beacons. 148

Ty Andrew Guest House, 33 Seymour Street, Aberdare, Mid-Glamorgan CF44 7BL

Tel: 01685 876603

Bed & Breakfast guest house with rooms (some en suite) ranging from singles to a family room. Drying facilities available.

The White Swan, Llanfrynach, Brecon, Powys LD3 7BZ

Tel: 01874 665276
website: www.the-white-swan.com
An excellent pub-restaurant in a row of smart black-and-white cottages. Sister establishment offering luxurious self-catering accommodation nearby. 150

Food and Drink

The Bulls Head Hotel, 86 The Street, Brecon, Powys LD3 7LS

Tel: 01874 622044 Fax: 01874 625321

Good-value overnight accommodation (2 rooms sleeping up to 6), pub grub and a great selection of real ales. Town-centre location.

The Tai'r Bull Inn, Libanus, Nr. Brecon, Powys LD3 8EL

Tel: 01874 625849

A very well-kept roadside inn offering good food, B&B accommodation and superb views of the Brecon Beacons. 148

The Wheatsheaf, Wheat Street, Brecon, Powys LD3 7DG

Tel: 01874 611109

A town-centre pub with a long, spacious bar. Pool table. Good bar food, good beer, young crowd.

The White Swan, Llanfrynach, Brecon, Powys LD3 7BZ

Tel: 01874 665276
website: www.the-white-swan.com
An excellent pub-restaurant in a row of smart black-and-white cottages. Sister establishment offering luxurious self-catering accommodation nearby. 150

Mountain Lakes Golf Club

Blaengwynlais, Caerphilly CF8 1NG

Tel: 02920 861128 Fax: 02920 863243

Sec/Manager: Phillip Pate

Professional: Sion Bedd

Directions: 1½ miles SW of Caerphilly. From M4 junction 32 take the A4054 north (Taff's Well), after ½ mile turn right onto minor road signed Castell Coch. Entrance after 2 miles on left hand side.

Visitors: Welcome: Contact Club in advance

Societies: Welcome: Contact Club in advance

Facilities: Putting Green, Chipping Green, Club Hire, Trolley Hire, Bar, Restaurant, Driving Range

Castle Heights

Date Founded: 1982

Type of Course: Mountain, Heathland, Parkland

No of Holes: 9

Length: 2800 yds (2584 mtrs)

Par: 34

SSS: 32

Green Fees: Weekdays: £7.50 per day;
Weekends/Bank Holidays:
£7.50 per day

Mountain Lake

Date Founded: 1989

Type of Course: Mountain

No of Holes: 18

Length: 6100 yds (5630 mtrs)

Par: 72

SSS: 71

Green Fees: Weekdays: £18 per day;
Weekends/Bank Holidays: £18
per day

Accommodation, Food and Drink

Reference numbers below refer to detailed
information provided in section 2

Accommodation

**The Greyhound Inn, Christchurch, Newport,
South Wales NP18 1JJ**

Tel: 01633 420306 Fax: 01633 430588

A handsome late 19th century gabled inn with a
proper village atmosphere, real ales and very good
food. Friendly and inviting.   109

**The Milton Hotel, Llanwern, Newport,
Gwent NP16 6DU**

Tel: 01633 412432

Home-cooked food, real ales and self-catering
accommodation in a former hunting lodge an easy
drive from exit 24 of the M4.   110

**The Priory Hotel & Restaurant, Caerleon,
South Wales NP18 1AG**

Tel: 01633 421241 Fax: 01633 421271

A historic hotel of exceptional quality and character,
set in its own secluded grounds in the Roman town of
Caerleon.   112

**The White Horse Inn, Davis Row, Pentwyn,
Nr. Fochriw, Bargoed, Mid-Glamorgan CF81 9NP**

Tel: 01685 841215

Popular inn open seven days a week for breakfast,
lunch and dinner. Super home-made pies and lots
more. Two B&B rooms planned.

Food and Drink

**Clawdd Coch Guest House, Pendoylan,
Vale of Glamorgan CF71 7UP**

Tel: 01446 760645

Versatile B&B facilities in a 17th century house with
five beautifully appointed bedrooms. Golfing breaks a
speciality.   115

**The Milton Hotel, Llanwern, Newport,
Gwent NP16 6DU**

Tel: 01633 412432

Home-cooked food, real ales and self-catering
accommodation in a former hunting lodge an easy
drive from exit 24 of the M4.   110

**The Priory Hotel & Restaurant, Caerleon,
South Wales NP18 1AG**

Tel: 01633 421241 Fax: 01633 421271

A historic hotel of exceptional quality and character,
set in its own secluded grounds in the Roman town of
Caerleon.   112

**The White Horse Inn, Davis Row, Pentwyn,
Nr. Fochriw, Bargoed, Mid-Glamorgan CF81 9NP**

Tel: 01685 841215

Popular inn open seven days a week for breakfast,
lunch and dinner. Super home-made pies and lots
more. Two B&B rooms planned.

Pontypridd Golf Club

Ty Hwyn Road, Pontypridd, CF37 4DJ

Tel: 01443 409904 Fax: 01443 491622

Pontypridd Golf Club, like the Whitehall club, is
situated just off the A470 road, and like the other
Rhondda clubs it is also a mountain course,

which, having been founded as long ago as 1905, has matured perfectly. Whereas the Rhondda Golf Club lies at the head of the great Rhondda Valleys, Pontypridd lies at the foot. The busy market town of Pontypridd is the hotbed of rugby in these parts, so don't be surprised if every other local golfer you happen to talk to at this golf club is either a former Welsh international rugby player, a present Welsh international player, a first class rugby player or is somehow involved with the Pontypridd Rugby Club. Like the rest of South Wales, rugby is a fervent religion here and usually everyone takes up the game of rugby at an early age, with golf taking its place as an active sport when the bones begin to creak and one finds the rugby wounds begin to take much longer to heal. This is why I wrote earlier in this guidebook the reason why the majority of golf courses in Wales (other than the links courses) are to be found alongside the slopes or on top of a mountain or hillside-the reason being that all the flat pieces of land were quickly snapped up for rugby grounds before golf courses became popular.

and quickly learned at an early age to accept them and go on to play the next hole without throwing a tantrum. Like I said, this course is a great character builder. It most certainly played its part in moulding Phillip Price into the fine professional player he is.

The course at Pontypridd is no exception to the rule. It's a mountain course with plenty of character, it's tough, it's got plenty of rough, it's often windy, the greens can be tricky and it requires ones full concentration on every shot. But it is also a wonderful course to play on. It's the gorgeous mountain turf which makes it so special. It's a delight to walk on and a delight to play a shot off, but the tricky greens are something you have to learn to overcome. The awkward stances you have to take and the rough you have to avoid, makes it a real character-building kind of challenge.

Phillip Price, the World Cup, Dunhill Cup and European Tour professional golfer, started his golf career here at Pontypridd (one of the rare exceptions from the Pontypridd area who chose golf as a career in preference to rugby), and represented the club as an amateur and also as a professional for a time. Anyone who has seen him play will realise why he is a cool character after they visit the Pontypridd course. He found every difficulty that could be thrown at him at his home club

Sec/Manager:	Vicky Hooley
Professional:	Wade Walters
Directions:	¾ mile E of Pontypridd. From M4 junction 32 take the A470 (Pontypridd) and exit after 6½ miles at Pontypridd taking the A4054 (Cilfynidd). After 100 yds turn right into Craig-yr-Halfa Rd, leading to Hospital Rd and then Ty Hwn Rd. Entrance after ¾ mile on right hand side.
Date Founded:	1906
Type of Course:	Mountainous
No of Holes:	18
Length:	5596 yds (5165 mtrs)
Par:	69
SSS:	69
Green Fees:	Under Review. Contact Club
Visitors:	Welcome: Weekends with member only.
Societies:	Welcome: Excluding weekends. Contact club by phone or in writing.
Facilities:	Putting Green, Chipping Green, Driving Range, Buggy Hire, Bar, Restaurant

Accommodation, Food and Drink

Reference numbers below refer to detailed information provided in section 2

Accommodation

The Crown Hotel, Varteg, Nr. Pontypool, Monmouthshire NP4 8UG

Tel: 01495 774312

Good atmosphere and good fun in a cheerful pub-hotel with B&B accommodation and evening meals with notice.

Ty Andrew Guest House, 33 Seymour Street, Aberdare, Mid-Glamorgan CF44 7BL

Tel: 01685 876603

Bed & Breakfast guest house with rooms (some en suite) ranging from singles to a family room. Drying facilities available.

Ty Shon Jacob Farm, Coch-y-North Lane, Tranch, Nr. Pontypool, Monmouthshire NP4 6BP

Tel/Fax: 01495 757536
e-mail: tyshonfarm@aol.com

Peace, quiet and great views on a 36-acre farm 1,250 feet above sea level. Three twin bedrooms for B&B: dinner by arrangement.

The White Horse Inn, Davis Row, Pentwyn, Nr. Fochriw, Bargoed, Mid-Glamorgan CF81 9NP

Tel: 01685 841215

Popular inn open seven days a week for breakfast, lunch and dinner. Super home-made pies and lots more. Two B&B rooms planned.

Food and Drink

The Crown Hotel, Varteg, Nr. Pontypool, Monmouthshire NP4 8UG

Tel: 01495 774312

Good atmosphere and good fun in a cheerful pub-hotel with B&B accommodation and evening meals with notice.

St Julian Inn, Newport, South Wales NP18 1QA

Tel: 01633 243548 Fax: 01633 243562

A welcoming old inn with the road on one side and the River Usk on the other. Bar-style menu, award-winning real ales.   108

The White Horse Inn, Davis Row, Pentwyn, Nr. Fochriw, Bargoed, Mid-Glamorgan CF81 9NP

Tel: 01685 841215

Popular inn open seven days a week for breakfast, lunch and dinner. Super home-made pies and lots more. Two B&B rooms planned.

from the fact that it is used for a section of the final qualifying rounds of the Amateur Championship whenever the great event is hosted by Royal Porthcawl. Designed by that great golf architect H. S. Colt in 1922, the course, like most seaside courses, is quite flattish and, I suppose, is best described as being partly a links course and partly downland.

Colt, almost certainly, took great and wicked delight in shaping the holes in the area of the linksland he was asked to design as part of the course. Here nature had created what can only be described as a perfect site for any sadistic tendencies lurking in a golf designers mind. Taking every advantage of what lay before him H. S. Colt produced a wonderful example of how to turn linksland with all the appearance of a Moonscape into a brute of a golf challenge. Huge sand dunes, similar to the ones to be found at Burnham and Berrow on the opposite side of the Bristol Channel, have been cleverly used to blind a hole or somehow guard a hole, with the thick, tufted grass growing on every inch of the dunes making it extremely difficult to satisfactorily remove any wayward golf ball. With a number of narrow burns and a few reedy wet patches to also negotiate, many a promising score has often suddenly turned into something of a nightmare over this demanding closing portion of ones round during many an important championship. The remainder of the course over the downland section has all the appearance of an easier challenge, but there

Pyle & Kenfig Golf Club

Waun-y-Mer, Kenfig, Bridgend CF33 4PU

Tel: **01656 783093** Fax: **01656 772822**

This is the third of the great coastal championship courses of Mid Glamorgan and one that is reckoned to be almost as tough as its two neighbours at Porthcawl and Southerndown. A measure of how tough the Pyle and Kenfig can be taken

is still gorse and bracken to overcome and a number of stony ruts and hollows to contend with. Being wide open to the elements, woe betide any smug look of a player who thought he was carving out a good score if the wind suddenly picks up and then howls in from the Bristol Channel, as it often so easily does. Then it can be a rather sad golfer who returns to the sanctuary of Pyle and Kenfig's large, comfortable and smart modern clubhouse to drown his sorrows.

Indeed, like every challenging course, one either loves it or hates it, depending on how well one performs on the day. For myself, I love the challenge of every top quality course after having played well or not. The course at Pyle and Kenfig is no exception.

Sec/Manager:	Stephen Anthony
Professional:	Robert Evans
Directions:	6 miles W of Bridgend centre. From M4 junction 37 take the A4229 (Porthcawl). After 1 mile at an Esso Service Station turn right into Heol Drewi Rd. Entrance after ¾ mile on left hand side.
Date Founded:	1926
Type of Course:	Links
No of Holes:	18
Length:	6278 yds (5795 mtrs)
Par:	71
SSS:	73
Green Fees:	Weekdays: £30 per day; Weekends/Bank Holidays: Unable to play
Visitors:	Welcome: Excluding weekends. Contact Club in advance
Societies:	Welcome: Contact Club in advance by phone
Facilities:	Putting Green, Chipping Green, Driving Range, Trolley Hire, Bar, Restaurant

Accommodation, Food and Drink

Reference numbers below refer to detailed information provided in section 2

Accommodation

Crossways House, Cowbridge, Vale of Glamorgan CF71 7LJ
Tel: 01446 773171 Fax: 01446 771707
e-mail: enquiries@crosswayshouse.co.uk
website: www.crosswayshouse.co.uk
Three B&B bedrooms and a self-catering flat in a

lovely country mansion set in 6 acres ¾ mile west of Cowbridge (B4270).

Drws Nesaf, Abergwrelych House, Pontwalby, Glynneath SA11 5LN
Tel: 01639 720035
A charming mid-Victorian cottage in beautiful walking country. Self-catering accommodation comprises sitting room/diner, kitchen, 2 bedrooms, shower room, patio.

Fairways Hotel, Porthcawl, South Glamorgan CF36 3LS
Tel: 01656 782085 Fax: 01656 785351
e-mail: fairwayshotel@aol.com
website: www.bridgend.gov.uk
Twenty-five en suite bedrooms in a smartly refurbished family-run hotel near the seafront. Restaurant, lounge bar, residents' lounge.   114

Hurst Dene Guest House, Uplands, Swansea SA2 0LJ
Tel/Fax: 01792 280920
website: www.hurstdene.co.uk
Ten bedrooms for Bed & Breakfast in a large Victorian terraced house. Also self-catering units. In a Swansea suburb near the sea.   124

Mair's Bed & Breakfast, 9 Coychurch Road, Bridgend, Mid Glamorgan CF31 3AR
Tel/Fax: 01656 654838
Homely Bed & Breakfast accommodation in six rooms (some en suite) in a private house. Disabled facilities on the ground floor.

Penuchadre Farm, St Brides Major, Bridgend, Mid Glamorgan CF32 0TE
Tel: 01656 880313
Bed & Breakfast accommodation in two single rooms and two doubles. There's a pub with excellent food next door.

Ty'n-y-Caeau, Margam Village, Port Talbot, West Glamorgan SA13 2NW
Tel: 01639 883897 Fax: 01639 895570
e-mail: gaen@tynycaeau.freeserve.co.uk
A large country house with superb gardens and comfortable en suite double or family rooms. Self catering also available.

Food and Drink

CJ's Wine Bar & Restaurant, Oystermouth, Swansea SA3 4DN
Tel: 01792 361246 Fax: 01792 419849
Cosy, friendly wine bar-café-restaurant in a row of shops close to the seafront. Varied menu with steaks and grill specialities and a vast cocktail list.   122

Fairways Hotel, Porthcawl, South Glamorgan CF36 3LS
Tel: 01656 782085 Fax: 01656 785351
e-mail: fairwayshotel@aol.com
website: www.bridgend.gov.uk

Twenty-five en suite bedrooms in a smartly refurbished family-run hotel near the seafront. Restaurant, lounge bar, residents' lounge.   114

The Mardy Hotel, 117 High Street, Gorseinon, Swansea SA4 2BT

Tel: 01792 892616

Snacks, burgers, scampi and steaks on the menu, with roasts on Sunday. Darts, pool, live entertainment three nights a week.

Rhondda Golf Club

Penrhys, Rhondda CF43 3PW

Tel: 01443 441384   Fax: 01443 441384

If Aberdare is "Queen of the Valleys" then Rhondda Golf Club must surely be the "King of the Valleys" as it stands majestically high above the two famous valleys that make up the Rhondda area, which once boasted more than a hundred high producing collieries that exported the best coal in the world to the rest of the world. The two valleys are named Rhondda Fawr and Rhondda Foch respectively (which translated means great, and small). Today there remains nothing but the derelict ruins of these great mineworks, and the great ugly scars are fast disappearing as the valleys become green again.

There is still much disrepair in the valleys, but don't let this deter you from visiting the Rhondda club where, like the rest of the Welsh valley folk, they are extremely friendly. The Rhondda club, like many other Welsh clubs, started out life as a nine-hole layout way back in 1910. Just a year later the president of the club, the wealthy Sir Leonard Wilkinson, used his influence and the backing of a few local business associates to successfully negotiate a leasing agreement to develop the course into 15-holes. At the same time, realising they were now going to stay, they also built a modest sort of clubhouse. The clubhouse remained as it was for many a long year, but a large and solid brick structure now stands proudly atop this high mountaintop site. By the mid-1930's the course had blossomed into a full-grown 18-hole course and was prospering, which meant that as the years went by the club was in the position to be able to purchase the land they leased. The club was able to do this in 1985, but the following summer on the eve of the club's qualifying rounds for their Club Championship, it was discovered that ten greens had been vandalised.

This, however, strangely proved a blessing in disguise because the Cardiff-based golf course designers and consultants MRM-Sandow, read of the club's plight and offered to repair the damage for free. As a result of this MRM-Sandow decided to become the main sponsors of Rhondda Golf Club's first ever pro-am event.

I was fortunate to be invited to play in the event, and the only regret was that I wish I had discovered the course many years earlier. The springy, mountain turf which had its roots in many inches of peaty soil, made every fairway shot a joy to hit as the ball stood as if on a tee waiting to be struck cleanly and without any effort. Being as high as you can get on this mountain top course and with nothing but open spaces, it is also an invigorating place to be now that the air is fresh and free from the grime of the once vast coalfields. There are many excellent holes to be found here, with the 18th being a good finishing hole as you drive from an elevated tee and hopefully find the rather small green with your approach shot. Being on a mountain top also means it is not too difficult a course to walk. However, there is always a catch somewhere to found and here it's the wind that blows over the two valleys, making it extremely difficult to score well on if one is unlucky enough to choose such a day to visit.

Sec/Manager:	G Rees
Professional:	G Bebb
Directions:	3 miles SW of Rhondda. From junction 32 of the M4 take the A470 to Pontypridd and then the A4058 towards Rhondda. Entrance is on the right 2 miles after Porth
Date Founded:	1904
Type of Course:	Mountain
No of Holes:	18
Length:	6205 yds (5670 mtrs)
Par:	70
SSS:	71
Green Fees:	Weekdays: £20 per day; Weekends/Bank Holidays: £25 per day
Visitors:	Welcome: Restricted weekends. Contact Club in advance
Societies:	Welcome: By arrangement. Contact Club in advance
Facilities:	Putting Green, Driving Range, Club Hire, Trolley Hire, Bar, Restaurant

Accommodation, Food and Drink

Reference numbers below refer to detailed information provided in section 2

Accommodation

The Crown Hotel, Varteg, Nr. Pontypool, Monmouthshire NP4 8UG

Tel: 01495 774312

Good atmosphere and good fun in a cheerful pub-hotel with B&B accommodation and evening meals with notice.

Fairways Hotel, Porthcawl,
South Glamorgan CF36 3LS

Tel: 01656 782085 Fax: 01656 785351
e-mail: fairwayshotel@aol.com
website: www.bridgend.gov.uk

Twenty-five en suite bedrooms in a smartly refurbished family-run hotel near the seafront. Restaurant, lounge bar, residents' lounge.　114

Ty Andrew Guest House, 33 Seymour Street,
Aberdare, Mid-Glamorgan CF44 7BL

Tel: 01685 876603

Bed & Breakfast guest house with rooms (some en suite) ranging from singles to a family room. Drying facilities available.

Ty Shon Jacob Farm, Coch-y-North Lane,
Tranch, Nr. Pontypool, Monmouthshire NP4 6BP

Tel/Fax: 01495 757536
e-mail: tyshonfarm@aol.com

Peace, quiet and great views on a 36-acre farm 1,250 feet above sea level. Three twin bedrooms for B&B: dinner by arrangement.

The White Horse Inn, Davis Row, Pentwyn,
Nr. Fochriw, Bargoed, Mid-Glamorgan CF81 9NP

Tel: 01685 841215

Popular inn open seven days a week for breakfast, lunch and dinner. Super home-made pies and lots more. Two B&B rooms planned.

Food and Drink

The Crown Hotel, Varteg, Nr. Pontypool,
Monmouthshire NP4 8UG

Tel: 01495 774312

Good atmosphere and good fun in a cheerful pub-hotel with B&B accommodation and evening meals with notice.

Fairways Hotel, Porthcawl,
South Glamorgan CF36 3LS

Tel: 01656 782085 Fax: 01656 785351
e-mail: fairwayshotel@aol.com
website: www.bridgend.gov.uk

Twenty-five en suite bedrooms in a smartly refurbished family-run hotel near the seafront. Restaurant, lounge bar, residents' lounge.　114

St Julian Inn, Newport, South Wales NP18 1QA

Tel: 01633 243548 Fax: 01633 243562

A welcoming old inn with the road on one side and the River Usk on the other. Bar-style menu, award-winning real ales.　108

The White Horse Inn, Davis Row, Pentwyn,
Nr. Fochriw, Bargoed, Mid-Glamorgan CF81 9NP

Tel: 01685 841215

Popular inn open seven days a week for breakfast,

lunch and dinner. Super home-made pies and lots more. Two B&B rooms planned.

Royal Porthcawl Golf Club

Rest Bay, Porthcawl CF36 3UW
Tel: 01656 782251 Fax: 01656 771687

One of only two Royal golf clubs in Wales, Royal Porthcawl Golf Club is often described as the premier club in Wales. Arguably, maybe this is so. Myself, however, having had a long love affair with the great golf courses to be found in both South Wales and North Wales, prefer to describe the Porthcawl club as the premier club in the south of the Principality, with Royal St David's Golf Club as the premier club of North Wales. I've known, visited, written about and played these two great clubs often enough to realise that they are both fantastic courses to play and delightful places at which to enjoy oneself. With this in mind I have long decided they both should stand on an equal footing. Royal Porthcawl is, indeed, the number one club in the south to play if one likes his or her golf challenge to be rough, tough and extremely difficult-even on a balmy summer's day. When the rain arrives to join the frequent strong winds, which blow off the Bristol Channel, it can be one of the toughest tests of golf in the world. The very strong USA Walker Cup team, which included the great Tiger Woods,

learned this the hard way when losing 14 matches to 10 against Great Britain and Ireland in horrendous weather during 1995.

On the eve of the Amateur Championship in 1988, the much-lamented Peter Dobereiner, the doyen of modern golf writers, described the Porthcawl links as being " at its scruffiest best". Some members took offence, but Peter was actually highly praising the condition of the course. His meaning being that the course had not been over manicured, or tarted up to use a better word, and therefore had been left as nature intended it to be as far as the rough was concerned-perfectly ideal for a prestigious event such as The Amateur. Believe me, the "Old Sages " of the famous club certainly knew what he was getting at in his description. The "Lovely Old Lady of the South" has hosted many prestigious events, amateur and professional, since being founded in 1891, but far too many to mention here.

A feature of this fascinating old links is that unlike many links the sea is in sight from every hole, as are the splendid views of Swansea Bay. The opening three holes run alongside the edge of Rest Bay and any violent hook-shot is in danger of finding the beach. Great character-building holes these. The 18th is one of the finest finishes to be found on a links. A par 4 with a downhill fairway all the way to the sea and into the prevailing wind, with a large and undulating green difficult to stop the ball on, makes it one of the great memorable holes in golf. A tough par 72 for the amateur golfer, but delightfully enjoyable. The old wooden clubhouse is not too bad either. Still in its original state, it creates a wonderful atmosphere of golf's early days in Wales, and I for one hope it never disappears.

Sec/Manager:	S.W Prescott
Professional:	Peter Evans
Directions:	6 miles W of Bridgend centre. From M4 junction 37 take the A4229 (Porthcawl). After 2½ miles at roundabout (Nottage) take third exit, Fulmar Rd. After 1 mile turn sharp right along West Bay Rd. Entrance after ½ mile at the end.
Date Founded:	1891
Type of Course:	Heathland
No of Holes:	18
Length:	6406 yds (5913 mtrs)
Par:	72
SSS:	74
Green Fees:	Weekdays: £45 per day; Weekends/Bank Holidays: £60 per day
Visitors:	Welcome: Restricted weekends. Contact Club in advance
Societies:	Welcome: By arrangement. Contact Club in writing
Facilities:	Putting Green, Chipping Green, Driving Range, Club Hire, Trolley Hire, Bar, Restaurant, Practice Area

Accommodation, Food and Drink

Reference numbers below refer to detailed information provided in section 2

Accommodation

Clawdd Coch Guest House, Pendoylan, Vale of Glamorgan CF71 7UP

Tel: 01446 760645

Versatile B&B facilities in a 17th century house with five beautifully appointed bedrooms. Golfing breaks a speciality. 115

Crossways House, Cowbridge, Vale of Glamorgan CF71 7LJ

Tel: 01446 773171 Fax: 01446 771707
e-mail: enquiries@crosswayshouse.co.uk
website: www.crosswayshouse.co.uk

Three B&B bedrooms and a self-catering flat in a lovely country mansion set in 6 acres ¾ mile west of Cowbridge (B4270).

Drws Nesaf, Abergwrelych House, Pontwalby, Glynneath SA11 5LN

Tel: 01639 720035

A charming mid-Victorian cottage in beautiful walking country. Self-catering accommodation comprises sitting room/diner, kitchen, 2 bedrooms, shower room, patio.

Fairways Hotel, Porthcawl,
South Glamorgan CF36 3LS

Tel: 01656 782085 Fax: 01656 785351
e-mail: fairwayshotel@aol.com
website: www.bridgend.gov.uk

Twenty-five en suite bedrooms in a smartly
refurbished family-run hotel near the seafront.
Restaurant, lounge bar, residents' lounge.   114

Hurst Dene Guest House, Uplands,
Swansea SA2 0LJ

Tel/Fax: 01792 280920
website: www.hurstdene.co.uk

Ten bedrooms for Bed & Breakfast in a large Victorian
terraced house. Also self-catering units. In a Swansea
suburb near the sea.   124

Mair's Bed & Breakfast, 9 Coychurch Road,
Bridgend, Mid Glamorgan CF31 3AR

Tel/Fax: 01656 654838

Homely Bed & Breakfast accommodation in six rooms
(some en suite) in a private house. Disabled facilities
on the ground floor.

Penuchadre Farm, St Brides Major, Bridgend,
Mid Glamorgan CF32 0TE

Tel: 01656 880313

Bed & Breakfast accommodation in two single rooms
and two doubles. There's a pub with excellent food
next door.

Ty'n-y-Caeau, Margam Village, Port Talbot,
West Glamorgan SA13 2NW

Tel: 01639 883897 Fax: 01639 895570
e-mail: gaen@tynycaeau.freeserve.co.uk

A large country house with superb gardens and
comfortable en suite double or family rooms. Self
catering also available.

Food and Drink

CJ's Wine Bar & Restaurant, Oystermouth,
Swansea SA3 4DN

Tel: 01792 361246 Fax: 01792 419849

Cosy, friendly wine bar-café-restaurant in a row of
shops close to the seafront. Varied menu with steaks
and grill specialities and a vast cocktail list.   122

Fairways Hotel, Porthcawl,
South Glamorgan CF36 3LS

Tel: 01656 782085 Fax: 01656 785351
e-mail: fairwayshotel@aol.com
website: www.bridgend.gov.uk

Twenty-five en suite bedrooms in a smartly
refurbished family-run hotel near the seafront.
Restaurant, lounge bar, residents' lounge.   114

The Mardy Hotel, 117 High Street, Gorseinon,
Swansea SA4 2BT

Tel: 01792 892616

Snacks, burgers, scampi and steaks on the menu, with
roasts on Sunday. Darts, pool, live entertainment
three nights a week.

Southerndown
Golf Club

Ewenny, Ogmore-by-Sea, Bridgend CF32 0QP
Tel: 01656 880326 Fax: 01656 880317

When I tell you that that some of the finest golfing brains over the last hundred years have each
in their turn played a part in moulding the lay-
out of the Southerndown course, you will quickly
realise why it has long held the reputation of being one of the outstanding natural downland
courses in the world and one which has been
enjoyed by countless thousands of visiting golfers in this golfing Mecca in the southern corner
of Mid Glamorgan. Willie Fernie set the pot boil-
ing when he was commissioned to design the
original in 1905. Harry Vardon and James Braid
then added their bit of spice to give the course an
extra satisfying bite. Then along came W. Herbert
Fowler in 1907, followed by Willie Park some six
years later, to add their special ingredients. Harry
Colt then appeared in 1918 with his mixture of
expertise, before Donald Steel recently came along
to stir the course up with excellent and extensive
alterations. Had all the experts been top-class
chefs the Southerndown course could have been
served up as a highly tasteful starter to the extra-
special main course of Royal Porthcawl, followed
by Pyle and Kenfig as the satisfying dessert of a
top quality Cordon Bleu Menu.

Sited high above the coastline and close to the
ruins of Ogmore Castle, the course is an absolute
delight to play, especially so on a calm and warm
summer's day with a light breeze coming off the
Bristol Channel. During my reporting days I liked
nothing better than making the journey to
Southerndown when the club was hosting the
prestigious Duncan Putter, because I found the
course equally enjoyable just to walk on and to
watch others playing as to play it myself. Held by
tradition over the Easter weekend, the Duncan
Putter has always attracted a high quality field of
amateur players since the trophy was put up for

competition by Colonel Anthony Duncan (known by all as Tony), who was a member of the great Duncan family of Southerndown Golf Club fame. Tony Duncan was one of the great amateurs golfers of Wales, having won the Welsh Amateur on three occasions (1938, 1948 and 1952), runner-up in the Amateur Championship in 1939, winner of the Presidents Putter in 1948 and 1958 and the non-playing captain of the Walker Cup in 1953. He inaugurated the Duncan Putter (which is always held at Southerndown) as a 72-hole event as a means of encouragement for up-and-coming young Welsh golfers and to provide early-season top-quality competition for more established players. It certainly served its purpose well because it has attracted the top players annually from the four home countries right up to this very day, as well as placing Southerndown well and truly on the golfing map. The main defence of its wide-open spaces is, of course, the wind, with the thick bracken and gorse proving powerful reinforcements, as are the gently undulating fairways which throw the ball unexpectedly into the soul destroying bunkers as well as the often unplayable rough. Indeed, a great test of golf and also of ones character, which is why it has hosted so many different top-quality events over the years, including the Piccadilly Masters and the Martini International. Many top amateur events have also been held there including the Welsh Amateur Championship and the Welsh Ladies' Amateur Championship.

Bernard Darwin, the Walker Cup player and greatest golf writer of all time, rated Southerndown as one of his top favourite courses. No better recommendation can you get, believe me!

Sec/Manager: Alan Hughes

Professional: D. McMonagle

Directions: 2½ miles SW of Bridgend centre. From M4 junction 35 take A473 (Bridgend), at second roundabout carry onto A48 (Laleston). Take first left into Ewenny Rd (A4265 Ogmore by Sea). After ½ mile turn right into Ogmore Rd. Entrance after 1¼ miles on left hand side opposite Ogmore Castle entance.

Date Founded: 1906

Type of Course: Downland

No of Holes: 18

Length: 6417 yds (5923 mtrs)

Par: 70

SSS: 72

Green Fees: Weekdays: £25 per day; Weekends/Bank Holidays: £35 per day

Visitors: Welcome: Contact Club in advance

Societies: Welcome: Contact Club in advance

Facilities: Putting Green, Chipping Green, Practice Area, Driving Range, Trolley Hire, Buggy Hire, Bar, Restaurant

Accommodation, Food and Drink

Reference numbers below refer to detailed information provided in section 2

Accommodation

Crossways House, Cowbridge, Vale of Glamorgan CF71 7LJ

Tel: 01446 773171 Fax: 01446 771707
e-mail: enquiries@crosswayshouse.co.uk
website: www.crosswayshouse.co.uk

Three B&B bedrooms and a self-catering flat in a lovely country mansion set in 6 acres ¾ mile west of Cowbridge (B4270).

Drws Nesaf, Abergwrelych House, Pontwalby, Glynneath SA11 5LN

Tel: 01639 720035

A charming mid-Victorian cottage in beautiful walking country. Self-catering accommodation comprises sitting room/diner, kitchen, 2 bedrooms, shower room, patio.

Fairways Hotel, Porthcawl, South Glamorgan CF36 3LS

Tel: 01656 782085 Fax: 01656 785351
e-mail: fairwayshotel@aol.com
website: www.bridgend.gov.uk

Twenty-five en suite bedrooms in a smartly refurbished family-run hotel near the seafront. Restaurant, lounge bar, residents' lounge.   114

Hurst Dene Guest House, Uplands, Swansea SA2 0LJ

Tel/Fax: 01792 280920

website: www.hurstdene.co.uk

Ten bedrooms for Bed & Breakfast in a large Victorian terraced house. Also self-catering units. In a Swansea suburb near the sea. 124

Mair's Bed & Breakfast, 9 Coychurch Road, Bridgend, Mid Glamorgan CF31 3AR

Tel/Fax: 01656 654838

Homely Bed & Breakfast accommodation in six rooms (some en suite) in a private house. Disabled facilities on the ground floor.

Penuchadre Farm, St Brides Major, Bridgend, Mid Glamorgan CF32 0TE

Tel: 01656 880313

Bed & Breakfast accommodation in two single rooms and two doubles. There's a pub with excellent food next door.

Ty'n-y-Caeau, Margam Village, Port Talbot, West Glamorgan SA13 2NW

Tel: 01639 883897 Fax: 01639 895570
e-mail: gaen@tynycaeau.freeserve.co.uk

A large country house with superb gardens and comfortable en suite double or family rooms. Self catering also available.

Food and Drink

CJ's Wine Bar & Restaurant, Oystermouth, Swansea SA3 4DN

Tel: 01792 361246 Fax: 01792 419849

Cosy, friendly wine bar-café-restaurant in a row of shops close to the seafront. Varied menu with steaks and grill specialities and a vast cocktail list. 122

Fairways Hotel, Porthcawl, South Glamorgan CF36 3LS

Tel: 01656 782085 Fax: 01656 785351
e-mail: fairwayshotel@aol.com
website: www.bridgend.gov.uk

Twenty-five en suite bedrooms in a smartly refurbished family-run hotel near the seafront. Restaurant, lounge bar, residents' lounge. 114

The Mardy Hotel, 117 High Street, Gorseinon, Swansea SA4 2BT

Tel: 01792 892616

Snacks, burgers, scampi and steaks on the menu, with roasts on Sunday. Darts, pool, live entertainment three nights a week.

and tennis courts. There is also a luxury country hotel converted from a 17th century farmhouse and which has 24 full-sized and luxurious bedrooms. Easy to find, this 10-year old complex lies directly off Junction 35 of the M4 Motorway and is also a Pay and Play complex.

Sec/Manager:	K. Brazell
Professional:	J.Peters
Directions:	4¼ miles E of Bridgend centre. From M4 junction 35 take the A473 (Pencoed) at the first roundabout turn right into Felindre Rd (Llanilid). Proceed for 1¼ miles and turn right into minor road, turn right after ½ mile at T-junction. Entrance after 200 yds on left hand side.
Visitors:	Welcome: Contact Club in advance. Restricted play if no handicap certificate.
Societies:	Welcome: Contact Club in advance.
Facilities:	Putting Green, Chipping Green, Club Hire, Trolley Hire, Buggy Hire, Bar, Restaurant, Driving Range

St Mary's Hotel Golf & Country Club

St Mary's Hill, Pencoed CF35 5EA

Tel: 01656 861100 Fax: 01656 863400

The St Mary's Hotel, Golf and Country Club, boasts both an 18-hole parkland course and a 9-hole course, plus a 15-bay floodlit driving range

St Mary's

Date Founded:	1989
Type of Course:	Parkland
No of Holes:	18
Length:	5073 yds (4682 mtrs)
Par:	67
SSS:	65
Green Fees:	Weekdays: £15 per day; Weekends/Bank Holidays: £17 per day

Seven Oaks

Date Founded:	1992
Type of Course:	Parkland
No of Holes:	9
Length:	2426 yds (2239 mtrs)
Par:	35
SSS:	34
Green Fees:	Weekdays: £5 per round; Weekends/Bank Holidays: £6 per round

Accommodation, Food and Drink

Reference numbers below refer to detailed information provided in section 2

Accommodation

Clawdd Coch Guest House, Pendoylan, Vale of Glamorgan CF71 7UP

Tel: 01446 760645

Versatile B&B facilities in a 17th century house with five beautifully appointed bedrooms. Golfing breaks a speciality.   115

Crossways House, Cowbridge, Vale of Glamorgan CF71 7LJ

Tel: 01446 773171 Fax: 01446 771707
e-mail: enquiries@crosswayshouse.co.uk website: www.crosswayshouse.co.uk

Three B&B bedrooms and a self-catering flat in a lovely country mansion set in 6 acres ¾ mile west of Cowbridge (B4270).

Fairways Hotel, Porthcawl, South Glamorgan CF36 3LS

Tel: 01656 782085 Fax: 01656 785351
e-mail: fairwayshotel@aol.com
website: www.bridgend.gov.uk

Twenty-five en suite bedrooms in a smartly refurbished family-run hotel near the seafront. Restaurant, lounge bar, residents' lounge.   114

The White Horse Inn, Davis Row, Pentwyn, Nr. Fochriw, Bargoed, Mid-Glamorgan CF81 9NP

Tel: 01685 841215

Popular inn open seven days a week for breakfast, lunch and dinner. Super home-made pies and lots more. Two B&B rooms planned.

Windmill Cottages, Llansannor, Cowbridge, Vale of Glamorgan CF71 7TF

Tel/Fax: 01446 772470
e-mail: rosser@globalnet.co.uk

Quality self-catering accommodation in 19th century barn conversions adjacent to a working farm. Lovely rural setting five minutes from Cowbridge.   116

Food and Drink

Fairways Hotel, Porthcawl, South Glamorgan CF36 3LS

Tel: 01656 782085 Fax: 01656 785351
e-mail: fairwayshotel@aol.com
website: www.bridgend.gov.uk

Twenty-five en suite bedrooms in a smartly refurbished family-run hotel near the seafront. Restaurant, lounge bar, residents' lounge.   114

St Julian Inn, Newport, South Wales NP18 1QA

Tel: 01633 243548 Fax: 01633 243562

A welcoming old inn with the road on one side and the River Usk on the other. Bar-style menu, award-winning real ales.   108

The White Horse Inn, Davis Row, Pentwyn, Nr. Fochriw, Bargoed, Mid-Glamorgan CF81 9NP

Tel: 01685 841215

Popular inn open seven days a week for breakfast, lunch and dinner. Super home-made pies and lots more. Two B&B rooms planned.

SOUTH GLAMORGAN

Of the three counties (West Glamorgan, Mid Glamorgan and South Glamorgan) which emerged from the break up of the ancient county of Glamorganshire during the administrative reconstruction of the 1970s, South Glamorgan proved to be the smallest in area size but the most important of the three. Indeed, the most important county in the whole of the Principality, because within it's confines stood not only the largest city in Wales but also the capital city of Wales, namely, of course, Cardiff. Just before the old century ended it increased its importance, along with Cardiff, when the National Assembly for Wales came into being and made its headquarters in Cardiff Bay. The countryside in South Glamorgan is of a more pastoral nature than visitors from outside of Wales imagine. Having been given the image over the years that everywhere in South Wales was heavily industrialised with mine workings and huge steel factories and ugly coal tips, people are pleasantly surprised to discover that South Wales is as beautiful and well worth visiting as the rest of the proud Principality. South Glamorgan does not have the spectacular Welsh mountains to boast about, but it does have the beautiful Vale of Glamorgan. This Vale is an excellent area to visit and can be found inside the A48 road and is bordered by the A426 and B4268 roads all the way to the Bristol Channel coastline. In the many lanes that cross one another throughout the vale are pretty villages and dreamy little hamlets, which you come upon quite unexpectedly. Forget the seaside resorts and golf courses in this county for a while and spend some time exploring along the tree-lined lanes with their miniature and picturesque valleys, because they are overflowing with ancient history.

The pride of the Vale of Glamorgan is the delightful little town of Cowbridge. Its coat of arms relates to a strange tale of how the town came by its name. What it shows is a cow crossing a bridge with a sheaf of corn held tightly in its mouth. It relates to the time when a cow got it's horns entangled in the balustrade of a new bridge built across the River Thaw and had to be slaughtered before anyone or anything could cross over and enter the town. When the wooden bridge came to be replaced by a stone one in 1321 it was given the Welsh name of Pont-faen. This means Cowbridge-hence the name the town is now called. Many picturesque old inns and shops run along its long and lovely main street.

In the centre of this street can be seen the old Town Hall and Market House, which also once served as a House of Correction for much of the old Glamorgan county. This fine old building still contains the old cells. When the Romans decided it was an ideal site for one of their stations, they surrounded the town with walls. Much later, when the conquering Normans arrived, they discovered that the ruined walls stood on such firm foundations they were also able to construct their defensive walls on them. Owen Glyndwr, however, soon made a sorry sight of the walls when he arrived on the scene, and the only remains now to be seen are around the South Gate. The church of the Holy Cross also has a huge 13th century embattled tower, a complicated building of outer stairways and mediaeval buttresses.

Llanblethian, the twin settlement of Cowbridge, can be found close by, and here you can see the gateway and ruins of St Quintin's Castle and also an interesting church. In 1400 the castle was attacked by Owen Glyndwr, who earlier had defeated the Anglo-Norman army in a bloodthirsty, fiercely fought battle on a moor-

Cardiff Bay

land above Cowbridge called Stalling Down. When the restoration of the church at Llanblethian was underway a sealed crypt was revealed under the south chapel. Inside the vault were discovered three hundred male skeletons, apparently thrown in without any thought of order. It is thought that this untidy heap of corpses were those slain in the bloody battle and dumped here unceremoniously.

Close by is the also historical village of St Hilary. A small and delightful place to visit, it has a number of well preserved and pretty thatched cottages as well as an excellent thatched inn, which, along with a 14th-century church, gives

Cardiff City Hall

the village an atmosphere of perfect tranquillity. Inside the church is a full-scale effigy of a knight in full battle armour. This is thought to represent Richard Basset, a member of a powerful local family who built the Old Beaupre Castle, which can be seen close by. Here it is claimed that the great and powerful Lords of the castle, joined the barons, along with a number of quite important Welshmen, in order to draft out the Magna Carta. No definite records have been found to support this claim. It seems, however, that King John did hide from his barons in a secret chamber at nearby Boverton Castle to avoid having to sign the all-important charter. Now only a ruin in the village, the castle was actually the residence of King John's divorced wife Haswise, so if he did actually persuade her to hide him there, it is quite possible that the story that has passed down through the ages of the drafting of the Magna Carta in Beaupre Castle is indeed true.

One of the most impressive ancient sights to be seen in the Vale of Glamorgan is the huge Tinkinswood Burial Chamber. This is one of the finest examples of megalithic Chambered tombs in Britain and, most certainly one of the largest and best preserved to be discovered anywhere. The giant capstone weighs around 40 tons and is over 3ft in thickness, which makes it a "must see" object to visit in this area. Being of the Neolithic period, it dates back to around 2500 BC and could only have been built by the early settlers who moved inland to discover this pleasant area after landing or being swept ashore from their unstable craft during a storm in the channel. Legend has it that the place is haunted and that a local drunkard used this place to sleep off the effects of his drinking spree one evening. Having chosen to shelter under the giant capstone, the ghosts which haunt this spot took umbrage that someone in such a state could treat the place where they had been laid to rest forever in such an uncaring fashion. Seizing the drunkard by his unkempt hair, they sent him spinning high in the Glamorgan sky until he was dropped into the centre of the local Dyffryn Woods. One wonders if this cured his taste for alcohol for all time! The quiet lane that leads to the burial chamber runs from the small hamlet of St Nicholas. Close by is St Lythan's, where another prehistoric tomb can be seen. The legend here is that once every year the tomb's large capstone moves off its supports like a hovercraft and whirls around three times before coming to rest in its original position. No reason has ever been given for this weird happening.

These are but a sample of the historical places to visit in the beautiful Vale of Glamorgan, before moving on to the many other attractions in this interesting county. One very special place to visit is St Fagan's on the western outskirts of Cardiff. It was here where one of the biggest and fiercest battles ever to be fought in Wales took place. This took place in 1648 when eight thousand Royalist soldiers - albeit ill equipped and poorly led - were almost totally massacred by Cromwell's highly-trained Roundheads during the Civil War. But this was not the first great battle to be fought at St Fagan's. Evidence has been dug up from the woods and fields here over the years that mighty clashes between the Saxons and invading Danes, followed by the Normans, have all taken place close to the village. Today the castle of St Fagan's houses the highly impressive National Folk Museum of Wales, depicting the folk culture of the proud Celtic nation throughout the ages, from Welsh love spoons to horrific and cruel instruments of War. There is also a new museum erected to hold relics too large and awkward to be shown inside the old castle. In the many acres surrounding the museums are old buildings showing the way the Welsh folk worked and lived around the Principality. There is a thatched cottage from the Flintshire region, a wonderful old woollen mill from Llanwrtyd Wells, in Powys, an old shop complete with many pre-war items, which was moved here from Abergavenny after the owner passed away just a few short years ago, and many more interesting buildings to see. A day, however, is not enough to spend at this very special place, which gives a fascinating look into bygone days.

The coastal region of South Glamorgan, although not as interesting as the Gower coastline, still has much to commend it. The town of Penarth, which lies just south of Cardiff, still retains an air of Edwardian times, and is a gorgeous place to be on a balmy summer's day and to stroll along the well-maintained promenade and spend some time on the beautifully preserved Victorian promenade. There is a delightful sort of genteel charm about Penarth, which is a rarity these days at many British seaside resorts.

There are also a number of colourful and pleasant parks to enjoy and a lovely cliff walk, with views of the small islands of Flat Holm and Steep Holm and beyond to the Somerset coast. Penarth also boasts the 400-berth Portway Marina, which is a beautiful transformation of the old coal-exporting dock that became redundant with the closing of the valleys pits. One extra attraction is the Paddle-steamer trips from the pier during the summer months. The Turner House Art Gallery, a branch of the National Museum of Wales has regular exhibitions from the National Museum. This can be found opposite the railway station. On the outskirts of the lovely old town and in the direction of Barry, is Comeston Lakes Country Park with its 200 acres of woodlands, lakes and meadows, where much bird life and plant life can be enjoyed. There is also an adventure playground, picnic sites and bridleways, not forgetting the 14th century mediaeval village. Reconstructed on its original foundations, there is much to be seen here, including farmyard animals.

Eight miles southwest of Cardiff and on the shoreline of the Bristol Channel, lies the town of Barry. Because of its position it grew into an important seaport when the high-quality Rhondda steam coal was in great demand during the industrial revolution. The huge railway sidings and marshalling yards were constantly in use as the coal poured in from the great valleys and was transported worldwide by ships of all nationalities. Many a young Welshman looking for adventure signed on his first merchant ship here at Barry Dock, preferring the challenge and dangers of the mighty oceans to that of the cramped and dirty conditions of toiling away beneath the surface of the Welsh mountains. The coal has now gone, as are the seemingly never-ending ending stream of coal steamers. Most of the ships that enter Barry these days belong to the West Indian banana importers. Barry Island, however, continues to bring in the customers. This bustling and lively seaside resort has catered for countless generations of Welsh valley folk looking for the fun and excitement of the seaside. In direct contrast to it's neighbour Penarth, Barry Island is a boisterous "kiss me quick" hats sort of a place, with lettered rock and cockle stalls and the largest funfair in the west of Britain. Add to this the bucket-and-spade beaches of Jackson's Bay, Whitmore Bay and The Knap, plus a grassy headland for walks and picnics and a huge outdoor swimming pool at Cold Knap, you quickly realise why this was a popular resort for day-trippers. Many youngsters throughout the generations, including myself, got their first view of the seaside when they came by coach to Barry Island during the eagerly awaited annual Sunday chapel outings, their one and only holiday trip of the year. How quickly times have changed!

Cardiff Castle

Last, but most certainly not least, we come to the great capital city of Cardiff. Only officially designated as the capital of the Principality by Queen Elizabeth II in 1955, Cardiff has quickly gone from strength to strength as the premier city in Wales. Still a busy and important seaport, the docks at Cardiff are not now constantly filled to overflowing with ships waiting to export the once precious "black diamonds" of the boom days of the South Wales coalfields, which caused the phenomenal growth of Cardiff and turned it overnight into a cosmopolitan city. People of many races have lived here happily side by side for over two centuries and have blended well into the culture of South Wales. Like a Japanese looking old man once said to me when we were watching Wales playing an international match at the old Arms Park many long years ago: "We Welshmen must stick together and shout loudly for our team to win, " And we did, and they did!

First time visitors to Cardiff are impressed with the spaciousness and cleanliness of its huge shopping centre, fashionable shops, arcades and excellent restaurants. This is nothing like the city they expected on the edge of a once vast industrial area. Who would have expected Cardiff to have one of the world's finest Civic Centres with buildings of white Portland stone, built with an elegance and design to match any such civic architecture in the world. Here one cannot fail to be impressed by the classic styles of such buildings as the City Hall, the Law Courts, the National Museum of Wales, the Temple of Peace and Health and the old Welsh Office, which along with the attractive parks gives the feeling of grandeur to the city centre. The majestic looking Cardiff Castle dominates the city centre, as can be expected having started life as a powerful Roman fortress. A large amount of the Roman walls can still be seen and the rest of the wall's outlines have been preserved. When the Normans arrived they added a motte and bailey inside the ruins of the old fort in 1091. In the 13th century the castle was enlarged to include the towers and a new walled surrounding. Then in stepped the 3rd Marquess of Bute, one of the richest men in the world with money made from the huge profits extracted from the creation of the huge and lucrative Cardiff docklands. Calling on William Burgess, a mid-Victorian genius of an architect, he transformed Cardiff Castle into the highly impressive building it is today. The interior is a glittering array of impressive rooms, with the elegant Banqueting Hall still in use for entertaining the important guests coming to the city. There is also a museum dedicated to the Welsh Regiment, and in the grounds of the castle peacocks strut. The castle park stretches alongside the River Taff (hence the nickname given to the Welsh people) towards the also impressive Llandaff Cathedral some miles away.

Close by the edge of the park is the headquarters and main ground of Glamorgan Cricket Club, the only first class cricket club in Wales. Cardiff is also the home of the massive Millennium Stadium, built by the Welsh Rugby Union to host the recent World Cup of Rugby, but now also in the limelight because of the staging of the FA Cup Final and the Worthington Football League Cup, while London's Wembley Stadium is being reconstructed. Wales may not now have a rugby team to match the great welsh teams of yesteryear, but they do now have one of the finest modern sporting arenas in the world.

The so-called notorious Tiger Bay and Bute Street areas have disappeared and have been replaced by the vibrant Cardiff Bay development with its Cardiff Bay Visitor Centre, The Welsh Industrial and Maritime Museum, the Norwegian Church and the National Assembly for Wales building, while the waterfront has been transformed into a marina and 8 miles of new waterfront, with a new freshwater lake being prepared. One can also see the architectural beauty of the ornate red-bricked Pierhead Building and the lovely old Victorian structures in nearby Mount Stuart Square, to remind one that the port at Cardiff was once rated among the world's wealthiest.

With only a population of around a third of a million, the city of Cardiff is not large when placed along many capital cities, but still caters for every need as far as entertainment and eating out is concerned. The highly rated Welsh National Opera performs seasonally at the New Theatre, which also puts on many leading plays and pantomimes throughout the year, whilst the other main theatre, The Sherman, also does many shows. The 2,000 seater St David's Hall and the 5,500 seated International Arena stage top class concerts and indoor sports events, whilst the Millennium Stadium has come into it's own by staging top singing artists such as Tina Turner and Cardiff's very own Shirley Bassey. As for eating there are many fine eating places to be found in and around the city, with the fashionable eating places to be found at the exciting new "Cafe Quarter" at Mill Lane Alfresco dining being the big attraction. The lovely city of Cardiff is a special Welsh delight and many will be surprised that it is so when they visit for the first time.

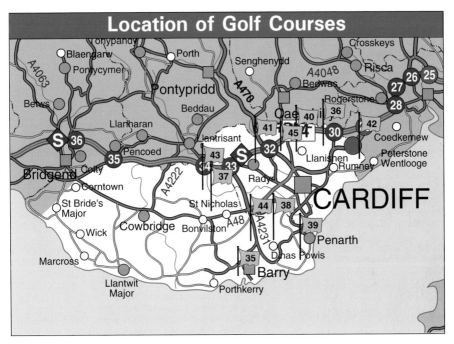

Location of Golf Courses

© MAPS IN MINUTES ™ 2001   © Crown Copyright, Ordnance Survey 2001

Brynhill Golf Club

Port Road, Barry CF62 8PN

Tel: 01446 720277 Fax: 01446 733660

On the A4050 road to Barry and not too far the Wenvoe Castle club, lies the Brynhill Golf Club founded in 1921, which has an amazing record of turning out junior golfers who go on to gain international honours and become professionals. One such player is Stephen Dodd, the former British Amateur Champion and Walker Cup player, who is now playing as a professional on the European Tour, and there are many other fine players, both male and female, who have achieved high honours and are still doing so. This has been achieved because of the painstaking work carried out by local member John Collins, who has formed a junior section with their very own clubhouse, which are both second to none inside the Principality. John Collins continues to work unstintingly to encourage the local youngsters to take the game up, and what a huge success rate this modest and popular man has achieved without any remuneration, but with the help of his long-suffering wife.

Sec/Manager:	Phil Gershenson
Professional:	Peter Fountain
Directions:	2 miles N of Barry. From M4 Junction 33 take A4232 to Culverhouse Cross then A4050 (Barry). Pass the Gulf Service Station and turn right after ½ mile into Little Brynhill Lane. Entrance is on right hand side.
Date Founded:	1923
Type of Course:	Parkland
No of Holes:	18
Length:	6200 yds (5723 mtrs)
Par:	72
SSS:	71
Green Fees:	Weekdays: £20 per day; Weekends/Bank Holidays: £25

	per day
Visitors:	Welcome: Excluding Tuesdays & Sundays. Contact Club in advance
Societies:	Welcome: Excluding Tuesdays & Sundays. Contact Club in advance
Facilities:	Putting Green, Chipping Green, Club Hire, Trolley Hire, Bar, Restaurant

Accommodation, Food and Drink

Reference numbers below refer to detailed information provided in section 2

Accommodation

Clawdd Coch Guest House, Pendoylan, Vale of Glamorgan CF71 7UP

Tel: 01446 760645

Versatile B&B facilities in a 17th century house with five beautifully appointed bedrooms. Golfing breaks a speciality. 115

Crossways House, Cowbridge, Vale of Glamorgan CF71 7LJ

Tel: 01446 773171 Fax: 01446 771707
e-mail: enquiries@crosswayshouse.co.uk website: www.crosswayshouse.co.uk

Three B&B bedrooms and a self-catering flat in a lovely country mansion set in 6 acres ¾ mile west of Cowbridge (B4270).

Fairways Hotel, Porthcawl, South Glamorgan CF36 3LS

Tel: 01656 782085 Fax: 01656 785351
e-mail: fairwayshotel@aol.com
website: www.bridgend.gov.uk

Twenty-five en suite bedrooms in a smartly refurbished family-run hotel near the seafront. Restaurant, lounge bar, residents' lounge. 114

The White Horse Inn, Davis Row, Pentwyn, Nr Fochriw, Bargoed, Mid-Glamorgan CF81 9NP

Tel: 01685 841215

Popular inn open seven days a week for breakfast, lunch and dinner. Super home-made pies and lots more. Two B&B rooms planned.

Windmill Cottages, Llansannor, Cowbridge, Vale of Glamorgan CF71 7TF

Tel/Fax: 01446 772470
e-mail: rosser@globalnet.co.uk

Quality self-catering accommodation in 19th century barn conversions adjacent to a working farm. Lovely rural setting five minutes from Cowbridge. 116

Food and Drink

St Julian Inn, Newport, South Wales NP18 1QA

Tel: 01633 243548 Fax: 01633 243562

A welcoming old inn with the road on one side and

the River Usk on the other. Bar-style menu, award-winning real ales.   108

The White Horse Inn, Davis Row, Pentwyn, Nr. Fochriw, Bargoed, Mid-Glamorgan CF81 9NP
Tel: 01685 841215
Popular inn open seven days a week for breakfast, lunch and dinner. Super home-made pies and lots more. Two B&B rooms planned.

Cardiff Golf Club

Sherbourne Avenue, Cyngoed,
Cardiff CF23 6SJ
Tel: 02920 753320 Fax: 02920 680011

Cardiff Golf Club, as the name implies, is the capital city's main golf club. Situated rather peacefully and perfectly out of sight in the rich residential area of Cyncoed, this glittering gem of a parkland course is extremely popular with golfers from every area of South Wales. Founded in 1921, its membership, as is expected, is drawn mainly from the professional and successful business people of the city, who reside from in and around the Cyncoed area. This, however, does not mean this is a snooty, unfriendly sort of club, Far from it. Whether you're a famous big fish or a mere minnow; a multi-millionaire or a struggling shopkeeper, golf is a great leveller and, like every golf club in Wales, if you play the game you are accepted. Nobody cares a damn as long as you behave yourself and not a cheat. The opening hole at Cardiff is a real beauty. A par 4 all down hill with the fairway bordered by trees, it can either make or break your round depending on how well your mind is focused on the job ahead. This is followed by a rather subtle little jewel of a par 3, which can also catch you unawares.

After this the courses open up in to a wide expanse of attractive parkland with a wonderful array of trees from ancient great oak to slimline silver birch lying in wait for the poorly directed shot. There is also a wide stream crossing a number of holes, which is the bane of the local

members and which many would love to see filled in!

The second half of this marvellous course has a number of excellent uphill and downhill holes (not too strenuous) before levelling out for some great finishing holes, with the par 3 eighteenth holding a reputation of often being responsible for suddenly changing the outcome of who the winner is of many an important championship which has been hosted here, including the Welsh Professional Championship. This hole looks quite benign, but possesses a rather wicked sting in its tail, believe me!

The old and quite respectable clubhouse has recently been replaced by a new and huge clubhouse, with full facilities and many excellent improvements to cater for the needs of the modern golfing fraternity.

Cardiff Golf Club is one of many excellent courses to found on the outskirts of the city, and an excellent introduction of what to expect from them all.

Sec/Manager:	Keith Lloyd
Professional:	Terry Hanson
Directions:	3½ miles N of Cardiff City Centre. From M4 junction take A4232 (south). At junction with A48 turn right into Pentwyn Rd, passing the Campanile Hotel and go 2 miles via Pentwyn Rd, Gwern Rhuddi Rd and Cyn Coed Rd. Turn left into Westminster Crescent and the entrance is on left hand side after 250 Yds.
Date Founded:	1922
Type of Course:	Parkland
No of Holes:	18
Length:	6016 yds (8446 mtrs)
Par:	70
SSS:	70
Green Fees:	Weekdays: £35 per day; Weekends/Bank Holidays: £40 per day
Visitors:	Welcome: Excluding Tuesday morning (weekends only with a member)
Societies:	Welcome: Excluding Thursdays
Facilities:	Putting Green, Practice Area, Trolley Hire, Bar, Restaurant

Accommodation, Food and Drink

Reference numbers below refer to detailed
information provided in section 2

Accommodation

**The Greyhound Inn, Christchurch, Newport,
South Wales NP18 1JJ**

Tel: 01633 420306 Fax: 01633 430588

A handsome late 19th century gabled inn with a
proper village atmosphere, real ales and very good
food. Friendly and inviting.   109

**The Milton Hotel, Llanwern, Newport,
Gwent NP16 6DU**

Tel: 01633 412432

Home-cooked food, real ales and self-catering
accommodation in a former hunting lodge an easy
drive from exit 24 of the M4.   110

**The Priory Hotel & Restaurant, Caerleon,
South Wales NP18 1AG**

Tel: 01633 421241 Fax: 01633 421271

A historic hotel of exceptional quality and character,
set in its own secluded grounds in the Roman town of
Caerleon.   112

**The White Horse Inn, Davis Row, Pentwyn,
Nr Fochriw, Bargoed, Mid-Glamorgan CF81 9NP**

Tel: 01685 841215

Popular inn open seven days a week for breakfast,
lunch and dinner. Super home-made pies and lots
more. Two B&B rooms planned.

Food and Drink

**Clawdd Coch Guest House, Pendoylan,
Vale of Glamorgan CF71 7UP**

Tel: 01446 760645

Versatile B&B facilities in a 17th century house with
five beautifully appointed bedrooms. Golfing breaks a
speciality.   115

**The Milton Hotel, Llanwern, Newport,
Gwent NP16 6DU**

Tel: 01633 412432

Home-cooked food, real ales and self-catering
accommodation in a former hunting lodge an easy
drive from exit 24 of the M4.   110

**The Priory Hotel & Restaurant, Caerleon,
South Wales NP18 1AG**

Tel: 01633 421241 Fax: 01633 421271

A historic hotel of exceptional quality and character,
set in its own secluded grounds in the Roman town of
Caerleon.   112

Cottrell Park Golf Club

St Nicolas, Cardiff CF5 6JY

Tel: 01446 781781 Fax: 01446 781187

Sec/Manager:	David Marchant
Professional:	Richard Herbert
Directions:	8 miles NW of Cardiff. From junction 33 of the M4 take the A4232 towards Cardiff. At the A48 roundabout turn right towards Cowbridge and follow this road through the village of St Nicholas. The entrance is on the right hand side 200 yds after you exit the village.
Visitors:	Welcome: Contact Club by telephone in advance.
Societies:	Welcome: Contact Club by telephone in advance. Unable to play at weekends and Bank Holidays
Facilities:	Putting Green, Trolley Hire, Buggy Hire, Bar, Restaurant, Driving Range

Macintosh

Date Founded:	1996
Type of Course:	Parkland
No of Holes:	18
Length:	6606 yds (6097 mtrs)
Par:	72
SSS:	72
Green Fees:	Weekdays: £25.00; Weekends/ Bank Holidays: £33.50

Button

Date Founded:	1996
Type of Course:	Parkland
No of Holes:	9
Length:	2807 yds (2591 mtrs)

Par:	35
SSS:	67
Green Fees:	Weekdays: £12.50; Weekends/ Bank Holidays: £16.75

Accommodation, Food and Drink

Reference numbers below refer to detailed information provided in section 2

Accommodation

Clawdd Coch Guest House, Pendoylan, Vale of Glamorgan CF71 7UP

Tel: 01446 760645

Versatile B&B facilities in a 17th century house with five beautifully appointed bedrooms. Golfing breaks a speciality.   115

Crossways House, Cowbridge, Vale of Glamorgan CF71 7LJ

Tel: 01446 773171 Fax: 01446 771707
e-mail: enquiries@crosswayshouse.co.uk
website: www.crosswayshouse.co.uk

Three B&B bedrooms and a self-catering flat in a lovely country mansion set in 6 acres ¾ mile west of Cowbridge (B4270).

Fairways Hotel, Porthcawl, South Glamorgan CF36 3LS

Tel: 01656 782085 Fax: 01656 785351
e-mail: fairwayshotel@aol.com
website: www.bridgend.gov.uk

Twenty-five en suite bedrooms in a smartly refurbished family-run hotel near the seafront. Restaurant, lounge bar, residents' lounge.   114

The White Horse Inn, Davis Row, Pentwyn, Nr Fochriw, Bargoed,Mid-Glamorgan CF81 9NP

Tel: 01685 841215

Popular inn open seven days a week for breakfast, lunch and dinner. Super home-made pies and lots more. Two B&B rooms planned.

Windmill Cottages, Llansannor, Cowbridge, Vale of Glamorgan CF71 7TF

Tel/Fax: 01446 772470
e-mail: rosser@globalnet.co.uk

Quality self-catering accommodation in 19th century barn conversions adjacent to a working farm. Lovely rural setting five minutes from Cowbridge.   116

Food and Drink

Fairways Hotel, Porthcawl, South Glamorgan CF36 3LS

Tel: 01656 782085 Fax: 01656 785351
e-mail: fairwayshotel@aol.com
website: www.bridgend.gov.uk

Twenty-five en suite bedrooms in a smartly refurbished family-run hotel near the seafront. Restaurant, lounge bar, residents' lounge.   114

St Julian Inn, Newport, South Wales NP18 1QA

Tel: 01633 243548 Fax: 01633 243562

A welcoming old inn with the road on one side and the River Usk on the other. Bar-style menu, award-winning real ales.   108

The White Horse Inn, Davis Row, Pentwyn, Nr Fochriw, Bargoed,Mid-Glamorgan CF81 9NP

Tel: 01685 841215

Popular inn open seven days a week for breakfast, lunch and dinner. Super home-made pies and lots more. Two B&B rooms planned.

Dinas Powis Golf Club

Old Highwalls, Dinas Powis CF64 4AJ

Tel: 02920 512727 Fax: 02920 512727

Three miles south-west of Cardiff and off the A4055 is the delightful 18-hole parkland course of Dinas Powis, which takes the name of the pleasant small and ancient village of Dinas Powis. An undulating course in peaceful surroundings and with a cosy little clubhouse, it is hard to believe it was taken over to the growing of vegetables for the war effort during the Second World War. Now fully recovered, this is a popular place to play, as can be vouched by the membership of some 700, which is amazing in a smallish county that can boast 14 good golf courses. Worth a visit.

Sec/Manager:	Jinny Golding
Professional:	Gareth Bennett
Directions:	4 miles SW of Cardiff City Centre. From M4 junction take A4232, then A4050 (Barry). Just past Wenvoe turn left (Dinas Powis) into St Andrews Rd, fork left into Britway Rd then left into Highwalls Rd. Entrance after 300 yds is on left hand side.
Date Founded:	1912
Type of Course:	Woodland/Parkland
No of Holes:	18
Length:	5486 yds (5064 mtrs)

Par:	67
SSS:	67
Green Fees:	Weekdays: £25 per day; Weekends/Bank Holidays: £30 per day
Visitors:	Welcome: Excluding Tuesdays & Saturdays
Societies:	Welcome: Excluding Tuesdays & Saturdays. Contact Club in advance
Facilities:	Putting Green, Chipping Green, Club Hire, Trolley Hire, Buggy Hire, Bar, Restaurant

Accommodation, Food and Drink

Reference numbers below refer to detailed
information provided in section 2

Accommodation

**Clawdd Coch Guest House, Pendoylan,
Vale of Glamorgan CF71 7UP**

Tel: 01446 760645

Versatile B&B facilities in a 17th century house with
five beautifully appointed bedrooms. Golfing breaks a
speciality.   115

**Crossways House, Cowbridge,
Vale of Glamorgan CF71 7LJ**

Tel: 01446 773171 Fax: 01446 771707
e-mail: enquiries@crosswayshouse.co.uk
website: www.crosswayshouse.co.uk

Three B&B bedrooms and a self-catering flat in a
lovely country mansion set in 6 acres ¾ mile west of
Cowbridge (B4270).

**Fairways Hotel, Porthcawl,
South Glamorgan CF36 3LS**

Tel: 01656 782085 Fax: 01656 785351
e-mail: fairwayshotel@aol.com
website: www.bridgend.gov.uk

Twenty-five en suite bedrooms in a smartly
refurbished family-run hotel near the seafront.
Restaurant, lounge bar, residents' lounge.   114

**The White Horse Inn, Davis Row, Pentwyn,
Nr Fochriw, Bargoed,Mid-Glamorgan CF81 9NP**

Tel: 01685 841215

Popular inn open seven days a week for breakfast,
lunch and dinner. Super home-made pies and lots
more. Two B&B rooms planned.

**Windmill Cottages, Llansannor, Cowbridge,
Vale of Glamorgan CF71 7TF**

Tel/Fax: 01446 772470
e-mail: rosser@globalnet.co.uk

Quality self-catering accommodation in 19th century
barn conversions adjacent to a working farm. Lovely
rural setting five minutes from Cowbridge.   116

Food and Drink

St Julian Inn, Newport,   South Wales NP18 1QA

Tel: 01633 243548 Fax: 01633 243562
A welcoming old inn with the road on one side and
the River Usk on the other. Bar-style menu, award-
winning real ales.   108

**The White Horse Inn, Davis Row, Pentwyn,
Nr Fochriw, Bargoed,Mid-Glamorgan CF81 9NP**

Tel: 01685 841215

Popular inn open seven days a week for breakfast,
lunch and dinner. Super home-made pies and lots
more. Two B&B rooms planned.

Glamorganshire Golf Club

Lavernock Road, Penarth CF64 5UP

Tel: 02920 701185 Fax: 02920701185

Having been founded as long ago as 1890, the
Glamorganshire Golf Club shares the distinction
with Conwy (Caernarvonshire) Golf Club of being the next two oldest constituted golf clubs after
Tenby Golf Club (1888) in Wales. This also makes
the Glamorganshire club the oldest official golf
club in South Wales, of which the members are
justly proud. They are also proud of the fact that
they had in the shape of Henry Howell the greatest amateur golfer ever to come out of Wales, at
least until the 1950s when Monmouthshire's
Iestyn Tucker and Llandrindod Wells's John
Morgan came into prominence. Of these three
outstanding amateur golfers, only Morgan had
the honour of making the Walker Cup team (the
first Welshman to do so), but to his credit he always insisted that Howell and Tucker, deserved
the honour before him. Incidentally, Iestyn
Tucker, the former president of the Welsh Golfing Union and current president of
Monmouthshire Golf Club, still plays golf regularly and often returns a gross score below his
age of 74. Just recently at his home club he won a
midweek competition with a gross 68, and he still
plays to a handicap of 5!

Henry Howell was Welsh Amateur Champion
no fewer than eight times, and in 1932 he proved
he was equal to any amateur in Britain by soundly
beating the champions of England, Scotland and
Ireland during the Home Internationals at Royal
Troon. Amazingly, he was not chosen for the
Walker Cup side that was played later that year.
A great betting man, in 1927 he covered three
bets of varying odds on how fast he could finish
a round in better or under par. 5 to 1 on shooting
72 or better in one and a half hours, 20 to 1 he
couldn't break 70 in the same time and 40 to 1
he couldn't break 65 in one hour and a quarter.
He accepted the challenge as long as the members accepted that the odds were for pounds
sterling and not mere shillings. Followed by a large
gallery of members and using a scorer with a stop-

ate a satisfactory score on your card. Equalling the par of 70 off your particular handicap on this delightful and tranquil course is a good achievement for the first-time visitor. Far better, perhaps, to play the Stableford system. After all that's what the good doctor successfully prescribed after long examination of this course!

watch, he completed the round in 63 shots in the amazing time of 68 minutes! Howell is just one of many great characters who have been members of the Glamorganshire club. Fellow golf writer and good friend Peter Corrigan, who wrote the excellent centenary book of the club, is one such character who now graces the club with his charm and good humour.

Glamorganshire also has a couple more claims to fame. First and foremost that the ingenious scoring system of Stableford, which is now enjoyed by millions of golfers around the world, was invented by club member Doctor Frank Stableford and tried out by fellow members for the first time ever at Glamorganshire in 1898. Much concerned and annoyed that one really bad hole out 18 could completely ruin an otherwise good card and spoil one's enjoyment, he finally found a solution. Proving a great success, it was not until he moved from Wales and became a member of Wallasey Golf Club in 1931 was his system fully approved and officially launched. Nevertheless, it remains a Welsh invention.

Secondly, when the famous Barbarians rugby team came on their annual Easter tour of South Wales, their first fixture was always against Penarth. With the Glamorganshire Golf Club being situated in this lovely old seaside town and with rugby and golf going together like fish and chips, the Barbarians made the golf club their official headquarters, and after the rough and tumble of the rugby game they enjoyed a spell of the more genteel and relaxing game of golf as a place to lick their wounds (as they often had to during the great days of Welsh rugby). Sadly, the rugby tour is no longer with us and the Barbarians visits are rather infrequent. The perfectly flat green of the 18th hole is situated directly outside the entrance of the clubhouse, so it is easy to imagine the banter from the rugby players as each member of their illustrious team was about to putt out!

The clubhouse still retains its old 1980 charm and is a pleasure to enjoy after one finishes a round over the old course. This delightful Penarth-based course is mainly parkland with lovely old trees playing a big part in the shaping of the holes over and around a gently sloping hill. At 6,091 yards, rather short by today's modern standards, it still takes a lot of guile and imagination to cre-

Sec/Manager:	Brian Williams
Professional:	Andrew Kerr
Directions:	4 miles S of Cardiff City Centre. From M4 junction 33 take A4232 (Barry, Penarth). At Culverhouse Cross take A4050, follow into B4267 (Lower Penarth). Entrance 250 yds past Gulf Service Station at outskirts of Lower Penarth on left hand side.
Date Founded:	1890
Type of Course:	Parkland
No of Holes:	18
Length:	6091 yds (5622 mtrs)
Par:	70
SSS:	70
Green Fees:	Weekdays: £30 per day; Weekends/Bank Holidays: £35 per day
Visitors:	Welcome: Excluding Tuesday Morning. Contact Club in advance
Societies:	Welcome: Excluding Monday - Wednesday & weekends. Contact Club in advance
Facilities:	Putting Green, Chipping Green, Practice Area, Club Hire, Trolley Hire, Buggy Hire, Bar, Restaurant

Accommodation, Food and Drink

Reference numbers below refer to detailed information provided in section 2

Accommodation

Clawdd Coch Guest House, Pendoylan, Vale of Glamorgan CF71 7UP

Tel: 01446 760645

Versatile B&B facilities in a 17th century house with five beautifully appointed bedrooms. Golfing breaks a speciality. 115

Crossways House, Cowbridge, Vale of Glamorgan CF71 7LJ

Tel: 01446 773171 Fax: 01446 771707
e-mail: enquiries@crosswayshouse.co.uk
website: www.crosswayshouse.co.uk

Three B&B bedrooms and a self-catering flat in a lovely country mansion set in 6 acres ¾ mile west of Cowbridge (B4270).

Fairways Hotel, Porthcawl, South Glamorgan CF36 3LS

Tel: 01656 782085 Fax: 01656 785351
e-mail: fairwayshotel@aol.com
website: www.bridgend.gov.uk
Twenty-five en suite bedrooms in a smartly refurbished family-run hotel near the seafront. Restaurant, lounge bar, residents' lounge.   114

The White Horse Inn, Davis Row, Pentwyn, Nr Fochriw, Bargoed, Mid-Glamorgan CF81 9NP

Tel: 01685 841215
Popular inn open seven days a week for breakfast, lunch and dinner. Super home-made pies and lots more. Two B&B rooms planned.

Windmill Cottages, Llansannor, Cowbridge, Vale of Glamorgan CF71 7TF

Tel/Fax: 01446 772470
e-mail: rosser@globalnet.co.uk
Quality self-catering accommodation in 19th century barn conversions adjacent to a working farm. Lovely rural setting five minutes from Cowbridge.   116

Food and Drink

St Julian Inn, Newport, South Wales NP18 1QA

Tel: 01633 243548 Fax: 01633 243562
A welcoming old inn with the road on one side and the River Usk on the other. Bar-style menu, award-winning real ales.   108

The White Horse Inn, Davis Row, Pentwyn, Nr Fochriw, Bargoed, Mid-Glamorgan CF81 9NP

Tel: 01685 841215
Popular inn open seven days a week for breakfast, lunch and dinner. Super home-made pies and lots more. Two B&B rooms planned.

Llanishen Golf Club

Heol Hir, Cardiff CF14 9UD
Tel: 029 2075 5078 Fax: 029 2075 5078

Just a couple of miles from Whitchurch, close to the village of Lisvane, lies the Llanishen Golf Club, which, having been founded in 1905, is older than

both the Cardiff and Whitchurch clubs and well worth a visit. This 18-hole course is divided by a road that leads to the cosy old clubhouse, with seven gently undulating holes to the left of the road as you enter, and the rest heading in the direction of the city. With a length of just 5,327 yards, par 68, it still proves difficult to score well on, as I discovered during my first visit in the 1970s.

Sec/Manager:	E Page
Professional:	A Jones
Directions:	5 miles N of Cardiff City Centre. From centre take the A470 leading into the A469 (Llanishen, Caerphilly). Turn right into minor road ½ mile after crossing M4 motorway. Entrance after ¾ mile on left hand side. If accessing from M4 leave at junction 32 taking the A48 (City Centre). After 2 miles join the A469 (Llanishen, Caerphilly)
Date Founded:	1905
Type of Course:	Parkland
No of Holes:	18
Length:	5327 yds (4917 mtrs)
Par:	68
SSS:	67
Green Fees:	Weekdays:£30
Visitors:	Welcome: Contact Club by telephone in advance. Unable to play at weekend's
Societies:	Welcome: Contact Club by telephone in advance
Facilities:	Putting Green, Chipping Green, Practice Area, Trolley Hire, Bar, Restaurant

Accommodation, Food and Drink

Reference numbers below refer to detailed information provided in section 2

Accommodation

The Greyhound Inn, Christchurch, Newport, South Wales NP18 1JJ
Tel: 01633 420306 Fax: 01633 430588
A handsome late 19th century gabled inn with a proper village atmosphere, real ales and very good food. Friendly and inviting.   109

The Milton Hotel, Llanwern, Newport, Gwent NP16 6DU
Tel: 01633 412432
Home-cooked food, real ales and self-catering

accommodation in a former hunting lodge an easy drive from exit 24 of the M4. 110

The Priory Hotel & Restaurant, Caerleon, South Wales NP18 1AG

Tel: 01633 421241 Fax: 01633 421271

A historic hotel of exceptional quality and character, set in its own secluded grounds in the Roman town of Caerleon. 112

The White Horse Inn, Davis Row, Pentwyn, Nr Fochriw, Bargoed, Mid-Glamorgan CF81 9NP

Tel: 01685 841215

Popular inn open seven days a week for breakfast, lunch and dinner. Super home-made pies and lots more. Two B&B rooms planned.

Food and Drink

Clawdd Coch Guest House, Pendoylan, Vale of Glamorgan CF71 7UP

Tel: 01446 760645

Versatile B&B facilities in a 17th century house with five beautifully appointed bedrooms. Golfing breaks a speciality. 115

The Milton Hotel, Llanwern, Newport, Gwent NP16 6DU

Tel: 01633 412432

Home-cooked food, real ales and self-catering accommodation in a former hunting lodge an easy drive from exit 24 of the M4. 110

The Priory Hotel & Restaurant, Caerleon, South Wales NP18 1AG

Tel: 01633 421241 Fax: 01633 421271

A historic hotel of exceptional quality and character, set in its own secluded grounds in the Roman town of Caerleon. 112

Radyr Golf Club

Drysgol Road, Raydr, Cardiff CF15 8BS

Tel: 02920 842408 Fax: 02920 843914

As the name suggests, this splendid golf club is situated close to the suburban and peaceful 13th century village of Radyr, an attractive little place, like the course itself, situated some 5 miles north-

west of Cardiff and off the A4119. Founded in 1902, it holds the honour of being the oldest of the Cardiff golf clubs and, in my opinion, the most charming location of them all. I'm sure John Moody, the former golf correspondent of the Western Mail, and a good friend, fully agrees with me because he chose to live at Radyr many, many years ago and is now happy in his retirement there with his wife, Joan. A former Welsh international amateur star, his golf career came to an abrupt halt following a painful back complaint that never left him.

Like Whitchurch and Cardiff, the Radyr club membership is made up of many professional and business people. One such member was Wallace Towers, who composed the song "Money is the root of all evil". Many from the clergy are also members, and a Catholic Archbishop of Wales was once a member. Again like Cardiff, many members are from the medical profession, as can be expected with The University Hospital for Wales based in Cardiff.

Radyr Golf Club came into existence when, in 1901, the Lisvane Golf Club and some members broke away to look for new pastures to build a golf course, the remainder staying to re-form the former Lisvane club into Llanishen Golf Club. Those who left searched and quickly found suitable and available land belonging to the Earl of Plymouth close to the peaceful old village of Radyr, and set about founding Radyr Golf Club in the aforementioned year of 1902. The lovely old clubhouse is situated in a perfect spot overlooking the first hole and the 18th green, where one can watch the play from a long sun lounge or out on the spacious patio. Apparently, this rather large old building replaced the original clubhouse after a fire in 1913, and was designed the way it is so that if the club ever folded the building could be sold as a semi-detached pair of quality dwellings in keeping with the prosperous area. Probably the thinking behind something like that happening was brought on by the start of the First World War in 1914 when the new clubhouse was about to be built. There is no threat of anything like that happening to the club these days, as the Radyr club is as popular as they come as far as visitors are concerned.

This lovely old parkland course really is an agreeable place to play a round of golf. The first hole takes you away from the clubhouse in a steady but not strenuous climb to a level green (nowhere on this course is there a tough climb) which is not too difficult to make a par 4 on. After this the course winds its way through and around delightful parkland before heading home with a great finishing hole, which demands a straight drive and an approach shot to a blind and sunken green close to the clubhouse. A good and enjoyable course to visit.

Sec/Manager:	Alan Edwards
Professional:	Robert Butterworth
Directions:	4 miles NW of Cardiff City Centre. From M4 junction 32 take the A470 (Pontypridd). After 1 mile turn right onto A4262 (Radyr). Pass under M4 and after 600 yds turn right into Drysgol Rd. Entrance after 250 yds on left hand side.
Date Founded:	1902
Type of Course:	Parkland
No of Holes:	18
Length:	6150 yds (5676 mtrs)
Par:	70
SSS:	70
Green Fees:	Weekdays: £38 per day; Weekends/Bank Holidays: £38 per day
Visitors:	Welcome: Excluding weekends. Contact Club in advance
Societies:	Welcome: Excluding Monday, Tuesday & weekends. Contact Club in advance
Facilities:	Putting Green, Chipping Green, Practice Area, Club Hire, Trolley Hire, Bar, Restaurant

Accommodation, Food and Drink

Reference numbers below refer to detailed information provided in section 2

Accommodation

The Greyhound Inn, Christchurch, Newport, South Wales NP18 1JJ

Tel: 01633 420306 Fax: 01633 430588

A handsome late 19th century gabled inn with a proper village atmosphere, real ales and very good food. Friendly and inviting.   109

The Milton Hotel, Llanwern, Newport, Gwent NP16 6DU

Tel: 01633 412432

Home-cooked food, real ales and self-catering accommodation in a former hunting lodge an easy drive from exit 24 of the M4.   110

The Priory Hotel & Restaurant, Caerleon, South Wales NP18 1AG

Tel: 01633 421241 Fax: 01633 421271

A historic hotel of exceptional quality and character, set in its own secluded grounds in the Roman town of Caerleon.   112

The White Horse Inn, Davis Row, Pentwyn, Nr Fochriw, Bargoed, Mid-Glamorgan CF81 9NP

Tel: 01685 841215

Popular inn open seven days a week for breakfast, lunch and dinner. Super home-made pies and lots more. Two B&B rooms planned.

Food and Drink

Clawdd Coch Guest House, Pendoylan, Vale of Glamorgan CF71 7UP

Tel: 01446 760645

Versatile B&B facilities in a 17th century house with five beautifully appointed bedrooms. Golfing breaks a speciality.   115

The Milton Hotel, Llanwern, Newport, Gwent NP16 6DU

Tel: 01633 412432

Home-cooked food, real ales and self-catering accommodation in a former hunting lodge an easy drive from exit 24 of the M4.   110

The Priory Hotel & Restaurant, Caerleon, South Wales NP18 1AG

Tel: 01633 421241 Fax: 01633 421271

A historic hotel of exceptional quality and character, set in its own secluded grounds in the Roman town of Caerleon.   112

The White Horse Inn, Davis Row, Pentwyn, Nr Fochriw, Bargoed, Mid-Glamorgan CF81 9NP

Tel: 01685 841215

Popular inn open seven days a week for breakfast, lunch and dinner. Super home-made pies and lots more. Two B&B rooms planned.

St Mellons Golf Club

St Mellons, Cardiff CF3 8XS

Tel: 01633 680401 Fax: 01633 681219

Another demanding parkland course that lies on the outskirts of Cardiff is St Mellons, which is easily reached from the Junctions 28 (West) or 30 (East) of the M4 Motorway and then just off the A48, 4 miles east of Cardiff. Situated in a beautiful parkland setting, this Par 70 course gently meanders its way in a wide circle around the large and impressive clubhouse, which has a rather pleasant interior and an excellent dining room. Again in a rather upmarket suburb of Cardiff, and a few short miles from Newport, thus catering for golfers of both areas, the club was founded in 1936

with little alteration since that time.

The opening hole, a par-4, which is perfectly flat and straight from tee to green, more often than not gives the first-time visitor a feeling of complacency. The same can also be said about the 2nd hole if you are not in the habit of slicing your tee-shot, which, although a dog-leg left, is another comparatively easy par-4. After this the course throws out a bit of an exciting challenge. Especially so at the slightly uphill par-3 third, which is guarded by some large bunkers and a grassy bank at the front and to the right of and undulating green. Not overlong, but a craftily designed hole. The remainder of the outward nine-holes go gently downhill and uphill with woods awaiting the sliced shots.

The inward half levels out somewhat, but has many trees to contend with. The two closing holes offer a tremendous, challenging finish. The 17th, a par-4, is a great hole. Dog-legging slightly to the left, with a copse of trees awaiting the hooked shot and a thickish wood waiting to catch the sliced shot, this hole is all about accuracy from the tee. The same can be said about the par-5 finishing hole. Although fairly straight from tee to green, the copse still awaits those golfers with a tendency to hook. For the slicers among you, there is the dreaded out of bounds roadway leading to the clubhouse. Add to this a couple of deep sand-traps guarding the tricky green, and you realise you have done rather well if only one shot has been dropped over these two excellent finishing holes. Definitely a course to visit!

Sec/Manager:	K. Newling
Professional:	B. Thomas
Directions:	5 miles NW of Cardiff City Centre. From M4 junction 28 take the A48 (St Mellons, Llanrumney). After 3¾ miles at roundabout turn left into Cyprus Drive then first left into Vaendre Close. Entrance is after 200 yds.
Date Founded:	1935
Type of Course:	Parkland
No of Holes:	18
Length:	6080 yds (5612 mtrs)

Par:	70
SSS:	70
Green Fees:	Weekdays: £32 per day; Weekends/Bank Holidays: Unable to play
Visitors:	Welcome: Excluding weekends. Contact Club in advance
Societies:	Welcome: Excluding weekends. Contact Club in advance
Facilities:	Putting Green, Chipping Green, Club Hire, Trolley Hire, Buggy Hire, Bar, Restaurant

Accommodation, Food and Drink

Reference numbers below refer to detailed information provided in section 2

Accommodation

Great House, Isca Road, Old Village, Caerleon, South Wales NP18 1QG

Tel: 01633 420216
e-mail: price.greathouse@tesco.net
website: www.visitgreathouse.co.uk

Three lovely letting bedrooms - two twins and a single - in a Grade 2, 16th century building of character with gardens overlooking the River Usk.

The Milton Hotel, Llanwern, Newport, Gwent NP16 6DU

Tel: 01633 412432

Home-cooked food, real ales and self-catering accommodation in a former hunting lodge an easy drive from exit 24 of the M4.   110

The Priory Hotel & Restaurant, Caerleon, South Wales NP18 1AG

Tel: 01633 421241 Fax: 01633 421271

A historic hotel of exceptional quality and character, set in its own secluded grounds in the Roman town of Caerleon.   112

The White Horse Inn, Davis Row, Pentwyn, Nr Fochriw, Bargoed, Mid-Glamorgan CF81 9NP

Tel: 01685 841215

Popular inn open seven days a week for breakfast, lunch and dinner. Super home-made pies and lots more. Two B&B rooms planned.

Food and Drink

The Greyhound Inn, Christchurch, Newport, South Wales NP18 1JJ

Tel: 01633 420306 Fax: 01633 430588

A handsome late 19th century gabled inn with a proper village atmosphere, real ales and very good food. Friendly and inviting.   109

The Milton Hotel, Llanwern, Newport, Gwent NP16 6DU

Tel: 01633 412432

Home-cooked food, real ales and self-catering

accommodation in a former hunting lodge an easy drive from exit 24 of the M4. 110

The Priory Hotel & Restaurant, Caerleon, South Wales NP18 1AG

Tel: 01633 421241 Fax: 01633 421271

A historic hotel of exceptional quality and character, set in its own secluded grounds in the Roman town of Caerleon. 112

St Julian Inn, Newport, South Wales NP18 1QA

Tel: 01633 243548 Fax: 01633 243562

A welcoming old inn with the road on one side and the River Usk on the other. Bar-style menu, award-winning real ales. 108

The White Horse Inn, Davis Row, Pentwyn, Nr Fochriw, Bargoed, Mid-Glamorgan CF81 9NP

Tel: 01685 841215

Popular inn open seven days a week for breakfast, lunch and dinner. Super home-made pies and lots more. Two B&B rooms planned.

Vale of Glamorgan Golf & Country Club

Hensol Park, Hensol CF7 8JY

Tel: 01443 665899 Fax: 01443 665890

Set in 200 acres of beautiful parkland, surrounded by woods and copses and with a challenging mixture of lakes and streams, this gorgeous venue is a must for the discerning holiday golfer who is planning to linger for some length of time in this excellent golfing county of South Glamorgan. When Peter Johnson, the former Cardiff club professional and official coach to the Welsh Golfing Union, acquired this wonderful site he realised a dream of creating a golf complex with the finest training facilities and a top-class championship course. Backed by local, enthusiastic business partners, he has seen the complex grow into something quite special. Not so "swish" and expansive as the magnificent Celtic Manor development at near by Newport, it, nevertheless, is a top quality establishment. Opened in 1995, it now features a 100 bedroom hotel and leisure centre, with swimming pool, squash, gymnasium, spa-baths, beauty clinic and solarium; while the Hensol Golf Academy with its 32-bay floodlit driving range and coffee shop does much to add to the enjoyment of the visitor. And then you have the two excellent golf courses. Yes, indeed, two golf courses. The 18-hole and aptly named *Lakes Course*, and the 9-hole layout of the *Hensol Course*. Rather demanding, the Lakes Course, is dominated by no less than a 20 acre lake, which allows water to come into play on 11 holes, with the 12th hole being situated on an island-shades of the famous island hole at Sawgrass in the USA-except that this hole at the Lakes is a dog-leg par 4, with the hole at Sawgrass being a par 3.

Designed by Peter Johnson, who is a stickler for everything being perfect, the Lakes course has developed rapidly since being laid down in 1994 and offers a tremendous challenge, so much so that it has hosted a number of West Region P. G. A. events since being opened.

The Hensol course is less demanding, but still offers much enjoyment to those who only wish to play nine-holes on occasion during their stay in this delightful part of South Glamorgan.

Incidentally, a measure of Peter Johnson's teaching ability can be taken from the fact that one of his two sons-Richard Johnson-is a regular and a winner on the American Buy. Com Professional Tour, which is the equivalent of our European Challenge Tour. Richard, now married and a resident of the USA, also gets the occasional invite to play the lucrative main tour. His last, invite at the time of writing, was the Bob Hope Event at Pebble Beach, in which he made the cut to the final stages.

Peter Johnson can be justly proud of his talented son and also of the superb Vale of Glamorgan complex.

Sec/Manager:	Peter Johnson
Professional:	Peter Johnson
Directions:	8 miles NW of Cardiff City Centre. From M4 junction 34 take minor exit from roundabout (Pendoylan, Barry). Entrance after ¾ mile.
Visitors:	Welcome: unable to play at weekends. Contact Club in advance
Societies:	Welcome: By arrangement. Contact Club in advance
Facilities:	Putting Green, Chipping Green, Club Hire, Trolley Hire, Buggy Hire, Bar, Restaurant, Driving Range

Lake

Date Founded: 1991
Type of Course: Parkland
No of Holes: 18
Length: 6507 yds (6006 mtrs)
Par: 72
SSS: 71
Green Fees: Weekdays: £30 per day; Weekends/Bank Holidays: Unable to play

Hensol

Date Founded: 1993
Type of Course: Parkland
No of Holes: 9

Length:	3115 yds (2875 mtrs)
Par:	71
SSS:	72
Green Fees:	Weekdays: £5 per day;
	Weekends/Bank Holidays:
	Unable to play

Accommodation, Food and Drink

Reference numbers below refer to detailed
information provided in section 2

Accommodation

**Clawdd Coch Guest House, Pendoylan,
Vale of Glamorgan CF71 7UP**

Tel: 01446 760645

Versatile B&B facilities in a 17th century house with
five beautifully appointed bedrooms. Golfing breaks a
speciality. 115

**Crossways House, Cowbridge,
Vale of Glamorgan CF71 7LJ**

Tel: 01446 773171 Fax: 01446 771707
e-mail: enquiries@crosswayshouse.co.uk website:
www.crosswayshouse.co.uk

Three B&B bedrooms and a self-catering flat in a
lovely country mansion set in 6 acres ¾ mile west of
Cowbridge (B4270).

**Fairways Hotel, Porthcawl,
South Glamorgan CF36 3LS**

Tel: 01656 782085 Fax: 01656 785351
e-mail: fairwayshotel@aol.com
website: www.bridgend.gov.uk

Twenty-five en suite bedrooms in a smartly
refurbished family-run hotel near the seafront.
Restaurant, lounge bar, residents' lounge. 114

St Julian Inn, Newport, South Wales NP18 1QA

Tel: 01633 243548 Fax: 01633 243562

A welcoming old inn with the road on one side and
the River Usk on the other. Bar-style menu, award-
winning real ales. 108

**The White Horse Inn, Davis Row, Pentwyn,
Nr. Fochriw, Bargoed, Mid-Glamorgan CF81 9NP**

Tel: 01685 841215

Popular inn open seven days a week for breakfast,
lunch and dinner. Super home-made pies and lots
more. Two B&B rooms planned.

**Windmill Cottages, Llansannor, Cowbridge,
Vale of Glamorgan CF71 7TF**

Tel/Fax: 01446 772470
e-mail: rosser@globalnet.co.uk

Quality self-catering accommodation in 19th century
barn conversions adjacent to a working farm. Lovely
rural setting five minutes from Cowbridge. 116

Food and Drink

**Fairways Hotel, Porthcawl,
South Glamorgan CF36 3LS**

Tel: 01656 782085 Fax: 01656 785351

e-mail: fairwayshotel@aol.com
website: www.bridgend.gov.uk

Twenty-five en suite bedrooms in a smartly
refurbished family-run hotel near the seafront.
Restaurant, lounge bar, residents' lounge. 114

**The White Horse Inn, Davis Row, Pentwyn,
Nr. Fochriw, Bargoed, Mid-Glamorgan CF81 9NP**

Tel: 01685 841215

Popular inn open seven days a week for breakfast,
lunch and dinner. Super home-made pies and lots
more. Two B&B rooms planned.

Wenvoe Castle Golf Club

Wenvoe, Cardiff CF5 6BE

Tel: 02920 594371 Fax: 02920 594371

James Braid always did his very best to design a
course that was not easy to play, and the course
he created at Wenvoe Castle is no exception. With
the land he had at his disposal here he clearly
put much thought into its planning and cleverly
created a lay-out which can only be described as
a course of two highly contrasting halves. The
club is situated south west of Cardiff, in the direction of Barry, and inside grounds that had for
centuries encircled Wenvoe Castle, which is not
actually a castle but a grand old mansion that
housed the well-known Jenner family for hundreds of years (Barry Town Football Club's ground
is named Jenner Park).

The Reverend Hugh Jenner was the last of the
Jenner family to live there, before moving to live
in England in 1926. Having been the golf club
president from when the club was founded in
1936, he remained so until he died at the ripe
old age of ninety-five.

Almost the whole of the interior of the grand
old clubhouse was destroyed by fire in 1960, but
was quickly renovated and redesigned into what
is now a comfortable and pleasant place to relax
after returning from a round of golf over the difficult and undulating parkland course, which
meanders three-quarters of the way around the
clubhouse. The opening hole is quite spectacular. From a lofty tee you drive into a valley and
then it's uphill to a tricky green to, hopefully, two
further shots and two putts for a par-5. After this
the remainder of the outward half has many trees
to negotiate and steep fairways, of which all but
one go downhill. I regard this half of the course
as one of the toughest I have encountered anywhere on a parkland course. After this you have
to negotiate a rather tough 10th hole, which is a
dog-leg with a difficult green to find with your
approach shot. A really good par-4 this. The course
then starts to flatten out and gets wider without
the trees of the opening half, but still a good test.
The finishing hole is a dog-leg downhill par 4,

where you get a fine view of the front of the old stone-built clubhouse with it's expansive patio terrace.

James Braid did a great job here. Enjoy the challenge!

Sec/Manager:	N. Simms
Professional:	J.D Harris
Directions:	4½ miles SW of Cardiff City Centre. From M4 junction 33 take the A4232 (Caerau). After 3½ miles at Culverhouse Cross turn right onto A4050 (Wenvoe). Go through Wenvoe, entrance after ½ mile on right hand side.
Date Founded:	1936
Type of Course:	Hilly Parkland
No of Holes:	18
Length:	6422 yds (5928 mtrs)
Par:	72
SSS:	71
Green Fees:	Weekdays: £32 per day; Weekends/Bank Holidays: Unable to play at weekends
Visitors:	Welcome: Unable to play at weekends. Contact Club in advance
Societies:	Welcome: Unable to play at weekends. Contact Club in advance
Facilities:	Putting Green, Chipping Green, Practice Area, Trolley Hire, Bar, Restaurant

Accommodation, Food and Drink

Reference numbers below refer to detailed information provided in section 2

Accommodation

Clawdd Coch Guest House, Pendoylan, Vale of Glamorgan CF71 7UP
Tel: 01446 760645
Versatile B&B facilities in a 17th century house with five beautifully appointed bedrooms. Golfing breaks a speciality. 115

Crossways House, Cowbridge, Vale of Glamorgan CF71 7LJ
Tel: 01446 773171 Fax: 01446 771707
e-mail: enquiries@crosswayshouse.co.uk website: www.crosswayshouse.co.uk
Three B&B bedrooms and a self-catering flat in a lovely country mansion set in 6 acres ¾ mile west of Cowbridge (B4270).

Fairways Hotel, Porthcawl, South Glamorgan CF36 3LS
Tel: 01656 782085 Fax: 01656 785351
e-mail: fairwayshotel@aol.com
website: www.bridgend.gov.uk
Twenty-five en suite bedrooms in a smartly refurbished family-run hotel near the seafront. Restaurant, lounge bar, residents' lounge. 114

The White Horse Inn, Davis Row, Pentwyn, Nr Fochriw, Bargoed, Mid-Glamorgan CF81 9NP
Tel: 01685 841215
Popular inn open seven days a week for breakfast, lunch and dinner. Super home-made pies and lots more. Two B&B rooms planned.

Windmill Cottages, Llansannor, Cowbridge, Vale of Glamorgan CF71 7TF
Tel/Fax: 01446 772470 e-mail: rosser@globalnet.co.uk
Quality self-catering accommodation in 19th century barn conversions adjacent to a working farm. Lovely rural setting five minutes from Cowbridge. 116

Food and Drink

St Julian Inn, Newport, South Wales NP18 1QA
Tel: 01633 243548 Fax: 01633 243562
A welcoming old inn with the road on one side and the River Usk on the other. Bar-style menu, award-winning real ales. 108

The White Horse Inn, Davis Row, Pentwyn, Nr Fochriw, Bargoed, Mid-Glamorgan CF81 9NP
Tel: 01685 841215
Popular inn open seven days a week for breakfast, lunch and dinner. Super home-made pies and lots more. Two B&B rooms planned.

Whitchurch Golf Club

Pantmawr Road, Ahitchurch, Cardiff CF4 6XD
Tel: 02920 620985 Fax: 02920 529860

Like the Cardiff club, Whitchurch Golf Club is a beautifully designed parkland course on the edge of the capital city and situated in a residential area, but perhaps not so richly endowed with the high class properties to be found in Cyncoed. Lying close to exit 32 of the M4 Motorway and alongside the A470, again like Cardiff, it has hosted many top class championships, including the Welsh Professional Championship, which was won here in their turn by Brian Hugget, David Llewellyn and Philip Parkin, all former European Tour players and World Cup players.

Founded in 1915 to accommodate the swelling number of well-off Cardiffian business people and their families who were being attracted to the game as it grew in popularity, and who were unable to gain entry to the other established golf clubs situated nearby at Llanishen, Radyr and the Cardiff club at Cyncoed, the Whitchurch course at first simply provided a number of holes to satisfy the golfing newcomers, but as it became more firmly established and prosperous the committee called on the talents of Open champion James Braid and Frank Johns to redesign the course into mainly what can be seen today. The opening holes drop down gently and away from the lovely old clubhouse, which started life as a farmhouse known as Pentwyn, and then winds it's way back and behind the clubhouse, before returning to the wide expanse in the direction of the city and then back again to finish close to the clubhouse. All in all the course is a memorable experience as it winds through the many lovely trees, which adds very much to the general character of the place.

Surprisingly, the course has the pleasing atmosphere of tranquillity, which with the course being bordered on one side by the M4 Motorway and the busy A470 road to the centre of Cardiff on the other, is totally unexpected. Cardiff is some three miles away, but the Whitchurch club lies close to the pleasant urban village of Whitchurch, from whence it got it's name. Like Cardiff Golf Club, the Whitchurch club is rather popular; therefore, it is advisable to book up a game before arriving.

Sec/Manager:	John King
Professional:	Eddy Clark
Directions:	3 miles NW of Cardiff City Centre. From M4 junction 32 take the A470 (Whitchurch, City Centre). Turn left off dual carriageway only 300 yds after slip road, into Pantmawr Rd. Entrance after 50 yds.
Date Founded:	1915
Type of Course:	Parkland
No of Holes:	18
Length:	6212 yds (5734 mtrs)
Par:	71
SSS:	70
Green Fees:	Weekdays: £35 per day; Weekends/Bank Holidays: £40 per day
Visitors:	Welcome: Unable to play on Tuesdays or Saturdays during the summer. Contact Club in advance
Societies:	Welcome: Parties over 20 only able to play on Thursdays. Parties under 20 only able to play Mondays, Wednesdays and Fridays. Contact Club in advance.
Facilities:	Putting Green, Chipping Green, Trolley Hire, Bar, Restaurant

Accommodation, Food and Drink

Reference numbers below refer to detailed information provided in section 2

Accommodation

The Greyhound Inn, Christchurch, Newport, South Wales NP18 1JJ

Tel: 01633 420306 Fax: 01633 430588

A handsome late 19th century gabled inn with a proper village atmosphere, real ales and very good food. Friendly and inviting.   109

The Milton Hotel, Llanwern, Newport, Gwent NP16 6DU

Tel: 01633 412432

Home-cooked food, real ales and self-catering accommodation in a former hunting lodge an easy drive from exit 24 of the M4.   110

The Priory Hotel & Restaurant, Caerleon, South Wales NP18 1AG

Tel: 01633 421241 Fax: 01633 421271

A historic hotel of exceptional quality and character, set in its own secluded grounds in the Roman town of Caerleon.   112

The White Horse Inn, Davis Row, Pentwyn, Nr Fochriw, Bargoed, Mid-Glamorgan CF81 9NP

Tel: 01685 841215

Popular inn open seven days a week for breakfast, lunch and dinner. Super home-made pies and lots more. Two B&B rooms planned.

Food and Drink

Clawdd Coch Guest House, Pendoylan, Vale of Glamorgan CF71 7UP

Tel: 01446 760645

Versatile B&B facilities in a 17th century house with five beautifully appointed bedrooms. Golfing breaks a speciality.   115

The Milton Hotel, Llanwern, Newport, Gwent NP16 6DU

Tel: 01633 412432

Home-cooked food, real ales and self-catering accommodation in a former hunting lodge an easy drive from exit 24 of the M4.   110

The Priory Hotel & Restaurant, Caerleon, South Wales NP18 1AG

Tel: 01633 421241 Fax: 01633 421271

A historic hotel of exceptional quality and character, set in its own secluded grounds in the Roman town of Caerleon.   112

WEST GLAMORGAN

This is another attractive Welsh county to visit and one that includes the fine city of Swansea within its boundaries and a beautiful coastline with a good selection of seaside golf courses to attract visiting golf fanatics. Swansea has been an important seaport for many centuries, and because of this suffered much bombing during the Second World War. Centuries before this the Vikings plundered the countryside and terrorised the inhabitants of Swansea and the nearby small villages as they made their way up the Bristol Channel. Later came the pirates to lie in wait to plunder the rich merchant ships sailing home to the Bristol Channel ports. The smuggling trade was also rampant in these parts. Now, however, the area is more famous as a tourist haunt. Rebuilt after the savage bombing raids, Swansea now has a swanky new shopping area to attract the holidaymaker, before they head off to discover the delights of the wonderful Gower Coast region.

Dylan Thomas was born in Swansea and there is now the newly built Dylan Thomas Centre, opened by former US president Jimmy Carter (who is a great lover of Dylan Thomas' work) as part of the 1995 International Year of Literature. The centre can be found in the Maritime Quarter of Swansea, housed in a wonderfully restored old building that celebrates not only Thomas' great and unusual literary talents but also that of its many other literary personage. Here in this delightful centre can be seen exhibitions of photography, art and literary readings, which are constantly changed. Indeed, Swansea is renowned for its excellent museums. The Glynn Vivian Art Gallery is noted as one of the best museums of fine and applied art inside the Principality. Rare collections of the famous Swansea porcelain ware, alongside other top quality Oriental and European ceramics, are permanently on show; as is some wonderful examples of paintings by Welsh artists and breathtaking maritime paintings of the 19th-century seascape artists.

Swansea Marina

On display at Swansea Museum is the mummy of an Egyptian priest named Hor, who is recorded as having died on the banks of the Nile in 2,000 BC. He now lies in an air-conditioned viewing chamber. The museum dates from 1841 and, as can be expected, displays many ancient artefacts of Swansea and the surrounding countryside. Like this museum, the Maritime and Industrial Museum is also located in the Maritime Quarter of the city. The highlight of this museum is the world's first passenger railway, which ran from Swansea to Mumbles from 1807. Situated on the waterfront, the museum is housed in a rather old warehouse inside the marina. An excellent place to visit for maritime history buffs. The city also has the remains of a castle close to its centre. Starting as a mott-and-bailey type of castle, it eventually became more of a fortress when it was rebuilt and strengthened during the 13th century. However, as the centuries passed by the castle suffered from the many conflicts of Welsh and British history, until eventually the northern block became notorious as a debtor's prison in the 18th century.

Further along the south Gower coast and standing above the old Victorian town of Mumbles, Oystermouth Castle is another impressive 13th century castle to visit. Built in 1280, this powerful fortress was host to Edward I when he decided to tour the Principality in 1284. Surprisingly, this castle took no part whatsoever in the Civil War-unlike every other castle throughout this area. Nowadays, because of its beautiful gardens and open-air spaces, the castle plays host to Shakespearian plays and opera. The castle's superb position overlooking Swansea Bay is a joy in itself.

The Gower Peninsula has long been a tourist attraction. The National Parks Commission rightly saw it fit, in 1957, to designate the wonderful place an" area of outstanding natural beauty", thus making it the first place in Britain to be given such a mark of approval. Many thousands of visitors who keep returning will readily agree that with its fine beaches, magnificent bays, rolling hills and exhilarating cliff top walks, contained in its length of some 14 miles and a width of 7 miles, still matches anywhere in the whole of the U. K. Nevertheless, during the severe winter months it is not called "The Wild Peninsular" for nothing, because here more shipwrecks have been recorded than at any other coastline in Brit-

Three Cliffs Bay, Parkmill

ain. Indeed, the Mumbles lifeboat has become famous worldwide for the daring rescue missions it has carried out over the last three centuries. Many heroic lifeboatmen from Mumbles have perished in saving some 500 lives, and the number of lives saved continues to rise yearly. A fascinating coastline, it has revealed pieces-of-eight, gold doubloons and other valuable items washed ashore from ancient treasure ships that became wrecked here.

Mumbles is a charming resort with a wonderfully restored Victorian pier, which celebrated its centenary in 1998. Named the "Pride of the Bay", the pier is an interesting place to take a stroll because the Mumbles lifeboat and its slipway are housed at the extreme end. The town itself is a delightful hotchpotch of inns, restaurants and rather quaint old shops. A short distance away at Mumbles Head stands a lighthouse. A tower to warn shipping has stood here since 1794 when fires were lit on its top for sailors to look out for. Then in 1800 an oil lantern stood the test of time until electricity arrived. The buildings adjoining the lighthouse were built in 1861 as a coastal fortress. Also on the island and just beneath the lighthouse is Bob's Cave, but visitors must beware as the large cave becomes flooded at high tide, and also be reminded here that the Bristol Channel has the second highest tidal level in the world, with the incoming tide travelling at a terrific speed. Please beware!

Between Mumbles and Pwll Du (Black Pool in Welsh) Bay and Head, there are a number of excellent coves and bays with wonderful names to explore, such as: Bracelet Bay, Limeslade Bay, Rotherslade, Brandy Cove and Langland Bay. The latter name being also the name of the fantastic golf course there, which also runs along the side of Caswell Bay. Indeed, when it comes to good courses, the Swansea area is, most certainly, the best kept secret in Britain. Here one can find a mixture of nine good courses, from links to parkland to cliff top venues, with only two being 9-hole layouts and one 12-holes. Whilst the rest of West Glamorgan has only a total of four courses!

Other good places to visit along this magnificent coastline are Oxwich with its gorgeous beaches at Oxwich Bay. The first aeroplane flight in Wales took place here on January 19th, 1911, when Mr E. Sutton flew his Bleriot monoplane to a height of 30 feet. The beach here is some two miles long and very safe for bathing. Oxwich Point and its neighbour Port Eynon Point are noted as being the most treacherous places for shipping in this area, because between them they are responsible for more shipwrecks than anywhere else along the Gower coast. The seaside village of Port Eynon is one of the loveliest places to visit in the Gower. In a peaceful location with large and safe sandy bay, excellent small shops, guesthouses and a good walking area, it is an ideal place to stay. Port Eynon was once famous for its huge oyster fishing industry, and oysters had been fished there since Roman times. But because of poaching by foreign trawlers the oyster catch declined to such an extent that the last haul of this great delicacy took place in 1879 and many oystermen and their families moved elsewhere, many of

Worms Head, nr Rhossili

Rhossili Beach

them to Mumbles, where oyster fishing continued until further decline in the 1930's.

Further west lies Rhossili Bay, three miles long and arguably the finest sands in Wales. Good for bathing and sea fishing, it also has lots of massive dunes in which to shelter when the winds blow in. Rhossili Downs also offers good walking and is a favourite place for picnics. The bay was also a favourite landing place for the Viking ships. Local archives record that these savage marauders destroyed the Priory at the village of Llangennith in 986 and slaughtered most of the inhabitants. Whilst this was happening the people of Rhossili retaliated and burnt three of the Viking ships lying beached at Burry Holmes. A famous true story of the Dollar Ship has been handed down through generations of Rhosseli people. A ship carrying silver was wrecked here during the 17th century, most certainly by wreckers who lured the ship on to the rocks. No record of the ship's name or the fate of its crew has been found. However, for generations since the tragedy many Spanish silver dollars and half dollars have been uncovered from the Rhossili sands. Most of the coins were dated 1625 and 1639, the reign of King Philip IV of Spain. Many locals benefited from their finds, but no coins have been discovered since 1833. Nevertheless, digging for the coins remains a favourite pastime of the youngsters in Rhosseli. Further along the coast and beyond Whitford Point, at a place called Llanrhidian Sands, a vessel called "Scanderoon Galley" sank with 12 chests of gold on board. All were salvaged except one, so there is a possibility of treasure also being found here. The Gower Coast really is a gem of a place to visit!

Moving much further inland in the county, the other main points of interest are to be found in the area of the Vale of Neath. This area has long been renowned for its stunning combination of woodlands and waterfalls. Here one can visit many places of interest. The most ancient of these being the remains of Neath Abbey. Founded in 1111 by Richard de Granville for the Cistercian Monks. Edward II sought asylum here after his escape from Caerphilly Castle and the wrath of his revolted barons. Henry Richmond also stayed here after landing at Milford Haven to dispute the crown with Richard the III.

The Gnoll Estate at Neath is also open to visitors wishing to explore the 200 acres of beautiful country parkland, woodland and lakes. An added bonus here is a nine-hole golf course. Set inside 9, 000 glorious acres of forest is the Afan Argoed Countryside Centre, offering guided walks, bicycle trails with bicycle hire, the South Wales Miners Museum and a small refreshment centre.

Then there is the Cefn Coed Colliery Museum. Cefn Coed was once renowned as the deepest anthracite mine in the world, and the museum splendidly portrays the hardships of the workers involved in extracting this once precious mineral from the bowels of the earth. One can also experience what it was like working below the surface by visiting the underground mining gallery, deep, dark, wet and with realistic sound recordings. By contrast, at Aberdulais Falls, near Neath, lies the remains of an old tinplate works, and copper was mined here as far back as 1584. The waterfall supplied the energy needed to drive the wheels of industry here for centuries and what was Europe's largest generating water-wheel is now in the care of the National Trust. Two good golf courses are also to be found in this area at Neath and Glyneath. The town of Neath was once an important iron and coal centre exporting vast quantities of both via the docks at Swansea, but is now a rather quiet place after the decline of the South Wales mining industry.

Further south lies Port Talbot and the mighty Margam steelworks. Just a few miles from this vast industrial area of noise and belching smoke lies the tranquil offering of Margam Park. Here in 800 acres of magnificent parkland is something for everyone to enjoy. The main feature being the 12th century Cistercian Abbey, Abbey Church and Stones Museum. Founded in 1147, the Abbey is still in remarkable good condition, thanks to some Victorian improvements by none other than Wiiliam Morris, the great architect of that time. The Tudor/Gothic mansion with its famous Orangery is a joy to behold, and oranges can still be seen growing there. Much more can be enjoyed here, including a giant hedge maze, a children's nursery rhyme village, ornamental gardens and a giant draughts and chess playing area. There's much fun to be found in glorious West Glamorgan.

Location of Golf Courses

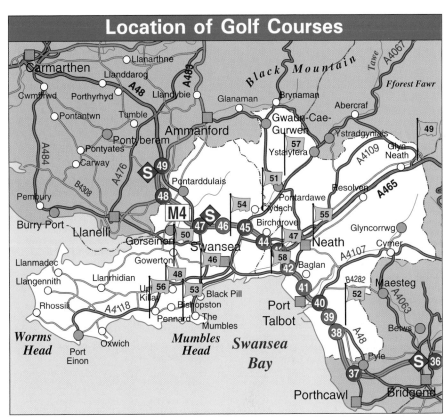

© MAPS IN MINUTES ™ 2001   © Crown Copyright, Ordnance Survey 2001

46 Clyne, West Glamorgan 80

47 Earlswood, West Glamorgan 81

48 Fairwood Park, West Glamorgan 82

49 Glynneath, West Glamorgan 83

50 Gower, West Glamorgan 84

51 Inco, West Glamorgan 86

52 Lakeside, West Glamorgan 87

53 Langland Bay, West Glamorgan 87

54 Morriston, West Glamorgan 89

55 Neath, West Glamorgan 90

56 Pennard, West Glamorgan 92

57 Pontardawe, West Glamorgan 93

58 Swansea Bay, West Glamorgan 94

Clyne Golf Club

**120 Owls Lodge Lane, Mayals,
Swansea SA3 5DP**
Tel: 01792 401989 Fax: 01792 401078

The Clyne course is another of the fine courses to be found in the Gower region. Like Fairwood Park it's slightly inland, but unlike Fairwood's parkland the terrain at Clyne is moorland, which of course, means a different type of rough for the golfer to contend with. Nothing, however, to frighten off the "rabbits" amongst you, simply a difference in challenge to your golfing skills and something extra to overcome in the search of golfing perfection. Yes, the courses on the Gower certainly has something for everyone to enjoy, whether it be the seaside links courses, the parkland at Fairwood Park or the moorland stretch which is Clyne.

Founded in 1920, Clyne Golf Club is the fifth oldest club in West Glamorgan, and one that has a long reputation of being an excellent course to play, with a warm and friendly atmosphere for visitors to enjoy in the spacious clubhouse. A measure of how popular the course is among the golfers of the area is the fact that the club can boast an enormous playing membership of close to 900 in number. An amazing number considering the many excellent courses in the Swansea area, and one which tells the visitor that Clyne must obviously be ranked highly by the golfing fraternity of Swansea. All in all a very good course to play. The views from the course are also something special, as is the good home cooking in the restaurant there!

Designed jointly by one of the great course architects, H. S. Colt and R. Harris, the 6,334 yards course is a splendid test of golf, with a demanding par of 70.

Sec/Manager:	Ray Thomson
Professional:	Jonathan Clewett
Directions:	4 miles SW of Swansea. From centre take the coast road A4067 (Mumbles). After 3 miles at Blackpill turn right onto B4436. After ½ mile turn right into Owls Lodge Lane. Entrance after 600 yds at the end.
Date Founded:	1920
Type of Course:	Links
No of Holes:	18
Length:	6334 yds (5846 mtrs)
Par:	70

SSS:	68
Green Fees:	Weekdays: £25 per day; Weekends/Bank Holidays: £30 per day
Visitors:	Welcome: Excluding Tuesday. Contact Club in advance
Societies:	Welcome: By arrangement. Contact Club in advance
Facilities:	Putting Green, Chipping Green, Practice Area, Club Hire, Trolley Hire, Bar, Restaurant

Accommodation, Food and Drink

Reference numbers below refer to detailed information provided in section 2

Accommodation

Bank Farm Leisure Park, Horton, Gower, Swansea SA3 1LL
Tel: 01792 390228/2390452 Fax: 01792 391282
e-mail: bankfarmleisure@cs.com
website: www.bankfarmleisure.co.uk
A perfect holiday base on the beautiful Gower Peninsula, with self-catering bungalows for rent and pitches for caravans and tents.   119

The Britannia Inn, Llanmadoc, Gower, Swansea SA3 1DB
Tel/Fax: 01792 386624   e-mail: mikdow@freeuk.com
A beautifully preserved 17th century inn on the northwestern tip of the Gower Peninsula, with a welcome for all ages, a menu to suit all tastes and three en suite bedrooms.   121

Devon View Hotel, 396 Oystermouth Road, Swansea SA1 3UL
Tel: 01792 462008
e-mail: joseph@devonview.co.uk
website: www.devonview.co.uk
Seafront hotel with 14 comfortable, high-ceilinged rooms. B&B, dinner by arrangement, packed lunches available.   117

Hurst Dene Guest House, Uplands, Swansea SA2 0LJ
Tel/Fax: 01792 280920 website: www.hurstdene.co.uk
Ten bedrooms for Bed & Breakfast in a large Victorian terraced house. Also self-catering units. In a Swansea suburb near the sea.   124

Little Haven Guest House, Oxwich, Gower, Swansea SA3 1LS
Tel: 01792 390940
Family-run guest house with a twin, two doubles and an en suite family room. Also self-catering bungalow. 11 miles from Swansea close to the sea.

Shoreline Hotel, Mumbles, Swansea SA3 4EA
Tel/Fax: 01792 366233
website: www.shorelinehotel.co.uk

A family-run hotel with 12 en suite bedrooms, bar and residents' lounge. Right on the seafront, with views across Swansea Bay. 118

Food and Drink

Bank Farm Leisure Park, Horton, Gower, Swansea SA3 1LL

Tel: 01792 390228/2390452 Fax: 01792 391282
e-mail: bankfarmleisure@cs.com
website: www.bankfarmleisure.co.uk
A perfect holiday base on the beautiful Gower Peninsula, with self-catering bungalows for rent and pitches for caravans and tents. 119

The Britannia Inn, Llanmadoc, Gower, Swansea SA3 1DB

Tel/Fax: 01792 386624   e-mail: mikdow@freeuk.com
A beautifully preserved 17th century inn on the northwestern tip of the Gower Peninsula, with a welcome for all ages, a menu to suit all tastes and three en suite bedrooms. 121

CJ's Wine Bar & Restaurant, Oystermouth, Swansea SA3 4DN

Tel: 01792 361246 Fax: 01792 419849
Cosy, friendly wine bar-café-restaurant in a row of shops close to the seafront. Varied menu with steaks and grill specialities and a vast cocktail list. 122

Earlswood Golf Club

Jersey Marine, Neath SA10 6JP
Tel: 01792 812198

Sec/Manager:	D Goatcher
Professional:	Mike Day
Directions:	3½ miles SW of Neath centre. From M4 junction 42 take the Fabian Way (A483, Swansea). After 1 mile at roundabout turn right onto B4290 (Skewen). Take first right after 200 yds then right at T-junction. Entrance after 250 yds at the end.
Date Founded:	1993

Type of Course:	Heathland
No of Holes:	18
Length:	5174 yds (4776 mtrs)
Par:	68
SSS:	68
Green Fees:	Weekdays: £8 per day; Weekends/Bank Holidays: £8 per day
Visitors:	Welcome
Societies:	Welcome
Facilities:	Putting Green, Chipping Green, Club Hire, Trolley Hire, Bar, Restaurant, Driving Range

Accommodation, Food and Drink

Reference numbers below refer to detailed information provided in section 2

Accommodation

Bank Farm Leisure Park, Horton, Gower, Swansea SA3 1LL

Tel: 01792 390228/2390452 Fax: 01792 391282
e-mail: bankfarmleisure@cs.com
website: www.bankfarmleisure.co.uk
A perfect holiday base on the beautiful Gower Peninsula, with self-catering bungalows for rent and pitches for caravans and tents. 119

The Britannia Inn, Llanmadoc, Gower, Swansea SA3 1DB

Tel/Fax: 01792 386624   e-mail: mikdow@freeuk.com
A beautifully preserved 17th century inn on the northwestern tip of the Gower Peninsula, with a welcome for all ages, a menu to suit all tastes and three en suite bedrooms. 121

Devon View Hotel, 396 Oystermouth Road, Swansea SA1 3UL

Tel: 01792 462008
e-mail: joseph@devonview.co.uk
website: www.devonview.co.uk
Seafront hotel with 14 comfortable, high-ceilinged rooms. B&B, dinner by arrangement, packed lunches available. 117

Drws Nesaf, Abergwrelych House, Pontwalby, Glynneath SA11 5LN

Tel: 01639 720035
A charming mid-Victorian cottage in beautiful walking country. Self-catering accommodation comprises sitting room/diner, kitchen, 2 bedrooms, shower room, patio.

Hurst Dene Guest House, Uplands, Swansea SA2 0LJ

Tel/Fax: 01792 280920 website: www.hurstdene.co.uk
Ten bedrooms for Bed & Breakfast in a large Victorian terraced house. Also self-catering units. In a Swansea suburb near the sea. 124

Little Haven Guest House, Oxwich, Gower, Swansea SA3 1LS

Tel: 01792 390940

Family-run guest house with a twin, two doubles and an en suite family room. Also self-catering bungalow. 11 miles from Swansea close to the sea.

Shoreline Hotel, Mumbles, Swansea SA3 4EA

Tel/Fax: 01792 366233

website: www.shorelinehotel.co.uk

A family-run hotel with 12 en suite bedrooms, bar and residents' lounge. Right on the seafront, with views across Swansea Bay.   118

Ty'n-y-Caeau, Margam Village, Port Talbot, West Glamorgan SA13 2NW

Tel: 01639 883897 Fax: 01639 895570

e-mail: gaen@tynycaeau.freeserve.co.uk

A large country house with superb gardens and comfortable en suite double or family rooms. Self catering also available.

Food and Drink

Bank Farm Leisure Park, Horton, Gower, Swansea SA3 1LL

Tel: 01792 390228/2390452 Fax: 01792 391282

e-mail: bankfarmleisure@cs.com

website: www.bankfarmleisure.co.uk

A perfect holiday base on the beautiful Gower Peninsula, with self-catering bungalows for rent and pitches for caravans and tents.   119

The Britannia Inn, Llanmadoc, Gower, Swansea SA3 1DB

Tel/Fax: 01792 386624   e-mail: mikdow@freeuk.com

A beautifully preserved 17th century inn on the northwestern tip of the Gower Peninsula, with a welcome for all ages, a menu to suit all tastes and three en suite bedrooms.   121

CJ's Wine Bar & Restaurant, Oystermouth, Swansea SA3 4DN

Tel: 01792 361246 Fax: 01792 419849

Cosy, friendly wine bar-café-restaurant in a row of shops close to the seafront. Varied menu with steaks and grill specialities and a vast cocktail list.   122

Fairwood Park Golf Club

Blackhills Lane, Upper Killay, Swansea SA2 7JN

Tel: 01792 203648 Fax: 01792 297849

Fairwood Park's claim to fame is that the club has twice successfully hosted the Welsh Professional Championship, and whilst doing so highlighted the fact that this beautifully laid out parkland course is one more West Glamorgan-based golf course which should be added to the visitors list of "must go and play" venues when staying in the area. Relatively unknown (even to many Welsh golfers) before first staging the prestigious Welsh Professional Championship in 1990, the course quickly gained prominence because of the huge media coverage (including Welsh television coverage) of the event and the glorious weather which attracted many people, who came, saw and very much liked what they saw to quickly return with their clubs ready for action. So successful was the staging of the event that the powers-that-were then of the PGA West Region, chose Fairwood Park as the championship's venue for the following year.

One professional golfer who found the course very much to his liking was Newport's Paul Mayo, who brilliantly won the prestigious Welsh professional title on both occasions, and afterwards highly praised the beautiful layout of the course.

Highly recommended to golfers with walking difficulties (I won't say seniors), the course is fairly flat but, nevertheless, not short and definitely not easy to score well on! Indeed, with its par of 72 and a length of 6754 yards, many a good quality professional failed to impress during the hosting of the Welsh Professional Championship-this when conditions were excellent.

Founded only in 1969 and well-designed by golf architects Hartree and Co. , the course has matured wonderfully well over the years and is a real pleasure to play on. Rather easy to find, it is situated off Blackhills Lane in Upper Killay, and opposite Swansea Airport.

Sec/Manager:	Christine Beer
Professional:	Gary Hughes
Directions:	4 miles SW of Swansea City Centre. From centre take Mansel St (A4118 Sketty, Port Eynon). After 4 miles turn left into Hen Parc Lane. Entrance after 1½ miles on left hand side.
Date Founded:	1969
Type of Course:	Parkland

No of Holes:	18
Length:	6754 yds (6234 mtrs)
Par:	72
SSS:	73
Green Fees:	Weekdays: £25 per day; Weekends/Bank Holidays: £30 per day
Visitors:	Welcome: By arrangement. Contact Club in advance
Societies:	Welcome: By arrangement. Contact Club in advance
Facilities:	Putting Green, Practice Ground, Club Hire, Trolley Hire, Buggy Hire, Bar, Restaurant

Accommodation, Food and Drink

Reference numbers below refer to detailed information provided in section 2

Accommodation

Bank Farm Leisure Park, Horton, Gower, Swansea SA3 1LL

Tel: 01792 390228/2390452 Fax: 01792 391282
e-mail: bankfarmleisure@cs.com
website: www.bankfarmleisure.co.uk
A perfect holiday base on the beautiful Gower Peninsula, with self-catering bungalows for rent and pitches for caravans and tents. 119

The Britannia Inn, Llanmadoc, Gower, Swansea SA3 1DB

Tel/Fax: 01792 386624   e-mail: mikdow@freeuk.com
A beautifully preserved 17th century inn on the northwestern tip of the Gower Peninsula, with a welcome for all ages, a menu to suit all tastes and three en suite bedrooms. 121

Culver House Hotel, Port Eynon, Gower, Swansea SA3 1NN

Tel: 01792 390755 Fax: 01792 390735
e-mail: info@culverhousehotel.co.uk
website: www.culverhousehotel.co.uk
Twelve en suite bedrooms in a friendly hotel idyllically situated right on the beach. Residents' lounge, bar, restaurant. Large car park. 120

Devon View Hotel, 396 Oystermouth Road, Swansea SA1 3UL

Tel: 01792 462008
e-mail: joseph@devonview.co.uk
website: www.devonview.co.uk
Seafront hotel with 14 comfortable, high-ceilinged rooms. B&B, dinner by arrangement, packed lunches available. 117

Hurst Dene Guest House, Uplands, Swansea SA2 0LJ

Tel/Fax: 01792 280920 website: www.hurstdene.co.uk
Ten bedrooms for Bed & Breakfast in a large Victorian

terraced house. Also self-catering units. In a Swansea suburb near the sea. 124

Parc-le-Breos, Parkmill, Gower, Swansea SA3 2HA

Tel: 01792 371636 Fax: 01792 371287
website: www.parc-le-breos.co.uk
Ten bedrooms including spacious family rooms in a 19th century hunting lodge in a rural setting on the Gower. Riding centre on site.

Shoreline Hotel, Mumbles, Swansea SA3 4EA

Tel/Fax: 01792 366233
website: www.shorelinehotel.co.uk
A family-run hotel with 12 en suite bedrooms, bar and residents' lounge. Right on the seafront, with views across Swansea Bay. 118

Food and Drink

Bank Farm Leisure Park, Horton, Gower, Swansea SA3 1LL

Tel: 01792 390228/2390452 Fax: 01792 391282
e-mail: bankfarmleisure@cs.com
website: www.bankfarmleisure.co.uk
A perfect holiday base on the beautiful Gower Peninsula, with self-catering bungalows for rent and pitches for caravans and tents. 119

The Britannia Inn, Llanmadoc, Gower, Swansea SA3 1DB

Tel/Fax: 01792 386624   e-mail: mikdow@freeuk.com
A beautifully preserved 17th century inn on the northwestern tip of the Gower Peninsula, with a welcome for all ages, a menu to suit all tastes and three en suite bedrooms. 121

Culver House Hotel, Port Eynon, Gower, Swansea SA3 1NN

Tel: 01792 390755 Fax: 01792 390735
e-mail: info@culverhousehotel.co.uk
website: www.culverhousehotel.co.uk
Twelve en suite bedrooms in a friendly hotel idyllically situated right on the beach. Residents' lounge, bar, restaurant. Large car park. 120

The Mardy Hotel, 117 High Street, Gorseinon, Swansea SA4 2BT

Tel: 01792 892616
Snacks, burgers, scampi and steaks on the menu, with roasts on Sunday. Darts, pool, live entertainment three nights a week.

Glynneath Golf Club

Penycraig, Pontneathvaughan SA11 5UH

Tel: 01639 720452 Fax: 01639 720452

Just a few miles from Neath is the "Royal" Glyneath Golf Club, who's president is that lovely character Max Boyce, the well known composer and singer of humorous rugby songs and a talented comedian. Max loves his golf as much as rugby, and runs an annual celebrity pro-am tournament at this pleasant 18-hole woodland cum parkland hilltop course, which is quite a riotous affair all in the aid of charity during the summer. A course well worth a visit, even more so when the approachable Max Boyce happens to be in attendance.

Sec/Manager:	David Fellowes
Professional:	None
Directions:	12 miles NE of Neath. From Neath take the A465 (Merthyr Tydfil). After 10 miles at Glynneath turn left onto the B4242 to Pont Nedd Fechan. Entrance just past Pont Nedd Fechan Tourist Information Centre.
Date Founded:	1931
Type of Course:	Parkland
No of Holes:	18
Length:	5656 yds (5220 mtrs)
Par:	69
SSS:	68
Green Fees:	Weekdays: £17 per day; Weekends/Bank Holidays: £22 per day
Visitors:	Welcome: By arrangement excluding weekends. Contact Club in advance
Societies:	Welcome: Excluding weekends. Contact Club in advance
Facilities:	Putting Green, Chipping Green, Practice Area, Club Hire, Trolley Hire, Bar, Restaurant

Accommodation, Food and Drink

Reference numbers below refer to detailed information provided in section 2

Accommodation

The County House, 100 The Street, Brecon, Powys LD3 7LS
Tel: 01874 625844 e-mail: countyhouse@ukworld.net
Licensed accommodation in a fine Georgian house. Three excellent en suite bedrooms: sitting room, dining room. B&B with dinner option.

Drws Nesaf, Abergwrelych House, Pontwalby, Glynneath SA11 5LN
Tel: 01639 720035
A charming mid-Victorian cottage in beautiful walking country. Self-catering accommodation comprises sitting room/diner, kitchen, 2 bedrooms, shower room, patio.

The Tai'r Bull Inn, Libanus, Nr. Brecon, Powys LD3 8EL
Tel: 01874 625849
A very well-kept roadside inn offering good food, B&B accommodation and superb views of the Brecon Beacons.   148

Ty Andrew Guest House, 33 Seymour Street, Aberdare, Mid-Glamorgan CF44 7BL
Tel: 01685 876603
Bed & Breakfast guest house with rooms (some en suite) ranging from singles to a family room. Drying facilities available.

The White Swan, Llanfrynach, Brecon, Powys LD3 7BZ
Tel: 01874 665276 website: www.the-white-swan.com
An excellent pub-restaurant in a row of smart black-and-white cottages. Sister establishment offering luxurious self-catering accommodation nearby.   150

Food and Drink

The Tai'r Bull Inn, Libanus, Nr. Brecon, Powys LD3 8EL
Tel: 01874 625849
A very well-kept roadside inn offering good food, B&B accommodation and superb views of the Brecon Beacons.   148

The Wheatsheaf, Wheat Street, Brecon, Powys LD3 7DG
Tel: 01874 611109
A town-centre pub with a long, spacious bar. Pool table. Good bar food, good beer, young crowd.

The White Swan, Llanfrynach, Brecon, Powys LD3 7BZ
Tel: 01874 665276 website: www.the-white-swan.com
An excellent pub-restaurant in a row of smart black-and-white cottages. Sister establishment offering luxurious self-catering accommodation nearby.   150

Gower Golf Club

Cefn Goleu, Three Crosses, Gowerton SA4 3HS
Tel: 01792 872480 Fax: 01792 872480

Just a few miles from Clyne can be found the newly-built Gower Golf Club, which lies close to Three Crosses and off the B4295 road to Penclawdd. Founded as recently as 1995, this 18-hole parkland course was designed by Donald Steel, the former Cambridge golfing blue, English international, fully qualified golf course architect, with a BA degree in agriculture, golf writer and fellow member of the Association of Golf Writers, and also its president. An excellent layout, the 6,441 yards, Par 71 course features a number of lakes and was chosen to host a Glamorgan Golf Union county match in 2001. Thus proving its rapid maturity.

Sec/Manager:	Adrian Richards
Professional:	Alan Williamson
Directions:	5 miles NW of Swansea City Centre. From M4 junction 47 take the A483 (Swansea). After 1½ miles turn right onto the A484 and after 1½ miles turn left onto the B4295. At Gowerton turn left onto the B4296, then via Mount St and Gae Marset Rd to entrance on right hand side 1mile from B4295.
Date Founded:	1995
Type of Course:	Parkland
No of Holes:	18
Length:	6441 yds (5945 mtrs)
Par:	71
SSS:	72
Green Fees:	Weekdays: £15 per day; Weekends/Bank Holidays: £17 per day
Visitors:	Welcome: By arrangement excluding weekends. Contact Club in advance
Societies:	Welcome: By arrangement. Contact Club in advance
Facilities:	Practice Area, Trolley Hire, Buggy Hire, Bar, Restaurant

Accommodation, Food and Drink

Reference numbers below refer to detailed information provided in section 2

Accommodation

Beachcomber Hotel, 364 Oystermouth Road, Swansea SA1 3UL

Tel: 01792 651380

Ten Bed & Breakfast rooms with shared bathrooms in a location handy for city and sea. Tv, tea-makers, ironing and drying facilities available.

The Britannia Inn, Llanmadoc, Gower, Swansea SA3 1DB

Tel/Fax: 01792 386624   e-mail: mikdow@freeuk.com

A beautifully preserved 17th century inn on the northwestern tip of the Gower Peninsula, with a welcome for all ages, a menu to suit all tastes and three en suite bedrooms.   121

Culver House Hotel, Port Eynon, Gower, Swansea SA3 1NN

Tel: 01792 390755 Fax: 01792 390735
e-mail: info@culverhousehotel.co.uk
website: www.culverhousehotel.co.uk

Twelve en suite bedrooms in a friendly hotel idyllically situated right on the beach. Residents' lounge, bar, restaurant. Large car park.   120

Devon View Hotel, 396 Oystermouth Road, Swansea SA1 3UL

Tel: 01792 462008
e-mail: joseph@devonview.co.uk
website: www.devonview.co.uk

Seafront hotel with 14 comfortable, high-ceilinged rooms. B&B, dinner by arrangement, packed lunches available.   117

Little Haven Guest House, Oxwich, Gower, Swansea SA3 1LS

Tel: 01792 390940

Family-run guest house with a twin, two doubles and an en suite family room. Also self-catering bungalow. 11 miles from Swansea close to the sea.

Parc-le-Breos, Parkmill, Gower, Swansea SA3 2HA

Tel: 01792 371636 Fax: 01792 371287
website: www.parc-le-breos.co.uk

Ten bedrooms including spacious family rooms in a 19th century hunting lodge in a rural setting on the Gower. Riding centre on site.

Food and Drink

The Britannia Inn, Llanmadoc, Gower, Swansea SA3 1DB

Tel/Fax: 01792 386624   e-mail: mikdow@freeuk.com

A beautifully preserved 17th century inn on the northwestern tip of the Gower Peninsula, with a welcome for all ages, a menu to suit all tastes and three en suite bedrooms.   121

CJ's Wine Bar & Restaurant, Oystermouth, Swansea SA3 4DN

Tel: 01792 361246 Fax: 01792 419849

Cosy, friendly wine bar-café-restaurant in a row of shops close to the seafront. Varied menu with steaks and grill specialities and a vast cocktail list.   122

Culver House Hotel, Port Eynon, Gower, Swansea SA3 1NN

Tel: 01792 390755 Fax: 01792 390735
e-mail: info@culverhousehotel.co.uk
website: www.culverhousehotel.co.uk

Twelve en suite bedrooms in a friendly hotel idyllically situated right on the beach. Residents' lounge, bar, restaurant. Large car park.   120

The Mardy Hotel, 117 High Street, Gorseinon, Swansea SA4 2BT

Tel: 01792 892616

Snacks, burgers, scampi and steaks on the menu, with roasts on Sunday. Darts, pool, live entertainment three nights a week.

Inco Golf Club

Clydach, Swansea SA6 5EU
Tel: 01792 844216

Sec/Manager:	Selwyn Murdock
Professional:	None
Directions:	5½ miles N of Swansea City Centre. From M4 junction 45 take the A4087 (Pontadawe). After 1¾ miles at roundabout turn left onto B4201 (Clydach). Entrance after 100 yds on right hand side.
Date Founded:	1964
Type of Course:	Meadowland
No of Holes:	18
Length:	6100 yds (5630 mtrs)
Par:	71
SSS:	70
Green Fees:	Weekdays: £10; Weekends/ Bank Holidays:£12.00-£15.00

Visitors:	Welcome: Contact Club by telephone in advance
Societies:	Welcome: Contact Club in advance, by arrangement only
Facilities:	Bar, Restaurant

Accommodation, Food and Drink

Reference numbers below refer to detailed information provided in section 2

Accommodation

Beachcomber Hotel, 364 Oystermouth Road, Swansea SA1 3UL

Tel: 01792 651380

Ten Bed & Breakfast rooms with shared bathrooms in a location handy for city and sea. Tv, tea-makers, ironing and drying facilities available.

Devon View Hotel, 396 Oystermouth Road, Swansea SA1 3UL

Tel: 01792 462008
e-mail: joseph@devonview.co.uk
website: www.devonview.co.uk

Seafront hotel with 14 comfortable, high-ceilinged rooms. B&B, dinner by arrangement, packed lunches available.   117

Drws Nesaf, Abergwrelych House, Pontwalby, Glynneath SA11 5LN

Tel: 01639 720035

A charming mid-Victorian cottage in beautiful walking country. Self-catering accommodation comprises sitting room/diner, kitchen, 2 bedrooms, shower room, patio.

Hurst Dene Guest House, Uplands, Swansea SA2 0LJ

Tel/Fax: 01792 280920 website: www.hurstdene.co.uk

Ten bedrooms for Bed & Breakfast in a large Victorian terraced house. Also self-catering units. In a Swansea suburb near the sea.   124

Wernoleu Hotel, Ammanford, Carmarthenshire SA18 2HX

Tel/Fax: 01269 592598

Warm and welcoming country hotel set in five acres of grounds, with seven spacious bedrooms, lots of real ales and a tasty bar menu.
125

Food and Drink

CJ's Wine Bar & Restaurant, Oystermouth, Swansea SA3 4DN

Tel: 01792 361246 Fax: 01792 419849

Cosy, friendly wine bar-café-restaurant in a row of shops close to the seafront. Varied menu with steaks and grill specialities and a vast cocktail list.   122

The Mardy Hotel, 117 High Street, Gorseinon, Swansea SA4 2BT

Tel: 01792 892616

Snacks, burgers, scampi and steaks on the menu, with roasts on Sunday. Darts, pool, live entertainment three nights a week.

Lakeside Golf Club

Water Street, Margam Port Talbot SA13 2PA
Tel: 01639 899959

Sec/Manager: D Thomas

Professional: M Wootton

Directions: 7 miles NW of Bridgend. From M4 junction 38 take the A40 (Pyle, Bridgend), after ½ mile turn right into Water Street. Entrance after ½ mile on left hand side.

Date Founded: 1992

Type of Course: Parkland

No of Holes: 18

Length: 4550 yds (4200 mtrs)

Par: 63

SSS: 63

Green Fees: Weekdays: £9.50; Weekends/Bank Holidays: £9.50

Visitors: Welcome: Welcome at all times

Societies: Welcome: Contact Club in advance, unable to play at certain weekend times

Facilities: Putting Green, Driving Range, Club Hire, Trolley Hire, Bar, Restaurant

Accommodation, Food and Drink

Reference numbers below refer to detailed information provided in section 2

Accommodation

Drws Nesaf, Abergwrelych House, Pontwalby, Glynneath SA11 5LN

Tel: 01639 720035

A charming mid-Victorian cottage in beautiful walking country. Self-catering accommodation comprises sitting room/diner, kitchen, 2 bedrooms, shower room, patio.

Fairways Hotel, Porthcawl, South Glamorgan CF36 3LS

Tel: 01656 782085 Fax: 01656 785351
e-mail: fairwayshotel@aol.com
website: www.bridgend.gov.uk

Twenty-five en suite bedrooms in a smartly refurbished family-run hotel near the seafront. Restaurant, lounge bar, residents' lounge.   114

Hurst Dene Guest House, Uplands, Swansea SA2 0LJ

Tel/Fax: 01792 280920
website: www.hurstdene.co.uk

Ten bedrooms for Bed & Breakfast in a large Victorian terraced house. Also self-catering units. In a Swansea suburb near the sea.   124

Ty'n-y-Caeau, Margam Village, Port Talbot, West Glamorgan SA13 2NW

Tel: 01639 883897 Fax: 01639 895570
e-mail: gaen@tynycaeau.freeserve.co.uk

A large country house with superb gardens and comfortable en suite double or family rooms. Self catering also available.

Food and Drink

CJ's Wine Bar & Restaurant, Oystermouth, Swansea SA3 4DN

Tel: 01792 361246 Fax: 01792 419849

Cosy, friendly wine bar-café-restaurant in a row of shops close to the seafront. Varied menu with steaks and grill specialities and a vast cocktail list.   122

Fairways Hotel, Porthcawl, South Glamorgan CF36 3LS

Tel: 01656 782085 Fax: 01656 785351
e-mail: fairwayshotel@aol.com
website: www.bridgend.gov.uk

Twenty-five en suite bedrooms in a smartly refurbished family-run hotel near the seafront. Restaurant, lounge bar, residents' lounge.   114

The Mardy Hotel, 117 High Street, Gorseinon, Swansea SA4 2BT

Tel: 01792 892616

Snacks, burgers, scampi and steaks on the menu, with roasts on Sunday. Darts, pool, live entertainment three nights a week.

Langland Bay Golf Club

Langland, Swansea SA3 4QR
Tel: 01792 361721

The members of the Langland Bay club consider themselves lucky through the fact that they have the best of both worlds on their wonderful course, they play on part parkland and part seaside links. One of the most attractive courses in this beautiful Gower Peninsular area, it was founded in 1904 by keen golfers who obviously knew their business when they set out to search for suitable land in which to indulge in their newly discovered sport-golf only becoming established in Wales six years previously. They could not have picked a better spot, because this is as perfect a place as can be found anywhere on which to build a golf course. Not a hidden gem by any means, but one that visitors tend to keep to themselves, and who can blame them? It's not everyday you come across such a treasure as this.

And it is not just the course that appeals to visitors. Here one can also find much enjoyment from its scenic and magnificent views of the Gower coast and over the Bristol Channel. Just 5,857 yards and a par of 70, not a long course by any means, but certainly one throwing out a stiff challenge. Indeed, a real toughie of a course, which will make you fight all the way in your attempt to conquer it.

Lots of rough, lots of sand traps, tricky greens, small greens, fast greens and horrible hazards, requires your full attention, so forget about the gorgeous scenery until your round ends. The 6th has the reputation of being the toughest hole on the Gower coast. Into the prevailing wind and an uphill trek, it really is a mighty par four. The 8th is also a bit of a test as you thread your way to the sanctuary of the green along a fearsome fairway close to the edge of Caswell Bay. The well-named "Death or Glory" 16th is a mere short hole, but it needs the correct club hit in the right direction with the correct distance to gain any glory from this sadistically designed hole. Otherwise, it's the death of any erstwhile promising scorecard!

Should you fall head over heels in love with this attractive course, and then you can romance with the lovely "Old Lady" by purchasing a weekly ticket (Mon-Fri) at a bargain price. Enjoy yourself!

Sec/Manager:	Lynn Coleman
Professional:	Mark Evans
Directions:	5 miles SW of Swansea City Centre. From centre take the coast road A4067 (Mumbles). At Mumbles outskirts turn right to Newton (B4593)and after ¾ mile at the Hillcrest House Hotel go straight into Langland Bay Rd. Entrance after ¾ mile.
Date Founded:	1904
Type of Course:	Seaside and Parkland
No of Holes:	18
Length:	5857 yds (5406 mtrs)
Par:	70
SSS:	69
Green Fees:	Weekdays: £28; Weekends/ Bank Holidays: £30
Visitors:	Welcome: Contact Club by telephone in advance.
Societies:	Welcome: Contact Club in advance. Unable tp play at weekends.
Facilities:	Putting Green, Chipping Green, Club Hire, Trolley Hire, Bar, Restaurant

Accommodation, Food and Drink

Reference numbers below refer to detailed information provided in section 2

Accommodation

Bank Farm Leisure Park, Horton, Gower, Swansea SA3 1LL

Tel: 01792 390228/2390452 Fax: 01792 391282
e-mail: bankfarmleisure@cs.com
website: www.bankfarmleisure.co.uk
A perfect holiday base on the beautiful Gower Peninsula, with self-catering bungalows for rent and pitches for caravans and tents.   119

Beachcomber Hotel, 364 Oystermouth Road, Swansea SA1 3UL

Tel: 01792 651380
Ten Bed & Breakfast rooms with shared bathrooms in a location handy for city and sea. Tv, tea-makers, ironing and drying facilities available.

The Britannia Inn, Llanmadoc, Gower, Swansea SA3 1DB

Tel/Fax: 01792 386624   e-mail: mikdow@freeuk.com
A beautifully preserved 17th century inn on the northwestern tip of the Gower Peninsula, with a welcome for all ages, a menu to suit all tastes and three en suite bedrooms.   121

Culver House Hotel, Port Eynon, Gower, Swansea SA3 1NN

Tel: 01792 390755 Fax: 01792 390735
e-mail: info@culverhousehotel.co.uk
website: www.culverhousehotel.co.uk
Twelve en suite bedrooms in a friendly hotel idyllically situated right on the beach. Residents' lounge, bar, restaurant. Large car park.   120

Devon View Hotel, 396 Oystermouth Road, Swansea SA1 3UL

Tel: 01792 462008
e-mail: joseph@devonview.co.uk
website: www.devonview.co.uk
Seafront hotel with 14 comfortable, high-ceilinged rooms. B&B, dinner by arrangement, packed lunches available.   117

Hurst Dene Guest House, Uplands, Swansea SA2 0LJ

Tel/Fax: 01792 280920 website: www.hurstdene.co.uk
Ten bedrooms for Bed & Breakfast in a large Victorian terraced house. Also self-catering units. In a Swansea suburb near the sea.   124

Little Haven Guest House, Oxwich, Gower, Swansea SA3 1LS

Tel: 01792 390940
Family-run guest house with a twin, two doubles and an en suite family room. Also self-catering bungalow. 11 miles from Swansea close to the sea.

Parc-le-Breos, Parkmill, Gower, Swansea SA3 2HA

Tel: 01792 371636 Fax: 01792 371287
website: www.parc-le-breos.co.uk
Ten bedrooms including spacious family rooms in a 19th century hunting lodge in a rural setting on the Gower. Riding centre on site.

Shoreline Hotel, Mumbles, Swansea SA3 4EA

Tel/Fax: 01792 366233
website: www.shorelinehotel.co.uk
A family-run hotel with 12 en suite bedrooms, bar and residents' lounge. Right on the seafront, with views across Swansea Bay.   118

Food and Drink

Bank Farm Leisure Park, Horton, Gower, Swansea SA3 1LL

Tel: 01792 390228/2390452 Fax: 01792 391282
e-mail: bankfarmleisure@cs.com
website: www.bankfarmleisure.co.uk
A perfect holiday base on the beautiful Gower Peninsula, with self-catering bungalows for rent and pitches for caravans and tents.   119

The Britannia Inn, Llanmadoc, Gower, Swansea SA3 1DB

Tel/Fax: 01792 386624   e-mail: mikdow@freeuk.com
A beautifully preserved 17th century inn on the northwestern tip of the Gower Peninsula, with a welcome for all ages, a menu to suit all tastes and three en suite bedrooms.   121

CJ's Wine Bar & Restaurant, Oystermouth, Swansea SA3 4DN

Tel: 01792 361246 Fax: 01792 419849
Cosy, friendly wine bar-café-restaurant in a row of shops close to the seafront. Varied menu with steaks and grill specialities and a vast cocktail list.   122

Culver House Hotel, Port Eynon, Gower, Swansea SA3 1NN

Tel: 01792 390755 Fax: 01792 390735
e-mail: info@culverhousehotel.co.uk
website: www.culverhousehotel.co.uk
Twelve en suite bedrooms in a friendly hotel idyllically situated right on the beach. Residents' lounge, bar, restaurant. Large car park.   120

Morriston Golf Club

160 Clasemont Road, Morriston,
Swansea SA6 6AJ
Tel: 01792 796528 Fax: 01792 795628

Sec/Manager:	V Thomas
Professional:	D Rees
Directions:	3½ miles N of Swansea centre. From M4 junction 46 take A48 (Morriston). Entrance after 1 mile on left hand side.
Date Founded:	1919
Type of Course:	Parkland
No of Holes:	18
Length:	5755 yds (5312 mtrs)
Par:	68
SSS:	68
Green Fees:	Weekdays: £18; Weekends/ Bank Holidays:£30
Visitors:	Welcome: Contact Club in advance. Unable to play on Saturday's in summer.
Societies:	Welcome: Contact Club in advance. Unable to play at weekend's.

Facilities: Putting Green, Chipping Green, Practice Area, Trolley Hire, Bar, Restaurant

Accommodation, Food and Drink

Reference numbers below refer to detailed information provided in section 2

Accommodation

Beachcomber Hotel, 364 Oystermouth Road, Swansea SA1 3UL

Tel: 01792 651380

Ten Bed & Breakfast rooms with shared bathrooms in a location handy for city and sea. Tv, tea-makers, ironing and drying facilities available.

Devon View Hotel, 396 Oystermouth Road, Swansea SA1 3UL

Tel: 01792 462008
e-mail: joseph@devonview.co.uk
website: www.devonview.co.uk

Seafront hotel with 14 comfortable, high-ceilinged rooms. B&B, dinner by arrangement, packed lunches available.   117

Drws Nesaf, Abergwrelych House, Pontwalby, Glynneath SA11 5LN

Tel: 01639 720035

A charming mid-Victorian cottage in beautiful walking country. Self-catering accommodation comprises sitting room/diner, kitchen, 2 bedrooms, shower room, patio.

Hurst Dene Guest House, Uplands, Swansea SA2 0LJ

Tel/Fax: 01792 280920 website: www.hurstdene.co.uk

Ten bedrooms for Bed & Breakfast in a large Victorian terraced house. Also self-catering units. In a Swansea suburb near the sea.   124

Wernoleu Hotel, Ammanford, Carmarthenshire SA18 2HX

Tel/Fax: 01269 592598

Warm and welcoming country hotel set in five acres of grounds, with seven spacious bedrooms, lots of real ales and a tasty bar menu.   125

Food and Drink

CJ's Wine Bar & Restaurant, Oystermouth, Swansea SA3 4DN

Tel: 01792 361246 Fax: 01792 419849

Cosy, friendly wine bar-café-restaurant in a row of shops close to the seafront. Varied menu with steaks and grill specialities and a vast cocktail list.   122

The Mardy Hotel, 117 High Street, Gorseinon, Swansea SA4 2BT

Tel: 01792 892616

Snacks, burgers, scampi and steaks on the menu, with roasts on Sunday. Darts, pool, live entertainment three nights a week.

Neath Golf Club

Cadoxton, Neath SA10 8AH

Tel: 01639 643615

If one is looking for a change from playing the seaside courses when visiting the West Glamorgan area, then Neath Golf Club is an excellent place to visit. In direct contrast to Swansea's great linkland clubs, the one at Neath sits majestically atop a high hill at Cadoxton and two miles from the bustling old town of Neath. Founded in 1934, the then committee members had the sense to commission a top quality golfer in the shape of Open champion James Braid to lay out the course from difficult terrain, and he most certainly came up trumps by creating a demanding course. The vistas of the Vale of Neath and the outstanding countryside beyond are something special. James Braid once wrote of the views: " I must say the views from every part of this course are truly magnificent". Henry Cotton also wrote a glowing tribute to the course when he penned a letter to a close friend: "I've travelled the entire golfing world but never before seen such golfing beauty as at Neath".

Another outstanding professional golfer who has fond memories of the Neath course is Welshman Brian Hugget, the former Ryder Cup captain, who's father was once the club professional here. Brian Hugget spent his boyhood here and learned to play and develop the game to a standard that served him well. Such is the character of Brian in not forgetting his grass roots, he presented a trophy in the shape of a silver plated putter to the club and also re-designed six of the holes at Neath. The splendid trophy now hangs proudly on a wall in the spacious clubhouse, and to show their appreciation the members graciously bestowed on Brian Hugget an honorary membership. The mercurial Welshman, who now lives in a Herefordshire village close to the Monmouthshire border, still has fond memories of his early days at Neath and is always ready to talk of them.

Many years have passed by since I last played the Neath course, but I still remember vividly the uphill climb of the two opening holes and the breathless gasp of amazement from my three golfing friends as they realised the course then flattened out and offered magnificent views. I also remember the thrill of standing on the tee of the par 4 15th hole, aptly named "The Pulpit". The green at this magnificent hole lies at what appears to be a mile below the green and within easy reach with a driver. I also remember we all opened our shoulders and failed miserably in our attempts to score what appeared an easy par!

The thick gorse and bracken, which wrecked my scorecard, is also a painful memory, but it is "The Pulpit" hole that will remain in my memory forever. As will the gorgeous views at this amazing inland course. Indeed the whole length of this 6,490 yards mountain course is unforgettable!

Sec/Manager:	M. Hughes
Professional:	E.M Bennet
Directions:	1½ miles N of Neath centre. From M4 junction 43 take A465 (Neath, Merthyr Tydfil), after 2¼ miles turn left onto the A4320 (Cadoxton), after ½ mile turn left into Cwmbach Rd. Entrance after ½ mile on right hand side.
Date Founded:	1934
Type of Course:	Heathland, Mountain
No of Holes:	18
Length:	6490 yds (5990 mtrs)
Par:	72
SSS:	72
Green Fees:	Weekdays: £20 per day; Weekends/Bank Holidays:£20 per day
Visitors:	Welcome: Except weekends. Contact Club in advance
Societies:	Welcome: Except weekends. Contact Club in advance
Facilities:	Putting Green, Chipping Green, Club Hire, Trolley Hire, Bar, Restaurant

Accommodation, Food and Drink

Reference numbers below refer to detailed information provided in section 2

Accommodation

Bank Farm Leisure Park, Horton, Gower, Swansea SA3 1LL

Tel: 01792 390228/2390452 Fax: 01792 391282

e-mail: bankfarmleisure@cs.com
website: www.bankfarmleisure.co.uk
A perfect holiday base on the beautiful Gower Peninsula, with self-catering bungalows for rent and pitches for caravans and tents. **119**

The Britannia Inn, Llanmadoc, Gower, Swansea SA3 1DB

Tel/Fax: 01792 386624   e-mail: mikdow@freeuk.com
A beautifully preserved 17th century inn on the northwestern tip of the Gower Peninsula, with a welcome for all ages, a menu to suit all tastes and three en suite bedrooms. **121**

Devon View Hotel, 396 Oystermouth Road, Swansea SA1 3UL

Tel: 01792 462008
e-mail: joseph@devonview.co.uk
website: www.devonview.co.uk
Seafront hotel with 14 comfortable, high-ceilinged rooms. B&B, dinner by arrangement, packed lunches available. **117**

Drws Nesaf, Abergwrelych House, Pontwalby, Glynneath SA11 5LN

Tel: 01639 720035
A charming mid-Victorian cottage in beautiful walking country. Self-catering accommodation comprises sitting room/diner, kitchen, 2 bedrooms, shower room, patio.

Hurst Dene Guest House, Uplands, Swansea SA2 0LJ

Tel/Fax: 01792 280920 website: www.hurstdene.co.uk
Ten bedrooms for Bed & Breakfast in a large Victorian terraced house. Also self-catering units. In a Swansea suburb near the sea. **124**

Little Haven Guest House, Oxwich, Gower, Swansea SA3 1LS

Tel: 01792 390940
Family-run guest house with a twin, two doubles and an en suite family room. Also self-catering bungalow. 11 miles from Swansea close to the sea.

Shoreline Hotel, Mumbles, Swansea SA3 4EA

Tel/Fax: 01792 366233
website: www.shorelinehotel.co.uk
A family-run hotel with 12 en suite bedrooms, bar and residents' lounge. Right on the seafront, with views across Swansea Bay. **118**

Food and Drink

Bank Farm Leisure Park, Horton, Gower, Swansea SA3 1LL

Tel: 01792 390228/2390452 Fax: 01792 391282
e-mail: bankfarmleisure@cs.com
website: www.bankfarmleisure.co.uk
A perfect holiday base on the beautiful Gower Peninsula, with self-catering bungalows for rent and pitches for caravans and tents. **119**

The Britannia Inn, Llanmadoc, Gower, Swansea SA3 1DB

Tel/Fax: 01792 386624   e-mail: mikdow@freeuk.com
A beautifully preserved 17th century inn on the
northwestern tip of the Gower Peninsula, with a
welcome for all ages, a menu to suit all tastes and
three en suite bedrooms.   121

CJ's Wine Bar & Restaurant, Oystermouth, Swansea SA3 4DN

Tel: 01792 361246 Fax: 01792 419849

Cosy, friendly wine bar-café-restaurant in a row of
shops close to the seafront. Varied menu with steaks
and grill specialities and a vast cocktail list.   122

Pennard Golf Club

2 Southgate Road, Southgate, Swansea SA3 2BT
Tel: 01792 233131 Fax: 01792 234797

Some 10 years ago, whilst on a Press trip to Arizona, I was invited to attend the beautiful Ventana
Canyon Golf Resort in Tucson, to listen to a talk
by Tom Doak, an American golf course architect,
who, although relatively young, had built up a
fine reputation of being one of the best at his
trade on that side of the Atlantic. During his talk
he also used slides to illustrate his thoughts on
what he considered the finest golf courses
throughout the world. To my complete surprise,
a picture of Pennard Golf Club suddenly appeared
on the screen along with the voice of Tom Doak
praising the excellence of the course to high
heaven. *"This"*, he enthused, *"Is one of the most
spectacular courses I have ever seen"*. He later said:
*"I now realise why Vicki Thomas, the Curtis Cup
player, is one of the finest amateur women golfers in
the world. If she can play to a plus handicap at
Pennard she must hold little or no fear whatsoever of
any other course in the world. Pennard is high on the
list of my all-time favourites"*. High praise indeed,
and I fully agree with what he said. How he came
to discover it, however, is beyond belief, because
all Welsh golf writers, including myself, have done
their very best to keep this rare treasure a closely
guarded secret over the long years since its creation. Now, however, with the secret out, Welsh
golfing scribes are reluctantly penning its praises
and bewailing the rising green fees as the invasion of the course swells to overflowing. Tom
Doaks, you have a lot to answer for!

It hurts me to tell you that the course can be
found just beyond the small village of Pennard
and is 8 miles west of Swansea via the A4607 and
the B4436. Founded in 1896, the majestic course
was laid out by James Braid-but not before he recovered from seeing the intoxicating stretch of
land waiting to be moulded into a golfing masterpiece. Over a century has now passed since that
day, but the course has seen little change and still
retains its old-fashioned charm, thanks to the re-

tention of the fearsome bracken, gorse and tumbling fairways awash with sand traps. Add to this
the great views of Three Cliff Bay and Mighty
Oxwich Bay, and you will quickly realise how
much a bargain the green fee was.

Like Langland Bay the course is not overlong
(6,265 yards, Par 71), but the rough and tricky
greens turns it into a formidable challenge and,
of course, being a seaside links you often have a
difficult wind to contend with. Most certainly a
course that remains in ones memory bank, with
the 7th, a shortish par four, being the most memorable. From the tee a deepish valley has to be
negotiated before you reach the fairway, which
runs alongside the ruins of Pennard Castle, built
by the Normans in the 12th century. The approach shot then has to find the craftily concealed
green. A wicked, cheeky hole this-as, of course, it
was meant to be.

Former club professional Bill Evans, and quite
a character to boot, once remarked: "The Pennard
course is St Andrews gone a bit mad. Every hole
takes some playing!" What more can I say?

Sec/Manager:	E.M Howell
Professional:	M.V Bennett
Directions:	7 miles SW of Swansea Town Centre. From M4 junction 42 take the A483 passing through Swansea and merge into the A4067 ((Mumbles). At Black Pill turn right onto the B4436. Go 1 mile past Bishopston and carry into Pennard Rd (signed Southgate). Entrance after 1 mile on right hand side.
Date Founded:	1896
Type of Course:	Links
No of Holes:	18
Length:	6265 yds (5783 mtrs)
Par:	71
SSS:	72
Green Fees:	Weekdays: £27 per day; Weekends/Bank Holidays: £35 per day
Visitors:	Welcome: Unable to play on Tuesday Morning. Contact Club in advance
Societies:	Welcome: unable to play at weekends. Contact Club in advance
Facilities:	Putting Green, Chipping Green, Club Hire, Trolley Hire, Bar, Restaurant

Accommodation, Food and Drink

Reference numbers below refer to detailed
information provided in section 2

Accommodation

Bank Farm Leisure Park, Horton, Gower, Swansea SA3 1LL

Tel: 01792 390228/2390452 Fax: 01792 391282
e-mail: bankfarmleisure@cs.com
website: www.bankfarmleisure.co.uk

A perfect holiday base on the beautiful Gower
Peninsula, with self-catering bungalows for rent and
pitches for caravans and tents.　　　　　119

Beachcomber Hotel, 364 Oystermouth Road, Swansea SA1 3UL

Tel: 01792 651380

Ten Bed & Breakfast rooms with shared bathrooms in
a location handy for city and sea. Tv, tea-makers,
ironing and drying facilities available.

The Britannia Inn, Llanmadoc, Gower, Swansea SA3 1DB

Tel/Fax: 01792 386624　e-mail: mikdow@freeuk.com

A beautifully preserved 17th century inn on the
northwestern tip of the Gower Peninsula, with a
welcome for all ages, a menu to suit all tastes and
three en suite bedrooms.　　　　　121

Culver House Hotel, Port Eynon, Gower, Swansea SA3 1NN

Tel: 01792 390755 Fax: 01792 390735
e-mail: info@culverhousehotel.co.uk
website: www.culverhousehotel.co.uk

Twelve en suite bedrooms in a friendly hotel
idyllically situated right on the beach. Residents'
lounge, bar, restaurant. Large car park.　　　120

Devon View Hotel, 396 Oystermouth Road, Swansea SA1 3UL

Tel: 01792 462008
e-mail: joseph@devonview.co.uk
website: www.devonview.co.uk

Seafront hotel with 14 comfortable, high-ceilinged
rooms. B&B, dinner by arrangement, packed lunches
available.　　　　　117

Hurst Dene Guest House, Uplands, Swansea SA2 0LJ

Tel/Fax: 01792 280920 website: www.hurstdene.co.uk

Ten bedrooms for Bed & Breakfast in a large Victorian
terraced house. Also self-catering units. In a Swansea
suburb near the sea.　　　　　124

Little Haven Guest House, Oxwich, Gower, Swansea SA3 1LS

Tel: 01792 390940

Family-run guest house with a twin, two doubles and
an en suite family room. Also self-catering bungalow.
11 miles from Swansea close to the sea.

Parc-le-Breos, Parkmill, Gower, Swansea SA3 2HA

Tel: 01792 371636 Fax: 01792 371287
website: www.parc-le-breos.co.uk

Ten bedrooms including spacious family rooms in a
19th century hunting lodge in a rural setting on the
Gower. Riding centre on site.

Shoreline Hotel, Mumbles, Swansea SA3 4EA

Tel/Fax: 01792 366233
website: www.shorelinehotel.co.uk

A family-run hotel with 12 en suite bedrooms, bar
and residents' lounge. Right on the seafront, with
views across Swansea Bay.　　　　　118

Food and Drink

Bank Farm Leisure Park, Horton, Gower, Swansea SA3 1LL

Tel: 01792 390228/2390452 Fax: 01792 391282
e-mail: bankfarmleisure@cs.com
website: www.bankfarmleisure.co.uk

A perfect holiday base on the beautiful Gower
Peninsula, with self-catering bungalows for rent and
pitches for caravans and tents.　　　　　119

The Britannia Inn, Llanmadoc, Gower, Swansea SA3 1DB

Tel/Fax: 01792 386624　e-mail: mikdow@freeuk.com

A beautifully preserved 17th century inn on the
northwestern tip of the Gower Peninsula, with a
welcome for all ages, a menu to suit all tastes and
three en suite bedrooms.　　　　　121

CJ's Wine Bar & Restaurant, Oystermouth, Swansea SA3 4DN

Tel: 01792 361246 Fax: 01792 419849

Cosy, friendly wine bar-café-restaurant in a row of
shops close to the seafront. Varied menu with steaks
and grill specialities and a vast cocktail list.　　122

Culver House Hotel, Port Eynon, Gower, Swansea SA3 1NN

Tel: 01792 390755 Fax: 01792 390735
e-mail: info@culverhousehotel.co.uk
website: www.culverhousehotel.co.uk

Twelve en suite bedrooms in a friendly hotel
idyllically situated right on the beach. Residents'
lounge, bar, restaurant. Large car park.　　　120

The Mardy Hotel, 117 High Street, Gorseinon, Swansea SA4 2BT

Tel: 01792 892616

Snacks, burgers, scampi and steaks on the menu, with
roasts on Sunday. Darts, pool, live entertainment
three nights a week.

Pontardwe Golf Club

Cefn Lian, Pontardwe, Swansea SA8 4SH

Tel: 01792 863118 **Fax:** 01792 830041

Sec/Manager:　M. Griffiths

Professional:　G. Hopkins

Directions: 9 miles NE of Swansea City Centre. From M4 junction 45 take the A4067 (Pontardawe). At Pontardawe turn left onto the A474 (Ammanford) skirting town. After almost 1¼ miles turn right into Cefn Llan Rd. Entrance after ¼ mile straight ahead.

Date Founded: 1924

Type of Course: Mountainous

No of Holes: 18

Length: 6038 yds (5573 mtrs)

Par: 70

SSS: 70

Green Fees: Weekdays: £22 per day; Weekends/Bank Holidays: Unable to play at weekends

Visitors: Welcome: Unable to play at weekends. Contact Club in advance.

Societies: Welcome: Contact Club in advance.

Facilities: Putting Green, Chipping Green, Trolley Hire, Bar, Restaurant

Accommodation, Food and Drink

Reference numbers below refer to detailed information provided in section 2

Accommodation

Beachcomber Hotel, 364 Oystermouth Road, Swansea SA1 3UL
Tel: 01792 651380
Ten Bed & Breakfast rooms with shared bathrooms in a location handy for city and sea. Tv, tea-makers, ironing and drying facilities available.

Devon View Hotel, 396 Oystermouth Road, Swansea SA1 3UL
Tel: 01792 462008
e-mail: joseph@devonview.co.uk
website: www.devonview.co.uk
Seafront hotel with 14 comfortable, high-ceilinged rooms. B&B, dinner by arrangement, packed lunches available.   117

Drws Nesaf, Abergwrelych House, Pontwalby, Glynneath SA11 5LN
Tel: 01639 720035
A charming mid-Victorian cottage in beautiful walking country. Self-catering accommodation comprises sitting room/diner, kitchen, 2 bedrooms, shower room, patio.

Hurst Dene Guest House, Uplands, Swansea SA2 0LJ

Tel/Fax: 01792 280920
website: www.hurstdene.co.uk
Ten bedrooms for Bed & Breakfast in a large Victorian terraced house. Also self-catering units. In a Swansea suburb near the sea.   124

Pemberton Arms, Burry Port, Swansea SA16 0RH
Tel: 01554 832129
A handsome late 19th century pub with two bars, lounge and beer garden. Food served all sessions except Wednesday and Sunday evenings.   123

Wernoleu Hotel, Ammanford, Carmarthenshire SA18 2HX
Tel/Fax: 01269 592598
Warm and welcoming country hotel set in five acres of grounds, with seven spacious bedrooms, lots of real ales and a tasty bar menu.   125

Food and Drink

CJ's Wine Bar & Restaurant, Oystermouth, Swansea SA3 4DN
Tel: 01792 361246 Fax: 01792 419849
Cosy, friendly wine bar-café-restaurant in a row of shops close to the seafront. Varied menu with steaks and grill specialities and a vast cocktail list.   122

The Mardy Hotel, 117 High Street, Gorseinon, Swansea SA4 2BT
Tel: 01792 892616
Snacks, burgers, scampi and steaks on the menu, with roasts on Sunday. Darts, pool, live entertainment three nights a week.

Swansea Bay Golf Club

Jersey Marine, Neath SA10 6JP

Tel: 01792 812198

Having been founded in 1892, this splendid links (yes, the golfers at Swansea are rather spoilt by the quality of their golf courses) holds the distinction of being the oldest club in the Swansea area, which is just one year later than the distinguished Royal Porthcawl Club-ranked as the premier golf club in South Wales. Indeed, in those halcyon days when golf was played only by the gentry, team matches were played between Swansea Bay and Royal Porthcawl (20 miles away), with the privileged members being conveyed by horse drawn carriages. Wonderful times were had by those players, who also enjoyed the luxury of having the courses practically to themselves. Today, especially during the summer months, the Swansea Bay links enjoys much popularity because it's the first course golfing visitors discover as they journey in search of the great courses in

Green, Club Hire, Trolley Hire,
Bar, Restaurant, Driving Range

Accommodation, Food and Drink

Reference numbers below refer to detailed
information provided in section 2

Accommodation

the Swansea area. Once found, once played, many players are more than content to travel no further, their reasoning being that when you're on to a good thing, stay with it! And who can blame them when accommodation is also plentiful close to this delightful links.

Sitting majestically close to the B4290 coast road at Jersey Marine, the links is exceptionally flat. This, however, does not mean the course is a "soft touch". Far from it, because there are some great and exciting holes to be found here. Just over a third of the holes run close to the sea, and are quite testing even without the wind that often blows in off the bay. When it does blow its like playing golf on a rollercoaster and equally exciting. Like St Andrews, the course also has a burn crossing through it to further tease and test one's ability to negotiate a links course with some satisfaction.

I love visiting the old place. I'm sure you will, too.

Sec/Manager:	D Goatcher
Professional:	Mike Day
Directions:	3½ miles SW of Neath centre. From M4 junction 42 take the Fabian Way (A483, Swansea). After 1 mile at roundabout turn right onto B4290 (Skewen). Take first right after 200 yds then right at T-junction. Entrance after 250 yds at the end.
Date Founded:	1892
Type of Course:	Links
No of Holes:	18
Length:	6605 yds (6096 mtrs)
Par:	72
SSS:	72
Green Fees:	Weekdays: £16 per day; Weekends/Bank Holidays: £22 per day
Facilities:	Putting Green, Chipping

Bank Farm Leisure Park, Horton, Gower, Swansea SA3 1LL

Tel: 01792 390228/2390452 Fax: 01792 391282
e-mail: bankfarmleisure@cs.com
website: www.bankfarmleisure.co.uk
A perfect holiday base on the beautiful Gower Peninsula, with self-catering bungalows for rent and pitches for caravans and tents.   119

Beachcomber Hotel, 364 Oystermouth Road, Swansea SA1 3UL

Tel: 01792 651380
Ten Bed & Breakfast rooms with shared bathrooms in a location handy for city and sea. Tv, tea-makers, ironing and drying facilities available.

The Britannia Inn, Llanmadoc, Gower, Swansea SA3 1DB

Tel/Fax: 01792 386624   e-mail: mikdow@freeuk.com
A beautifully preserved 17th century inn on the northwestern tip of the Gower Peninsula, with a welcome for all ages, a menu to suit all tastes and three en suite bedrooms.   121

Devon View Hotel, 396 Oystermouth Road, Swansea SA1 3UL

Tel: 01792 462008
e-mail: joseph@devonview.co.uk
website: www.devonview.co.uk
Seafront hotel with 14 comfortable, high-ceilinged rooms. B&B, dinner by arrangement, packed lunches available.   117

Drws Nesaf, Abergwrelych House, Pontwalby, Glynneath SA11 5LN

Tel: 01639 720035
A charming mid-Victorian cottage in beautiful walking country. Self-catering accommodation comprises sitting room/diner, kitchen, 2 bedrooms, shower room, patio.

Hurst Dene Guest House, Uplands, Swansea SA2 0LJ

Tel/Fax: 01792 280920 website: www.hurstdene.co.uk
Ten bedrooms for Bed & Breakfast in a large Victorian terraced house. Also self-catering units. In a Swansea suburb near the sea.   124

Little Haven Guest House, Oxwich, Gower, Swansea SA3 1LS

Tel: 01792 390940
Family-run guest house with a twin, two doubles and an en suite family room. Also self-catering bungalow. 11 miles from Swansea close to the sea.

Shoreline Hotel, Mumbles, Swansea SA3 4EA

Tel/Fax: 01792 366233
website: www.shorelinehotel.co.uk
A family-run hotel with 12 en suite bedrooms, bar
and residents' lounge. Right on the seafront, with
views across Swansea Bay.   118

Ty'n-y-Caeau, Margam Village, Port Talbot, West Glamorgan SA13 2NW

Tel: 01639 883897 Fax: 01639 895570
e-mail: gaen@tynycaeau.freeserve.co.uk
A large country house with superb gardens and
comfortable en suite double or family rooms. Self
catering also available.

Food and Drink

Bank Farm Leisure Park, Horton, Gower, Swansea SA3 1LL

Tel: 01792 390228/2390452 Fax: 01792 391282
e-mail: bankfarmleisure@cs.com
website: www.bankfarmleisure.co.uk
A perfect holiday base on the beautiful Gower
Peninsula, with self-catering bungalows for rent and
pitches for caravans and tents.   119

The Britannia Inn, Llanmadoc, Gower, Swansea SA3 1DB

Tel/Fax: 01792 386624   e-mail: mikdow@freeuk.com
A beautifully preserved 17th century inn on the
northwestern tip of the Gower Peninsula, with a
welcome for all ages, a menu to suit all tastes and
three en suite bedrooms.   121

CJ's Wine Bar & Restaurant, Oystermouth, Swansea SA3 4DN

Tel: 01792 361246 Fax: 01792 419849
Cosy, friendly wine bar-café-restaurant in a row of
shops close to the seafront. Varied menu with steaks
and grill specialities and a vast cocktail list.   122

CARMARTHENSHIRE

Visitors entering the historical county of Carmarthenshire for the very first time are more often than not ignorant of the fact that they are entering the magical homeland of the celebrated Merlin the Wizard, the legendary wonder man whose fame is widespread throughout the world. Tell visitors this and they look at you with an unbelieving smile, which suggests they think he was merely the mythical forerunner of the wizards in the Harry Potter fictional books, written by J. K. Rowling. (who, incidentally, was born close to Chepstow, in Monmouthshire). Nevertheless, the most famous wizard in the world was an actual person.

Born in the old county town of Carmarthen, he fled to the Caledonian Forest in the Lowlands of Scotland (which was then a Welsh speaking area) after being defeated at the Battle of Arfderydd in 573. It is written that he roamed this area in solitude for some 50 years, with only wild animals to keep him company, but most stories of Merlin's prophecies are connected with the town of his birth-the most famous being that of Carmarthen's old oak tree in the centre of the town. Merlin predicted that should this Druidic oak fall then shall Carmarthen town be flooded. During the 1980's the old tree was removed to the Carmarthen museum. True enough the old town suffered se-

Llyn Brianne

vere floods a few years later. It has been passed down through the ages that Merlin spent much time with King Arthur as his advisor, but the legends of Arthur are reckoned to be mythical-or are they? Merlin was a real person and maybe only a talented magician, conjuror, hypnotist or a more than just lucky prophet who was clever enough to dupe the simple people of his time. We shall never know, but he must have been a bit of a genius for his reputation to have lasted to this very day! It could have been he who invented the legend of King Arthur, which was then continued in the works of Nennius, a 9th-century Bangor monk; followed by Geoffrey of Monmouth in the 12th century, then Sir Thomas Malory in 1470 and Tennyson in 1869, with the myth being much romanticised as each of the authors took up their pens.

But it is not only Merlin that gives Carmarthen its historical fame, because the town was once the most westerly outpost of the Romans. Then called Maridunum, it was one of their most important towns and was at the junction of two of their huge highways. Alas, nothing remains of the Roman occupation other than a varied amount of small antiquities discovered throughout the years. At the Carmarthen Heritage Centre can be seen a mock up of a Roman kitchen and also demonstrations of coracle fishing from the Towy quayside. Coracles can still be seen in use by fisherman on the River Teifi at the picturesque village of Cenarth and above the famous Cenarth Falls, which are noted for their salmon leap. The coracles were first used as small fishing vessels by the ancient Britons and have seen little change in design over the centuries. Carmarthen now has a much-modernised shopping centre but has somehow managed to retain a charm and cosiness to attract visitors to linger awhile. Carmathen also boasts an excellent 18-hole golf club just a few miles away and high in the hills of the beautiful countryside.

At Middleton Hall, just a few miles from Carmarthen, is the rather impressive National Botanic Gardens of Wales with its very own dome, which houses hundreds of tropical plants. Opened in the spring of 2000, the site also offers many acres of beautiful outdoor gardens and something of interest for all ages. A remarkable "must visit" venue.

National Botanic Gardens

A few miles from Carmarthen in the direction of St Clears, lies the sleepy and rather quirky old coastal town of Laugharne (pronounced Larne), which took its name from general Laugharne, the "turncoat", who seized the old Norman castle in the town for Parliament in 1647 and afterwards deserted to the King. However, it was thanks to Dylan Thomas, Wales's great writer and poet, that the town became immortalized. After leaving his birthplace in Swansea as a 20-year-old reporter to work in London, Thomas married three years later and decided to settle down in Laugharne. The atmosphere of the place most certainly proved a great inspiration; because it was here that he wrote his finest works and what was regarded as his masterpiece, *Under Milk Wood*. He spent much of the last four years of his life in a seaside cottage known as the "Boat House". Overlooking a small estuary off Carmarthen Bay and set amongst the rocks below Milk Wood (yes, such a place does exist), this is a delightful spot to visit and I can think of no better place to be on a calm sunny day than walking through Milk Wood and soaking up the atmosphere that much inspired the rumbustious Welsh genius.

The old Boat House has now become a memorial and museum of Thomas's works and the Brown's Hotel, where he drank himself silly with the characters of the town, still stands untouched by time. During a lecture tour of the USA, three months after completing Under Milk Wood, Thomas died after a somewhat heavy drinking spell. His grave in the main churchyard of Laugharne is marked by a small, white wooden cross simply stating his name. He was aged just 43.

Along the coast from Laugharne is the village of Pendine with its great expanse of hard sandy beach where the land speed records were once attempted. It was here that J. G. Parry-Thomas was decapitated when his car, named Babs, crashed while he was attempting to break the record in 1927. His car was later buried in the sands, but was dug up by enthusiasts in 1971 and restored. Now one can visit the Babs Museum of Speed dedicated to the world land speed record, or take a drive along the mighty sands. East of Carmarthen lies the small and quiet rural town of Llandeilo, which is an ideal spot to stay if one wishes to visit the nearby Black Mountains. A visit to Dinefwr Park on the outskirts of the town is recommended. Owned by the National Trust, the Park is home to the ancient herd of Dinefwr White Park Cattle, a rare breed, and one can also visit the fine house, which was built in 1660, and admire the stunning views of the Towy Valley. The first building on this site was built in 876 by Roderick the Great as a palace and stronghold for his son Cadell. Three miles southeast of the town is the truly impressive Carreg-Cennen Castle, Wales' most dramatically situated castle. Standing on an isolated

Laugharne

Dylan Thomas Boathouse

limestone rock, some 300 feet high, overlooking the River Cennen, the origin of the this castle remains something of a mystery. It is thought to have been started by the ancient Britons and improved upon by the Romans, but the towers that remain are said to be no older than the time of Edward I. The views from the castle are some of the finest in the county with extensive panoramic views as far as the Irish Sea. Glynhir Golf Club, a good golfing venue with a full-sized course is also but a few miles from the town and set in superb surroundings.

A few miles north is the town of Llandovery, which is famous for its old public school that turned out many famous international rugby players. But the town's most famous figure is the 17th century vicar, Rhys Pritchard, who was the author of the famous book: *Welshman's Candle*.

At Carmarthenshire's southern tip lies the ancient town of Kidwelly with its Industrial Museum. Here an original tinplate works has been converted into the museum, which displays old and varied engines of the industrial era. Kidwelly Castle is also a fine place to visit. Still in fairly sound condition, the castle was built in 1094 by William de Londres as a stockaded fortress and rebuilt and strengthened during the 12th century to such an extent that it withstood a determined siege by Owain Glyndwr in 1403. Still well preserved there is much of interest to be explored at this historic castle.

The most important town in this area is the famous rugby town of Llanelli, renowned for its long association with the steel, tinplate and coal mining industries. The town now boasts an excellent new shopping centre and is an ideal location for touring this area of West Wales. Within easy reach from the M4 motorway, the area offers a delightful choice of woodland, fine beaches and rolling open countryside, with the Pembrey Country Park being the main attraction. This magnificent country park features a large forest rolling down to the spectacular Cefn Sidan beach, which stretches, unspoilt, for seven miles along Carmarthen Bay. Close by lies the attractive small seaside town of Burry Port, with its busy, picturesque harbour. Burry Port's claim to fame is that it was the place where the "Friendship", flown by the American aviation pioneer landed on June 18, 1928, to become the first seaplane to fly the Atlantic non-stop. The flight took 20 hours 40 minutes, and Amelia Earhart, who was a passenger, created another piece of

Carreg Cennen Castle

history by becoming the first women to cross the mighty Atlantic in an aeroplane. In close proximity to Burry Port is situated Ashburnham golf links-one of Welsh golf's glittering hidden gems. Pembrey, however, is the nearest town to the links, and in the tiny churchyard here is the grave of Napolean Bonaparte's niece, whilst alongside are buried German airmen shot down during the Second World War.

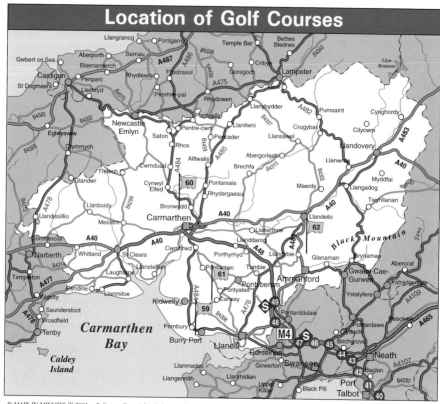

© MAPS IN MINUTES ™ 2001   © Crown Copyright, Ordnance Survey 2001

Ashburnham Golf Club

Cliff Terrace, Burry Port SA16 0HN

Tel: 01554 832269

Ranked as one of the finest courses on the Welsh golfing scene, I must admit that the old established and wonderful Ashburnham links is one of my favourite places to visit and to test out my ability as a golfer. Founded in 1894, it is one of the oldest clubs in the Principality and the oldest to be found in Carmarthenshire. Lying close to the Burry Estuary and Worm's Head and edging the Pembrey Country Park, the old course has seen a number of changes over the years, being extended from its original 9 holes to 18 in 1902, then altered by J. H. Taylor in 1914. Then along came F. H. Hawtree in 1923 to do his best to improve on Taylor's expertise, and between them they succeeded rather well in creating one of Wales' golfing masterpieces. In typical links fashion, many of the holes run out as far as possible before the course takes a turn homewards, with every hole out and in throwing out a tough challenge to the best of golfers-even more so when the wind howls across Carmarthen Bay. In contrast to this stretch of rugged linksland, the opening two holes and the final closing holes are inland and close to the impressive clubhouse, with an old, grassed over railway embankment, which was once a rail link from a coalmine to the ancient Pembrey Port, forming a boundary between the last two holes.

During its centenary celebrations the old club staged the British Home International Team Championship, to add to the many important events staged here over its long history. It was here that Europe's present Ryder Cup captain, Sam Torrance, gained his first professional title, the 1976 Martini tournament. Bernard Gallagher, the former Europe Ryder Cup captain, also has fond memories of Ashburnham, because his first success in the paid ranks also took place here when he won the 1969 Schweppes event. Ashburnham was also much liked by the great Harry Vardon- he once declared: "*Of all the courses in Wales, this is the one I like best*". During my reporting days I was privileged to cover many important amateur events at Ashburnham, with the last one being the 1989 British Youth's Open Amateur Championship, which resulted in Andrew Coltart, now a successful tournament professional and Ryder Cup player, losing in a play-off to M. Smith, of Brokenhurst Park. One of the joys of visiting this old club was meeting up with John Treharne, the former club secretary of Ashburnham and also the Welsh Golfing Union, for whom he worked

long hours from a makeshift office at his home and on the road with major Welsh amateur events, using nothing but an old fountain pen and a battered old typewriter, before retiring in the mid 1980's. How different now with all the electronic aids and a permanent headquarters at Celtic Manor, plus a good salary, for the also hardworking and dedicated present secretary, Richard Dixon. John Treharne will talk all day about his golfing memories, but what he does not mention is that he was a school chum of none other than the great Dylan Thomas! A modest man, a nice man and a great character is John, and a man who knows more than anyone about the past happenings at Ashburnham Golf Club. Another interesting member is Terry Griffiths, the former world professional snooker champion, who has a fine house close to the course. I once asked him if he found it hard work travelling around the world and playing high pressure snooker under the hot lights, week in and week out? He replied: "*After working as a postman for many years, getting up at 4am every morning and trudging through snow, ice and freezing conditions to deliver letters during the winter months. That was hard work and pressure. I now count my blessings after every match is completed, win or lose*". And he loves playing golf at Ashburnham, too.

There are lots more friendly characters to be found and willing to chat over a drink in Ashburnham's large and homely clubhouse or during a round on the great links. Believe me, you will regret if you pass the historic old place by.

Sec/Manager:	D.K Williams
Professional:	R.A Ryder
Directions:	1 mile SW of Burry Port centre. From M4 junction 48 take the A4138 (Llanelli, Burry Port). After 4 miles turn right onto A484 (Burry Port). After 4½ miles turn left at BP Service Station at outskirts of Burry Port into Church Rd (B4311). Entrance after 1¼ miles in Cliffe Terrace on left hand side.
Date Founded:	1894
Type of Course:	Links
No of Holes:	18
Length:	6916 yds (6319 mtrs)
Par:	72
SSS:	74
Green Fees:	Weekdays: £27.50 per day; Weekends/Bank Holidays: £32.50 per day

Visitors:	Welcome: By arrangement. Contact Club in advance
Societies:	Welcome: Excluding weekends. Contact Club in advance
Facilities:	Putting Green, Chipping Green, Club Hire, Trolley Hire, Bar, Restaurant

Accommodation, Food and Drink

Reference numbers below refer to detailed information provided in section 2

Accommodation

Bryncoch Farm Guest House, Llandyfan, Ammanford, Carmarthenshire SA18 2TY

Tel: 01269 850480 Fax: 01269 850888
e-mail:bryncoch@tesco.net

Farmhouse Bed & Breakfast accommodation in a lovely setting high above the Amman Valley. Craft shop and coffee shop on site.   126

Bryngwenyn Farm, Pontberem, Llanelli, Carmarthenshire SA15 5NG

Tel/Fax: 01269 843990
e-mail: lizhedges@ic24.net

Comfortable, well-appointed holiday cottages in the grounds of a substantial 17th century farmhouse in the heart of the country. Meals by arrangement.   128

Caernewydd Farm, Kidwelly, Carmarthenshire SA17 4TF

Tel: 01554 890729 Fax: 01554 891407

Much modernised late 19th century farmhouse in open countryside. Six luxurious en suite bedrooms for Bed & Breakfast, separate lounge/diner, packed lunches available. Swimming pool.   130

Greenfield Cottage, Ferryside, Carmarthenshire SA17 5UE

Tel: 01267 267815 Fax: 01267 267934
e-mail: pmagor99@hotmail.com
website: www.greenfield1@currantbun.com

1950s cottage and Victorian-style conservatory restaurant in two acres of grounds with great views. Three spacious bedrooms. Large car park.   131

Pemberton Arms, Burry Port, Swansea SA16 0RH

Tel: 01554 832129

A handsome late 19th century pub with two bars, lounge and beer garden. Food served all sessions except Wednesday and Sunday evenings.   123

Red Lion Hotel, Pembrey, Carmarthenshire SA16 0UB

Tel: 01554 832724
website: www.the-redlionhotel.co.uk

Bed & Breakfast accommodation and a varied choice of bar food in a 16th century inn on the village square. Beer garden.   127

Tanylan Farm Holidays, Tanylan Farm, Kidwelly, Carmarthenshire SA17 5HJ

Tel/Fax: 01267 267306
e-mail: tanylanfarm@aol.com
website: www.tanylanfarmholidays.co.uk

A beautifully situated farmhouse with six bedrooms for B&B, and nearby touring and camping site 200 yards from Carmarthen Bay.   129

Food and Drink

Greenfield Cottage, Ferryside, Carmarthenshire SA17 5UE

Tel: 01267 267815 Fax: 01267 267934
e-mail: pmagor99@hotmail.com
website: www.greenfield1@currantbun.com

1950s cottage and Victorian-style conservatory restaurant in two acres of grounds with great views. Three spacious bedrooms. Large car park.   131

Pemberton Arms, Burry Port, Swansea SA16 0RH

Tel: 01554 832129

A handsome late 19th century pub with two bars, lounge and beer garden. Food served all sessions except Wednesday and Sunday evenings.   123

Red Lion Hotel, Pembrey, Carmarthenshire SA16 0UB

Tel: 01554 832724
website: www.the-redlionhotel.co.uk

Bed & Breakfast accommodation and a varied choice of bar food in a 16th century inn on the village square. Beer garden.   127

Carmarthen Golf Club

Blaenycoed Road, Carmarthen SA33 6EH

Tel: 01267 281588 Fax: 01267 281493

Set high on a hill some 4 miles northwest of Carmarthen town, it is hard to believe that Carmarthen Golf Club is now at its fifth location since being formed in 1907. Standing proudly in its lofty position at the top of Foel Hill at Rhydymarchog, and at a height of 1,000 feet above sea level, this superb parkland course is in

such a wonderful location one wonders why the place was not chosen in the first place. The stunning views of the magnificent Welsh countryside alone, is worth considerably more than the cost of the modest green fees, whilst the exhilarating clean air also makes it well worth the visit.

When the course was designed by J. H. Taylor in 1928, the fairways were littered by so many stones that it proved impossible to have them mown without serious damage to the mechanical cutters. However, the club captain quickly found a solution by getting his members to stand in lines across the fairways and, armed with buckets, to pick up the stones. Records tell us that the job was completed quite satisfactorily in less than two days!

The length of the course - 6,245 yards, Par 71 - gives a false impression of being an easy challenge, but beware of complacency. J. H. Taylor never believed in designing courses that were easy to conquer; he took as much care in designing courses that offered a good challenge as he did in attempting to overcome their challenge when playing. His course at Carmarthen is no exception. The first here is typical-uphill, long and difficult-it's a tough and frustrating par four, and it doesn't get any easier as the round continues. Anyone beating their handicap here performed rather well-or had more than a few lucky breaks! The clubhouse is a bit of a gem, too, offering further outstanding views and good Welsh cooking.

Sec/Manager:	Jonathan Coe
Professional:	Pat Gillis
Directions:	3¼ miles N of Carmarthen.

From the eastern end of Carmarthen or the A40, take the A484 (Newcastle Emlyn) after 2 miles turn left onto minor road (Newchurch). Entrance on the right hand side after another 2 miles.

Date Founded:	1929
Type of Course:	Heathland
No of Holes:	18
Length:	6245 yds (5764 mtrs)
Par:	71
SSS:	71
Green Fees:	Weekdays: £20 per day; Weekends/Bank Holidays: £20 per day
Visitors:	Welcome: By arrangement. Contact Club in advance
Societies:	Welcome: Excluding weekends. Contact Club in advance
Facilities:	Putting Green, Chipping Green, Practice Area, Club Hire, Trolley Hire, Bar, Restaurant

Accommodation, Food and Drink

Reference numbers below refer to detailed information provided in section 2

Accommodation

Bryncoch Farm Guest House, Llandyfan, Ammanford, Carmarthenshire SA18 2TY

Tel: 01269 850480 Fax: 01269 850888
e-mail:bryncoch@tesco.net

Farmhouse Bed & Breakfast accommodation in a lovely setting high above the Amman Valley. Craft shop and coffee shop on site. 126

Bryngwenyn Farm, Pontberem, Llanelli, Carmarthenshire SA15 5NG

Tel/Fax: 01269 843990
e-mail: lizhedges@ic24.net

Comfortable, well-appointed holiday cottages in the grounds of a substantial 17th century farmhouse in the heart of the country. Meals by arrangement. 128

Caernewydd Farm, Kidwelly, Carmarthenshire SA17 4TF

Tel: 01554 890729 Fax: 01554 891407

Much modernised late 19th century farmhouse in open countryside. Six luxurious en suite bedrooms for Bed & Breakfast, separate lounge/diner, packed lunches available. Swimming pool. 130

Greenfield Cottage, Ferryside, Carmarthenshire SA17 5UE

Tel: 01267 267815 Fax: 01267 267934
e-mail: pmagor99@hotmail.com

website: www.greenfield1@currantbun.com
1950s cottage and Victorian-style conservatory restaurant in two acres of grounds with great views. Three spacious bedrooms. Large car park. 131

Pemberton Arms, Burry Port, Swansea SA16 0RH

Tel: 01554 832129

A handsome late 19th century pub with two bars, lounge and beer garden. Food served all sessions except Wednesday and Sunday evenings. 123

Red Lion Hotel, Pembrey, Carmarthenshire SA16 0UB

Tel: 01554 832724
website: www.the-redlionhotel.co.uk
Bed & Breakfast accommodation and a varied choice of bar food in a 16th century inn on the village square. Beer garden. 127

Tanylan Farm Holidays, Tanylan Farm, Kidwelly, Carmarthenshire SA17 5HJ

Tel/Fax: 01267 267306
e-mail: tanylanfarm@aol.com
website: www.tanylanfarmholidays.co.uk
A beautifully situated farmhouse with six bedrooms for B&B, and nearby touring and camping site 200 yards from Carmarthen Bay. 129

Food and Drink

Greenfield Cottage, Ferryside, Carmarthenshire SA17 5UE

Tel: 01267 267815 Fax: 01267 267934
e-mail: pmagor99@hotmail.com
website: www.greenfield1@currantbun.com
1950s cottage and Victorian-style conservatory restaurant in two acres of grounds with great views. Three spacious bedrooms. Large car park. 131

Pemberton Arms, Burry Port, Swansea SA16 0RH

Tel: 01554 832129

A handsome late 19th century pub with two bars, lounge and beer garden. Food served all sessions except Wednesday and Sunday evenings. 123

Red Lion Hotel, Pembrey, Carmarthenshire SA16 0UB

Tel: 01554 832724
website: www.the-redlionhotel.co.uk
Bed & Breakfast accommodation and a varied choice of bar food in a 16th century inn on the village square. Beer garden. 127

Glyn Abbey Golf Club

Glyn Abbey, Trimsaran SA17 4LB
Tel: 01554 810278 Fax: 01554 810278

Sec/Manager:	John Smith
Professional:	Neil Evans
Directions:	5 miles NW of Llanelli. From centre take the A484 then turn right onto the B4308 to Trimsaran. At Trimsaran turn right onto B4317. Entrance after 2 miles just before Carway on left hand side.
Date Founded:	1992
Type of Course:	Parkland
No of Holes:	18
Length:	6173 yds (5698 mtrs)
Par:	70
SSS:	70
Green Fees:	Weekdays: £15.00 (Summer) £10 (Winter); Weekends/Bank Holidays: £18.00 (Summer) £12.00 (Winter)
Visitors:	Welcome: Contact Club by telephone in advance.
Societies:	Welcome: Contact Club by telephone in advance.
Facilities:	Putting Green, Chipping Green, Driving Range, Club Hire, Trolley Hire, Buggy Hire, Bar, Restaurant

Accommodation, Food and Drink

Reference numbers below refer to detailed information provided in section 2

Accommodation

Bryncoch Farm Guest House, Llandyfan, Ammanford, Carmarthenshire SA18 2TY

Tel: 01269 850480 Fax: 01269 850888
e-mail:bryncoch@tesco.net
Farmhouse Bed & Breakfast accommodation in a lovely setting high above the Amman Valley. Craft shop and coffee shop on site. 126

Bryngwenyn Farm, Pontberem, Llanelli, Carmarthenshire SA15 5NG

Tel/Fax: 01269 843990
e-mail: lizhedges@ic24.net
Comfortable, well-appointed holiday cottages in the grounds of a substantial 17th century farmhouse in the heart of the country. Meals by arrangement.   128

**Caernewydd Farm, Kidwelly,
Carmarthenshire SA17 4TF**

Tel: 01554 890729 Fax: 01554 891407
Much modernised late 19th century farmhouse in open countryside. Six luxurious en suite bedrooms for Bed & Breakfast, separate lounge/diner, packed lunches available. Swimming pool.   130

**Greenfield Cottage, Ferryside,
Carmarthenshire SA17 5UE**

Tel: 01267 267815 Fax: 01267 267934
e-mail: pmagor99@hotmail.com
website: www.greenfield1@currantbun.com
1950s cottage and Victorian-style conservatory restaurant in two acres of grounds with great views. Three spacious bedrooms. Large car park.   131

**Red Lion Hotel, Pembrey,
Carmarthenshire SA16 0UB**

Tel: 01554 832724
website: www.the-redlionhotel.co.uk
Bed & Breakfast accommodation and a varied choice of bar food in a 16th century inn on the village square. Beer garden.   127

**Tanylan Farm Holidays, Tanylan Farm, Kidwelly,
Carmarthenshire SA17 5HJ**

Tel/Fax: 01267 267306
e-mail: tanylanfarm@aol.com
website: www.tanylanfarmholidays.co.uk
A beautifully situated farmhouse with six bedrooms for B&B, and nearby touring and camping site 200 yards from Carmarthen Bay.   129

Food and Drink

**Greenfield Cottage, Ferryside,
Carmarthenshire SA17 5UE**

Tel: 01267 267815 Fax: 01267 267934
e-mail: pmagor99@hotmail.com
website: www.greenfield1@currantbun.com
1950s cottage and Victorian-style conservatory restaurant in two acres of grounds with great views. Three spacious bedrooms. Large car park.   131

**The Mardy Hotel, 117 High Street, Gorseinon,
Swansea SA4 2BT**

Tel: 01792 892616
Snacks, burgers, scampi and steaks on the menu, with roasts on Sunday. Darts, pool, live entertainment three nights a week.

**Pemberton Arms, Burry Port,
Swansea SA16 0RH**

Tel: 01554 832129
A handsome late 19th century pub with two bars, lounge and beer garden. Food served all sessions except Wednesday and Sunday evenings.   123

**Red Lion Hotel, Pembrey,
Carmarthenshire SA16 0UB**

Tel: 01554 832724
website: www.the-redlionhotel.co.uk
Bed & Breakfast accommodation and a varied choice of bar food in a 16th century inn on the village square. Beer garden.   127

Glynhir Golf Club

**Glynhir Road, Llandybie,
Ammanford SA18 2TF**

Tel: 01269 850472 Fax: 01269 851365

This is another fine 18-hole parkland course set in beautiful, idyllic surroundings close to the River Loughor, in the foothills of the awe inspiring Black Mountains. Located some 3 miles from the market town of Ammanford and close to the small town of Llandeilo, Glynhir Golf Club was founded in 1909.

With golf increasing in popularity during the 1960's, the club's membership increased so rapidly that land had to be found suitable for an 18-hole course. This resulted in the purchase of a farm and 105 acres, which was to the satisfaction of the architect Fred Hawtree. A huge bonus in the purchase was a huge stone barn just asking to be created into what is now reality - a magnificent and roomy clubhouse. All this came about because of a government grant, a bank loan, an investment loan draw and twenty-six members laying out £1,000 each.

The members now have a club to be proud of at Glynhir, which means "the long dell". The excellent clubhouse and locker rooms have recently undergone refurbishment, and the club now offers a "Summer Special" during Mondays (April to October), whereby visitors get reduced green fees until 4.00pm. This par 69, 6,000 yards course is, indeed, a worthwhile place to visit.

Sec/Manager: Dennis Kenchington
Professional: Duncan Prior

Directions: 3 miles NE of Ammanford. From centre take the A483 (Llandeilo) for 2 miles. At Llandybie turn right into Glynhir Road. Entrance after 1½ miles on right hand side.

Date Founded: 1967

Type of Course: Parkland

No of Holes: 18

Length: 6000 yds (5538 mtrs)

Par: 69

SSS: 69

Green Fees: Weekdays: £16 per day; Weekends/Bank Holidays: £22 per day

Visitors: Welcome: Excluding Sunday. Contact Club in advance

Societies: Welcome: By arrangement. Contact Club in advance

Facilities: Putting Green, practice Area, Club Hire, Trolley Hire, Bar, Restaurant

Accommodation, Food and Drink

Reference numbers below refer to detailed information provided in section 2

Accommodation

Bryncoch Farm Guest House, Llandyfan, Ammanford, Carmarthenshire SA18 2TY

Tel: 01269 850480 Fax: 01269 850888
e-mail:bryncoch@tesco.net
Farmhouse Bed & Breakfast accommodation in a lovely setting high above the Amman Valley. Craft shop and coffee shop on site.   126

Bryngwenyn Farm, Pontberem, Llanelli, Carmarthenshire SA15 5NG

Tel/Fax: 01269 843990
e-mail: lizhedges@ic24.net
Comfortable, well-appointed holiday cottages in the grounds of a substantial 17th century farmhouse in the heart of the country. Meals by arrangement.   128

Caernewydd Farm, Kidwelly, Carmarthenshire SA17 4TF

Tel: 01554 890729 Fax: 01554 891407
Much modernised late 19th century farmhouse in open countryside. Six luxurious en suite bedrooms for Bed & Breakfast, separate lounge/diner, packed lunches available. Swimming pool.   130

Greenfield Cottage, Ferryside, Carmarthenshire SA17 5UE

Tel: 01267 267815 Fax: 01267 267934
e-mail: pmagor99@hotmail.com
website: www.greenfield1@currantbun.com

1950s cottage and Victorian-style conservatory restaurant in two acres of grounds with great views. Three spacious bedrooms. Large car park.   131

Red Lion Hotel, Pembrey, Carmarthenshire SA16 0UB

Tel: 01554 832724
website: www.the-redlionhotel.co.uk
Bed & Breakfast accommodation and a varied choice of bar food in a 16th century inn on the village square. Beer garden.   127

Tanylan Farm Holidays, Tanylan Farm, Kidwelly, Carmarthenshire SA17 5HJ

Tel/Fax: 01267 267306
e-mail: tanylanfarm@aol.com
website: www.tanylanfarmholidays.co.uk
A beautifully situated farmhouse with six bedrooms for B&B, and nearby touring and camping site 200 yards from Carmarthen Bay.   129

Wernoleu Hotel, Ammanford, Carmarthenshire SA18 2HX

Tel/Fax: 01269 592598
Warm and welcoming country hotel set in five acres of grounds, with seven spacious bedrooms, lots of real ales and a tasty bar menu.
125

Food and Drink

Greenfield Cottage, Ferryside, Carmarthenshire SA17 5UE

Tel: 01267 267815 Fax: 01267 267934
e-mail: pmagor99@hotmail.com
website: www.greenfield1@currantbun.com

1950s cottage and Victorian-style conservatory restaurant in two acres of grounds with great views. Three spacious bedrooms. Large car park.   *131*

Pemberton Arms, Burry Port, Swansea SA16 0RH

Tel: 01554 832129
A handsome late 19th century pub with two bars, lounge and beer garden. Food served all sessions except Wednesday and Sunday evenings.   123

Red Lion Hotel, Pembrey, Carmarthenshire SA16 0UB

Tel: 01554 832724
website: www.the-redlionhotel.co.uk
Bed & Breakfast accommodation and a varied choice of bar food in a 16th century inn on the village square. Beer garden.   127

PEMBROKESHIRE

Visitors to the beautiful county of Pembrokeshire are often left wondering why it ever became known as "Little England beyond Wales", even more so when they hear the lilting Welsh language being regularly spoken in the northern areas of the county. The truth of the matter is that the title stuck after the county became colonised largely by the English and Flemish settlers in the Middle Ages, who established many wool factories in the south. Indeed, the rather attractive seaside town of Tenby earned its early prosperity on account of the huge trade in Welsh wool. Like the rest of Pembrokeshire, Tenby now relies on its huge popularity as a tourist attraction to maintain its prosperity. It is hardly surprising that holidaymakers continue to flock to Tenby and the rest of Pembrokeshire when one considers that all year round it has something to offer everyone who visits this unique and beautiful corner of Wales-unique because it has the best beaches in the whole of Britain. No other region can boast of so many Blue Flag beaches, Green Coast awards or Seaside Award beaches, and there are over 50 to choose from! Barafundle Bay in South Pembrokeshire continues to be voted one of the most attractive beaches in Britain, while Caerfai near to St David's was recently chosen by a national newspaper as one of the finest beaches in the

Whitesand Bay, nr St David's

world. For surfers some of the best beaches in Wales in which to enjoy their sport can be found at Newgale, Manorbier and Freshwater West, whilst windsurfers will delight in discovering the ideal waters at Dale and Newport. The unpronounceable and small resorts of Cwm-yr-eglwys, Pwll Gwaaelod and Traethllfyn offer a mixture of sand dunes, rock pools and quiet beaches, and these are but a few of the fantastic seaside places to be found. Pembrokeshire is also unique inasmuch as it boasts the only coastal National Park in Britain. And what a breathtaking coastline it is with its National Trail which provides magnificent and inspiring walking with only the wildlife and fellow walkers to share the peace and quite. Offshore are a number of islands, which offer sanctuary to some of the most important sea bird colonies in the world. The islands of Skokholm and Skomer share the world's largest colony of Manx Shearwaters (over 150, 000 pairs), whilst Grassholm is the world's fourth largest gannetry. As if this is not enough to delight the birdwatching brigades, there are also oystercatchers, storm petrels, peregrine falcons, cormorants, choughs, razorbills, puffins and many other seabirds doing their best to cause traffic jams in the skies above the Pembrokeshire coastal area.

Boat trips are available to Skomer, Skokholm and Grassholm from Martin Haven, whilst trips to Ramsey Island, which has the second largest Atlantic grey seal colony in southern Britain, can be found at St David's. Picturesque Caldey Island, which lies southeast of Tenby's superb North Beach, is, without question, the most frequently visited island. Take a boat from Tenby to enjoy the many pleasures of this fascinating island, which has long been inhabited by the Cistercian Monks at their medieval priory and monastery. Visit also their interesting museum and perfumery before going to the beaches to round off a memorable day. Pembrokeshire is also noted for a few historical castles, with none better than the mighty Pembroke Castle. Set high on a cliff face on the bank of the River Cleddau and overlooking the historic town of Pembroke, the castle is a fine example of Norman architecture with its five-storey, 75 feet high circular Great Tower reputed to be

St David's Cathedral

the finest of its kind in Britain. It is also noted as the birthplace of the Tudor Dynasty after Jasper Tudor was granted the castle and earldom in 1454, whereupon his nephew, the future Henry VII, was born there. Many other unique facts make Pembroke Castle a special place to visit. When the castle was under attack during the Civil Wars, Oliver Cromwell actually arrived in person to conduct the siege which finally led to its surrender, and there is a huge natural cavern to be found inside the castle, where many flint tools have been discovered, suggesting it was occupied during the Stone Age, many centuries before the Norman fortress was built. Other fine castles can be found at Manorbier, Carew (Milford Haven), which also features the only working tidal mill in Wales, whilst the village of Cilgerran has the remains of its castle standing on a rock above the charming River Teifi. Badly damaged during the Civil War and allowed to fall into ruin, the castle became immortalised by Turner when he made it the subject of one of his fine paintings. Pembrokeshire also boasts of having the smallest city in the world, which is named St David's after the patron saint of Wales, who was born in this area during the 10th century. This is most certainly justified by the fact that there is a huge cathedral, which was built in 1340 by Bishop Gower for the many pilgrims who came to this pretty town (sorry, city) to visit the shrine of St David. There is also a fine nine-hole golf course close by which is, of course, called St David's City. Founded in 1902, it is to be found 2 miles west of St David's at Whitesands Bay. Presently preparing for its centenary, the club lies on a breezy headland overlooking the Irish Sea, which is almost the most westerly point of Wales. Further north is the delightful small town of Newport, which is well worth a visit because not only is it a rather tranquil spot but it also has an excellent nine-hole golf course just two miles away on linksland close to the impressive Newport Beach. Reasonably flat and designed by

Fishguard Harbour

James Braid, this is a delightful seaside links with every hole as good as they come. With magnificent views over Newport Bay and an excellent clubhouse, plus accommodation available on site at four purpose built flats, it's well worth a visit. Close to Newport one can visit the reconstructed Iron Age Settlement at Castell Henllys and the impressive Ancient Burial Chamber in the hills at Pentre Ifan, which dates back over 5, 000 years. It was also from the local Preseli Hills that the bluestones of Stonehenge were transported to Salisbury Plain. Another fine nine-hole course can also be found just 2 miles, off the A40 at Letterston, near Fishguard. Known as Priskilly Forest Golf Club, it was founded in 1992 and is set in rolling parkland with a par of 70. Good accommodation is also available here in a 3-star country house. The last of the short courses is to be found at Rosemarket, near Milford Haven. Rosemarket Golf Club boasts that it has the longest nine-hole course in Wales, but this is about to be extended to 18-holes. The venue is also ideal for beginners because no handicap certificate is required, despite the fact that it recently became affiliated to the Welsh Golfing Union.

Before departing this wonderful county of legends, visitors may be interested to learn that Pembrokeshire was also the location for the last ever invasion of Britain. This took place near Strumble Head, Fishguard, on the 22nd February 1797, when the army of Republican France decided to undertake a second Norman Conquest. Believing it to be better to surprise the British by entering through the back door, they sailed quietly up the Irish Sea and made a landing in West Wales. Seventeen boats put soldiers ashore at Fishguard Bay, but during the night Jemima Nicholas, a doughty Welsh farmer's wife, rallied hundreds of Pembroke women to her side on a nearby hill to help Lord Cawdor and his handful of yeomanry. With the women clad in their scarlet shawls and high black hats (a Welsh women's national dress), the invaders mistakenly thought they were a division of British soldiers, and quickly threw down their arms and surrendered.

The fascinating and historic town of Tenby, once an important medieval trading port, a fortress, a highly fashionable Georgian resort and a major fishing port, also holds a prominent and proud position in Welsh golfing history because in 1888 it became the birthplace of Welsh golf. Yes, indeed, this "Little England beyond Wales" truly is a unique place to visit whatever the season, whatever the reason and for whatever fires the imagination.

Tenby Harbour

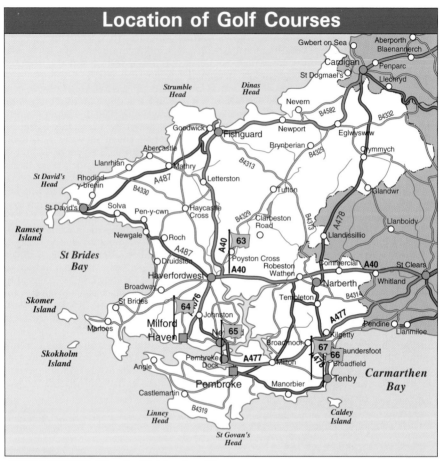

Location of Golf Courses

© MAPS IN MINUTES ™ 2001   © Crown Copyright, Ordnance Survey 2001

Haverfordwest Golf Club

Arnolds Down, Haverfordwest SA61 2XQ
Tel: 01437 763565 Fax: 01437 764143

Sitting rather peacefully inside the glorious setting of the Pembrokeshire National Park, yet only one mile along the A40 road from the bustling and historic market town of Haverfordwest, the pleasant 18-hole parkland course of Haverfordwest Golf Club has been catering for the golfing needs of the local communities since as far back as 1904, which makes it the second oldest 18-hole course in the county and one of the more older clubs in the West Wales area. One of its most important changes, however, is the magnificent new clubhouse, which was erected in 1994 and which provides for all the golfers needs, including excellent changing facilities and a fine selection of home cooked food to attract the holiday visitor.

Although the attractive course is a rather easy walk, this does not mean that its 6,005 yards, par 70, length is anything like an easy "pushover" of a course. Indeed, there are quite a number of excellent tests of your skills to be found along the fairways. The 8th-hole, in particular, at only 180 yards, offers a truly stiff challenge. Here you have to carry a valley with a somewhat nasty pond lying in its lower reaches just waiting to drown the hopes of those foolish enough to underclub from the tee. A good holiday course this, and one which offers reduced green fees to visiting societies.

Sec/Manager:	John Solly
Professional:	Alex Pile
Directions:	1 mile E of Haverfordwest. From centre take the A40 (Narbeth, Carmarthen).

Entrance after 1 mile from centre on left hand side.

Date Founded:	1904
Type of Course:	Parkland
No of Holes:	18
Length:	6005 yds (5542 mtrs)
Par:	70
SSS:	69
Green Fees:	Weekdays: £19; Weekends/ Bank Holidays: £22
Visitors:	Welcome: Contact Club by telephone in advance, play by arrangement only
Societies:	Welcome: Contact Club by telephone in advance, play by arrangement only
Facilities:	Putting Green, Practice Area, Club Hire, Trolley Hire, Buggy Hire, Bar, Restaurant

Accommodation, Food and Drink

Reference numbers below refer to detailed information provided in section 2

Accommodation

Blue Dolphin Hotel, Tenby, Pembrokeshire SA70 7HW
Tel: 01834 842590
Eleven letting bedrooms in a friendly hotel within the old town walls. B&B, plus packed lunches and evening meals by arrangement.   140

Brongwyn Cottages, Brongwyn Mawr, Penparc, Cardiganshire SA43 1SA
Tel: 01239 613644 Fax: 01239 615725
Six pretty cottages surrounding flower filled courtyard. 5 star accommodation, indoor pool. Magnificent coastline nearby.

Castlemead Hotel, Manorbier, Nr. Tenby, Pembrokeshire SA70 7TA
Tel/Fax: 01834 871358
e-mail: castlemeadhotel@aol.com
Eight comfortable en suite rooms in an Edwardian residence with an excellent reputation for good food. Peaceful setting near the sea.   135

Clarence House Hotel, Tenby, Pembrokeshire SA70 7DU
Tel: 01834 844371 Fax: 01834 844372
Sixty-eight en suite bedrooms in a seafront hotel that offers traditional standards of hospitality and service. Lifts to all floors. Patio/garden.   139

Cleddau Bridge Hotel, Pembroke Dock, Pembrokeshire SA72 6EG
Tel: 01646 685961 Fax: 01646 685746
e-mail: information@cleddaubridge.co.uk

website: cleddaubridgehotel.co.uk
Twenty-two double rooms, two suites and two
restaurants in a modern hotel scenically set by the
famous Cleddau Bridge. 132

Giltar Hotel, Tenby, Pembrokeshire SA70 7DU

Tel: 01834 842507/843424 Fax: 01834 845480
website: www.giltar-hotel.co.uk
A friendly family-run hotel in a fine position on the
esplanade above South Beach. 75 en suite rooms, lifts
to all floors, air-conditioned seaview restaurant. 138

Hammonds Park Hotel, Narberth Road, Tenby, Pembrokeshire SA70 8HT

Tel: 01834 842696 Fax: 01834 844295
14 bedrooms including family rooms in a delightful,
quiet hotel just north of the town. The hotel is non-
smoking except for the tv lounge. Off-road parking.
Use of spa.

Heywood Mount Hotel, Tenby, Pembrokeshire SA70 8DA

Tel: 01834 842087 Fax: 01834 842113
e-mail: reception@heywoodmount.co.uk
website: www.heywoodmount.co.uk
Country house hotel in attractive grounds half a mile
from the centre of town. 21 well-equipped en suite
guest rooms: restaurant, lounge bar and leisure
facilities. 137

Highgate Inn Hotel, Hundleton, Pembrokeshire SA71 5RD

Tel: 01646 685904 Fax: 01646 681888
e-mail: windy.gail@virgin.net
Village local and comfortable hotel all in one. Five en
suite, non-smoking bedrooms: bar and restaurant
menus: draught and keg ales.

Kinloch Court Hotel, Tenby, Pembrokeshire SA70 7EG

Tel: 01834 842777 Fax: 01834 843097
e-mail: kinlochhotel@aol.com
website: kinlochcourt-hotel.co.uk
The former Tenby Rectory is now a fine private hotel
with 14 en suite bedrooms and an excellent name for
food and hospitality. 134

Penwern Fach Holiday Cottages, Pont Hirwuan, Ceredigion SA43 2RL

Tel: 01239 710694 Fax: 01239 710854
Spacious, well-equipped self-catering cottages in a
lovely secluded setting near Cenarth. Exclusive use of
driving range. 159

West Hall, St Florence, Nr. Tenby, Pembrokeshire SA70 8LW

Tel/Fax: 01834 871336
Comfortable self-catering accommodation in six
bedrooms for up to 16 guests in a three-storey
Pembrokeshire farmhouse in the centre of a
picturesque village.

Food and Drink

Castlemead Hotel, Manorbier, Nr. Tenby, Pembrokeshire SA70 7TA

Tel/Fax: 01834 871358
e-mail: castlemeadhotel@aol.com
Eight comfortable en suite rooms in an Edwardian
residence with an excellent reputation for good food.
Peaceful setting near the sea. 135

Clarence House Hotel, Tenby, Pembrokeshire SA70 7DU

Tel: 01834 844371 Fax: 01834 844372
Sixty-eight en suite bedrooms in a seafront hotel that
offers traditional standards of hospitality and service.
Lifts to all floors. Patio/garden. 139

Cleddau Bridge Hotel, Pembroke Dock, Pembrokeshire SA72 6EG

Tel: 01646 685961 Fax: 01646 685746
e-mail: information@cleddaubridge.co.uk
website: cleddaubridgehotel.co.uk
Twenty-two double rooms, two suites and two
restaurants in a modern hotel scenically set by the
famous Cleddau Bridge. 132

Cross Inn, Penally, Tenby, Pembrokeshire SA70 7PU

Tel: 01834 844665
Freshly cooked pub fare and two real ales in a pleasant
inn overlooking Tenby Golf Club. Closed Monday
lunchtime.

Giltar Hotel, Tenby, Pembrokeshire SA70 7DU

Tel: 01834 842507/843424 Fax: 01834 845480
website: www.giltar-hotel.co.uk
A friendly family-run hotel in a fine position on the
esplanade above South Beach. 75 en suite rooms, lifts
to all floors, air-conditioned seaview restaurant. 138

Hammonds Park Hotel, Narberth Road, Tenby, Pembrokeshire SA70 8HT

Tel: 01834 842696 Fax: 01834 844295
14 bedrooms including family rooms in a delightful,
quiet hotel just north of the town. The hotel is non-
smoking except for the tv lounge. Off-road parking.
Use of spa.

Heywood Mount Hotel, Tenby, Pembrokeshire SA70 8DA

Tel: 01834 842087 Fax: 01834 842113
e-mail: reception@heywoodmount.co.uk
website: www.heywoodmount.co.uk
Country house hotel in attractive grounds half a mile
from the centre of town. 21 well-equipped en suite
guest rooms: restaurant, lounge bar and leisure
facilities. 137

Highgate Inn Hotel, Hundleton, Pembrokeshire SA71 5RD

Tel: 01646 685904 Fax: 01646 681888
e-mail: windy.gail@virgin.net
Village local and comfortable hotel all in one. Five en
suite, non-smoking bedrooms: bar and restaurant
menus: draught and keg ales.

The Navy Inn, Pembroke Dock, Pembrokeshire SA72 6XS

Tel: 01646 682300

Spacious public house with two bars, a beer garden and an extensive choice of snacks and meals. Close to the waterfront.   133

The Sherlock Holmes Inn, 19 Military Road, Pennar, Pembroke Dock, Pembrokeshire SA72 6SH

Tel: 01646 687526

Get on the trail of this friendly pub for a good selection of traditional bar food and some wicked desserts.

Milford Haven Golf Club

Hubberston, Milford Havern SA72 3RX

Tel: 01646 697822 Fax: 01646 697870

Now a superb and thriving 18-hole course overlooking the busy shipping lanes of the magnificent Haven waterway, the early Milford Haven golfing fraternity were more than content with the nine-hole layout they founded in 1913. However, the prestigious and international sea town of Milford Haven, once challenging Grimsby as Britain's leading fishing port before falling into recession between the two World Wars, suddenly regained its prosperity after the 1939-1945 World War. Being one of the finest and sheltered inland harbours in Europe, the mighty oil companies recognised its huge potential and built their oil refineries and sailed their giant oil tankers into the harbours of the great estuary.

This led to a large increase in membership of the golf club and with it the need for a full-sized course, which quickly bore fruition. Today, members and visitors delight in the challenges of the rolling meadow-land course with its breathtaking panoramic views across the mighty waterway and beyond. All the holes are delightfully and individually named to describe their characteristics, such as the Valley and Orchard holes, whilst the attractive clubhouse matches the quality of the course and visitors are assured of a real warm and friendly Pembrokeshire welcome, with the

first floor lounge offering not only a comforting atmosphere but also stunning scenic views of this truly remarkable corner of West Wales.

Sec/Manager:	Mike Flood
Professional:	Dillon Williams
Directions:	1 mile W of Milford Haven centre. From centre take the Herbrandston road. Entrance on the outskirts on left hand side.
Date Founded:	1913
Type of Course:	Seaside
No of Holes:	18
Length:	6035 yds (5570 mtrs)
Par:	71
SSS:	70
Green Fees:	Weekdays:£15; Weekends/Bank Holidays:£20
Visitors:	Welcome: Contact Club by telephone in advance
Societies:	Welcome: Contact Club by telephone or writing in advance
Facilities:	Putting Green, Chipping Green, Driving Range, Club Hire, Trolley Hire, Buggy Hire, Bar, Restaurant

Accommodation, Food and Drink

Reference numbers below refer to detailed information provided in section 2

Accommodation

Blue Dolphin Hotel, Tenby, Pembrokeshire SA70 7HW

Tel: 01834 842590

Eleven letting bedrooms in a friendly hotel within the old town walls. B&B, plus packed lunches and evening meals by arrangement.   140

Brongwyn Cottages, Brongwyn Mawr, Penparc, Cardiganshire SA43 1SA

Tel: 01239 613644 Fax: 01239 615725

Six pretty cottages surrounding flower filled courtyard. 5 star accommodation, indoor pool. Magnificent coastline nearby.

Castlemead Hotel, Manorbier, Nr. Tenby, Pembrokeshire SA70 7TA

Tel/Fax: 01834 871358

e-mail: castlemeadhotel@aol.com

Eight comfortable en suite rooms in an Edwardian residence with an excellent reputation for good food. Peaceful setting near the sea.   135

**Clarence House Hotel, Tenby,
Pembrokeshire SA70 7DU**

Tel: 01834 844371 Fax: 01834 844372

Sixty-eight en suite bedrooms in a seafront hotel that
offers traditional standards of hospitality and service.
Lifts to all floors. Patio/garden.   139

**Cleddau Bridge Hotel, Pembroke Dock,
Pembrokeshire SA72 6EG**

Tel: 01646 685961 Fax: 01646 685746
e-mail: information@cleddaubridge.co.uk
website: cleddaubridgehotel.co.uk

Twenty-two double rooms, two suites and two
restaurants in a modern hotel scenically set by the
famous Cleddau Bridge.   132

**The Dial Inn, Lamphey,
Pembrokeshire SA71 5NU**

Tel/Fax: 01646 672426
website: www.dialinnpembroke@barbox.net

Spacious, tastefully decorated en suite bedrooms and
a superb restaurant in a former dower house. Squash
courts adjoining.   136

Giltar Hotel, Tenby, Pembrokeshire SA70 7DU

Tel: 01834 842507/843424 Fax: 01834 845480
website: www.giltar-hotel.co.uk

A friendly family-run hotel in a fine position on the
esplanade above South Beach. 75 en suite rooms, lifts
to all floors, air-conditioned seaview restaurant. 138

**Hammonds Park Hotel, Narberth Road, Tenby,
Pembrokeshire SA70 8HT**

Tel: 01834 842696 Fax: 01834 844295

14 bedrooms including family rooms in a delightful,
quiet hotel just north of the town. The hotel is non-
smoking except for the tv lounge. Off-road parking.
Use of spa.

**Heywood Mount Hotel, Tenby,
Pembrokeshire SA70 8DA**

Tel: 01834 842087 Fax: 01834 842113
e-mail: reception@heywoodmount.co.uk
website: www.heywoodmount.co.uk

Country house hotel in attractive grounds half a mile
from the centre of town. 21 well-equipped en suite
guest rooms: restaurant, lounge bar and leisure
facilities.   137

**Highgate Inn Hotel, Hundleton,
Pembrokeshire SA71 5RD**

Tel: 01646 685904 Fax: 01646 681888
e-mail: windy.gail@virgin.net

Village local and comfortable hotel all in one. Five en
suite, non-smoking bedrooms: bar and restaurant
menus: draught and keg ales.

**Kinloch Court Hotel, Tenby,
Pembrokeshire SA70 7EG**

Tel: 01834 842777 Fax: 01834 843097
e-mail: kinlochhotel@aol.com
website: kinlochcourt-hotel.co.uk

The former Tenby Rectory is now a fine private hotel
with 14 en suite bedrooms and an excellent name for
food and hospitality.   134

**Penwern Fach Holiday Cottages, Pont Hirwuan,
Ceredigion SA43 2RL**

Tel: 01239 710694 Fax: 01239 710854

Spacious, well-equipped self-catering cottages in a
lovely secluded setting near Cenarth. Exclusive use of
driving range.   159

Food and Drink

**Castlemead Hotel, Manorbier, Nr. Tenby,
Pembrokeshire SA70 7TA**

Tel/Fax: 01834 871358
e-mail: castlemeadhotel@aol.com

Eight comfortable en suite rooms in an Edwardian
residence with an excellent reputation for good food.
Peaceful setting near the sea.   135

**Clarence House Hotel, Tenby,
Pembrokeshire SA70 7DU**

Tel: 01834 844371 Fax: 01834 844372

Sixty-eight en suite bedrooms in a seafront hotel that
offers traditional standards of hospitality and service.
Lifts to all floors. Patio/garden.   139

**Cleddau Bridge Hotel, Pembroke Dock,
Pembrokeshire SA72 6EG**

Tel: 01646 685961 Fax: 01646 685746
e-mail: information@cleddaubridge.co.uk
website: cleddaubridgehotel.co.uk

Twenty-two double rooms, two suites and two
restaurants in a modern hotel scenically set by the
famous Cleddau Bridge.   132

**The Dial Inn, Lamphey,
Pembrokeshire SA71 5NU**

Tel/Fax: 01646 672426
website: www.dialinnpembroke@barbox.net

Spacious, tastefully decorated en suite bedrooms and
a superb restaurant in a former dower house. Squash
courts adjoining.   136

Giltar Hotel, Tenby, Pembrokeshire SA70 7DU

Tel: 01834 842507/843424 Fax: 01834 845480
website: www.giltar-hotel.co.uk

A friendly family-run hotel in a fine position on the
esplanade above South Beach. 75 en suite rooms, lifts
to all floors, air-conditioned seaview restaurant. 138

**Hammonds Park Hotel, Narberth Road, Tenby,
Pembrokeshire SA70 8HT**

Tel: 01834 842696 Fax: 01834 844295

14 bedrooms including family rooms in a delightful,
quiet hotel just north of the town. The hotel is non-
smoking except for the tv lounge. Off-road parking.
Use of spa.

**Heywood Mount Hotel, Tenby,
Pembrokeshire SA70 8DA**

Tel: 01834 842087 Fax: 01834 842113
e-mail: reception@heywoodmount.co.uk
website: www.heywoodmount.co.uk

Country house hotel in attractive grounds half a mile
from the centre of town. 21 well-equipped en suite
guest rooms: restaurant, lounge bar and leisure
facilities.   137

**Highgate Inn Hotel, Hundleton,
Pembrokeshire SA71 5RD**

Tel: 01646 685904 Fax: 01646 681888
e-mail: windy.gail@virgin.net

Village local and comfortable hotel all in one. Five en suite, non-smoking bedrooms: bar and restaurant menus: draught and keg ales.

**The Sherlock Holmes Inn, 19 Military Road,
Pennar, Pembroke Dock,
Pembrokeshire SA72 6SH**

Tel: 01646 687526

Get on the trail of this friendly pub for a good selection of traditional bar food and some wicked desserts.

South Pembrokeshire Golf Club

Military Road, Pembroke Dock SA72 6SE
Tel: **01646 621453** Fax: **01646 621453**

Located above the town of Pembroke Dock and on the opposite side of the mighty waterway from Milford Haven, the South Pembrokeshire Golf Club started life as a small nine-hole course just over 20 years ago, but recent years have seen it blossom into a rather pleasant 18-hole layout. Situated on top of what is known as Barrack Hill, the course offers superb scenic views of the great estuary and the Irish Sea beyond. It is also situated close to the only Royal Naval Dockyard to be found in Wales and is but a five minute car drive from the Irish Ferries terminal at Pembroke Dock, as well as being on the edge of the beautiful surroundings of the Pembrokeshire Coastal Path. Not overlong at 6,158 yards, the course, nevertheless, has a fair number of testing holes to contend with.

The par-3 third looks a rather easy hole to negotiate with its length of only 122 yards and all downhill, but the locals will tell you it can be a real card wrecker unless treated with the utmost respect. Quite a number of the remaining holes leaves one wondering if they were designed by a sadist, most notably the wicked fifth and sixteenth ball-swallowing holes with so much rough lying in wait for any wayward shot. Also, a grant-aid project has resulted in the planting of over 20,000 trees and a tastefully-built new clubhouse offering excellent catering and hospitality. For visitors wishing to stay awhile at this charming spot, suitable accommodation can be arranged by the steward. What more could one ask for from good Welsh hospitality?

Sec/Manager: Don Owen
Professional: None

Directions: Western outskirts of Pembroke Dock. If entering Pembroke Dock on the A477, at the roundabout on the outskirts take London Rd (A4139) and follow round turning left into Victoria Rd at first T-junction. At the junction with High St carry straight on into Treowen Rd, then take the third right into Military Rd. Entrance after ½ mile on left hand side.

Date Founded: 1969
Type of Course: Clifftop/Parkland
No of Holes: 18
Length: 6158 yds (5684 mtrs)
Par: 72
SSS: 70
Green Fees: Weekdays: £15 per day; Weekends/Bank Holidays: £20 per day
Visitors: Welcome: By arrangement. Contact Club in advance
Societies: Welcome: By arrangement. Contact Club in advance
Facilities: Putting Green, Practice Area, Trolley Hire, Buggy Hire, Bar, Restaurant

Accommodation, Food and Drink

Reference numbers below refer to detailed information provided in section 2

Accommodation

**Cleddau Bridge Hotel, Pembroke Dock,
Pembrokeshire SA72 6EG**

Tel: 01646 685961 Fax: 01646 685746
e-mail: information@cleddaubridge.co.uk
website: cleddaubridgehotel.co.uk

Twenty-two double rooms, two suites and two restaurants in a modern hotel scenically set by the famous Cleddau Bridge.   132

**The Dial Inn, Lamphey,
Pembrokeshire SA71 5NU**

Tel/Fax: 01646 672426
website: www.dialinnpembroke@barbox.net

Spacious, tastefully decorated en suite bedrooms and a superb restaurant in a former dower house. Squash courts adjoining.   136

**High Noon Guest House, Lower Lamphey Road,
Pembroke, Pembrokeshire SA71 4AB**

Tel/Fax: 01646 683736
e-mail: info@highnoon.co.uk
website: www.highnoon.co.uk

Nine bedrooms, most en suite, including family

rooms in a pleasant guest house well placed for exploring the Pembrokeshire Coast National Park.

Highgate Inn Hotel, Hundleton, Pembrokeshire SA71 5RD

Tel: 01646 685904 Fax: 01646 681888
e-mail: windy.gail@virgin.net

Village local and comfortable hotel all in one. Five en suite, non-smoking bedrooms: bar and restaurant menus: draught and keg ales.

Food and Drink

Bay Tree Restaurant, Tredegar House, Tudor Square, Tenby, Pembrokeshire SA70 7AJ

Tel: 01834 843516 Fax: 01834 845866

A restaurant of real character and great atmosphere, with a long menu of home-cooked dishes using fresh local produce wherever possible.

Cleddau Bridge Hotel, Pembroke Dock, Pembrokeshire SA72 6EG

Tel: 01646 685961 Fax: 01646 685746
e-mail: information@cleddaubridge.co.uk website: cleddaubridgehotel.co.uk

Twenty-two double rooms, two suites and two restaurants in a modern hotel scenically set by the famous Cleddau Bridge.   132

The Dial Inn, Lamphey, Pembrokeshire SA71 5NU

Tel/Fax: 01646 672426
website: www.dialinnpembroke@barbox.net

Spacious, tastefully decorated en suite bedrooms and a superb restaurant in a former dower house. Squash courts adjoining.   136

Highgate Inn Hotel, Hundleton, Pembrokeshire SA71 5RD

Tel: 01646 685904 Fax: 01646 681888
e-mail: windy.gail@virgin.net

Village local and comfortable hotel all in one. Five en suite, non-smoking bedrooms: bar and restaurant menus: draught and keg ales.

The Navy Inn, Pembroke Dock, Pembrokeshire SA72 6XS

Tel: 01646 682300

Spacious public house with two bars, a beer garden and an extensive choice of snacks and meals. Close to the waterfront.   133

The Sherlock Holmes Inn, 19 Military Road, Pennar, Pembroke Dock, Pembrokeshire SA72 6SH

Tel: 01646 687526

Get on the trail of this friendly pub for a good selection of traditional bar food and some wicked desserts.

Tenby Golf Club

The Burrows, Tenby SA70 7NP

Tel: **01834 842978** Fax: **01834 844447**

Members of Tenby Golf Club are more than justified in being highly proud of their wonderful club because of the fact that it proved to be the official birthplace of Welsh golf during the month of September 1888. The game of golf was probably played in many parts of the Principality before this date, but it was here on the charming old links that the first officially constituted club in Wales was founded. Indeed, records in the Town Clerks office show proof that golf was played on "The Burrows"-the name the ancient linksland has long been known by-when it was recorded that the Mayor of Tenby adjourned a court to go and play a game in 1875! The old club and, of

course, Welsh golf must also feel proud that the year of their birth is one that they share with the USA, because although golf had long been played in fits and starts in America, it was actually a Scotsman, John Reid, from Dunfermline, and four enthusiastic friends, who officially founded the first golf club in the USA, which they named the St Andrews Club of Yonkers, with Reid becoming its first president, on 14 November, 1888.

The enthusiasm for golf amongst the upper class residents of Tenby must have been sparked off by the many English holidaymakers who saw it fashionable to flock to Tenby because of its fine beaches. It is obvious that many of them brought along their clubs because "The Burrows" was crying out that it was made for golf, what with its many high sand dunes, beautiful rolling turf, natural grassy bunkers and stunning views across Carmarthen Bay. Once the locals caught the golf

bug it was only a matter of time before a longing for a proper golf course became reality. And, without doubt, Wales could not have asked for a better birthplace. A beautiful resort in a beautiful country and a beautiful place to lay out its first golf course, shows that the pioneers of Welsh golf most certainly had their wits about them. Much credit must go to James Braid for his expertise as a course designer because almost all of the original design still exists. The creating of a loftier tee at the 18th and on top of the Black Rock, to give a more exciting finish to ones round, and the two pot bunkers in front of the 13th hole instead of the long single bunker is about as far as any major changes goes. The only other major change of note is the building of the huge new clubhouse at the entrance of the course, which replaces the old clubhouse that nestled alongside the Black Rock at the 18th tee.

I must admit I have rather a soft spot for this Old Master of a course, because it was here that I got my first taste of playing a links course shortly after taking up the game in 1963; and it has left me with many fine memories of my many visits there during my reporting days. I can still recall the day when Philip Price, now a fine European Tour professional, announced on the terrace of the Tenby clubhouse to the powers-that-then-were of the Welsh Golfing Union during the close of the Welsh Amateur Strokeplay Championship, in 1988, that he was going to join the paid ranks because he could no longer afford to remain an amateur, despite being on the verge of Walker Cup selection. The Welsh golfing gods must surely have been listening and took pity on him, because he has since amassed over £2 million in official earnings as a professional and twice been a tournament winner.

Yes, indeed, the oldest course in Wales is a wonderful and magical place to visit.

Sec/Manager:	Jeff Pearson
Professional:	Mark Hawkey
Directions:	1 mile S of Tenby centre. Entrance on the right hand side just before the Kinloch

Hotel, Battery Rd, on the southern outskirts.

Date Founded:	1888
Type of Course:	Links
No of Holes:	18
Length:	6337 yds (5849 mtrs)
Par:	69
SSS:	71
Green Fees:	Weekdays: £26 per day; Weekends/Bank Holidays:£32 per day; Twilight Ticket after 4.30 pm daily, 30% discount
Visitors:	Welcome: Anytime by arrangement. Contact Club in advance
Societies:	Welcome: Excluding Saturdays, Sundays, Mondays & Tuesdays. Contact Club in advance
Facilities:	Putting Green, Chipping Green, Practice Tee, Club Hire, Trolley Hire, Bar, Restaurant, Private Rooms

Accommodation, Food and Drink

Reference numbers below refer to detailed information provided in section 2

Accommodation

Blue Dolphin Hotel, Tenby, Pembrokeshire SA70 7HW

Tel: 01834 842590

Eleven letting bedrooms in a friendly hotel within the old town walls. B&B, plus packed lunches and evening meals by arrangement. 140

Castlemead Hotel, Manorbier, Nr. Tenby, Pembrokeshire SA70 7TA

Tel/Fax: 01834 871358
e-mail: castlemeadhotel@aol.com

Eight comfortable en suite rooms in an Edwardian residence with an excellent reputation for good food. Peaceful setting near the sea. 135

Clarence House Hotel, Tenby, Pembrokeshire SA70 7DU

Tel: 01834 844371 Fax: 01834 844372

Sixty-eight en suite bedrooms in a seafront hotel that offers traditional standards of hospitality and service. Lifts to all floors. Patio/garden. 139

Cleddau Bridge Hotel, Pembroke Dock, Pembrokeshire SA72 6EG

Tel: 01646 685961 Fax: 01646 685746
e-mail: information@cleddaubridge.co.uk
website: cleddaubridgehotel.co.uk

Twenty-two double rooms, two suites and two restaurants in a modern hotel scenically set by the famous Cleddau Bridge. 132

The Dial Inn, Lamphey,
Pembrokeshire SA71 5NU

Tel/Fax: 01646 672426
website: www.dialinnpembroke@barbox.net
Spacious, tastefully decorated en suite bedrooms and
a superb restaurant in a former dower house. Squash
courts adjoining.   136

Giltar Hotel, Tenby, Pembrokeshire SA70 7DU

Tel: 01834 842507/843424 Fax: 01834 845480
website: www.giltar-hotel.co.uk
A friendly family-run hotel in a fine position on the
esplanade above South Beach. 75 en suite rooms, lifts
to all floors, air-conditioned seaview restaurant.   138

Hammonds Park Hotel, Narberth Road, Tenby,
Pembrokeshire SA70 8HT

Tel: 01834 842696 Fax: 01834 844295
14 bedrooms including family rooms in a delightful,
quiet hotel just north of the town. The hotel is non-
smoking except for the tv lounge. Off-road parking.
Use of spa.

Heywood Mount Hotel, Tenby,
Pembrokeshire SA70 8DA

Tel: 01834 842087 Fax: 01834 842113
e-mail: reception@heywoodmount.co.uk
website: www.heywoodmount.co.uk
Country house hotel in attractive grounds half a mile
from the centre of town. 21 well-equipped en suite
guest rooms: restaurant, lounge bar and leisure
facilities.   137

High Noon Guest House, Lower Lamphey Road,
Pembroke, Pembrokeshire SA71 4AB

Tel/Fax: 01646 683736
e-mail: info@highnoon.co.uk
website: www.highnoon.co.uk
Nine bedrooms, most en suite, including family
rooms in a pleasant guest house well placed for
exploring the Pembrokeshire Coast National Park.

Kinloch Court Hotel, Tenby,
Pembrokeshire SA70 7EG

Tel: 01834 842777 Fax: 01834 843097
e-mail: kinlochhotel@aol.com
website: kinlochcourt-hotel.co.uk
The former Tenby Rectory is now a fine private hotel
with 14 en suite bedrooms and an excellent name for
food and hospitality.   134

West Hall, St Florence, Nr. Tenby,
Pembrokeshire SA70 8LW

Tel/Fax: 01834 871336
Comfortable self-catering accommodation in six
bedrooms for up to 16 guests in a three-storey
Pembrokeshire farmhouse in the centre of a
picturesque village.

Food and Drink

Bay Tree Restaurant, Tredegar House,Tudor
Square, Tenby, Pembrokeshire SA70 7AJ

Tel: 01834 843516 Fax: 01834 845866

A restaurant of real character and great atmosphere,
with a long menu of home-cooked dishes using fresh
local produce wherever possible.

Castlemead Hotel, Manorbier, Nr. Tenby,
Pembrokeshire SA70 7TA

Tel/Fax: 01834 871358
e-mail: castlemeadhotel@aol.com
Eight comfortable en suite rooms in an Edwardian
residence with an excellent reputation for good food.
Peaceful setting near the sea.   135

Clarence House Hotel, Tenby,
Pembrokeshire SA70 7DU

Tel: 01834 844371 Fax: 01834 844372
Sixty-eight en suite bedrooms in a seafront hotel that
offers traditional standards of hospitality and service.
Lifts to all floors. Patio/garden.   139

Cleddau Bridge Hotel, Pembroke Dock,
Pembrokeshire SA72 6EG

Tel: 01646 685961 Fax: 01646 685746
e-mail: information@cleddaubridge.co.uk
website: cleddaubridgehotel.co.uk
Twenty-two double rooms, two suites and two
restaurants in a modern hotel scenically set by the
famous Cleddau Bridge.   132

Cross Inn, Penally, Tenby,
Pembrokeshire SA70 7PU

Tel: 01834 844665
Freshly cooked pub fare and two real ales in a pleasant
inn overlooking Tenby Golf Club. Closed Monday
lunchtime.

The Dial Inn, Lamphey,
Pembrokeshire SA71 5NU

Tel/Fax: 01646 672426
website: www.dialinnpembroke@barbox.net
Spacious, tastefully decorated en suite bedrooms and
a superb restaurant in a former dower house. Squash
courts adjoining.   136

Giltar Hotel, Tenby, Pembrokeshire SA70 7DU

Tel: 01834 842507/843424 Fax: 01834 845480
website: www.giltar-hotel.co.uk
A friendly family-run hotel in a fine position on the
esplanade above South Beach. 75 en suite rooms, lifts
to all floors, air-conditioned seaview restaurant.   138

Hammonds Park Hotel, Narberth Road, Tenby,
Pembrokeshire SA70 8HT

Tel: 01834 842696 Fax: 01834 844295
14 bedrooms including family rooms in a delightful,
quiet hotel just north of the town. The hotel is non-
smoking except for the tv lounge. Off-road parking.
Use of spa.

Heywood Mount Hotel, Tenby,
Pembrokeshire SA70 8DA

Tel: 01834 842087 Fax: 01834 842113
e-mail: reception@heywoodmount.co.uk
website: www.heywoodmount.co.uk
Country house hotel in attractive grounds half a mile
from the centre of town. 21 well-equipped en suite

guest rooms: restaurant, lounge bar and leisure facilities. 137

The Navy Inn, Pembroke Dock, Pembrokeshire SA72 6XS

Tel: 01646 682300

Spacious public house with two bars, a beer garden and an extensive choice of snacks and meals. Close to the waterfront. 133

Trefloyne Golf Club

Trefloyne Park, Penally, Tenby SA70 7RG

Tel: 01834 842165 Fax: 01834 842165

Sec/Manager:	None
Professional:	S. Laidler
Directions:	1 mile SW of Tenby centre. From centre take the A4139 Marsh Rd (Pembroke). After 1 mile turn right into Trefloyne Lane. Entrance after 100 yds on left hand side.
Date Founded:	1996
Type of Course:	Parkland
No of Holes:	18
Length:	6635 yds (6124 mtrs)
Par:	71
SSS:	73
Green Fees:	Weekdays: £20 per day; Weekends/Bank Holidays: £25 per day
Visitors:	Welcome: Contact Club in advance
Societies:	Welcome: Contact Club in advance
Facilities:	Putting Green, Chipping Green, Club Hire, Trolley Hire, Buggy Hire

Accommodation, Food and Drink

Reference numbers below refer to detailed information provided in section 2

Accommodation

Blue Dolphin Hotel, Tenby, Pembrokeshire SA70 7HW

Tel: 01834 842590

Eleven letting bedrooms in a friendly hotel within the old town walls. B&B, plus packed lunches and evening meals by arrangement. 140

Castlemead Hotel, Manorbier, Nr. Tenby, Pembrokeshire SA70 7TA

Tel/Fax: 01834 871358
e-mail: castlemeadhotel@aol.com

Eight comfortable en suite rooms in an Edwardian residence with an excellent reputation for good food. Peaceful setting near the sea. 135

Clarence House Hotel, Tenby, Pembrokeshire SA70 7DU

Tel: 01834 844371 Fax: 01834 844372

Sixty-eight en suite rooms in a seafront hotel that offers traditional standards of hospitality and service. Lifts to all floors. Patio/garden. 139

Cleddau Bridge Hotel, Pembroke Dock, Pembrokeshire SA72 6EG

Tel: 01646 685961 Fax: 01646 685746
e-mail: information@cleddaubridge.co.uk
website: cleddaubridgehotel.co.uk

Twenty-two double rooms, two suites and two restaurants in a modern hotel scenically set by the famous Cleddau Bridge. 132

The Dial Inn, Lamphey, Pembrokeshire SA71 5NU

Tel/Fax: 01646 672426
website: www.dialinnpembroke@barbox.net

Spacious, tastefully decorated en suite bedrooms and a superb restaurant in a former dower house. Squash courts adjoining. 136

Giltar Hotel, Tenby, Pembrokeshire SA70 7DU

Tel: 01834 842507/843424 Fax: 01834 845480
website: www.giltar-hotel.co.uk

A friendly family-run hotel in a fine position on the esplanade above South Beach. 75 en suite rooms, lifts to all floors, air-conditioned seaview restaurant. 138

Hammonds Park Hotel, Narberth Road, Tenby, Pembrokeshire SA70 8HT

Tel: 01834 842696 Fax: 01834 844295

14 bedrooms including family rooms in a delightful, quiet hotel just north of the town. The hotel is non-smoking except for the tv lounge. Off-road parking. Use of spa.

Heywood Mount Hotel, Tenby, Pembrokeshire SA70 8DA

Tel: 01834 842087 Fax: 01834 842113
e-mail: reception@heywoodmount.co.uk

website: www.heywoodmount.co.uk
Country house hotel in attractive grounds half a mile from the centre of town. 21 well-equipped en suite guest rooms: restaurant, lounge bar and leisure facilities. 137

High Noon Guest House, Lower Lamphey Road, Pembroke, Pembrokeshire SA71 4AB

Tel/Fax: 01646 683736
e-mail: info@highnoon.co.uk
website: www.highnoon.co.uk
Nine bedrooms, most en suite, including family rooms in a pleasant guest house well placed for exploring the Pembrokeshire Coast National Park.

Kinloch Court Hotel, Tenby, Pembrokeshire SA70 7EG

Tel: 01834 842777 Fax: 01834 843097
e-mail: kinlochhotel@aol.com
website: kinlochcourt-hotel.co.uk
The former Tenby Rectory is now a fine private hotel with 14 en suite bedrooms and an excellent name for food and hospitality. 134

West Hall, St Florence, Nr. Tenby, Pembrokeshire SA70 8LW

Tel/Fax: 01834 871336
Comfortable self-catering accommodation in six bedrooms for up to 16 guests in a three-storey Pembrokeshire farmhouse in the centre of a picturesque village.

Food and Drink

Bay Tree Restaurant, Tredegar House, Tudor Square, Tenby, Pembrokeshire SA70 7AJ

Tel: 01834 843516 Fax: 01834 845866
A restaurant of real character and great atmosphere, with a long menu of home-cooked dishes using fresh local produce wherever possible.

Castlemead Hotel, Manorbier, Nr. Tenby, Pembrokeshire SA70 7TA

Tel/Fax: 01834 871358
e-mail: castlemeadhotel@aol.com
Eight comfortable en suite rooms in an Edwardian residence with an excellent reputation for good food. Peaceful setting near the sea. 135

Clarence House Hotel, Tenby, Pembrokeshire SA70 7DU

Tel: 01834 844371 Fax: 01834 844372
Sixty-eight en suite bedrooms in a seafront hotel that offers traditional standards of hospitality and service. Lifts to all floors. Patio/garden. 139

Cleddau Bridge Hotel, Pembroke Dock, Pembrokeshire SA72 6EG

Tel: 01646 685961 Fax: 01646 685746
e-mail: information@cleddaubridge.co.uk
website: cleddaubridgehotel.co.uk
Twenty-two double rooms, two suites and two restaurants in a modern hotel scenically set by the famous Cleddau Bridge. 132

Cross Inn, Penally, Tenby, Pembrokeshire SA70 7PU

Tel: 01834 844665
Freshly cooked pub fare and two real ales in a pleasant inn overlooking Tenby Golf Club. Closed Monday lunchtime.

The Dial Inn, Lamphey, Pembrokeshire SA71 5NU

Tel/Fax: 01646 672426
website: www.dialinnpembroke@barbox.net
Spacious, tastefully decorated en suite bedrooms and a superb restaurant in a former dower house. Squash courts adjoining. 136

Giltar Hotel, Tenby, Pembrokeshire SA70 7DU

Tel: 01834 842507/843424 Fax: 01834 845480
website: www.giltar-hotel.co.uk
A friendly family-run hotel in a fine position on the esplanade above South Beach. 75 en suite rooms, lifts to all floors, air-conditioned seaview restaurant. 138

Hammonds Park Hotel, Narberth Road, Tenby, Pembrokeshire SA70 8HT

Tel: 01834 842696 Fax: 01834 844295
14 bedrooms including family rooms in a delightful, quiet hotel just north of the town. The hotel is non-smoking except for the tv lounge. Off-road parking. Use of spa.

Heywood Mount Hotel, Tenby, Pembrokeshire SA70 8DA

Tel: 01834 842087 Fax: 01834 842113
e-mail: reception@heywoodmount.co.uk
website: www.heywoodmount.co.uk
Country house hotel in attractive grounds half a mile from the centre of town. 21 well-equipped en suite guest rooms: restaurant, lounge bar and leisure facilities. 137

The Navy Inn, Pembroke Dock, Pembrokeshire SA72 6XS

Tel: 01646 682300
Spacious public house with two bars, a beer garden and an extensive choice of snacks and meals. Close to the waterfront. 133

CARDIGANSHIRE (CEREDIGION)

The old county of Cardiganshire has a wonderful coastline which runs from its shire town of Cardigan in the south, which borders Pembrokeshire, to the small and uninteresting town of Borth in the north of the county. The major seaside resorts that are sandwiched between these two towns are Newquay, Aberaeron and the famous university town of Aberystwyth. Also along this charming coastline are many pretty villages just waiting to be discovered by the relatively few visitors who decide to explore this area in search of new places for some peace and quiet from the city life they have to endure during their busy and stressful working days.

Cardigan, situated on the northern side of the Teifi (hence its Welsh name Aberteifi - "*mouth of the Teifi*") is today a busy, bustling market town, but was once an important seaport until the River Teifi silted up and forced the ships elsewhere. Cardigan Town has a real bloody past, because here, in 1135, a fierce battle took place between the Normans and the Welsh, which saw the Normans defeated in a battle so ferocious that the river ran red with the blood of three thousand Norman soldiers. It is recorded that their bodies provided a human bridge for the victorious Welshmen to cross the river and take the castle and town. Now a quaint and quiet small town, Cardigan's charm

Aberaeron

comes from its narrow and twisting streets and the historic ruins of a Norman castle. All that remains of this castle are two towers and a fragment of wall, but like every Welsh castle it has a story behind it.

It was from this castle that Owain ap Cadwgan rode off to Pembroke Castle to abduct the Lady Nest, the wife of Gerald de Windsor, who was the custodian of Pembroke Castle. Owain ap Cadwgan and the quite willing Nest then went to live together in a castle near Llangollen until King Henry I, whose mistress Lady Nest had been, took umbrage, banished Owain and took from his father, Prince Cadwgan, much land and many of his possessions. The king also replaced Gerald de Windsor as the custodian of all his Welsh Castles with Gilbert de Clare. History tells us that the promiscuous Lady Nest had countless affairs and that her many descendants figure prominently in Welsh history. The old seven-arched Cardigan Bridge, which spans the River Teifi, is rather attractive and one can watch the annual Regatta from this bridge and the banks of the Teifi. One of the main attractions is the coracle race-the old-fashioned and quaint boats of the Ancient Britons, which are still used in this area of Wales. The River Teifi is some 50 miles long and starts as a small stream, which runs through the beautiful Teifi Valley before entering into Cardigan Bay, some 3 miles from Cardigan. With the river and the valley beloved by fisherman and artists alike, it is a favourite place for the fishermen more so because the stream-cum-river is noted for some of the finest salmon and trout in Wales.

The nearby village of St Dogmaels, which is officially in Pembrokeshire because it lies on that side of the river, is, nevertheless, still regarded as a suburb of Cardigan, and here is often seen the lovely sight of fisherman paddling along in the ancient coracles. Also at St Dogmaels is Sealyham Hall, the place where the first Welsh Corgi and Sealyham terriers were bred. In the grounds of the vicarage are the remains of a 12th century abbey and nearby an Early English style parish church with a 7ft stone pillar reputed to date from the 6th century.

A few miles from St Dogmaels at the mouth of the Teifi Estuary, is Poppit Sands, a lovely peaceful spot with good dunes offering excellent windbreaking relief when the gusts blow in off the sea. Across the other side of the estuary and back into Cardiganshire, the delightful Cardigan Bay offers Britain's first Marine Heritage Coast, with stunning beaches and seals, porpoises and dolphins to be seen offshore. The small sea-

Teifi Valley, nr Cenarth

side villages of Aberporth, Tresaith and Penybryn offer seclusion and award-winning golden beaches, which includes the 18th century smuggler's beach at Penybryn. The beautiful surrounding countryside also offers glorious walking opportunities along the Heritage Coastal Path. Further along this golden coastline are the larger resorts of New Quay and Llangrannog, both extremely popular with South Walians because of the expansive sandy beaches and the nearby-secluded bays. Llangrannog is the home of the Welsh League of Youth's residential centre, which includes among its leisure and sports facilities a dry ski-slope-all open to visitors. Move on to the resort of Aberaeron and you will be surprised with its Georgian appearance and the excellent stone-walled harbour. Indeed, it is regarded as one of Wales's most picturesque coastal towns. One of Wales's first specially planned towns; many of the buildings are of special historic or architectural interest. If it's scenic countryside you are after, then inland and extending to the villages of Felinfach, Talsarn and upwards beyond Llangeitho is the tranquil Vale of Aeron.

Onwards along this wonderful coastline you will discover many other small seaside villages with beaches and coves from where you can continue to spot the seals, porpoises and dolphins along with the other wild life. Many of these villages have names beginning with LLan (Welsh for enclosure or church) so don't get confused and lost if you happen to stop over for a few days at one of them. The major resort and most important town on this coast is the university town of Aberystwyth, known and loved by countless British people who studied at the University College of Wales. The town gives out a distinct feeling of the Victorian and Georgian era's because of the many fine buildings from those times, but history tells us the town dates back through many more centuries. King Edward I erected one of his many Welsh castles here, in 1277, and before that Gilbert Strongbow built a castle at the mouth of the River Ystwyth in 1109. Going even further back in time, a prehistoric camp was erected by the early coastal dwellers of the region, indicated by the discovery of their earthworks on a nearby hilltop known as Pen Dinas (Top Fort).

Tresaith, nr Aberporth

Overlooking the old town from a high hill are the modern buildings of the University College of Wales, and alongside stands the National Library of Wales. Many rare books and ancient manuscripts are contained here. Indeed, the oldest Welsh manuscript in existence, The Black Book of Carmarthen, is one of many priceless written works contained securely within this most important of Welsh libraries. A collection of strange tales, passed down through word of mouth until becoming recorded in the Middle Ages, became entitled: "Mabinogion". The oldest known copy of this important collection of tales is also housed here. This book inspired Lord Tennyson and Malory to write their tales of courageous knights and famous saints. Who knows, perhaps many of this collection of strange tales originated with the great Welsh wizard, Merlin!

The Norman castle close to the town's foreshore is now nothing but a stumpy old ruin lying close to the original buildings of the university, which was founded in 1872. Aberystwyth, with its award-winning beach and many attractions, also offers an excellent and mixed accommodation to suit every pocket, and for the golfing visitor a fine meadowland-cum-links full-sized golf course. One of the main features of the town is the famous Vale of Rheidol Narrow Gauge Railway (the River Rheidol, like the Ystwyth, empties into Cardigan Bay at Aberystwyth), which links Aberystwyth to Devil's Bridge. After enjoying the wonderful views of this beautiful Vale of Rheidol, when you step off the train at Devil's Bridge you will not believe the spectacular scenery and the dramatic waterfalls which lie amidst the Plynlimon Hills region. The only residential hotel in this unique location, is the famous Hafod Arms Hotel, which because of it's design and the gorgeous location, gives one a feeling of being in the Swiss Alpine region or maybe parts of Austria. Myself, I regard this area among the most spectacular and tranquil regions of the Principality. The railway through this exquisite valley was originally laid down in 1902 to transport mineral from the lead mines to the awaiting ships at Aberystwyth. Thankfully, it was later restored for the enjoyment of the many tourists who visit the area. The Mynach and the Rhiedol, just gushing streams at this point, dramatically descend into the gorge below, and three bridges and a number of footpaths have been created to allow visitors to also descend the gorge to view the spectacular falls. An amazing magical place is Devil's Bridge. Not too far away is the equally famous Elan Valley, with its huge dams holding back the wonderful Welsh water which flows through the taps of many households in the Midland region of England!

South from Devil' Bridge is the market town of Tregaron, which is situated close to the mountainous source of the Teifi. You are now in the famous Red Kite country, a rare bird of prey that is much protected in this area. At Red Kite feeding centres, you have a chance to see as many as 60 of these agile and beautifully coloured birds swooping down to catch their food. It's great fun watching them competing with the Buzzards and Ravens, both of whom are quite common in this area. At Tregaron there is a Kite Country Centre and Museum, where you can learn much about these rare and graceful birds. There are many of these centres to be found throughout the Mid-Wales counties.

The heather clad uplands close to Tregaron, were once the haunt of the famous Welsh character Twm Sion Cati, Wales's answer to the Englishman, Robin Hood. There are many stories told in the locality of this lovable Welsh character. Also in this area are the interesting ruins of Strata Florida Abbey. Once a famous Welsh monastery, it is believed to have been founded by Rhys ap Gryffydd, Prince of South Wales, for the Cistercians in 1164. Several Cambrian princes are buried here, and it once housed the Welsh National Records. It is also reputed as the burial place of the great 14th century Welsh poet, Daffyd ap Gwilym. King Henry IV and his son, the future Henry V, once used the abbey as headquarters when in pursuit of Owain Glendwr, and when attacking Aberystwyth in 1408. Glendwr continued to be a thorn in Henry V's side throughout his reign.

Back along the coastline this delightful county comes to an end along a scenic coastline in the direction of Borth, and on to Ynyslas on the southern shores of the beautiful Dyfi Estuary with its glorious sand dunes. In this area you are rewarded with an excellent 18-hole championship links course, called Borth and Ynyslas.

This historic county of Cardiganshire (Ceredigion) should not be missed.

Aberporth

Location of Golf Courses

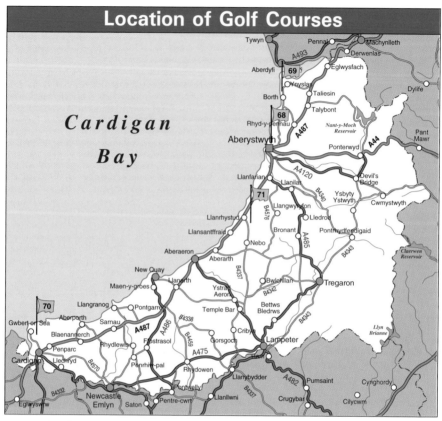

Cardigan Bay

© MAPS IN MINUTES ™ 2001   © Crown Copyright, Ordnance Survey 2001

Aberystwyth Golf Club

Bryn-y-Mor, Aberystwyth SY23 2HY
Tel: 01970 615104 Fax: 01970 626622

The golf club at Aberystwyth has served local golfers, the university golfers and holiday golfers really well since Harry Vardon poured his expertise into its creation way back in 1911. Although overlooking the ancient university town and offering glorious views of the town, Cardigan Bay and the harbour in one direction and panoramic scenery of the mountains and countryside in other directions, surprisingly it is only a short and not too difficult walk to reach from the town centre at the road adjacent to the famous Cliff Railway, which is another feature of Aberystwyth. Adding to the charm of the course is the cosy bungalow-type clubhouse, with picture windows overlooking the 18th green and also a small and attractive pavilion section to view from. At almost every hole of this delightful lay-out can be seen wonderful views, with the 17th giving you a perfect birds-eye view of Aberystwyth Town. The course itself is also rather pleasant to the eye with its beautifully manicured fairways and greens, along with neatly trimmed sand traps and bunkers all adding to the glorious spot carefully chosen by the discerning founders of the club al-

most a century ago. Like most of Vardon's creations, the course opens up in challenging fashion with a long and uphill par-4, and is then followed by another longish par-4 to keep even the better players well and truly on their toes for what lies ahead. Each September, the West Region PGA club professionals join forces with the amateurs for one of the largest Pro-am events in their busy calendar. No-one has yet brought the course to its knees, despite many of these professionals being former European Tour players.

After playing the fourth and fifth holes, the visitor will perhaps realise why this is so. The fourth has a nasty ditch across the fairway-nasty because it has an awful habit of attracting one's golf ball like a magnet that has been somehow modified to attract rubber! But it is the frightening 520 yards par-5 10th that does most damage to promising scorecards. The hole now differs from the original design in as much that it has been upgraded into a mighty challenge by water surrounding the green. Aberystwyth may be a pleasant meadowland-cum-parkland stretching modestly to just 6,110 yards with a par of 70, but it still throws out a mighty and exciting challenge-as many good professional golfers have discovered to their cost. Just enjoy it!

Sec/Manager:	Jim Mcleod
Professional:	None
Directions:	¾ mile NE of Aberystwith. From center take Morfa Mowr Rd, north and parallel with the coast, near the end turn right into Bryn-Y-Mor Rd. Entrance after a sharp right bend on the right.
Date Founded:	1911
Type of Course:	Meadowland
No of Holes:	18
Length:	6110 yds (5640 mtrs)
Par:	70
SSS:	70
Green Fees:	Weekdays: Summer £18 per day, Winter £15 per day; Weekends/Bank Holidays: Summer £15 per day, Winter £18 per day
Visitors:	Welcome: Contact Club in advance
Societies:	Welcome: Contact Club in advance
Facilities:	Putting Green, Chipping Green, Practice Area, Trolley Hire, Caddy Service, Bar, Restaurant

Accommodation, Food and Drink

Reference numbers below refer to detailed information provided in section 2

Accommodation

Aberystwyth Park Lodge, Parc-y-Llyn, Aberystwyth, Ceredigion SY23 3TL

Tel: 01970 636333 Fax: 01970 636334
e-mail: aberparklodge.co.uk
Very modern (June 2000), spacious hotel with 36 en suite bedrooms, all with tv, telephone and modem point. Café and restaurant.   157

Awel Y Môr, 4 Bodfor Terrace, Aberdovey, Gwynedd LL35 0EA

Tel/Fax: 01654 767058
e-mail: awlymor@lineone.net
website: http://website.lineone.net/~awelymor
Victorian seaside guest house with seven comfortable bedrooms, most with double and single beds. Good Welsh breakfast.

The Dovey Inn, Aberdovey, Gwynedd LL35 0EF

Tel: 01654 767332 Fax: 01654 767996
e-mail: rk@doveyinn.com
website: www.doveyinn.com
Handsome 18th century seafront inn with eight letting bedrooms, three bars and a 30-seat dining room with a long menu.   170

Dyffryn Castell Hotel, Ponterwyd, Aberystwyth, Ceredigion SY23 3LB

Tel/Fax: 01970 890237
e-mail: dyffryncastell.hotel.activebooking.com
website: www.smoothhound.co.uk/hotels/dyffryn.html
A family-run hotel at the foot of the slopes of Plynlimon, with eight bedrooms, a cosy bar and an extensive menu.   158

Penycastell Farm Hotel, Llanrhystud, Ceredigion, SY23 5BZ

Tel/Fax: 01974 272622
e-mail: penycastellhotel@faxvia.net
Terrific views from a peacefully located farmhouse with very comfortable en suite bedrooms, including a four-poster room.   156

Plas Penhelig Country House Hotel, Aberdovey, Gwynedd LL35 0NA

Tel: 01654 767676 Fax: 01654 767783
A distinguished country house hotel in a glorious setting with views over the Dovey estuary. 14 quiet, comfortable en suite rooms, superb food.   168

Trefeddian Hotel, Aberdovey, Gwynedd LL35 0SB

Tel: 01654 767213 Fax: 01654 767777
A distinguished hotel in a lovely secluded setting with fine views across Cardigan Bay. Attractive bedrooms, spacious lounges.   160

Y Gelli, Lovesgrove, Aberystwyth, Ceredigion SY23 3HP

Tel: 01970 617834 e-mail: pat.twigg@virgin.net
Six bedrooms ranging from a single to a family suite in Y Gelli guest house: accommodation for up to 40 (B&B, full board or self-catering) in Plas Dolau hostel.

Food and Drink

Aberystwyth Park Lodge, Parc-y-Llyn, Aberystwyth, Ceredigion SY23 3TL

Tel: 01970 636333 Fax: 01970 636334
e-mail: aberparklodge.co.uk
Very modern (June 2000), spacious hotel with 36 en suite bedrooms, all with tv, telephone and modem point. Café and restaurant.   157

The Dovey Inn, Aberdovey, Gwynedd LL35 0EF

Tel: 01654 767332 Fax: 01654 767996
e-mail: rk@doveyinn.com
website: www.doveyinn.com
Handsome 18th century seafront inn with eight letting bedrooms, three bars and a 30-seat dining room with a long menu.   170

Plas Penhelig Country House Hotel, Aberdovey, Gwynedd LL35 0NA

Tel: 01654 767676 Fax: 01654 767783
A distinguished country house hotel in a glorious setting with views over the Dovey estuary. 14 quiet, comfortable en suite rooms, superb food.   168

Trefeddian Hotel, Aberdovey, Gwynedd LL35 0SB

Tel: 01654 767213 Fax: 01654 767777
A distinguished hotel in a lovely secluded setting with fine views across Cardigan Bay. Attractive bedrooms, spacious lounges.   160

Yr Hen Lew Du, 16 Bridge Street, Aberystwyth, Ceredigion SY23 1PZ

Tel: 01970 615378 Fax: 01970 627775
Traditional town centre Public House with bar menus and daily blackboard specials. Good food and beer.
B&B

Borth & Ynslas Golf Club

Borth, Ceredigion SY24 5JS
Tel: 01970 871202 Fax: 01970 871202

Just 8 miles north of Aberystwyth and on the opposite side of the Dyfi Estuary to the renowned Aberdovey links course, lies the mysterious old course of Borth and Ynylas-thus named because of the small villages of Borth and Ynylas which it lies between-and mysterious because the oldest golf club in Wales, recognised by all and sundry governing bodies who determine such important matters of the Royal and Ancient game and record the facts, is that of Tenby Golf Club-officially founded in 1888. Yet at Borth and Ynylas they continue to insist that they were in existence in 1885, and I am certainly not going to dispute this fact, because there is something in the atmosphere at Borth which reeks of old age, even more so than Tenby! And I'm not talking about the splendidly atmospheric old wooden clubhouse, which once stood proudly in defiance of being replaced by a young impostor until mysteriously being burnt to the ground some years ago.

Whenever I visit this old masterpiece I always have a strange feeling that I am at the old course of St Andrews without the famous old clubhouse and other famous buildings that overlook it.

Nevertheless, I love visiting the "lonely old lady" and the wicked tricks she plays with one's confidence as her humps and bumps and sneaky sand traps stretched across her ageing fairways, constantly grabs hold of a seemingly perfectly struck shot. Then there's the wind that whips in off the estuary with the roar of a cavalry charge and the typical linksland rough that adds to the torture of playing a links course. But visit her on a gorgeous summer's day and she may let you off lightly like a long lost sibling coming home to stay. A great but often ignored Welsh masterpiece.

Borth and Ynylas, indeed, has great character, and I only wish someone could come up with authentic documented evidence to actually prove the date when this grand old course was officially founded. There is recorded proof of golf being played on the site where the Tenby course lies, many years before their official opening, but they-rightly so-cannot lay claim to this earlier (and actually recorded) date of some sort of unofficial golf club being in existence at Tenby. So until Borth and Ynylas come up trumps with the proof, they are, I'm afraid, sadly out on a lonely limb.

Sec/Manager:	Sue Wilson
Professional:	J.G Lewis
Directions:	6 miles NE of Aberystwyth or 1 mile N of Borth. From Aberystwyth take A487 (Machynlleth). After 3 miles turn left onto B4353 to Borth. Go through Borth and entrance is on the right hand side ¼ mile beyond the Glanmor Hotel.
Date Founded:	1885
Type of Course:	Links
No of Holes:	18
Length:	6116 yds (5645 mtrs)
Par:	70
SSS:	70
Green Fees:	Weekdays: Summer £22 per day, Winter £15 per day;

Weekends/Bank Holidays: Summer £30 per day, Winter £18 per day

Visitors: Welcome: Unable to play on weekend mornings before 10.15 am

Societies: Welcome: Unable to play on weekend mornings

Facilities: Putting Green, Practice Ground, Club Hire, Trolley Hire, Buggy Hire, Bar, Restaurant

Accommodation, Food and Drink

Reference numbers below refer to detailed information provided in section 2

Accommodation

Aberystwyth Park Lodge, Parc-y-Llyn, Aberystwyth, Ceredigion SY23 3TL
Tel: 01970 636333 Fax: 01970 636334
e-mail: aberparklodge.co.uk
Very modern (June 2000), spacious hotel with 36 en suite bedrooms, all with tv, telephone and modem point. Café and restaurant. 157

Awel Y Môr, 4 Bodfor Terrace, Aberdovey, Gwynedd LL35 0EA
Tel/Fax: 01654 767058
e-mail: awlymor@lineone.net
website: http://website.lineone.net/~awelymor
Victorian seaside guest house with seven comfortable bedrooms, most with double and single beds. Good Welsh breakfast.

Caethle Chalet & Caravan Park, Tywyn, Gwynedd LL36 9HS
Tel/Fax: 01654 710587
Extensive, unspoilt country setting with pitches for touring caravans, and three chalets for self-catering accommodation.

Cranbourne Hotel, Barmouth, Gwynedd LL42 1NA
Tel/Fax: 01341 280202
Recently refurbished seaside hotel in a Victorian terrace. Two single bedrooms, eight doubles and six twins including family rooms. Bar snacks. 182

The Dovey Inn, Aberdovey, Gwynedd LL35 0EF
Tel: 01654 767332 Fax: 01654 767996
e-mail: rk@doveyinn.com
website: www.doveyinn.com
Handsome 18th century seafront inn with eight letting bedrooms, three bars and a 30-seat dining room with a long menu. 170

Dyffryn Castell Hotel, Ponterwyd, Aberystwyth, Ceredigion SY23 3LB
Tel/Fax: 01970 890237
e-mail: dyffryncastell.hotel.activebooking.com

website: www.smoothhound.co.uk/hotels/ dyffryn.html
A family-run hotel at the foot of the slopes of Plynlimon, with eight bedrooms, a cosy bar and an extensive menu. 158

Pant-y-Neuadd, Aberdyfi Road, Tywyn, Gwynedd LL36 9HW
Tel/Fax: 01654 711393
website: www.pant-y-neuadd@lineone.net
A park that offers pitches for touring caravans, static caravans for rent and two stone cottages for self-catering holidays. Close to a safe, sandy beach.

Penycastell Farm Hotel, Llanrhystud, Ceredigion, SY23 5BZ
Tel/Fax: 01974 272622
e-mail: penycastellhotel@faxvia.net
Terrific views from a peacefully located farmhouse with very comfortable en suite bedrooms, including a four-poster room. 156

Pen-y-Bont Hotel, Tal-y-Llyn, Tywyn, Gwynedd LL36 9AJ
Tel: 01654 782285
e-mail: penybonthotel@btinternet.com
website: www.smoothhound.co.uk/hotels/ penybont.html
Former 16th century coaching inn situated on the edge of the beautiful Tal-y-Llyn Lake. Five en suite bedrooms, two bars, old-world restaurant (non-smoking) with extensive menus.

Plas Penhelig Country House Hotel, Aberdovey, Gwynedd LL35 0NA
Tel: 01654 767676 Fax: 01654 767783
A distinguished country house hotel in a glorious setting with views over the Dovey estuary. 14 quiet, comfortable en suite rooms, superb food. 168

Trefeddian Hotel, Aberdovey, Gwynedd LL35 0SB
Tel: 01654 767213 Fax: 01654 767777
A distinguished hotel in a lovely secluded setting with fine views across Cardigan Bay. Attractive bedrooms, spacious lounges. 160

Wavecrest Hotel, 8 Marine Parade, Barmouth, Gwynedd LL42 1NA
Tel: 01341 280330
Nine comfortable en suite bedrooms with tv in a family-run Victorian terrace hotel on the seafront. Good home-cooked food, cheerful bar with 64 malt whiskies.

Y Gelli, Lovesgrove, Aberystwyth, Ceredigion SY23 3HP
Tel: 01970 617834 e-mail: pat.twigg@virgin.net
Six bedrooms ranging from a single to a family suite in Y Gelli guest house: accommodation for up to 40 (B&B, full board or self-catering) in Plas Dolau hostel.

Food and Drink

Aberystwyth Park Lodge, Parc-y-Llyn, Aberystwyth, Ceredigion SY23 3TL

Tel: 01970 636333 Fax: 01970 636334
e-mail: aberparklodge.co.uk
Very modern (June 2000), spacious hotel with 36 en
suite bedrooms, all with tv, telephone and modem
point. Café and restaurant.   157

The Dovey Inn, Aberdovey, Gwynedd LL35 0EF
Tel: 01654 767332 Fax: 01654 767996
e-mail: rk@doveyinn.com
website: www.doveyinn.com
Handsome 18th century seafront inn with eight
letting bedrooms, three bars and a 30-seat dining
room with a long menu.   170

**Pen-y-Bont Hotel, Tal-y-Llyn, Tywyn,
Gwynedd LL36 9AJ**
Tel: 01654 782285
e-mail: penybonthotel@btinternet.com
website: www.smoothhound.co.uk/hotels/
penybont.html
Former 16th century coaching inn situated on the
edge of the beautiful Tal-y-Llyn Lake. Five en suite
bedrooms, two bars, old-world restaurant (non-
smoking) with extensive menus.

**Plas Penhelig Country House Hotel, Aberdovey,
Gwynedd LL35 0NA**
Tel: 01654 767676 Fax: 01654 767783
A distinguished country house hotel in a glorious
setting with views over the Dovey estuary. 14 quiet,
comfortable en suite rooms, superb food.   168

**Trefeddian Hotel, Aberdovey,
Gwynedd LL35 0SB**
Tel: 01654 767213 Fax: 01654 767777
A distinguished hotel in a lovely secluded setting
with fine views across Cardigan Bay. Attractive
bedrooms, spacious lounges.   160

**The Whitehall Hotel, Corbett Square, Tywyn,
Gwynedd LL36 9DF**
Tel/Fax: 01654 710212
A friendly pub with a good bar menu. Hot baguettes,
jacket potatoes, toasted sandwiches, steaks, pies,
curries - and lots more. Children welcome.

Cardigan Golf Club

Gwbert-on-Sea SA43 1PR
Tel: 01239 621775 Fax: 01239 621775
Once one of Wales's best kept secrets as the perfect place to visit for a blissful weekend of golf
away from the maddening crowds of golfers who
swarmed to other more reachable courses for a
quick round or two before returning to their work
places for another week of toil, The secret was
well and truly blown apart after American golf
writer Furman Bisher, discovered the old Cardigan course and quickly let the proverbial cat out
of the bag when he informed his many readers in
the Atlanta Journal that during his visit to Wales,
one of the highlights was playing golf at the Cardigan Golf Club. Having never previously been

to Wales, he made the trip in 1993 to take a good
look at Royal Porthcawl-possibly with the 1995
Walker Cup match quickly approaching. Originally only a short trip, he was so taken by the
beauty of Wales that he decided that he and his
wife would stay on for a ten-day tour of the Principality. Being the doyen of American golf writers,
what he wrote about the Cardigan course certainly
placed it firmly on the golfing map. He described
the view from the top of the course as the finest
he had seen anywhere in golf, with the exception of Pebble Beach. High praise, indeed! And it
could not have come at a better time for the Cardigan club, with its centenary year of 1995 so near
to being entered.

The Cardigan Golf Club started out as nine-
holes, but slowly grew into an 18-hole lay-out as
the club grew more prosperous. A mixture of
meadowland and linksland, this impressive course
is set on a hill high above the Teifi Estuary and
two miles from the historic town of Cardigan.
Spectacular views are everywhere on this enjoyable course, and if anyone's swing could match
the quality of these views he would be a better
player than Tiger Woods. Quite long at 6,687 yards
(par 72) the course provides a memorable finish
over the final three holes with the troublesome
bracken and typical linksland.

The best time to visit is during August when
the club stages a match between members and
any visitors who care to take them on-the more
visitors the better. One word of warning, Make
sure you have a willing chauffeur to transport you
back to your place of accommodation. This match
has been played for countless years-at least since
the end of the Second World War-and the mighty
sing-song that follows during the evening, does
tend to give one a huge thirst!

Sec/Manager:	John Jones
Professional:	Colin Parson
Directions:	2¾ miles NW of Cardigan. From centre take B4548 Gwbert Rd, leading to Coronation Drive. Entrance is on the right hand side after a sharp bend at the end of Coronation Drive.
Date Founded:	1895
Type of Course:	Links
No of Holes:	18
Length:	6687 yds (6172 mtrs)
Par:	72
SSS:	73
Green Fees:	Weekdays: £20 per day; Weekends/Bank Holidays: £25 per day
Visitors:	Welcome: Contact Club in

advance

Societies: Welcome: contact Club in advance

Facilities: Putting Green, Chipping Green, Practice Area, Club Hire, Trolley Hire, Buggy Hire, Bar, Restaurant

Accommodation, Food and Drink

Reference numbers below refer to detailed information provided in section 2

Accommodation

Brongwyn Cottages, Brongwyn Mawr, Penparc, Cardiganshire SA43 1SA

Tel: 01239 613644 Fax: 01239 615725

Six pretty cottages surrounding flower filled courtyard. 5 star accommodation, indoor pool. Magnificent coastline nearby.

Clarence House Hotel, Tenby, Pembrokeshire SA70 7DU

Tel: 01834 844371 Fax: 01834 844372

Sixty-eight en suite bedrooms in a seafront hotel that offers traditional standards of hospitality and service. Lifts to all floors. Patio/garden.   139

Giltar Hotel, Tenby, Pembrokeshire SA70 7DU

Tel: 01834 842507/843424 Fax: 01834 845480
website: www.giltar-hotel.co.uk

A friendly family-run hotel in a fine position on the esplanade above South Beach. 75 en suite rooms, lifts to all floors, air-conditioned seaview restaurant. 138

Penwern Fach Holiday Cottages, Pont Hirwuan, Ceredigion SA43 2RL

Tel: 01239 710694 Fax: 01239 710854

Spacious, well-equipped self-catering cottages in a lovely secluded setting near Cenarth. Exclusive use of driving range.   159

Penycastell Farm Hotel, Llanrhystud, Ceredigion, SY23 5BZ

Tel/Fax: 01974 272622
e-mail: penycastellhotel@faxvia.net

Terrific views from a peacefully located farmhouse with very comfortable en suite bedrooms, including a four-poster room.   156

Food and Drink

Clarence House Hotel, Tenby, Pembrokeshire SA70 7DU

Tel: 01834 844371 Fax: 01834 844372

Sixty-eight en suite bedrooms in a seafront hotel that offers traditional standards of hospitality and service. Lifts to all floors. Patio/garden.   139

Giltar Hotel, Tenby, Pembrokeshire SA70 7DU

Tel: 01834 842507/843424 Fax: 01834 845480
website: www.giltar-hotel.co.uk

A friendly family-run hotel in a fine position on the

esplanade above South Beach. 75 en suite rooms, lifts to all floors, air-conditioned seaview restaurant.   138

Penrhos Golf & Country Club

Llanrhystud, Aberystwyth S123 5AY
Tel: 01974 202999 Fax: 01974 202999

As far as golf clubs are concerned in Cardiganshire, the Penrhos Golf and Country Club is the new boy on the block and as precocious and ambitious as any ten-year-old youngster around. In a mere 10 years this bubbly and bouncing newcomer (I won't call it an upstart) has done it's very best to steal a march on its considerably more mature counterparts in the county of Cardiganshire-and is certainly making a huge impression as it continues to develop. Situated 9 miles south of Aberystwyth at Llanrhystyd, the club is set in a beautiful position overlooking Cardigan Bay and offering some magnificent panoramic views of the surrounding countryside. Since it's insignificant birth in 1991, this progressive club has grown from something of an ugly duckling into an attractive complex with nothing left to chance. Not allowing one single blade of fairway grass to grow under their busy feet, the proud proprietors have seen the club grow into the big apple of their eye that they originally intended, and one that has attracted a large membership. Now boasting an 18-hole championship length course as well as a new 9-hole lay-out and an excellent driving range, the club also consists of a comfortable and extensive clubhouse with full leisure facilities, a conference centre and first class restaurant, a fully-stocked professional shop and a recently opened hotel with 15 en-suite rooms. The 18-hole course offers a fine challenge through its entire length of 6,321 yards, which is parkland with a number of wooded areas bordering the fairways to add to the challenge of its par 72 lay-out. Being in a rather unspoilt area of the Principality, The Penrhos Golf and Country Club is a welcome addition to the Welsh golfing scene.

Sec/Manager: R. Rees-Evans
Professional: Paul Diamond

Directions:	8 miles S of Aberystwyth near the coast. From Aberystwyth take the A487 (Cardigan). At Llanrhystud turn left onto the B4337 (Cross Inn), go ½ mile and turn left into minor road (Llangwyryfon). Entrance after ¼ mile on left hand side.
Visitors:	Welcome: Unable to play on Sunday morning. Contact Club in advance.
Societies:	Welcome: Contact Club in advance
Facilities:	Putting Green, Chipping Green, Club Hire, Trolley Hire, Buggy Hire, Bar, Restaurant, Driving Range

18 Hole

Date Founded: 1991

Type of Course: Parkland

No of Holes: 18

Length: 6321 yds (5834 mtrs)

Par: 72

SSS: 73

Green Fees: Weekdays: £18 per day; Weekends/Bank Holidays: £24 per day

9 Hole

Date Founded: 1994

Type of Course: Parkland

No of Holes: 9

Length: 1827 yds (1686 mtrs)

Par: 31

SSS: None

Green Fees: Weekdays: £4 per day; Weekends/Bank Holidays: £4 per day

Accommodation, Food and Drink

Reference numbers below refer to detailed information provided in section 2

Accommodation

Aberystwyth Park Lodge, Parc-y-Llyn, Aberystwyth, Ceredigion SY23 3TL

Tel: 01970 636333 Fax: 01970 636334
e-mail: aberparklodge.co.uk

Very modern (June 2000), spacious hotel with 36 en suite bedrooms, all with tv, telephone and modem point. Café and restaurant. 157

Dyffryn Castell Hotel, Ponterwyd, Aberystwyth, Ceredigion SY23 3LB

Tel/Fax: 01970 890237
e-mail: dyffryncastell.hotel.activebooking.com
website: www.smoothhound.co.uk/hotels/
dyffryn.html

A family-run hotel at the foot of the slopes of Plynlimon, with eight bedrooms, a cosy bar and an extensive menu. 158

Penycastell Farm Hotel, Llanrhystud, Ceredigion, SY23 5BZ

Tel/Fax: 01974 272622
e-mail: penycastellhotel@faxvia.net

Terrific views from a peacefully located farmhouse with very comfortable en suite bedrooms, including a four-poster room. 156

Plas Penhelig Country House Hotel, Aberdovey, Gwynedd LL35 0NA

Tel: 01654 767676 Fax: 01654 767783

A distinguished country house hotel in a glorious setting with views over the Dovey estuary. 14 quiet, comfortable en suite rooms, superb food. 168

Y Gelli, Lovesgrove, Aberystwyth, Ceredigion SY23 3HP

Tel: 01970 617834 e-mail: pat.twigg@virgin.net

Six bedrooms ranging from a single to a family suite in Y Gelli guest house: accommodation for up to 40 (B&B, full board or self-catering) in Plas Dolau hostel.

Yr Hen Lew Du, 16 Bridge Street, Aberystwyth, Ceredigion SY23 1PZ

Tel: 01970 615378 Fax: 01970 627775

Traditional town centre Public House with bar menus and daily blackboard specials. Good food and beer.
B&B

Food and Drink

Aberystwyth Park Lodge, Parc-y-Llyn, Aberystwyth, Ceredigion SY23 3TL

Tel: 01970 636333 Fax: 01970 636334
e-mail: aberparklodge.co.uk

Very modern (June 2000), spacious hotel with 36 en suite bedrooms, all with tv, telephone and modem point. Café and restaurant. 157

Plas Penhelig Country House Hotel, Aberdovey, Gwynedd LL35 0NA

Tel: 01654 767676 Fax: 01654 767783

A distinguished country house hotel in a glorious setting with views over the Dovey estuary. 14 quiet, comfortable en suite rooms, superb food. 168

Yr Hen Lew Du, 16 Bridge Street, Aberystwyth, Ceredigion SY23 1PZ

Tel: 01970 615378 Fax: 01970 627775

Traditional town centre Public House with bar menus and daily blackboard specials. Good food and beer.
B&B

POWYS

Entering the huge county of Powys from the south via the pleasant market town of Abergavenny, Monmouthshire, one quickly discovers the small and delightful town of Crickhowell, which lies east of the magnificent River Usk and in the foothills of the imposing Black Mountains. With its abundance of good inns-the most famous being the ancient coaching inn, The Bear, and a number of attractive shops, a caravan site, and attractive riverside walks, this a an excellent place to stay awhile. An attractive nine-hole golf course is also available nearby just a couple of miles away over the Usk river bridge and on the edge of the village of Llangattock. Forming part of the Old Rectory Hotel, the course is open to non residents at a modest green fee, and is well worth a visit.

Llyn y Fan Fawr, Black Mountains

The county of Powys came into being when a number of small Welsh counties and parts of counties came to be amalgamated in a general streamlining by the government some years ago. Indeed, the ancient name Powys goes back to shortly after the Roman evacuation in the year 420, when the principality of Powys was formed during the tri-partition of Wales. For centuries after, Powys witnessed much struggle and strife as lords and barons and princes and kings fought over the fertile lands of Mid-Wales. The Norman knight Baldwyn, Roger de Mongomery, Rufus (the Red King), Henry III and Hubert de Burgh, struggled and counter-struggled to gain victory. The gallant men of Powys bitterly resented any invasion of their land, and William the Conqueror's men and those of many monarchs came to grief when batting with the fiery Welshmen of the tiny Principality. Today, as one travels through this peaceful and enchanting part of Wales, it is hard to imagine the cruel and bloody battlefields that once littered the area.

Travelling north from Crickhowell in the direction of Brecon , the ancient shire town of the disbanded county of Breconshire, one travels through one the most beautiful and picturesque areas of the United Kingdom. A bustling market town with plenty of character, Brecon lies at the heart of the Brecon Beacons. Composed mainly of sandstone the mountains rise to a height of almost 3,000 feet and are the highest mountain group in South Wales. Welsh speakers may sometimes be heard calling them by their old name of *Cader-Arthan*, which means Arthur's Chair. The slopes on the northern side are mainly quite steep and dangerous during the winter months and are used by the Hereford-based SAS Regiment for their hazardous and enduring training exercises, but the southern side offer a more gentle and safer landscape for ordinary walkers. There is also the exceptional Brecon Mountain Centre, which attracts many visitors looking to savour the atmosphere of being among the peaks, whilst just a few miles away in the direction of Sennybridge can be found the famous prehistoric caves known as Dany-y-Ogof.

Brecon is also famous for its indoor market, its two boating areas, an excellent public library, its annual jazz festival and for being the garrison town of the South Wales Borders Regiment of Rorkes Drift fame. Indeed, the old town also had a millitary importance in early times when it was a Roman garrison town. Nothing remains of the Roman occupation, but Bernard de Newmarch used the stone from the Roman fort to build a castle in Brecon at the end of the eleventh century. All that now remains is the Ely tower in the grounds of the old Castle Hotel. This tower is named after Morton, Bishop of Ely who was imprisoned there by Richard III, his custodian being the notorious Duke of Buckinghamwho later lost his head for plotting with his prisoner the dethronement of the King. Morton , however, escaped to France to persuade Henry Tudor to claim the throne. This chain of events finally led to the Battle of Bosworth. Another ancient building worth visiting is the eleventh century Norman church, which lies close to the old regimental barracks. Brecon is also justly proud of being the birthplace in 1755 of Sarah Kemble, who as Sarah Siddons went on to become one of the greatest of British actresses.

Golfers will be pleased to hear that two golf courses are to be found close to the ancient town. The James Braid designed Brecon Golf Club lies west on the A40 and less than a mile from the town. A pleasant nineholer, it was founded in 1902. One of Wales' greatest amateur golfers, the late Albert Evans , was born at Newton Farm, right in the middle of this course- The more later Cradoc Golf Club (founded in 1967) lies in Penoyre Park close to the village of Cradocwhich is high above Brecon in a truly spectacular area.

Builth Wells

Before heading north for Builth Wells, one would do well to pay a visit to the sleepy old town of Talgarth with its somewhat single fourteenth century single tower, and then further east to the world renowned town of Hay-on-Wye. For collectors and lovers of old books this magical, bustling old town is awash with old printers ink. Truly a book person's dream place, with practically every shop bursting at the seams with collectable old books. During a Press trip to Arizona some twelve years ago, l was amazed to hear Canada's top golf writer, Lorne Bernstien, (an avid collector of old and rare golf books, like myself), telling a Swiss journalist that one of his remaining ambitions was to spend a week visiting Hay-on-Wye, in Wales! Hay is also famous for its annual Festival of Literature, when famous authors hold talks, lectures and forums about the art of the written word.

Powys is famous for having the upper reaches of two of the finest salmon fishing rivers in Britain-the River Usk and the River Wye-within its boundaries. Whereas Brecon lies alongside the Usk, the market town of Builth Wells is blessed by being alongside the equally beautiful Wye.

As the name suggests, Builth Wells was once famous for its health-giving waters which poured from the natural springs outside the town. Scores of people once flocked to the town to take the waters during the Victorian era, but the modern day tourist comes for the peace and quiet and beautiful scenery of the area, for the good fishing, excellent hill-walking, water sports, a spot of golf and the annual Royal Welsh Agricultural Show, which sees the attractive town full to overflowing. Close by and well worth a visit are Llangammarch Wells and Llanwrtyd Wells, both also once famous for springs rich in chalybeate and sulphur.

Over the Wye Bridge and in a northerly direction from Builth Wells is the delightful old town of Llandrindod Wells. Regarded as the major spa town in Mid Wales by the Victorians it rose to some importance and enjoyed great prosperity, as can still be seen by the many Victorian-built hotels and other fine buildings there. The Victorians, including royalty, came in their droves, not only to take the waters but also for the huge and still attractive boating lake, good bowling greens, the ex-

Craig Goch Reservoir, Elan Valley

cellent golf course above the town and the breathtaking walks among the many rolling hills. Still an excellent holiday place for those searching for solitude from the busy cities, Llandrindod (known by the locals as Llandod) is still a place where the healthgiving waters can be sampled and where the atmosphere of Victorian times can be experienced. During each August visitors arrive to take part in the Victorian Week, when the locals all dress in Victorian costumes and provide entertainment in the style of the 'Good Old Days'. A truly unforgettable week!

Pen y Garreg Resevoir, Elan Valley

Tranquil towns are abound in Powys, and Rhyader is no exception. The trip northwards from Llandrindod to Rhyader is truly memorable as you drive along the edge of the Radnor forests. Rhyader lies at the entrance of the magnificent Elan Valley with its mighty Dams and reservoirs, used by the famous Dambusters squadron to perfect the raids on the dams of the Rhur Valley. To the east lies the small town of Llanidloes, and here above the town can be found the pleasant nine-hole course of St Idloes. Blessed with a small membership and a friendly, pleasant clubhouse it is quite an enjoyable place to play. A little further north is another attractive nine-hole layout known as St. Giles, Newtown. Situated one mile east of Newtown on the A483, this course has been played on since 1890, but before that the land was used for horseracing. In the early days one of the great characters was the Reverend Stanley Phillips who, about to tee off for his second nine, luckily remembered he had a funeral to attend to. Removing his shoes, socks and trousers, he took a short cut to the church by wading over the wide stream and returned after the funeral to join his pals over the last three holes. Philip Parkin, another great character and former European Tour member, Dunhill Cup and World Cup player, plus an amateur record which equals that of Newport's Paul Mayo, honed his golfing skills here and still resides in the area. Newtown itself, a busy town with much light industry, is famous as the birthplace of Robert Owen, who started the co-operative movement in Scotland and founded a communist colony in America. Welshpool just 14 miles northeast of Newtown, is a large ancient agricultural town situated in the wide valley of the upper River Severn. Overlooked by the peaks of the Breidden Hills, where one can see the obelisk erected to commemorate the defeat of the, French navy off the Domincan Islands by Admiral Rodney, Welshpool lies close to the border with Shropshire and is mainly English speaking. The impressive Powis Castle, now privately owned and used as a hotel, was erected in the seventeenth century on the site of a much older castle and sits proudly above the old town. Welshpool also boasts a fine mountain golf course some four miles west of the town.

Machynlleth, on the western edge of the county is, without doubt, the most historical town to be found in Mid-Wales. Here in 1402 Owen Glyndwr, Wales' most fervant patriot, was crowned Prince of Wales and remained the scourge of the English. The house in Eastern Street where he held his parliament can still be visited. Lying deep in the Dovey valley, amidst picturesque countryside, this delightful market town also boasts an interesting nine-hole course (yes, there are lots of nine-holes courses inside Powys), which lies atop the mountain just one mile east of the town on the A489, and which offers some magnificent views. By the way, the tongue-twisting word Machynlleth is pronounced Machuncleth.

Powis Castle, Welshpool

Location of Golf Courses

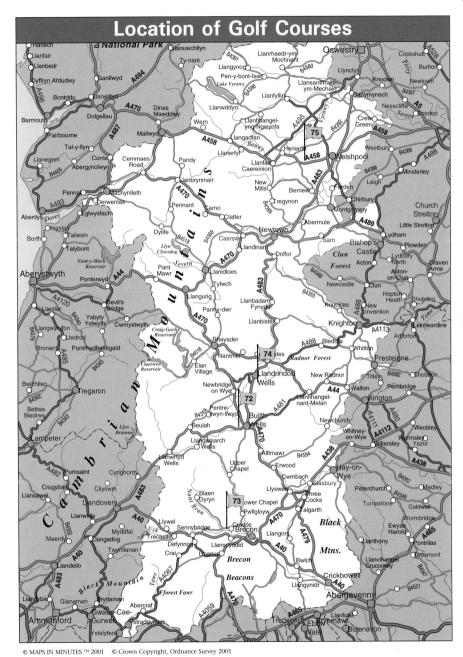

© MAPS IN MINUTES ™ 2001   © Crown Copyright, Ordnance Survey 2001

Builth Wells Golf Club

Golf Club Road, Builth Wells CD2 3NF
Tel: 01982 553296 Fax: 01982 551064

Like the Llandrindod club, Builth Wells Golf Club has some rare golfing characters, who are also extremely friendly and rather canny (don't offer to play them for high stakes!). Situated close to the town on the A483 in the direction of Llandovery, this attractive parkland course first came into being in 1923 as an extra attraction (like Llandrindod Wells) for the many visitors who flocked to the town to take the medicinal waters. Then the club could only find enough land to accomodate nine-holes, but in the late 1960's further land became available which contained the once much sought after health-giving springs. With the popular modern-day belief in alternative medicines who knows, the members may now be sitting (or should I say playing ?) on a liquid goldmine!

Offering panoramic all-round views, this well maintained eighteen-hole, par 66, course is unique inasmuch as there are no par 5s to be found, hence the low par figure. Therefore, it can be quite an interesting challenge to get round close to one's handicap.

An interesting feature of the club is its sixteenth century charming and cosy clubhouse. Offering a warm welcome, good home cooking and a pleasant atmosphere, it's a place where visitors tend to linger a little longer than originally intended.

Sec/Manager:	John Jones
Professional:	Simon Edwards
Directions:	½ mile NW of Builth Wells. From center take the A483 and on the Western outskirts turn right into Golf Links Rd. The entrance is on the left hand side after about 400 yds.
Date Founded:	1923
Type of Course:	Parkland
No of Holes:	18
Length:	5197 yds (4797 mtrs)
Par:	66
SSS:	66
Green Fees:	Weekdays: Summer £16 per day, Winter £12 per day; Weekends/Bank Holidays: Summer £22 per day, Winter £17 per day
Visitors:	Welcome: Excluding Saturdays 8.30 - 9.30 am & 1.30 -2.30 pm.
Societies:	Welcome: Contact Club by phone or in writing
Facilities:	Putting Green , Club Hire, Trolley Hire, Bar, Restaurant

Accommodation, Food and Drink

Reference numbers below refer to detailed information provided in section 2

Accommodation

The Bell Country Inn, Llanyre,
Llandrindod Wells, Powys LD1 6DY
Tel: 01597 823959 Fax: 01597 825899

e-mail: dgj.jones@virgin.net
website: www.thebellcountryinn.com
Friendly, family run inn with lovely views. 9 en suite
rooms and restaurant serving traditional and
international dishes as well as a good wine list. 144

Bucks Head House, School Farm, Upper Hergest, Kington, Herefordshire HR5 3EW
Tel: 01544 231063
Six bedrooms ona 290-acre working farm with
magnificent views. Lounge, sun room. B&B or B,B &
Dinner. 6-berth static caravan also available.

The Bulls Head Hotel, 86 The Street, Brecon, Powys LD3 7LS
Tel: 01874 622044 Fax: 01874 625321
Good-value overnight accommodation (2 rooms
sleeping up to 6), pub grub and a great selection of
real ales. Town-centre location.

The Cedars, Builth Wells, Powys LD2 3PB
Tel: 01982 553356
website: www.cedars.ltd.co.uk
A comfortable family residence, circa 1880, with
seven letting bedrooms, lounge and restaurant.
Overlooks the River Wye. 149

Corven Hall,Howey, Llandrindod Wells, Powys LD1 5RE
Tel: 01597 823368
Six spacious bedrooms (most en suite) for Bed &
Breakfast in a Victorian house with lovely gardens
and fine views. 151

The County House, 100 The Street, Brecon, Powys LD3 7LS
Tel: 01874 625844
e-mail: countyhouse@ukworld.net
Licensed accommodation in a fine Georgian house.
Three excellent en suite bedrooms: sitting room,
dining room. B&B with dinner option.

Gwystre Inn, Gwystre, Llandrindod Wells, Powys LD1 6RM
Tel: 01597 851650
A 300-year-old pub with three en suite twin rooms
and good-value home-cooked food. Local ales. Darts
and pool.

Kincoed Hotel, Temple Street, Llandrindod Wells, Powys LD1 5HF
Tel: 01597 822656
Arrive as a guest, leave as a friend. Ten rooms for B&B,
with evening meals by arrangement. Breakfasts fit for
a king.

Llandetty Hall Farm, Talybont-on-Usk, Powys LD3 7YR
Tel: 01874 676415
A Grade ll listed farmhouse in the Brecon Beacons
National Park, offering non-smoking B&B accommo-
dation in three spacious bedrooms. 145

The Llanerch Inn, Llandrindod Wells, Powys LD1 6BG

Tel: 01597 822086 Fax: 01597 824618
e-mail: llanerchinn@ic24.net
Family-owned 16th century inn of great character,
with 12 en suite rooms. Snacks and meals. Residents'
lounge, patio, garden, play area. 152

The Montpellier Hotel, Llandrindod Wells, Powys LD1 5HW
Tel: 01597 822388 Fax: 01597 825600
A handsome redbrick Victorian building in the town
centre. Eleven well-furnished en suite bedrooms, 30-
cover brasserie, lounge bar. 155

The Old Ford Inn, Llanhamlach, Nr. Brecon, Powys LD3 7YB
Tel/Fax: 01874 665220
e-mail: enquiries@theoldfordinn.co.uk
website: www.theoldfordinn.co.uk
A fine old country inn offering wonderful views, a
warm ambience, excellent food and drink and very
comfortable B&B accommodation. 147

Red House Farm, Howey, Llandrindod Wells, Powys LD1 5PP
Tel: 01597 822973
website: http://www.lineone.net/~redhousefarm
A traditional stone farmhouse with exposed beams
and old-world character providing warm, comfortable
Bed & Breakfast accommodation in three spacious
bedrooms. 154

The Royal Oak, Gladestry, Powys HR5 3NR
Tel: 01544 370669
Sixteenth century village pub offering real ales, home-
cooked food, a good selection of wine and four
comfortable letting bedrooms. 142

Seland Newydd, Pwllgloyw, Nr. Brecon, Powys LD3 9PY
Tel: 01874 690282
website: www.selandnewydd.co.uk
Real ales, excellent wines, fine food and comfortable
new en suite bedrooms in a country inn halfway
between Builth Wells and Cradoc. 146

The Tai'r Bull Inn, Libanus, Nr. Brecon, Powys LD3 8EL
Tel: 01874 625849
A very well-kept roadside inn offering good food, B&B
accommodation and superb views of the Brecon
Beacons. 148

The Vulcan Arms, Llanwrthwl, Llandrindod Wells, Powys LD1 6NN
Tel: 01597 811180 Fax: 01597 811152
e-mail: Vulcan.arms@virgin.net
A delighful inn on the A470 Rhayader-Builth Wells
road. Food is served all day, starting with an early
morning breakfast. 153

The White Swan, Llanfrynach, Brecon, Powys LD3 7BZ
Tel: 01874 665276
website: www.the-white-swan.com
An excellent pub-restaurant in a row of smart black-

and-white cottages. Sister establishment offering luxurious self-catering accommodation nearby.   150

Food and Drink

The Barley Mow, 1 West Street, Builth Wells, Powys LD2 3AH

Tel: 01982 553648

One of the oldest pubs in town, with a sporting owner and a sporting clientele. Excellent value meals. Book for Sunday lunch.

The Bell Country Inn, Llanyre, Llandrindod Wells, Powys LD1 6DY

Tel: 01597 823959 Fax: 01597 825899
e-mail: dgj.jones@virgin.net
website: www.thebellcountryinn.com

Friendly, family run inn with lovely views. 9 en suite rooms and restaurant serving traditional and international dishes as well as a good wine list.   144

The Bulls Head Hotel, 86 The Street, Brecon, Powys LD3 7LS

Tel: 01874 622044 Fax: 01874 625321

Good-value overnight accommodation (2 rooms sleeping up to 6), pub grub and a great selection of real ales. Town-centre location.

The Cedars, Builth Wells, Powys LD2 3PB

Tel: 01982 553356
website: www.cedars.ltd.co.uk

A comfortable family residence, circa 1880, with seven letting bedrooms, lounge and restaurant. Overlooks the River Wye.   149

Gwystre Inn, Gwystre, Llandrindod Wells, Powys LD1 6RM

Tel: 01597 851650

A 300-year-old pub with three en suite twin rooms and good-value home-cooked food. Local ales. Darts and pool.

The Llanerch Inn, Llandrindod Wells, Powys LD1 6BG

Tel: 01597 822086 Fax: 01597 824618
e-mail: llanerchinn@ic24.net

Family-owned 16th century inn of great character, with 12 en suite rooms. Snacks and meals. Residents' lounge, patio, garden, play area.   152

The Montpellier Hotel, Llandrindod Wells, Powys LD1 5HW

Tel: 01597 822388 Fax: 01597 825600

A handsome redbrick Victorian building in the town centre. Eleven well-furnished en suite bedrooms, 30-cover brasserie, lounge bar.   155

The Old Ford Inn, Llanhamlach, Nr. Brecon, Powys LD3 7YB

Tel/Fax: 01874 665220
e-mail: enquiries@theoldfordinn.co.uk
website: www.theoldfordinn.co.uk

A fine old country inn offering wonderful views, a warm ambience, excellent food and drink and very comfortable B&B accommodation.   147

The Prince Llewellyn Inn, Cilmery, Brecon, Powys LD2 3NU

Tel: 01982 552694

A friendly inn four miles west of Builth Wells on the A483, with a lovely garden, comfortable bars, good beer and an excellent restaurant.

The Royal Oak, Gladestry, Powys HR5 3NR

Tel: 01544 370669

Sixteenth century village pub offering real ales, home-cooked food, a good selection of wine and four comfortable letting bedrooms.   142

Seland Newydd, Pwllgloyw, Nr. Brecon, Powys LD3 9PY

Tel: 01874 690282
website: www.selandnewydd.co.uk

Real ales, excellent wines, fine food and comfortable new en suite bedrooms in a country inn halfway between Builth Wells and Cradoc.   146

The Tai'r Bull Inn, Libanus, Nr. Brecon, Powys LD3 8EL

Tel: 01874 625849

A very well-kept roadside inn offering good food, B&B accommodation and superb views of the Brecon Beacons.   148

The Vulcan Arms, Llanwrthwl, Llandrindod Wells, Powys LD1 6NN

Tel: 01597 811180 Fax: 01597 811152
e-mail: Vulcan.arms@virgin.net

A delighful inn on the A470 Rhayader-Builth Wells road. Food is served all day, starting with an early morning breakfast.   153

The Wheatsheaf, Wheat Street, Brecon, Powys LD3 7DG

Tel: 01874 611109

A town-centre pub with a long, spacious bar. Pool table. Good bar food, good beer, young crowd.

The White Pheasant, 9 High Street, Kington, Herefordshire HR5 3AX

Tel: 01544 231291

A 60-cover licensed restaurant serving great value dinners and Sunday lunch. Top-quality steaks (up to 24oz!) and delicious desserts.

The White Swan, Llanfrynach, Brecon, Powys LD3 7BZ

Tel: 01874 665276
website: www.the-white-swan.com

An excellent pub-restaurant in a row of smart black-and-white cottages. Sister establishment offering luxurious self-catering accommodation nearby.   150

Cradoc Golf Club

Penoyre Park, Cradoc, Brecon LD3 9LP

Tel: 01874 623658 Fax: 01874 623658

When a few members of Brecon Golf Club decided their was an urgent need for an 18-hole course for the growing town, Leslie Watkins, the Brecon captain, and vice-captain John Morrell, were in complete agreement and started searching for suitable ground. Discovering that Penoyre Park, along with its fine mansion house was available, they quickly went into action. In less than a month they managed to raise £80,000 and the purchase was completed in April 1967. Naming it Penoyre Golf and Country Club, the club quickly attracted over 400 members, Starting with 9-holes and 9 holes in the pipeline, the club was in business. Sadly, in the mid 1970's, the club suffered some serious financial difficulties and lost the old mansion house. Determined not to lose the course, the enthusiastic committee set up a huge fund-raising scheme and incuded in this was a raffle for a brand new motor car. Proving a huge success, they managed not only to save the course but also built a large and comfortable clubhouse

Directions:	2 miles NW of Brecon. From centre take the B4520 (Builth Wells) and after 2 miles turn left onto minor road. Entrance after ¾ mile on right hand side.
Date Founded:	1969
Type of Course:	Parkland
No of Holes:	18
Length:	5923 yds (5467 mtrs)
Par:	72
SSS:	72
Green Fees:	Weekdays:£20 Weekends/Bank Holidays:£25.00
Visitors:	Welcome: Contact Club by telephone in advance.
Societies:	Welcome: Contact Club in writing or telephone in advance.
Facilities:	Putting Green, Driving Range, Club Hire, Trolley Hire, Buggy Hire, Bar, Restaurant

Accommodation, Food and Drink

Reference numbers below refer to detailed information provided in section 2

Accommodation

close to the entrance of the old park, and renamed the club Cradoc after the small village there. A splendid parkland course just two miles from Brecon, the layout is in a magnificent setting in the Brecon Beacons National Park with such breathtaking views one could well believe this was Swiss country! Another attraction is the excellent Welsh cooking, so much so that the club boasts over 1,000 social members who merely arrive for eating purposes. A most enjoyable course and a memorable experience.

Sec/Manager: Lynn Price

Professional: Richard Davies

The Bulls Head Hotel, 86 The Street, Brecon, Powys LD3 7LS

Tel: 01874 622044 Fax: 01874 625321

Good-value overnight accommodation (2 rooms sleeping up to 6), pub grub and a great selection of real ales. Town-centre location.

The Cedars, Builth Wells, Powys LD2 3PB

Tel: 01982 553356

website: www.cedars.ltd.co.uk

A comfortable family residence, circa 1880, with seven letting bedrooms, lounge and restaurant. Overlooks the River Wye.

The County House, 100 The Street, Brecon, Powys LD3 7LS

Tel: 01874 625844
e-mail: countyhouse@ukworld.net

Licensed accommodation in a fine Georgian house. Three excellent en suite bedrooms: sitting room, dining room. B&B with dinner option.

Llandetty Hall Farm, Talybont-on-Usk, Powys LD3 7YR

Tel: 01874 676415

A Grade ll listed farmhouse in the Brecon Beacons National Park, offering non-smoking B&B accommodation in three spacious bedrooms.   145

The Montpellier Hotel, Llandrindod Wells, Powys LD1 5HW

Tel: 01597 822388 Fax: 01597 825600

A handsome redbrick Victorian building in the town centre. Eleven well-furnished en suite bedrooms, 30-cover brasserie, lounge bar.   155

The Old Ford Inn, Llanhamlach, Nr. Brecon, Powys LD3 7YB

Tel/Fax: 01874 665220
e-mail: enquiries@theoldfordinn.co.uk
website: www.theoldfordinn.co.uk

A fine old country inn offering wonderful views, a warm ambience, excellent food and drink and very comfortable B&B accommodation.   147

Red House Farm, Howey, Llandrindod Wells, Powys LD1 5PP

Tel: 01597 824973
website: http://www.lineone.net/~redhousefarm

A traditional stone farmhouse with exposed beams and old-world character providing warm, comfortable Bed & Breakfast accommodation in three spacious bedrooms.   154

Seland Newydd, Pwllgloyw, Nr. Brecon, Powys LD3 9PY

Tel: 01874 690282
website: www.selandnewydd.co.uk

Real ales, excellent wines, fine food and comfortable new en suite bedrooms in a country inn halfway between Builth Wells and Cradoc.   146

The Tai'r Bull Inn, Libanus, Nr. Brecon, Powys LD3 8EL

Tel: 01874 625849

A very well-kept roadside inn offering good food, B&B accommodation and superb views of the Brecon Beacons.   148

The Vulcan Arms, Llanwrthwl, Llandrindod Wells, Powys LD1 6NN

Tel: 01597 811180 Fax: 01597 811152
e-mail: Vulcan.arms@virgin.net

A delightful inn on the A470 Rhayader-Builth Wells road. Food is served all day, starting with an early morning breakfast.   153

The Wenallt, Gilwern, Nr. Abergavenny, Gwent NP7 0HP

Tel: 01873 830694
e-mail: thewenallt@talk21.com

A 16th century Welsh longhouse in a superb hillside setting in the Brecon Beacons National Park. Large, comfortable bedrooms: three-course dinners.   107

The White Swan, Llanfrynach, Brecon, Powys LD3 7BZ

Tel: 01874 665276
website: www.the-white-swan.com

An excellent pub-restaurant in a row of smart black-and-white cottages. Sister establishment offering luxurious self-catering accommodation nearby.   150

Food and Drink

The Barley Mow, 1 West Street, Builth Wells, Powys LD2 3AH

Tel: 01982 553648

One of the oldest pubs in town, with a sporting owner and a sporting clientele. Excellent value meals. Book for Sunday lunch.

The Bulls Head Hotel, 86 The Street, Brecon, Powys LD3 7LS

Tel: 01874 622044 Fax: 01874 625321

Good-value overnight accommodation (2 rooms sleeping up to 6), pub grub and a great selection of real ales. Town-centre location.

The Cedars, Builth Wells, Powys LD2 3PB

Tel: 01982 553356
website: www.cedars.ltd.co.uk

A comfortable family residence, circa 1880, with seven letting bedrooms, lounge and restaurant. Overlooks the River Wye.   149

The Montpellier Hotel, Llandrindod Wells, Powys LD1 5HW

Tel: 01597 822388 Fax: 01597 825600

A handsome redbrick Victorian building in the town centre. Eleven well-furnished en suite bedrooms, 30-cover brasserie, lounge bar.   155

The Old Ford Inn, Llanhamlach, Nr. Brecon, Powys LD3 7YB

Tel/Fax: 01874 665220
e-mail: enquiries@theoldfordinn.co.uk
website: www.theoldfordinn.co.uk

A fine old country inn offering wonderful views, a warm ambience, excellent food and drink and very comfortable B&B accommodation.   147

The Prince Llewellyn Inn, Cilmery, Brecon, Powys LD2 3NU

Tel: 01982 552694

A friendly inn four miles west of Builth Wells on the A483, with a lovely garden, comfortable bars, good beer and an excellent restaurant.

Seland Newydd, Pwllgloyw, Nr. Brecon, Powys LD3 9PY

Tel: 01874 690282
website: www.selandnewydd.co.uk

Real ales, excellent wines, fine food and comfortable

new en suite bedrooms in a country inn halfway between Builth Wells and Cradoc.   146

The Tai'r Bull Inn, Libanus, Nr. Brecon, Powys LD3 8EL

Tel: 01874 625849

A very well-kept roadside inn offering good food, B&B accommodation and superb views of the Brecon Beacons.   148

The Vulcan Arms, Llanwrthwl, Llandrindod Wells, Powys LD1 6NN

Tel: 01597 811180 Fax: 01597 811152
e-mail: Vulcan.arms@virgin.net

A delighful inn on the A470 Rhayader-Builth Wells road. Food is served all day, starting with an early morning breakfast.   153

The Wheatsheaf, Wheat Street, Brecon, Powys LD3 7DG

Tel: 01874 611109

A town-centre pub with a long, spacious bar. Pool table. Good bar food, good beer, young crowd.

The White Swan, Llanfrynach, Brecon, Powys LD3 7BZ

Tel: 01874 665276
website: www.the-white-swan.com

An excellent pub-restaurant in a row of smart black-and-white cottages. Sister establishment offering luxurious self-catering accommodation nearby.   150

Llandrindod Golf Club

Llandrindod Wells, Powys LD1 5NY

Tel: 01597 823873 Fax: 01597 823873

Harry Vardon could not have believed his luck when asked to create a golf course on mountain land above the splendid spa town of Llandrindod Wells to accommodate the many Victorians who flocked to the town to sample the health-giving waters and enjoy their leisure pursuits. No easier and more pleasant task had ever arisen for the English golfing maestro. God has done such such a perfect job in creating this part of the universe, that it appears that Vardon simply had to mark where he required the tee-markers to be placed

and the hole to be cut at each hole, then quietly left the rest to a man with a lawnmover. Never was their such a natural place just asking to become a golf course! In another four years the club celebrates its centenary, but amazingly the old course has seen little change except for the removal of the sheep and the introduction of a small reservoir to supply the greens during the summer months. Offering peace and solitude equal to that of the Rolls of Monmouth course, and with glorious vistas of the Radnor forests to the east, the Plynlimon Hills to the west, and southwards the Brecon Beacons and the Black Mountains beyond, it's like God's heaven on earth on a balmy summer's day, with the nesting skylarks, plovers and other birdlife singing their merry songs. Added to this, there are no dreaded sand bunkers to worry about! I have often described the 'Llandod' course as the nearest thing to a links course that can be found anwhere inland, what with its blind holes, severe rough, hidden grassy hollows, fast natural greens, rocky valley's to carry and occasional strong winds to contend with.

The Llandrindod course now boasts a superb brick and stone built bungalow-styled clubhouse with a golf shop attached, which has replaced the wooden Victorian cricket pavilion-like building. Wondering how best to get rid of the old clubhouse, which had outlived its usefullness, one bright committee member suggested setting it alight and celebrating an early bonfire night with a summer barbecue to follow. All went well until

a wind came up and threatened the stewards quarters and a liquid gas tank close by. It most certainly ended on a memorable note when the local fire brigade had to be called in!

Many memorable holes are to be found on this exhilarating course, but the most famous is the aptly name" Death or Glory" 18th hole. A short par four of 297 yards, there is practically no fairway between tee and green, which lie either side of a deep valley at the foot of which is a ravine crossed by a wooden bridge erected by the then club president (recently retired from the post) and long-standing member, "Bud" Bottomley, to replace the decaying Harry Vardon Bridge during the 1980's. There's a friendly bunch of characters to be found at Llandrindod, which could leave you wondering if the English translation of Llandrindod Wells may well mean friendship. Especially so if you happen to be there for the Annual Open Weekwhich takes place every summer and attracts male and female golfers of all handicap categories and from all parts of the UK.

Sec/Manager:	Graham Harris
Professional:	None
Directions:	1 mile SE of Llandrindod Wells. From centre take Temple St (A483 Builth Wells) after 300 yds turn left into Grosvenor Rd. Entrance after ¾ mile on left hand side.
Date Founded:	1905
Type of Course:	Moorland
No of Holes:	18
Length:	5759 yds (5316 mtrs)
Par:	69
SSS:	69
Green Fees:	Weekdays:£15.00 per round, £20 per day Weekends/Bank Holidays: £20 per round, £25.00 per day
Visitors:	Welcome: Contact Club by telephone in advance
Societies:	Welcome: Contact Club in advance
Facilities:	Putting Green, Chipping Green, Club Hire, Trolley Hire, Buggy Hire, Bar, Restaurant

Accommodation, Food and Drink

Reference numbers below refer to detailed information provided in section 2

Accommodation

The Bell Country Inn, Llanyre, Llandrindod Wells, Powys LD1 6DY
Tel: 01597 823959 Fax: 01597 825899
e-mail: dgj.jones@virgin.net
website: www.thebellcountryinn.com
Friendly, family run inn with lovely views. 9 en suite rooms and restaurant serving traditional and international dishes as well as a good wine list.   144

The Cedars, Builth Wells, Powys LD2 3PB
Tel: 01982 553356
website: www.cedars.ltd.co.uk
A comfortable family residence, circa 1880, with seven letting bedrooms, lounge and restaurant. Overlooks the River Wye.   149

Corven Hall,Howey, Llandrindod Wells, Powys LD1 5RE
Tel: 01597 823368
Six spacious bedrooms (most en suite) for Bed & Breakfast in a Victorian house with lovely gardens and fine views.   151

Gwystre Inn, Gwystre, Llandrindod Wells, Powys LD1 6RM
Tel: 01597 851650
A 300-year-old pub with three en suite twin rooms and good-value home-cooked food. Local ales. Darts and pool.

The Harp Inn, Old Radnor, Presteigne, Powys LD8 2RH
Tel/Fax: 01544 350655
A beautifully restored 15th century inn with exposed stone walls and beamed ceilings, set in a pretty village. Excellent home cooking and five guest bedrooms enjoying lovely views.   141

Kincoed Hotel, Temple Street, Llandrindod Wells, Powys LD1 5HF
Tel: 01597 822656
Arrive as a guest, leave as a friend. Ten rooms for B&B, with evening meals by arrangement. Breakfasts fit for a king.

The Llanerch Inn, Llandrindod Wells, Powys LD1 6BG
Tel: 01597 822086 Fax: 01597 824618
e-mail: llanerchinn@ic24.net
Family-owned 16th century inn of great character, with 12 en suite rooms. Snacks and meals. Residents' lounge, patio, garden, play area.   152

The Montpellier Hotel, Llandrindod Wells, Powys LD1 5HW
Tel: 01597 822388 Fax: 01597 825600
A handsome redbrick Victorian building in the town centre. Eleven well-furnished en suite bedrooms, 30-cover brasserie, lounge bar.   155

Red House Farm, Howey, Llandrindod Wells, Powys LD1 5PP
Tel: 01597 824973
website: http://www.lineone.net/~redhousefarm
A traditional stone farmhouse with exposed beams

and old-world character providing warm, comfortable Bed & Breakfast accommodation in three spacious bedrooms. 154

The Royal Oak, Gladestry, Powys HR5 3NR

Tel: 01544 370669

Sixteenth century village pub offering real ales, home-cooked food, a good selection of wine and four comfortable letting bedrooms. 142

The Talbot Hotel, Kington, Herefordshire HR5 3DJ

Tel: 01544 231744

A 16th century coaching inn on a corner site in the town centre. Cosy bars, home cooking, four refurbished bedrooms. 221

The Vulcan Arms, Llanwrthwl, Llandrindod Wells, Powys LD1 6NN

Tel: 01597 811180 Fax: 01597 811152
e-mail: Vulcan.arms@virgin.net

A delighful inn on the A470 Rhayader-Builth Wells road. Food is served all day, starting with an early morning breakfast. 153

Food and Drink

The Barley Mow, 1 West Street, Builth Wells, Powys LD2 3AH

Tel: 01982 553648

One of the oldest pubs in town, with a sporting owner and a sporting clientele. Excellent value meals. Book for Sunday lunch.

The Bell Country Inn, Llanyre, Llandrindod Wells, Powys LD1 6DY

Tel: 01597 823959 Fax: 01597 825899
e-mail: dgj.jones@virgin.net
website: www.thebellcountryinn.com

Friendly, family run inn with lovely views. 9 en suite rooms and restaurant serving traditional and international dishes as well as a good wine list. 144

The Cedars, Builth Wells, Powys LD2 3PB

Tel: 01982 553356

website: www.cedars.ltd.co.uk

A comfortable family residence, circa 1880, with seven letting bedrooms, lounge and restaurant. Overlooks the River Wye. 149

Gwystre Inn, Gwystre, Llandrindod Wells, Powys LD1 6RM

Tel: 01597 851650

A 300-year-old pub with three en suite twin rooms and good-value home-cooked food. Local ales. Darts and pool.

The Harp Inn, Old Radnor, Presteigne, Powys LD8 2RH

Tel/Fax: 01544 350655

A beautifully restored 15th century inn with exposed stone walls and beamed ceilings, set in a pretty village. Excellent home cooking and five guest bedrooms enjoying lovely views. 141

The Llanerch Inn, Llandrindod Wells, Powys LD1 6BG

Tel: 01597 822086 Fax: 01597 824618
e-mail: llanerchinn@ic24.net

Family-owned 16th century inn of great character, with 12 en suite rooms. Snacks and meals. Residents' lounge, patio, garden, play area. 152

The Montpellier Hotel, Llandrindod Wells, Powys LD1 5HW

Tel: 01597 822388 Fax: 01597 825600

A handsome redbrick Victorian building in the town centre. Eleven well-furnished en suite bedrooms, 30-cover brasserie, lounge bar. 155

The Royal Oak, Gladestry, Powys HR5 3NR

Tel: 01544 370669

Sixteenth century village pub offering real ales, home-cooked food, a good selection of wine and four comfortable letting bedrooms. 142

The Talbot Hotel, Kington, Herefordshire HR5 3DJ

Tel: 01544 231744

A 16th century coaching inn on a corner site in the town centre. Cosy bars, home cooking, four refurbished bedrooms. 221

The Vulcan Arms, Llanwrthwl, Llandrindod Wells, Powys LD1 6NN

Tel: 01597 811180 Fax: 01597 811152
e-mail: Vulcan.arms@virgin.net

A delighful inn on the A470 Rhayader-Builth Wells road. Food is served all day, starting with an early morning breakfast. 153

Welshpool Golf Club

Golfa Hill, Welshpool SY21 9AQ

Tel: 01938 850249

The records will tell you that Welshpool Golf Club became established in 1929. Never the less, the Royal and Ancient game was actually introduced to this delightfully quiet and peaceful corner of the Principality in 1894, the nine-hole course being laid out in the Deer Park. Some 14 years later the course was moved to the Red Bank, which was part of a windy common above the town of Welshpool that Owen de la Pola, Prince Of Powis, gifted to the town in 1290, and which still belongs to the local community.

Come the spring of 1927, the club's finances made miserable reading with the balance sheet showing a deficit of £34 11s 5p. Uneasy about the situation, several members began looking for more suitable land with the possibility of creating an 18-hole layout, and when the committee met during October of the following year it became known that another area of the huge common, aptly named The Golfa, was an ideal

crossroads, signed Golfa Hill. Entrance after ½ mile.

Date Founded: 1894

Type of Course: Mountainous

No of Holes: 18

Length: 5708 yds (5268 mtrs)

Par: 70

SSS: 68

Green Fees: Weekdays: £12.50 per day all year. Weekends/Bank Holidays: Winter £15.50 per day. Summer £20.50 per day

Visitors: Welcome: Contact Club in advance

Societies: Welcome: Contact Club in advance

Facilities: Putting Green, Club Hire, Trolley Hire, Bar, Restaurant

site, and the Town Surveyor had stated that an access road offered no problem. A Major Marriot, agent to Lord Powis, indicated that he saw no reason for planning permission being refused. In no time at all the enthusiastic committee went into action to terminate the lease of the Red Barn site, wrote to members for financial help, and at a special meeting in November, recommended the forming of a limited company with a working capital of £4,500. Leaving nothing to chance, the site was secured and James Braid was commissioned to create a full-sized golf course. The summer of 1929 then saw the affairs of the earlier club wound up, with the assets and the remaining balance transferred to the Welshpool Golf Club Limited. The first official meeting of the new club was held during that September, and play finally commenced on New Year's Day, 1930.

The present members of Welshpool Golf Club must be eternally grateful for the enthusiasm and foresight of that past committee and members, because they now have a golf course to be extremely proud of. Visitors will surely also be thankful after playing a round on this memorable course set on a mountain top-even more so when they discover the realistic prices for playing and for the fine food on offer in the cosy clubhouse afterwards!

Sec/Manager: Don Lewis

Professional: Bob Barlow

Directions: 3 miles W of Welshpool centre. From centre take the A458 (Heniarth, Dolgellau), after 4 miles turn right at staggered

Accommodation, Food and Drink

Reference numbers below refer to detailed information provided in section 2

Accommodation

The Church Inn, Ludlow, Shropshire SY8 1AW

Tel: 01584 872174 Fax: 01584 877146
e-mail: reception@thechurchinn.com
website: www.thechurchinnludlow.co.uk

A venerable hostelry with a history spanning seven centuries. Bar and restaurant menus, nine en suite bedooms including family rooms.   214

The Cock Hotel, Forden, Welshpool, Powys SY21 8LX

Tel: 01938 580226

Late-19th century village inn serving a good choice of freshly prepared food, from sandwiches to mighty mixed grills. Also two guest rooms for B&B.   143

Number Twenty Eight, Ludlow, Shropshire SY8 1PQ

Tel: 01584 876996 Fax: 01584 876860
Reservations: 0800 081 5000
e-mail: ross@no28.co.uk
website: www.no28.co.uk

Characterful accommodation in six period houses in Lower Broad Street: early Georgian, Tudor, late Victorian. Breakfast at Number 28.   212

Plas Penhelig Country House Hotel, Aberdovey, Gwynedd LL35 0NA

Tel: 01654 767676 Fax: 01654 767783

A distinguished country house hotel in a glorious setting with views over the Dovey estuary. 14 quiet, comfortable en suite rooms, superb food.   168

Food and Drink

The Black Horse Inn, Maesbrook, Oswestry, Shropshire SY10 8QG

Tel: 01691 682472 Fax: 01691 682872

A great pub for food, with a menu that offers an excellent choice for all tastes. Shropshire sirloin, with mushrooms and local blue cheese, is a favourite.

The Bradford Arms, Knockin, Nr. Oswestry, Shropshire SY10 8HJ

Tel: 01691 682358

A fine black-and-white roadside inn serving an excellent selection of home-cooked food for country appetites. Smart bar, non-smoking restaurant, beer garden. 210

The Church Inn, Ludlow, Shropshire SY8 1AW

Tel: 01584 872174 Fax: 01584 877146
e-mail: reception@thechurchinn.com
website: www.thechurchinnludlow.co.uk

A venerable hostelry with a history spanning seven centuries. Bar and restaurant menus, nine en suite bedooms including family rooms. 214

The Cock Hotel, Forden, Welshpool, Powys SY21 8LX

Tel: 01938 580226

Late-19th century village inn serving a good choice of freshly prepared food, from sandwiches to mighty mixed grills. Also two guest rooms for B&B. 143

The Henllan, Llangyniew, Welshpool, Powys SY21 9EJ

Tel: 01938 810343

Popular licensed premises serving bar and restaurant meals - roast beef dinners among the favourites - and Sunday lunches. Country & Western music most Saturday nights.

Plas Penhelig Country House Hotel, Aberdovey, Gwynedd LL35 0NA

Tel: 01654 767676 Fax: 01654 767783

A distinguished country house hotel in a glorious setting with views over the Dovey estuary. 14 quiet, comfortable en suite rooms, superb food. 168

Ye Olde Bull Ring Tavern, Ludlow, Shropshire SY8 1AB

Tel: 01584 872311

An amazing black and white timbered building dating from 1385. Two bars, stunning restaurant. 213

GWYNEDD

The historical county of Gwynedd is renowned for having some of the finest golf courses to be found in the North Wales region of the Principality. Stretching from Aberdovey in the southern end of this vast county to St. Deinol, near Bangor, in the north, this is the discerning golfer's dream of a place. But more about the golfing delights to be found in Gwynedd later.

If travelling to North Wales from the direction of Aberystwyth, the A487 coastal road turns inland from the Dyfi Estuary (Dovey Estuary in English) and turns left over a bridge at the northern end of Machynlleth before moving in a northerly direction to Caernarvon. However, for golfing visitors to this part of the Principality it is best to turn left after crossing the bridge and take the A493 to Aberdovey. The most southerly resort in Gwynedd is the charming and picturesque seaside town of Aberdovey, which lies at the northern end of the Dyfi Estuary. Once a prosperous fishing harbour and a shelter for ships from the south-westerly storms in Cardigan Bay, the town is now a popular stopping place for golfers, seascape artists and casual holidaymakers. A delightful mixture of small shops, cosy inns and restaurants, guesthouses and small hotels, all adds to the pleasant atmosphere of this small resort. The well known old Welsh song "The Bells of Aberdovey", tells of the legend of Cantre'r Gwaelod, which stood on the site where Aberdovey now stands until the sadly neglected dykes broke away to allow the sea from Cardigan bay to rush in and drown it. Over the centuries since this disaster the locals have often sworn they have heard the bells chiming from the city lost beneath the waves-hence the composing of this lovely sounding Welsh ballad. A short distance along the coastal road is Towyn, a quiet holiday town with a long main street and a number of interesting shops. Outside the town on the other side of the coastal road is a sandy beach, which stretches right back to Aberdovey Golf Club and on to Aberdovey itself. From Towyn the miniature Talyllyn Railway runs inland to the edge of the Dovey Forest and the foothills of Cader Idris, where beyond lies the beautiful Tal-y-llyn Lake. During the summer countless visitors travel on this line before alighting at Dolgoch Halt. From here a short walk takes you beneath a waterfall, which is one of three to be seen as you continue your walk through beautiful countryside before

Aberdovey

returning to the train. This is a memorable experience and one which I cannot resist repeating whenever I visit this area close to the Cambrian coastline.

From Towyn the coastal road will take you to the interesting seaside town of Barmouth, but the scenic route to this resort is much more enjoyable. This route is along the B4405, which runs alongside the Talyllyn Railway before connecting to the A487 trunk road at Tal-y-llyn Lake that will take you through to the town of Dolgellau-a magnificent tourist centre. On the way to Dolgellau the scenery is quite outstanding. After passing the lake the trunk road continues alongside the foothills of Cader Idris and rises in a long ascent of Bwlchllyn Bach and high above the lake, from where you find yourself in one of the most beautiful spots in Wales and in an area which matches anywhere in Europe, which is hardly surprising when I tell you that you are now journeying through a section of the Snowdonia National Park-one of the world's great natural and unspoilt areas. At the T-junction where the road takes you left to Dolgellau or right to Welshpool along the A470, you will find the famous Cross Foxes Hotel. Take a stop here and follow the signs to the "Torrent Walk" and you will be rewarded with breathtaking views in every direction. Dolgellau lies in the Wnion Valley and was once the county town of Merionethshire, before this county was swallowed up in the reconstruction of the sadly missed smaller counties. What is considered the most attractive walk in this area is along the "Precipice Walk", which is exactly what it says. Rising to the north of Dolgellau, it skirts the steep Moel Cynwch mountain in a winding stony pathway giving fantastic views of Cader Idris and the town of Barmouth beyond. There are many other fine walks from the excellent tourist centre of Dolgellau.

Barmouth is a pretty and popular seaside resort situated at the mouth of the Mawddach Estuary, and travelling through the beautiful Mawddach Valley on your way to Barmouth is a joy to behold and a journey one never forgets in a hurry. In the mountains north of the estuary are the famous Welsh goldmines. It is known that the Romans mined for gold here first and used the local population to do the hard labour. The interpretation of the name Dolgellau perfectly sums up the extent of the slavery used here.

It interprets as "Meadow of the Slaves", which leaves nothing much for the imagination. The Clogau gold mine at the village of Bont-Ddu is open to visitors and well worth a visit. In the area of the old county of Merionthshire there are also lead, manganese and copper mines to be found.

At Barmouth the coastal road northwards passes straight through the centre of the town and onwards to the small village of Talybont. In the hills close to Talybont are the remains of the hill fort of Craig y Dinas and nearby the remains of a mysterious stone circle. Further along is a Neolithic burial chamber, giving proof of prehistoric settlements in this area.

Harlech Castle

The next village northwards along the A496 is Llanbedr, which is close to a strip of land known locally as Mochras, but to others as Shell Island, where can be found over a couple of hundred different seashells. Further northwards is Harlech, the small town with a huge historical background. This quaint old town is dominated by Harlech Castle. This mighty fortress was built by Edward I after he had finally conquered the powerful and troublesome Llewellyn, last of the ancient Welsh princes. The most formidable fortress in Wales, it was built on a towering rock with the sea to the front and a huge rock ditch with a width of almost 50ft guarding the otherwise vulnerable point at the side. The castle has never been breached, despite being pounded relentlessly over the centuries of ancient conflict. Queen Margaret of Anjou once took refuge there, and Daffyd ap Einon, her Welsh general managed to keep the fortress intact for eight years against the army of the Earl of Pembroke. Owain Glendwr failed to gain an entry by force in 1404, and it was only after a long seige and starvation that the handful of men in the garrison surrendered. Charles I's general did likewise when Oliver Cromwell's brother adopted the same tactics during the Civil War.

The famous Welsh song "Men of Harlech", tells the story of how Daffyd ap Einon held out for eight years during the War of the Roses and only agreed to surrender if he and his seventeen remaining men were promised they would not be killed. The song tells how the English, honouring his bravery, gave their promise and allowed him to proudly march out of the castle, followed by his brave men. Today the castle stands proudly intact and overlooks flat lands, which once formed part of the seabed of the mighty Cardigan Bay.

Continuing to motor along the coast road to Porthmadog, one reaches the fascinating village of Portmeirion, built by the famous Welsh architect, Glough Williams-Ellis, who having fallen in love with the Italian Riviera-based village of Portofino, set out to find a site in his native land suitable to build a similar Italian-styled village. Now some eighty years old, Portmeirion is a magical place to visit with its beautiful coastal setting overlooking the waters of Traeth Bach and a secluded sandy beach. One has to pay a fee to enter this gorgeous village, but every penny paid is amply paid back in bucketfuls of breathtaking beauty from the handsome buildings and the

Portmeirion

atmosphere of the place. Noel Coward was attracted to the place by its peaceful solitude, and was so inspired he wrote his famous play "Blithe Spirit" there during his brief stay of one week. The famous television cult series "The Prisoner" was also filmed here. Keen followers of this strange series now treat Portmeirion as a pilgrimage. The famous and much collected Portmeirion pottery is also produced here and provides a showroom to purchase the many designs. A short distance away is the attractive holiday town of Porthmadog, which is entered by paying a small toll to cross a narrow causeway over the mouth of the Afon Glaslyn. Portmadog has a small harbour once used to export the famous Welsh slate to the rest of the world, but is now used mainly by the holidaymakers. The same can be said of the old narrow-gauge railway that brought the slates from the Ffestiniog mines to the harbour. Now it transports thousands of visitors annually through the scenic Moelwyn hills. Portmadog is said to be named after Madwg ap Owain Gwynedd, a Welsh prince, who sailed from Wales to discover America some three hundred years before Christopher Columbus.

South of Porthmadog is the quiet and pretty village of Borth-y-Gwest lying in a secluded cove overlooking Tremadog Bay. Close to this village are the sands at Black Rock, where one can travel on by car. Here also are a number of caves to be explored by those with a sense of adventure in their veins. The next village is Tremadog, named after William Alexander Madocks who was responsible for bridging the Glaswyn Estuary with a causeway at Porthmadog. What is not generally known is that Tremadog is the birthplace of T. E. Lawrence (Lawrence of Arabia), who was born here in 1888 at a house called "The Woodlands". Shelley, the poet, also lived at Tremadog for a number of years after discovering it as a place perfectly suited to his writing skills. Shelley supported Madocks when the Welshman set out plans, which reclaimed the marshland above the causeway, such was his love of the area. Just a few miles west of Tremadog is the popular holiday resort of Criccieth. Sheltered by the Snowdonia mountain range, the climate here is as mild as you can get in Britain. Arguably Wales's finest politician, David Lloyd George, spent his boyhood at Criccieth and was brought up by his uncle, Richard Lloyd, the local shoemaker. The former British Prime Minister is buried close to Criccieth in the village of Llanystumdwy. At this village can be seen the small cottage of Richard Lloyd, where David Lloyd George lived during his youth. Close by is a museum dedicated to the great man by the local people. Long before the Normans arrived at Criccieth the Welsh built a fine castle. Edward I once had control of the castle, and Glyndwr failed to conquer it when deciding an assault whilst on the way to his main objective Caernarfon Castle. For the holidaymaker, Criccieth

Porthmadog Harbour

has a fine sandy beach and is crowned by a dramatic headland.

Further westwards is the large holiday resort of Pwllheli, known to thousands of people in Britain because it was probably where they spent their first ever holiday as youngsters after Sir Billy Butlin built one of his highly popular holiday camps close by. This coastal market town was granted a charter by the Black Prince in 1355. Today it boasts a much-used yachting marina, and this, along with the fine sandy beach, still attracts many visitors to the town. Of a more quiet nature

Criccieth Castle

is the resort of Llanbredrog. Less crowded, but with good beaches and hidden coves, it is ideal for a more relaxing break. As you travel further along this wonderful Lleyn Peninsular, which is renowned for its fine beaches and excellent golf courses, you reach the equally delightful resort of Abersoch. An attractive place to stay (yes, it has a golf course), Abersoch is a real bustling sort of seaside village, with an extensive and beautifully sheltered stretch of sands. It also boasts an excellent water sports centre. Some three miles offshore are the St Tudwal's Islands, both of which have a mediaeval background. The westerly island has a lighthouse built on it, while on the other island is a chapel built by St Tudfal, which has a number of artefacts on show from the long gone abbey which once stood on Bardsey Island.

Moving south you find a remote area with a number of good camping sites, but the westerly section of the headland is prone to the savagery of the south-westerly winds. A good stretch of beach is to be found here, but the bay was not called Hell's Mouth for nothing! Heading towards the extreme end of the mighty peninsular, the main village here is Aberdaron, the old "Pilgrim Way" to the remote and sacred island of Bardsey. The "Holy Island" of Wales lies a few miles off the "Land's End" of Wales and the village of Aberdaron once saw a thick continuous queue of pilgrims patiently waiting their turn to board the vessels, which conveyed them through treacherous seas to visit the famous Abbey of St Mary on Bardsey. The abbey was founded by St Cadfan in the 6th century. A number of monasteries during this time were being sacked by the Saxons and the only safe haven for these unfortunate Christians was at Bardsey Island, which led to the island becoming known as "The Isle of Saints", where it is claimed that as many as 20, 000 holy men came to be buried there. Little remains of the abbey now, but the outline of St Mary's church where the pilgrims made their final prayers before visiting the abbey can still be seen. Legend has it that Bardsey is also Avalon, the island where King Arthur was taken after his last battle and where the great Welsh wizard, Merlin, is also buried. Another interesting story of Aberdaron is that of "Jack of Aberdaron" who, in the early part of the 19th century, put Aberdaron on the map with his amazing linguistic capabilities. It is said he was able to absorb foreign languages and immediately speak them without any learning difficulties. Apparently, he lived and died in poverty, which most certainly would not have happened these days.

From Aberdaron the road takes you back north along the north-western coast of the peninsular. Here you are offered fine sea views of Caernarfon Bay and the Irish Sea. A good stopping point here is at Morfa Nefyn, a good centre for walkers and anyone interested in a spot of climbing. A few miles away, at Llithfaen, is the first of the three peaks known as the "the Rivals" an Anglo-Saxon corruption of "Yr Eifl. Two miles away, at Llanaelhaearn, are the two other peaks. At the summit of one of these peaks is Tre'r Ceiri (The Giants Town), once the most important prehistoric settlement in North Wales. Enclosed by giant stone walls-some rising to 15ft-it is claimed that more than a hundred hut circles lay protected by these walls. Fragments of these walls are still to be seen. When the Romans discovered this town they added to its fortifications and used it as a safe haven against the fierce local tribes. Going back to Morfa Nefyn, the nearby fields are said to have been used in 1284 by Edward I to hold a jousting tournament to prematurely celebrate his conquest of Wales after his victory over Llewelyn. In this area, close to the B4417 road, is the outstanding Nefyn Golf Club, one of the most fantastic sites in the world to lay-out a golf course. The small resort of

Porth Dinllaen, Nefyn

Nefyn is one of the most popular spots on this coastline for the holiday visitor in search of a small and quaint village to stay at.

Further up the coast can be found the also attractive village of Clynnog-fawr, with its church of St Beuno being of interest to anyone interested in fine architectural work. The Perpendicular work here is a fine example of the great skills of bygone craftsmen. There is much of interest for the visitor to see in this wonderful place of worship. Adjoining the church is the much more ancient church of Eglwys Beuno, where, it is reputed, that St Beuno lies buried. St Beuno is said to have a left a well by the roadside for parishioners to cleanse themselves before kneeling in prayer on the saint's altar tomb, afterwards any affliction they suffered from was cured. As this tale of miraculous healing spread, it thus became another place of pilgrimage on the peninsular and also where the two pilgrimage routes met.

As you continue towards the end of the peninsular, there are many fine stretches of sand to be found and a number of camp and caravan sites. As for the inland section of the Lleyn Peninsular, except for the "The Rivals", the place is mainly flat and uninteresting, but there are a number of small villages where accommodation may be found, and also a few caravan sites. Leaving the peninsular region, the next major place is that of Caernarfon, the ancient fortress town with an equally ancient castle, which is lapped by the waters of the Menai Strait and whose walls are amazingly well preserved. Built by Edward I in 1285, outwardly Caernarfon Castle remains practically intact, mainly because it has been considerably restored throughout the years. Inside, however, much has been demolished but the outline of the original ground floor plan is clearly visible. The most imposing of the Welsh castles built by Edward I, it is also the birthplace of Edward II, born in 1284, who was responsible for its completion in 1322. In modern times, of course, it set the scene for the investiture of Prince Charles as Prince of Wales in 1969, and before that, in 1911, Edward, Duke of Windsor, was also invested there as Prince of Wales. The most imposing feature of this ancient castle is its seven towers, which adds to the majesty of the immense fortress-a fortress so impregnable it defied the many onslaughts from Owain Glendower in the 15th century and although changing hands a number of times during the Civil War, it survived any serious damage. Now a busy tourist centre and a bustling town, there is much to be seen regarding its long history, which dates back to the time when the Romans built an important stronghold called Segontium on the edge of the town. The old town also has a fine full-sized parkland golf course on its outskirts to tempt you to prolong your stay.

The A487 road north-eastwards straddles the mighty Menai Strait until it turns slightly inland a mile or two past Port Dinorwic. Once an important port for shipping away the quality slate brought in from the huge quarries in the Llanberis Valley, the port found fame when one of its ships, The Mary Mitchell, was used during the First World War to attract over-confident German submarines to surface thinking the British ship was unarmed. Proving the perfect decoy, the Mary Mitchell's concealed guns opened fire and often sank the unsuspecting enemy vessels from close range.

From Port Dinorwic you journey on to Bangor, which lies at the extreme north of the large county of Gwynedd. Situated on the eastern entrance of the Menai Strait, Bangor faces the Isle Of Anglesey, which is joined to the mainland by Telford's well-constructed Menai suspension bridge. Bangor is the seat of the University of North Wales and is Britain's oldest Cathedral City, albeit a rather small city but a city of character and a pleasant shopping centre. Bangor's cathedral was founded before that of Canterbury, because a church existed there as long ago as the 6th century. Leaving this ancient seat of learning and heading back southwards to explore the remainder of Gwynedd, the first town along the A5 road is Bethesda. Here can be seen the terraced slate quarries of Penrhyn. Slate has been quarried here for centuries and many of Britain's historic houses as far back as Elizabeth I have Welsh slate from these quarries still defying the elements on their rooftops. Penrhyn Castle, which is close to Bangor and overlooking Conwy Bay, is a magnificent building to visit and includes an impressive four-poster bed made of slate from the quarries at Penrhyn amongst its many original furnishings. A collection of dolls from many countries and a fine collection of old locomotive engines are also on show at this fine castle.

Continuing to travel south from Bethesda, one picks up the A4086 at Capel Curig and heads west in the direction of Llanberis via the dramatic Pass of Llanberis. One is now in the centre of the wild and craggy countryside of the breathtaking Snowdonia National Park. Along the Pass of Llanberis you are never without a sight of Mount Snowdon, the highest mountain with its summit of 3,560ft above sea level, in Wales and England. No matter which direction you travel in this outstanding area of Wales, you will not be disappointed. Travel in any direction and you will be rewarded with some of the finest mountain scenery and vistas of great lakes to be found in Britain. At the village of Llanberis one is able to get to Snowdon's summit by taking the famous Snowdon Mountain Railway. No visit to North Wales is complete without a visit to the summit of this majestic mountain. The all round view from the summit is truly remarkable and more descriptive passages than I can write in this guide would still fail to do justice to the magnificent views. There are many, many more places to visit in this great park, such as beautiful Btews-y-Coed with its amazing Swallow Falls, the vast Bala Lake at Bala and the slate mines of Blaenau Ffestiniog. The other Ffestiniog just a few miles south is where the Ffestiniog Narrow Gauge Railway stops for tourists from Porthmadog to alight to admire the scenery. That then is the county of Gwynedd, arguably the most dramatic county in the whole of the proud Principality.

Sunrise from Snowdon

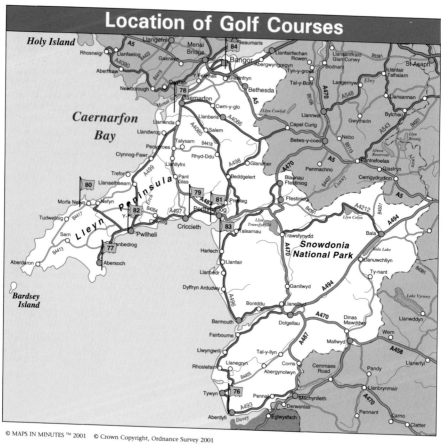

© MAPS IN MINUTES ™ 2001   © Crown Copyright, Ordnance Survey 2001

Aberdovey Golf Club

Aberdovey, Gwynedd LL35 0RT
Tel: 01654 767210 Fax: 01654 767027

This fabulous links course on the edge of the Dyfi (Dovey) Estuary began it's existence in rather a simple fashion when a group of enthusiasts eager to take up the game, cut some holes on land that was known as the Marsh and planted flowerpots in them. This happened towards the end of the 1880's and one of the group, Colonel Arthur Ruck, was the uncle of Bernard Darwin, the doyen of golf writers. Darwin spent much of his boyhood at Aberdovey during this time and often played golf there with his uncle, years before the club was officially formed in 1892. The first tournament took place in April of that year and involved a dozen or so competitors, which was won by the precocious young Darwin with a gross score of exactly 100. In his wonderful writings about the great game, Darwin described Aberdovey as, "*The course that my soul loves best of all the courses in the world*". Many generations later another golfing great in the shape of Ian Woosnam, arguably the greatest ever golfer to come out of Wales, had a caravan parked close to Aberdovey's original clubhouse and spent as much time as he could visiting and playing the course with his close friends, and still goes there to keep

his game in trim whenever his busy tournament schedule allows it. Both of these great golfing characters fell head-over-heels in love with Aberdovey after just one visit, and countless other golfers have also done likewise. Three famous architects, Braid, Colt and Fowler, each did their bit to fashion the course into what can be seen today. In typical links fashion the course follows a narrow route out and back, with giant sand dunes guarding the course from the sea and a railway and small hills on the opposite side, thus creating a small valley which acts as a highly troublesome wind tunnel when the wind blows in from the north and makes the outward section extremely tough. The third hole, once completely blind but now only partially so, is as tough a par-3 as can be found anywhere. Named "The Cader" it is a wicked challenge over a huge sandhill to a switchback green guarded by vicious bunkers. Just the type of hole you don't need at the start of a round. Believe me, there is not an easy hole on this course. Hit any hole in regulation and you still have difficulty getting the ball into the hole on the fast and tricky greens. Many major amateur tournaments have been played over this great links and it is now the home of the Welsh Seniors' Amateur Championship, which has been won by many of Wales's former great amateur golfers, including Iestyn Tucker from the Monmouthshire Golf Club, who represented Wales in international matches from 1949 to 1975, a record of which he is justly proud.

The cosy old clubhouse has recently been replaced by a new building, but still offers a warm welcome to visitors and gives one a chance to take a look at the clubs Bernard Darwin used so expertly when playing his beloved course about which he also wrote, "*About this one course in the world I am a hopeless and shameful sentimentalist and I glory in my shame.* "

One amusing memory I have of Darwin's beloved Aberdovey is of the time when I was reporting on the Welsh Seniors event and alighting from my car in the car park I met a good friend from the Pontypool club in Monmouthshire-the late lamented Bill Howells. When I enquired

about what score he had returned, he replied, " *I shot an 84 and it reminds me of my war service-out in 39 and back in 45.*" A great character and a good golfer was Bill, like many others in golf I have been privileged to know.

Aberdovey and Royal St David's have two things in common. One that they are each amongst the finest links courses in the world and, secondly, they are both blessed by having a railway station next to their car parks, with the added bonus that they are linked by this railway line. What more can a golfing enthusiast ask for?

Sec/Manager:	John Griffiths
Professional:	John Davis
Directions:	½ mile W of Aberdovey. Take A493 (West) and turn left 900 yds after Bodfer Hotel. Entrance is at the end.
Date Founded:	1892
Type of Course:	Links
No of Holes:	18
Length:	6445 yds (5949 mtrs)
Par:	71
SSS:	71
Green Fees:	Weekdays: Summer £30 per day, Winter £24 per day; Weekends/Bank Holidays: Summer £35 per day, Winter £26 per day
Visitors:	Welcome: Some restrictions apply. Contact Club in advance.
Societies:	Welcome: By arrangement. Contact Club in advance
Facilities:	Putting Green, Chipping Green, Club Hire, Trolley Hire, Buggy Hire, Bar, Restaurant

Accommodation, Food and Drink

Reference numbers below refer to detailed information provided in section 2

Accommodation

Awel Y Môr, 4 Bodfor Terrace, Aberdovey, Gwynedd LL35 0EA
Tel/Fax: 01654 767058
e-mail: awlymor@lineone.net
website: http://website.lineone.net/~awelymor
Victorian seaside guest house with seven comfortable bedrooms, most with double and single beds. Good Welsh breakfast.

Caethle Chalet & Caravan Park, Tywyn, Gwynedd LL36 9HS

Tel/Fax: 01654 710587
Extensive, unspoilt country setting with pitches for touring caravans, and three chalets for self-catering accommodation.

Cranbourne Hotel, Barmouth, Gwynedd LL42 1NA
Tel/Fax: 01341 280202
Recently refurbished seaside hotel in a Victorian terrace. Two single bedrooms, eight doubles and six twins including family rooms. Bar snacks.   182

The Dovey Inn, Aberdovey, Gwynedd LL35 0EF
Tel: 01654 767332 Fax: 01654 767996
e-mail: rk@doveyinn.com
website: www.doveyinn.com
Handsome 18th century seafront inn with eight letting bedrooms, three bars and a 30-seat dining room with a long menu.   170

Morlyn Restaurant & Guest House, Llandanwg, Harlech, Gwynedd LL46 2SB
Tel: 01341 241298
e-mail: info@northwales-holidays.com
website: www.northwales-holidays.com
Choice of Bed & Breakfast and self-catering accommodation with superb mountain and sea views. Bistro-style restaurant.

Pant-y-Neuadd, Aberdyfi Road, Tywyn, Gwynedd LL36 9HW
Tel/Fax: 01654 711393
website: www.pant-y-neuadd@lineone.net
A park that offers pitches for touring caravans, static caravans for rent and two stone cottages for self-catering holidays. Close to a safe, sandy beach.

Plas Penhelig Country House Hotel, Aberdovey, Gwynedd LL35 0NA
Tel: 01654 767676 Fax: 01654 767783
A distinguished country house hotel in a glorious setting with views over the Dovey estuary. 14 quiet, comfortable en suite rooms, superb food.   168

Rhinog Park, Dyffryn Ardudwy, Gwynedd LL44 2HA
Tel: 01341 247652 Fax: 01531 640280
e-mail: rhinogpark@countryparks.com
website: www.countryparks.com
Self-catering lodges in a lovely scenic setting within Snowdonia National Park. Short walk to beach.   169

Trefeddian Hotel, Aberdovey, Gwynedd LL35 0SB
Tel: 01654 767213 Fax: 01654 767777
A distinguished hotel in a lovely secluded setting with fine views across Cardigan Bay. Attractive bedrooms, spacious lounges.   160

Wavecrest Hotel, 8 Marine Parade, Barmouth, Gwynedd LL42 1NA
Tel: 01341 280330
Nine comfortable en suite bedrooms with tv in a family-run Victorian terrace hotel on the seafront.

Good home-cooked food, cheerful bar with 64 malt whiskies.

Food and Drink

The Dovey Inn, Aberdovey, Gwynedd LL35 0EF
Tel: 01654 767332 Fax: 01654 767996
e-mail: rk@doveyinn.com
website: www.doveyinn.com
Handsome 18th century seafront inn with eight letting bedrooms, three bars and a 30-seat dining room with a long menu.   170

Morlyn Restaurant & Guest House, Llandanwg, Harlech, Gwynedd LL46 2SB
Tel: 01341 241298
e-mail: info@northwales-holidays.com
website: www.northwales-holidays.com
Choice of Bed & Breakfast and self-catering accommodation with superb mountain and sea views. Bistro-style restaurant.

Pen-y-Bont Hotel, Tal-y-Llyn, Tywyn, Gwynedd LL36 9AJ
Tel: 01654 782285
e-mail: penybonthotel@btinternet.com
website: www.smoothhound.co.uk/hotels/
penybont.html
Former 16th century coaching inn situated on the edge of the beautiful Tal-y-Llyn Lake. Five en suite bedrooms, two bars, old-world restaurant (non-smoking) with extensive menus.

Plas Penhelig Country House Hotel, Aberdovey, Gwynedd LL35 0NA
Tel: 01654 767676 Fax: 01654 767783
A distinguished country house hotel in a glorious setting with views over the Dovey estuary. 14 quiet, comfortable en suite rooms, superb food.   168

Trefeddian Hotel, Aberdovey, Gwynedd LL35 0SB
Tel: 01654 767213 Fax: 01654 767777
A distinguished hotel in a lovely secluded setting with fine views across Cardigan Bay. Attractive bedrooms, spacious lounges.   160

The Whitehall Hotel, Corbett Square, Tywyn, Gwynedd LL36 9DF
Tel/Fax: 01654 710212
A friendly pub with a good bar menu. Hot baguettes, jacket potatoes, toasted sandwiches, steaks, pies, curries - and lots more. Children welcome.

Abersoch Golf Club

Golf Road, Abersoch, Gwynedd LL53 7EY
Tel: **01758 712622** Fax: **01758 712777**

Sec/Manager:	Alan Jones
Professional:	Alan Jones
Directions:	½ mile S Abersoch. From

centre take Stryd Fawr, leading into Lon Sam Bach. Turn left into Golf Road. Entrance after ¼ mile on right hand side

Date Founded:	1907
Type of Course:	Links/Parkland
No of Holes:	18
Length:	5008 yds (4622 mtrs)
Par:	69
SSS:	68
Green Fees:	Weekdays: £20 per day; Weekends/Bank Holidays: £24 per day
Visitors:	Welcome: Contact Club in advance
Societies:	Welcome: Contact Club in advance
Facilities:	Putting Green, Chipping Green, Club Hire, Trolley Hire, Buggy Hire, Bar, Restaurant

Accommodation, Food and Drink

Reference numbers below refer to detailed information provided in section 2

Accommodation

The Carisbrooke Hotel, Abersoch, Gwynedd LL53 7DY
Tel: 01758 712526 Fax: 01758 713666
e-mail: davies@abersoch-carisbrookehotel.co.uk
A small, neat, family-run hotel with seven bedrooms and a family suite. Lounge, bar.   175

The Cliffs Inn, Morfa Nefyn, Nr. Pwllheli, Gwynedd LL53 6BY
Tel: 01758 720356 Fax: 01758 720544
e-mail: enquiries@cliffs-inn.co.uk
White-painted hotel offering self-catering accommodation, excellent food and magnificent views across to Anglesey. Fifty yards from the beach.   180

The Crown Hotel, High Street, Pwllheli, Gwynedd LL53 5RT
Tel/Fax: 01758 612664
Family-run town centre hotel with 12 en suite rooms (tv, tea-makers), a lively bar (pool, darts, bar football) and good food.

Harbour Hotel, Abersoch, Gwynedd LL53 7HR
Tel: 01758 712406 Fax: 01758 713826 e-mail: mail@harbour-hotel.com
website: www.harbour-hotel.com
Fourteen en suite bedrooms in a seaside Bed & Breakfast hotel, café-bar, wine bar and disco.   172

Plas Bodegroes, Pwllheli, Gwynedd LL53 5TH
Tel: 01758 612363 Fax: 01758 701247
e-mail: gunna@bodegroes.co.uk

website: www.bodegroes.co.uk
A Georgian manor house in a superb secluded setting is the finest restaurant with rooms in Wales. Eight lovely bedrooms, wonderful food. 173

St Tudwals Inn, Abersoch, Gwynedd LL53 7DS

Tel: 01758 712539

Five en suite bedrooms, all-day bar snacks and an à la carte restaurant in one of Abersoch's most popular meeting places. 161

The White House Hotel & Restaurant, Abersoch, Gwynedd LL53 7AG

Tel: 01758 713427 Fax: 01758 713512
e-mail: whitehousehotel@btinternet.com
A fine hotel in a magnificent setting looking out over Cardigan Bay. Thirteen well-equipped en suite bedrooms, lounge, bar, top-class restaurant. 162

Food and Drink

The Cliffs Inn, Morfa Nefyn, Nr. Pwllheli, Gwynedd LL53 6BY

Tel: 01758 720356 Fax: 01758 720544
e-mail: enquiries@cliffs-inn.co.uk
White-painted hotel offering self-catering accommodation, excellent food and magnificent views across to Anglesey. Fifty yards from the beach. 180

The Crown Hotel, High Street, Pwllheli, Gwynedd LL53 5RT

Tel/Fax: 01758 612664

Family-run town centre hotel with 12 en suite rooms (tv, tea-makers), a lively bar (pool, darts, bar football) and good food.

The Galley Restaurant, Lon Nant-Iago, Llanbedrog, Pwllheli, Gwynedd LL53 7TR

Tel: 01758 740730

Popular licenced restaurant with sheltered terraces overlooking the National Trust beach. Snack menu 11-6.30: full menu 6.30 till late. Booking advisable.

Harbour Hotel, Abersoch, Gwynedd LL53 7HR

Tel: 01758 712406 Fax: 01758 713826
e-mail: mail@harbour-hotel.com
website: www.harbour-hotel.com
Fourteen en suite bedrooms in a seaside Bed & Breakfast hotel, café-bar, wine bar and disco. 172

Plas Bodegroes, Pwllheli, Gwynedd LL53 5TH

Tel: 01758 612363 Fax: 01758 701247
e-mail: gunna@bodegroes.co.uk
website: www.bodegroes.co.uk
A Georgian manor house in a superb secluded setting is the finest restaurant with rooms in Wales. Eight lovely bedrooms, wonderful food. 173

St Tudwals Inn, Abersoch, Gwynedd LL53 7DS

Tel: 01758 712539

Five en suite bedrooms, all-day bar snacks and an à la carte restaurant in one of Abersoch's most popular meeting places. 161

The White House Hotel & Restaurant, Abersoch, Gwynedd LL53 7AG

Tel: 01758 713427 Fax: 01758 713512
e-mail: whitehousehotel@btinternet.com
A fine hotel in a magnificent setting looking out over Cardigan Bay. Thirteen well-equipped en suite bedrooms, lounge, bar, top-class restaurant. 162

Royal Town of Caernarfon Golf Club

Aberforeshore, Llanfaglan,
Caernarfon LL54 5RP

Tel: 01286 673783 Fax: 01286 672535

Sec/Manager:	Gren Jones
Professional:	Aled Owen
Directions:	1¼ miles SW of Caernafon. From the center take the A487(Bontnewydd). At southern outskirts turn right just after crossing the river into Aber Foreshore Rd. Entrance on the right hand side after 1¾ miles.
Date Founded:	1909
Type of Course:	Parkland
No of Holes:	18
Length:	5891 yds (5437 mtrs)
Par:	69
SSS:	68
Green Fees:	Weekdays: Summer £15 per day, Winter £10 per day; Weekends/Bank Holidays: Summer £20 per day, Winter £10 per day
Visitors:	Welcome: Excluding Tuesdays. Contact Club in advance
Societies:	Welcome: Contact Club by phone or in writing

Facilities: Putting Green, Practice
                  Ground, Trolley Hire, Buggy
                  Hire, Bar, Restaurant

Accommodation, Food and Drink

Reference numbers below refer to detailed
information provided in section 2

Accommodation

**Celtic Royal Hotel, Caernarfon,
Gwynedd LL55 1AY**

Tel: 01286 674477 Fax: 01286 674139
e-mail: enquiries@celtic-royal.co.uk
website: www.celtic-royal.co.uk
110 fully equipped en suite bedrooms in a newly
refurbished town centre hotel near the Castle.
Restaurant, bar, gym, swimming pool.   166

**Menai Bank Hotel, Caernarfon,
Gwynedd LL55 1BD**

Tel/Fax: 01286 673297
e-mail: menaibankhotel@tesconet.co.uk
website: www.menaibankhotel.co.uk
Excellent food and comfortable accommodation in a
turn-of-the-century hotel with many original
features. Sixteen en suite bedrooms.   163

The Menai Hotel, Bangor, Gwynedd LL57 2BG

Tel: 01248 354200 Fax: 01248 354512
e-mail: info@themenai33.freeserve.co.uk
Nine en suite rooms, lively modern bar, snack and bar
meals, evening à la carte. Good views over the Menai
Straits.   165

**The Royal Oak, Malltraeth, Bodorgan,
Anglesey LL62 5AS**

Tel: 01407 840015
Former cottages make a delightful village pub with
coal fires warming a cosy bar and lounge. Excellent
food includes local seafood and game. Four letting
bedrooms.   191

St Tudwals Inn, Abersoch, Gwynedd LL53 7DS

Tel: 01758 712539
Five en suite bedrooms, all-day bar snacks and an à la
carte restaurant in one of Abersoch's most popular
meeting places.   161

**Tegfan Guest House, 4 Church Street,
Caernarfon, Gwynedd LL55 1SW**

Tel: 01286 673703
Very friendly family-run B&B two minutes from the
harbour and castle, with five comfortable bedrooms,
some en suite. Excellent breakfast.

**The Three Crowns Inn, Bangor,
Gwynedd LL57 1HB**

Tel: 01248 351138
A quiet location in the town centre for an inn with
three well-furnished B&B guest rooms and a menu of
home-cooked dishes. Beer garden.   164

**The White House Hotel & Restaurant, Abersoch,
Gwynedd LL53 7AG**

Tel: 01758 713427 Fax: 01758 713512
e-mail: whitehousehotel@btinternet.com
A fine hotel in a magnificent setting looking out over
Cardigan Bay. Thirteen well-equipped en suite
bedrooms, lounge, bar, top-class restaurant.   162

Food and Drink

**Celtic Royal Hotel, Caernarfon,
Gwynedd LL55 1AY**

Tel: 01286 674477 Fax: 01286 674139
e-mail: enquiries@celtic-royal.co.uk
website: www.celtic-royal.co.uk
110 fully equipped en suite bedrooms in a newly
refurbished town centre hotel near the Castle.
Restaurant, bar, gym, swimming pool.   166

**Menai Bank Hotel, Caernarfon,
Gwynedd LL55 1BD**

Tel/Fax: 01286 673297
e-mail: menaibankhotel@tesconet.co.uk
website: www.menaibankhotel.co.uk
Excellent food and comfortable accommodation in a
turn-of-the-century hotel with many original
features. Sixteen en suite bedrooms.   163

The Menai Hotel, Bangor, Gwynedd LL57 2BG

Tel: 01248 354200 Fax: 01248 354512
e-mail: info@themenai33.freeserve.co.uk
Nine en suite rooms, lively modern bar, snack and bar
meals, evening à la carte. Good views over the Menai
Straits.   165

**The Royal Oak, Malltraeth, Bodorgan,
Anglesey LL62 5AS**

Tel: 01407 840015
Former cottages make a delightful village pub with
coal fires warming a cosy bar and lounge. Excellent
food includes local seafood and game. Four letting
bedrooms.   191

St Tudwals Inn, Abersoch, Gwynedd LL53 7DS

Tel: 01758 712539
Five en suite bedrooms, all-day bar snacks and an à la
carte restaurant in one of Abersoch's most popular
meeting places.   161

**The Three Crowns Inn, Bangor,
Gwynedd LL57 1HB**

Tel: 01248 351138
A quiet location in the town centre for an inn with
three well-furnished B&B guest rooms and a menu of
home-cooked dishes. Beer garden.   164

**The White House Hotel & Restaurant, Abersoch,
Gwynedd LL53 7AG**

Tel: 01758 713427 Fax: 01758 713512
e-mail: whitehousehotel@btinternet.com
A fine hotel in a magnificent setting looking out over
Cardigan Bay. Thirteen well-equipped en suite
bedrooms, lounge, bar, top-class restaurant.   162

Criccieth Golf Club

Ednyfed Hill, Criccieth LL52
Tel: 01766 522154

Situated on a hilltop known as Ednyfed Hill and just one mile inland from the centre of the seaside town of Criccieth, the 18-hole lay-out of Criccieth Golf Club was founded in 1905 mainly for the benefit of holidaymakers who were beginning to catch the golf bug which was beginning to spread across Wales as a result of its popularity in other parts of Great Britain. This pleasant hilltop course gently undulating along the high ground and offering stunning views of the Lleyn Peninsular, Cardigan Bay and across to the mountains of Snowdonia, is the ideal lay-out for golfing holidaymakers who are looking to play a pleasant round of golf without having to over-stretch themselves in an attempt to bring in a satisfying score and without having to stretch their holiday budget to extremes. Measuring a mere 5,535 yards (par-68), the course offers an exhilarating experience when the gentle summer breezes blow across the fairways with the faint smell of the sea from Cardigan Bay.

The town of Criccieth was the boyhood home of Lloyd George, Prime Minister of Britain during the First World War, and, I am told, he used to quietly sneak a round of golf on the Criccieth course, whenever he returned to North Wales and could spare the time.

A rather small and friendly club with full bar and catering facilities and moderate green fees, visitors are made most welcome at Criccieth Golf Club, as they are, of course, throughout the entire golf clubs in Wales.

Sec/Manager:	Mancolm Hamleton
Professional:	None
Directions:	¾ mile E of Criccieth centre. From centre take the High St

(A497, Porthmadog). Entrance after ¾ mile on left hand side.

Date Founded:	1905
Type of Course:	Mountainous
No of Holes:	18
Length:	5535 yds (5109 mtrs)
Par:	68
SSS:	67
Green Fees:	Weekdays: £13.00; Weekends/ Bank Holidays: £16.00
Visitors:	Welcome: Contact Club by telephone in advance. Unable to play on Wednesday, Saturday and Sunday afternoons.
Societies:	Welcome: Contact Club in writing or by telephone in advance.
Facilities:	Putting Green, Trolley Hire, Buggy Hire, Bar, Restaurant

Accommodation, Food and Drink

Reference numbers below refer to detailed information provided in section 2

Accommodation

Awel Mór Hotel, Criccieth, Gwynedd LL52 0EL
Tel: 01766 522086
e-mail: sue.petch@virgin.net
website: www.cricciethaccommodation.co.uk/
Nine en suite bedrooms on three floors in a recently renovated hotel on the seafront near the Castle. Guest lounge and bar. 179

The Crown Hotel, High Street, Pwllheli, Gwynedd LL53 5RT
Tel/Fax: 01758 612664
Family-run town centre hotel with 12 en suite rooms (tv, tea-makers), a lively bar (pool, darts, bar football) and good food.

Gwynfryn Farm, Llanbedr, Gwynedd LL45 2NY
Tel/Fax: 01341 241381
website: www.lokalink.co.uk/harlech/gwynfrynfarm/ homepage.htm
Stone-built self-catering cottages on a 20-acre farm in Snowdonia National Park. Also en suite B&B room in 16th century farmhouse. 171

Hafod Wen Guest House, Harlech, Gwynedd LL46 2RA
Tel: 01766 780356
e-mail: hafodwen@enterprise.net
website: www.hafodwen.co.uk
Edwardian house set in eight acres of clifftop gardens, with tremendous views, seven well-appointed en suite bedrooms and superb home cooking. 177

Marine Hotel, Criccieth, Gwynedd LL52 0EA

Tel: 01766 522946 Fax: 01766 522216
e-mail: marinecriccieth@lineone.net
Fifteen en suite rooms in a traditional hotel opposite
the castle and only 50 yards from the sea. Bar and
restaurant, tv lounge. 174

The White House Hotel & Restaurant, Abersoch, Gwynedd LL53 7AG

Tel: 01758 713427 Fax: 01758 713512
e-mail: whitehousehotel@btinternet.com
A fine hotel in a magnificent setting looking out over
Cardigan Bay. Thirteen well-equipped en suite
bedrooms, lounge, bar, top-class restaurant. 162

Yr Hen Fecws, Porthmadog, Gwynedd LL49 9AP

Tel: 01766 514625
An 18th century Welsh-stone building of great
charcater, 'The Old Bakery' is a bistro-style restaurant
with four letting bedrooms. 167

Food and Drink

The Bryn Hir Arms, Criccieth, Gwynedd LL52 0BT

Tel: 01766 522493
High-street pub with two bars and a bistro using
mostly local produce. Patio garden. 183

The Crown Hotel, High Street, Pwllheli, Gwynedd LL53 5RT

Tel/Fax: 01758 612664
Family-run town centre hotel with 12 en suite rooms
(tv, tea-makers), a lively bar (pool, darts, bar football)
and good food.

Marine Hotel, Criccieth, Gwynedd LL52 0EA

Tel: 01766 522946 Fax: 01766 522216
e-mail: marinecriccieth@lineone.net
Fifteen en suite rooms in a traditional hotel opposite
the castle and only 50 yards from the sea. Bar and
restaurant, tv lounge. 174

The Plas Restaurant, Harlech, Gwynedd LL46 2YA

Tel: 01766 780204
A late-Victorian building in a spectacular location
overlooking Royal St David's Golf Course and the sea.
Open 9-8 for snacks, from noon for full menu. 178

Ponds Bistro, Porthmadog, Gwynedd LL49 9LR

Tel: 01766 512333
website: www.ponds-bistro.co.uk
A stylish high-street bistro open seven evenings a
week and for Sunday lunch. Excellent home cooking
using prime local produce. 176

The White House Hotel & Restaurant, Abersoch, Gwynedd LL53 7AG

Tel: 01758 713427 Fax: 01758 713512
e-mail: whitehousehotel@btinternet.com
A fine hotel in a magnificent setting looking out over

Cardigan Bay. Thirteen well-equipped en suite
bedrooms, lounge, bar, top-class restaurant. 162

Yr Hen Fecws, Porthmadog, Gwynedd LL49 9AP

Tel: 01766 514625
An 18th century Welsh-stone building of great
charcater, 'The Old Bakery' is a bistro-style restaurant
with four letting bedrooms. 167

Yr Hen Feudy Restaurant, Llanbedr, Gwynedd LL45 2NH

Tel/Fax: 01341 241555
An Excellent restaurant open all day from May to
October in a modern conversion of a farm building.
Steaks and fresh fish among the specialities. 181

Nefyn & District Golf Club

Morfa Nefyn, Pwllheli LL53 6DA

Tel: 01758 720966 Fax: 01758 720476

One of eleven golf clubs in Gwynedd that was
founded before the outbreak of the First World
War, the Nefyn course is another rare jewel in
the crown of Welsh golf. One of Wales's best kept
secrets, even from many Welsh golfers who play
in the south of the Principality, this gorgeous
course in a magical setting is truly laid out in a
wonderland of a place, with magnificent views
to be seen of the Irish Sea from every hole. I have
been told that a former honorary secretary once
described the second nine holes as, " *Like playing
from the upper deck of an aircraft carrier*", a description
that perfectly sums up those holes that jut
out on a narrow finger of land from the mighty
Lleyn Peninsular. Golf here is a great adventure,
a thrill a minute and a problem every second as
you attempt to thread your way along the top of
the cliffs on a seemingly perilous journey to every
green. Without a doubt the Nefyn course is the
nearest thing in the entire golfing world to America's
famous Pebble Beach course. Members tell
me that Nefyn was once known locally as the

"hush-hush club", because when discovered by visitors they tended to keep quiet about the place and keep it as their very own "Shangrila".

Founded in 1907, the architect James Braid must have thought he had been sent to heaven when he arrived at Nefyn to lay out the new course and saw the beauty and felt the wonderful tranquillity of the place. Indeed, judging by the large membership at Nefyn, many others are of the same opinion and many others are on a long waiting list waiting to get in! No fewer than ten of the holes run alongside the sea, and if you have never before played golf on holes which run along the edge of a clifftop you will get the golfing thrill of a lifetime. Along every yard of the par-5 12th you can experience a thrill a minute. First you have a blind tee-shot, then a blind second shot and a huge, mighty huge, pothole to hopefully avoid, a public footpath to keep a wary eye on

and, best of all, the Ty Coch (Red House) Inn on the gorgeous beach below, which is accessible from the 12th hole should you need a reviving drink. The beautiful seaside village of Portdinllaen, which lies directly below the course is such a stunning place it has been preserved by the National Trust. Lying in a quiet cove with its aforementioned beach, it sits below the course like the final brushwork of a rare masterpiece. Here you also have a lifeboat station and a light-house visited by many holidaymakers making their way from the public footpath that cuts across the 12th hole. Not the longest of challenges at 6,332 yards from the old lay-out, but the club has recently extended the course so that a choice of two homeward routes are on offer, with the new lay-out giving a complete length of 6,548 yards. Nevertheless, both lay-outs carry a par of 71, and both are as tough as they come when the wind blows from any direction. On a calm and clear day when the views are far-reaching and the seabirds are singing their choruses and your swing is in harmony with the peaceful atmosphere, it is hard to believe that many of my fellow Welsh-men spend thousands of pounds sterling to leave Wales and go to foreign countries in search of a golfing paradise during the summer months, when right on their doorsteps is a heavenly course named Nefyn.

Sec/Manager:	Barry Owens
Professional:	John Froom
Directions:	7 miles NW of Pwllheli. From centre take the A498 (Nefyn), after 5 miles join the B4412 (Morfa Nefyn). Go straight through Morfa Nefyn on Lon Golff (still B4412). Entrance on right hand side.
Visitors:	Welcome: By arrangement. Contact Club in advance
Societies:	Welcome: Contact Club in advance

Facilities: Putting Green, Chipping Green, Club Hire, Trolley Hire, Buggy Hire, Bar, Restaurant, Snooker Room, Practice Area

Old

Date Founded: 1907
Type of Course: Clifftop
No of Holes: 18
Length: 6201 yds (5724 mtrs)
Par: 71
SSS: 71
Green Fees: Weekdays: £26 per day; Weekends/Bank Holidays: £31 per day

New

Date Founded: 1993
Type of Course: Clifftop
No of Holes: 18
Length: 6548 yds (6044 mtrs)
Par: 71
SSS: 71
Green Fees: Weekdays: £26 per day; Weekends/Bank Holidays: £31 per day

Accommodation, Food and Drink

Reference numbers below refer to detailed information provided in section 2

Accommodation

Awel Mór Hotel, Criccieth, Gwynedd LL52 0EL
Tel: 01766 522086 e-mail: sue.petch@virgin.net
website: www.cricciethaccommodation.co.uk/
Nine en suite bedrooms on three floors in a recently renovated hotel on the seafront near the Castle. Guest lounge and bar.   179

Caeau Capel Hotel, Nefyn, Gwynedd LL53 6EB
Tel: 01758 720240
Late 19th century country house in a garden setting on the Llyn Peninsula. 18 en suite bedrooms, home-cooked traditional food. Bar, lounge, games room.184

The Carisbrooke Hotel, Abersoch, Gwynedd LL53 7DY
Tel: 01758 712526 Fax: 01758 713666
e-mail: davies@abersoch-carisbrookehotel.co.uk
A small, neat, family-run hotel with seven bedrooms and a family suite. Lounge, bar.   175

Celtic Royal Hotel, Caernarfon, Gwynedd LL55 1AY
Tel: 01286 674477 Fax: 01286 674139
e-mail: enquiries@celtic-royal.co.uk
website: www.celtic-royal.co.uk
110 fully equipped en suite bedrooms in a newly refurbished town centre hotel near the Castle. Restaurant, bar, gym, swimming pool.   166

Harbour Hotel, Abersoch, Gwynedd LL53 7HR
Tel: 01758 712406 Fax: 01758 713826
e-mail: mail@harbour-hotel.com
website: www.harbour-hotel.com
Fourteen en suite bedrooms in a seaside Bed & Breakfast hotel, café-bar, wine bar and disco.   172

Marine Hotel, Criccieth, Gwynedd LL52 0EA
Tel: 01766 522946 Fax: 01766 522216
e-mail: marinecriccieth@lineone.net
Fifteen en suite rooms in a traditional hotel opposite the castle and only 50 yards from the sea. Bar and restaurant, tv lounge.   174

Menai Bank Hotel, Caernarfon, Gwynedd LL55 1BD
Tel/Fax: 01286 673297
e-mail: menaibankhotel@tesconet.co.uk
website: www.menaibankhotel.co.uk
Excellent food and comfortable accommodation in a turn-of-the-century hotel with many original features. Sixteen en suite bedrooms.   163

Mynydd Ednyfed Country House Hotel, Criccieth, Gwynedd LL52 0PH
Tel: 01766 523269 Fax: 01766 522929
e-mail: mynydd-ednyfed@criccieth.net
website: www.criccieth.net
400-year-old stone-built country house set in seven acres, with eight en suite rooms, fine home cooking and a variety of sporting facilities.   185

Plas Bodegroes, Pwllheli, Gwynedd LL53 5TH
Tel: 01758 612363 Fax: 01758 701247
e-mail: gunna@bodegroes.co.uk
website: www.bodegroes.co.uk
A Georgian manor house in a superb secluded setting is the finest restaurant with rooms in Wales. Eight lovely bedrooms, wonderful food.   173

St Tudwals Inn, Abersoch, Gwynedd LL53 7DS
Tel: 01758 712539
Five en suite bedrooms, all-day bar snacks and an à la carte restaurant in one of Abersoch's most popular meeting places.   161

Tegfan Guest House, 4 Church Street, Caernarfon, Gwynedd LL55 1SW
Tel: 01286 673703
Very friendly family-run B&B two minutes from the harbour and castle, with five comfortable bedrooms, some en suite. Excellent breakfast.

The White House Hotel & Restaurant, Abersoch, Gwynedd LL53 7AG
Tel: 01758 713427 Fax: 01758 713512
e-mail: whitehousehotel@btinternet.com
A fine hotel in a magnificent setting looking out over

Cardigan Bay. Thirteen well-equipped en suite bedrooms, lounge, bar, top-class restaurant. 162

Food and Drink

The Bryn Hir Arms, Criccieth, Gwynedd LL52 0BT

Tel: 01766 522493

High-street pub with two bars and a bistro using mostly local produce. Patio garden. 183

Celtic Royal Hotel, Caernarfon, Gwynedd LL55 1AY

Tel: 01286 674477 Fax: 01286 674139
e-mail: enquiries@celtic-royal.co.uk
website: www.celtic-royal.co.uk

110 fully equipped en suite bedrooms in a newly refurbished town centre hotel near the Castle. Restaurant, bar, gym, swimming pool. 166

The Galley Restaurant, Lon Nant-Iago, Llanbedrog, Pwllheli, Gwynedd LL53 7TR

Tel: 01758 740730

Popular licenced restaurant with sheltered terraces overlooking the National Trust beach. Snack menu 11-6.30: full menu 6.30 till late. Booking advisable.

Harbour Hotel, Abersoch, Gwynedd LL53 7HR

Tel: 01758 712406 Fax: 01758 713826
e-mail: mail@harbour-hotel.com
website: www.harbour-hotel.com

Fourteen en suite bedrooms in a seaside Bed & Breakfast hotel, café-bar, wine bar and disco. 172

Marine Hotel, Criccieth, Gwynedd LL52 0EA

Tel: 01766 522946 Fax: 01766 522216
e-mail: marinecriccieth@lineone.net

Fifteen en suite rooms in a traditional hotel opposite the castle and only 50 yards from the sea. Bar and restaurant, tv lounge. 174

Menai Bank Hotel, Caernarfon, Gwynedd LL55 1BD

Tel/Fax: 01286 673297
e-mail: menaibankhotel@tesconet.co.uk
website: www.menaibankhotel.co.uk

Excellent food and comfortable accommodation in a turn-of-the-century hotel with many original features. Sixteen en suite bedrooms. 163

Mynydd Ednyfed Country House Hotel, Criccieth, Gwynedd LL52 0PH

Tel: 01766 523269 Fax: 01766 522929
e-mail: mynydd-ednyfed@criccieth.net
website: www.criccieth.net

400-year-old stone-built country house set in seven acres, with eight en suite rooms, fine home cooking and a variety of sporting facilities. 185

Plas Bodegroes, Pwllheli, Gwynedd LL53 5TH

Tel: 01758 612363 Fax: 01758 701247
e-mail: gunna@bodegroes.co.uk
website: www.bodegroes.co.uk

A Georgian manor house in a superb secluded setting

is the finest restaurant with rooms in Wales. Eight lovely bedrooms, wonderful food. 173

St Tudwals Inn, Abersoch, Gwynedd LL53 7DS

Tel: 01758 712539

Five en suite bedrooms, all-day bar snacks and an à la carte restaurant in one of Abersoch's most popular meeting places. 161

The White House Hotel & Restaurant, Abersoch, Gwynedd LL53 7AG

Tel: 01758 713427 Fax: 01758 713512
e-mail: whitehousehotel@btinternet.com

A fine hotel in a magnificent setting looking out over Cardigan Bay. Thirteen well-equipped en suite bedrooms, lounge, bar, top-class restaurant. 162

Porthmadog Golf Club

Morfa Bychan, Porthmadog LL49 9UU

Tel: **01766 514124** Fax: **01766 514638**

Another one of James Braid's creations and another one of the very good golf courses to be found on the Lleyn Peninsular, the Porthmadog Golf Club first saw the light of day when local businessmen joined forces and went in search of a suitable site in which to build the seaside town's very own course as an added attraction to lure the discerning visitor to Porthmadog. In no time at all they discovered a vacant site just two miles south of the town and close to the famous and broad expanse of Black Rock Sands. Calling on the expertise of the then current Open Champion, James Braid, in 1901, to give his thoughts on the stretch of vacant land, he declared it a perfect spot for a golf course to be laid out. The satisfied band of Porthmadog businessmen then proposed that Braid would be its creator.

A quiet and pleasant man but not a great talker, Braid set about his task with the quiet thoroughness he adopted when competing in tournaments, and came up trumps with a stunning and challenging golf course. Built on a mixture of links and heathland and with rough typical of both terrains, the Porthmadog course offers eighteen holes of sheer delight for those golfers who like a bit of a "bite" in the golf courses they attempt to conquer. Measuring 6,363 yards, with a par of 71, the course offers excellent views of Cardigan Bay, Snowdonia and the surrounding countryside, which all adds up to a an enjoyable place to visit. Founded in 1902, the ideal time to visit this James Braid creation is during the first week of each July when the club puts on an Open Week featuring many and varied competitions from the Saturday to the following Sunday, which is a memorable occasion for golfing visitors. In the town of Porthmadog, at Pensamer Road, is the Porthmadog Driving Range for those who like a warm-up before a round, and the Criccieth Golf Club lies just a few short miles west of Porthmadog Golf Club.

Sec/Manager:	Mrs A Richardson
Professional:	Peter Bright
Directions:	1¼ miles SW of Portmadog. From centre take Borth Rd to the South, after 300 yds fork right into Morfa Bychan. Entrance after 1 mile on left hand side.
Date Founded:	1905
Type of Course:	Links
No of Holes:	18
Length:	6363 yds (5873 mtrs)
Par:	71
SSS:	71
Green Fees:	Weekdays: £25 per day; Weekends/Bank Holidays: £30 per day
Visitors:	Welcome: Contact Club in advance
Societies:	Welcome: Contact Club in advance
Facilities:	Putting Green, Practice ground, Trolley Hire, Buggy Hire, Bar, Restaurant

Accommodation, Food and Drink

Reference numbers below refer to detailed information provided in section 2

Accommodation

Awel Môr Hotel, Criccieth, Gwynedd LL52 0EL
Tel: 01766 522086
e-mail: sue.petch@virgin.net
website: www.cricciethaccommodation.co.uk/

Nine en suite bedrooms on three floors in a recently renovated hotel on the seafront near the Castle. Guest lounge and bar.   179

Caeau Capel Hotel, Nefyn, Gwynedd LL53 6EB
Tel: 01758 720240
Late 19th century country house in a garden setting on the Llyn Peninsula. 18 en suite bedrooms, home-cooked traditional food. Bar, lounge, games room.184

The Carisbrooke Hotel, Abersoch, Gwynedd LL53 7DY
Tel: 01758 712526 Fax: 01758 713666
e-mail: davies@abersoch-carisbrookehotel.co.uk
A small, neat, family-run hotel with seven bedrooms and a family suite. Lounge, bar.   175

Gwynfryn Farm, Llanbedr, Gwynedd LL45 2NY
Tel/Fax: 01341 241381
website: www.lokalink.co.uk/harlech/ gwynfrynfarm/homepage.htm
Stone-built self-catering cottages on a 20-acre farm in Snowdonia National Park. Also en suite B&B room in 16th century farmhouse.   171

Hafod Wen Guest House, Harlech, Gwynedd LL46 2RA
Tel: 01766 780356
e-mail: hafodwen@enterprise.net
website: www.hafodwen.co.uk
Edwardian house set in eight acres of clifftop gardens, with tremendous views, seven well-appointed en suite bedrooms and superb home cooking.   177

Harbour Hotel, Abersoch, Gwynedd LL53 7HR
Tel: 01758 712406 Fax: 01758 713826
e-mail: mail@harbour-hotel.com
website: www.harbour-hotel.com
Fourteen en suite bedrooms in a seaside Bed & Breakfast hotel, café-bar, wine bar and disco.   172

Marine Hotel, Criccieth, Gwynedd LL52 0EA
Tel: 01766 522946 Fax: 01766 522216
e-mail: marinecriccieth@lineone.net
Fifteen en suite rooms in a traditional hotel opposite the castle and only 50 yards from the sea. Bar and restaurant, tv lounge.   174

Morlyn Restaurant & Guest House, Llandanwg, Harlech, Gwynedd LL46 2SB
Tel: 01341 241298
e-mail: info@northwales-holidays.com
website: www.northwales-holidays.com
Choice of Bed & Breakfast and self-catering accommodation with superb mountain and sea views. Bistro-style restaurant.

Mynydd Ednyfed Country House Hotel, Criccieth, Gwynedd LL52 0PH
Tel: 01766 523269 Fax: 01766 522929
e-mail: mynydd-ednyfed@criccieth.net
website: www.criccieth.net
400-year-old stone-built country house set in seven acres, with eight en suite rooms, fine home cooking and a variety of sporting facilities.   185

Rhinog Park, Dyffryn Ardudwy, Gwynedd LL44 2HA

Tel: 01341 247652 Fax: 01531 640280
e-mail: rhinogpark@countryparks.com
website: www.countryparks.com

Self-catering lodges in a lovely scenic setting within Snowdonia National Park. Short walk to beach. 169

Yr Hen Fecws, Porthmadog, Gwynedd LL49 9AP

Tel: 01766 514625

An 18th century Welsh-stone building of great charcater, 'The Old Bakery' is a bistro-style restaurant with four letting bedrooms. 167

Food and Drink

The Bryn Hir Arms, Criccieth, Gwynedd LL52 0BT

Tel: 01766 522493

High-street pub with two bars and a bistro using mostly local produce. Patio garden. 183

Harbour Hotel, Abersoch, Gwynedd LL53 7HR

Tel: 01758 712406 Fax: 01758 713826
e-mail: mail@harbour-hotel.com
website: www.harbour-hotel.com

Fourteen en suite bedrooms in a seaside Bed & Breakfast hotel, café-bar, wine bar and disco. 172

Marine Hotel, Criccieth, Gwynedd LL52 0EA

Tel: 01766 522946 Fax: 01766 522216
e-mail: marinecriccieth@lineone.net

Fifteen en suite rooms in a traditional hotel opposite the castle and only 50 yards from the sea. Bar and restaurant, tv lounge. 174

Morlyn Restaurant & Guest House, Llandanwg, Harlech, Gwynedd LL46 2SB

Tel: 01341 241298
e-mail: info@northwales-holidays.com
website: www.northwales-holidays.com

Choice of Bed & Breakfast and self-catering accommodation with superb mountain and sea views. Bistro-style restaurant.

Mynydd Ednyfed Country House Hotel, Criccieth, Gwynedd LL52 0PH

Tel: 01766 523269 Fax: 01766 522929
e-mail: mynydd-ednyfed@criccieth.net
website: www.criccieth.net

400-year-old stone-built country house set in seven acres, with eight en suite rooms, fine home cooking and a variety of sporting facilities. 185

The Plas Restaurant, Harlech, Gwynedd LL46 2YA

Tel: 01766 780204

A late-Victorian building in a spectacular location overlooking Royal St David's Golf Course and the sea. Open 9-8 for snack, from noon for full menu. 178

Ponds Bistro, Porthmadog, Gwynedd LL49 9LR

Tel: 01766 512333
website: www.ponds-bistro.co.uk

A stylish high-street bistro open seven evenings a week and for Sunday lunch. Excellent home cooking using prime local produce. 176

Yr Hen Fecws, Porthmadog, Gwynedd LL49 9AP

Tel: 01766 514625

An 18th century Welsh-stone building of great charcater, 'The Old Bakery' is a bistro-style restaurant with four letting bedrooms. 167

Yr Hen Feudy Restaurant, Llanbedr, Gwynedd LL45 2NH

Tel/Fax: 01341 241555

An Excellent restaurant open all day from May to October in a modern conversion of a farm building. Steaks and fresh fish among the specialities. 181

Pwllheli Golf Club

Golf Road, Pwllheli LL53 5PS

Tel: 01758 701644 Fax: 01758 701644

The oldest of the golf clubs on the Lleyn Peninsular, Pwllheli Golf Club was founded in 1900 and designed by none other than Old Tom Morris of St Andrews fame. A few years later it was decided that the course needed to be extended somewhat and along came another Open Champion by the name of James Braid to do his bit and also leave his mark on the lovely old seaside course. As can be expected from two top-class golfers who knew everything there was to know about how a seaside course should be laid out, they produced a course that the local Pwllheli golfers have ever since been proud of.

In the 6,200 yards they had to fit in an 18-hole lay-out, they certainly played a big part in encouraging tourism to the charming resort of Pwllheli, which has continued for over a century. Many thousands of visitors flocked to Pwllheli following the 1939-45 War years to stay at the Butlin Holiday Camp on the edge of the town, and the golfers among them must have been overjoyed to discover a golfing paradise close by, while many others probably played their first tentative shots and decided to take up the great game after being bitten by the golfing bug that lies in wait on every type of golf course for the unwary.

Carved out of a delightful mixture of parkland and linksland, this enjoyable par-69 small course-like its near neighbours along this beautiful coastline-offers the added delights of the gorgeous views across Cardigan Bay and beyond to the spectacular Snowdonia mountain range.

With a cosy clubhouse offering full facilities and a fully stocked golf shop-plus a seaside course designed by two multiple winners of the Open

Championship, the Pwllheli Golf Club is a special place to visit.

Sec/Manager:	Emlyn Pritchard
Professional:	John Pilkington
Directions:	1 mile SW of Pwllheli. From Ala Rd in centre take Penrhydliniog Rd, leading to Fford Glancymeran Rd then Golf Rd. Entrance is at the end.
Date Founded:	1900
Type of Course:	Links/Parkland
No of Holes:	18
Length:	6108 yds (5638 mtrs)
Par:	69
SSS:	69
Green Fees:	Weekdays: Summer £22 per day, Winter £27 per day; Weekends/Bank Holidays: Summer £15 per day, Winter £15 per day
Visitors:	Welcome: Excluding Tuesday, Thursday & weekends
Societies:	Welcome: By arrangement. Contact Club in advance
Facilities:	Putting Green, Chipping Green, Driving Range, Club Hire, Trolley Hire, Buggy Hire, Caddy Service, Bar, Restaurant, Private Rooms

Accommodation, Food and Drink

Reference numbers below refer to detailed information provided in section 2

Accommodation

Awel Mór Hotel, Criccieth, Gwynedd LL52 0EL

Tel: 01766 522086 e-mail: sue.petch@virgin.net
website: www.cricciethaccommodation.co.uk/
Nine en suite bedrooms on three floors in a recently renovated hotel on the seafront near the Castle. Guest lounge and bar. 179

Caeau Capel Hotel, Nefyn, Gwynedd LL53 6EB

Tel: 01758 720240
Late 19th century country house in a garden setting on the Llyn Peninsula. 18 en suite bedrooms, home-cooked traditional food. Bar, lounge, games room.184

The Carisbrooke Hotel, Abersoch, Gwynedd LL53 7DY

Tel: 01758 712526 Fax: 01758 713666
e-mail: davies@abersoch-carisbrookehotel.co.uk
A small, neat, family-run hotel with seven bedrooms and a family suite. Lounge, bar. 175

The Cliffs Inn, Morfa Nefyn, Nr. Pwllheli, Gwynedd LL53 6BY

Tel: 01758 720356 Fax: 01758 720544
e-mail: enquiries@cliffs-inn.co.uk
White-painted hotel offering self-catering accommodation, excellent food and magnificent views across to Anglesey. Fifty yards from the beach. 180

The Crown Hotel, High Street, Pwllheli, Gwynedd LL53 5RT

Tel/Fax: 01758 612664
Family-run town centre hotel with 12 en suite rooms (tv, tea-makers), a lively bar (pool, darts, bar football) and good food.

Harbour Hotel, Abersoch, Gwynedd LL53 7HR

Tel: 01758 712406 Fax: 01758 713826
e-mail: mail@harbour-hotel.com
website: www.harbour-hotel.com
Fourteen en suite bedrooms in a seaside Bed & Breakfast hotel, café-bar, wine bar and disco. 172

Marine Hotel, Criccieth, Gwynedd LL52 0EA

Tel: 01766 522946 Fax: 01766 522216
e-mail: marinecriccieth@lineone.net
Fifteen en suite rooms in a traditional hotel opposite the castle and only 50 yards from the sea. Bar and restaurant, tv lounge. 174

Mynydd Ednyfed Country House Hotel, Criccieth, Gwynedd LL52 0PH

Tel: 01766 523269 Fax: 01766 522929
e-mail: mynydd-ednyfed@criccieth.net
website: www.criccieth.net
400-year-old stone-built country house set in seven acres, with eight en suite rooms, fine home cooking and a variety of sporting facilities. 185

Plas Bodegroes, Pwllheli, Gwynedd LL53 5TH

Tel: 01758 612363 Fax: 01758 701247
e-mail: gunna@bodegroes.co.uk
website: www.bodegroes.co.uk
A Georgian manor house in a superb secluded setting is the finest restaurant with rooms in Wales. Eight lovely bedrooms, wonderful food. 173

St Tudwals Inn, Abersoch, Gwynedd LL53 7DS

Tel: 01758 712539
Five en suite bedrooms, all-day bar snacks and an à la carte restaurant in one of Abersoch's most popular meeting places. 161

Food and Drink

The Bryn Hir Arms, Criccieth, Gwynedd LL52 0BT

Tel: 01766 522493
High-street pub with two bars and a bistro using mostly local produce. Patio garden. 183

The Cliffs Inn, Morfa Nefyn, Nr. Pwllheli, Gwynedd LL53 6BY

Tel: 01758 720356 Fax: 01758 720544
e-mail: enquiries@cliffs-inn.co.uk
White-painted hotel offering self-catering accommo-

dation, excellent food and magnificent views across to Anglesey. Fifty yards from the beach.   180

The Crown Hotel, High Street, Pwllheli, Gwynedd LL53 5RT

Tel/Fax: 01758 612664

Family-run town centre hotel with 12 en suite rooms (tv, tea-makers), a lively bar (pool, darts, bar football) and good food.

The Galley Restaurant, Lon Nant-Iago, Llanbedrog, Pwllheli, Gwynedd LL53 7TR

Tel: 01758 740730

Popular licenced restaurant with sheltered terraces overlooking the National Trust beach. Snack menu 11-6.30: full menu 6.30 till late. Booking advisable.

Harbour Hotel, Abersoch, Gwynedd LL53 7HR

Tel: 01758 712406 Fax: 01758 713826
e-mail: mail@harbour-hotel.com
website: www.harbour-hotel.com
Fourteen en suite bedrooms in a seaside Bed & Breakfast hotel, café-bar, wine bar and disco.   172

Marine Hotel, Criccieth, Gwynedd LL52 0EA

Tel: 01766 522946 Fax: 01766 522216
e-mail: marinecriccieth@lineone.net
Fifteen en suite rooms in a traditional hotel opposite the castle and only 50 yards from the sea. Bar and restaurant, tv lounge.   174

Mynydd Ednyfed Country House Hotel, Criccieth, Gwynedd LL52 0PH

Tel: 01766 523269 Fax: 01766 522929
e-mail: mynydd-ednyfed@criccieth.net
website: www.criccieth.net
400-year-old stone-built country house set in seven acres, with eight en suite rooms, fine home cooking and a variety of sporting facilities.   185

Plas Bodegroes, Pwllheli, Gwynedd LL53 5TH

Tel: 01758 612363 Fax: 01758 701247
e-mail: gunna@bodegroes.co.uk
website: www.bodegroes.co.uk
A Georgian manor house in a superb secluded setting is the finest restaurant with rooms in Wales. Eight lovely bedrooms, wonderful food.   173

St Tudwals Inn, Abersoch, Gwynedd LL53 7DS

Tel: 01758 712539

Five en suite bedrooms, all-day bar snacks and an à la carte restaurant in one of Abersoch's most popular meeting places.   161

Royal St Davids Golf Club

Harlech LL46 2UB

Tel: 01766 780203 Fax: 01766 781110

Without a doubt the premier golf club in North Wales is the majestic Royal St. David's Golf Club

at Harlech. This magnificent links course is to North Wales what Royal Porthcawl is to South Wales-the brightest jewel in the crown of their particular region. Together they share the honour of being the only Royal clubs in Wales, therefore sharing the distinction of being Number One of all the golf courses in Wales. Lying in the great shadow of the imposing Harlech Castle, Royal St. David's was founded in 1894, two years later than Royal Porthcawl, and is laid out on linksland, which was once part of the seabed of Cardigan Bay when it lapped the great walls of Harlech Castle. Long receded, the waters left behind flat layers of sand and scrub and sandhills to provide the perfect setting for a great championship links course amidst on the great beauty spots of North Wales. The then Prince of Wales (later King Edward VII) accepted the patronage quite soon after the formation of the club, but it was not before 10 years later that the Royal charter was actually granted to the club, who had prematurely and proudly used the prestigious "Royal" prefix ever since the Prince of Wales had accepted the patronage! Later, in 1934, King George V was patron and in 1935 when the Duke of Windsor was the Prince of Wales, he accepted the Captaincy of the club, thus extending the Royal connections with the great club and adding much more to its prestige. First impressions, like St. Andrews, gives one a feeling that the course will not be too difficult to conquer, but complacency can lead to total collapse of one's

confidence. Therefore it is best to treat this Welsh masterpiece with the respect it deserves, even on the kindest of summer days. Indeed, it has been described by professionals who have played there as the world's toughest par 69.

Over the years of reporting the Royal and Ancient game, I have been privileged to witness many top class amateurs competing over this great links and saw many go away with "their tail between their legs", while others played the course with respect and walked away contented. In 1988 the club professionals arrived to compete in the Wilson Club Professional Championship and were warned on the eve of the tournament by the P. G. A. Captain David Huish, who talked of it being the world's toughest par 69. At the completion of the 72-hole tournament the majority of the professionals agreed with him. Scotsman Russell Weir was the only player to beat par in every round to win with eight shots to spare, and that year he was playing some of the finest golf of his professional career. Had the wind really picked up during that sunny week in June everyone would have been struggling.

Only twice do successive holes head in the same direction so the wind causes havoc as it swirls and gusts through the sandhills, making club selection something of a lottery. With only two par fives on the course there is little chance of retrieving a dropped shot by the big hitters, whilst the par threes are mostly guarded by dunes and thick rough waiting to gather up the wayward tee-shot. The par-4 15th is a tough nut to crack. At 427-yards the dog-legged fairway requires an accurate drive to avoid the sandhills and grassy hollows. If the prevailing wind is at full force it is best not to strive at getting home in two. Many have tried and ending up regretting it. The course finishes with a par three, but the penultimate 17th hole requires full concentration to avoid the thickish rough, which borders both edges of the narrow fairway. When I tell you that the SSS is 73 (par 69) you will quickly realise that this course really does pose a few problems along its 6,552 yards. John Barnett, a cheery character and long-standing club professional is as happy

as a sand boy in his well-stocked shop overlooking the sandhills, which is not surprising when living in such a beautiful environment and with good home cooking at the charming old clubhouse. With such a splendid course and plenty of good accommodation, the charming town of Harlech is an excellent centre for golfing visitors wishing to visit the other great courses of Gwynedd.

Sec/Manager:	David Morkill
Professional:	John Barnett
Directions:	At NW outskirts of Harlech. Entrance on the A496 Barmouth to Blaenau Ffestiniog road close to where Railway crosses over the road.

Date Founded: 1894

Type of Course: Links

No of Holes: 18

Length: 6552 yds (6048 mtrs)

Par: 69

SSS: 73

Green Fees:	Weekdays: Summer £30 per day. Winter contact Club in advance; Weekends/Bank Holidays: Summer £30 per day. Winter contact Club in advance
Visitors:	Welcome: Contact Club in advance
Societies:	Welcome: By arrangement. Contact Club in advance
Facilities:	Putting Green, Chipping Green, Practice Ground, Trolley Hire, Buggy Hire, Bar, Restaurant

Accommodation, Food and Drink

Reference numbers below refer to detailed information provided in section 2

Accommodation

Awel Mór Hotel, Criccieth, Gwynedd LL52 0EL

Tel: 01766 522086
e-mail: sue.petch@virgin.net
website: www.cricciethaccommodation.co.uk/
Nine en suite bedrooms on three floors in a recently renovated hotel on the seafront near the Castle. Guest lounge and bar.   179

Caeau Capel Hotel, Nefyn, Gwynedd LL53 6EB

Tel: 01758 720240
Late 19th century country house in a garden setting

on the Llyn Peninsula. 18 en suite bedrooms, home-cooked traditional food. Bar, lounge, games room.184

Caethle Chalet & Caravan Park, Tywyn, Gwynedd LL36 9HS

Tel/Fax: 01654 710587
Extensive, unspoilt country setting with pitches for touring caravans, and three chalets for self-catering accommodation.

The Cliffs Inn, Morfa Nefyn, Nr. Pwllheli, Gwynedd LL53 6BY

Tel: 01758 720356 Fax: 01758 720544
e-mail: enquiries@cliffs-inn.co.uk
White-painted hotel offering self-catering accommo-dation, excellent food and magnificent views across to Anglesey. Fifty yards from the beach.   180

Cranbourne Hotel, Barmouth, Gwynedd LL42 1NA

Tel/Fax: 01341 280202
Recently refurbished seaside hotel in a Victorian terrace. Two single bedrooms, eight doubles and six twins including family rooms. Bar snacks.   182

The Dovey Inn, Aberdovey, Gwynedd LL35 0EF

Tel: 01654 767332 Fax: 01654 767996
e-mail: rk@doveyinn.com
website: www.doveyinn.com
Handsome 18th century seafront inn with eight letting bedrooms, three bars and a 30-seat dining room with a long menu.   170

Gwynfryn Farm, Llanbedr, Gwynedd LL45 2NY

Tel/Fax: 01341 241381
website: www.lokalink.co.uk/harlech/
  gwynfrynfarm/homepage.htm
Stone-built self-catering cottages on a 20-acre farm in Snowdonia National Park. Also en suite B&B room in 16th century farmhouse.   171

Hafod Wen Guest House, Harlech, Gwynedd LL46 2RA

Tel: 01766 780356
e-mail: hafodwen@enterprise.net
website: www.hafodwen.co.uk
Edwardian house set in eight acres of clifftop gardens, with tremendous views, seven well-appointed en suite bedrooms and superb home cooking.   177

Morlyn Restaurant & Guest House, Llandanwg, Harlech, Gwynedd LL46 2SB

Tel: 01341 241298
e-mail: info@northwales-holidays.com
website: www.northwales-holidays.com
Choice of Bed & Breakfast and self-catering accommodation with superb mountain and sea views. Bistro-style restaurant.

Mynydd Ednyfed Country House Hotel, Criccieth, Gwynedd LL52 0PH

Tel: 01766 523269 Fax: 01766 522929
e-mail: mynydd-ednyfed@criccieth.net
website: www.criccieth.net
400-year-old stone-built country house set in seven

acres, with eight en suite rooms, fine home cooking and a variety of sporting facilities.   185

Pant-y-Neuadd, Aberdyfi Road, Tywyn, Gwynedd LL36 9HW

Tel/Fax: 01654 711393
website: www.pant-y-neuadd@lineone.net
A park that offers pitches for touring caravans, static caravans for rent and two stone cottages for self-catering holidays. Close to a safe, sandy beach.

Plas Bodegroes, Pwllheli, Gwynedd LL53 5TH

Tel: 01758 612363 Fax: 01758 701247
e-mail: gunna@bodegroes.co.uk
website: www.bodegroes.co.uk
A Georgian manor house in a superb secluded setting is the finest restaurant with rooms in Wales. Eight lovely bedrooms, wonderful food.   173

Plas Penhelig Country House Hotel, Aberdovey, Gwynedd LL35 0NA

Tel: 01654 767676 Fax: 01654 767783
A distinguished country house hotel in a glorious setting with views over the Dovey estuary. 14 quiet, comfortable en suite rooms, superb food.   168

Rhinog Park, Dyffryn Ardudwy, Gwynedd LL44 2HA

Tel: 01341 247652 Fax: 01531 640280
e-mail: rhinogpark@countryparks.com
website: www.countryparks.com
Self-catering lodges in a lovely scenic setting within Snowdonia National Park. Short walk to beach.   169

Trefeddian Hotel, Aberdovey, Gwynedd LL35 0SB

Tel: 01654 767213 Fax: 01654 767777
A distinguished hotel in a lovely secluded setting with fine views across Cardigan Bay. Attractive bedrooms, spacious lounges.   160

Wavecrest Hotel, 8 Marine Parade, Barmouth, Gwynedd LL42 1NA

Tel: 01341 280330
Nine comfortable en suite bedrooms with tv in a family-run Victorian terrace hotel on the seafront. Good home-cooked food, cheerful bar with 64 malt whiskies.

Yr Hen Fecws, Porthmadog, Gwynedd LL49 9AP

Tel: 01766 514625
An 18th century Welsh-stone building of great charcater, 'The Old Bakery' is a bistro-style restaurant with four letting bedrooms.   167

Food and Drink

The Cliffs Inn, Morfa Nefyn, Nr. Pwllheli, Gwynedd LL53 6BY

Tel: 01758 720356 Fax: 01758 720544
e-mail: enquiries@cliffs-inn.co.uk
White-painted hotel offering self-catering accommo-dation, excellent food and magnificent views across to Anglesey. Fifty yards from the beach.   180

The Dovey Inn, Aberdovey, Gwynedd LL35 0EF

Tel: 01654 767332 Fax: 01654 767996
e-mail: rk@doveyinn.com
website: www.doveyinn.com
Handsome 18th century seafront inn with eight
letting bedrooms, three bars and a 30-seat dining
room with a long menu.   170

Morlyn Restaurant & Guest House, Llandanwg, Harlech, Gwynedd LL46 2SB

Tel: 01341 241298
e-mail: info@northwales-holidays.com
website: www.northwales-holidays.com
Choice of Bed & Breakfast and self-catering
accommodation with superb mountain and sea views.
Bistro-style restaurant.

Mynydd Ednyfed Country House Hotel, Criccieth, Gwynedd LL52 0PH

Tel: 01766 523269 Fax: 01766 522929
e-mail: mynydd-ednyfed@criccieth.net
website: www.criccieth.net
400-year-old stone-built country house set in seven
acres, with eight en suite rooms, fine home cooking
and a variety of sporting facilities.   185

Pen-y-Bont Hotel, Tal-y-Llyn, Tywyn, Gwynedd LL36 9AJ

Tel: 01654 782285
e-mail: penybonthotel@btinternet.com
website: www.smoothhound.co.uk/hotels/
      penybont.html
Former 16th century coaching inn situated on the
edge of the beautiful Tal-y-Llyn Lake. Five en suite
bedrooms, two bars, old-world restaurant (non-
smoking) with extensive menus.

Plas Bodegroes, Pwllheli, Gwynedd LL53 5TH

Tel: 01758 612363 Fax: 01758 701247
e-mail: gunna@bodegroes.co.uk
website: www.bodegroes.co.uk
A Georgian manor house in a superb secluded setting
is the finest restaurant with rooms in Wales. Eight
lovely bedrooms, wonderful food.   173

Plas Penhelig Country House Hotel, Aberdovey, Gwynedd LL35 0NA

Tel: 01654 767676 Fax: 01654 767783
A distinguished country house hotel in a glorious
setting with views over the Dovey estuary. 14 quiet,
comfortable en suite rooms, superb food.   168

The Plas Restaurant, Harlech, Gwynedd LL46 2YA

Tel: 01766 780204
A late-Victorian building in a spectacular location
overlooking Royal St David's Golf Course and the sea.
Open 9-8 for snacks, from noon for full menu.   178

Ponds Bistro, Porthmadog, Gwynedd LL49 9LR

Tel: 01766 512333
website: www.ponds-bistro.co.uk
A stylish high-street bistro open seven evenings a
week and for Sunday lunch. Excellent home cooking
using prime local produce.   176

Trefeddian Hotel, Aberdovey, Gwynedd LL35 0SB

Tel: 01654 767213 Fax: 01654 767777
A distinguished hotel in a lovely secluded setting
with fine views across Cardigan Bay. Attractive
bedrooms, spacious lounges.   160

The Whitehall Hotel, Corbett Square, Tywyn, Gwynedd LL36 9DF

Tel/Fax: 01654 710212
A friendly pub with a good bar menu. Hot baguettes,
jacket potatoes, toasted sandwiches, steaks, pies,
curries - and lots more. Children welcome.

Yr Hen Fecws, Porthmadog, Gwynedd LL49 9AP

Tel: 01766 514625
An 18th century Welsh-stone building of great
charcater, 'The Old Bakery' is a bistro-style restaurant
with four letting bedrooms.   167

Yr Hen Feudy Restaurant, Llanbedr, Gwynedd LL45 2NH

Tel/Fax: 01341 241555
An Excellent restaurant open all day from May to
October in a modern conversion of a farm building.
Steaks and fresh fish among the specialities.   181

St Deiniol Golf Club

Penbryn, Bangor LL57 1PX
Tel: 01248 353098

Sec/Manager:	Bob Thomas
Professional:	None
Directions:	1 mile E of Bangor centre. From the A55 approaching Bangor take the A5122 (Bangor, Port Penrhyn), At Port Penrhyn keep on Ffordd Llandegai (A5122) and turn left into Penybryn Rd at a crossroads. Follow Penybryn Rd for 350 yds entrance is at the end.

Date Founded: 1906

Type of Course: Hilly Parkland

No of Holes: 18

Length: 5423 yds (5005 mtrs)

Par: 68

SSS: 68

Green Fees: Weekdays: £14 per day ; Weekends/Bank Holidays: £18 per day

Visitors: Welcome: Contact Club in advance

Societies: Welcome: Contact Club in advance

Facilities: Putting Green, Trolley Hire, Bar, Restaurant

Accommodation, Food and Drink

Reference numbers below refer to detailed information provided in section 2

Accommodation

Celtic Royal Hotel, Caernarfon, Gwynedd LL55 1AY

Tel: 01286 674477 Fax: 01286 674139
e-mail: enquiries@celtic-royal.co.uk
website: www.celtic-royal.co.uk
110 fully equipped en suite bedrooms in a newly refurbished town centre hotel near the Castle. Restaurant, bar, gym, swimming pool.   166

The Gazelle Hotel, Glyn Garth, Menai Bridge, Anglesey LL59 5PD

Tel: 01248 713364 Fax: 01248 713167
website: www.gazellehotel.fsnet.co.uk
Nine rooms in a little gem of a hotel in a picturesque setting at the water's edge. Bar snacks and à la carte selection.   187

Menai Bank Hotel, Caernarfon, Gwynedd LL55 1BD

Tel/Fax: 01286 673297
e-mail: menaibankhotel@tesconet.co.uk
website: www.menaibankhotel.co.uk
Excellent food and comfortable accommodation in a turn-of-the-century hotel with many original features. Sixteen en suite bedrooms.   163

The Menai Hotel, Bangor, Gwynedd LL57 2BG

Tel: 01248 354200 Fax: 01248 354512
e-mail: info@themenai33.freeserve.co.uk
Nine en suite rooms, lively modern bar, snack and bar meals, evening à la carte. Good views over the Menai Straits.   165

Tegfan Guest House, 4 Church Street, Caernarfon, Gwynedd LL55 1SW

Tel: 01286 673703
Very friendly family-run B&B two minutes from the

harbour and castle, with five comfortable bedrooms, some en suite. Excellent breakfast.

The Three Crowns Inn, Bangor, Gwynedd LL57 1HB

Tel: 01248 351138
A quiet location in the town centre for an inn with three well-furnished B&B guest rooms and a menu of home-cooked dishes. Beer garden.   164

Food and Drink

Celtic Royal Hotel, Caernarfon, Gwynedd LL55 1AY

Tel: 01286 674477 Fax: 01286 674139
e-mail: enquiries@celtic-royal.co.uk
website: www.celtic-royal.co.uk
110 fully equipped en suite bedrooms in a newly refurbished town centre hotel near the Castle. Restaurant, bar, gym, swimming pool.   166

The Gazelle Hotel, Glyn Garth, Menai Bridge, Anglesey LL59 5PD

Tel: 01248 713364 Fax: 01248 713167
website: www.gazellehotel.fsnet.co.uk
Nine rooms in a little gem of a hotel in a picturesque setting at the water's edge. Bar snacks and à la carte selection.   187

The Marquis, Rhosybol, Nr Amlwch, Anglesey LL68 9PT

Tel: 01407 380283
Friendly pub with good beers and a varied range of bar snacks and main meals. Beer garden, pool table, darts, live weekend entertainment.

Menai Bank Hotel, Caernarfon, Gwynedd LL55 1BD

Tel/Fax: 01286 673297
e-mail: menaibankhotel@tesconet.co.uk
website: www.menaibankhotel.co.uk
Excellent food and comfortable accommodation in a turn-of-the-century hotel with many original features. Sixteen en suite bedrooms.   163

The Menai Hotel, Bangor, Gwynedd LL57 2BG

Tel: 01248 354200 Fax: 01248 354512
e-mail: info@themenai33.freeserve.co.uk
Nine en suite rooms, lively modern bar, snack and bar meals, evening à la carte. Good views over the Menai Straits.   165

The Three Crowns Inn, Bangor, Gwynedd LL57 1HB

Tel: 01248 351138
A quiet location in the town centre for an inn with three well-furnished B&B guest rooms and a menu of home-cooked dishes. Beer garden.   164

ANGLESEY

Many of the visitors entering the Isle of Anglesey from the northern areas of Britain merely have a passing affair with this lovely Welsh island or, to put it more bluntly, have a one-night stand before embarking or disembarking from the Irish Ferry at Holyhead in search of other more lasting attractions across the Irish Sea or further inland through Wales and beyond. But for the discerning traveller to the island, they linger much longer and fall passionately in love with the place as they meander round the beautiful coastline enjoying the scenery and the good beaches. As for the golfing visitors, they hang around to savour the delights of the excellent golf courses on this ancient island, such as Bull Bay, Anglesey and Holyhead.

To reach the island motorists have to cross over the Menai Strait by way of one of the two historical bridges that span the strait. The old Menai Suspension Bridge, which is situated close to the university town of Bangor, was built by Telford in 1819, and was the first bridge of its kind in the world. Still on display at Ban-gor Museum are the drawings prepared by Telford when he designed the famous bridge. A short distance away is the Britannia Bridge, which carries the railway over the Menai Strait. The original bridge was damaged by fire in 1970 and was replaced by this more modern and stronger structure. After crossing the Menai Bridge the first town you enter is that of Menai Bridge, the small Victorian town named after Telford's historic suspension bridge. Close by lies the village with the longest name in the world, marked on the maps as Llanfair P. G, but given it's correct

Menai Bridge

name of Llanfairpwllgwyngyllgogerychwyrnddrobwllllandysiliogogoch, it is the best tongue-twister in the world. Near that mouthful of a village is Plas Newydd, once the stately home of the Marquess of Anglesey, whose family member Lord Paget (the first holder of the Anglesey title) distinguished himself in the Napoleonic Wars when commanding the cavalry first at Corunna and then, as the Earl of Uxbridge, at the famous Battle of Waterloo. The Marquess finally gave the impressive 18th century mansion to the National Trust, which is now open to the public. This idyllic building is situated on the banks of the Menai Strait, and contains Rex Whistler's largest wall painting, which alone makes the visit well worthwhile.

Keeping the Menai Strait to your right and taking the A545 road, the next town is Beaumaris, which stands on the shore of the narrow Strait. A town of much historical interest, it has many fine buildings. Beaumaris Castle was built by King Edward I in 1295 to guard the town from the Welsh who attempted to cross the Menai Strait. A formidable fortress, it withheld attacks from the Welsh and the Normans and is still in a remarkably good state, despite being captured in 1646 by General Mytton from the Royalist soldiers. Much of the castle is now covered in ivy and other similar foliage, which gives it a rather sombre appearance, but there is much to explore there.

Other places of interest include the Victorian Gaol House in Steeple Street. Here can be seen the place of execution and an old wooden treadmill amongst other things of interest. Beaumaris Church has in its porch a coffin lid with an effigy inscribed on it said to be Joan the unfaithful wife of Prince Llywelyn and daughter of King John. The coffin itself was found in the 19th century after being used on a farm as a water-trough! Beaumaris Town also has a good selection of inns, shops, cosy tearooms and restaurants to enjoy.

Further along the coast is the village of Penmon, which has the remains of a primitive fort, a wishing well and, most importantly, the ruins of an abbey founded by St Seriol in the sixth century. A few miles offshore is the famous Puffin Island, which as the name suggests, is an important breeding ground for that dumpy bird the Puffin. In ancient times a monastery stood on this small island, which was built by monks who decided to settle there. It was used as a burial place for the monks of Penmon Abbey, and Madgwyn, the Ruler of Gwynedd, is also recorded as

Beaumaris Castle

being interned there in 547. The marauding Danes, however, destroyed the monastery in ad 853 and named the island Priestholm.

Heading north-west from Beaumaris you reach the inland market town of Llangefni, Anglesey's centre of administration, because of its central location on the island. A small farmhouse close to Llangefni and known as Penmynydd, is recorded as being the home of Owen Tudor who courted and married the widow of Henry V. Edmund, one of their three sons, then married the daughter of John of Gaunt. They became the parents of Henry VII, who later became the first Tudor King of England. Who would have thought that this obscure farmhouse in the Anglesey countryside would play such a prominent and important role in the history of this small island of ours? If you are interested in this part of our history I recommend you read the wonderful historical novels of American author Sharon Penman.

Back towards the coast in an easterly direction is the splendidly located Red Wharf Bay. Here lies the tiny and peaceful hamlet of Red Wharf, situated at the end of a glorious stretch of sand that sweeps eastwards for five miles. Further north from Red Wharf are the two small but popular seaside resorts of Bennllech and Moelfre. Both resorts are renowned for the firm sands on their lovely beaches, but Moelfre has a sad tale to tell. In October 1859 the Australian ship Royal Charter was heading for the port of Liverpool, not too many miles away, but got into difficulties and sank close to the beach at Moelfre with a cargo of gold valued at a quarter of a million pounds sterling, but the great tragedy was that 465 people were drowned. It is said that many local people became rich overnight from the fact that many of those drowned wore money pouches filled with much gold. A sad tale but apparently quite true. Eighty years later the area witnessed another great tragedy when the submarine HMS Thetis, failed to surface when on trials close to Traeth Bychan Beach. Later the unfortunate vessel was beached at Traeth Bychan with the loss of ninety-nine submariners. Today at Llangallgo stands a memorial in the shape of an obelisk for those unfortunate sailors. As for the village of Moelfre, it now has a very fine lifeboat station to hopefully avoid any more such tragedies.

In the area between Moelfre and its more northern neighbour Amlwch, there are a good number of camp and caravan sites to be found close to the coastline. All in all the Anglesey coastline stretches for 125 miles and is classified as an Area of Outstanding Natural Beauty, with 24 of its fine beaches holding awards. The old market town of Amlwch lies among the rugged landscape of the north eastern end of Anglesey and boasts a fine Heritage Museum in its port area. It also has an interesting Catholic Church known as Our Lady Star of the Sea and is built in the shape of an upturned keel of a boat. The best day to visit Amlwch is on a Friday, which is Market Day. There is also excellent sea fishing among the rocks close to the port area, and not too far away is the splendid Bull Bay Golf Club with 18-holes of splendid heathland on top of a cliff.

The Romans discovered copper in the nearby Parys Mountain, and the remains of a Roman bathhouse can still be seen close to Amlwch. Copper continued to be mined here in the 18th century, and the port at Amlych is recorded as having loaded into ships more than eighty thousand tons of copper annually. The town was also made famous because of its tobacco-processing, and the then widely known Amlwch Shag was a favourite among pipe smokers. However, Amlwch had its moment of shame when one of the locals brought home a red cap, which he had taken from a corpse that had been thrown overboard from a ship off Bull Bay. The unfortunate seaman had been suffering from the dreaded plague and the local man who, after wearing the cap for a number of days, was infected with the disease and became responsible for the disease spreading through the island. Locally it was talked about as the "Plague of the Red Cap", from which many islanders failed to survive.

As you travel westwards to the village of Cemaes you will find that the coastline gives out a more rugged and rocky appearance and the sea in this area is rather treacherous because of the very strong currents. Cemaes is unique inasmuch that it has the only church in Wales dedicated to Ireland's St Patrick. It appears that the patron saint of Ireland landed safely close by Cemaes after crossing the rough Irish Sea in a coracle without any oars or sails to assist him. To mark this amazing journey there is also a small island close by which is known as the Island of St Patrick.

Continue southwards along the A5025 and you reach a place known simply as Valley, where the road meets a junction of the A5 trunk road. Just off the A5025 at Llanddeusant is the only working windmill in the Principality. Built during the time of the Napoleonic Wars it was restored and opened in 1986, from which time visitors have been able to purchase genuine stoneground flour. From Valley the A5 road crosses the Beddmanarch Bay into Holy Island. Here the road and railway line ends at Holyhead for the ferry terminal to Dublin. Holyhead is the largest town on Anglesey and one that is usually ignored by people more concerned with boarding or disembarking from the ferry. Close by, however, there are excellent sailing, golfing and fishing facilities. South of Holyhead at Trearddur Bay is the very fine Holyhead Golf Club. The town of Holyhead boasts a covered market, cinema and theatre, whilst rest of the Holy Island boasts a number of award winning beaches and a spectacular coastline. Less than half an hour from Holyhead by road is North Stack Point, which offers excellent scenery from the clifftop. Above the point is the summit of Holyhead Mountain, where can be seen impressive views of Snowdonia, the Isle of Man, and the Irish coast. On a clear day one can also see the mountains of the Lake District, whilst on the lower slope can be found the remains of the ancient fort of Gaer-y-Twr.

Along this coastline of the Holy Island which reaches out into the Irish Sea, can be seen many varieties of bird life. At South Stack there are spectacular colonies of many sea birds, including Puffins, Razorbills and Guillemots. Grey Seals are also very much in evidence. Along these cliffs excavated rock dwellings of prehistoric times, known as "Huts of the Irish", are to be found. Heading back inland past Valley on the A5 and then turning south along the A4080, you reach Rhosneigr where you find the Anglesey Golf Club and some excellent beaches. Continue to journey southeast and the next place of interest after crossing the River Cefni is the village of Newborough. Close by is the Malltraeth Sands, a wide inlet consisting of sand and marshland with a number of camp sites nearby. On the A4080 signposted from Newborough, lies the Newborough Forest, a Forest Enterprise site of pine forest with many miles of walks and rides.

Here can be spotted many waterfowl, ravens, crossbills and siskins. Good car parking, toilet facilities, an information centre and dog-walking paths are also available.

Between Newborough and the Menai Bridge there is much of interest to be seen, including the Bryn Celli Ddu prehistoric burial chamber, the finest of all the burial chambers within the Principality. If you have time to visit the inland regions of Anglesey there are more interesting places, including Cefni Reservoir and the much larger Alaw Reservoir, near Llanerchymedd. Indeed, the lovely Isle of Anglesey has much to offer the more discerning visitor. Crossing the Irish Sea can maybe wait a while.

South Stack, Holyhead

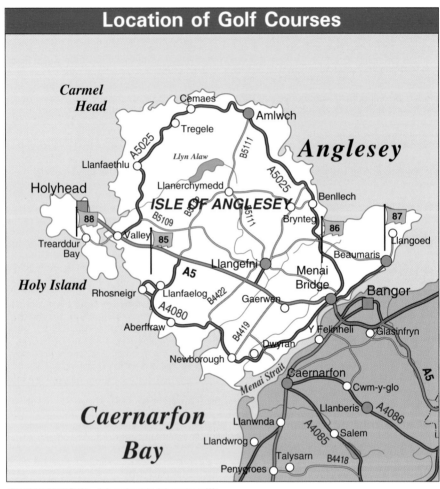

Location of Golf Courses

Anglesey Golf Club

Station Road, Rhosneigr, LL64 5QX
Tel: 01407 811202 Fax: 01407 810219

The Anglesey Golf Club is situated at Rhosneigr, some 8 miles southeast from Holyhead and off the A408 road on the main island of Anglesey. Another course with a good age after being founded in 1914, the course was later improved upon by George Duncan, who remodelled a number of holes only to be left fuming when the R. A. F. decided they needed a section of the course for their requirements and rapidly requisitioned such land. Nevertheless, the Anglesey course still retained plenty of space to continue the Royal and Ancient Game as it originally started in Scotland in 1454 when seeing the light of day on seaside linksland. The Anglesey course is layed out on such typical terrain, flattish seaside land with tough patches of heather and troublesome sand dunes to negotiate, which all add to the enjoyment of playing a truly genuine links course. Like many other links lay-outs, trouble can lie at every hole and at places on the course where you least expect it. The cosy clubhouse offers full facilities; the railway stops close-by and there are a number of caravan and camping sites along the pleasant beach areas to attract the holiday golfer.

Sec/Manager:	Claire Preece
Professional:	P. Lovell
Directions:	½ mile N of Rhosneigr. From center take Station Rd (A4080) north. Entrance after ½ mile on left hand side near sharp right hand bend.
Date Founded:	1914
Type of Course:	Parkland
No of Holes:	18
Length:	6300 yds (5815 mtrs)
Par:	68

SSS:	68
Green Fees:	Weekdays: Winter £10 per day, Summer £15 per day; Weekends/Bank Holidays: Winter £15 per day, Summer £20 per day.
Visitors:	Welcome: Contact Club in advance.
Societies:	Welcome: Contact Club in advance.
Facilities:	Putting Green, Club Hire, Trolley Hire, Buggy Hire, Restaurant

Accommodation, Food and Drink

Reference numbers below refer to detailed information provided in section 2

Accommodation

Bull Bay Hotel, Bull Bay, Anglesey LL68 9SH
Tel/Fax: 01407 830223
A fine hotel overlooking Bull Bay, with gardens running down to the beach. Ten comfortable en suite rooms: bar and restaurant menus.   188

The Kings Arms, Holyhead, Anglesey LL65 1DL
Tel: 01407 762528
Ten en suite bedrooms have just been added to this fine old pub. Good home cooking, with snacks served all day and a good-value carte.   190

Lastra Farm Hotel, Amlwch, Anglesey LL68 9TF
Tel: 01407 830906 Fax: 01407 832522
e-mail: booking@lastra-hotel.com
website: www.lastra-hotel.com
A beautifully restored 17th century farmhouse a mile inland from Bull Bay, with tastefully appointed bedrooms and a top-class restaurant.   186

Menai Bank Hotel, Caernarfon, Gwynedd LL55 1BD
Tel/Fax: 01286 673297
e-mail: menaibankhotel@tesconet.co.uk
website: www.menaibankhotel.co.uk
Excellent food and comfortable accommodation in a turn-of-the-century hotel with many original features. Sixteen en suite bedrooms.   163

The Menai Hotel, Bangor, Gwynedd LL57 2BG
Tel: 01248 354200 Fax: 01248 354512
e-mail: info@themenai33.freeserve.co.uk
Nine en suite rooms, lively modern bar, snack and bar meals, evening à la carte. Good views over the Menai Straits.   165

Penrhos Country Guest House, Gwalchmai, Anglesey LL65 4PW
Tel: 01407 720508
A former farmhouse standing in delightful gardens on the Holyhead – Menai Bridge road. Four large rooms

with sea views. Lounge with Sky TV and excellent breakfasts.   192

The Royal Oak, Malltraeth, Bodorgan, Anglesey LL62 5AS

Tel: 01407 840015

Former cottages make a delightful village pub with coal fires warming a cosy bar and lounge. Excellent food includes local seafood and game. Four letting bedrooms.   191

Trecastell Hotel, Bull Bay, Anglesey LL68 9SA

Tel: 01407 830651 Fax: 01407 832114
e-mail: trecastell@aol.com
A classic seaside hotel overlooking the bay, with 14 well-appointed en suite bedrooms and excellent eating in the lounge-café and non-smoking restaurant.   189

Food and Drink

Bull Bay Hotel, Bull Bay, Anglesey LL68 9SH

Tel/Fax: 01407 830223
A fine hotel overlooking Bull Bay, with gardens running down to the beach. Ten comfortable en suite rooms: bar and restaurant menus.   188

The Kings Arms, Holyhead, Anglesey LL65 1DL

Tel: 01407 762528
Ten en suite bedrooms have just been added to this fine old pub. Good home cooking, with snacks served all day and a good-value carte.   190

Lastra Farm Hotel, Amlwch, Anglesey LL68 9TF

Tel: 01407 830906 Fax: 01407 832522
e-mail: booking@lastra-hotel.com
website: www.lastra-hotel.com
A beautifully restored 17th century farmhouse a mile inland from Bull Bay, with tastefully appointed bedrooms and a top-class restaurant.   186

Menai Bank Hotel, Caernarfon, Gwynedd LL55 1BD

Tel/Fax: 01286 673297
e-mail: menaibankhotel@tesconet.co.uk
website: www.menaibankhotel.co.uk
Excellent food and comfortable accommodation in a turn-of-the-century hotel with many original features. Sixteen en suite bedrooms.   163

The Menai Hotel, Bangor, Gwynedd LL57 2BG

Tel: 01248 354200 Fax: 01248 354512
e-mail: info@themenai33.freeserve.co.uk
Nine en suite rooms, lively modern bar, snack and bar meals, evening à la carte. Good views over the Menai Straits.   165

The Royal Oak, Malltraeth, Bodorgan, Anglesey LL62 5AS

Tel: 01407 840015
Former cottages make a delightful village pub with coal fires warming a cosy bar and lounge. Excellent food includes local seafood and game. Four letting bedrooms.   191

Trecastell Hotel, Bull Bay, Anglesey LL68 9SA

Tel: 01407 830651 Fax: 01407 832114
e-mail: trecastell@aol.com
A classic seaside hotel overlooking the bay, with 14 well-appointed en suite bedrooms and excellent eating in the lounge-café and non-smoking restaurant.   189

Bull Bay Golf Club

Beaumaris LL58 8YW

Tel: 01407 830960 Fax: 01407 832612

The golf course at Bull Bay lies close to the small town of Amlwch and on clifftops, which command far seeing views of the mountains of Snowdonia and the Isle of Man. The most northerly golf course in Wales, it is laid out on tough and rugged heathland which was provided by the Marquess of Anglesey, who not only paid for the entire cost of creating the course but also for the original clubhouse. The designer was Herbert Fowler of Walton Heath fame, who worked miracles on this windswept headland terrain that overlooks a rocky coastline. An exhibition match between James Braid and J. H. Taylor heralded the opening of the course in 1913, and was memorable from the fact that the highly-talented James Braid took an eight at the short third hole after failing to negotiate a smallish ravine.

During that period David Lloyd George regarded the course as one of his favourites and often played there, no doubt cursing in his strong Welsh language whenever he found trouble amongst the thick gorse, which is prevalent at Bull Bay. Parts of the course, however, give the appearance of a parkland course with the trees that edge the greens. During the 1960's the course was a mere 5,700 yards but has since been extended to 6, 276 yards and a tough par of 70.

A feature of the course is that 11 of the holes are above your eyeline as you attempt to play your approach shot, which of course gives you a feeling of uncertainty on how to play the shot. As for the tee shots, you find that the fairways lie below you, which tempts you to open your shoulders, often with disastrous results because of the heavy rough that edges a number of the fairways. The long par-4 18th hole is a great challenge. Downhill all the way, the views from the tee can distract you from your shot if you are not careful. This friendly old club now boasts a fine new clubhouse with a balcony overlooking the final green. On a lovely summer's day it is the perfect spot to relax after enjoying your round, which you will not fail to do no matter how badly you played this delightful clifftop course. The clubhouse also has an excellent restaurant and a fully stocked golf shop.

Sec/Manager:	Mr Furlong
Professional:	John Burns
Directions:	1 mile SW of Beaumaris. From centre take the A545 to the SW outskirts and turn right into Allt Goch Bach. Entrance is on right hand side after ½ mile.
Date Founded:	1913
Type of Course:	Heathland
No of Holes:	18
Length:	6276 yds (5793 mtrs)
Par:	70
SSS:	70
Green Fees:	Weekdays:£20 per day; Weekends/Bank Holidays: £25 per day
Visitors:	Welcome: By arrangement. Contact Club in advance
Societies:	Welcome: By arrangement. Contact Club in advance
Facilities:	Putting Green, Practice Ground, Trolley Hire, Buggy Hire, Bar, Restaurant

Accommodation, Food and Drink

Reference numbers below refer to detailed information provided in section 2

Accommodation

Bull Bay Hotel, Bull Bay, Anglesey LL68 9SH
Tel/Fax: 01407 830223
A fine hotel overlooking Bull Bay, with gardens running down to the beach. Ten comfortable en suite rooms: bar and restaurant menus.   188

The Gazelle Hotel, Glyn Garth, Menai Bridge, Anglesey LL59 5PD
Tel: 01248 713364 Fax: 01248 713167
website: www.gazellehotel.fsnet.co.uk
Nine rooms in a little gem of a hotel in a picturesque setting at the water's edge. Bar snacks and à la carte selection.   187

The Kings Arms, Holyhead, Anglesey LL65 1DL
Tel: 01407 762528
Ten en suite bedrooms have just been added to this fine old pub. Good home cooking, with snacks served all day and a good-value carte.   190

Lastra Farm Hotel, Amlwch, Anglesey LL68 9TF
Tel: 01407 830906 Fax: 01407 832522
e-mail: booking@lastra-hotel.com
website: www.lastra-hotel.com
A beautifully restored 17th century farmhouse a mile inland from Bull Bay, with tastefully appointed bedrooms and a top-class restaurant.   186

The Menai Hotel, Bangor, Gwynedd LL57 2BG
Tel: 01248 354200 Fax: 01248 354512
e-mail: info@themenai33.freeserve.co.uk
Nine en suite rooms, lively modern bar, snack and bar meals, evening à la carte. Good views over the Menai Straits.   165

Penrhos Country Guest House, Gwalchmai, Anglesey LL65 4PW
Tel: 01407 720508
A former farmhouse standing in delightful gardens on the Holyhead – Menai Bridge road. Four large rooms with sea views. Lounge with Sky TV and excellent breakfasts.   192

The Three Crowns Inn, Bangor, Gwynedd LL57 1HB
Tel: 01248 351138
A quiet location in the town centre for an inn with three well-furnished B&B guest rooms and a menu of home-cooked dishes. Beer garden.   164

Trecastell Hotel, Bull Bay, Anglesey LL68 9SA
Tel: 01407 830651 Fax: 01407 832114
e-mail: trecastell@aol.com
A classic seaside hotel overlooking the bay, with 14 well-appointed en suite bedrooms and excellent eating in the lounge-café and non-smoking restaurant.   189

Food and Drink

Bull Bay Hotel, Bull Bay, Anglesey LL68 9SH

Tel/Fax: 01407 830223

A fine hotel overlooking Bull Bay, with gardens
running down to the beach. Ten comfortable en suite
rooms: bar and restaurant menus.   188

**The Gazelle Hotel, Glyn Garth, Menai Bridge,
Anglesey LL59 5PD**

Tel: 01248 713364 Fax: 01248 713167
website: www.gazellehotel.fsnet.co.uk

Nine rooms in a little gem of a hotel in a picturesque
setting at the water's edge. Bar snacks and à la carte
selection.   187

The Kings Arms, Holyhead, Anglesey LL65 1DL

Tel: 01407 762528

Ten en suite bedrooms have just been added to this
fine old pub. Good home cooking, with snacks served
all day and a good-value carte.   190

Lastra Farm Hotel, Amlwch, Anglesey LL68 9TF

Tel: 01407 830906 Fax: 01407 832522
e-mail: booking@lastra-hotel.com
website: www.lastra-hotel.com

A beautifully restored 17th century farmhouse a mile
inland from Bull Bay, with tastefully appointed
bedrooms and a top-class restaurant.   186

**The Marquis, Rhosybol, Nr Amlwch,
Anglesey LL68 9PT**

Tel: 01407 380283

Friendly pub with good beers and a varied range of
bar snacks and main meals. Beer garden, pool table,
darts, live weekend entertainment.

The Menai Hotel, Bangor, Gwynedd LL57 2BG

Tel: 01248 354200 Fax: 01248 354512
e-mail: info@themenai33.freeserve.co.uk

Nine en suite rooms, lively modern bar, snack and bar
meals, evening à la carte. Good views over the Menai
Straits.   165

**The Three Crowns Inn, Bangor,
Gwynedd LL57 1HB**

Tel: 01248 351138

A quiet location in the town centre for an inn with
three well-furnished B&B guest rooms and a menu of
home-cooked dishes. Beer garden.   164

Trecastell Hotel, Bull Bay, Anglesey LL68 9SA

Tel: 01407 830651 Fax: 01407 832114
e-mail: trecastell@aol.com

A classic seaside hotel overlooking the bay, with 14
well-appointed en suite bedrooms and excellent
eating in the lounge-café and non-smoking
restaurant.   189

Henllys Hall Golf Club

Llanfaes, Beaumaris LL58 8HU

Tel: 01248 811717 Fax: 01248 811511

Sec/Manager:	Peter Maton
Professional:	None
Directions:	4 miles NE of Menai Bridge. From Menai Bridge take the A545 (Beaumaris). On entering Beaumaris turn right onto the B1509 and follow for 1 mile, turn left onto minor road (Llan-Faes). Henllys Hall Hotel is signed with entrance on left hand side.
Date Founded:	1997
Type of Course:	Parkland
No of Holes:	18
Length:	5766 yds (5322 mtrs)

Par:	72
SSS:	70
Green Fees:	Weekdays:£18.00; Weekends/ Bank Holidays: £24.00
Visitors:	Welcome: Contact Club by telephone in advance
Societies:	Welcome: Contact Club by telephone in advance
Facilities:	Chipping Green, Practice Ground, Trolley Hire, Buggy Hire, Bar, Restaurant

Accommodation, Food and Drink

Reference numbers below refer to detailed information provided in section 2

Accommodation

Bull Bay Hotel, Bull Bay, Anglesey LL68 9SH

Tel/Fax: 01407 830223

A fine hotel overlooking Bull Bay, with gardens running down to the beach. Ten comfortable en suite rooms: bar and restaurant menus. 188

The Gazelle Hotel, Glyn Garth, Menai Bridge, Anglesey LL59 5PD

Tel: 01248 713364 Fax: 01248 713167
website: www.gazellehotel.fsnet.co.uk

Nine rooms in a little gem of a hotel in a picturesque setting at the water's edge. Bar snacks and à la carte selection. 187

Lastra Farm Hotel, Amlwch, Anglesey LL68 9TF

Tel: 01407 830906 Fax: 01407 832522
e-mail: booking@lastra-hotel.com
website: www.lastra-hotel.com

A beautifully restored 17th century farmhouse a mile inland from Bull Bay, with tastefully appointed bedrooms and a top-class restaurant. 186

Penrhos Country Guest House, Gwalchmai, Anglesey LL65 4PW

Tel: 01407 720508

A former farmhouse standing in delightful gardens on the Holyhead – Menai Bridge road. Four large rooms with sea views. Lounge with Sky TV and excellent breakfasts. 192

Trecastell Hotel, Bull Bay, Anglesey LL68 9SA

Tel: 01407 830651 Fax: 01407 832114
e-mail: trecastell@aol.com

A classic seaside hotel overlooking the bay, with 14 well-appointed en suite bedrooms and excellent eating in the lounge-café and non-smoking restaurant. 189

Food and Drink

Bull Bay Hotel, Bull Bay, Anglesey LL68 9SH

Tel/Fax: 01407 830223

A fine hotel overlooking Bull Bay, with gardens running down to the beach. Ten comfortable en suite rooms: bar and restaurant menus. 188

The Gazelle Hotel, Glyn Garth, Menai Bridge, Anglesey LL59 5PD

Tel: 01248 713364 Fax: 01248 713167
website: www.gazellehotel.fsnet.co.uk

Nine rooms in a little gem of a hotel in a picturesque setting at the water's edge. Bar snacks and à la carte selection. 187

Lastra Farm Hotel, Amlwch, Anglesey LL68 9TF

Tel: 01407 830906 Fax: 01407 832522
e-mail: booking@lastra-hotel.com
website: www.lastra-hotel.com

A beautifully restored 17th century farmhouse a mile inland from Bull Bay, with tastefully appointed bedrooms and a top-class restaurant. 186

The Marquis, Rhosybol, Nr Amlwch, Anglesey LL68 9PT

Tel: 01407 380283

Friendly pub with good beers and a varied range of bar snacks and main meals. Beer garden, pool table, darts, live weekend entertainment.

Trecastell Hotel, Bull Bay, Anglesey LL68 9SA

Tel: 01407 830651 Fax: 01407 832114
e-mail: trecastell@aol.com

A classic seaside hotel overlooking the bay, with 14 well-appointed en suite bedrooms and excellent eating in the lounge-café and non-smoking restaurant. 189

Holyhead Golf Club

Trearddur Bay, Holyhead, Anglesey LL65 2YL

Tel: 01407 763279 Fax: 01407 763279

Linked by a causeway to the main island of Anglesey, this highly popular heathland course is situated on the northern end of Holy Island overlooking the beautiful Trearddur Bay. Another of James Braid's quality creations - he designed the course in 1912 - the course has great character and offers a daunting challenge, even more so when the Irish Sea releases the mighty southwest gales which the course has no defence against. If you have never played a seaside course before, when such winds blow you will realise why the Open Championship is always played on a links course and is regarded as the greatest major golf championship in the world - only the greatest golfers in the field survive those conditions. As for yourself you a may find it a tough struggle, but it's nevertheless a memorable and exhilarating experience. A wonderful and intriguing course, Holyhead has hosted a number of quality amateur tournaments including the Welsh Amateur Strokeplay Championship, The Welsh Ladies' Amateur Championship, and both Welsh Boys' and Welsh Girls' Amateur Championship.

Quite undulating with steep hummocks, thickish heather and gorse and with fairways which force the ball to go right, this delightful venue is not as easy as it appears when seen for the first time, but a course which is made for the holiday golfer when the conditions are perfect. For myself I find it one of my favourite places to play during the summer months because of its glorious views and the peaceful atmosphere of the place. The view from the elevated tee at the 10th hole is quite stunning. Here you have totally uninterrupted all round panoramic views of the Irish Sea, The Lleyn Peninsular and Snowdonia. Boasting also an excellent clubhouse, there is the added attraction of the club having its very own accommodation and special arrangements with local guest houses so that holiday golfers have the opportunity of staying close to the course.

There is rather a strange tale in how the Holyhead club came into being. A Commander Holland, who was a superintendent in the marine section of the old London and North Western railway, often wondered what his seamen did to pass their leisure time when waiting a day for their vessels to return to Holyhead. He discovered that mostly they went and played golf and decided to try out the game for himself. Becoming totally addicted to the game he set about persuading the

railway to build a golf course close to Holyhead, whereby railway guests at the nearby railway hotel would boost the hotel takings by staying longer. To cut a long story short, the railway company built the course, the hotel prospered until the London to Dun Laoghaire express train came into being and whisked the travellers to Ireland and vice versa in double quick time to their intended destination without having to linger. Therefore, the golf course became a "white elephant" and was offered to the local club members for £11,000. Together they somehow scraped up the amount and later recouped some of the money by selling some of the precious land as individual bungalow-building sites. The present club members have, indeed, a lot to thank Commander Holland for.

Recently re-routing two holes-the 9th has now become a par five - the course now stretches to 6,080 yards with a par of 71. I am certain you will enjoy it.

Sec/Manager:	None
Professional:	Steve Williams
Directions:	1½ miles S of Holyhead. From centre take the B4545 (Trearddur) after 1¼ miles turn left into Lon Garrog Fawr. Entrance is on right hand side.
Date Founded:	1912
Type of Course:	Heathland
No of Holes:	18
Length:	6080 yds (5612 mtrs)
Par:	71
SSS:	71
Green Fees:	Weekdays:£19.00; Weekends/ Bank Holidays:£25.00
Visitors:	Welcome: Contact Club by telephone in advance, unable to play on Saturday's
Societies:	Welcome: Contact Club in advance
Facilities:	Putting Green, Chipping Green, Club Hire, Trolley Hire, Bar, Restaurant

Accommodation, Food and Drink

Reference numbers below refer to detailed information provided in section 2

Accommodation

Bull Bay Hotel, Bull Bay, Anglesey LL68 9SH
Tel/Fax: 01407 830223

A fine hotel overlooking Bull Bay, with gardens running down to the beach. Ten comfortable en suite rooms: bar and restaurant menus. 188

The Gazelle Hotel, Glyn Garth, Menai Bridge, Anglesey LL59 5PD

Tel: 01248 713364 Fax: 01248 713167
website: www.gazellehotel.fsnet.co.uk
Nine rooms in a little gem of a hotel in a picturesque setting at the water's edge. Bar snacks and à la carte selection. 187

The Kings Arms, Holyhead, Anglesey LL65 1DL

Tel: 01407 762528
Ten en suite bedrooms have just been added to this fine old pub. Good home cooking, with snacks served all day and a good-value carte. 190

Lastra Farm Hotel, Amlwch, Anglesey LL68 9TF

Tel: 01407 830906 Fax: 01407 832522
e-mail: booking@lastra-hotel.com
website: www.lastra-hotel.com
A beautifully restored 17th century farmhouse a mile inland from Bull Bay, with tastefully appointed bedrooms and a top-class restaurant. 186

Penrhos Country Guest House, Gwalchmai, Anglesey LL65 4PW

Tel: 01407 720508
A former farmhouse standing in delightful gardens on the Holyhead – Menai Bridge road. Four large rooms with sea views. Lounge with Sky TV and excellent breakfasts. 192

The Royal Oak, Malltraeth, Bodorgan, Anglesey LL62 5AS

Tel: 01407 840015
Former cottages make a delightful village pub with coal fires warming a cosy bar and lounge. Excellent food includes local seafood and game. Four letting bedrooms. 191

Trecastell Hotel, Bull Bay, Anglesey LL68 9SA

Tel: 01407 830651 Fax: 01407 832114
e-mail: trecastell@aol.com
A classic seaside hotel overlooking the bay, with 14 well-appointed en suite bedrooms and excellent eating in the lounge-café and non-smoking restaurant. 189

The Kings Arms, Holyhead, Anglesey LL65 1DL

Tel: 01407 762528
Ten en suite bedrooms have just been added to this fine old pub. Good home cooking, with snacks served all day and a good-value carte. 190

Lastra Farm Hotel, Amlwch, Anglesey LL68 9TF

Tel: 01407 830906 Fax: 01407 832522
e-mail: booking@lastra-hotel.com
website: www.lastra-hotel.com
A beautifully restored 17th century farmhouse a mile inland from Bull Bay, with tastefully appointed bedrooms and a top-class restaurant. 186

The Royal Oak, Malltraeth, Bodorgan, Anglesey LL62 5AS

Tel: 01407 840015
Former cottages make a delightful village pub with coal fires warming a cosy bar and lounge. Excellent food includes local seafood and game. Four letting bedrooms. 191

Trecastell Hotel, Bull Bay, Anglesey LL68 9SA

Tel: 01407 830651 Fax: 01407 832114
e-mail: trecastell@aol.com
A classic seaside hotel overlooking the bay, with 14 well-appointed en suite bedrooms and excellent eating in the lounge-café and non-smoking restaurant. 189

Food and Drink

Bull Bay Hotel, Bull Bay, Anglesey LL68 9SH

Tel/Fax: 01407 830223
A fine hotel overlooking Bull Bay, with gardens running down to the beach. Ten comfortable en suite rooms: bar and restaurant menus. 188

The Gazelle Hotel, Glyn Garth, Menai Bridge, Anglesey LL59 5PD

Tel: 01248 713364 Fax: 01248 713167
website: www.gazellehotel.fsnet.co.uk
Nine rooms in a little gem of a hotel in a picturesque setting at the water's edge. Bar snacks and à la carte selection. 187

CONWY

As I mentioned in the introduction I am not writing about the counties as they are officially recognized but as they are broken down in the Golfer's Handbook. Therefore, this Conwy section is actually part of the vast county of Gwynedd and writing of it as Conwy allows me to feature more of the excellent courses in North Wales. The area I am mainly concentrating on is the north coastal section, which carries the A55 Expressway road system, and the inland area behind it. Starting at the villages of Llanfairfechan and Penmaenmawr-interesting tongue-twisters to anyone not used to the Welsh pronunciations-which lie west of the town of Conwy, these were favourite holiday haunts of Prime Minister W. E. Gladstone. Both these villages have wonderful views of Conwy Bay and Puffin Island beyond. Behind these villages there are some pleasant walks and even better views of the sea, but to the south are a number of wind farms with their countless wind machines looking like something out of space and helping to spoil the views beyond. But away from these frightful things is some beautiful countryside to explore and also a top class caravan site. Near Penmaenmawr is a delightful golf course of the same name. The club was founded way back in 1910, and has an attractive nine-hole course created on pleasant parkland and well worth a visit. The ancient town of Conwy is famous for its magnificent and well preserved castle, its quaint streets and shops and the massive stone walls which surrounds it. First time visitors cannot fail to be impressed by this wonderful old and charming town.

Conwy Castle

Indeed, it has often been described as the Welsh Carcassonne, and it is easy to see why this is so. As you enter the town through one of its Norman gateways you will realise that is was obviously one of the best well-protected towns in Britain and, perhaps, in Europe. This magnificent fortress was rated by King Edward I as the second in importance to Caernarvon Castle of the many fine castles he built to defend North Wales. Started in 1285 by Henry de Elverton it took a mere five years to complete. Indeed, the Norman stonemasons somehow completed ten castles in North Wales in just eighteen years-an amazing feat, even with the help of local conscripted labour. A measure of the expertise of their craft can be taken from the fact that the castles which escaped the destruction of Cromwell's armies still stand in impressive fashion and with just a mere hint of restoration. Adding to the charm of this great fortress at Conwy is the early 19th century suspension bridge built by Telford and designed to appear part of the mediaeval castle.

Dominating the Conway Estuary the castle suffered many attacks and Edward I was besieged here in 1294. King Richard II sought refuge on his way from Ireland in 1399, but was betrayed and captured by Bolingbroke and confined in a tower of nearby Flint Castle. Following the Civil War the Earl of Conwy was given permission by Charles II to dismantle the castle in 1665, but he only succeeded in destroying a small portion thanks to his ship carrying the materials to Ireland for him to build himself a fine mansion there, suffered in a violent storm and sank beneath the waves. The castle walls surrounding the town are open to the public along with the castle and make an interesting walk above the old town. As well as the castle there are many other things of interest for the visitor to see. The Tudor mansion of Plas Mawr, a fine example of Elizabethan architecture, was built in 1585 by Robert Wynne, and is worthy of a visit from not only its architectural interest but also because of the antique artefacts on display. Another timbered building close by on the corner of Castle Street and High Street throws out a claim that it is the oldest house in Conwy. Make your way down to the attractive and interesting quayside and you will also discover what is claimed to be the smallest dwelling in the world. Having been inside (I won't add the word 'squeezed"), I would not dispute this claim. I have a soft spot for this lovely old-fashioned town, and so will you when you get there.

After moving east out of Conwy it is best to leave the A55 and take the A549 to the grand old town of Llandudno, which lies between the

Llandudno

two imposing headlands of Great Orme and Little Orme. Once known as the "Queen of Welsh Watering-places, " the town of Llandudno is Wales' largest seaside resort and one which has retained its charm and dignity, which is sadly lacking at a number of British resorts. Here there is no "over the top" noise and brashness or rundown appearance which detracts many visitors. The town has a long, wide frontage overlooking the award-winning North Beach. Many good Victorian-built hotels are to be found along this quiet front, which backs on to the main shopping centre and which is an interesting, bustling and buzzing sort of place. Facing directly west of the town is the West Beach with its quiet sand dunes behind more fine hotels. Llandudno, of course does have many attractions to delight the youngsters, but it tastefully still retains the elegance and splendour of its Edwardian and Victorian era. During the first week of June the resort stages an annual Victorian Extravaganza Weekend to recreate its Victorian past. This spectacular show attracts visitors from all parts of Britain, who enjoy a steam funfair, vintage car displays, street entertainment and attractions, shop stalls, music and locals dressed in Victorian costumes, to name but a few at the fun-filled weekend which continues into the following Monday. During the last week of June there is also staged a Midsummer Musical Festival. At the foot of the Great Orme there is a natural small amphitheatre which has been turned into a beautiful flower-filled garden which is known as "Happy Valley". For the garden enthusiasts there is also the internationally renowned Bodnant Gardens just outside of Llandudno. One can take a trip to the top of the Great Orme to view the stunning scenery of the North Wales coastline and mountains. But long before the Victorians took over Llandudno, the Vikings arrived and liked what they saw of this wonderful spot and stayed to build their settlements. Indeed, it was these mighty warriors who named the Great Orme and Little Orme headlands that stand either side of the long curving bay which takes in the North Beach.

Another point of interest in this elegant resort is the memorial stone with a white rabbit checking the time of day with his watch. This was installed to mark the time when Lewis Carroll spent a holiday at Llandudno, and in doing so was inspired to write the famous children's story Alice in Wonderful. A "must visit" place is Llandudno.

Further along the coast is the small and charming resort of Rhos-on-Sea. Another clean and bustling town with a charm of its very own. Here you will find a sheltered harbour used by a fleet of fishing boats. Having chosen Rhos-on-Sea as a quiet place to stay during my reporting days of covering many Welsh golfing events, I hold a special regard for the small town, which is shared by my long suffering golf widow of a wife who fell in love with Rhos-on-Sea when she first saw it on a fine summer's day. A friendly place with good shops and restaurants, hotels and guest houses, it also has an excellent golf course overlooking Penrhyn Bay. Just a short distance away is the resort of Colwyn Bay, where you rejoin the A55 Expressway. Colwyn Bay is renowned as a paradise for watersport enthusiasts because of its 3 miles of good sands and safe waters. Once a small fishing village it has since grown into a popular holiday resort for families because of the beaches, family holiday attractions and a coastal cycle route. High above Colwyn Bay there is the Welsh Mountain Zoo, a conservation zoo set in garden surroundings. Here there are many endangered and rare animals from throughout the world. Mid-way between Colwyn Bay and Rhyl are the small resorts of Llanddulas and Abergele. Between these two resorts run 7 miles of excellent beach, whilst Abergele also boasts a quality full-sized parkland golf course. Between the villages of

Colwyn Bay

Pensarn Towyn and Kinmel Bay, the good beaches continue and there are a number of caravan and camp sites to be found close to the sea. Heading back to Conwy along the busy A55, when you come to the village of Llandudno Junction take the B5106 which follows the River Conwy through the beautiful Vale of Conwy. Here you will pass close by the aforementioned Bodnant Gardens as you continue on your journey. Pull off the road at the village of Tal-y-cafn and cross over the river and you will discover the ruins of the Roman fort of Canovium. Along a nearby mountain track is an Iron Age Fort, and close by a Youth Hostel.

Along the A470 is the ancient market town of Llanrwst, a pleasant and quiet town with a charming river bridge of some antiquity. This bridge dates back to 1536, which is confirmed in a carving on one side of the bridge. In the parish church one can see the massive stone-tomb of Llywelyn the Great, who was originally buried in 1240 at Aberconwy Abbey. The best time to visit Llanrwst is Wednesday when market day sees the old town bustling with Welsh-speaking shoppers. Further south on the River Conwy and in the valley of the Gwydr Forest, lies the picturesque village of Betws-y-Coed. A popular tourist attraction, it can become somewhat crowded in the summer months but, nevertheless, should be visited because of the natural attractions to be seen in this beautiful location renowned for its picturesque wooded glens and streams. The many and varied beauty-spots are indeed breathtaking. Among the most famous of these is the enchanting Swallow Falls, one of the finest to be seen in Wales. Situated some 2 miles from Betws-y-Coed, the falls occur in the River Llugwy and is bordered by tree-grown slopes and rocks. The Fairy Glen, or given its Welsh name "Ffos Noddyn" (Ditch of the Chasm), is renowned as one

Rhyl Harbour

of the most famous beauty-spots in Britain. A beautifully wooded narrow gorge through which the River Conwy passes, it is situated close to Betws-y-Coed. These are but two of the many enchanting places for which Betws-y-Coed is famed. What makes Betws-y-Coed such an attractive location is the fact that the town has been built at the meeting place of three perfectly clean rivers-the Conwy, the Lledr and the Llugy.

Of interest to golfers is the charming Betws-y-Coed Golf Club. Situated on the outskirts of this charming village, the course is a nine-hole lay-out with full clubhouse facilities and, to state the obvious, is set in beautiful surroundings.

Location of Golf Courses

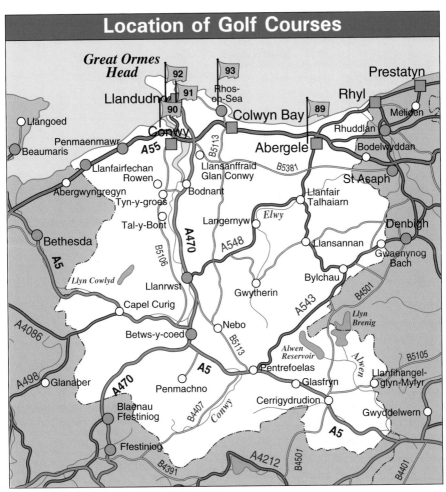

Great Ormes Head

92

93

Prestatyn

Llandudno

91

Rhos-on-Sea

Rhyl

90

Meliden

Llangoed

Colwyn Bay

89

Conwy

Rhuddlan

Penmaenmawr

A55

B5113

Abergele

Bodelwyddan

Beaumaris

Llanfairfechan

Llansanffraid

B5381

St Asaph

Rowen

Glan Conwy

Abergwyngregyn

Bodnant

Llanfair Talhaiarn

Tyn-y-groes

Tal-y-Bont

Langernyw

Elwy

Denbigh

Bethesda

A470

A548

Llansannan

Gwaenynog Bach

A5

B5106

Llyn Cowlyd

Llanrwst

Gwytherin

Bylchau

B4501

Capel Curig

A543

Llyn Brenig

A4086

Betws-y-coed

Nebo

B5113

Alwen Reservoir

A498

Glanaber

A470

A5

Pentrefoelas

Alwen

Llanfihangel-glyn-Myfyr

B5105

Penmachno

Glasfryn

Blaenau Ffestiniog

B4407

Conwy

Cerrigydrudion

A5

Gwyddelwern

Ffestiniog

A4212

B4501

B4401

B4391

© MAPS IN MINUTES ™ 2001   © Crown Copyright, Ordnance Survey 2001

Abergele & Pensarn Golf Club

Tan-y-Gopa Road, Abergele,
Denbighshire LL22 8DS
Tel: 01745 824034 Fax: 01745 824034

Yet another of my North Wales favourite golf courses, and not only because I have a few old golfing friends who are members of Abergele but also because it is a delightful parkland course to play and a friendly clubhouse to relax in after one's round. Situated close to the sea and in the grounds of Gwrych Castle, a magnificent 19th century mock castle which was built by the Countess of Dundonald and which dominates the section of the A55 Expressway bordering the course. The club was actually founded in 1910, but the present course was designed at a later date by Hawtree and Sons, the then well known and prestigious firm of golf architects. A charming easy walking course with a testing par of 72, it meanders through a splendid array of trees and along fairly flat fairways bordered by grassy rough that at least offers a playable shot which although not too easy is also not too difficult. Where the difficulty lies is when the wayward shot gets blocked by the many bushes and trees that add to the beauty of the course but which brings forth words of frustration rather than praise from golfers who are suffering from a constant lack of accuracy. Nevertheless, laid out on the coastal plain and beneath rolling, tree-filled Welsh hills and backed by the lovely old castle, no-one ever leaves Abergele with bad memories because every bad round is quickly forgotten on entering the friendly

clubhouse and enjoying the traditional Welsh fayre it has to offer. Definitely not a club to overlook.

Sec/Manager:	Chris Langdon
Professional:	Ian Runge
Directions:	On the SW outskirts of Abergele. From center take A547 (West) Market St, after ½ mile turn left into Tan-Y- Gopa Rd. Entrance after ½ mile on left hand side
Date Founded:	1910
Type of Course:	Parkland
No of Holes:	18
Length:	6520 yds (6018 mtrs)
Par:	72
SSS:	71
Green Fees:	Weekdays: £25.00; Weekends/ Bank Holidays: £30
Visitors:	Welcome: Contact Club by telephone in advance. Unable to play on Saturdays.
Societies:	Welcome: Contact Club in advance. Unable to play on Saturdays.
Facilities:	Putting Green, Indoor Practice Area, Trolley Hire, Buggy Hire, Bar, Restaurant

Accommodation, Food and Drink

Reference numbers below refer to detailed information provided in section 2

Accommodation

Caerlyr Hall Hotel, Conwy Old Road, Penmaenmawr, Conwy LL34 6SW
Tel: 01492 623518
Nine twin/family rooms in a Victorian country house hotel with bar and restaurant. Golf breaks arranged.

Cayo Guest House, 74 Vale Street, Denbigh, Denbighshire LL16 3BW
Tel: 01745 812686
A friendly guest house with six letting bedrooms, most en suite. Bed & Breakfast, with packed lunches and evening meals by arrangement.

Graig Park Hotel & Country Club, Dyserth, Denbighshire LL18 6DX
Tel: 01745 571022 Fax: 01745 571024
Hotel & Country Club set among lawns and woodland near the North Wales coast. Hotel accommodation or fully equipped log cabins. Sports and leisure facilities, restaurant. 199

The Grosvenor Hotel, Colwyn Bay, Conwy LL29 7PS

Tel: 01492 530798 Fax: 01492 531586
e-mail: thegrosvenor@freenetname.co.uk
website: www.hotel-grosvenor.co.uk

A friendly, relaxing hotel with 18 bedrooms, many of family size. A la carte menu and bar snacks. Bar, lounge, pool table.   193

The Old Rectory Country House, Llansanffraid Glan Conwy, Conwy LL28 5LP

Tel: 01492 580611 Fax: 01492 584555
e-mail: info@oldrectorycountryhouse.co.uk
website: www.oldrectorycountryhouse.co.uk

A small country house in a secluded setting with Snowdonian vistas. Six splendid en suite rooms (some half-testers or four-poster) and outstanding food from a Michelin starred chef.

Plas Elwy Hotel, The Roe, St Asaph, Denbighshire LL17 0LT

Tel: 01745 582263 Fax: 01745 583864
e-mail: plaselwy@gtleisure.co.uk
website: www.gtleisure.co.uk/plaselwy

Thirteen en suite bedrooms with tv and telephone in an 1850s building and adjacent lodge. Beamed restaurant, steaks a speciality.

Food and Drink

Caerlyr Hall Hotel, Conwy Old Road, Penmaenmawr, Conwy LL34 6SW

Tel: 01492 623518

Nine twin/family rooms in a Victorian country house hotel with bar and restaurant. Golf breaks arranged.

Graig Park Hotel & Country Club, Dyserth, Denbighshire LL18 6DX

Tel: 01745 571022 Fax: 01745 571024

Hotel & Country Club set among lawns and woodland near the North Wales coast. Hotel accommodation or fully equipped log cabins. Sports and leisure facilities, restaurant.   199

The Grosvenor Hotel, Colwyn Bay, Conwy LL29 7PS

Tel: 01492 530798 Fax: 01492 531586
e-mail: thegrosvenor@freenetname.co.uk
website: www.hotel-grosvenor.co.uk

A friendly, relaxing hotel with 18 bedrooms, many of family size. A la carte menu and bar snacks. Bar, lounge, pool table.   193

Lakeside Inn, Tan-y-Mynydd, Moelfre, Abergele, Conwy LL22 9RF

Tel: 01745 823691

Good choice of lunch and evening food in a country pub that's part of a leisure complex. Pool room, beer garden.

The Old Rectory Country House, Llansanffraid Glan Conwy, Conwy LL28 5LP

Tel: 01492 580611 Fax: 01492 584555
e-mail: info@oldrectorycountryhouse.co.uk

website: www.oldrectorycountryhouse.co.uk

A small country house in a secluded setting with Snowdonian vistas. Six splendid en suite rooms (some half-testers or four-poster) and outstanding food from a Michelin starred chef.

Plas Elwy Hotel, The Roe, St Asaph, Denbighshire LL17 0LT

Tel: 01745 582263 Fax: 01745 583864
e-mail: plaselwy@gtleisure.co.uk
website: www.gtleisure.co.uk/plaselwy

Thirteen en suite bedrooms with tv and telephone in an 1850s building and adjacent lodge. Beamed restaurant, steaks a speciality.

Conwy Golf Club (Caernarvonshire)

Morfa, Conwy LL32 8ER
Tel: 01492 593400 Fax: 01492 593363

Situated on the western edge of the fascinating old town of Conwy and offering superb views of Llandudno's Great Orme and the Isle of Anglesey, the exciting Conwy course (or Caernarvonshire to give it the old name it is also known by) is rated by many golfers as tougher than even the Royal St David's course. Laid out on the Morfa Peninsular when the Conwy club was founded in 1890, records tell us that golf was actually played on the Morfa as far back as 1869 when three Scots golfing enthusiasts laid out a few holes to practice the game while away from home. Indeed, a visitor's book which somehow escaped when the original clubhouse burnt down with all the club records suggests that the club was alive and booming in an unofficial capacity a little time later from that date. It is also recorded that by 1875 a few members from the Royal Liverpool Club at Hoylake visited the Morfa, liked what they saw and brought in an expert to build a 12-hole course on this beautiful piece of linksland, and much later the course gained quite a reputation after being extended to 18-holes when the club became officially formed, and as a

result hosted many championship events until the First World War cast a dark shadow over civilisation during 1914-18 and the club was taken by the government for an army training establishment. George Duncan, an Aberdonian, was appointed the club's first professional in 1910, and he proved to be such a great talent that not only did he create a new professional record of 65 shortly after joining the club but he also went on to win The Open Championship in 1920 and become a Ryder Cup player-beating the legendary American player Walter Hagen by 10 and 8 in 1929 at Moortown, Leeds, thus repeating the win he had over Hagen by 6 and 5 in a match between the American and British professionals in 1926. Many famous people have graced the Conwy fairways including the actor Trevor Howard, whose father-in-law, Captain John Cherry was a member and club captain in 1934-35. He lived near the course and his daughter was the famous actress Helen Cherry.

Having suffered during the World War, the club received another setback when, under great secrecy, it was decided to build the now famous "Mulberry Harbours" for the D-Day invasion of Europe in 1944 on a site which is now part of the second green but was then the 9th green and which was totally lost. Today a commemorative memorial stands on the site where they were constructed and successfully launched on the Conwy Estuary for transport to the invasion beaches. The third oldest club in Wales, a distinction it shares with the Glamorganshire club, this is one of the great British links with a finish that is as tough as they come. Thick gorse grows in profusion along-

side the fairways of the final three holes and I have witnessed and written about many fine players of both sexes who have thrown away certain championship-winning positions when coming to grief by losing a ball in these dense gorse thickets. The 18th also has a nasty ridge crossing it and a few awkward bunkers to contend with. As for the rest of the holes on this wide open and unsheltered links, there is trouble everywhere along the humps and hollows of this outstanding course. Just short of 7, 000 yards, the par 72 is a mighty challenge for even the classiest of golfers, but is always a joy to play. A very friendly club, I can also recommend the fine cooking inside the lovely old clubhouse, which has stood since fire destroyed the original in 1933. Should you be a visiting society the long-standing club professional and genial character, Peter Lees, not only has a superb golf shop but is also available as an after-dinner speaker of some excellence. Conwy Golf Club is a great place to visit.

Sec/Manager:	D Brown
Professional:	P Lees
Directions:	2 miles W of Conwy. From centre take Bangor Rd (A547), pass under the A55 dual carriageway and carry into Meiron Drive, after ½ mile turn left at mini roundabout. Entrance after 100 yds on the left hand side.
Date Founded:	1890
Type of Course:	Links
No of Holes:	18
Length:	6647 yds (6135 mtrs)
Par:	72
SSS:	72
Green Fees:	Weekdays:£25.00; Weekends/ Bank Holidays:£32.00
Visitors:	Welcome: Contact Club by telephone in advance.
Societies:	Welcome: Contact Club in advance. Unable to play on Thursdays
Facilities:	Putting Green, Practice Area, Trolley Hire, Buggy Hire, Bar, Restaurant

Accommodation, Food and Drink

Reference numbers below refer to detailed information provided in section 2

Accommodation

Alexandra Hotel, Clonmel Street, Llandudno,

Conwy LL30 2LE

Tel: 01492 876670 Fax: 01492 872282
Public house with nine en suite family rooms and a
residents' bar. Restaurant. Drying facilities.

**Berthlwyd Hall, Llechwedd, Conwy,
Carnarvonshire LL32 8DQ**

Tel: 01492 592409 Fax: 01492 572290
e-mail: berthlwydhall@hotmail.com
website: www.berthlwydhall.com
Four beautifully appointed bedrooms in a country
manor house with a fine restaurant and an elegant
residents' lounge.   194

**Bryn Arthur, Tabor Hill, Great Orme, Llandudno,
Conwy LL30 2QW**

Tel: 01492 876278
e-mail: brynarthur-guesthouse@supanet.com
website: www.llandudno.com/bryn.html
Comfortable country guest house with six non-
smoking bedrooms from single to family size. B&B,
packed lunches, evening meals or snacks, drying
facilities. Parking available.

**Bulkeley Mill B&B, Bulkeley Mill, Rowen,
Conwy LL32 8TS**

Tel: 01492 650481
Picturesque valley setting for a B&B with two letting
rooms, one with a balcony over the old water wheel.
No smoking.

**Caerlyr Hall Hotel, Conwy Old Road,
Penmaenmawr, Conwy LL34 6SW**

Tel: 01492 623518
Nine twin/family rooms in a Victorian country house
hotel with bar and restaurant. Golf breaks arranged.

**Dwygyfylchi Hotel, Conwy Old Road,
Dwygyfylchi, Penmaenmawr, Conwy LL34 6SP**

Tel: 01492 623395
A friendly little hotel with two letting bedrooms, a
twin and a family room, both en suite. Full menu of
snacks and main meals.

**Glan Heulog Guest House, Llanrwst Road,
Conwy LL32 8LT**

Tel: 01492 593845
e-mail: glanheulog@no1guesthouse.freeserve.co.uk
website: www.snowdoniabandb.co.uk
Family-run guest house with with six double rooms, a
twin and a family room en suite, and a further room
not en suite. Car parking. Drying facilities.

**The Grosvenor Hotel, Colwyn Bay,
Conwy LL29 7PS**

Tel: 01492 530798 Fax: 01492 531586
e-mail: thegrosvenor@freenetname.co.uk
website: www.hotel-grosvenor.co.uk
A friendly, relaxing hotel with 18 bedrooms, many of
family size. A la carte menu and bar snacks. Bar,
lounge, pool table.   193

**Hotel Messina, Great Orme, Llandudno,
Conwy LL30 2LS**

Tel/Fax: 01492 875260

e-mail: Catherine.Murphy@talk21.com
Ten bedrooms, most en suite, in an 1890s building on
the lower slopes of the Great Orme. Room only plus
continental breakfast.   197

**The Old Rectory Country House, Llansanffraid
Glan Conwy, Conwy LL28 5LP**

Tel: 01492 580611 Fax: 01492 584555
e-mail: info@oldrectorycountryhouse.co.uk
website: www.oldrectorycountryhouse.co.uk
A small country house in a secluded setting with
Snowdonian vistas. Six splendid en suite rooms
(some half-testers or four-poster) and outstanding
food from a Michelin starred chef.

**Orotava Hotel, 105 Glan Y Mor Road,
Penrhyn Bay, Llandudno, Conwy LL30 3PH**

Tel: 01492 549780
Four double and two twin rooms, all en suite, most
with sea views. Restaurant open to non-residents at
weekends.

**The Queen Victoria, Llandudno,
Conwy LL30 2HL**

Tel: 01492 860949 Fax: 01492 878032
e-mail: tony@queenvictoriaf.s.life.co.uk
A bright, cheerful public house/restaurant close to the
pier and beach. Good choice of food and wine, four
real ales. B&B next door.   198

The Risboro Hotel, Llandudno, Conwy LL30 2ED

Tel: 01492 876343/4 Fax: 01492 879881
e-mail: hotelrisboro@ukonline.co.uk
website: www.risboro-hotel.co.uk
Bright, cheerful hotel close to shops, the beach and
several golf courses. 63 en suite rooms, lounge, bars,
restaurants, health club, swimming pool.   196

Rosedene Hotel, Llandudno, Conwy LL30 2DY

Tel: 01492 876491 Fax: 01492 872150
e-mail: janet@hodgett97.freeserve.co.uk
A well-appointed hotel in a row of elegant late-19th
century houses. Eleven en suite rooms, B&B, dinner
for residents and their guests.   195

Food and Drink

**Alexandra Hotel, Clonmel Street, Llandudno,
Conwy LL30 2LE**

Tel: 01492 876670 Fax: 01492 872282
Public house with nine en suite family rooms and a
residents' bar. Restaurant. Drying facilities.

**Caerlyr Hall Hotel, Conwy Old Road,
Penmaenmawr, Conwy LL34 6SW**

Tel: 01492 623518
Nine twin/family rooms in a Victorian country house
hotel with bar and restaurant. Golf breaks arranged.

**The Grosvenor Hotel, Colwyn Bay,
Conwy LL29 7PS**

Tel: 01492 530798 Fax: 01492 531586
e-mail: thegrosvenor@freenetname.co.uk
website: www.hotel-grosvenor.co.uk
A friendly, relaxing hotel with 18 bedrooms, many of

family size. A la carte menu and bar snacks. Bar, lounge, pool table.   193

The Old Rectory Country House, Llansanffraid Glan Conwy, Conwy LL28 5LP

Tel: 01492 580611 Fax: 01492 584555
e-mail: info@oldrectorycountryhouse.co.uk
website: www.oldrectorycountryhouse.co.uk
A small country house in a secluded setting with Snowdonian vistas. Six splendid en suite rooms (some half-testers or four-poster) and outstanding food from a Michelin starred chef.

Orotava Hotel, 105 Glan Y Mor Road, Penrhyn Bay, Llandudno, Conwy LL30 3PH

Tel: 01492 549780
Four double and two twin rooms, all en suite, most with sea views. Restaurant open to non-residents at weekends.

The Queen Victoria, Llandudno, Conwy LL30 2HL

Tel: 01492 860949 Fax: 01492 878032
e-mail: tony@queenvictoriaf.s.life.co.uk
A bright, cheerful public house/restaurant close to the pier and beach. Good choice of food and wine, four real ales. B&B next door.   198

The Risboro Hotel, Llandudno, Conwy LL30 2ED

Tel: 01492 876343/4 Fax: 01492 879881
e-mail: hotelrisboro@ukonline.co.uk
website: www.risboro-hotel.co.uk
Bright, cheerful hotel close to shops, the beach and several golf courses. 63 en suite rooms, lounge, bars, restaurants, health club, swimming pool.   196

Maesdu Golf Club

Hospital Road, Llandudno LL30 1HU
Tel: 01492 876450 Fax: 01492 871570

Another of my favourite North Wales courses, The Maesdu club lies almost directly opposite the North Wales club, but is different inasmuch as it is more of a parkland lay-out than a links course. Founded in 1915, nineteen years after its North Wales neighbour, the founding members suffered agonizing opposition from the non-golfing townsfolk to such an extent that a protest meeting was held at the Llandudno Town Hall. All this, it should be noted, was at the height of the First World War, but surprisingly the local council decided that another golf course was needed to attract tourism to the town-obviously giving no thought that maybe it would be used by occupying foreign armies. The Maesdu (Black Meadow) course is laid out on land between the Wardre Hills and the Irish Sea. This was part of the land that witnessed a tremendous battle when, in 1098AD, the marauding and cruel Vikings landed from the sea and huge losses of men on both sides left the site being named Maedu. Many more bat-

tles were also fought throughout the centuries around this area, which overlooks the village of Deganwy until Edward I destroyed Deganwy Castle and replaced it with the great castle at Conwy. Now the only battles fought here are of the golfing kind on an excellent course which was laid by the celebrated Tom Jones, the first professional of the Maesdu club-a reign which lasted for 53 years. He was also steward and greenkeeper and

finally captain of the club. A portrait of him wearing his red coat now hangs proudly in the clubhouse as a tribute to his services to the club. His daughter went on to become an international and captain of the Welsh ladies Golf Union, while her husband John Brown was club captain and their son, Clive Brown, is a former Welsh amateur international and was the successful captain of the GB&I Walker Cup team in 1995. The course which Tom Jones laid out proved good enough to host many top events and regularly hosted the famous Penfold tournament in the 1950s and 60, s. Henry Cotton, Peter Aliss, Harry Weetman, Peter Butler and Harry Bradshaw all emerged triumphant when the Penfold was held at Maesdu, and Mr Penfold, the owner of the great golf ball manufacturing company actually opened Maesdu's new and impressive clubhouse which still serves the golfing clientele. The course, which gently slopes in an up-and-down fashion has also hosted many important Welsh amateur events and like its neighbour across the road offers fine views and is extremely popular among holiday golfers. Don't miss it.

Sec/Manager:	George Dean
Professional:	Simon Boulden
Directions:	1 mile S of Llandudno centre. From centre take the A546 (Deganwy), At outskirts of Llandudno turn left into Hospital Rd. Entrance after 150 yds on left hand side.
Date Founded:	1915
Type of Course:	Parkland
No of Holes:	18
Length:	6225 yds (5746 mtrs)
Par:	72
SSS:	71
Green Fees:	Weekdays:£25.00 per day, £20 per afternoon; Weekends/Bank Holidays: £30 per day, £25.00 per afternoon
Visitors:	Welcome: Contact Club by telephone in advance
Societies:	Welcome: Contact Club in writing or telephone in advance
Facilities:	Putting Green, Chipping Green, Club Hire, Trolley Hire, Buggy Hire, Bar, Restaurant

Accommodation, Food and Drink

Reference numbers below refer to detailed information provided in section 2

Accommodation

Alexandra Hotel, Clonmel Street, Llandudno, Conwy LL30 2LE

Tel: 01492 876670 Fax: 01492 872282

Public house with nine en suite family rooms and a residents' bar. Restaurant. Drying facilities.

Berthlwyd Hall, Llechwedd, Conwy, Carnarvonshire LL32 8DQ

Tel: 01492 592409 Fax: 01492 572290
e-mail: berthlwydhall@hotmail.com
website: www.berthlwydhall.com

Four beautifully appointed bedrooms in a country manor house with a fine restaurant and an elegant residents' lounge. 194

Bryn Arthur, Tabor Hill, Great Orme, Llandudno, Conwy LL30 2QW

Tel: 01492 876278
e-mail: brynarthur-guesthouse@supanet.com
website: www.llandudno.com/bryn.html

Comfortable country guest house with six non-smoking bedrooms from single to family size. B&B, packed lunches, evening meals or snacks, drying facilities. Parking available.

Bulkeley Mill B&B, Bulkeley Mill, Rowen, Conwy LL32 8TS

Tel: 01492 650481

Picturesque valley setting for a B&B with two letting rooms, one with a balcony over the old water wheel. No smoking.

Caerlyr Hall Hotel, Conwy Old Road, Penmaenmawr, Conwy LL34 6SW

Tel: 01492 623518

Nine twin/family rooms in a Victorian country house hotel with bar and restaurant. Golf breaks arranged.

Celtic Royal Hotel, Caernarfon, Gwynedd LL55 1AY

Tel: 01286 674477 Fax: 01286 674139
e-mail: enquiries@celtic-royal.co.uk
website: www.celtic-royal.co.uk

110 fully equipped en suite bedrooms in a newly refurbished town centre hotel near the Castle. Restaurant, bar, gym, swimming pool. 166

Dwygyfylchi Hotel, Conwy Old Road, Dwygyfylchi, Penmaenmawr, Conwy LL34 6SP

Tel: 01492 623395

A friendly little hotel with two letting bedrooms, a twin and a family room, both en suite. Full menu of snacks and main meals.

Glan Heulog Guest House, Llanrwst Road, Conwy LL32 8LT

Tel: 01492 593845
e-mail: glanheulog@no1guesthouse.freeserve.co.uk
website: www.snowdoniabandb.co.uk

Family-run guest house with with six double rooms, a twin and a family room en suite, and a further room not en suite. Car parking. Drying facilities.

The Grosvenor Hotel, Colwyn Bay, Conwy LL29 7PS

Tel: 01492 530798 Fax: 01492 531586
e-mail: thegrosvenor@freenetname.co.uk
website: www.hotel-grosvenor.co.uk
A friendly, relaxing hotel with 18 bedrooms, many of family size. A la carte menu and bar snacks. Bar, lounge, pool table.   193

Hotel Messina, Great Orme, Llandudno, Conwy LL30 2LS

Tel/Fax: 01492 875260
e-mail: Catherine.Murphy@talk21.com
Ten bedrooms, most en suite, in an 1890s building on the lower slopes of the Great Orme. Room only plus continental breakfast.   197

The Old Rectory Country House, Llansanffraid Glan Conwy, Conwy LL28 5LP

Tel: 01492 580611 Fax: 01492 584555
e-mail: info@oldrectorycountryhouse.co.uk
website: www.oldrectorycountryhouse.co.uk
A small country house in a secluded setting with Snowdonian vistas. Six splendid en suite rooms (some half-testers or four-poster) and outstanding food from a Michelin starred chef.

Orotava Hotel, 105 Glan Y Mor Road, Penrhyn Bay, Llandudno, Conwy LL30 3PH

Tel: 01492 549780
Four double and two twin rooms, all en suite, most with sea views. Restaurant open to non-residents at weekends.

The Queen Victoria, Llandudno, Conwy LL30 2HL

Tel: 01492 860949 Fax: 01492 878032
e-mail: tony@queenvictoriaf.s.life.co.uk
A bright, cheerful public house/restaurant close to the pier and beach. Good choice of food and wine, four real ales. B&B next door.   198

The Risboro Hotel, Llandudno, Conwy LL30 2ED

Tel: 01492 876343/4 Fax: 01492 879881
e-mail: hotelrisboro@ukonline.co.uk
website: www.risboro-hotel.co.uk
Bright, cheerful hotel close to shops, the beach and several golf courses. 63 en suite rooms, lounge, bars, restaurants, health club, swimming pool.   196

Rosedene Hotel, Llandudno, Conwy LL30 2DY

Tel: 01492 876491 Fax: 01492 872150
e-mail: janet@hodgett97.freeserve.co.uk
A well-appointed hotel in a row of elegant late-19th century houses. Eleven en suite rooms, B&B, dinner for residents and their guests.   195

Food and Drink

Alexandra Hotel, Clonmel Street, Llandudno, Conwy LL30 2LE

Tel: 01492 876670 Fax: 01492 872282
Public house with nine en suite family rooms and a residents' bar. Restaurant. Drying facilities.

Caerlyr Hall Hotel, Conwy Old Road, Penmaenmawr, Conwy LL34 6SW

Tel: 01492 623518
Nine twin/family rooms in a Victorian country house hotel with bar and restaurant. Golf breaks arranged.

Celtic Royal Hotel, Caernarfon, Gwynedd LL55 1AY

Tel: 01286 674477 Fax: 01286 674139
e-mail: enquiries@celtic-royal.co.uk
website: www.celtic-royal.co.uk
110 fully equipped en suite bedrooms in a newly refurbished town centre hotel near the Castle. Restaurant, bar, gym, swimming pool.   166

The Grosvenor Hotel, Colwyn Bay, Conwy LL29 7PS

Tel: 01492 530798 Fax: 01492 531586
e-mail: thegrosvenor@freenetname.co.uk
website: www.hotel-grosvenor.co.uk
A friendly, relaxing hotel with 18 bedrooms, many of family size. A la carte menu and bar snacks. Bar, lounge, pool table.   193

The Old Rectory Country House, Llansanffraid Glan Conwy, Conwy LL28 5LP

Tel: 01492 580611 Fax: 01492 584555
e-mail: info@oldrectorycountryhouse.co.uk
website: www.oldrectorycountryhouse.co.uk
A small country house in a secluded setting with Snowdonian vistas. Six splendid en suite rooms (some half-testers or four-poster) and outstanding food from a Michelin starred chef.

Orotava Hotel, 105 Glan Y Mor Road, Penrhyn Bay, Llandudno, Conwy LL30 3 PH

Tel: 01492 549780
Four double and two twin rooms, all en suite, most with sea views. Restaurant open to non-residents at weekends.

The Queen Victoria, Llandudno, Conwy LL30 2HL

Tel: 01492 860949 Fax: 01492 878032
e-mail: tony@queenvictoriaf.s.life.co.uk
A bright, cheerful public house/restaurant close to the pier and beach. Good choice of food and wine, four real ales. B&B next door.   198

The Risboro Hotel, Llandudno, Conwy LL30 2ED

Tel: 01492 876343/4 Fax: 01492 879881
e-mail: hotelrisboro@ukonline.co.uk
website: www.risboro-hotel.co.uk
Bright, cheerful hotel close to shops, the beach and several golf courses. 63 en suite rooms, lounge, bars, restaurants, health club, swimming pool.   196

North Wales Golf Club

72 Bryniau Road, West Shore,
Llandudno LL30 2DZ
Tel: 01492 875325

The North Wales Golf Club is one of the three very fine seaside courses which caters for the holiday golfers who descend on the seaside resorts of Llandudno and Rhos-on-Sea during the summer months and which are also popular during the other seasons. Here at the North Wales club you will find another typical links course with great natural beauty and offering spectacular views over Conwy Sands and beyond to Puffin Island and the Isle of Anglesey. Situated on Llandudno's glorious West Shore on the A546 and two miles from the A55 Expressway, the course is yet another of North Wales's 19th century classic seaside courses, but one which is not so demanding as Harlech or Conwy. Nevertheless, it provides a fine testing challenge for the visitor partial to seaside courses. Following in the footsteps of its near neighbour Conwy, it was laid out on genuine links terrain almost directly opposite that of Conwy, but a few miles away from the actual mouth of the Conwy Estuary.

Designed by Tancred Cummins, this delightful links has a par of 71 and is 6,294 yards in length. The course offers an interesting variety of holes with small and tricky greens and fairways which run close to the seashore and are fairly undulating. As is expected from a seaside course the rough can be troublesome and the wind can cause a few problems, but don't let this put you off. The club has a pleasing clubhouse with full catering facilities and the professional shop is well stocked. Founded in 1894, the North Wales Golf Club has long been a popular venue for holiday golfers because of its close proximity to Llandudno, and really is a joy to play. Being so popular, I recommend you ring and book a starting time.

Sec/Manager:	W Williams
Professional:	R Bradbury
Directions:	On SW outskirts of Llandudno. From seafront take The Parade (A546) west or anti clockwise past the Karden Hotel, after ½ mile into Bryniau Rd, entrance on right hand side.
Date Founded:	1894
Type of Course:	Links
No of Holes:	18
Length:	6294 yds (5809 mtrs)
Par:	71
SSS:	71
Green Fees:	Weekdays:£25.00; Weekends/ Bank Holidays:£35.00
Visitors:	Welcome: Contact Club in advance. Unable to play on Wednesday morning.
Societies:	Welcome: Contact Club by telephone in advance.
Facilities:	Putting Green, Chipping Green, Practice Ground, Club Hire, Trolley Hire, Buggy Hire, Caddy Service, Bar, Restaurant

Accommodation, Food and Drink

Reference numbers below refer to detailed information provided in section 2

Accommodation

Alexandra Hotel, Clonmel Street, Llandudno, Conwy LL30 2LE
Tel: 01492 876670 Fax: 01492 872282
Public house with nine en suite family rooms and a residents' bar. Restaurant. Drying facilities.

Berthlwyd Hall, Llechwedd, Conwy, Carnarvonshire LL32 8DQ
Tel: 01492 592409 Fax: 01492 572290
e-mail: berthlwydhall@hotmail.com
website: www.berthlwydhall.com
Four beautifully appointed bedrooms in a country manor house with a fine restaurant and an elegant residents' lounge. 194

Bryn Arthur, Tabor Hill, Great Orme, Llandudno, Conwy LL30 2QW
Tel: 01492 876278

e-mail: brynarthur-guesthouse@supanet.com
website: www.llandudno.com/bryn.html
Comfortable country guest house with six non-smoking bedrooms from single to family size. B&B, packed lunches, evening meals or snacks, drying facilities. Parking available.

Bulkeley Mill B&B, Bulkeley Mill, Rowen, Conwy LL32 8TS
Tel: 01492 650481
Picturesque valley setting for a B&B with two letting rooms, one with a balcony over the old water wheel. No smoking.

Caerlyr Hall Hotel, Conwy Old Road, Penmaenmawr, Conwy LL34 6SW
Tel: 01492 623518
Nine twin/family rooms in a Victorian country house hotel with bar and restaurant. Golf breaks arranged.

Celtic Royal Hotel, Caernarfon, Gwynedd LL55 1AY
Tel: 01286 674477 Fax: 01286 674139
e-mail: enquiries@celtic-royal.co.uk
website: www.celtic-royal.co.uk
110 fully equipped en suite bedrooms in a newly refurbished town centre hotel near the Castle. Restaurant, bar, gym, swimming pool.   166

Dwygyfylchi Hotel, Conwy Old Road, Dwygyfylchi, Penmaenmawr, Conwy LL34 6SP
Tel: 01492 623395
A friendly little hotel with two letting bedrooms, a twin and a family room, both en suite. Full menu of snacks and main meals.

Glan Heulog Guest House, Llanrwst Road, Conwy LL32 8LT
Tel: 01492 593845
e-mail: glanheulog@no1guesthouse.freeserve.co.uk
website: www.snowdoniabandb.co.uk
Family-run guest house with with six double rooms, a twin and a family room en suite, and a further room not en suite. Car parking. Drying facilities.

The Grosvenor Hotel, Colwyn Bay, Conwy LL29 7PS
Tel: 01492 530798 Fax: 01492 531586
e-mail: thegrosvenor@freenetname.co.uk
website: www.hotel-grosvenor.co.uk
A friendly, relaxing hotel with 18 bedrooms, many of family size. A la carte menu and bar snacks. Bar, lounge, pool table.   193

Hotel Messina, Great Orme, Llandudno, Conwy LL30 2LS
Tel/Fax: 01492 875260
e-mail: Catherine.Murphy@talk21.com
Ten bedrooms, most en suite, in an 1890s building on the lower slopes of the Great Orme. Room only plus continental breakfast.   197

The Old Rectory Country House, Llansanffraid Glan Conwy, Conwy LL28 5LP
Tel: 01492 580611 Fax: 01492 584555

e-mail: info@oldrectorycountryhouse.co.uk
website: www.oldrectorycountryhouse.co.uk
A small country house in a secluded setting with Snowdonian vistas. Six splendid en suite rooms (some half-testers or four-poster) and outstanding food from a Michelin starred chef.

Orotava Hotel, 105 Glan Y Mor Road, Penrhyn Bay, Llandudno, Conwy LL30 3PH
Tel: 01492 549780
Four double and two twin rooms, all en suite, most with sea views. Restaurant open to non-residents at weekends.

The Queen Victoria, Llandudno, Conwy LL30 2HL
Tel: 01492 860949 Fax: 01492 878032
e-mail: tony@queenvictoriaf.s.life.co.uk
A bright, cheerful public house/restaurant close to the pier and beach. Good choice of food and wine, four real ales. B&B next door.   198

The Risboro Hotel, Llandudno, Conwy LL30 2ED
Tel: 01492 876343/4 Fax: 01492 879881
e-mail: hotelrisboro@ukonline.co.uk
website: www.risboro-hotel.co.uk
Bright, cheerful hotel close to shops, the beach and several golf courses. 63 en suite rooms, lounge, bars, restaurants, health club, swimming pool.   196

Rosedene Hotel, Llandudno, Conwy LL30 2DY
Tel: 01492 876491 Fax: 01492 872150
e-mail: janet@hodgett97.freeserve.co.uk
A well-appointed hotel in a row of elegant late-19th century houses. Eleven en suite rooms, B&B, dinner for residents and their guests.   195

Food and Drink

Alexandra Hotel, Clonmel Street, Llandudno, Conwy LL30 2LE
Tel: 01492 876670 Fax: 01492 872282
Public house with nine en suite family rooms and a residents' bar. Restaurant. Drying facilities.

Caerlyr Hall Hotel, Conwy Old Road, Penmaenmawr, Conwy LL34 6SW
Tel: 01492 623518
Nine twin/family rooms in a Victorian country house hotel with bar and restaurant. Golf breaks arranged.

Celtic Royal Hotel, Caernarfon, Gwynedd LL55 1AY
Tel: 01286 674477 Fax: 01286 674139
e-mail: enquiries@celtic-royal.co.uk
website: www.celtic-royal.co.uk
110 fully equipped en suite bedrooms in a newly refurbished town centre hotel near the Castle. Restaurant, bar, gym, swimming pool.   166

The Grosvenor Hotel, Colwyn Bay, Conwy LL29 7PS
Tel: 01492 530798 Fax: 01492 531586
e-mail: thegrosvenor@freenetname.co.uk
website: www.hotel-grosvenor.co.uk

A friendly, relaxing hotel with 18 bedrooms, many of family size. A la carte menu and bar snacks. Bar, lounge, pool table.   193

The Old Rectory Country House, Llansanffraid Glan Conwy, Conwy LL28 5LP

Tel: 01492 580611 Fax: 01492 584555
e-mail: info@oldrectorycountryhouse.co.uk
website: www.oldrectorycountryhouse.co.uk
A small country house in a secluded setting with Snowdonian vistas. Six splendid en suite rooms (some half-testers or four-poster) and outstanding food from a Michelin starred chef.

Orotava Hotel, 105 Glan Y Mor Road, Penrhyn Bay, Llandudno, Conwy LL30 3 PH

Tel: 01492 549780
Four double and two twin rooms, all en suite, most with sea views. Restaurant open to non-residents at weekends.

The Queen Victoria, Llandudno, Conwy LL30 2HL

Tel: 01492 860949 Fax: 01492 878032
e-mail: tony@queenvictoriaf.s.life.co.uk
A bright, cheerful public house/restaurant close to the pier and beach. Good choice of food and wine, four real ales. B&B next door.   198

The Risboro Hotel, Llandudno, Conwy LL30 2ED

Tel: 01492 876343/4 Fax: 01492 879881
e-mail: hotelrisboro@ukonline.co.uk
website: www.risboro-hotel.co.uk
Bright, cheerful hotel close to shops, the beach and several golf courses. 63 en suite rooms, lounge, bars, restaurants, health club, swimming pool.   196

Rhos-on-Sea Golf Club

Penrhyn Bay, Llandudno LL30 3PU

Tel: **01492 549641**

The Rhos-on-Sea club is another of the old-established golf clubs in Wales and was created in the late 19th century just eleven years after Tenby set the ball rolling inside the Principality in 1888. Lying slightly inland from Penrhyn Bay and at the edge of the charming seaside town from where

it gained its name, The Rhos-on-Sea club came into existence mainly to cater for the many visitors who were fast becoming addicted to the game of golf and also to keep them from going elsewhere for their holiday golf. Situated in walking distance of the hotels and guest houses in the village, it is indeed in an ideal location for a holiday golf club. The locals like the place, too, because the club boasts well over 600 playing members and a local bookshop owner and keen member I met there some years ago had nothing but praise for the old club where he had first learned to play golf.

A parkland course with a demanding par of 68, it is mainly flat except for a few small inclines and the greens there are excellent to putt on. As can be expected from a seaside course, there are fine views of Penrhyn Bay and along the coast to the Little Orme and the Great Orme in one direction and across to Rhyl and Prestatyn in the other. Mike Macara, the club professional, was a fine amateur international player for Wales from 1983 to 1993 when a member of the Maesdu club. With Maesdu being some six miles away to the west he has obviously decided he is not yet ready to leave his beloved North Wales. And who can blame him with so many fine courses in close proximity?

Sec/Manager:	John Leigh
Professional:	Mike Macara
Directions:	1¾ miles NW of Colwyn Bay centre. From the A55 take the Rhos-on-Sea turn off (B1115, Rhos-on-Sea, Penrhyn Bay), after nearly ¾ mile turn right into Church Rd, go the end (½ m) and turn left onto Marine Drive. Entrance after ½ mile on left hand side.

Date Founded: 1899

Type of Course: Parkland

No of Holes: 18

Length: 5612 yds (5180 mtrs)

Par: 68

SSS: 68

Green Fees:	Weekdays: £20 per day; Weekends/Bank Holidays: £28 per day
Visitors:	Welcome: Contact Club in advance
Societies:	Welcome: Contact Club in advance
Facilities:	Putting Green, Chipping Green, Club Hire, Trolley Hire, Bar, Restaurant

Accommodation, Food and Drink

Reference numbers below refer to detailed information provided in section 2

Accommodation

Alexandra Hotel, Clonmel Street, Llandudno, Conwy LL30 2LE

Tel: 01492 876670 Fax: 01492 872282

Public house with nine en suite family rooms and a residents' bar. Restaurant. Drying facilities.

Berthlwyd Hall, Llechwedd, Conwy, Carnarvonshire LL32 8DQ

Tel: 01492 592409 Fax: 01492 572290
e-mail: berthlwydhall@hotmail.com
website: www.berthlwydhall.com

Four beautifully appointed bedrooms in a country manor house with a fine restaurant and an elegant residents' lounge.   194

Bryn Arthur, Tabor Hill, Great Orme, Llandudno, Conwy LL30 2QW

Tel: 01492 876278
e-mail: brynarthur-guesthouse@supanet.com
website: www.llandudno.com/bryn.html

Comfortable country guest house with six non-smoking bedrooms from single to family size. B&B, packed lunches, evening meals or snacks, drying facilities. Parking available.

Bulkeley Mill B&B, Bulkeley Mill, Rowen, Conwy LL32 8TS

Tel: 01492 650481

Picturesque valley setting for a B&B with two letting rooms, one with a balcony over the old water wheel. No smoking.

Caerlyr Hall Hotel, Conwy Old Road, Penmaenmawr, Conwy LL34 6SW

Tel: 01492 623518

Nine twin/family rooms in a Victorian country house hotel with bar and restaurant. Golf breaks arranged.

Dwygyfylchi Hotel, Conwy Old Road, Dwygyfylchi, Penmaenmawr, Conwy LL34 6SP

Tel: 01492 623395

A friendly little hotel with two letting bedrooms, a twin and a family room, both en suite. Full menu of snacks and main meals.

Glan Heulog Guest House, Llanrwst Road, Conwy LL32 8LT

Tel: 01492 593845
e-mail: glanheulog@no1guesthouse.freeserve.co.uk
website: www.snowdoniabandb.co.uk

Family-run guest house with with six double rooms, a twin and a family room en suite, and a further room not en suite. Car parking. Drying facilities.

The Grosvenor Hotel, Colwyn Bay, Conwy LL29 7PS

Tel: 01492 530798 Fax: 01492 531586
e-mail: thegrosvenor@freenetname.co.uk
website: www.hotel-grosvenor.co.uk

A friendly, relaxing hotel with 18 bedrooms, many of family size. A la carte menu and bar snacks. Bar, lounge, pool table.   193

Hotel Messina, Great Orme, Llandudno, Conwy LL30 2LS

Tel/Fax: 01492 875260
e-mail: Catherine.Murphy@talk21.com

Ten bedrooms, most en suite, in an 1890s building on the lower slopes of the Great Orme. Room only plus continental breakfast.   197

The Old Rectory Country House, Llansanffraid Glan Conwy, Conwy LL28 5LP

Tel: 01492 580611 Fax: 01492 584555
e-mail: info@oldrectorycountryhouse.co.uk
website: www.oldrectorycountryhouse.co.uk

A small country house in a secluded setting with Snowdonian vistas. Six splendid en suite rooms (some half-testers or four-poster) and outstanding food from a Michelin starred chef.

Orotava Hotel, 105 Glan Y Mor Road, Penrhyn Bay, Llandudno, Conwy LL30 3PH

Tel: 01492 549780

Four double and two twin rooms, all en suite, most with sea views. Restaurant open to non-residents at weekends.

The Queen Victoria, Llandudno, Conwy LL30 2HL

Tel: 01492 860949 Fax: 01492 878032
e-mail: tony@queenvictoriaf.s.life.co.uk

A bright, cheerful public house/restaurant close to the pier and beach. Good choice of food and wine, four real ales. B&B next door.   198

The Risboro Hotel, Llandudno, Conwy LL30 2ED

Tel: 01492 876343/4 Fax: 01492 879881
e-mail: hotelrisboro@ukonline.co.uk
website: www.risboro-hotel.co.uk

Bright, cheerful hotel close to shops, the beach and several golf courses. 63 en suite rooms, lounge, bars, restaurants, health club, swimming pool.   196

Rosedene Hotel, Llandudno, Conwy LL30 2DY

Tel: 01492 876491 Fax: 01492 872150
e-mail: janet@hodgett97.freeserve.co.uk

A well-appointed hotel in a row of elegant late-19th century houses. Eleven en suite rooms, B&B, dinner for residents and their guests.   195

Food and Drink

Alexandra Hotel, Clonmel Street, Llandudno, Conwy LL30 2LE
Tel: 01492 876670 Fax: 01492 872282

Public house with nine en suite family rooms and a residents' bar. Restaurant. Drying facilities.

Caerlyr Hall Hotel, Conwy Old Road, Penmaenmawr, Conwy LL34 6SW
Tel: 01492 623518

Nine twin/family rooms in a Victorian country house hotel with bar and restaurant. Golf breaks arranged.

The Grosvenor Hotel, Colwyn Bay, Conwy LL29 7PS
Tel: 01492 530798 Fax: 01492 531586
e-mail: thegrosvenor@freenetname.co.uk
website: www.hotel-grosvenor.co.uk

A friendly, relaxing hotel with 18 bedrooms, many of family size. A la carte menu and bar snacks. Bar, lounge, pool table.   193

The Old Rectory Country House, Llansanffraid Glan Conwy, Conwy LL28 5LP
Tel: 01492 580611 Fax: 01492 584555
e-mail: info@oldrectorycountryhouse.co.uk
website: www.oldrectorycountryhouse.co.uk

A small country house in a secluded setting with Snowdonian vistas. Six splendid en suite rooms (some half-testers or four-poster) and outstanding food from a Michelin starred chef.

Orotava Hotel, 105 Glan Y Mor Road, Penrhyn Bay, Llandudno, Conwy LL30 3PH
Tel: 01492 549780

Four double and two twin rooms, all en suite, most with sea views. Restaurant open to non-residents at weekends.

The Queen Victoria, Llandudno, Conwy LL30 2HL
Tel: 01492 860949 Fax: 01492 878032
e-mail: tony@queenvictoriaf.s.life.co.uk

A bright, cheerful public house/restaurant close to the pier and beach. Good choice of food and wine, four real ales. B&B next door.   198

The Risboro Hotel, Llandudno, Conwy LL30 2ED
Tel: 01492 876343/4 Fax: 01492 879881
e-mail: hotelrisboro@ukonline.co.uk
website: www.risboro-hotel.co.uk

Bright, cheerful hotel close to shops, the beach and several golf courses. 63 en suite rooms, lounge, bars, restaurants, health club, swimming pool.   196

DENBIGHSHIRE

The ancient county of Denbighshire is one of two northern Welsh counties known as "The Borderlands of North Wales", the other being the neighbouring county of Flintshire. Denbighshire runs from the shores of the Irish Sea at Rhyl and the extreme edge of the Principality to the beautiful Ceirog Valley on the borders of the English county of Shropshire. Close by is the famous town of Llangollen and the picturesque Vale of Llangollen. Lying at the foot of the breathtaking Horseshoe Pass and beneath wooded slopes that adds to its attractive appearance, Llangollen is immensely popular with visitors from all corners of the world, who first came to discover it when attending the world famous Llangollen International Musical Festival, which attracts thousands of musicians, folk dancers and artists from the entire planet and all dressed in their national dress. It is certainly a splendid and happy place to be during that wonderful week of music. Set in an area of natural outstanding beauty the lovely old town exudes a wonderful atmosphere of pastoral tranquillity that often permeates into the very soul of the casual visitor and forces them to remain much longer than intended. This obviously happened to two eccentric Irish ladies, the Honourable Sarah Ponsonby and Lady Eleanor Butler, who made a brief visit to Llangollen in 1779, liked very much what they saw and decided to stay on a while. The "while" being a lifetime because they purchased a beautiful house on the outskirts of the town which was called Plas Newydd (New Mansion). Here they promised each other to devote their lives to celibacy, friendship, the knitting of blue stockings, and to be good hosts to their famous friends whenever they came to visit them. Among their visitors were Sir Walter Scott, the Duke of Wellington and William Wordsworth. Indeed, the eccentric ladies took great objection to a sonnet the great poet wrote about them. As time went by the fame of their eccentricity spread far and wide and they became known as the "Ladies of Llangollen", and the lovely old house where they lived out their lives with their faithful servant, Mary Carryl, remains something of a shrine for the countless visitors attracted to the magnificent Eliabethan-styled mansion and its gorgeous garden and grounds. The two famous old ladies and their loyal servant now lie buried in the churchyard of Llangollen Church, where they regularly worshipped at their very own special pew, part of which now forms one of the window recesses at Plas Newydd.

The famous Llangollen Canal is one of Britain's most picturesque cruising canals. Stretching for a length of some 46 miles it leaves the Shropshire Union Canal at Hurleston and winds its silent way through the English counties of Cheshire and Shropshire before entering the Principality. One of its spectacular spots is Thomas Telford's spectacular Froncysllte Aqueduct, which stands 126ft above the Welsh meadows. This wonderful aqueduct has been nominated for World Heritage status. Along the canal there are numerous quaint pubs to visit and on the restaurant boats and horse-drawn barges you will also pass by locks, country cottages, tunnels and other delights. A 19th century rhyme tells us there are "Seven Wonders of Wales" and all, with the exception of Snowdon, are to be found in the North Wales Borderlands. The old rhyme goes:

Pistyll Rhaiadr and Wrexham Steeple,
Snowdon's Mountain without the people,
Overton yew-trees, St Winefrides Wells,
Llangollen Bridge and Gresford Bells.

Not spectacular wonders by today's standards, but something to look out for on your travels through Denbighshire and Flintshire. Llangollen Bridge crosses the River Dee and the townsfolk are immensely proud of their "Welsh Wonder" bridge. Originally built by Henry I and reconstructed in 1346, the bridge is now a scheduled ancient monument. Travel-

Llangollen

Plas Newydd, Llangollen

ling from Llangollen southwards to Pistyll Rhaidr in the beautiful Ceirog Valley you will pass through the picture-postcard hamlet of Llanarmon Dyffryn Ceirog. Head for Llanrhaeadr and turn right down the well-signposted "Waterfall Road". This narrow road brings you to the foot of Pistyll Rhaeadr in the beautiful Tanat Valley. A slow and winding journey, but well rewarded by the spectacular sight of the highest waterfall in Wales and England- 240ft of tumbling white water and a wonderful climax to the difficult drive.

The third of the "Seven Welsh Wonders" close to this area is at Overton a mere 8 miles from Llangollen. Well worth seeing the 21 tall and dark Yew trees in the churchyard of the Parish Church of St Mary are some of the oldest trees in Britain and date back to medieval times. The charming village of Overton is also as old and is mentioned in the Doomsday Book. St Giles Parish Church, which dominates the Wrexham skyline, is another of the wonders. (described in the Flintshire section of this guide, along with the Gresford Bells and Holywell's St Winifride's Well).

About two miles north of Llangollen on the A542 are the ruins of Valle Crucis Abbey (Vale of the Cross) founded by the Cistercians in 1200 and once one of the most important religious centres in Wales. A burial place of many Welsh princes, it is also regarded by many historians as the resting place of Owain Glyndwr because this was the last place he is recorded as being seen. A short distance from the abbey is a stone pillar known as "Eliseg's Pillar", which is actually the remains of a cross erected in memory of the Welsh prince Eliiseg who ruled this area during the eighth century and who was killed in a fierce battle close to Chester. Destroyed during the Civil War it was later re-erected in 1779, at which time a skeleton was discovered beneath the mound and believed to be that of the ancient prince. Continuing northwards along the A542 you continue to climb towards the famous "Horseshoe Pass", a spectacular part of the lower regions of the Llantysilio Mountain. From here can be seen some stunning scenery to the south of the Vale of Llangollen and beyond. Continuing northwards through this beautiful area, the next important Denbighshire town worth exploring is that of Ruthin (pronounced Rithin). Lying peacefully now in the impressive Vale of Clwyd, Ruthin once witnessed the cruel savagery of Owain Glyndwr's forces when the Welsh prince burned the town in 1400 after failing to conquer Ruthin Castle, which was built by Edward I in 1281. A few centuries later Oliver Cromwell was more successful and all but completely destroyed the great fortress in 1646. During the 19th century, however, the old castle had a new lease of life and was reconstructed and converted into a fine

Pistyll Rhaeadr

mansion and is now a luxurious hotel! There is an eerie tale connected with the old castle. There were many sightings over the centuries of a ghostly figure of a man fully armed but only wearing one gauntlet. In proof of this strange tale a single mediaeval gauntlet was unearthed during excavations for new and stronger footings to the mansion.

There is much of architectural interest to be discovered in this charming old town, including the wonderful oak roof on the north side of St Peter's Church. This was a gift from Henry VII in appreciation of the Welsh support at the Battle of Bosworth. A delightful town of great character, Ruthin is pleasantly surrounded by a pastoral landscape.

Further north is Denbigh, which is full of historical interest. A pleasant walled market town, Denbigh was originally called Caledfwyn (Rocky Hill) because of its steep sloping position over-looking the Vale of Clwyd. Dominating the town is the almost 900 year old Denbigh Castle. Charles I took refuge in the castle in 1645 and over the centuries of conflict the castle suffered from many attacks and sieges but today its ruins are a favourite spot with visitors because of its great views. The remains of a 13th century Carmelite Friary destroyed by fire in 1898 can be also seen as well as the ruins of a mediaeval unfinished church begun by the Earl of Leicester in the castle grounds during 1579 and now known as "Leicester's Folly. There is also the remains of St Hilary's Church, a garrison church built in 1334. In more modern times Denbigh's claim to fame is that it is the birthplace of H. M. Stanley, the explorer who went in search of David Livingstone lost in Africa. Although born in the town, Stanley was actually brought up in a workhouse at nearby St Asaph. The town of St Asaph is situated in a delightful part of the Vale of Clwyd and claims to have the smallest cathedral in Wales and England.

Continuing north is the interesting small town of Rhuddlan, dominated by the final chain of castle strongholds built by Edward I. Rhuddlan Castle is quite an impressive sight as you enter the town. Erected by Edward on a site that originally contained a motte and bailey Saxon

Rhuddlan Castle

structure, it has stood proudly guarding the old town since being built in 1277. Many battles have been fought around the site known as Rhuddlan Marsh, with the first recorded conflict being that between the mighty Celtic leader Caradoc and the Saxon ruler King Offa. King Harold captured the old "castle" in 1063 and it changed hands many more times before Edward I erected his mighty stronghold. Today Rhuddlan, on the banks of the River Clwyd, is a charming and friendly place to visit, especially so for golfers because of the fine parkland course to be found there.

Another golf course-albeit just 9 holes-is to be found on the outskirts of the seaside town of Rhyl, just a few miles north of Rhuddlan. Rhyl, with its three miles of good beach, a marine lake and plenty to entertain the youngsters, is doing its very best to retain its popularity of the early post-war years and looks to be succeeding in good fashion. Eastwards along the coast from Rhyl is the other Denbighshire seaside resort of Prestatyn. Much smaller than Rhyl, it was occupied in Neolothic times and then by the Romans. Close to Prestatyn is where King Offa decided to start his famous Offa's Dyke, a massive earthworks built as a boundary between Wales and England and which stretches the entire length of the Principality and is now a famous walk for the more energetic lovers of nature. A pleasant and bustling small town, Prestatyn is among my favourite places to visit, mainly because of its excellent championship links golf course.

There is much to see and do in Denbighshire, the choice is yours.

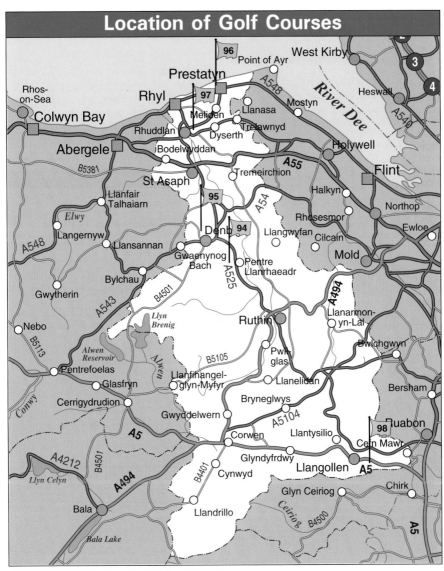

Location of Golf Courses

© MAPS IN MINUTES ™ 2001   © Crown Copyright, Ordnance Survey 2001

Bryn Morfydd Hotel & Golf Club

Llanrhaeadr, Denbigh, Denbighshire LL16 4NP
Tel: 01745 890280 Fax: 01745 890488

The club was founded in 1982, with the course of similar length and par as the Denbigh club. Designed by the well-known professionals Peter Aliss and Dave Thomas, like its neighbour it is a mature parkland layout. Since 1992 the club has also been able to boast a 9-hole par-3 course designed by Muirhead and C. S. Henderson-the latter being the club's Director of Golf. The courses are named the Duchess Course and Dukes Course respectively. There is also a full-sized clubhouse and a 3-Star hotel on site.

Sec/Manager:	Mrs S. Williams
Professional:	Richard Hughes
Directions:	3 miles S of Denbigh. Take A525 (Ruthin) from Denbigh and turn right at Pentre on Pant-pastynog road. Entrance after ½ mile.
Sec/Manager:	Mrs. S. Williams
Professional:	Richard Hughes
Directions:	3 miles S of Denbigh. Take A525 (Ruthin) from Denbigh and turn right at Pentre on Pant-pastynog road. Entrance after ½ mile.
Visitors:	Welcome: Contact Club in advance
Societies:	Welcome: Contact Club in advance
Facilities:	Club Hire, Trolley Hire, Buggy Hire, Bar, Restaurant

Dukes

Date Founded:	1990
Type of Course:	Parkland
No of Holes:	18
Length:	5637 yds (5203 mtrs)
Par:	70
SSS:	67
Green Fees:	Weekdays: £15 per day; Weekends/Bank Holidays: £20 per day

Duchess

Date Founded:	1970
Type of Course:	Parkland
No of Holes:	18
Length:	1146 yds (1057 mtrs)
Par:	27
SSS:	Not Known
Green Fees:	Weekdays: £5 per day; Weekends/Bank Holidays: £5 per day

Accommodation, Food and Drink

Reference numbers below refer to detailed information provided in section 2

Accommodation

Cayo Guest House, 74 Vale Street, Denbigh, Denbighshire LL16 3BW
Tel: 01745 812686
A friendly guest house with six letting bedrooms, most en suite. Bed & Breakfast, with packed lunches and evening meals by arrangement.

The Old Mill Private Hotel, Melin-y-Wern, Denbigh Road, Nannerch, Mold, Flintshire CH7 5RH
Tel: 01352 741542 Fax: 01352 740254
e-mail: welcome@old-mill.co.uk
website: www.old-mill.co.uk
'Warmest Welcome' Award-winning hotel with six en suite bedrooms and a restaurant. Craft shop on site.

Plas Elwy Hotel, The Roe, St Asaph, Denbighshire LL17 0LT
Tel: 01745 582263 Fax: 01745 583864
e-mail: plaselwy@gtleisure.co.uk
website: www.gtleisure.co.uk/plaselwy
Thirteen en suite bedrooms with tv and telephone in an 1850s building and adjacent lodge. Beamed restaurant, steaks a speciality.

The Three Pigeons Inn, Graigfechan, Ruthin, Denbighshire LL15 2EU
Tel: 01824 703178 Fax: 01824 703812
17th century drovers inn with two bars, a games room and a non-smoking dining room, plus two spacious bedrooms. Also a caravan and camping site. 202

Food and Drink

The Drover's Arms, Rhewl, Nr. Ruthin, Denbighshire LL15 2UD
Tel: 01824 703163
website: www.droversarms.co.uk
A pretty pub dating from the 16th century, located on the A525. Large bar with dining, lounge and games area. Beer garden. 201

The Old Mill Private Hotel, Melin-y-Wern, Denbigh Road, Nannerch, Mold, Flintshire CH7 5RH

Tel: 01352 741542 Fax: 01352 740254
e-mail: welcome@old-mill.co.uk
website: www.old-mill.co.uk
'Warmest Welcome' Award-winning hotel with six en suite bedrooms and a restaurant. Craft shop on site.

Plas Elwy Hotel, The Roe, St Asaph, Denbighshire LL17 0LT

Tel: 01745 582263 Fax: 01745 583864
e-mail: plaselwy@gtleisure.co.uk
website: www.gtleisure.co.uk/plaselwy
Thirteen en suite bedrooms with tv and telephone in an 1850s building and adjacent lodge. Beamed restaurant, steaks a speciality.

The Three Pigeons Inn, Graigfechan, Ruthin, Denbighshire LL15 2EU

Tel: 01824 703178 Fax: 01824 703812
17th century drovers inn with two bars, a games room and a non-smoking dining room, plus two spacious bedrooms. Also a caravan and camping site.   202

Denbigh Golf Club

Henllan Road, Denbigh LL16 5AA
Tel: 01745 814159 Fax: 01745 814888

Denbigh Golf Club is situated just one mile north-west of the ancient county town of Denbigh on the B5382 road, and has been serving the needs of the local golfing fraternity for almost 80 years. It was founded in 1922 after a few local golf en-thusiasts decided it was about time the old town followed the example of other Welsh agricultural towns by boasting a golf course as one of its amenities. Seeking a suitable piece of land for a golf course, they were fortunate to acquire a per-fect site so close to the town (Remember, most people had to walk to get anywhere in those days), and over the years they patiently (with the help of John Stockton who designed the course) nur-tured the course into the pleasant parkland lay-out

that can be seen at the present time and which is much appreciated by the 600 or so members that are there today. Not over-long at 5,712 yards, the course is nevertheless laid-out in a way to offer a testing challenge to most average golfers, with the SSS of 68 not often threatened.

Offering full facilities in the cosy clubhouse, the course is an ideal place for the holiday golfer because of its close proximity to the interesting and historic hillside town of Denbigh and also because of its beautiful setting in the picturesque Vale of Clywd. Indeed, it is well worth the golf-ing visitor to plan a stopover in the old town because it now also boasts another good 18-hole golf club at the opposite end to that of the Denbigh Golf Club, named Bryn Morfydd Hotel.

Sec/Manager:	John Raine
Professional:	Mike Jones
Directions:	1½ miles NW of Denbigh. From centtre take A543 (Bylchau) and on outskirts turn right onto B5382 (Henllan). From outskirts entrance after ½ mile on left hand side.
Date Founded:	1922
Type of Course:	Parkland
No of Holes:	18
Length:	5712 yds (5272 mtrs)
Par:	69
SSS:	68
Green Fees:	Weekdays: £24 per day; Weekends/Bank Holidays: £30 per day
Visitors:	Welcome: Contact Club in advance
Societies:	Welcome: Excluding 12.30-2.30 weekdays & 11.30-2.30 weekends. Contact Club in advance by phone or in writing
Facilities:	Putting Green, Chipping Green, Club Hire, Trolley Hire, Bar, Restaurant

Accommodation, Food and Drink

Reference numbers below refer to detailed information provided in section 2

Accommodation

Cayo Guest House, 74 Vale Street, Denbigh, Denbighshire LL16 3BW

Tel: 01745 812686
A friendly guest house with six letting bedrooms, most en suite. Bed & Breakfast, with packed lunches and evening meals by arrangement.

The Old Mill Private Hotel, Melin-y-Wern, Denbigh Road, Nannerch, Mold, Flintshire CH7 5RH

Tel: 01352 741542 Fax: 01352 740254
e-mail: welcome@old-mill.co.uk
website: www.old-mill.co.uk
'Warmest Welcome' Award-winning hotel with six en suite bedrooms and a restaurant. Craft shop on site.

Plas Elwy Hotel, The Roe, St Asaph, Denbighshire LL17 0LT

Tel: 01745 582263 Fax: 01745 583864
e-mail: plaselwy@gtleisure.co.uk
website: www.gtleisure.co.uk/plaselwy
Thirteen en suite bedrooms with tv and telephone in an 1850s building and adjacent lodge. Beamed restaurant, steaks a speciality.

Food and Drink

The Drover's Arms, Rhewl, Nr. Ruthin, Denbighshire LL15 2UD

Tel: 01824 703163
website: www.droversarms.co.uk
A pretty pub dating from the 16th century, located on the A525. Large bar with dining, lounge and games area. Beer garden.　　　201

Lakeside Inn, Tan-y-Mynydd, Moelfre, Abergele, Conwy LL22 9RF

Tel: 01745 823691
Good choice of lunch and evening food in a country pub that's part of a leisure complex. Pool room, beer garden.

The Old Mill Private Hotel, Melin-y-Wern, Denbigh Road, Nannerch, Mold, Flintshire CH7 5RH

Tel: 01352 741542 Fax: 01352 740254
e-mail: welcome@old-mill.co.uk
website: www.old-mill.co.uk
'Warmest Welcome' Award-winning hotel with six en suite bedrooms and a restaurant. Craft shop on site.

Plas Elwy Hotel, The Roe, St Asaph, Denbighshire LL17 0LT

Tel: 01745 582263 Fax: 01745 583864
e-mail: plaselwy@gtleisure.co.uk
website: www.gtleisure.co.uk/plaselwy
Thirteen en suite bedrooms with tv and telephone in an 1850s building and adjacent lodge. Beamed restaurant, steaks a speciality.

Prestatyn Golf Club

Marine Road East, Prestatyn LL19 7HS

Tel: 01745 888353 Fax: 01745 888353

Another of the great championship courses to be found in North Wales and, like the Conwy course on the same coastline, the Prestatyn club is laid out on gorgeous linksland known as "Morfa",

meaning bog or sea-marsh in the Welsh tongue. Founded in 1905, the course is laid out between the coastal railway and the Irish Sea and within sight of the western coastline of northern England. A feature of this demanding links course is a canal, which crosses the links and is known as the infamous "Prestatyn Gutter", which has suffered the wrath of countless frustrated golfers. In the early days the course was leased by a hotel, which offered accommodation to the holiday golfers. The land, however, was owned by Lord Aberconwy, whose death duties in the early 1960's put an end to the hotel and the golf course, with the land eventually becoming the property of a non-golfing businessman in payment of a large debt. He decided there was much money to be made by putting a housing estate on the precious Morfa. The local authorities, however, were either keen local golfers or people with good sense, because they refused to allow houses to be erected on the land. The then club president, Jim Corson,

decided to pester the owner into doing a deal with the hopeful Prestatyn Club. To his credit Corson eventually traced the owner at the dog races in Manchester and clinched the deal on the spot. The triumphant club was back in business and has never looked back. With the help of enthusiastic fellow member and businessman, Harry Griffiths, who sold his engineering business when still in his thirties, they brought the old course back up to scratch to the undying thanks of all members who have since followed. Today the course is as good as it has ever been and boasts a fine two-storied clubhouse with a huge upstairs lounge area. There is not an easy hole to be found at Prestatyn, and the sandhills which border many of the holes are thick with tufted sea-grass, which plays havoc with the confidence of any golfer who possesses a few wayward shots within his game. Another wide open typical links course it is an absolute delight to play on a glorious summer's day, but when the wind whips off the Irish Sea it can be a "wicked witch" of a course to play.

Situated close to the pleasant small town of Prestatyn and close to the splendid beaches, it is an excellent holiday course for the discerning golfer. As one Australian visitor once said to me: It's a real beaut of a course, and the beer's not too bad either, old Mate!" Which is as good a compliment as a Welshman will ever get from an Aussie golfer. Indeed, it does offer a great but fair challenge with its par of 73, tricky greens and rolling fairways stretching to a length of 6,808 yards of sheer delight.

Sec/Manager:	Roy Woodfruff
Professional:	Malcolm Staton
Directions:	1¼ miles NE of Prestatyn centre. From centre go north via Gronan Rd and turn left into Prestatyn Rd (A548). After ½ mile turn right on a sharp bend into Marine Rd East. Entrance after 300 yds on left hand side.
Date Founded:	1905
Type of Course:	Links
No of Holes:	18
Length:	6808 yds (6283 mtrs)
Par:	73
SSS:	73
Green Fees:	Weekdays: £22 per day; Weekends/Bank Holidays: £27 per day
Visitors:	Welcome: Excluding Saturday. Contact Club in advance
Societies:	Welcome: Excluding Saturday & Tuesday. Contact Club in advance
Facilities:	Putting Green, Chipping Green, Club Hire, Trolley Hire, Buggy Hire, Bar, Restaurant

Accommodation, Food and Drink

Reference numbers below refer to detailed information provided in section 2

Accommodation

Cayo Guest House, 74 Vale Street, Denbigh, Denbighshire LL16 3BW
Tel: 01745 812686
A friendly guest house with six letting bedrooms, most en suite. Bed & Breakfast, with packed lunches and evening meals by arrangement.

Cheshire Farm, Papermill Lane, Oakenholt, Flint CH6 5SU
Tel/Fax: 01244 830295
A delightful B&B on an 18th century working dairy farm with three letting bedrooms including a family room. Set in beautiful gardens. Children and pets welcome.

Graig Park Hotel & Country Club, Dyserth, Denbighshire LL18 6DX
Tel: 01745 571022 Fax: 01745 571024
Hotel & Country Club set among lawns and woodland near the North Wales coast. Hotel accommodation or fully equipped log cabins. Sports and leisure facilities, restaurant.   199

Plas Elwy Hotel, The Roe, St Asaph, Denbighshire LL17 0LT
Tel: 01745 582263 Fax: 01745 583864
e-mail: plaselwy@gtleisure.co.uk
website: www.gtleisure.co.uk/plaselwy
Thirteen en suite bedrooms with tv and telephone in an 1850s building and adjacent lodge. Beamed restaurant, steaks a speciality.

Food and Drink

The Drover's Arms, Rhewl, Nr. Ruthin, Denbighshire LL15 2UD
Tel: 01824 703163
website: www.droversarms.co.uk
A pretty pub dating from the 16th century, located on the A525. Large bar with dining, lounge and games area. Beer garden.   201

Graig Park Hotel & Country Club, Dyserth, Denbighshire LL18 6DX
Tel: 01745 571022 Fax: 01745 571024
Hotel & Country Club set among lawns and woodland near the North Wales coast. Hotel accommodation or fully equipped log cabins. Sports and leisure facilities, restaurant.   199

Lakeside Inn, Tan-y-Mynydd, Moelfre, Abergele, Conwy LL22 9RF
Tel: 01745 823691
Good choice of lunch and evening food in a country pub that's part of a leisure complex. Pool room, beer garden.

Plas Elwy Hotel, The Roe, St Asaph, Denbighshire LL17 0LT
Tel: 01745 582263 Fax: 01745 583864
e-mail: plaselwy@gtleisure.co.uk
website: www.gtleisure.co.uk/plaselwy
Thirteen en suite bedrooms with tv and telephone in an 1850s building and adjacent lodge. Beamed restaurant, steaks a speciality.

Rhuddlan Golf Club

Meliden Road, Rhuddlan LL18 6LB
Tel: 01745 590217 Fax: 01745 590472

In direct contrast to the Prestatyn links the course at Rhuddlan is pure parkland with the only sand in sight being that contained in the bunkers and sand traps. At the other end of the town to Rhuddlan Castle, it is a beautifully groomed course with much attention given to the greens.

Designed by Fred Hawtree and founded in 1930, it is situated in the beautiful Vale of Clwyd and offers attractive views of the surrounding countryside. One cannot fail to be impressed by the large clubhouse as you enter the spacious car-parking area. Inside the main lounge is as comfortable and attractive as any I have had the privilege of entering. Over the years the club has organised a splendid Charity Pro-Am which has raised huge sums of money for children's charities and which I have had the pleasure of being invited to play in. A gently undulating parkland course of 6,471 yards it meanders among the many fine bushes and trees that are a delight to set eyes on during the summer months. Never wind-lashed the attractive course is finely protected from the worst of the weathers by the Clwydian Range of mountains. The par of the course is 70, providing an excellent test of one's golf abilities in peaceful surroundings. Having hosted a number of county and national championships the club is the perfect holiday place to visit and to play some memorable golf.

Sec/Manager:	David Morris
Professional:	Andrew Carr
Directions:	3 miles S of Rhyl centre. From the A55 at St Asaph take the A525 (Rhyl), after 2 miles turn right into Rhuddlan continuing on A525. At first roundabout, after ¾ mile, take the A547 (Prestatyn). Entrance after 150 yds on right hand side.
Date Founded:	1930
Type of Course:	Parkland
No of Holes:	18

Length:	6471 yds (5973 mtrs)
Par:	70
SSS:	71
Green Fees:	Weekdays: £26 per day; Weekends/Bank Holidays: £30 per day
Visitors:	Welcome: Contact Club in advance, unable to play on Sundays
Societies:	Welcome: Contact Club in advance, unable to play at weekends
Facilities:	Putting Green, Chipping Green, Club Hire, Trolley Hire, Buggy Hire, Bar, Restaurant

Accommodation, Food and Drink

Reference numbers below refer to detailed information provided in section 2

Accommodation

Cayo Guest House, 74 Vale Street, Denbigh, Denbighshire LL16 3BW
Tel: 01745 812686
A friendly guest house with six letting bedrooms, most en suite. Bed & Breakfast, with packed lunches and evening meals by arrangement.

Cheshire Farm, Papermill Lane, Oakenholt, Flint CH6 5SU
Tel/Fax: 01244 830295
A delightful B&B on an 18th century working dairy farm with three letting bedrooms including a family room. Set in beautiful gardens. Children and pets welcome.

Graig Park Hotel & Country Club, Dyserth, Denbighshire LL18 6DX
Tel: 01745 571022 Fax: 01745 571024
Hotel & Country Club set among lawns and woodland near the North Wales coast. Hotel accommodation or fully equipped log cabins. Sports and leisure facilities, restaurant.   199

Plas Elwy Hotel, The Roe, St Asaph, Denbighshire LL17 0LT
Tel: 01745 582263 Fax: 01745 583864
e-mail: plaselwy@gtleisure.co.uk
website: www.gtleisure.co.uk/plaselwy
Thirteen en suite bedrooms with tv and telephone in an 1850s building and adjacent lodge. Beamed restaurant, steaks a speciality.

Food and Drink

The Drover's Arms, Rhewl, Nr. Ruthin, Denbighshire LL15 2UD
Tel: 01824 703163
website: www.droversarms.co.uk
A pretty pub dating from the 16th century, located on

the A525. Large bar with dining, lounge and games area. Beer garden.   201

Graig Park Hotel & Country Club, Dyserth, Denbighshire LL18 6DX

Tel: 01745 571022 Fax: 01745 571024

Hotel & Country Club set among lawns and woodland near the North Wales coast. Hotel accommodation or fully equipped log cabins. Sports and leisure facilities, restaurant.   199

Lakeside Inn, Tan-y-Mynydd, Moelfre, Abergele, Conwy LL22 9RF

Tel: 01745 823691

Good choice of lunch and evening food in a country pub that's part of a leisure complex. Pool room, beer garden.

Plas Elwy Hotel, The Roe, St Asaph, Denbighshire LL17 0LT

Tel: 01745 582263 Fax: 01745 583864
e-mail: plaselwy@gtleisure.co.uk
website: www.gtleisure.co.uk/plaselwy

Thirteen en suite bedrooms with tv and telephone in an 1850s building and adjacent lodge. Beamed restaurant, steaks a speciality.

Vale of Llangollen Golf Club

Holyhead Road, Llangollen LL20 7PR

Tel: 01978 860906 Fax: 01978 860906

The Vale of Llangollen Golf Club lies in one of the most beautiful places imaginable for an inland course to be located. Sitting at the bottom of the bowl of the highly picturesque and green valley from whence it got its name, the Llangollen course is one of the outstanding hidden treasures of the Welsh golf scene. Approaching the equally gorgeous town of Llangollen in a westerly direction from the A5, you will get a panoramic view of the course before you turn off to enter the club's car park, which is just off the road. The charming clubhouse lies next to the car park and overlooking the course where it slopes down to the flat plain of the stunning vale. Gently flowing past five of Llangollen's attractive holes is the delightful River Dee; not so delightful, however, close to three of the holes if you are not a straight hitter of the ball. Run out of golf balls at these holes and you fancy your chances at fishing instead, there is some consolation to be had because the river is renowned for its fine salmon.

Founded in 1908, the Llangollen members were content with just 9 holes for over sixty years, but decided to purchase further land from a local farmer at the end of the 1960's after much fund raising to produce the necessary money. The club president came up trumps by providing hundreds of special young trees for the new course and other

enthusiastic members added their input to the new and exciting development. Today their enthusiasm has paid off handsomely with an 18-hole course to be proud of. The many trees that were planted have successfully taken root to transform the terrain into a magnificent parkland course of some quality. The River Dee offers its most troublesome spot at the 9th River Hole where it flows alongside the right-hand fairway. With the hole taking a vicious dog-leg left you have to place your drive as right as possible to have an opportunity of finding the green with your second. Too far right and your ball joins many others in a deep watery graveyard. Too far left and you can forget about making par at this great and challenging 425 yards hole. Little wonder that it is rated by many as the best golf hole in North Wales. In saying that, it is also one of the best inland golf courses in North Wales.

The likeable David Vaughan, a former European Tour player and now trying his luck on the Seniors Tour, has long played his trade here as a club professional, and who can blame him for not wanting to leave this most heavenly of locations.

Sec/Manager:	David Black
Professional:	David Vaugh
Directions:	½ mile E of Llangollen centre. From centre take the A5 (Froncysyllte). Entrance after ½ mile on left hand side.
Date Founded:	1908
Type of Course:	Parkland
No of Holes:	18
Length:	6656 yds (6144 mtrs)
Par:	72
SSS:	73
Green Fees:	Weekdays: £20 per day; Weekends/Bank Holidays: £25 per day
Visitors:	Welcome: Unable to play at weekends. Contact Club in advance
Societies:	Welcome: Unable to play at weekends. Contact Club in advance
Facilities:	Putting Green, Chipping Green, Club Hire, Bar, Restaurant

Accommodation, Food and Drink

Reference numbers below refer to detailed information provided in section 2

Accommodation

Bridge End Hotel, Llangollen, Denbighshire LL20 8RY

Tel: 01978 860634
e-mail: bridge-endhotel@btconnect.com
A handsome former coaching inn in the town centre, with nine comfortable guest rooms (some en suite) and bar and restaurant menus.   200

Elgar House, 16 Elgar Close, Oswestry, Shropshire SY11 2LZ

Tel: 01691 661323 mob: 07879 462813
A conservatory-fronted bungalow with three en suite bedrooms (two family size), guest bar and pleasant gardens. B&B: dinner with notice. AA 4 Diamonds.

Glen Helen Holiday Cottages, Pant, Oswestry, Shropshire SY10 9QN

Tel/Fax: 01691 830094
e-mail: gaskill@globalnet.co.uk
website: www.glenhelen.co.uk
High-class self-catering accommodation in two holiday cottages, each with two bedrooms, bath/shower, kitchen-diner, lounge and garden.   211

The Hand Hotel, Llanarmon Dyffryn Ceiriog, Clwyd LL20 7LD

Tel: 01691 600666 Fax: 01691 600262
e-mail: handllandcb@netscapeonline.co.uk
Built in the late 16th century, the Hand stands in beautiful countryside at the head of the Ceiriog Valley. 13 en suite bedrooms, bar and restaurant meals.   203

Sebastians Restaurant & Hotel, 45 Willow Street, Oswestry, Shropshire SY11 1AQ

Tel: 01691 655444 Fax: 01691 653452
e-mail: sebastians.rest@virgin.net
website: www.sebastians-hotel.co.uk
Individually appointed en suite bedrooms of great charm, plus fine French cuisine in an atmospheric 16th century setting. Private car park.

The Three Pigeons Inn, Graigfechan, Ruthin, Denbighshire LL15 2EU

Tel: 01824 703178 Fax: 01824 703812
17th century drovers inn with two bars, a games room and a non-smoking dining room, plus two spacious bedrooms. Also a caravan and camping site.   202

The West Arms Hotel, Llanarmon Dyffryn Ceiriog, Ceiriog Valley, Clwyd LL20 7LD

Tel: 01691 600665 Fax: 01691 600622
e-mail: booking@thewestarms.co.uk
website: www.thewestarms.co.uk
A charming, old-world country inn nestling in the lovely, peaceful Ceiriog Valley. Sixteen en suite bedrooms including two large suites. Bar and restaurant meals.   204

Food and Drink

The Black Horse Inn, Maesbrook, Oswestry, Shropshire SY10 8QG

Tel: 01691 682472 Fax: 01691 682872
A great pub for food, with a menu that offers an

excellent choice for all tastes. Shropshire sirloin, with mushrooms and local blue cheese, is a favourite.

The Bradford Arms, Knockin, Nr. Oswestry, Shropshire SY10 8HJ

Tel: 01691 682358
A fine black-and-white roadside inn serving an excellent selection of home-cooked food for country appetites. Smart bar, non-smoking restaurant, beer garden.   210

Bridge End Hotel, Llangollen, Denbighshire LL20 8RY

Tel: 01978 860634 e-mail: bridge-endhotel@btconnect.com
A handsome former coaching inn in the town centre, with nine comfortable guest rooms (some en suite) and bar and restaurant menus.   200

The Hand Hotel, Llanarmon Dyffryn Ceiriog, Clwyd LL20 7LD

Tel: 01691 600666 Fax: 01691 600262
e-mail: handllandcb@netscapeonline.co.uk
Built in the late 16th century, the Hand stands in beautiful countryside at the head of the Ceiriog Valley. 13 en suite bedrooms, bar and restaurant meals.   203

The New Inn, Corwen Road, Pontblyddyn, Mold, Flintshire CH7 4HR

Tel: 01352 771459
A friendly inn serving traditional home-cooked food from noon every day. Quick snacks to full meals on a varied menu with a children's section.

Sebastians Restaurant & Hotel, 45 Willow Street, Oswestry, Shropshire SY11 1AQ

Tel: 01691 655444 Fax: 01691 653452
e-mail: sebastians.rest@virgin.net
website: www.sebastians-hotel.co.uk
Individually appointed en suite bedrooms of great charm, plus fine French cuisine in an atmospheric 16th century setting. Private car park.

The Three Pigeons Inn, Graigfechan, Ruthin, Denbighshire LL15 2EU

Tel: 01824 703178 Fax: 01824 703812
17th century drovers inn with two bars, a games room and a non-smoking dining room, plus two spacious bedrooms. Also a caravan and camping site.   202

The West Arms Hotel, Llanarmon Dyffryn Ceiriog, Ceiriog Valley, Clwyd LL20 7LD

Tel: 01691 600665 Fax: 01691 600622
e-mail: booking@thewestarms.co.uk
website: www.thewestarms.co.uk
A charming, old-world country inn nestling in the lovely, peaceful Ceiriog Valley. Sixteen en suite bedrooms including two large suites. Bar and restaurant meals.

FLINTSHIRE

Despite being one of the smallest counties in North Wales the county of Flintshire has the distinction of having the largest town (Wrexham) in the northern areas of the Principality. Once one of the most important industrial centres in North Wales, all that remains as a reminder of these prosperous times are a handful of tourist attractions that complements the industrial past. Wrexham also has a fine Arts Centre in its extensive library building and an interesting County Borough Museum. A lovely bustling sort of town with many fine architectural buildings-of which one of the most historic is the St Giles Parish Church. One of the "Seven Wonders of Wales" the church has a tower known as the "Wrexham Steeple" which dominates the skyline of Wrexham town and which is regarded as the finest example of Gothic architecture in North Wales. Also of historic interest is the fact that a replica of the 136ft high tower has been built into the Yale University in America. This is to commemorate a famous Welshman named Elihu Yale, who was the benefactor of the world famous university and who now lies in the churchyard at St Giles. An ideal centre from which to visit the charming English border town of Chester and the North Wales coastline, Wrexham town is situated in the beautiful Clwedog Valley and is also close to the Clwydian Hill Range, which run between Flintshire and Denbighshire and are famous for their ancient hillforts and a section of Offa's Dyke. At the village of Holt, a short distance from Wrexham, can be seen the Roman tile factory. On the banks of the River Dee is Bangor-on-Dee, near Wrexham, famous for its National Hunt racecourse and where can also be seen the mediaeval St Dunawd's Church in a picturesque setting overlooking the Dee. Moving south on the A483 you come to the ancient border town of Chirk where runs a section of the Shropshire Canal, carried across the Ceirog valley by an aqueduct, which runs alongside the railway viaduct.

Chirk Castle is in a remarkable good condition and appears to be untouched by the ravages of conflict throughout the centuries. This, however, is a false impression because Cromwell's soldiers breached the walls and left behind a bit of a ruin. After the Civil War came to an end the castle was restored to much of its former glory by Sir Thomas Middleton, but further restorers did their best to alter it into a luxurious mansion and in doing so spoiled its appearance. Indoors, however, there is much of interest to be seen including a pair of jackboots belonging to Oliver Cromwell and a four-poster bed where King Charles I once slept. Built to guard the entrance of the secret Ceirog Valley below the imposing Berwyn Mountains, the castle is well worth visiting. Chirk, like Wrexham, also boasts an excellent full-sized golf course, while close to the English/ Welsh border is the unique Llanymynech Golf Club, where Ian Woosnam learned the game that brought him much fame and fortune. Moving back north and beyond Wrexham, the next important town is that of Mold, a pleasant market town and an excellent shopping centre. Wednesdays and Saturdays are the market days and when the locals come to town to add to the Welshness of the place. Near Mold is the popular Loggerheads Country Park, which provides a rewarding day out for all the family. Set in the heart of the Clwydian Range and near the quietness of the beautiful River Alyn, there is much to do here including walks along the nature trails and inside the woodland areas, picnic areas, a countryside centre, displays, a cafe and a restaurant and all in an award winning area of outstanding natural beauty offering breathtaking views. Open all the year round, the admission is free.

North-eastwards the town of Flint stands proudly overlooking the Dee Estuary and beyond to the Wirral Peninsular and Merseyside. The Dee Estuary-the eastern edge of the Irish Sea-has long been renowned as of international importance for fauna, flora and birdlife, while the huge wide beach area at Talacre, north of Flint, holds a Yellow Flag Rural Seaside Award and is a popular holiday destination, especially so for caravanners who have a good choice of caravan parks. Returning to Flint, the old county town is renowned for its 13th century castle, because this is where King Richard II was confined after being moved from Conwy Castle in 1399. It was here that Richard, disguised as a priest, managed to be received by Bolingbroke before eventually being forced to abdicate and afterwards meeting a violent death. Built by Edward I in 1277, the castle was once a formidable fortress and part of the mighty chain of strongholds built by Edward after his conquest of Wales. Now in ruins the castle is still of architectural interest because of its circular towers, one of which possesses two concentric walls two yards thick divided by a space of 21ft.

Holywell (pronounced Hollywell) is also an ancient town and derives its name from the Holy St Winifred's Well. Another of the "Seven Wonders of Wales" it has long been the "Welsh Lourdes" to many afflicted pilgrims who once arrived in their thousands looking for an instant cure. The legend began in the seventh-century when the fierce and cruel Caradoc, the Welsh Prince, fell madly in love with St Winifred, who firmly rejected his wooing and was disgusted with his rough approaches to her. To cut a long story short, his temper at being rejected got the better of him and he decapitated the unfortunate Winifred. The head rolled away, came to rest by a church and lo and behold the pool of blood turned into a vast spring. After much praying by her family the saintly lady returned from the dead and the legend was born. The magical spring continued to flow and the pilgrims continued to flock to Holywell so much so that centuries later the Countess of Richmond, Henry VII's mother, built the beautiful St Winifred's Chapel and Plunge Bath around the sacred well, which still stands in all its glory at Holywell.

Flintshire's other claim to fame is that William Gladstone, who was four times the Prime Minister of Britain, made the 18th century Hawarden Castle his country home and spent much of his leisure time there in the country that he much loved. Situated in a pleasant part of Flintshire, the town of Hawarden is a peaceful sort of place and boasts a full-sized parkland golf course. The historic town of Caerwys and the quiet town of Buckley are also places well worth visiting, with Buckley of interest to golfers because of its pleasant parkland course. All in all Flintshire has much more to offer the discerning visitor than described in this guide and being so close to the English border is in an ideal location for being explored.

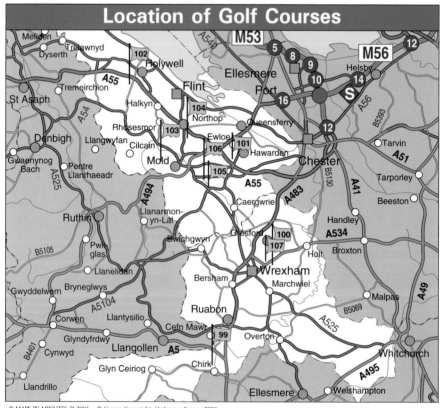

© MAPS IN MINUTES ™ 2001   © Crown Copyright, Ordnance Survey 2001

Chirk Golf Club

Chirk, Wrexham LL14 5AD

Tel: 01691 774407 Fax: 01691 773878

The golf club of Chirk may be one of the youngsters on the Welsh golfing scene, but it certainly hasn't been shy in telling the rest of the Welsh clubs that it has a course to be reckoned with and one that is certainly no pushover. Founded in 1991, it quickly found the attention of the golfing pundits by announcing (a clever way to announce its arrival) that two of the holes on its demanding course had a greater length than 600 yards! It goes without saying that both holes are mean and mighty par 5s and a great attraction to those golfers who fancy their chances as big hitters of the poor little golf ball. The 9th is certainly a massive hole, measuring a mighty 664 yards, giving Wales the distinction of having the longest golf hole in Britain. If you are thinking this is a stupid and impossible hole for amateurs to attempt to birdie, there has already been an eagle three recorded here-and this by one of Chirk's junior members!

The other long par 5 measures (I won't say a mere) just 632 yards, which must be a relief to the local members who only have another 300 plus yards to reach in the hope of a making a par after their drives! These two monster holes help to give the course a tough competitive length of 7,045 yards and a par of 72.

Nevertheless, the course has the full approval of the members because the club can boast a playing membership of well over 900. The club may be a precocious youngster with an age of just 11 years, but one that has obviously become a welcome addition to the Chirk community.

A parkland course close to Llangollen, Wrexham and the border county of Shropshire, Chirk has proved to be an excellent venue for holiday golfers. With an excellent clubhouse, featuring a spike bar and a good restaurant, a driving range with 15 undercover and floodlit bays, practice bunkers and a 9-hole par3 course, it is little wonder that the young club has proved to be a big hit in such a short time.

Sec/Manager:	Mark Maddison
Professional:	Mark Maddison
Directions:	9 miles S of Wrexham. From centre take A5152 leading to A483 (Oswestry). After 5 miles turn right onto A5 (Llangollen). Turn left after 1 mile onto minor road. Entrance after 800 yds.

Visitors:	Welcome: Contact Club in advance
Societies:	Welcome: Contact Club in advance
Facilities:	Putting Green, Chipping Green, Trolley Hire, Buggy Hire, Bar, Restaurant, Driving Range

18 Hole

Date Founded:	1991
Type of Course:	Parkland
No of Holes:	18
Length:	7045 yds (6503 mtrs)
Par:	72
SSS:	74
Green Fees:	Weekdays: £18 per day; Weekends/Bank Holidays: £25 per day

9 Hole

Date Founded:	1991
Type of Course:	Parkland
No of Holes:	9
Length:	6541 yds (6037 mtrs)
Par:	72
SSS:	73
Green Fees:	Weekdays: £5 per day; Weekends/Bank Holidays: £7.50 per day

Accommodation, Food and Drink

Reference numbers below refer to detailed information provided in section 2

Accommodation

Bridge End Hotel, Llangollen, Denbighshire LL20 8RY
Tel: 01978 860634
e-mail: bridge-endhotel@btconnect.com
A handsome former coaching inn in the town centre, with nine comfortable guest rooms (some en suite) and bar and restaurant menus.   200

The Cock Hotel, Forden, Welshpool, Powys SY21 8LX
Tel: 01938 580226
Late-19th century village inn serving a good choice of freshly prepared food, from sandwiches to mighty mixed grills. Also two guest rooms for B&B.   143

Elgar House, 16 Elgar Close, Oswestry, Shropshire SY11 2LZ
Tel: 01691 661323 mob: 07879 462813

A conservatory-fronted bungalow with three en suite bedrooms (two family size), guest bar and pleasant gardens. B&B: dinner with notice. AA 4 Diamonds.

Glen Helen Holiday Cottages, Pant, Oswestry, Shropshire SY10 9QN

Tel/Fax: 01691 830094
e-mail: gaskill@globalnet.co.uk
website: www.glenhelen.co.uk
High-class self-catering accommodation in two holiday cottages, each with two bedrooms, bath/shower, kitchen-diner, lounge and garden.   211

The Hand Hotel, Llanarmon Dyffryn Ceiriog, Clwyd LL20 7LD

Tel: 01691 600666 Fax: 01691 600262
e-mail: handllandcb@netscapeonline.co.uk
Built in the late 16th century, the Hand stands in beautiful countryside at the head of the Ceiriog Valley. 13 en suite bedrooms, bar and restaurant meals.   203

Sebastians Restaurant & Hotel, 45 Willow Street, Oswestry, Shropshire SY11 1AQ

Tel: 01691 655444 Fax: 01691 653452
e-mail: sebastians.rest@virgin.net
website: www.sebastians-hotel.co.uk
Individually appointed en suite bedrooms of great charm, plus fine French cuisine in an atmospheric 16th century setting. Private car park.

The Three Pigeons Inn, Graigfechan, Ruthin, Denbighshire LL15 2EU

Tel: 01824 703178 Fax: 01824 703812
17th century drovers inn with two bars, a games room and a non-smoking dining room, plus two spacious bedrooms. Also a caravan and camping site.   202

Food and Drink

The Black Horse Inn, Maesbrook, Oswestry, Shropshire SY10 8QG

Tel: 01691 682472 Fax: 01691 682872
A great pub for food, with a menu that offers an excellent choice for all tastes. Shropshire sirloin, with mushrooms and local blue cheese, is a favourite.

The Bradford Arms, Knockin, Nr. Oswestry, Shropshire SY10 8HJ

Tel: 01691 682358
A fine black-and-white roadside inn serving an excellent selection of home-cooked food for country appetites. Smart bar, non-smoking restaurant, beer garden.   210

Bridge End Hotel, Llangollen, Denbighshire LL20 8RY

Tel: 01978 860634
e-mail: bridge-endhotel@btconnect.com
A handsome former coaching inn in the town centre, with nine comfortable guest rooms (some en suite) and bar and restaurant menus.   200

The Cock Hotel, Forden, Welshpool, Powys SY21 8LX

Tel: 01938 580226
Late-19th century village inn serving a good choice of freshly prepared food, from sandwiches to mighty mixed grills. Also two guest rooms for B&B.   143

The Hand Hotel, Llanarmon Dyffryn Ceiriog, Clwyd LL20 7LD

Tel: 01691 600666 Fax: 01691 600262
e-mail: handllandcb@netscapeonline.co.uk
Built in the late 16th century, the Hand stands in beautiful countryside at the head of the Ceiriog Valley. 13 en suite bedrooms, bar and restaurant meals.   203

The New Inn, Corwen Road, Pontblyddyn, Mold, Flintshire CH7 4HR

Tel: 01352 771459
A friendly inn serving traditional home-cooked food from noon every day. Quick snacks to full meals on a varied menu with a children's section.

Sebastians Restaurant & Hotel, 45 Willow Street, Oswestry, Shropshire SY11 1AQ

Tel: 01691 655444 Fax: 01691 653452
e-mail: sebastians.rest@virgin.net
website: www.sebastians-hotel.co.uk
Individually appointed en suite bedrooms of great charm, plus fine French cuisine in an atmospheric 16th century setting. Private car park.

The Three Pigeons Inn, Graigfechan, Ruthin, Denbighshire LL15 2EU

Tel: 01824 703178 Fax: 01824 703812
17th century drovers inn with two bars, a games room and a non-smoking dining room, plus two spacious bedrooms. Also a caravan and camping site.   202

Clays Farm Golf Club

Bryn Estyn Road, Wrexham LL13 9UB

Tel: 01978 661406 Fax: 01978 661417

Sec/Manager:	Steve Williams
Professional:	David Larvin
Directions:	2 miles E of Wrexham. From centre take A5152 then join A534 (Nantwich). After ½ mile from the outskirts of Wrexham turn right onto minor road and then right into Bryn Ested Rd. Entrance on right hand side after ¼ mile.
Date Founded:	1991
Type of Course:	Parkland
No of Holes:	27
Length:	6000 yds (5538 mtrs)
Par:	69

SSS: 67

Green Fees: Weekdays:£13.00; Weekends/ Bank Holidays:£18.50

Visitors: Welcome: Contact Club by telephone in advance.

Societies: Welcome: Contact Club by telephone in advance.

Facilities: Putting Green, Chipping Green, Driving Range, Club Hire, Trolley Hire, Caddy Service, Bar, Restaurant

Accommodation, Food and Drink

Reference numbers below refer to detailed information provided in section 2

Accommodation

Bridge End Hotel, Llangollen, Denbighshire LL20 8RY
Tel: 01978 860634
e-mail: bridge-endhotel@btconnect.com
A handsome former coaching inn in the town centre, with nine comfortable guest rooms (some en suite) and bar and restaurant menus. 200

The Hand Hotel, Llanarmon Dyffryn Ceiriog, Clwyd LL20 7LD
Tel: 01691 600666 Fax: 01691 600262
e-mail: handllandcb@netscapeonline.co.uk
Built in the late 16th century, the Hand stands in beautiful countryside at the head of the Ceiriog Valley. 13 en suite bedrooms, bar and restaurant meals. 203

The Three Pigeons Inn, Graigfechan, Ruthin, Denbighshire LL15 2EU
Tel: 01824 703178 Fax: 01824 703812
17th century drovers inn with two bars, a games room and a non-smoking dining room, plus two spacious bedrooms. Also a caravan and camping site. 202

The West Arms Hotel, Llanarmon Dyffryn Ceiriog, Ceiriog Valley, Clwyd LL20 7LD
Tel: 01691 600665 Fax: 01691 600622
e-mail: booking@thewestarms.co.uk
website: www.thewestarms.co.uk
A charming, old-world country inn nestling in the lovely, peaceful Ceiriog Valley. Sixteen en suite bedrooms including two large suites. Bar and restaurant meals. 204

Food and Drink

Bridge End Hotel, Llangollen, Denbighshire LL20 8RY
Tel: 01978 860634
e-mail: bridge-endhotel@btconnect.com
A handsome former coaching inn in the town centre, with nine comfortable guest rooms (some en suite) and bar and restaurant menus. 200

The Hand Hotel, Llanarmon Dyffryn Ceiriog, Clwyd LL20 7LD
Tel: 01691 600666 Fax: 01691 600262
e-mail: handllandcb@netscapeonline.co.uk
Built in the late 16th century, the Hand stands in beautiful countryside at the head of the Ceiriog Valley. 13 en suite bedrooms, bar and restaurant meals. 203

The New Inn, Corwen Road, Pontblyddyn, Mold, Flintshire CH7 4HR
Tel: 01352 771459
A friendly inn serving traditional home-cooked food from noon every day. Quick snacks to full meals on a varied menu with a children's section.

The Three Pigeons Inn, Graigfechan, Ruthin, Denbighshire LL15 2EU
Tel: 01824 703178 Fax: 01824 703812
17th century drovers inn with two bars, a games room and a non-smoking dining room, plus two spacious bedrooms. Also a caravan and camping site. 202

The West Arms Hotel, Llanarmon Dyffryn Ceiriog, Ceiriog Valley, Clwyd LL20 7LD
Tel: 01691 600665 Fax: 01691 600622
e-mail: booking@thewestarms.co.uk
website: www.thewestarms.co.uk
A charming, old-world country inn nestling in the lovely, peaceful Ceiriog Valley. Sixteen en suite bedrooms including two large suites. Bar and restaurant meals. 204

Hawarden Golf Club

Groomsdale Lane, Hawarden Deeside CH5 3EH

Tel: 01244 531447 Fax: 01244 536901

Close to the borders of the English county of Cheshire and a mere six miles from the charming and atmospheric old city of Chester, playing golf at Hawarden could not be more ideal for golfers wishing to include a bit of nightlife or eating at top-class restaurants after a day on the golf course. Founded in 1911 on meadowland which has matured by careful planning and much patience into an attractive parkland course with a good showing of many and varied trees, the Hawarden course throws out an excellent challenge throughout its entire length of 5,900 yards. With the par of 69 exactly matching the standard scratch score the members find they have their

work cut out to reduce their handicaps on a regular basis. Indeed, a number of members are only too glad to tell you that their handicaps remain dormant or spiral upwards rather than in the opposite direction. Nevertheless, golf is not all about pursuing a prestigious low handicap but also about enjoying oneself with good friends, which is what many members prefer to do at the very friendly Hawarden club. A pleasing place to be, the course is undulating in parts but not too tiring to play. Ideal for holiday golfers and visiting societies, who are made most welcome, except on Saturdays when it is a competition day, the club offers full catering in its comfortable clubhouse and green fees which are rather modest.

Sec/Manager:	M Coppack
Professional:	B Rowlands
Directions:	6 miles W of Chester City Centre. From centre take Grosvenor Rd (A483) to the A55. Turn onto the A55 (St Asaph) and after 5 miles turn right onto the A550, Hawarden. After 1 mile turn right onto The Highway (B5125), then after 600 yds turn left into Groomsdale Lane. Entrance after 150 yds on left hand side.
Date Founded:	1911
Type of Course:	Parkland
No of Holes:	18
Length:	5900 yds (5446 mtrs)
Par:	69
SSS:	68
Green Fees:	Weekdays: £16.00; Weekends/ Bank Holidays:£20
Visitors:	Welcome: Contact Club in advance, unable to play on Saturday and Wednesday
Societies:	Welcome: Contact Club by telephone in advance, unable to play on Monday, Wednesday and Saturday
Facilities:	Putting Green, Trolley Hire, Buggy Hire, Bar, Restaurant

Accommodation, Food and Drink

Reference numbers below refer to detailed information provided in section 2

Accommodation

The Antelope, Rhydymwyn, Mold, Flintshire CH7 5HE

Tel: 01352 741247 Fax: 01352 741933
Former coaching inn on the A541 Mold-Denbigh road. Two bars, dining room, bar snacks and restaurant menus. Four letting bedrooms.   205

Cheshire Farm, Papermill Lane, Oakenholt, Flint CH6 5SU

Tel/Fax: 01244 830295
A delightful B&B on an 18th century working dairy farm with three letting bedrooms including a family room. Set in beautiful gardens. Children and pets welcome.

The Glann Hotel, 2 Stone Place, Hoole, Chester, Cheshire CH2 3NR

Tel: 01244 344800
e-mail: glannhot@supernet.com
Bed & Breakfast hotel in the suburbs of Chester, with six double rooms, two twins, one single and a family room.

Graig Park Hotel & Country Club, Dyserth, Denbighshire LL18 6DX

Tel: 01745 571022 Fax: 01745 571024
Hotel & Country Club set among lawns and woodland near the North Wales coast. Hotel accommodation or fully equipped log cabins. Sports and leisure facilities, restaurant.   199

Greyhound Hotel, Farndon, Cheshire CH3 6PU

Tel/Fax: 01829 270244
e-mail: greyhound-farndon@lineone.net
An attractive late-19th century pub in the village centre, with wholesome pub food and three letting bedrooms for B&B.   208

Mitchell's of Chester Guest House, 28 Hough Green, Chester, Cheshire CH4 8JQ

Tel: 01244 679004 Fax: 01244 659567
e-mail: mitoches@dialstart.net
website: www.mitchellsofchester.com
An elegantly restored Victorian house in the south of the city, with seven well-appointed non-smoking bedrooms and a lounge overlooking the garden. B&B.

Food and Drink

The Antelope, Rhydymwyn, Mold, Flintshire CH7 5HE

Tel: 01352 741247 Fax: 01352 741933
Former coaching inn on the A541 Mold-Denbigh road. Two bars, dining room, bar snacks and restaurant menus. Four letting bedrooms.   205

Graig Park Hotel & Country Club, Dyserth, Denbighshire LL18 6DX

Tel: 01745 571022 Fax: 01745 571024
Hotel & Country Club set among lawns and woodland near the North Wales coast. Hotel accommodation or fully equipped log cabins. Sports and leisure facilities, restaurant.   199

Greyhound Hotel, Farndon, Cheshire CH3 6PU

Tel/Fax: 01829 270244

e-mail: greyhound-farndon@lineone.net

An attractive late-19th century pub in the village centre, with wholesome pub food and three letting bedrooms for B&B. 208

The New Inn, Corwen Road, Pontblyddyn, Mold, Flintshire CH7 4HR

Tel: 01352 771459

A friendly inn serving traditional home-cooked food from noon every day. Quick snacks to full meals on a varied menu with a children's section.

Holywell Golf Club

Brynford, Holywell CA18 8LQ

Tel: 01352 710040 Fax: 01352 713937

Sharing with Wrexham the honour of being one of the oldest clubs in the borderland county of Flintshire, Holywell was founded in 1906 and lies on a mixture of natural moorland, parkland and linksland terrain, which offers an excellent challenge for the holiday golfer, with little climbing to add to the many hazards this pleasant and peaceful course throws at the unwary or first time visiting player. Set in one of the most pleasant and picturesque areas of Flintshire, the course is situated close to the hamlet of Brynford and a mere 2 miles south of the lovely old town of Holywell, from whence its name is derived.

For those of you who prefer the courses you play to have a bigger challenge than just natural rough and sand traps to overcome, then the Holywell lay-out will surely be your "cup of tea" because the par of 70 is definitely not a "piece of cake" course with a good score simply handed to you on a dinner plate. Indeed, the hazards here will set your pulse racing with a number of the holes laid around rocky quarries and others with water to contend with. However, if your golf and your confidence suffers after playing these holes then you can always visit the sacred, healing well at the nearby shrine of St Winifreds in the hope of an instant cure!

With a cosy clubhouse offering a warm and friendly atmosphere, a good practice area and buggies for hire, Holywell Golf Club is well worth a visit.

Sec/Manager:	Steve Roberts
Professional:	Matt Parsley
Directions:	1 mile SW of Holywell centre. From centre take Brynford St (B5121, Brynford), after 1m pass under the A55 and turn right at crossroads. Entrance after ¼ mile on right hand side.

Date Founded:	1906
Type of Course:	Heathland
No of Holes:	18
Length:	5636 yds (5202 mtrs)
Par:	70
SSS:	71
Green Fees:	Weekdays:£18.00; Weekends/ Bank Holidays:£23.00
Visitors:	Welcome: Contact Club by telephone in advance, unable to play on Saturday
Societies:	Welcome: Contact Club in writing or telephone in advance
Facilities:	Putting Green, Chipping Green, Trolley Hire, Buggy Hire, Bar, Restaurant

Accommodation, Food and Drink

Reference numbers below refer to detailed information provided in section 2

Accommodation

The Antelope, Rhydymwyn, Mold, Flintshire CH7 5HE

Tel: 01352 741247 Fax: 01352 741933

Former coaching inn on the A541 Mold-Denbigh road. Two bars, dining room, bar snacks and restaurant menus. Four letting bedrooms. 205

Cheshire Farm, Papermill Lane, Oakenholt, Flint CH6 5SU

Tel/Fax: 01244 830295

A delightful B&B on an 18th century working dairy farm with three letting bedrooms including a family room. Set in beautiful gardens. Children and pets welcome.

Graig Park Hotel & Country Club, Dyserth, Denbighshire LL18 6DX

Tel: 01745 571022 Fax: 01745 571024

Hotel & Country Club set among lawns and woodland near the North Wales coast. Hotel accommodation or fully equipped log cabins. Sports and leisure facilities, restaurant. 199

The Old Mill Private Hotel, Melin-y-Wern, Denbigh Road, Nannerch, Mold, Flintshire CH7 5RH

Tel: 01352 741542 Fax: 01352 740254
e-mail: welcome@old-mill.co.uk
website: www.old-mill.co.uk

'Warmest Welcome' Award-winning hotel with six en suite bedrooms and a restaurant. Craft shop on site.

Food and Drink

The Antelope, Rhydymwyn, Mold, Flintshire CH7 5HE

Tel: 01352 741247 Fax: 01352 741933
Former coaching inn on the A541 Mold-Denbigh road. Two bars, dining room, bar snacks and restaurant menus. Four letting bedrooms.   205

Graig Park Hotel & Country Club, Dyserth, Denbighshire LL18 6DX

Tel: 01745 571022 Fax: 01745 571024
Hotel & Country Club set among lawns and woodland near the North Wales coast. Hotel accommodation or fully equipped log cabins. Sports and leisure facilities, restaurant.   199

The Old Mill Private Hotel, Melin-y-Wern, Denbigh Road, Nannerch, Mold, Flintshire CH7 5RH

Tel: 01352 741542 Fax: 01352 740254
e-mail: welcome@old-mill.co.uk
website: www.old-mill.co.uk
'Warmest Welcome' Award-winning hotel with six en suite bedrooms and a restaurant. Craft shop on site.

Mold Golf Club

Cilcain Road, Pantymwyn, Mold CH7 5EH
Tel: 01352 740318 Fax: 01352 741517

The third oldest golf club in Flintshire, Mold has one of the shorter 18-hole courses in a county which is much blessed by a wonderful array of golf courses suited to the casual visitor who combines a few rounds of golf with other interesting aspects of a short stay. Founded in 1909 and designed by Hawtree, the course is an attractive and undulating parkland lay-out, which is situated some four miles west of the ancient town of Mold and close to the impressive Clwydian Hills. An excellent little holiday course it offers picturesque views of the Clwydian countryside and, lying close to the two courses at Padeswood, it could quite easily be included into the itinerary of golfers planning to visit those courses. Being only 5,512 yards, with a par of 67, the course is not

too difficult to walk or play but, nevertheless, offers an enjoyable challenge to the average amateur golfer.

With full clubhouse facilities, an excellent practice ground and fairly moderate green fees, the Mold club is certainly well worth a visit.

Sec/Manager:	Peter Mather
Professional:	Mark Jordan
Directions:	2 miles W of Mold centre. From the top of High St take Gwernaffield Rd to Gwernaffield. Go straight on into Cilcain Rd. Entrance after ¾ mile at brow of hill on left hand side.
Date Founded:	1909
Type of Course:	Upland
No of Holes:	18
Length:	5512 yds (5088 mtrs)
Par:	67
SSS:	67
Green Fees:	Weekdays:£18.00 (Summer) £12.00 (Winter); Weekends/ Bank Holidays: £20 (Summer) £17.00 (Winter)
Visitors:	Welcome: Contact Club by telephone in advance
Societies:	Welcome: Contact Club by telephone in advance
Facilities:	Putting Green, Practice Ground, Club Hire, Trolley Hire, Buggy Hire, Bar, Restaurant

Accommodation, Food and Drink

Reference numbers below refer to detailed information provided in section 2

Accommodation

The Antelope, Rhydymwyn, Mold,

Flintshire CH7 5HE

Tel: 01352 741247 Fax: 01352 741933
Former coaching inn on the A541 Mold-Denbigh
road. Two bars, dining room, bar snacks and
restaurant menus. Four letting bedrooms.   205

**Cheshire Farm, Papermill Lane, Oakenholt,
Flint CH6 5SU**

Tel/Fax: 01244 830295
A delightful B&B on an 18th century working dairy
farm with three letting bedrooms including a family
room. Set in beautiful gardens. Children and pets
welcome.

**The Old Mill Private Hotel, Melin-y-Wern,
Denbigh Road, Nannerch, Mold,
Flintshire CH7 5RH**

Tel: 01352 741542 Fax: 01352 740254
e-mail: welcome@old-mill.co.uk
website: www.old-mill.co.uk
'Warmest Welcome' Award-winning hotel with six en
suite bedrooms and a restaurant. Craft shop on site.

**The Three Pigeons Inn, Graigfechan, Ruthin,
Denbighshire LL15 2EU**

Tel: 01824 703178 Fax: 01824 703812
17th century drovers inn with two bars, a games room
and a non-smoking dining room, plus two spacious
bedrooms. Also a caravan and camping site.   202

Food and Drink

**The Antelope, Rhydymwyn, Mold,
Flintshire CH7 5HE**

Tel: 01352 741247 Fax: 01352 741933
Former coaching inn on the A541 Mold-Denbigh
road. Two bars, dining room, bar snacks and
restaurant menus. Four letting bedrooms.   205

**The Drover's Arms, Rhewl, Nr. Ruthin,
Denbighshire LL15 2UD**

Tel: 01824 703163
website: www.droversarms.co.uk
A pretty pub dating from the 16th century, located on
the A525. Large bar with dining, lounge and games
area. Beer garden.   201

**The New Inn, Corwen Road, Pontblyddyn, Mold,
Flintshire CH7 4HR**

Tel: 01352 771459
A friendly inn serving traditional home-cooked food
from noon every day. Quick snacks to full meals on a
varied menu with a children's section.

**The Old Mill Private Hotel, Melin-y-Wern,
Denbigh Road, Nannerch, Mold,
Flintshire CH7 5RH**

Tel: 01352 741542 Fax: 01352 740254
e-mail: welcome@old-mill.co.uk
website: www.old-mill.co.uk
'Warmest Welcome' Award-winning hotel with six en
suite bedrooms and a restaurant. Craft shop on site.

**The Three Pigeons Inn, Graigfechan, Ruthin,
Denbighshire LL15 2EU**

Tel: 01824 703178 Fax: 01824 703812
17th century drovers inn with two bars, a games room
and a non-smoking dining room, plus two spacious
bedrooms. Also a caravan and camping site.   202

Northop Country Park Golf Club

Northop, Chester CH7 6WA
Tel: 01244 816181 Fax: 01244 814661

Founded in 1993, the Northrop Country Park club
has quickly built a reputation of being one of the
finest inland golf venues for visitors to North
Wales. Designed by John Jacobs, recognised as
one of the world's finest teachers of golf and a
former Ryder Cup player, who has fond memories of North Wales after having finished
runner-up to the great Henry Cotton in the
Penfold event at Maesdu in the 1950's, the course
is laid out in 272 acres of truly magnificent parkland, featuring a wonderful array of tall and
mature trees. A credit to John Jacobs and the expertise of the greenkeeping staff, the course found
instant fame by hosting the Welsh PGA National
Championship in its first full year of opening in
1994 and received much praise from the competing professionals. Proving to be no "flash in the
pan" type of course it increased its reputation by
not only hosting the Welsh professional tournament again in 1995 and 1996 but also the 1995
British Girls Championship and the Girls Internationals. Now firmly established as an excellent
place to visit, golf at Northrop has been under
the watchful eye of none other than David
Llewellyn, the former European Tour star who,
along with his famous partner Ian Woosnam,
lifted the 1987 World Cup trophy for Wales. Now
taking a back seat and keeping an eye on the
magnificent place, he has handed over the reins
of club professional to the more than capable
Matthew Pritchard. Mainly flat, the course me-

anders around the fine old trees which reminds one of the Old Course at St Pierre in the south of the Principality. With a par of 72 and a length of 6,750 yards, it offers a fine and exciting challenge to even the best of golfers, with the 380-yard dog-legged par four 16th being, arguably, the best of the challenges. Here one has a wide expanse of water to contend with to the right, troublesome trees to the left and a wicked stream guarding the front of the green, thus proving that holes do not have to be overlong to become great challenging holes. As well as an excellent championship course to attract even the most discerning of golfers, Northrop Country Park also has a beautifully-designed and Georgian-styled red-bricked clubhouse, complete with a full length balcony terrace, a first class restaurant, two all-weather tennis courts, a gymnasium, sauna baths, an eight-bay driving range and a fully stocked professional shop. Situated just off the A55 Expressway 3 miles south of Flint and close to the magnificent border town of Chester, you will have no trouble finding this excellent and enjoyable golf complex.

Sec/Manager:	Paul Fletcher
Professional:	Mathew Pritchard
Directions:	10 miles W of Chester centre. From centre take the A483 (Wrexham) and join the A55 (St Asaph, Colwyn Bay), after 9 miles turn right onto B5126 (Northop). After 200 yds turn left into minor road. Entrance after ½ mile on right hand side.
Date Founded:	1994
Type of Course:	Parkland
No of Holes:	18
Length:	6750 yds (6230 mtrs)
Par:	72
SSS:	73
Green Fees:	Weekdays: £30 per day; Weekends/Bank Holidays: £35 per day
Visitors:	Welcome: Contact Club in advance
Societies:	Welcome: Unable to play weekend mornings. Contact Club by phone and in writing
Facilities:	Putting Green, Chipping Green, Driving Range, Club Hire, Trolley Hire, Buggy Hire, Caddy Service, Bar, Restaurant, Private Rooms

Accommodation, Food and Drink

Reference numbers below refer to detailed information provided in section 2

Accommodation

The Antelope, Rhydymwyn, Mold, Flintshire CH7 5HE

Tel: 01352 741247 Fax: 01352 741933

Former coaching inn on the A541 Mold-Denbigh road. Two bars, dining room, bar snacks and restaurant menus. Four letting bedrooms.   205

Cheshire Farm, Papermill Lane, Oakenholt, Flint CH6 5SU

Tel/Fax: 01244 830295

A delightful B&B on an 18th century working dairy farm with three letting bedrooms including a family room. Set in beautiful gardens. Children and pets welcome.

The Old Mill Private Hotel, Melin-y-Wern, Denbigh Road, Nannerch, Mold, Flintshire CH7 5RH

Tel: 01352 741542 Fax: 01352 740254
e-mail: welcome@old-mill.co.uk
website: www.old-mill.co.uk
'Warmest Welcome' Award-winning hotel with six en suite bedrooms and a restaurant. Craft shop on site.

The Three Pigeons Inn, Graigfechan, Ruthin, Denbighshire LL15 2EU

Tel: 01824 703178 Fax: 01824 703812

17th century drovers inn with two bars, a games room and a non-smoking dining room, plus two spacious bedrooms. Also a caravan and camping site.   202

Food and Drink

The Antelope, Rhydymwyn, Mold, Flintshire CH7 5HE

Tel: 01352 741247 Fax: 01352 741933

Former coaching inn on the A541 Mold-Denbigh road. Two bars, dining room, bar snacks and restaurant menus. Four letting bedrooms.   205

The Drover's Arms, Rhewl, Nr. Ruthin, Denbighshire LL15 2UD

Tel: 01824 703163
website: www.droversarms.co.uk
A pretty pub dating from the 16th century, located on the A525. Large bar with dining, lounge and games area. Beer garden.   201

The New Inn, Corwen Road, Pontblyddyn, Mold, Flintshire CH7 4HR

Tel: 01352 771459

A friendly inn serving traditional home-cooked food from noon every day. Quick snacks to full meals on a varied menu with a children's section.

The Old Mill Private Hotel, Melin-y-Wern, Denbigh Road, Nannerch, Mold, Flintshire CH7 5RH

Tel: 01352 741542 Fax: 01352 740254
e-mail: welcome@old-mill.co.uk
website: www.old-mill.co.uk
'Warmest Welcome' Award-winning hotel with six en
suite bedrooms and a restaurant. Craft shop on site.

The Three Pigeons Inn, Graigfechan, Ruthin, Denbighshire LL15 2EU

Tel: 01824 703178 Fax: 01824 703812
17th century drovers inn with two bars, a games room
and a non-smoking dining room, plus two spacious
bedrooms. Also a caravan and camping site.   202

Old Padeswood Golf Club

Station Road, Padeswood, Mold CH7 4JL
Tel: 01244 547701 Fax: 01244 545082

This club was founded in 1933 and reformed in
1978, after being designed by Arthur Joseph. A
rolling meadowland type course set in a tree-lined
valley, the Old Padeswood course, at 6,685 yards,
is longer than its Padeswood and Buckley neighbour and has a demanding par of 72. There is
also the attraction of a par-3 course for the beginners in your party to enjoy, a pleasant clubhouse
with full facilities and an excellent practice area.
Indeed an excellent spot for visiting parties.

Sec/Manager: John Witfield
Professional: Tony Davies

Directions: 3 miles SE of Mold centre.
From centre take the A541
(Wrexham), after 2 miles bear
left onto the A5118. Entrance
after 1¼ miles on right hand
side.

Date Founded: 1978
Type of Course: Meadowland
No of Holes: 18
Length: 6685 yds (6171 mtrs)
Par: 72
SSS: 71
Green Fees: Weekdays: £20 per day;
Weekends/Bank Holidays: £25
per day
Visitors: Welcome: Contact Club in
advance
Societies: Welcome: Contact Club in
advance
Facilities: Putting Green, Trolley Hire,
Buggy Hire, Bar, Restaurant

Accommodation, Food and Drink

Reference numbers below refer to detailed
information provided in section 2

Accommodation

**The Antelope, Rhydymwyn, Mold,
Flintshire CH7 5HE**
Tel: 01352 741247 Fax: 01352 741933
Former coaching inn on the A541 Mold-Denbigh
road. Two bars, dining room, bar snacks and
restaurant menus. Four letting bedrooms.   205

**Cheshire Farm, Papermill Lane, Oakenholt,
Flint CH6 5SU**
Tel/Fax: 01244 830295
A delightful B&B on an 18th century working dairy
farm with three letting bedrooms including a family
room. Set in beautiful gardens. Children and pets
welcome.

**Graig Park Hotel & Country Club, Dyserth,
Denbighshire LL18 6DX**
Tel: 01745 571022 Fax: 01745 571024
Hotel & Country Club set among lawns and
woodland near the North Wales coast. Hotel
accommodation or fully equipped log cabins. Sports
and leisure facilities, restaurant.   199

**The Old Mill Private Hotel, Melin-y-Wern,
Denbigh Road, Nannerch, Mold,
Flintshire CH7 5RH**
Tel: 01352 741542 Fax: 01352 740254
e-mail: welcome@old-mill.co.uk
website: www.old-mill.co.uk
'Warmest Welcome' Award-winning hotel with six en
suite bedrooms and a restaurant. Craft shop on site.

Food and Drink

**The Antelope, Rhydymwyn, Mold,
Flintshire CH7 5HE**

Tel: 01352 741247 Fax: 01352 741933
Former coaching inn on the A541 Mold-Denbigh
road. Two bars, dining room, bar snacks and
restaurant menus. Four letting bedrooms. 205

**Graig Park Hotel & Country Club, Dyserth,
Denbighshire LL18 6DX**

Tel: 01745 571022 Fax: 01745 571024
Hotel & Country Club set among lawns and
woodland near the North Wales coast. Hotel
accommodation or fully equipped log cabins. Sports
and leisure facilities, restaurant. 199

**The New Inn, Corwen Road, Pontblyddyn, Mold,
Flintshire CH7 4HR**

Tel: 01352 771459
A friendly inn serving traditional home-cooked food
from noon every day. Quick snacks to full meals on a
varied menu with a children's section.

**The Old Mill Private Hotel, Melin-y-Wern,
Denbigh Road, Nannerch, Mold,
Flintshire CH7 5RH**

Tel: 01352 741542 Fax: 01352 740254
e-mail: welcome@old-mill.co.uk
website: www.old-mill.co.uk
'Warmest Welcome' Award-winning hotel with six en
suite bedrooms and a restaurant. Craft shop on site.

Padeswood & Buckley Golf Course

The Caia, Station Lane, Padeswood,
Mold CH7 4JD

Tel: 01244 550537 Fax: 01244 541600

The first time I had the pleasure of visiting the
Padeswood and Buckley Golf Club was when I
went there to report on the 1990 Welsh Girls
Championship. I was then pleasantly surprised

to discover the course was a highly attractive and
beautifully groomed parkland lay-out with much
character. Situated within the splendid Clwydian
countryside with charming and picturesque views
and close to the quiet village of Padeswood, this
delightful 18-hole course was founded in 1933, a
rare time for golf courses to be created because it
was the years of the great economic depression
that swept in from the USA.

Designed by the A. Williams Partnership company, the course, which is splendidly situated
alongside the peaceful River Alyn, stretches for
just under 6,000 yards of delightful undulating
and lush countryside with every hole bordered
by attractive and flowering trees, which adds to
the peaceful atmosphere of the whole place. Add
to this the small and cosy clubhouse with excellent catering and a warm welcome given to
visitors, it is an excellent club for societies of 15
or more to pencil in for future visits, because packages include 27 holes of golf, coffee on arrival,
light lunch and a three course evening meal. All
this for a modest price on a pleasant untiring type
of course is a bargain to be considered. Close to
good accommodation and in a splendid part of
Flintshire, the village of Padeswood is a good place
for a stopover because quite close to the
Padeswood and Buckley course lies the also excellent Old Padeswood Golf Club.

Sec/Manager:	Malcolm Conway
Professional:	David Ashton
Directions:	3½ miles SE of Mold. From centre take the A541 (Wrexham), after 2 miles bear left onto the A5118, turn right after 1¼ miles into minor road. Entrance after ½ mile on right hand side.
Date Founded:	1933
Type of Course:	Parkland
No of Holes:	18
Length:	5982 yds (5521 mtrs)
Par:	70
SSS:	70
Green Fees:	Weekdays: £20 per day; Weekends/Bank Holidays:£25 per day
Visitors:	Welcome: Excluding Sunday. Contact Club in advance
Societies:	Welcome: Excluding weekends. Contact Club in advance
Facilities:	Putting Green, Chipping Green, Practice Area, Club Hire, Trolley Hire, Buggy Hire, Bar, Restaurant

Accommodation, Food and Drink

Reference numbers below refer to detailed
information provided in section 2

Accommodation

**The Antelope, Rhydymwyn, Mold,
Flintshire CH7 5HE**

Tel: 01352 741247 Fax: 01352 741933

Former coaching inn on the A541 Mold-Denbigh
road. Two bars, dining room, bar snacks and
restaurant menus. Four letting bedrooms.   205

**Cheshire Farm, Papermill Lane, Oakenholt,
Flint CH6 5SU**

Tel/Fax: 01244 830295

A delightful B&B on an 18th century working dairy
farm with three letting bedrooms including a family
room. Set in beautiful gardens. Children and pets
welcome.

**Graig Park Hotel & Country Club, Dyserth,
Denbighshire LL18 6DX**

Tel: 01745 571022 Fax: 01745 571024

Hotel & Country Club set among lawns and
woodland near the North Wales coast. Hotel
accommodation or fully equipped log cabins. Sports
and leisure facilities, restaurant.   199

**The Old Mill Private Hotel, Melin-y-Wern,
Denbigh Road, Nannerch, Mold,
Flintshire CH7 5RH**

Tel: 01352 741542 Fax: 01352 740254
e-mail: welcome@old-mill.co.uk
website: www.old-mill.co.uk

'Warmest Welcome' Award-winning hotel with six en
suite bedrooms and a restaurant. Craft shop on site.

Food and Drink

**The Antelope, Rhydymwyn, Mold,
Flintshire CH7 5HE**

Tel: 01352 741247 Fax: 01352 741933

Former coaching inn on the A541 Mold-Denbigh
road. Two bars, dining room, bar snacks and
restaurant menus. Four letting bedrooms.   205

**Graig Park Hotel & Country Club, Dyserth,
Denbighshire LL18 6DX**

Tel: 01745 571022 Fax: 01745 571024

Hotel & Country Club set among lawns and
woodland near the North Wales coast. Hotel
accommodation or fully equipped log cabins. Sports
and leisure facilities, restaurant.   199

**The New Inn, Corwen Road, Pontblyddyn, Mold,
Flintshire CH7 4HR**

Tel: 01352 771459

A friendly inn serving traditional home-cooked food
from noon every day. Quick snacks to full meals on a
varied menu with a children's section.

**The Old Mill Private Hotel, Melin-y-Wern,
Denbigh Road, Nannerch, Mold,**

Flintshire CH7 5RH

Tel: 01352 741542 Fax: 01352 740254
e-mail: welcome@old-mill.co.uk
website: www.old-mill.co.uk

'Warmest Welcome' Award-winning hotel with six en
suite bedrooms and a restaurant. Craft shop on site.

Wrexham Golf Club

Holt Road, Wrexham LL13 9SB

Tel: 01978 364268 Fax: 01978 364268

The Wrexham club was founded in 1906 on a
piece of land on the other side of the town to
where it now lies 2 miles northeast of Wrexham
on the A534. Come 1924 the members felt that
the club had outgrown the original course and
accepted the opportunity of moving to the present
site, where they called on the expertise of James
Braid to lay-out a quality course, and there they
have remained happily ever since. Now a delightful full-sized course on a base of sandy soil and
gravel, it has matured into a rather pleasant parkland lay-out. What is assumed as being unique to
the club, the daunting task for the incoming club
captain of having to drive himself into office from
the first tee while watched by the fellow members, is even more so for the poor incoming
Wrexham captain each year because for well over
five decades it has been the tradition for the club
professional to stand behind the new captain and
fire a shotgun at the exact moment that the
clubhead impacts the ball and sends it on its
merry way, but not always on a straight flight
path. Which is not unexpected when you think
of what the poor unfortunate new captain must
be suffering at that particular moment!

During the latter part of the 1960's the
Wrexham club celebrated the opening of their
new and large splendid single-storey clubhouse
by arranging an exhibition match with Welsh-
men Dai Rees and Dave Thomas taking on their
Ryder Cup colleagues Peter Aliss and Bernard
Hunt. At the time the club president was James
McAlpine, the chairman of the giant Sir Robert
McAlpine building construction company, who

obviously had something to do with the club-house being such a sumptuous creation.

The course comprises five par-3s, three par-5s and ten par-4s, which are all excellently drained because of the nature of the sub soil, and the terrain is gently undulating with no excessive climbs to endure. With a length of 6,250 yards, the par of 70 looks comparatively easy for the golfing "tigers" but at the recent Clwyd Open event the lowest scratch scores returned were two of 69-this on a beautiful sunny and windless summer's day speaks volumes about how difficult the course does play from the back tee blocks. On most courses the old saying of "conquer the par-3, s and you conquer the course" rings true, but when you have five of these short holes, like Wrexham, you have to have much finesse in your game to score well. Therefore, Wrexham's subtle five short-ies reduce the threat of the "master blasters" among you. A number of the long holes have out of bounds to pose an extra problem for the un-wary, with the 7th-a dog-leg par-4-being regarded the most difficult despite the fact of no out of bounds to worry about. A channelled fairway with trees and thick bushes to contend with and a steep slope to the right, the fairway then dog-legs left with a steep slope guarding the green on its left, which tends to throw the approach shot beyond and below the green, from where a devilish chip shot has to be played to the green. A great hole and one of many on this interesting course. A very friendly club is Wrexham and one you will certainly enjoy.

Sec/Manager:	Pamela Oldfield
Professional:	Paul Williams
Directions:	2 miles E of Wrexham centre. From centre take Rhosnesni Lane (B5100) for 1 mile to roundabout. Turn left onto A534 (Nantwich). Entrance after ¾ mile, just after next roundabout, on left hand side.
Date Founded:	1924
Type of Course:	Parkland
No of Holes:	18
Length:	6250 yds (5769 mtrs)
Par:	70
SSS:	70
Green Fees:	Weekdays: £22 per day; Weekends/Bank Holidays: £27 per day
Visitors:	Welcome: Except Tuesdays. Contact Club in advance
Societies:	Welcome: except Tuesdays.

	Contact Club in advance
Facilities:	Putting Green, Chipping Green, Practice Ground, Club Hire, Trolley Hire, Buggy Hire, Bar, Restaurant

Accommodation, Food and Drink

Reference numbers below refer to detailed information provided in section 2

Accommodation

Bridge End Hotel, Llangollen, Denbighshire LL20 8RY
Tel: 01978 860634
e-mail: bridge-endhotel@btconnect.com
A handsome former coaching inn in the town centre, with nine comfortable guest rooms (some en suite) and bar and restaurant menus.   200

The Cock Hotel, Forden, Welshpool, Powys SY21 8LX
Tel: 01938 580226
Late-19th century village inn serving a good choice of freshly prepared food, from sandwiches to mighty mixed grills. Also two guest rooms for B&B.   143

Greyhound Hotel, Farndon, Cheshire CH3 6PU
Tel/Fax: 01829 270244 e-mail: greyhound-farndon@lineone.net
An attractive late-19th century pub in the village centre, with wholesome pub food and three letting bedrooms for B&B.   208

The Hand Hotel, Llanarmon Dyffryn Ceiriog, Clwyd LL20 7LD
Tel: 01691 600666 Fax: 01691 600262
e-mail: handllandcb@netscapeonline.co.uk
Built in the late 16th century, the Hand stands in beautiful countryside at the head of the Ceiriog Valley. 13 en suite bedrooms, bar and restaurant meals.   203

Sebastians Restaurant & Hotel, 45 Willow Street, Oswestry, Shropshire SY11 1AQ
Tel: 01691 655444 Fax: 01691 653452
e-mail: sebastians.rest@virgin.net
website: www.sebastians-hotel.co.uk
Individually appointed en suite bedrooms of great charm, plus fine French cuisine in an atmospheric 16th century setting. Private car park.

The Three Pigeons Inn, Graigfechan, Ruthin, Denbighshire LL15 2EU
Tel: 01824 703178 Fax: 01824 703812
17th century drovers inn with two bars, a games room and a non-smoking dining room, plus two spacious bedrooms. Also a caravan and camping site.   202

The West Arms Hotel, Llanarmon Dyffryn Ceiriog, Ceiriog Valley, Clwyd LL20 7LD
Tel: 01691 600665 Fax: 01691 600622
e-mail: booking@thewestarms.co.uk

website: www.thewestarms.co.uk
A charming, old-world country inn nestling in the lovely, peaceful Ceiriog Valley. Sixteen en suite bedrooms including two large suites. Bar and restaurant meals. 204

Food and Drink

The Black Horse Inn, Maesbrook, Oswestry, Shropshire SY10 8QG

Tel: 01691 682472 Fax: 01691 682872
A great pub for food, with a menu that offers an excellent choice for all tastes. Shropshire sirloin, with mushrooms and local blue cheese, is a favourite.

Bridge End Hotel, Llangollen, Denbighshire LL20 8RY

Tel: 01978 860634
e-mail: bridge-endhotel@btconnect.com
A handsome former coaching inn in the town centre, with nine comfortable guest rooms (some en suite) and bar and restaurant menus. 200

The Cock Hotel, Forden, Welshpool, Powys SY21 8LX

Tel: 01938 580226
Late-19th century village inn serving a good choice of freshly prepared food, from sandwiches to mighty mixed grills. Also two guest rooms for B&B. 143

Greyhound Hotel, Farndon, Cheshire CH3 6PU

Tel/Fax: 01829 270244
e-mail: greyhound-farndon@lineone.net
An attractive late-19th century pub in the village centre, with wholesome pub food and three letting bedrooms for B&B. 208

The Hand Hotel, Llanarmon Dyffryn Ceiriog, Clwyd LL20 7LD

Tel: 01691 600666 Fax: 01691 600262
e-mail: handllandcb@netscapeonline.co.uk
Built in the late 16th century, the Hand stands in beautiful countryside at the head of the Ceiriog Valley. 13 en suite bedrooms, bar and restaurant meals. 203

The New Inn, Corwen Road, Pontblyddyn, Mold, Flintshire CH7 4HR

Tel: 01352 771459
A friendly inn serving traditional home-cooked food from noon every day. Quick snacks to full meals on a varied menu with a children's section.

Sebastians Restaurant & Hotel, 45 Willow Street, Oswestry, Shropshire SY11 1AQ

Tel: 01691 655444 Fax: 01691 653452
e-mail: sebastians.rest@virgin.net
website: www.sebastians-hotel.co.uk
Individually appointed en suite bedrooms of great charm, plus fine French cuisine in an atmospheric 16th century setting. Private car park.

The Three Pigeons Inn, Graigfechan, Ruthin, Denbighshire LL15 2EU

Tel: 01824 703178 Fax: 01824 703812

17th century drovers inn with two bars, a games room and a non-smoking dining room, plus two spacious bedrooms. Also a caravan and camping site. 202

The West Arms Hotel, Llanarmon Dyffryn Ceiriog, Ceiriog Valley, Clwyd LL20 7LD

Tel: 01691 600665 Fax: 01691 600622
e-mail: booking@thewestarms.co.uk
website: www.thewestarms.co.uk
A charming, old-world country inn nestling in the lovely, peaceful Ceiriog Valley. Sixteen en suite bedrooms including two large suites. Bar and restaurant meals. 204

Location of Golf Courses

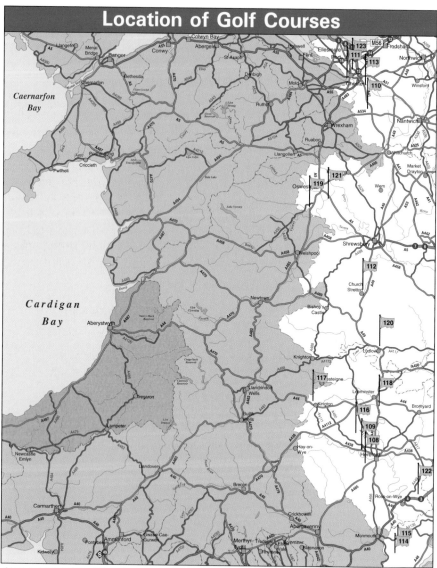

© MAPS IN MINUTES ™ 2001   © Crown Copyright, Ordnance Survey 2001

WELSH BORDERS

In addition to 18 hole courses in Wales *The Golfers Guide to Wales* includes a small selection of golf clubs which are actually in the English counties of Cheshire, Shropshire and Herefordshire.

There are relatively few golf clubs on the eastern borders of Wales although the courses are located in some splendid Welsh countryside. Those golfers who like to play 2 or more rounds of golf during their travels and who wish to enjoy some of the more isolated Welsh courses will be able to do this by including both Welsh and English border clubs in their golfing itinerary. The English clubs selected are close to the Welsh border, offer a stimulating golfing challenge and indeed many have Welsh members.

Belmont Lodge Golf Club

Belmont, Hereford HR2 9SA
Tel: 01432 352666 Fax: 01432 358090

Having been involved with Belmont Golf Club (its original title) even before it was created, when I was invited by the partnership to work on publicising the venture and later when I had the honour of becoming the club captain in its second year of trading, I must admit to having something of a soft spot for the Herefordshire-based club. Founded in 1983, when William Chicester inherited the Belmont Estate from his father, the club has witnessed some troubled times but, thankfully, is now very much alive and kicking. William Chichester and his two partners had ambitious plans to turn the old estate into a thriving golf and hotel complex, which, to their credit, they almost succeeded in doing. Golf designer and former professional golfer, Robert Sandow (who was one of the partners) created a long and demanding parkland course of some beauty to attract a large club membership, and the old Belmont Mansion House was refurbished into an extensive clubhouse. With famous film star Sean Connery invited to open the complex along with a host of well-known celebrities also turning up to play with the members in a charity tourna-

ment, the club seemed to be prospering. However, the cost of getting the complex off the ground was underestimated and some years later the partnership had to sell. Bad luck also saw the new owner getting into money troubles and the club looked doomed to becoming part housing estate and part sand and gravel quarry because it lay on some of the richest sand and gravel land in the south of England. Thankfully, the present owners stepped in with a rescue plan, sold some of the land, re-designed part of the course and have never looked back. Today Belmont is thriving and now boasts full clubhouse facilities and self-catering accommodation on site at Belmont Lodge. Situated just two miles from the centre of Hereford and off the A436 road to Abergavenny, which lies over the Welsh border in Monmouthshire, the Belmont complex is overlooked by the famous Belmont Abbey. In a gorgeous parkland setting, the course offers beautiful views of the lovely River Wye, with the back nine holes actually bordering the peaceful river. With a SSS of 72, the demanding course has a length of 6,511 yards, with many good holes on which to test your golfing skills.

The club professional, Mike Welsh, is an Englishman (despite his surname) with a great sense of humour and a friendly disposition, which makes visiting his well stocked shop something to look forward to. Having been at Belmont since its creation, he obviously loves the place. So will you when you decide to make a visit.

Sec/Manager:	Alan Carver
Professional:	Mike Welsh
Directions:	2¼ miles SW of Hereford. From centre take the A49 then the A465 (Abergavenney), after 2¼ miles turn right, signed Belmont Abbey. Entrance after ¾ mile.
Date Founded:	1983
Type of Course:	Parkland
No of Holes:	18
Length:	6511 yds (5949 mtrs)
Par:	72
SSS:	72
Green Fees:	Weekdays: £14; Weekends/ Bank Holidays: £25
Visitors:	Welcome: Contact Club in advance
Societies:	Welcome: Contact Club in advance
Facilities:	Putting Green, Practice Area, Trolley Hire, Buggy Hire, Bar, Restaurant

Accommodation, Food and Drink

Reference numbers below refer to detailed
information provided in section 2

Accommodation

**Belmont Lodge & Golf Course, Belmont,
Hereford HR2 9SA**

Tel: 01432 352666 Fax: 01432 358090
e-mail: info@belmontlodge.co.uk
website: www.belmontlodge.co.uk
Thirty purpose-built modern rooms in the grounds of
18th century Belmont House, with a golf course by
the River Wye.   216

**The Black Swan, Much Dewchurch,
Herefordshire HR2 8DJ**

Tel: 01981 540295
Delightful 14th century hostelry serving excellent
food - pies and quiches a speciality. Real ales.
Accommodation available at local farms.

**New Priory Hotel, Stretton Sugwas,
Herefordshire HR4 7AR**

Tel: 01432 760264 Fax: 01432 761809
Ten very comfortable bedrooms in a handsome 19th
century country house set in landscaped grounds.
Two restaurants, lounge bars.   218

**Ye Olde Crown Inn, Pant-y-Gelli,
Monmouthshire NP7 7HR**

Tel/Fax: 01873 853314
e-mail: yeoldcrown@aol.com
An attractive and very popular 15th century inn on a
hillside north of Abergavenny. Real ales, very good
food and excellent overnight accommodation.   103

Food and Drink

**The Axe & Cleaver, Much Birch, Nr. Hereford,
Herefordshire HR2 8HU**

Tel/Fax: 01981 540203
An attractive black and white pub on the A49 south
of Hereford, with lovely gardens and a great
reputation for the quality of its food and drink.   223

**Belmont Lodge & Golf Course, Belmont,
Hereford HR2 9SA**

Tel: 01432 352666 Fax: 01432 358090
e-mail: info@belmontlodge.co.uk
website: www.belmontlodge.co.uk
Thirty purpose-built modern rooms in the grounds of
18th century Belmont House, with a golf course by
the River Wye.   216

**The Black Swan, Much Dewchurch,
Herefordshire HR2 8DJ**

Tel: 01981 540295
Delightful 14th century hostelry serving excellent
food - pies and quiches a speciality. Real ales.
Accommodation available at local farms.

The Comet Inn, Madley, Herefordshire HR2 9NJ

Tel: 01981 250600 e-mail: cometinn@madley

Large white-painted pub with a traditional ambience
and lovely gardens. Bar meals, à la carte, real ales.
Four miles from Hereford off the B4352 Hay road. 220

**The Fountain Inn, Orcup Hill,
Herefordshire HR2 8EP**

Tel: 01981 540304
A friendly country pub in a hilltop setting south of
Hereford. Splendid home cooking, excellent wine list,
real ales.   217

**The Horse & Groom, Hereford,
Herefordshire HR4 0AP**

Tel: 01432 355026 Fax: 01432 269242
website: www.dave@thehorseandgroom.fsnet.co.uk
Traditional decor in a lovely old pub close to the city
centre. Real ales, home-cooked bar snacks and meals.
The owner is a keen golfer.   219

**The New Harp Inn, Hoarwithy, Nr. Hereford,
Herefordshire HR2 6QH**

Tel: 01432 840213
Seventeenth century pub near the River Wye serving
good bar snacks and full meals. Three letting
bedrooms, large gardens.   215

**New Priory Hotel, Stretton Sugwas,
Herefordshire HR4 7AR**

Tel: 01432 760264 Fax: 01432 761809
Ten very comfortable bedrooms in a handsome 19th
century country house set in landscaped grounds.
Two restaurants, lounge bars.   218

**Ye Olde Crown Inn, Pant-y-Gelli,
Monmouthshire NP7 7HR**

Tel/Fax: 01873 853314
e-mail: eoldcrown@aol.com
An attractive and very popular 15th century inn on a
hillside north of Abergavenny. Real ales, very good
food and excellent overnight accommodation.   103

Burghill Valley
Golf Club

Tillington Road, Burghill, Hereford HR4 7RW

Tel: 01432 760456 Fax: 01432 761654

Situated at the opposite end of Hereford to that
of Belmont Lodge, The Burghill Valley Golf Club
can be found 4 miles northwest of the historic
city and close to the village of Burghill.

Founded in 1991 the club has quickly gained a
reputation of being an excellent venue for golfing societies and holiday golfers to visit. Set within
the beautiful Herefordshire countryside amidst a
charming background of small hills and woodland, with the distant views of the Welsh
mountains adding to the gorgeous pastoral setting, the course is very easy on the eye and fairly

easy to walk. Gently rolling fairways, bordered by young trees that will make the 6,239 yards, par 71, course more formidable when they mature, meander their way around two sizeable lakes, which are the main threats to a satisfying scorecard at the moment and throw out a good challenge to those golfers who like to attack a course.

A special feature of the course is where you have to play through mature cider apple orchids, cider, of course, being an important product of the rich Herefordshire countryside. A fair but interesting course for every class of golfer, the greens and fairways are in excellent condition with every hole full of interest and needing some thought to negotiate successfully. Representing the Burghill Valley club on a worldwide basis is the successful European Tour professional, David Park, the club's tournament professional. A Welshman, David resides in the Herefordshire area and can often be spotted at practice when taking a break from tournaments. The club professional, who has an excellent golf shop and available to give tuition, is the friendly Nigel Clarke. The attractive and excellent clubhouse at Burghill Valley has a warm and friendly atmosphere, with a large terrace overlooking the 18th green and offering magnificent views of the course and Hay Bluff beyond. With a bar and a good restaurant leading onto the terrace there is as much to enjoy when off the course as when treading the rolling fairways.

Sec/Manager:	Keith Smith
Professional:	Nigel Clarke
Directions:	4 miles NW of Hereford. From centre take the A438 (Swainshill), at Swainshill turn right onto A480, after 1½ miles turn right onto B road signed Burghhill. At second crossroads turn left. Entrance after 200 yds.
Date Founded:	1989
Type of Course:	Parkland
No of Holes:	18
Length:	6239 yds (5701 mtrs)
Par:	71
SSS:	70
Green Fees:	Weekdays: £20; Weekends/ Bank Holidays: £ 25
Visitors:	Welcome: Contact Club in advance – before 11.00 at weekends
Societies:	Welcome: Contact Club in advance

Facilities:	Putting Green, Chipping Green, Club Hire, Trolley Hire, Buggy Hire, Bar, Restaurant

Accommodation, Food and Drink

Reference numbers below refer to detailed information provided in section 2

Accommodation

Belmont Lodge & Golf Course, Belmont, Hereford HR2 9SA

Tel: 01432 352666 Fax: 01432 358090
e-mail: info@belmontlodge.co.uk
website: www.belmontlodge.co.uk

Thirty purpose-built modern rooms in the grounds of 18th century Belmont House, with a golf course by the River Wye. 216

The Black Swan, Much Dewchurch, Herefordshire HR2 8DJ

Tel: 01981 540295

Delightful 14th century hostelry serving excellent food - pies and quiches a speciality. Real ales. Accommodation available at local farms.

New Priory Hotel, Stretton Sugwas, Herefordshire HR4 7AR

Tel: 01432 760264 Fax: 01432 761809

Ten very comfortable bedrooms in a handsome 19th century country house set in landscaped grounds. Two restaurants, lounge bars. 218

Ye Olde Crown Inn, Pant-y-Gelli, Monmouthshire NP7 7HR

Tel/Fax: 01873 853314
e-mail: yeoldcrown@aol.com

An attractive and very popular 15th century inn on a hillside north of Abergavenny. Real ales, very good food and excellent overnight accommodation. 103

Ye Olde Salutation Inn, Weobley, Herefordshire HR4 8SJ

Tel: 01544 318443 Fax: 01544 318216
e-mail: salutationinn@btinternet.com

A classic English country pub in one of the county's prettiest vilages. Three charming bedrooms, top-class cuisine. 224

Food and Drink

The Axe & Cleaver, Much Birch, Nr. Hereford, Herefordshire HR2 8HU

Tel/Fax: 01981 540203

An attractive black and white pub on the A49 south of Hereford, with lovely gardens and a great reputation for the quality of its food and drink. 223

Belmont Lodge & Golf Course, Belmont, Hereford HR2 9SA

Tel: 01432 352666 Fax: 01432 358090
e-mail: info@belmontlodge.co.uk
website: www.belmontlodge.co.uk

Thirty purpose-built modern rooms in the grounds of 18th century Belmont House, with a golf course by the River Wye.   216

The Black Swan, Much Dewchurch, Herefordshire HR2 8DJ

Tel: 01981 540295

Delightful 14th century hostelry serving excellent food - pies and quiches a speciality. Real ales. Accommodation available at local farms.

The Comet Inn, Madley, Herefordshire HR2 9NJ

Tel: 01981 250600 e-mail: cometinn@madley

Large white-painted pub with a traditional ambience and lovely gardens. Bar meals, à la carte, real ales. Four miles from Hereford off the B4352 Hay road. 220

The Fountain Inn, Orcup Hill, Herefordshire HR2 8EP

Tel: 01981 540304

A friendly country pub in a hilltop setting south of Hereford. Splendid home cooking, excellent wine list, real ales.   217

The Horse & Groom, Hereford, Herefordshire HR4 0AP

Tel: 01432 355026 Fax: 01432 269242
website: www.dave@thehorseandgroom.fsnet.co.uk

Traditional decor in a lovely old pub close to the city centre. Real ales, home-cooked bar snacks and meals. The owner is a keen golfer.   219

The Kites Nest Inn, Swainshill, Herefordshire HR4 7QA

Tel/Fax: 01981 590217

Fine home cooking - both restaurant and bar menus - in a popular pub by the A438 west of Hereford. Also good wines, beers, soft drinks.   222

The New Harp Inn, Hoarwithy, Nr. Hereford, Herefordshire HR2 6QH

Tel: 01432 840213

Seventeenth century pub near the River Wye serving good bar snacks and full meals. Three letting bedrooms, large gardens.   215

New Priory Hotel, Stretton Sugwas, Herefordshire HR4 7AR

Tel: 01432 760264 Fax: 01432 761809

Ten very comfortable bedrooms in a handsome 19th century country house set in landscaped grounds. Two restaurants, lounge bars.   218

Ye Olde Crown Inn, Pant-y-Gelli, Monmouthshire NP7 7HR

Tel/Fax: 01873 853314
e-mail: yeoldcrown@aol.com

An attractive and very popular 15th century inn on a hillside north of Abergavenny. Real ales, very good food and excellent overnight accommodation.   103

Ye Olde Salutation Inn, Weobley, Herefordshire HR4 8SJ

Tel: 01544 318443 Fax: 01544 318216
e-mail: salutationinn@btinternet.com

A classic English country pub in one of the county's prettiest vilages. Three charming bedrooms, top-class cuisine.   224

Carden Park Golf Club

Carden Park, Chester CH3 9DQ

Tel: 01829 731600 Fax: 01829 731032

Sec/Manager:	Dave Llewelyn
Professional:	Simon Edwards
Directions:	9 miles S of Chester. From E side of Chester take the A41 (Whitchurch), after 8 miles turn right onto the A534 (Wrexham), then after ¾ mile turn left onto B road signed Tilston. Entrance on right hand side after ½ mile.
Visitors:	Welcome: Contact Club in advance
Societies:	Welcome: Contact Club in advance
Facilities:	Putting Green, Chipping Green, Driving Range, Club Hire, Trolley Hire, Buggy Hire, Bar, Restaurant, Private Rooms

Chester

Date Founded:	1993
Type of Course:	Parkland
No of Holes:	19
Length:	6348 yds (5800 mtrs)
Par:	72
SSS:	72
Green Fees:	Weekdays: £40; Weekends/ Bank Holidays: £40

Nicklaus

Date Founded: 1998

Type of Course: Parkland

No of Holes: 18

Length: 6302 yds (5758 mtrs)

Par: 72

SSS: 72

Green Fees: Weekdays: £60; Weekends/
Bank Holidays: £60

Accommodation, Food and Drink

Reference numbers below refer to detailed
information provided in section 2

Accommodation

**The Duke of Wellington, Marsh Lane, Ince,
Nr. Chester, Cheshire CH2 4NR**

Tel: 0151 356 0222

Public house serving bar meals and snacks: jacket
potatoes, salads, burgers, chilli, sausages with beans
and chips. Functions by arrangement.

**The Glann Hotel, 2 Stone Place, Hoole, Chester,
Cheshire CH2 3NR**

Tel: 01244 344800
e-mail: glannhot@supernet.com
Bed & Breakfast hotel in the suburbs of Chester, with
six double rooms, two twins, one single and a family
room.

**Greyhound Hotel, Farndon,
Cheshire CH3 6PU**

Tel/Fax: 01829 270244
e-mail: greyhound-farndon@lineone.net
An attractive late-19th century pub in the village
centre, with wholesome pub food and three letting
bedrooms for B&B.　　　　　　　　　　　　　208

**Mitchell's of Chester Guest House,
28 Hough Green, Chester, Cheshire CH4 8JQ**

Tel: 01244 679004 Fax: 01244 659567
e-mail: mitoches@dialstart.net
website: www.mitchellsofchester.com
An elegantly restored Victorian house in the south of
the city, with seven well-appointed non-smoking
bedrooms and a lounge overlooking the garden. B&B.

Food and Drink

**Cheshire Farm Ice Cream, Drumlan Hall,
Newton Lane, Tattenhall, Chester,
Cheshire CH3 9NE**

Tel: 01829 770995 Fax: 01829 770856
e-mail: cfic@btconnect.com
Splendid tea rooms serving snacks, cream teas and
their own range of top-quality Cheshire Farm ice
creams. Also close to Portal championship course at
Tarporley.

**The Copper Mine, Broxton, Nr. Chester,
Cheshire CH3 9JH**

Tel: 01829 782293 Fax: 01829 782183
e-mail: coppermineinn@cs.com
A handsome country pub on the A534 Nantwich-
Wrexham road, with two bars, two non-smoking
eating areas and a large garden. Bar and restaurant
menus, extensive choice of wines.　　　　　207

**Greyhound Hotel, Farndon,
Cheshire CH3 6PU**

Tel/Fax: 01829 270244
e-mail: greyhound-farndon@lineone.net
An attractive late-19th century pub in the village
centre, with wholesome pub food and three letting
bedrooms for B&B.　　　　　　　　　　　　　208

**The Sportsmans Arms, Tattenhall,
Cheshire CH3 9QF**

Tel: 01829 770233 Fax: 01829 771886
A charming village pub serving a good selection of
light bites and full meals from noon onwards. Pool,
darts, golf corner, patio.　　　　　　　　　206

Chester Golf Club

Curzon Park North, Chester CH4 8AR

Tel: 01244 677760 Fax: 01244 676667

Sec/Manager: V Wood

Professional: G Parton

Directions: ½ mile of Church Stretton
centre. From centre take
Shrewsbury Rd (B4370), after
500 yds turn left into Carding
Mill Valley, then first right into
Trevor Hill. Entrance on right
hand side after 300 yds.

Date Founded: 1901

Type of Course: Parkland

No of Holes: 18

Length: 6508 yds (5946 mtrs)

Par: 72

SSS: 71

Green Fees: Weekdays: £23 per day;
Weekends/Bank Holidays: £28
per day

Visitors: Welcome: Contact Club in
advance

Societies: Welcome: Contact Club in
advance

Facilities: Putting Green, Club Hire,
Trolley Hire, Bar, Restaurant

Accommodation, Food and Drink

Reference numbers below refer to detailed
information provided in section 2

Accommodation

**The Duke of Wellington, Marsh Lane, Ince,
Nr. Chester, Cheshire CH2 4NR**

Tel: 0151 356 0222
Public house serving bar meals and snacks: jacket
potatoes, salads, burgers, chilli, sausages with beans
and chips. Functions by arrangement.

**The Glann Hotel, 2 Stone Place, Hoole, Chester,
Cheshire CH2 3NR**

Tel: 01244 344800
e-mail: glannhot@supernet.com
Bed & Breakfast hotel in the suburbs of Chester, with
six double rooms, two twins, one single and a family
room.

Greyhound Hotel, Farndon, Cheshire CH3 6PU

Tel/Fax: 01829 270244
e-mail: greyhound-farndon@lineone.net
An attractive late-19th century pub in the village
centre, with wholesome pub food and three letting
bedrooms for B&B.   208

**Mitchell's of Chester Guest House, 28 Hough
Green, Chester, Cheshire CH4 8JQ**

Tel: 01244 679004 Fax: 01244 659567
e-mail: mitoches@dialstart.net
website: www.mitchellsofchester.com
An elegantly restored Victorian house in the south of
the city, with seven well-appointed non-smoking
bedrooms and a lounge overlooking the garden. B&B.

Food and Drink

**Cheshire Farm Ice Cream, Drumlan Hall,
Newton Lane, Tattenhall, Chester,
Cheshire CH3 9NE**

Tel: 01829 770995 Fax: 01829 770856
e-mail: cfic@btconnect.com
Splendid tea rooms serving snacks, cream teas and
their own range of top-quality Cheshire Farm ice
creams. Also close to Portal championship course at
Tarporley.

**The Copper Mine, Broxton, Nr. Chester,
Cheshire CH3 9JH**

Tel: 01829 782293 Fax: 01829 782183
e-mail: coppermineinn@cs.com
A handsome country pub on the A534 Nantwich-
Wrexham road, with two bars, two non-smoking
eating areas and a large garden. Bar and restaurant
menus, extensive choice of wines.   207

**Greyhound Hotel, Farndon,
Cheshire CH3 6PU**

Tel/Fax: 01829 270244
e-mail: greyhound-farndon@lineone.net
An attractive late-19th century pub in the village
centre, with wholesome pub food and three letting

bedrooms for B&B.   208

**The Sportsmans Arms, Tattenhall,
Cheshire CH3 9QF**

Tel: 01829 770233 Fax: 01829 771886
A charming village pub serving a good selection of
light bites and full meals from noon onwards. Pool,
darts, golf corner, patio.   206

Church Stretton Golf Club

Trevor Hill, Church Stretton SY6 6JH

Tel: 01694 722281

Sec/Manager:	Ron Broughton
Professional:	James Townsend
Directions:	½ mile of Church Stretton centre. From centre take Shrewsbury Rd (B4370), after 500 yds turn left into Carding Mill Valley, then first right into Trevor Hill. Entrance on right hand side after 300 yds.
Date Founded:	1898
Type of Course:	Moorland
No of Holes:	18
Length:	5026 yds (4592 mtrs)
Par:	66
SSS:	65
Green Fees:	Weekdays: £18; Weekends/ Bank Holidays: £26
Visitors:	Welcome: Contact Club in advance – some weekend restrictions
Societies:	Welcome: Contact Club in advance – some weekend restrictions
Facilities:	Putting Green, Bar, Restaurant

Accommodation, Food and Drink

Reference numbers below refer to detailed
information provided in section 2

Accommodation

The Church Inn, Ludlow, Shropshire SY8 1AW

Tel: 01584 872174 Fax: 01584 877146
e-mail: reception@thechurchinn.com
website: www.thechurchinnludlow.co.uk
A venerable hostelry with a history spanning seven
centuries. Bar and restaurant menus, nine en suite
bedooms including family rooms.   214

The Cock Hotel, Forden, Welshpool,
Powys SY21 8LX

Tel: 01938 580226

Late-19th century village inn serving a good choice of freshly prepared food, from sandwiches to mighty mixed grills. Also two guest rooms for B&B. 143

Number Twenty Eight, Ludlow,
Shropshire SY8 1PQ

Tel: 01584 876996 Fax: 01584 876860 Reservations: 0800 081 5000

e-mail: ross@no28.co.uk

website: www.no28.co.uk

Characterful accommodation in six period houses in Lower Broad Street: early Georgian, Tudor, late Victorian. Breakfast at Number 28. 212

Pulpits Farm, Field Lane, Little Hereford,
Nr Ludlow, Shropshire SY8 4AU

Tel: 01584 711356

e-mail: wilcoxrichard15@btinternet.com

Farmhouse Bed & Breakfast (evening meal optional) in lovely peaceful countryside. Two rooms, one en suite, one with private bathroom. Lounge with tv.

The Royal Oak, Clee Hill, Nr. Ludlow,
Shropshire SY8 3PE

Tel: 01584 890405

e-mail: 2toes.leisure@barbox.com

website: www.2toesleisure.com

17th century pub rich in atmosphere. Bar snacks and restaurant meals, excellent ales, pub games, jazz and R&B nights. 209

Food and Drink

The Boot Inn, Orleton, Ludlow,
Shropshire SY8 4HN

Tel: 01568 780228

Lovely old black and white country inn 5 miles south of Ludlow. Home-cooked bar snacks and full meals, good selection of real ales and wines.

The Church Inn, Ludlow, Shropshire SY8 1AW

Tel: 01584 872174 Fax: 01584 877146

e-mail: reception@thechurchinn.com

website: www.thechurchinnludlow.co.uk

A venerable hostelry with a history spanning seven centuries. Bar and restaurant menus, nine en suite bedooms including family rooms. 214

The Cock Hotel, Forden, Welshpool,
Powys SY21 8LX

Tel: 01938 580226

Late-19th century village inn serving a good choice of freshly prepared food, from sandwiches to mighty mixed grills. Also two guest rooms for B&B. 143

The Royal Oak, Clee Hill, Nr. Ludlow,
Shropshire SY8 3PE

Tel: 01584 890405

e-mail: 2toes.leisure@barbox.com

website: www.2toesleisure.com

17th century pub rich in atmosphere. Bar snacks and

restaurant meals, excellent ales, pub games, jazz and R&B nights. 209

The Salwey Arms, Woofferton, Ludlow,
Shropshire SY8 4AZ

Tel: 01584 711203

Home-cooked food, cask ales and well-kept bedrooms (including a large family room) in a welcoming inn.

Ye Olde Bull Ring Tavern, Ludlow,
Shropshire SY8 1AB

Tel: 01584 872311

An amazing black and white timbered building dating from 1385. Two bars, stunning restaurant. 213

Eaton Golf Club

Guy Lane, Waverton, Chester CH3 7PH

Tel: **01244 335885** Fax: **01244 335782**

Sec/Manager:	Kerry Brown
Professional:	Bill Tye
Directions:	4 miles SE of Chester. From centre take Boughton (A51) leading to A5115 and A41 (Whitchurch). Go under A55 dual carriageway, after 1¼ miles turn left into Eggsbridge Lane, leading to Guy Lane. Entrance on right hand side ¾ mile from A41.
Date Founded:	1993
Type of Course:	Parkland
No of Holes:	18
Length:	6562 yds (5996 mtrs)
Par:	72
SSS:	71
Green Fees:	Weekdays: £30; Weekends/ Bank Holidays: £35
Visitors:	Welcome: Contact Club in advance; Weekends and Weds morning only
Societies:	Welcome: Contact Club in advance; Weekends and Weds morning only
Facilities:	Putting Green, Trolley Hire, Buggy Hire, Bar, Restaurant

Accommodation, Food and Drink

Reference numbers below refer to detailed information provided in section 2

Accommodation

The Duke of Wellington, Marsh Lane, Ince, Nr. Chester, Cheshire CH2 4NR

Tel: 0151 356 0222

Public house serving bar meals and snacks: jacket potatoes, salads, burgers, chilli, sausages with beans and chips. Functions by arrangement.

The Glann Hotel, 2 Stone Place, Hoole, Chester, Cheshire CH2 3NR

Tel: 01244 344800
e-mail: glannhot@supernet.com

Bed & Breakfast hotel in the suburbs of Chester, with six double rooms, two twins, one single and a family room.

Greyhound Hotel, Farndon, Cheshire CH3 6PU

Tel/Fax: 01829 270244
e-mail: greyhound-farndon@lineone.net

An attractive late-19th century pub in the village centre, with wholesome pub food and three letting bedrooms for B&B.   208

Mitchell's of Chester Guest House, 28 Hough Green, Chester, Cheshire CH4 8JQ

Tel: 01244 679004 Fax: 01244 659567
e-mail: mitoches@dialstart.net
website: www.mitchellsofchester.com

An elegantly restored Victorian house in the south of the city, with seven well-appointed non-smoking bedrooms and a lounge overlooking the garden. B&B.

Food and Drink

Cheshire Farm Ice Cream, Drumlan Hall, Newton Lane, Tattenhall, Chester, Cheshire CH3 9NE

Tel: 01829 770995 Fax: 01829 770856
e-mail: cfic@btconnect.com

Splendid tea rooms serving snacks, cream teas and their own range of top-quality Cheshire Farm ice

creams. Also close to Portal championship course at Tarporley.

The Copper Mine, Broxton, Nr. Chester, Cheshire CH3 9JH

Tel: 01829 782293 Fax: 01829 782183
e-mail: coppermineinn@cs.com

A handsome country pub on the A534 Nantwich-Wrexham road, with two bars, two non-smoking eating areas and a large garden. Bar and restaurant menus, extensive choice of wines.   207

Greyhound Hotel, Farndon, Cheshire CH3 6PU

Tel/Fax: 01829 270244
e-mail: greyhound-farndon@lineone.net

An attractive late-19th century pub in the village centre, with wholesome pub food and three letting bedrooms for B&B.   208

The Sportsmans Arms, Tattenhall, Cheshire CH3 9QF

Tel: 01829 770233 Fax: 01829 771886

A charming village pub serving a good selection of light bites and full meals from noon onwards. Pool, darts, golf corner, patio.

Forest Hills Golf Club

Mile End Road, Coleford GL16 7BY

Tel: **01594 810620** Fax: **01594 810823**

Sec/Manager:	Colin Revill
Professional:	Richard Ballard
Directions:	1 mile NE of Coleford. From centre take Bakers Hill (B4028, Mile End) after ¾ mile turn right onto B4432 (Broadwell). Entrance closeby junction.
Date Founded:	1992
Type of Course:	Parkland
No of Holes:	18
Length:	6300 yds (5756 mtrs)
Par:	72
SSS:	71
Green Fees:	Weekdays: £17; Weekends/ Bank Holidays: £22
Visitors:	Welcome: Contact Club in advance
Societies:	Welcome: Contact Club in advance
Facilities:	Putting Green, Chipping Green, Driving Range, Club

Hire, Trolley Hire, Buggy Hire,
Bar, Restaurant

Accommodation, Food and Drink

Reference numbers below refer to detailed
information provided in section 2

Accommodation

**The Black Swan, Much Dewchurch,
Herefordshire HR2 8DJ**

Tel: 01981 540295

Delightful 14th century hostelry serving excellent
food - pies and quiches a speciality. Real ales.
Accommodation available at local farms.

**The Crown at Whitebrook, Whitebrook,
Nr. Monmouth, Monmouthshire NP25 4TX**

Tel: 01600 860254 Fax: 01600 860607
e-mail: crown@whitebrook.demon.co.uk website:
www.crownatwhitebrook.co.uk

A superb restaurant and hotel in a lovely secluded
Wye Valley setting. The food is outstanding, the
bedrooms well equipped and full of character. 101

**Forest House Hotel, Cinderhill, Coleford,
Gloucestershire GL16 8HQ**

Tel: 01594 832424

Situated in the ancient woodlands of the Forest of
Dean, with eight well appointed en suite rooms.
Comfortable lounge and a dining room serving a la
carte with fine wines. 225

**Mill End House, Newland, Coleford,
Gloucestershire GL16 8NF**

Tel: 01594 832128   e-mail: apriljohnt@aol.com

An 18th century house with lovely gardens and
splendid views. Three en suite bedrooms, excellent
breakfasts. Two miles west of Coleford, signposted
from the town square. Four golf courses within 15
minutes.

**Poolway House Hotel, Gloucester Road,
Coleford, Gloucestershire GL16 8BN**

Tel: 01594 833937
e-mail: poolway@btinternet.com

16th century country house with seven comfortable
en suite rooms, good home cooking and a well-
chosen wine list. Pleasant garden setting.

Food and Drink

**The Black Swan, Much Dewchurch,
Herefordshire HR2 8DJ**

Tel: 01981 540295

Delightful 14th century hostelry serving excellent
food - pies and quiches a speciality. Real ales.
Accommodation available at local farms.

**The Crown at Whitebrook, Whitebrook,
Nr. Monmouth, Monmouthshire NP25 4TX**

Tel: 01600 860254 Fax: 01600 860607
e-mail: crown@whitebrook.demon.co.uk

website: www.crownatwhitebrook.co.uk

A superb restaurant and hotel in a lovely secluded
Wye Valley setting. The food is outstanding, the
bedrooms well equipped and full of character. 101

**Forest House Hotel, Cinderhill, Coleford,
Gloucestershire GL16 8HQ**

Tel: 01594 832424

Situated in the ancient woodlands of the Forest of
Dean, with eight well appointed en suite rooms.
Comfortable lounge and a dining room serving a la
carte with fine wines. 225

Forest of Dean
Golf Club

Lords Hill, Coleford GL16 8BE

Tel: 01594 832583 Fax: 01594 832584

Sec/Manager:	Steve Hosford
Professional:	Andy Grey
Directions:	¼ mile.s NE of Coleford. From centre take Old Station Way, after 150 yds turn right into Lords Hill. Entrance on right hand side after 300 yds.
Date Founded:	1973
Type of Course:	Parkland
No of Holes:	18
Length:	6033 yds (5512 mtrs)
Par:	70
SSS:	69
Green Fees:	Weekdays: £15; Weekends/ Bank Holidays: £25
Visitors:	Welcome: Contact Club in advance
Societies:	Welcome: Contact Club in advance; not Fri, Sat or Sun
Facilities:	Putting Green, Chipping Green, Club Hire, Trolley Hire, Buggy Hire, Bar, Restaurant

Accommodation, Food and Drink

Reference numbers below refer to detailed
information provided in section 2

Accommodation

**The Black Swan, Much Dewchurch,
Herefordshire HR2 8DJ**

Tel: 01981 540295

Delightful 14th century hostelry serving excellent
food - pies and quiches a speciality. Real ales.
Accommodation available at local farms.

**The Crown at Whitebrook, Whitebrook,
Nr. Monmouth, Monmouthshire NP25 4TX**

Tel: 01600 860254 Fax: 01600 860607
e-mail: crown@whitebrook.demon.co.uk
website: www.crownatwhitebrook.co.uk

A superb restaurant and hotel in a lovely secluded
Wye Valley setting. The food is outstanding, the
bedrooms well equipped and full of character.   101

**Forest House Hotel, Cinderhill, Coleford,
Gloucestershire GL16 8HQ**

Tel: 01594 832424

Situated in the ancient woodlands of the Forest of
Dean, with eight well appointed en suite rooms.
Comfortable lounge and a dining room serving a la
carte with fine wines.   225

**Mill End House, Newland, Coleford,
Gloucestershire GL16 8NF**

Tel: 01594 832128   e-mail: apriljohnt@aol.com

An 18th century house with lovely gardens and
splendid views. Three en suite bedrooms, excellent
breakfasts. Two miles west of Coleford, signposted
from the town square. Four golf courses within 15
minutes.

**Poolway House Hotel, Gloucester Road,
Coleford, Gloucestershire GL16 8BN**

Tel: 01594 833937
e-mail: poolway@btinternet.com

16th century country house with seven comfortable
en suite rooms, good home cooking and a well-
chosen wine list. Pleasant garden setting.

Food and Drink

**The Black Swan, Much Dewchurch,
Herefordshire HR2 8DJ**

Tel: 01981 540295

Delightful 14th century hostelry serving excellent
food - pies and quiches a speciality. Real ales.
Accommodation available at local farms.

**The Crown at Whitebrook, Whitebrook,
Nr. Monmouth, Monmouthshire NP25 4TX**

Tel: 01600 860254 Fax: 01600 860607
e-mail: crown@whitebrook.demon.co.uk
website: www.crownatwhitebrook.co.uk

A superb restaurant and hotel in a lovely secluded
Wye Valley setting. The food is outstanding, the
bedrooms well equipped and full of character.   101

**Forest House Hotel, Cinderhill, Coleford,
Gloucestershire GL16 8HQ**

Tel: 01594 832424

Situated in the ancient woodlands of the Forest of
Dean, with eight well appointed en suite rooms.
Comfortable lounge and a dining room serving a la
carte with fine wines.   225

Herefordshire Golf Club

Ravens Causeway, Wormsley,
Hereford HR4 8LY

Tel: 01432 830219

Sec/Manager:	Terry Horobin
Professional:	David Hemming
Directions:	7½ miles NW of Hereford. From centre take the A438 (Willersley), after 3 miles turn right onto the A480 (Sarnesfield), after another 3 miles turn right onto B road signed Wormsley, Tillington Common. After 1¼ miles turn left at T junction. Entrance on left hand side after 1¼ miles.
Date Founded:	1932
Type of Course:	Parkland
No of Holes:	18
Length:	6078 yds (5554 mtrs)
Par:	70
SSS:	69
Green Fees:	Weekdays: £20 per round; £25 per day; Weekends/Bank Holidays: £25 per round; £32 per day
Visitors:	Welcome: Contact Club in advance; not Mon-Fri mornings

Societies: Welcome: Contact Club in
              advance

Facilities: Putting Green, Chipping
              Green, Club Hire, Trolley Hire,
              Buggy Hire, Bar, Restaurant

Accommodation, Food and Drink

Reference numbers below refer to detailed
information provided in section 2

Accommodation

**Belmont Lodge & Golf Course, Belmont,
Hereford HR2 9SA**

Tel: 01432 352666 Fax: 01432 358090
e-mail: info@belmontlodge.co.uk
website: www.belmontlodge.co.uk

Thirty purpose-built modern rooms in the grounds of
18th century Belmont House, with a golf course by
the River Wye.   216

**Bucks Head House, School Farm,
Upper Hergest, Kington,
Herefordshire HR5 3EW**

Tel: 01544 231063

Six bedrooms ona 290-acre working farm with
magnificent views. Lounge, sun room. B&B or B,B &
Dinner. 6-berth static caravan also available.

**New Priory Hotel, Stretton Sugwas,
Herefordshire HR4 7AR**

Tel: 01432 760264 Fax: 01432 761809

Ten very comfortable bedrooms in a handsome 19th
century country house set in landscaped grounds.
Two restaurants, lounge bars.   218

**Ye Olde Salutation Inn, Weobley,
Herefordshire HR4 8SJ**

Tel: 01544 318443 Fax: 01544 318216
e-mail: salutationinn@btinternet.com

A classic English country pub in one of the county's
prettiest vilages. Three charming bedrooms, top-class
cuisine.   224

Food and Drink

**Belmont Lodge & Golf Course, Belmont,
Hereford HR2 9SA**

Tel: 01432 352666 Fax: 01432 358090
e-mail: info@belmontlodge.co.uk
website: www.belmontlodge.co.uk

Thirty purpose-built modern rooms in the grounds of
18th century Belmont House, with a golf course by
the River Wye.   216

**The Horse & Groom, Hereford,
Herefordshire HR4 0AP**

Tel: 01432 355026 Fax: 01432 269242
website: www.dave@thehorseandgroom.fsnet.co.uk

Traditional decor in a lovely old pub close to the city
centre. Real ales, home-cooked bar snacks and meals.
The owner is a keen golfer.   219

**The Kites Nest Inn, Swainshill,
Herefordshire HR4 7QA**

Tel/Fax: 01981 590217

Fine home cooking - both restaurant and bar menus -
in a popular pub by the A438 west of Hereford. Also
good wines, beers, soft drinks.

                                            222

**New Priory Hotel, Stretton Sugwas,
Herefordshire HR4 7AR**

Tel: 01432 760264 Fax: 01432 761809

Ten very comfortable bedrooms in a handsome 19th
century country house set in landscaped grounds.
Two restaurants, lounge bars.   218

**The White Pheasant, 9 High Street, Kington,
Herefordshire HR5 3AX**

Tel: 01544 231291

A 60-cover licensed restaurant serving great value
dinners and Sunday lunch. Top-quality steaks (up to
24oz!) and delicious desserts.

**Ye Olde Salutation Inn, Weobley,
Herefordshire HR4 8SJ**

Tel: 01544 318443 Fax: 01544 318216
e-mail: salutationinn@btinternet.com

A classic English country pub in one of the county's
prettiest vilages. Three charming bedrooms, top-class
cuisine.   224

Kington Golf Club

Bradnor Hill, Kington HR5 3RE

Tel: 01544 230340 Fax: 01544 231320

Sec/Manager: Glyn Witcome

Professional: Dean Oliver

Directions: 12½ miles W of Leominster.
               From centre take Bargates
               (A44, Kington). At Kington
               follow A44 short distance and
               turn right onto B4355
               (Presteigne), after 150 yds only
               turn left into Barton Lane.
               Entrance after 1 mile.

Date Founded: 1926

Type of Course: Heathland (highest course in
England)

No of Holes: 18

Length: 5753 yds (5257 mtrs)

Par: 70

SSS: 68

Green Fees: Weekdays: £15; Weekends/
Bank Holidays: £20

Visitors: Welcome: Contact Club in
advance

Societies: Welcome: Contact Club in
advance

Facilities: Putting Green, Practice Area,
Club Hire, Trolley Hire, Bar,
Restaurant

Accommodation, Food and Drink

Reference numbers below refer to detailed
information provided in section 2

Accommodation

**The Bell Country Inn, Llanyre,
Llandrindod Wells, Powys LD1 6DY**

Tel: 01597 823959 Fax: 01597 825899
e-mail: dgj.jones@virgin.net
website: www.thebellcountryinn.com
Friendly, family run inn with lovely views. 9 en suite
rooms and restaurant serving traditional and
international dishes with good wine list.   144

**Bucks Head House, School Farm,
Upper Hergest, Kington,
Herefordshire HR5 3EW**

Tel: 01544 231063
Six bedrooms ona 290-acre working farm with
magnificent views. Lounge, sun room. B&B or B,B &
Dinner. 6-berth static caravan also available.

The Church Inn, Ludlow, Shropshire SY8 1AW

Tel: 01584 872174 Fax: 01584 877146
e-mail: reception@thechurchinn.com
website: www.thechurchinnludlow.co.uk
A venerable hostelry with a history spanning seven
centuries. Bar and restaurant menus, nine en suite
bedooms including family rooms.   214

**Corven Hall,Howey, Llandrindod Wells,
Powys LD1 5RE**

Tel: 01597 823368
Six spacious bedrooms (most en suite) for Bed &
Breakfast in a Victorian house with lovely gardens
and fine views.   151

**Gwystre Inn, Gwystre, Llandrindod Wells,
Powys LD1 6RM**

Tel: 01597 851650
A 300-year-old pub with three en suite twin rooms
and good-value home-cooked food. Local ales. Darts
and pool.

**The Harp Inn, Old Radnor, Presteigne,
Powys LD8 2RH**

Tel/Fax: 01544 350655
A beautifully restored 15th century inn with exposed
stone walls and beamed ceilings, set in a pretty
village. Excellent home cooking and five guest
bedrooms enjoying lovely views.   141

**Kincoed Hotel, Temple Street,
Llandrindod Wells, Powys LD1 5HF**

Tel: 01597 822656
Arrive as a guest, leave as a friend. Ten rooms for B&B,
with evening meals by arrangement. Breakfasts fit for
a king.

**The Llanerch Inn, Llandrindod Wells,
Powys LD1 6BG**

Tel: 01597 822086 Fax: 01597 824618
e-mail: llanerchinn@ic24.net
Family-owned 16th century inn of great character,
with 12 en suite rooms. Snacks and meals. Residents'
lounge, patio, garden, play area.   152

**New Priory Hotel, Stretton Sugwas,
Herefordshire HR4 7AR**

Tel: 01432 760264 Fax: 01432 761809
Ten very comfortable bedrooms in a handsome 19th
century country house set in landscaped grounds.
Two restaurants, lounge bars.   218

**Number Twenty Eight, Ludlow,
Shropshire SY8 1PQ**

Tel: 01584 876996 Fax: 01584 876860
Reservations: 0800 081 5000
e-mail: ross@no28.co.uk
website: www.no28.co.uk
Characterful accommodation in six period houses in
Lower Broad Street: early Georgian, Tudor, late
Victorian. Breakfast at Number 28.   212

**Pulpits Farm, Field Lane, Little Hereford,
Nr. Ludlow, Shropshire SY8 4AU**

Tel: 01584 711356

e-mail: wilcoxrichard15@btinternet.com
Farmhouse Bed & Breakfast (evening meal optional)
in lovely peaceful countryside. Two rooms, one en
suite, one with private bathroom. Lounge with tv.

The Royal Oak, Clee Hill, Nr. Ludlow, Shropshire SY8 3PE

Tel: 01584 890405
e-mail: 2toes.leisure@barbox.com
website: www.2toesleisure.com

17th century pub rich in atmosphere. Bar snacks and
restaurant meals, excellent ales, pub games, jazz and
R&B nights. 209

The Royal Oak, Gladestry, Powys HR5 3NR

Tel: 01544 370669
Sixteenth century village pub offering real ales, home-
cooked food, a good selection of wine and four
comfortable letting bedrooms. 142

The Talbot Hotel, Kington, Herefordshire HR5 3DJ

Tel: 01544 231744
A 16th century coaching inn on a corner site in the
town centre. Cosy bars, home cooking, four
refurbished bedrooms. 221

Ye Olde Salutation Inn, Weobley, Herefordshire HR4 8SJ

Tel: 01544 318443 Fax: 01544 318216
e-mail: salutationinn@btinternet.com
A classic English country pub in one of the county's
prettiest vilages. Three charming bedrooms, top-class
cuisine. 224

Food and Drink

The Bell Country Inn, Llanyre, Llandrindod Wells, Powys LD1 6DY

Tel: 01597 823959 Fax: 01597 825899
e-mail: dgj.jones@virgin.net
website: www.thebellcountryinn.com

Friendly, family run inn with lovely views. 9en suite
rooms and restaurant serving traditional and
international dishes with good wine list. 144

The Boot Inn, Orleton, Ludlow, Shropshire SY8 4HN

Tel: 01568 780228
Lovely old black and white country inn 5 miles south
of Ludlow. Home-cooked bar snacks and full meals,
good selection of real ales and wines.

The Church Inn, Ludlow, Shropshire SY8 1AW

Tel: 01584 872174 Fax: 01584 877146
e-mail: reception@thechurchinn.com
website: www.thechurchinnludlow.co.uk
A venerable hostelry with a history spanning seven
centuries. Bar and restaurant menus, nine en suite
bedooms including family rooms. 214

The Comet Inn, Madley, Herefordshire HR2 9NJ

Tel: 01981 250600 e-mail: cometinn@madley
Large white-painted pub with a traditional ambience

and lovely gardens. Bar meals, à la carte, real ales.
Four miles from Hereford off the B4352 Hay road. 220

Gwystre Inn, Gwystre, Llandrindod Wells, Powys LD1 6RM

Tel: 01597 851650
A 300-year-old pub with three en suite twin rooms
and good-value home-cooked food. Local ales. Darts
and pool.

The Harp Inn, Old Radnor, Presteigne, Powys LD8 2RH

Tel/Fax: 01544 350655
A beautifully restored 15th century inn with exposed
stone walls and beamed ceilings, set in a pretty
village. Excellent home cooking and five guest
bedrooms enjoying lovely views. 141

The Kites Nest Inn, Swainshill, Herefordshire HR4 7QA

Tel/Fax: 01981 590217
Fine home cooking - both restaurant and bar menus -
in a popular pub by the A438 west of Hereford. Also
good wines, beers, soft drinks. 222

The Llanerch Inn, Llandrindod Wells, Powys LD1 6BG

Tel: 01597 822086 Fax: 01597 824618
e-mail: llanerchinn@ic24.net
Family-owned 16th century inn of great character,
with 12 en suite rooms. Snacks and meals. Residents'
lounge, patio, garden, play area. 152

New Priory Hotel, Stretton Sugwas, Herefordshire HR4 7AR

Tel: 01432 760264 Fax: 01432 761809
Ten very comfortable bedrooms in a handsome 19th
century country house set in landscaped grounds.
Two restaurants, lounge bars. 218

The Royal Oak, Clee Hill, Nr. Ludlow, Shropshire SY8 3PE

Tel: 01584 890405
e-mail: 2toes.leisure@barbox.com
website: www.2toesleisure.com

17th century pub rich in atmosphere. Bar snacks and
restaurant meals, excellent ales, pub games, jazz and
R&B nights. 209

The Royal Oak, Gladestry, Powys HR5 3NR

Tel: 01544 370669
Sixteenth century village pub offering real ales, home-
cooked food, a good selection of wine and four
comfortable letting bedrooms. 142

The Salwey Arms, Woofferton, Ludlow, Shropshire SY8 4AZ

Tel: 01584 711203
Home-cooked food, cask ales and well-kept bedrooms
(including a large family room) in a welcoming inn.

The Talbot Hotel, Kington, Herefordshire HR5 3DJ

Tel: 01544 231744
A 16th century coaching inn on a corner site in the

town centre. Cosy bars, home cooking, four refurbished bedrooms. 221

The White Pheasant, 9 High Street, Kington, Herefordshire HR5 3AX

Tel: 01544 231291

A 60-cover licensed restaurant serving great value dinners and Sunday lunch. Top-quality steaks (up to 24oz!) and delicious desserts.

Ye Olde Bull Ring Tavern, Ludlow, Shropshire SY8 1AB

Tel: 01584 872311

An amazing black and white timbered building dating from 1385. Two bars, stunning restaurant. 213

Ye Olde Salutation Inn, Weobley, Herefordshire HR4 8SJ

Tel: 01544 318443 Fax: 01544 318216

e-mail: salutationinn@btinternet.com

A classic English country pub in one of the county's prettiest vilages. Three charming bedrooms, top-class cuisine. 224

Leominster Golf Club

Ford Bridge, Leominster, Herefordshire HR6 OLE

Tel: 01568 610055 Fax: 01568 610055

Sec/Manager:	Jessica Kingwood
Professional:	Andrew Ferriday
Directions:	2½ miles S of Leominster. From centre take Mill St, at roundabout turn right onto A49 (Hereford), after 2½ miles turn left onto B road signed Stoke Prior. Entrance on right hand side after ¼ mile.
Date Founded:	1967
Type of Course:	Parkland
No of Holes:	18
Length:	6026 yds (5506 mtrs)
Par:	70

SSS:	69
Green Fees:	Weekdays: Various; contact club; Weekends/Bank Holidays: Various; contact club
Visitors:	Welcome: Contact Club in advance
Societies:	Welcome: Contact Club in advance
Facilities:	Putting Green, Trolley Hire, Bar, Restaurant

Accommodation, Food and Drink

Reference numbers below refer to detailed information provided in section 2

Accommodation

The Church Inn, Ludlow, Shropshire SY8 1AW

Tel: 01584 872174 Fax: 01584 877146

e-mail: reception@thechurchinn.com

website: www.thechurchinnludlow.co.uk

A venerable hostelry with a history spanning seven centuries. Bar and restaurant menus, nine en suite bedooms including family rooms. 214

The Harp Inn, Old Radnor, Presteigne, Powys LD8 2RH

Tel/Fax: 01544 350655

A beautifully restored 15th century inn with exposed stone walls and beamed ceilings, set in a pretty village. Excellent home cooking and five guest bedrooms enjoying lovely views. 141

New Priory Hotel, Stretton Sugwas, Herefordshire HR4 7AR

Tel: 01432 760264 Fax: 01432 761809

Ten very comfortable bedrooms in a handsome 19th century country house set in landscaped grounds. Two restaurants, lounge bars. 218

Number Twenty Eight, Ludlow, Shropshire SY8 1PQ

Tel: 01584 876996 Fax: 01584 876860

Reservations: 0800 081 5000

e-mail: ross@no28.co.uk website: www.no28.co.uk

Characterful accommodation in six period houses in Lower Broad Street: early Georgian, Tudor, late Victorian. Breakfast at Number 28. 212

Pulpits Farm, Field Lane, Little Hereford, Nr. Ludlow, Shropshire SY8 4AU

Tel: 01584 711356

e-mail: wilcoxrichard15@btinternet.com

Farmhouse Bed & Breakfast (evening meal optional) in lovely peaceful countryside. Two rooms, one en suite, one with private bathroom. Lounge with tv.

The Royal Oak, Clee Hill, Nr. Ludlow, Shropshire SY8 3PE

Tel: 01584 890405

e-mail: 2toes.leisure@barbox.com

website: www.2toesleisure.com

17th century pub rich in atmosphere. Bar snacks and restaurant meals, excellent ales, pub games, jazz and R&B nights. 209

The Talbot Hotel, Kington, Herefordshire HR5 3DJ

Tel: 01544 231744

A 16th century coaching inn on a corner site in the town centre. Cosy bars, home cooking, four refurbished bedrooms. 221

Food and Drink

The Boot Inn, Orleton, Ludlow, Shropshire SY8 4HN

Tel: 01568 780228

Lovely old black and white country inn 5 miles south of Ludlow. Home-cooked bar snacks and full meals, good selection of real ales and wines.

The Church Inn, Ludlow, Shropshire SY8 1AW

Tel: 01584 872174 Fax: 01584 877146
e-mail: reception@thechurchinn.com
website: www.thechurchinnludlow.co.uk

A venerable hostelry with a history spanning seven centuries. Bar and restaurant menus, nine en suite bedrooms including family rooms. 214

The Harp Inn, Old Radnor, Presteigne, Powys LD8 2RH

Tel/Fax: 01544 350655

A beautifully restored 15th century inn with exposed stone walls and beamed ceilings, set in a pretty village. Excellent home cooking and five guest bedrooms enjoying lovely views. 141

New Priory Hotel, Stretton Sugwas, Herefordshire HR4 7AR

Tel: 01432 760264 Fax: 01432 761809

Ten very comfortable bedrooms in a handsome 19th century country house set in landscaped grounds. Two restaurants, lounge bars. 218

The Royal Oak, Clee Hill, Nr. Ludlow, Shropshire SY8 3PE

Tel: 01584 890405
e-mail: 2toes.leisure@barbox.com
website: www.2toesleisure.com

17th century pub rich in atmosphere. Bar snacks and restaurant meals, excellent ales, pub games, jazz and R&B nights. 209

The Salwey Arms, Woofferton, Ludlow, Shropshire SY8 4AZ

Tel: 01584 711203

Home-cooked food, cask ales and well-kept bedrooms (including a large family room) in a welcoming inn.

The Talbot Hotel, Kington, Herefordshire HR5 3DJ

Tel: 01544 231744

A 16th century coaching inn on a corner site in the town centre. Cosy bars, home cooking, four refurbished bedrooms. 221

Ye Olde Bull Ring Tavern, Ludlow, Shropshire SY8 1AB

Tel: 01584 872311

An amazing black and white timbered building dating from 1385. Two bars, stunning restaurant. 213

Llanymynech Golf Club

Pant, nr Oswestry, Shropshire SY10 8LB
Tel: 01691 830542

If you are one of those potential big-hitters and think you are capable of hitting the golf ball a "country mile", then Llanymynech is the place for you to visit, because the Llanymynech Golf Club is in the unique position of having the border between Wales and England running through its course, thus making it intentionally possible to drive off in Wales and then find your ball on the fairway in England. To record this unique happening you may wish to take the photographic opportunity where a small plaque at the dog-leg fourth informs the golfer of what has been achieved. Actually, the boundary is part of Offa's Dyke, which was built by King Offa to keep the Welsh out of England. Had he known that one day a golf course would be built through it, the famous old dyke would have certainly been widened considerably. Five holes later you return to the Principality after teeing off from an elevated tee at the challenging par-5 ninth. Founded in 1933, the club is also famous for being the place where Welshman and golfing superstar Ian Woosnam first took an interest in the game and played as a member before deciding to chance his arm among the professional big guns. Once playing at Ludlow with a group of former clubmates and county player colleagues of Woosnam, they explained to me that when the Welsh wizard announced his intention of becoming a touring professional in the 1970s, they spent days pleading with him not to take such a drastic step because they reckoned he was no better than

Date Founded:	1933
Type of Course:	Upland
No of Holes:	18
Length:	6047 yds (5525 mtrs)
Par:	70
SSS:	69
Green Fees:	Weekdays: £20 per round; £25 per day; Weekends/Bank Holidays: £25 per round
Visitors:	Welcome: Contact Club in advance
Societies:	Welcome: Contact Club in advance
Facilities:	Putting Green, Chipping Green, Trolley Hire, Bar, Restaurant

thousands of other single player amateurs, including themselves, and one day would come to regret the foolish decision. To their credit they readily admitted they were left with much egg on their faces when, in the early 1980's, Woosnam broke away from the regular also-rans on the tough professional circuit to record his first of many titles, including the US Masters title.

After an easy opening two holes, this splendid upland course rises through foothills and opens up some rather spectacular views of the two countries from the inward nine holes. After crossing the small stream at the par-5 ninth the course starts to rise further with the 10th, a par-3, split by an awesome valley that has to be carried from an elevated tee, with the small green lying on the opposite side guarded by shrubs.

My favourite hole, however, is the 12th, where from another elevated tee you are looking down on stunning panoramic views of the Shropshire flatlands on one side and the glory of Wales in the other direction. A magnificent hole to play on a glorious and clear summer's day. Indeed, a magnificent course to play no matter which hole! Not a huge and spacious clubhouse here, but one that is cosy, comforting, and which features a framed professional course record of 65 by you know who! If you want to know more about "Woosie" then talk to the competent club professional Andy Griffiths, a great and friendly character and a long-standing chum of the Welsh golfing genius.

Sec/Manager:	David Thomas
Professional:	Andrew Griffiths
Directions:	4¾ miles S of Oswestry. From centre take Shrewsbury Rd (B4579), at Travelodge (roundabout) turn right onto A483 (Welshpool), after 4¼ miles take first right just after Pant Tourist Infromation and follow for ½ mile. Entrance on right hand side.

Accommodation, Food and Drink

Reference numbers below refer to detailed information provided in section 2

Accommodation

The Cock Hotel, Forden, Welshpool, Powys SY21 8LX

Tel: 01938 580226

Late-19th century village inn serving a good choice of freshly prepared food, from sandwiches to mighty mixed grills. Also two guest rooms for B&B.   143

Elgar House, 16 Elgar Close, Oswestry, Shropshire SY11 2LZ

Tel: 01691 661323 mob: 07879 462813

A conservatory-fronted bungalow with three en suite bedrooms (two family size), guest bar and pleasant gardens. B&B: dinner with notice. AA 4 Diamonds.

Glen Helen Holiday Cottages, Pant, Oswestry, Shropshire SY10 9QN

Tel/Fax: 01691 830094
e-mail: gaskill@globalnet.co.uk
website: www.glenhelen.co.uk

High-class self-catering accommodation in two holiday cottages, each with two bedrooms, bath/shower, kitchen-diner, lounge and garden.   211

The Hand Hotel, Llanarmon Dyffryn Ceiriog, Clwyd LL20 7LD

Tel: 01691 600666 Fax: 01691 600262
e-mail: handllandcb@netscapeonline.co.uk

Built in the late 16th century, the Hand stands in beautiful countryside at the head of the Ceiriog Valley. 13 en suite bedrooms, bar and restaurant meals.   203

Sebastians Restaurant & Hotel, 45 Willow Street, Oswestry, Shropshire SY11 1AQ

Tel: 01691 655444 Fax: 01691 653452
e-mail: sebastians.rest@virgin.net

website: www.sebastians-hotel.co.uk
Individually appointed en suite bedrooms of great charm, plus fine French cuisine in an atmospheric 16th century setting. Private car park.

The West Arms Hotel, Llanarmon Dyffryn Ceiriog, Ceiriog Valley, Clwyd LL20 7LD
Tel: 01691 600665 Fax: 01691 600622
e-mail: booking@thewestarms.co.uk
website: www.thewestarms.co.uk
A charming, old-world country inn nestling in the lovely, peaceful Ceiriog Valley. Sixteen en suite bedrooms including two large suites. Bar and restaurant meals.   204

Food and Drink

The Black Horse Inn, Maesbrook, Oswestry, Shropshire SY10 8QG
Tel: 01691 682472 Fax: 01691 682872
A great pub for food, with a menu that offers an excellent choice for all tastes. Shropshire sirloin, with mushrooms and local blue cheese, is a favourite.

The Bradford Arms, Knockin, Nr. Oswestry, Shropshire SY10 8HJ
Tel: 01691 682358
A fine black-and-white roadside inn serving an excellent selection of home-cooked food for country appetites. Smart bar, non-smoking restaurant, beer garden.   210

The Cock Hotel, Forden, Welshpool, Powys SY21 8LX
Tel: 01938 580226
Late-19th century village inn serving a good choice of freshly prepared food, from sandwiches to mighty mixed grills. Also two guest rooms for B&B.   143

The Hand Hotel, Llanarmon Dyffryn Ceiriog, Clwyd LL20 7LD
Tel: 01691 600666 Fax: 01691 600262
e-mail: handllandcb@netscapeonline.co.uk
Built in the late 16th century, the Hand stands in beautiful countryside at the head of the Ceiriog Valley. 13 en suite bedrooms, bar and restaurant meals.   203

The Henllan, Llangyniew, Welshpool, Powys SY21 9EJ
Tel: 01938 810343
Popular licensed premises serving bar and restaurant meals - roast beef dinners among the favourites - and Sunday lunches. Country & Western music most Saturday nights.

Sebastians Restaurant & Hotel, 45 Willow Street, Oswestry, Shropshire SY11 1AQ
Tel: 01691 655444 Fax: 01691 653452
e-mail: sebastians.rest@virgin.net
website: www.sebastians-hotel.co.uk
Individually appointed en suite bedrooms of great charm, plus fine French cuisine in an atmospheric 16th century setting. Private car park.

The West Arms Hotel, Llanarmon Dyffryn Ceiriog, Ceiriog Valley, Clwyd LL20 7LD
Tel: 01691 600665 Fax: 01691 600622
e-mail: booking@thewestarms.co.uk
website: www.thewestarms.co.uk
A charming, old-world country inn nestling in the lovely, peaceful Ceiriog Valley. Sixteen en suite bedrooms including two large suites. Bar and restaurant meals.   204

Ludlow Golf Club

Bromfield, Ludlow SY8 2BT
Tel: 01584 856285

There are many golf courses throughout England that are sited at racecourses, and the course at Ludlow Racecourse is one of the better ones. Situated 2 miles north of the charming and historical town of Ludlow, and just off the A49, the Ludlow club is as old as they come in this part of the pleasant English countryside. Founded as long ago as 1889, the club has done remarkably well in having to endure days when countless racing fans flock to see the "Sport of Kings". Built around the racecourse, the golf course is laid on attractive heathland that provides easy walking and which stretches to 6,277 yards (SSS 70) of pure excellence.

One of my favourite courses outside of Wales, The Ludlow Golf Club is situated in a beautiful area of the Shropshire countryside and quite close to the Mid Wales border, which makes it an ideal and extra venue for visiting golfers concentrating their itinerary on that part of the Principality. A delightfully designed course for golfers who like

a good challenge at every hole, there are blind holes, dog-legged holes, and holes that slowly eat away your confidence. Indeed, there are some great holes to be found on the Ludlow course, including one or two of the short holes. The front nine offers a tremendous challenge, with much gorse and small and rocky valleys to negotiate. Every shot provides a thrill a second as you hold your breath awaiting its eventual outcome, and is worth more than the modest green fee you paid out for the exhilarating experience. As if deciding to let you off the hook and give you some respite, the inward half opens out into more open fairways at the far end of the racecourse, but still requires your full attention as you breath more easily. A great little course with a cosy and welcoming clubhouse. Certainly not to be missed.

Sec/Manager:	Roger Heath
Professional:	Russell Price
Directions:	2½ miles NW of Ludlow. From centre take Bromfield Rd (A4361) and join A49 (Shrewsbury), after ¾ mile turn right onto B4365 (Culmington). Turn left onto B road after 150 yds just past railway line. Entrance on right hand side after ½ mile at first crossroads.
Date Founded:	1889
Type of Course:	Heathland
No of Holes:	18
Length:	6277 yds (5735 mtrs)
Par:	70
SSS:	70
Green Fees:	Weekdays: £18.50 per round; £24.50 per day; Weekends/ Bank Holidays: £24.50 per round
Visitors:	Welcome: Contact Club in advance
Societies:	Welcome: Contact Club in advance
Facilities:	Putting Green, Chipping Green, Trolley Hire, Bar, Restaurant

Accommodation, Food and Drink

Reference numbers below refer to detailed information provided in section 2

Accommodation

The Church Inn, Ludlow, Shropshire SY8 1AW

Tel: 01584 872174 Fax: 01584 877146
e-mail: reception@thechurchinn.com
website: www.thechurchinnludlow.co.uk

A venerable hostelry with a history spanning seven centuries. Bar and restaurant menus, nine en suite bedooms including family rooms. 214

Number Twenty Eight, Ludlow, Shropshire SY8 1PQ

Tel: 01584 876996 Fax: 01584 876860
Reservations: 0800 081 5000
e-mail: ross@no28.co.uk website: www.no28.co.uk

Characterful accommodation in six period houses in Lower Broad Street: early Georgian, Tudor, late Victorian. Breakfast at Number 28. 212

Pulpits Farm, Field Lane, Little Hereford, Nr. Ludlow, Shropshire SY8 4AU

Tel: 01584 711356
e-mail: wilcoxrichard15@btinternet.com

Farmhouse Bed & Breakfast (evening meal optional) in lovely peaceful countryside. Two rooms, one en suite, one with private bathroom. Lounge with tv.

The Royal Oak, Clee Hill, Nr. Ludlow, Shropshire SY8 3PE

Tel: 01584 890405
e-mail: 2toes.leisure@barbox.com
website: www.2toesleisure.com

17th century pub rich in atmosphere. Bar snacks and restaurant meals, excellent ales, pub games, jazz and R&B nights. 209

Food and Drink

The Boot Inn, Orleton, Ludlow, Shropshire SY8 4HN

Tel: 01568 780228

Lovely old black and white country inn 5 miles south of Ludlow. Home-cooked bar snacks and full meals, good selection of real ales and wines.

The Church Inn, Ludlow, Shropshire SY8 1AW

Tel: 01584 872174 Fax: 01584 877146
e-mail: reception@thechurchinn.com
website: www.thechurchinnludlow.co.uk

A venerable hostelry with a history spanning seven centuries. Bar and restaurant menus, nine en suite bedooms including family rooms. 214

The Royal Oak, Clee Hill, Nr. Ludlow, Shropshire SY8 3PE

Tel: 01584 890405
e-mail: 2toes.leisure@barbox.com
website: www.2toesleisure.com
17th century pub rich in atmosphere. Bar snacks and restaurant meals, excellent ales, pub games, jazz and R&B nights.   209

The Salwey Arms, Woofferton, Ludlow, Shropshire SY8 4AZ
Tel: 01584 711203
Home-cooked food, cask ales and well-kept bedrooms (including a large family room) in a welcoming inn.

Ye Olde Bull Ring Tavern, Ludlow, Shropshire SY8 1AB
Tel: 01584 872311
An amazing black and white timbered building dating from 1385. Two bars, stunning restaurant.   213

Oswestry Golf Club

Aston Park, Oswestry SY11 4JJ
Tel: **01691 610535** Fax: **01691 670580**

Sec/Manager:	Arthur Jennings
Professional:	David Skelton
Directions:	3¼ miles SE of Oswestry. From centre take Salop Rd (B4579) and join A5 (Shrewsbury) at Travelodge on roundabout. Entrance after 2 miles just before junction with B5009 (Whittington).
Date Founded:	1930
Type of Course:	Parkland
No of Holes:	18
Length:	6024 yds (5504 mtrs)
Par:	70
SSS:	69
Green Fees:	Weekdays: £23 per round, £28 per day; Weekends/Bank Holidays: £31 per round, £36 per day
Visitors:	Welcome: Contact Club in advance
Societies:	Welcome: Contact Club in advance – Wed and Fri only
Facilities:	Putting Green, Practice Area, Trolley Hire, Bar, Restaurant

Accommodation, Food and Drink

Reference numbers below refer to detailed information provided in section 2

Accommodation

The Cock Hotel, Forden, Welshpool, Powys SY21 8LX
Tel: 01938 580226
Late-19th century village inn serving a good choice of freshly prepared food, from sandwiches to mighty mixed grills. Also two guest rooms for B&B.   143

Elgar House, 16 Elgar Close, Oswestry, Shropshire SY11 2LZ
Tel: 01691 661323 mob: 07879 462813
A conservatory-fronted bungalow with three en suite bedrooms (two family size), guest bar and pleasant gardens. B&B: dinner with notice. AA 4 Diamonds.

Glen Helen Holiday Cottages, Pant, Oswestry, Shropshire SY10 9QN
Tel/Fax: 01691 830094
e-mail: gaskill@globalnet.co.uk
website: www.glenhelen.co.uk
High-class self-catering accommodation in two holiday cottages, each with two bedrooms, bath/ shower, kitchen-diner, lounge and garden.   211

The Hand Hotel, Llanarmon Dyffryn Ceiriog, Clwyd LL20 7LD
Tel: 01691 600666 Fax: 01691 600262
e-mail: handllandcb@netscapeonline.co.uk
Built in the late 16th century, the Hand stands in beautiful countryside at the head of the Ceiriog Valley. 13 en suite bedrooms, bar and restaurant meals.   203

Sebastians Restaurant & Hotel, 45 Willow Street, Oswestry, Shropshire SY11 1AQ
Tel: 01691 655444 Fax: 01691 653452
e-mail: sebastians.rest@virgin.net
website: www.sebastians-hotel.co.uk
Individually appointed en suite bedrooms of great charm, plus fine French cuisine in an atmospheric 16th century setting. Private car park.

The West Arms Hotel, Llanarmon Dyffryn Ceiriog, Ceiriog Valley, Clwyd LL20 7LD
Tel: 01691 600665 Fax: 01691 600622
e-mail: booking@thewestarms.co.uk
website: www.thewestarms.co.uk
A charming, old-world country inn nestling in the lovely, peaceful Ceiriog Valley. Sixteen en suite bedrooms including two large suites. Bar and restaurant meals.   204

Food and Drink

The Black Horse Inn, Maesbrook, Oswestry, Shropshire SY10 8QG
Tel: 01691 682472 Fax: 01691 682872
A great pub for food, with a menu that offers an excellent choice for all tastes. Shropshire sirloin, with mushrooms and local blue cheese, is a favourite.

The Bradford Arms, Knockin, Nr. Oswestry, Shropshire SY10 8HJ
Tel: 01691 682358
A fine black-and-white roadside inn serving an excellent selection of home-cooked food for country

appetites. Smart bar, non-smoking restaurant, beer garden.   210

The Cock Hotel, Forden, Welshpool, Powys SY21 8LX

Tel: 01938 580226

Late-19th century village inn serving a good choice of freshly prepared food, from sandwiches to mighty mixed grills. Also two guest rooms for B&B.   143

The Hand Hotel, Llanarmon Dyffryn Ceiriog, Clwyd LL20 7LD

Tel: 01691 600666 Fax: 01691 600262
e-mail: handllandcb@netscapeonline.co.uk

Built in the late 16th century, the Hand stands in beautiful countryside at the head of the Ceiriog Valley. 13 en suite bedrooms, bar and restaurant meals.   203

The Henllan, Llangyniew, Welshpool, Powys SY21 9EJ

Tel: 01938 810343

Popular licensed premises serving bar and restaurant meals - roast beef dinners among the favourites - and Sunday lunches. Country & Western music most Saturday nights.

Sebastians Restaurant & Hotel, 45 Willow Street, Oswestry, Shropshire SY11 1AQ

Tel: 01691 655444 Fax: 01691 653452
e-mail: sebastians.rest@virgin.net
website: www.sebastians-hotel.co.uk

Individually appointed en suite bedrooms of great charm, plus fine French cuisine in an atmospheric 16th century setting. Private car park.

The West Arms Hotel, Llanarmon Dyffryn Ceiriog, Ceiriog Valley, Clwyd LL20 7LD

Tel: 01691 600665 Fax: 01691 600622
e-mail: booking@thewestarms.co.uk
website: www.thewestarms.co.uk

A charming, old-world country inn nestling in the lovely, peaceful Ceiriog Valley. Sixteen en suite bedrooms including two large suites. Bar and restaurant meals.   204

Ross-on-Wye
Golf Club

Two Park, Gursley, Ross-on-Wye HR6 7UT

Tel: 01989 720267 Fax: 01989 720212

A favourite among South Walians, not only because of its easy accessibility from the Monmouthshire border and into Herefordshire, but also because of its excellence. Situated some 5 miles northwest of the rather attractive old market town of Ross-on-Wye and close to the small town of Newent, the Ross club lies just off Junction 3 of the M50 motorway, but is delightfully hidden from the sight and sound of the traffic. Founded in 1903, the club has a course that has developed into a fine championship venue-as can be expected from a C. K. Cotton designed lay-out.

Purely parkland and edged by woodland, the Ross course is well known for its narrow fairways, which call for good accuracy from the tee to green, speaking volumes for the talent of Isteyn Tucker, the former Welsh international and former president of the Welsh Golfing Union, who is now president of the Monmouthshire Golf Club at nearby Abergavenny. A legend in Welsh amateur circles, he competed in a senior event at Ross-on-Wye two years ago and won the competition by equalling his age of 72 with a brilliant score of Gross 72. Once a plus handicap golfer, he still maintains a single handicap figure of 5 while close to his 75th birthday!

One of the classic inland courses, Ross-on-Wye has a number of undulating fairways and many mature trees and bushes to add to its impressive challenge. Nevertheless, treat it with the respect it deserves and this excellent championship lay-out will reward you. Arrive with the expectation of losing many golf balls, then you will. Concentration is very much the key on this great old course.

The Ross-on-Wye club also boasts an elegant and impressive clubhouse to add to the peaceful atmosphere of the place. Quite spacious, rather comfortable and with an elegance of the pre-war years, it has a wide terrace overlooking the 18th green and excellent catering on offer in the pleasant dining room. Before going out to play this excellent 6,451 parkland course, there is a driving range and a good practice area to work out at and a well-stocked professional shop for your equipment needs, with the likeable club professional, Nick Catchpole, available for any needed tuition. This is a course that is well recommended.

Sec/Manager:	Peter Plumb
Professional:	Nick Catchpole
Directions:	4¼ miles NE of Ross-on-Wye. From centre take Over Ross St (B4234) to M50 (Worcester, M5) after 4 miles at junction 3 turn onto B4221. Entrance is 200 yds N of junction via a minor road.
Date Founded:	1903
Type of Course:	Parkland
No of Holes:	18
Length:	6451 yds (5894 mtrs)
Par:	72
SSS:	73

Green Fees: Weekdays: Various; £36 - £46;
Weekends/Bank Holidays:
Various; £36 - £46

Visitors: Welcome: Contact Club in
advance

Societies: Welcome: Contact Club in
advance – Wed-Fri only

Facilities: Putting Green, Chipping
Green, Driving Range, Club
Hire, Trolley Hire, Bar,
Restaurant

Accommodation, Food and Drink

Reference numbers below refer to detailed
information provided in section 2

Accommodation

**The Black Swan, Much Dewchurch,
Herefordshire HR2 8DJ**

Tel: 01981 540295

Delightful 14th century hostelry serving excellent
food - pies and quiches a speciality. Real ales.
Accommodation available at local farms.

**Forest House Hotel, Cinderhill, Coleford,
Gloucestershire GL16 8HQ**

Tel: 01594 832424

Situated in the ancient woodlands of the Forest of
Dean, with eight well appointed en suite rooms.
Comfortable lounge and a dining room serving a la
carte with fine wines.   225

**Mill End House, Newland, Coleford,
Gloucestershire GL16 8NF**

Tel: 01594 832128   e-mail: apriljohnt@aol.com

An 18th century house with lovely gardens and
splendid views. Three en suite bedrooms, excellent
breakfasts. Two miles west of Coleford, signposted
from the town square. Four golf courses within 15
minutes.

Food and Drink

**The Axe & Cleaver, Much Birch, Nr. Hereford,
Herefordshire HR2 8HU**

Tel/Fax: 01981 540203

An attractive black and white pub on the A49 south
of Hereford, with lovely gardens and a great
reputation for the quality of its food and drink.   223

**The Black Swan, Much Dewchurch,
Herefordshire HR2 8DJ**

Tel: 01981 540295

Delightful 14th century hostelry serving excellent
food - pies and quiches a speciality. Real ales.
Accommodation available at local farms.

**Forest House Hotel, Cinderhill, Coleford,
Gloucestershire GL16 8HQ**

Tel: 01594 832424

Situated in the ancient woodlands of the Forest of

Dean, with eight well appointed en suite rooms.
Comfortable lounge and a dining room serving a la
carte with fine wines.   225

**The Fountain Inn, Orcup Hill,
Herefordshire HR2 8EP**

Tel: 01981 540304

A friendly country pub in a hilltop setting south of
Hereford. Splendid home cooking, excellent wine list,
real ales.   217

**The Horse & Groom, Hereford,
Herefordshire HR4 0AP**

Tel: 01432 355026 Fax: 01432 269242
website: www.thehorseandgroom.fsnet.co.uk
Traditional decor in a lovely old pub close to the city
centre. Real ales, home-cooked bar snacks and meals.
The owner is a keen golfer.   219

**The New Harp Inn, Hoarwithy, Nr. Hereford,
Herefordshire HR2 6QH**

Tel: 01432 840213

Seventeenth century pub near the River Wye serving
good bar snacks and full meals. Three letting
bedrooms, large gardens.   215

Upton by Chester
Golf Club

Upton Lane, Upton by Chester, Chester CH2 1EE
Tel: 01244 381183 Fax: 01244 381333

Sec/Manager: Fred Hopley

Professional: Peter Gardner

Directions: 1½ miles N of Chester. From
centre take St Oswalds Way
and turn right into Liverpool
Rd (A5116), after 1½ miles turn
right, crossing dual carriageway, into Upton Lane. Then
take second right after 350 yds.
Entrance on right hand side.

Date Founded: 1934

Type of Course: Parkland

No of Holes:	18
Length:	5850 yds (5345 mtrs)
Par:	69
SSS:	68
Green Fees:	Weekdays: £20; Weekends/ Bank Holidays: £20
Visitors:	Welcome: Contact Club in advance
Societies:	Welcome: Contact Club in advance; Wed – Fri only
Facilities:	Putting Green, Chipping Green, Trolley Hire, Buggy Hire, Bar, Restaurant

Accommodation, Food and Drink

Reference numbers below refer to detailed information provided in section 2

Accommodation

The Duke of Wellington, Marsh Lane, Ince, Nr. Chester, Cheshire CH2 4NR

Tel: 0151 356 0222

Public house serving bar meals and snacks: jacket potatoes, salads, burgers, chilli, sausages with beans and chips. Functions by arrangement.

The Glann Hotel, 2 Stone Place, Hoole, Chester, Cheshire CH2 3NR

Tel: 01244 344800
e-mail: glannhot@supernet.com

Bed & Breakfast hotel in the suburbs of Chester, with six double rooms, two twins, one single and a family room.

Greyhound Hotel, Farndon, Cheshire CH3 6PU

Tel/Fax: 01829 270244
e-mail: greyhound-farndon@lineone.net

An attractive late-19th century pub in the village centre, with wholesome pub food and three letting bedrooms for B&B.   208

Mitchell's of Chester Guest House, 28 Hough Green, Chester, Cheshire CH4 8JQ

Tel: 01244 679004 Fax: 01244 659567
e-mail: mitoches@dialstart.net
website: www.mitchellsofchester.com

An elegantly restored Victorian house in the south of the city, with seven well-appointed non-smoking bedrooms and a lounge overlooking the garden. B&B.

Food and Drink

Cheshire Farm Ice Cream, Drumlan Hall, Newton Lane, Tattenhall, Chester, Cheshire CH3 9NE

Tel: 01829 770995 Fax: 01829 770856
e-mail: cfic@btconnect.com

Splendid tea rooms serving snacks, cream teas and their own range of top-quality Cheshire Farm ice creams. Also close to Portal championship course at Tarporley.

The Copper Mine, Broxton, Nr. Chester, Cheshire CH3 9JH

Tel: 01829 782293 Fax: 01829 782183
e-mail: coppermineinn@cs.com

A handsome country pub on the A534 Nantwich-Wrexham road, with two bars, two non-smoking eating areas and a large garden. Bar and restaurant menus, extensive choice of wines.   207

Greyhound Hotel, Farndon, Cheshire CH3 6PU

Tel/Fax: 01829 270244
e-mail: greyhound-farndon@lineone.net

An attractive late-19th century pub in the village centre, with wholesome pub food and three letting bedrooms for B&B.   208

The Sportsmans Arms, Tattenhall, Cheshire CH3 9QF

Tel: 01829 770233 Fax: 01829 771886

A charming village pub serving a good selection of light bites and full meals from noon onwards. Pool, darts, golf corner, patio.   206

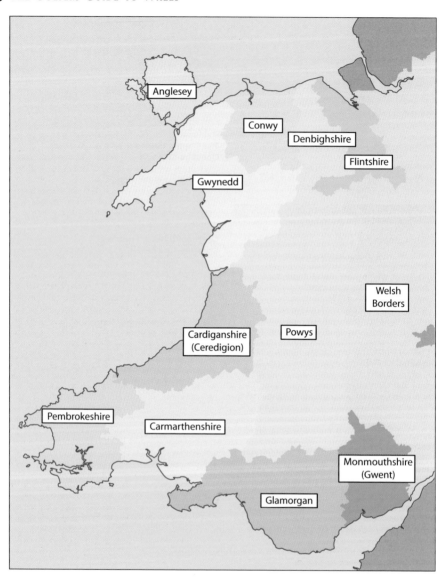

Anglesey

Conwy

Denbighshire

Flintshire

Gwynedd

Welsh Borders

Cardiganshire (Ceredigion)

Powys

Pembrokeshire

Carmarthenshire

Monmouthshire (Gwent)

Glamorgan

Accommodation, Food and Drink

THE CROWN AT WHITEBROOK `101`

Whitebrook, Nr. Monmouth, Monmouthshire NP25 4TX
Tel: 01600 860254 Fax: 01600 860607
e-mail: crown@whitebrook.demon.co.uk
website: www.crownatwhitebrook.co.uk

Angela and Elizabeth Barbara own and run an outstanding restaurant with rooms in a lovely secluded Wye Valley setting. The original inn has been modernised and converted into a romantic auberge offering very high standards of cuisine allied to comfortable, characterful accommodation. The pick of local produce combines with the best traditions of French cuisine to conceive and execute top-quality dishes on an inventive menu with choices such as roast mignonette of monk fish served with salted scallops and sesame oil, or free range Welsh rose veal fillet. Meals end with the finest British farmhouse cheeses and a tempting selection of hot and cold desserts. To complement the superb food is a wine list from the top drawer, with over 150 well-chosen labels.

The 10 bedrooms, all with bathrooms en suite, individually controlled central heating, tv, telephone and radio-alarm, are let on either Bed & Breakfast or Dinner, Bed & Breakfast terms. The pick of the rooms is a Manor Room with a four-poster bed and whirlpool bath. The location, not far from Brecon Beacons National Park, Tintern Abbey and the renowned beauty spot of Symonds Yat, is a tremendous asset, and when the sun shines the patio is a delightful spot for enjoying a quiet drink. In the evening, or when the wind blows, the charming lounge is an equally pleasant rendezvous.

Restaurant with Rooms
Top-quality food and wine; 10 en suite bedrooms

Credit Cards: All the major cards

Local Golf Courses: Forest of Dean, The Rolls of Monmouth, Ross-on-Wye

BROOKLANDS FARM `102`

Chepstow Road, Raglan, Monmouthshire NP1 2EN
Tel: 01291 690782 e-mail: brooklandsfarm@raglanfsbusiness.co.uk

Stones from nearby Raglan Castle, whose surrender in 1646 marked the end of the Civil War, were used in the building of a cottage which has been extended down the years to form a much larger property. The Price family, who run a dairy farm on the 97-acre site, welcome B&B guests with four letting bedrooms (one en suite) with washbasins, tea-makers, radios and alarm clocks. An excellent breakfast starts the day, and evening meals are available by arrangement (or there are pubs and restaurants in the village, which is only 200 yards away). The tv lounge and dining room overlook the garden, where chairs and tables are set out in fine weather.

Farmhouse B&B
Four bedrooms, 1 en suite; tv lounge, dinner by arrangement

Credit Cards: None

Local Golf Courses: Alice Springs, Raglan Park, The Rolls of Monmouth

YE OLDE CROWN INN `103`

Old Hereford Road, Pant-y-Gelli, Nr. Abergavenny, Monmouthshire NP7 7HR
Tel/Fax: 01873 853314 e-mail: yeoldcrown@aol.com

Visit our renowned 15th century coaching inn and restaurant situated within the Brecon Beacons National Park, less than two miles from Abergavenny. Take in the magnificent views of the Holy Mountain, browse over our extensive bar, special and restaurant menus featuring old favourites along with more exotic and international dishes. Sample our range of real ales or try one of our numerous Malts (CAMRA 2001 Beer Guide Entry). Bed & Breakfast is available from our 4 bedrooms (1 double, 2 twin and 1 single with private bathroom). All bedrooms have tea & coffee facilities and enjoy beautiful views of the Skirrid. Mel & Rosemary Mitchell

Inn, Food & Accommodation
Four B&B bedrooms; bar and restaurant menus

Credit Cards: Mastercard, Visa

Local Golf Courses: Wernddu, Monmouthshire, Belmont Lodge

MONMOUTHSHIRE

Farmhouse B&B

Four antique-furnished en suite rooms; heated indoor pool

Credit Cards: None

MILL FARM 104

Denbridge Road, Cwmafon, Nr. Pontypool, South Wales NP4 8XJ
Tel/Fax: 01495 774588

Old-world charm and modern comfort combine delightfully in a 15th century farmhouse run by Caroline and Clive Jayne. The four bedrooms are furnished with antiques (some four-posters) and all have en suite facilities, tv and tea-making kit. Relaxing is the name of the game, and breakfast is served until noon - packed lunches and evening meals by arrangement. Log fires, beams, oak panelling and spiral stone staircases present a traditional scene, but in contrast there's a heated swimming pool in the lounge, with robes and towels provided - a feature possibly unique to Mill Farm! In the garden is the croquet lawn and boules pitch.

Local Golf Courses: Pontypool, Monmouthshire, St Pierre

Pub with Food

Bar food served lunchtime and evening

Credit Cards: None

THE LANCASTER ARMS 105

Old Hereford Road, Pandy, Nr. Abergavenny,
Monmouthshire NP7 8DW Tel: 01873 890699

A sizeable cottage built in 1843 has been converted into a most agreeable pub standing five miles north of Abergavenny on the A465 road that leads up to Hereford. Inside, it's small, cosy and inviting, a good place to pause for a drink and a meal. The food, served every lunchtime and evening, is home-cooked and hearty, and the daily specials, including curries and hotpots, are guaranteed to satisfy. Golfers are very welcome, and there's even a separate side room for golf parties. Owner Sandra Lyon knows the area well and will point out the local walks and sights - the River Monnow runs nearby and the Black Mountains are practically on the doorstep.

Local Golf Courses: Monmouthshire, The Rolls of Monmouth, Wernddu

Pub, Food & Accommodation

Bar meals; two bedrooms for B&B

Credit Cards: None

THE BELMONT INN 106

22 Monmouth Road, Abergavenny, Monmouthshire NP7 5HH
Tel: 01873 850074

David and Rita Collins put out the welcome mat at their cheerful pub on the A40 just a short walk from the town centre. A good choice of beers is served in the roomy, comfortable bar, where the locals play pool and darts. Home-cooked food, including excellent grills and fish specials, is served most sessions (not Wednesday night) and there's a well-chosen selection of wines to accompany. Special meals can be arranged for golfing groups. The Belmont has a pleasant patio garden at the side, and two twin bedrooms for guests staying overnight.

Local Golf Courses: Wernddu, Monmouthshire, West Monmouthshire

Country Hotel

10 bedrooms, most en suite; B&B and evening meal

Credit Cards: None

THE WENALLT 107

Gilwern, Nr. Abergavenny, Gwent NP7 0HP
Tel: 01873 830694 e-mail: thewenallt@talk21.com

A 16th century Welsh longhouse in an unrivalled hilltop location that affords breathtaking views over the Usk Valley. The Harris family take excellent care of their guests and offer exceptional value for money in terms of both accommodation and food. The bedrooms are large and comfortably furnished, some with en suite or private bathroom, all with washbasins and tea-makers. There's a television room, and an oak-beamed drawing room for planning the next day's outings or chatting with the other guests. A splendid three-course dinner is served in the traditionally appointed dining room.

Local Golf Courses: Cradoc, Alice Springs, Monmouthshire, Wernddu

ST JULIAN INN 108

Caerleon Road, Newport, South Wales NP18 1QA
Tel: 01633 243548 Fax: 01633 243562

Steve Williams and his business partner Mary run a most welcoming old inn standing between the main road and the River Usk. Traditional ales are something of a speciality, and bar-style food (jacket potatoes, burgers, scampi, chilli, lasagne) is served lunchtime and evening. Church pews have found a new home in the bar, which is divided into several sections - one has darts, pool and a big tv screen. There's also a skittle alley-cum-function room, while outside is a pleasant balcony overlooking the river, an area for playing boules and a large off-road car park.

Pub with Food

Riverside pub serving lunches and dinners
Credit Cards: Access, Mastercard, Visa

Local Golf Courses: Celtic Manor, Llanwern, St Pierre, The Newport

THE GREYHOUND INN 109

Christchurch, Newport, South Wales NP18 1JJ
Tel: 01633 420306 Fax: 01633 430588

A handsome gabled building dating from 1890. Built as a private residence, it soon became an inn, replacing the adjacent coaching inn, and for the last five years has been thriving in the ownership of David and Shirley Potts. The owners and their friendly staff offer a proper village atmosphere along with well-kept real ales and an exceptional choice of very good food, from light snacks to three-course meals. The newly opened conservatory is proving a great success - it's the ideal place for a party or a special golfing dinner. The inn stands opposite the church and memorial cross in lovely countryside on the eastern outskirts of Newport. Leave the M4 at J24.

Inn with Food

Inn with snack and restaurant menus
Credit Cards: Access, Amex, Mastercard, Visa

Local Golf Courses: Celtic Manor, Llanwern, St Pierre

THE MILTON HOTEL 110

Milton Hill, Llanwern, Newport, Gwent NP16 6DU
Tel: 01633 412432

Leave the M4 at exit 24 and follow the signs to Llanwern to find this former hunting lodge run by Kelvin Picks and his mother Elaine. Real ales are served in the bars, and there's a separate 40-seat restaurant which doubles as a function room with its own bar. Visitors can eat and drink well here, and they can also stay overnight. Accommodation comprises ten self-catering lodges adjoining the main building; each lodge can sleep up to four people. The Milton has a pleasant little terrace and its own large car park.

Hotel, Self-Catering, Restaurant

10 self-catering lodges; bars and restaurant
Credit Cards: Access, Mastercard, Visa

Local Golf Courses: Llanwern, Celtic Manor, Shirenewton

THE NEW INN 111

Pwllmeyric, Chepstow, Monmouthshire NP16 6LF
Tel: 01291 622670
e-mail: liz-avent@hotmail.com

New in 1745, when it replaced a coaching inn, this handsome stone-built hostelry is owned by experienced publicans Liz and Steve Avent-Frampton. It stands off the A48 Chepstow-Newport road in a part of the world that is rich in history, and should not be missed by anyone looking for a good meal. Chef Tim James uses top-quality ingredients in preparing a wide range of dishes, from paté-stuffed mushrooms to grilled trout, local pork with a cheese and mushroom sauce, and several succulent ways with steak. Real ales. Large car park.

Country Inn with Food

Country Inn with à la carte menu and real ales
Credit Cards: Access, Mastercard, Visa

Local Golf Courses: Shirenewton, St Pierre, Dewstow, Raglan Parc

MONMOUTHSHIRE

THE PRIORY HOTEL & RESTAURANT 112

Caerleon, South Wales NP18 1AG
Tel: 01633 421241 Fax: 01633 421271

The Priory is a hotel of great quality and character set in secluded grounds in the historic town of Caerleon on the River Usk. The grand, handsome building, which dates back to 1180, was originally a monastery and later became a nunnery. Many of the best features from the 14th century have been preserved, including the ancient flagstones and the very rare 16th century glass medallions surrounding the Nun's Court. The Oak Room, which has 16th century panelling and stained glass windows throughout, is used as part of the main restaurant and as a conference room.

In the main restaurant, a massive chill cabinet displays a wonderful selection of seafood, shellfish, meat and game, salads and fruit - all ready to be prepared for the day's dishes, which are chalked up on boards behind the cabinets. The soft oak bar boasts one of the largest selections of Spanish wines in Britain - two of the directors are Spanish, and their influence shows strongly in the food, the wine and the hospitality.

Antique furniture is found throughout the 22 bedrooms, all of which have en suite bathrooms and showers, satellite tv, direct-dial telephone, tea/coffee-makers, minibars etc. Accommodation ranges from singles to triples/family rooms, some of which are adapted for wheelchair access. The Blue Room, which was originally the master bedroom dating back to the 17th centruy, is now back to its former glory boasting a huge four poster bed and glamorous marble bathroom.

The hotel is situated in the centre of the idyllic town, with many places of interest nearby. Within walking distance are the Roman Legionary Museum, the ancient Church of St Cadoc, the 18th century Charity School, the Roman baths and the ampitheatre - one of the best preserved forms in Europe. The Romans arrived in 75AD and developed Caerleon, then known as Isca Silurium, into a major rest and recreation town. In the dark ages, Caerleon was known as the court of King Arthur, the amphitheatre being the round table. This romantic mysterious town is perceived by many to be the true Camelot. Icons of the Arthurian legends may be seen at Ffwrwm arts, crafts and sculpture garden.

The town is just minutes away from Newport and very close to the M4 motorway (junction 25 westbound and 26 eastbound).

For further information on rates and weekend breaks, please contact our friendly reception desk at any time, on the phone or fax numbers above and they will be happy to help you.

Hotel & Restaurant
22 en suite bedrooms with satellite tv, phone; bars and restaurant

Credit Cards: All the major cards	Local Golf Courses: Celtic Manor, St Pierre, Llanwern, The Newport

MONMOUTHSHIRE

THE BOAT INN · 113

The Back, Chepstow, Monmouthshire NP16 5HH
Tel: 01291 628192 Fax: 01291 628193
e-mail: boat@inn.net

Mark, Pat, daughter Lisa and son-in-law Phil make a great team at this really delightful inn by the River Wye. An inn for 400 years - and a shipyard building before that - it has great charm, and when the weather permits, the beer garden right on the river is the place to be. Four real ales are served in the comfortable bar, while upstairs in the restaurant an extensive à la carte menu is available every evening from 6.30 to 10, offering dishes to suit all tastes and appetites. Check directions when booking.

Inn with Food

Riverside inn serving dinner daily

Credit Cards: Access, Amex, Mastercard, Visa

Local Golf Courses: Shirenewton, Monmouth, Raglan

FAIRWAYS HOTEL · 114

West Drive, Porthcawl, Mid Glamorgan CF36 3LS
Tel: 01656 782085 Fax: 01656 785351
e-mail: fairwayshotel@aol.com website: www.bridgend.gov.uk

Built at the end of the 19th century and recently tastefully refurbished, Fairways enjoys a prime position overlooking the Heritage Coast. This family run hotel provides comfortable, up-to-date accommodation in 25 en suite bedrooms, including four family rooms; all have tv and telephone. Full à la carte and table d'hote menus are served in the restaurant, while lighter lunches can be taken in the lounge bar. Leave the M4 at exit 37 on the A4229 to Porthcawl promenade. Ample parking spaces.

Hotel with Restaurant

25 en suite rooms with tv and phone; snacks and full meals

Credit Cards: All the major cards

Local Golf Courses: Royal Porthcawl, Pyle & Kenfig, Southerndown

CLAWDD COCH GUEST HOUSE · 115

Clawdd Coch, Pendoylan, Vale of Glamorgan CF71 7UP
Tel: 01446 760645

Golfing breaks are a speciality at Peter and Marilyn Roe's 17th century Welsh longhouse, which enjoys lovely views across the Vale of Glamorgan. Built as a farmhouse and also used as a prayer house by the local community, it was renovated and extended by the present owners into a comfortable, characterful guest house. Bed & Breakfast accommodation comprises five beautifully appointed en suite bedrooms with teletext tv and tea/coffee-making facilities. The 'zip and link' beds can be arranged to suit individual requirements by offering single, twin, double and family rooms. A full breakfast is served, and the nearby village inn provides very good evening meals. M4, junction 34, head towards Pendoylan.

Bed & Breakfast

5 en suite bedrooms with tv; golfing breaks arranged

Credit Cards: None

Local Golf Courses: Cottrell Park, Southerndown, Celtic Manor.

WINDMILL COTTAGES · 116

Llansannor, Nr Cowbridge, Vale of Glamorgan CF71 7TF
Tel: 01446 772470 e-mail: rosser@globalnet.co.uk

John and Claire Rosser have been farming here for 25 years, and in 1999 they converted some of the outbuildings into self-catering accommodation. They did a superb job, and the five self-contained units have great character, with feature stone walls, heavy beams and handsome country furniture. They have either one or two bedrooms, bathroom or shower room, kitchen-diner and lounge. An optional breakfast package is available. There are plenty of shops and pubs in the locality, and the old market town of Cowbridge is only five minutes away by car. For Windmill Cottages take J35 off the M4.

Self-Catering

Five 1- or 2-bedroom cottages for self-catering

Credit Cards: None

Local Golf Courses: Cottrell Park, Vale of Glamorgan, St Mary's

GLAMORGAN

Seafront Guest House

Sixteen rooms, en suite; B&B, dinner by arrangement

Credit Cards: All major cards

DEVON VIEW GUEST HOUSE 117

396 Oystermouth Road, Swansea, West Glamorgan SA1 3UL
Tel: 01792 462008   www. devonview.co.uk
e-mail: joseph@devonview.co.uk

Overlooking the seafront and only 30 metres from the glorious Swansea Bay beach, the Devon View Guest House was built as a mine captain's residence in the 1900s. It has been run since 1999 by Joseph and Alison Carr-Frost, in whose family it has been for 18 years. The accommodation comprises capacity for 37 people in single, twin, double and family rooms with en suite facilities available, tastefully furnished, with typical Victorian high ceilings. Day rooms, lounge/ bar and 32 cover non-smoking dining room, are equally traditional. Limited parking front and rear, free council car park nearby. Swansea in Bloom winner.

Local Golf Courses: Langland, Clyne, Pennard, Fairwood Park

B&B Hotel

12 en suite bedrooms with tv; newly refurbished
Credit Cards: Access, Diners, Mastercard, Visa

SHORELINE HOTEL 118

648 Mumbles Road, Southend, Mumbles, Swansea SA3 4EA
Tel/Fax: 01792 366233
website: www. shorelinehotel.co.uk

Nicola and Nicholas Round run a most delightful small hotel in a row of houses, shops and restaurants on the seafront, with the beach directly opposite. The Shoreline has 12 letting bedrooms, all of them with en suite facilities, tv, tea-makers and central heating. There's a comfortable residents' lounge, a well-stocked bar and a dining room. The views stretching across Swansea Bay are splendid and it's only a short walk to the centre of Mumbles, known as the Gateway to the Gower Peninsula.

Local Golf Courses: Clyne, Fairwood Park, Langland, Pennard

Leisure Park

Self-catering Bungalows, static homes, pitches for caravans and tents
Credit Cards: All the major cards

BANK FARM LEISURE PARK 119

Bank Farm, Horton, Gower, Swansea SA3 1LL
Tel: 01792 390228/390452 Fax: 01792 391282
e-mail: bankfarmleisure@cs.com website: www.bankfarmleisure.co.uk

The Richards family's holiday and leisure complex sits above one of the Gower Peninsula's loveliest beaches. Six self-catering bungalows, each sleeping 4-5 and all fully equipped, are supplemented by static holiday homes and by pitches for caravans and tents, with optional electrical hook-up and a central block with showers, toilets and laundry. Amenities include a swimming pool, children's playground and playroom, licensed bar, coffee shop, restaurant and general store. The sandy beach is on the doorstep, the views are stunning, and there are lots of places to visit in the vicinity.

Local Golf Courses: Pennard, Langland Bay, Clyne, Fairwood Park

Hotel & Restaurant

12 rooms with en suite or private facilities; restaurant, bar, lounge
Credit Cards: Access, Mastercard, Visa

CULVER HOUSE HOTEL 120

Port Eynon, Gower, Swansea SA3 1NN
Tel: 01792 390755 e-mail: info@culverhousehotel.co.uk
Fax: 01792 390735 www.culverhousehotel.co.uk

In an idyllic location 100yds from the beautiful Blue Flag beach at Port Eynon, this quiet and friendly hotel offers personal service. The restaurant is of an exceptionally high standard. Interesting menus provide for all tastes including a wide vegetarian choice, and focus on freshly prepared dishes using local produce. Singles are welcomed with no supplement. All twelve bedrooms have en-suite or private facilities with TV and tea & coffee making facilities. Most have sea views and the hotel is non-smoking . Ground floor rooms available. Contact Susan or Mark Cottell for details.

Local Golf Courses: Fairwood Park, Pennard, Langland Bay, Gower

GLAMORGAN

THE BRITANNIA INN | 121

Llanmadoc, Gower, Swansea SA3 1DB
Tel/Fax: 01792 386624   e-mail: mikdow@freeuk.com

For more than 20 years Mike and Pearl Downie have owned and run this beautifully preserved 17th century inn on the remote north-western tip of the lovely Gower Peninsula. Many original features survive, including the fireplace and bread oven, and the beams in the lounge were taken from ships which were 'lanterned' ashore and wrecked for their cargoes. The inn has the best selection of real ales in the area, and a very varied menu of snacks and main dishes is served in the bars or out in the garden. The upstairs has been converted into three comfortable en suite bedrooms with tv and tea-making facilities. The garden has a children's play area and small menagerie.

Inn, Food & Accommodation

Three en suite bedrooms; full menu, garden with menagerie
Credit Cards: Access, Mastercard, Visa

Local Golf Courses: Gower, Fairwood Park, Langland Bay, Clyne

CJ'S WINE BAR & RESTAURANT | 122

135 Mumbles Road, Oystermouth, Swansea SA3 4DN
Tel: 01792 361246 Fax: 01792 419849

A friendly wine bar, café and restaurant in a row of shops close to the seafront. Behind a modern redbrick facade keen golfer Roger Roberts, here for 20 years, runs a neat, cosy venue with a warm, welcoming atmosphere. Open every lunchtime except Monday and every evening, CJ's serves a nicely varied menu of starters, salads, burgers, fish dishes and speciality steaks and grills. The blackboard always lists some extra dishes, including vegetarian main courses. There's an extensive wine list and a prodigious cocktail list - well over 50, including CJ's Crunch with peach schnapps, Jack Daniels and orange juice. Parties for up to 30; outdoor eating in the summer.

Wine Bar & Restaurant

Full menu and extensive wine and cocktail lists
Credit Cards: Access, Amex, Mastercard, Visa

Local Golf Courses: Langland Bay, Pennard, Swansea Bay, Clyne

PEMBERTON ARMS | 123

Colby Road, Burry Port, Swansea SA16 0RH
Tel: 01554 832129

A handsome cream-painted, half-timbered pub, with a colourful flower display in summer, on the main A484 Llanelli-Carmarthen road. It's the first venture into the licensed trade for Paul Marsh, whose son works behind the bar. The pub's interior is roomy and comfortable, and in the public bar darts and pool are played, with a trophy cabinet advertising the skills of the local players. All this activity can generate a hunger, and the Pemberton Arms offers a menu of classic pub favourites - steaks, grills, sausages, scampi, jacket potatoes - and a popular traditional Sunday lunch (no food Wednesday or Sunday evenings). The pub has it own golfing society and is very near Ashburnham Golf Course.

Pub with Food

Traditional pub food

Credit Cards: None

Local Golf Courses: Ashburnham, Carmarthen, Pontardawe

HURST DENE GUEST HOUSE | 124

10 Sketty Road, Uplands, Swansea SA2 0LJ
Tel/Fax: 01792 280920 website: www.hurstdene.co.uk

From the M4 at junction 42 take the A483 towards Swansea to find this pleasant suburban guest house run by the Hefferman family. Tastefully appointed accommodation comprises ten bedrooms, most en suite, with tv and tea-makers. Cots, hairdryers, ironing facilities and packed lunches can all be provided, and there's private parking at the back of the building. Self-catering accommodation is also available, next door in seven self-contained units, some suitable for families. Hurst Dene is a good base for visits to the city, several golf courses and the scenic delights of the Gower Peninsula.

Guest House

Ten B&B rooms + self-catering units; evening meals by arrangement
Credit Cards: All the major cards

Local Golf Courses: Clyne, Langland, Fairwood Park, Pennard

GLAMORGAN

WERNOLEU HOTEL   125

31 Pontamman Road, Ammanford, Carmarthenshire SA18 2HX
Tel/Fax: 01269 592598

Christine and James Kinch offer a real home from home at their splendid hotel set in five well-tended acres just off the A474. The building is part 17th century and part late-Victorian, and behind the cheerful red-and-white frontage there's a warm welcome and plenty of room to relax. The seven double bedrooms all have en suite facilities, tv and tea-makers, and open fires keep things cosy in the lounge and bar, where guests can enjoy a fine selection of real ales. The evening bar menu includes grills, curries, scampi, omelettes and savoury pies, with sandwiches for lighter snacks. Large car park, patio and garden.

Country Hotel

Seven en suite double rooms; bar menu

Credit Cards: Mastercard, Visa

Local Golf Courses: Glynhir, Pontardawe, Morriston

BRYNCOCH FARM GUEST HOUSE   126

Llandyfan, Ammanford, Carmarthenshire SA18 2TY
Tel: 01269 850480 Fax: 01269 850888
e-mail: bryncoch@tesco.net

Bryncoch Farm enjoys a scenic setting in open countryside high above the Amman Valley on the edge of the Black Mountains. It's very much a family affair, with Mary and Graham Richardson running a Bed & Breakfast business and son Robert in charge of the craft centre. Tastefully appointed guest accommodation consists of three en suite bedrooms - a double and two twins - with tv and tea/coffee-making facilities. Amenities include a residents' lounge and a children's play area. Packed lunches can be provided and the family can arrange free transport to local pubs and golf courses.

Farmhouse B&B

Three en suite rooms with tv; craft centre, coffee shop

Credit Cards: None

Local Golf Courses: Glynhir, Glyn Abbey, Ashburnham, Carmarthen

RED LION HOTEL   127

24 Randell Square, Pembrey, Carmarthenshire SA16 0UB
Tel: 01554 832724 website: www.the-redlionhotel.co.uk

Enter Pembrey on the A484 LLanelli-Carmarthen road to find the Red Lion Hotel next to the 11th century church on the square in the heart of the village. Diana and Robert Spittles run a most sociable inn that caters well for both local residents and visitors to the region. Pool and darts are played in the L-shaped bar, where a very varied menu runs from quick and simple bar snacks to full meals. The real ale on offer changes regularly, and there's a small, select wine list. Visitors staying overnight will find comfortable accommodation in three double rooms and a single. The inn has a small garden, and motorists will find ample parking space on the square.

Hotel with Bar Meals

Three double rooms and a single for B&B; snacks and meals

Credit Cards: None

Local Golf Courses: Ashburnham, Carmarthen, Glyn Abbey

BRYNGWENYN FARM   128

Pontyberem, Llanelli, Carmarthenshire SA15 5NG
Tel/Fax: 01269 843990   e-mail: lizhedges@ic24.net

Liz and Simon Hedges have recently taken over the ownership and running of comfortable, well-appointed holiday accommodation a short drive from the end of the M4. In the grounds of a substantial 17th century farmhouse on a working sheep farm, old barns have been expertly converted to provide three holiday cottages for either self-catering or Bed & Breakfast accommodation, with other meals by arrangement. Each has a large lounge with patio, kitchen/diner, bathroom and two or three bedrooms. Additionally there is an en suite double bedroom with tv for B&B in the farmhouse. Children are welcome as are well-behaved dogs.

Farmhouse Accommodation

Three cottages (self-catering or B&B) + 1 farmhouse B&B room

Credit Cards: None

Local Golf Courses: Ashburnham, Carmarthen, Glynhir, Glyn Abbey

TANYLAN FARM HOLIDAYS 129

Tanylan Farm, Kidwelly, Carmarthenshire SA17 5HJ
Tel/Fax: 01267 267306 e-mail: tanylanfarm@aol.com
website: www.tanylanfarmholidays.co.uk
Set in beautiful countryside 200 yards from Carmarthen Bay,
Tanylan Farm Holidays provides a superb base for exploring the
region. The heart of the operation is a mid-Victorian farmhouse
with six large en suite bedrooms. Owner Barbara Evans offers an
alternative in the nearby Carmarthen Bay Touring and Camping
Park, where there are pitches for touring caravans, motor caravans

Farmhouse B&B, Caravan Park

Six en suite rooms; pitches for
caravans and tents

and tents. Amenities include showers, toilet and laundry facilities,
water points and a children's adventure playground. Close by are a
leisure-oriented holiday park and a health suite; evening meals can
be arranged at a local country club.

Credit Cards: None

Local Golf Courses:Ashburnham, Carmarthen, Glynhir, Glyn Abbey

CAERNEWYDD FARM 130

Pembrey Road, Kidwelly, Carmarthenshire SA17 4TF
Tel: 01554 890729 Fax: 01554 891407
Set in open countryside just off the A484, this spick-and-span farmhouse has been much modernised since being built at the end of
the 19th century. It is now run as a Bed & Breakfast business by
Beryl Beynon, who was born in the house, together with her husband Brian and daughters Alison and Victoria. Three double bedrooms and three twins, all en suite, provide very comfortable over-

Farmhouse B&B

Six en suite bedrooms with tv;
heated swimming pool

night accommodation. They all have tv and tea-makers, and breakfast is served in the lounge/dining room. Packed lunches can be
provided, and the house has washing/drying facilities. Adjoining
the house are a heated swimming pool and a large car park.

Credit Cards: None

Local Golf Courses:Ashburnham, Carmarthen, Glynhir, Glyn Abbey

GREENFIELD COTTAGE 131

Ferryside, Carmarthenshire SA17 5UE Tel: 01267 267815
Fax: 01267 267934 e-mail: pmagor99@hotmail.com
website: www.greenfield1@currantbun.com
Set in glorious countryside with lovely views in all directions,
Greenfield Cottage is a mid-1950s house with an adjoining Victorian-style conservatory. Cecilia and Phil Magor are the resident proprietors, welcoming visitors of all ages for a meal or an overnight
stay. They have three spacious letting bedrooms with king-size beds
and tea/coffee trays. There's a tv lounge for residents, a large car

Guest House, café & restaurant

3 bedrooms; tv lounge. Snack and
full menus
Credit Cards: Access, Mastercard,
Visa

park and safe storage for bicycles. The conservatory restaurant, The
Meadows, serves home-cooked food at prettily laid tables in a lovely
relaxed ambience: full breakfast, morning coffee, cream teas and
evening meals.

Local Golf Courses:Carmarthen, Glynhir, Glyn Abbey, Ashburnham

CLEDDAU BRIDGE HOTEL 132

Essex Road, Pembroke Dock, Pembrokeshire SA72 6EG
Tel: 01646 685961 e-mail:
information@cleddaubridgehotel.co.uk
Fax: 01646 685746 website: cleddaubridgehotel.co.uk
The Cleddau Bridge Hotel stands in three acres of grounds a few
hundred yards from one of the area's best-known landmarks, the
Cleddau Bridge, and enjoys fine views over the river. The 24 letting
bedrooms - recently refurbished along with the rest of the hotel -
range from singles to a family suite; all have full en suite bath-

Hotel

24 en suite rooms including 2
suites; bar and restaurant menus

rooms, satellite tv, radio, telephone and tea-makers. A bar meal
menu is served in the Alberta Bar or through room service, while
in the elegant Royal Restaurant there's a choice of à la carte or
table d'hote menu. Popular venue for functions and conferences.

Credit Cards: All the major cards

Local Golf Courses: Tenby, Haverfordwest, Milford Haven

CARMARTHENSHIRE

PEMBROKSHIRE

PEMBROKESHIRE

THE NAVY INN — 133

Melville Street, Pembroke Dock, Pembrokeshire SA72 6XS
Tel: 01646 682300

Dating from the end of the 19th century, the Navy Inn is a substantial building on a corner site near the waterfront. Behind the stone facade - painted navy blue in parts - there's plenty of space inside, and a beer garden with a safe children's play area at the back. There are two bars, one with pool, darts and a wide-screen tv for sporting events, the other with seats for 60 used mainly by customers enjoying a quiet drink or a meal. Peter Schaaf, who recently took over after 15 years experience in the trade, offers a menu to suit all appetites, from ciabatta sandwiches and jacket potatoes to spaghetti bolognese, lamb kebabs, grilled shark steak, oriental beef stir-fry and a mighty 24oz gammon steak.

Inn with Food
Snack and full menus

Credit Cards: Mastercard, Visa

Local Golf Courses: South Pembrokeshire, Haverfordwest, Tenby

KINLOCH COURT HOTEL — 134

Queens Parade, Tenby, Pembrokeshire SA70 7EG
Tel: 01834 842777 Fax: 01834 843097
e-mail: kinlochhotel@aol.com web: www.kinlochcourt-hotel.co.uk

The former Tenby Rectory is now a fine private hotel in a commanding position with great views both inland and out to sea. Personally run by owners Lee and Jenny Davies, the hotel has 14 centrally heated en suite bedrooms, including triple and family rooms, all with tv, telephone, radio, hairdryer and tea-making facilities. The extensive 3- or 4-course dinner menu changes daily, and lunch, morning coffee and afternoon tea are also available. There's a convivial, well-stocked bar and a comfortable residents' lounge. Ample parking spaces.

Hotel
14 en suite rooms; daily-changing dinner menu

Credit Cards: All the major cards

Local Golf Courses: Tenby, Trefloyne, Milford Haven, Haverfordwest

CASTLEMEAD HOTEL — 135

Manorbier, Nr. Tenby, Pembrokeshire SA70 7TA
Tel/Fax: 01834 871358 e-mail: castlemeadhotel@aol.com

Geoff and Lorna Greasley, here for 15 years, take excellent care of guests at their charming Edwardian residence at the head of a wooded valley. Eight en suite bedrooms with tv and tea-makers provide quiet, comfortable overnight accommodation; three of the rooms are on the ground floor of a converted coach house. In the restaurant (open also to non-residents) a daily-changing four-course dinner is served. The restaurant, lounge and cosy bar-sunroom all enjoy the views and have direct access to the garden, where light lunches and cream teas are served in fine weather. A great place to relax, and perfect for walkers, birdwatchers and nature-lovers - and there's safe bathing from the beach just a stone's throw away.

Country Hotel
Eight en suite bedrooms with tv; daily-changing dinner menu

Credit Cards: Mastercard, Visa

Local Golf Courses: Tenby, Trefloyne, Milford Haven, Haverfordwest

THE DIAL INN — 136

Lamphey, Pembrokeshire SA71 5NU
Tel/Fax: 01646 672426 website: www.dialinnpembroke@barbox.net

Just a stone's throw from the Bishop's Palace, this former dower house dating from 1820 offers very high standards of food and accommodation. Open for coffee, lunch, dinner and bar meals, Granville and Ruth Hill's inn has earned a great reputation with the quality and variety of its cooking. The choice runs from bar food to a daily blackboard menu and an imaginative dining room menu. t The accommodation comprises five spacious en suite bedrooms with tv and tea-makers. Pool and darts are played in the games room, and more serious exercise can be taken on the two adjacent squash courts.

Inn, Food & Accommodation
5 en suite rooms; bar and restaurant menus

Credit Cards: Mastercard, Visa

Local Golf Courses: Tenby, Trefloyne, Milford Haven

HEYWOOD MOUNT HOTEL & SPA LEISURE SUITE 137

Heywood Lane, Tenby, Pembrokeshire SA70 8DA
Tel: 01834 842087   e-mail: reception@heywoodmount.co.uk
Fax: 01834 842113   website: www.heywoodmount.co.uk

Standing in one acre of landscaped gardens in a quiet residential part of Tenby with ample safe parking for all. You are invited to dine in the elegant Meadow's Restaurant which has an excellent evening menu with a wine list which will delight you. The extremely comfortable Stables Bar is the perfect place to rest in after a hard days golf! The large reading lounge looks onto the terrace patio and rear sun trapped lawn. All the bedrooms are en suite, comprehensively equipped and tastefully decorated. Newly opened August 2001 is an indoor swimming pool, sauna, solarium, jacuzzi and fitness suite. Every comfort under one roof, plus concessional rates at all our golf courses.

Hotel and Leisure Club

21 en suite bedrooms with tv and telephone; table d'hote dinner
Credit Cards: Amex, Mastercard, Visa

Local Golf Courses: Tenby, Trefloyne, Haverfordwest, Milford Haven

---

GILTAR HOTEL 138

The Esplanade, Tenby, Pembrokeshire SA70 7DU
Tel: 01834 842507/843424 Fax: 01834 845480
website: www.giltar-hotel.co.uk

Miguel Gonzalez and his staff welcome guests of all ages to the Giltar Hotel, which enjoys a commanding position on the esplanade above South Beach at Tenby. The substantial premises, built in 1830 and sympathetically modernised down the years, contain 75 comfortable bedrooms, all with bath or shower en suite, tv and tea-making facilities. Children are welcome at reduced rates, and cots and high chairs are available. Lifts serve all floors. Snacks are served at lunchtime, and a good dinner in the seaview restaurant. Lively cellar bar, tv lounges, pool table. Near to golf club.

Seaside Hotel

75 en suite rooms with tv;

Credit Cards: Amex, Mastercard, Visa

Local Golf Courses: Tenby, Trefloyne, Milford Haven, Haverfordwest

---

CLARENCE HOUSE HOTEL 139

The Esplanade, Tenby, Pembrokeshire SA70 7DU
Tel: 01834 844371 e-mail: clarencehotel@freeuk.com
Fax: 01834 844372 website: www.clarencehotel-tenby.co.uk

In the same family for 60 years, Clarence House Hotel offers carefree holidays by the sea combining old-world charm and civility with modern comfort and amenities. The building, which dates from 1860, enjoys a prime position on the esplanade, with easy access on the level to the town's facilities and a slipway or a few steps down to safe, sandy South Beach. Loz and Penny Phillips are the current owner-managers, maintaining a long tradition of hospitality that begins as soon as guests enter through the splendid revolving oak door into the reception ;lounge. A lift provides access to the 68 bedrooms, all of which have private bath/ shower and toilet, tv, tea-maker and individually controlled heating. Rooms at the front enjoy superb sea views.

The Seagull Bar has different roles to play throughout the day, from mid-morning coffee to lunchtime snacks, afternoon tea, pre-dinner happy hour, after-dinner coffee and drinks and late-evening bar and nightcap service. In the non-smoking ground-floor seaview restaurant a table d'hote menu is served from 6.30 to 7.30. The choice, which changes daily, typically includes tried-and-tested favourites such as minestrone, roast lamb, spaghetti bolognese and poached haddock. The hotel can organise golfing holidays, golf society lunches are catered for, and there's even a power point for recharging the batteries of golf buggies. The lounge opens on to a pretty rose garden, and on the seafront opposite the hotel is a small, private paved garden for taking the sun and for access to the steps down to the beach.

Seaside Hotel

Seaside hotel with 68 en suite rooms; bar, lounge, table d'hote restaurant
Credit Cards: All the major cards

Local Golf Courses: Tenby, Trefloyne, Milford Haven, Haverfordwest

PEMBROKESHIRE

BLUE DOLPHIN HOTEL 140

St Mary's Street, Tenby, Pembrokeshire SA70 7HW
Tel: 01834 842590 Fax: 01834 844877

Roger Bannister's friendly Blue Dolphin Hotel is located in a quaint street within the medieval town walls about 100 yards from the South Beach at Tenby. Eleven letting bedrooms comprise single, double, twin and family rooms, and cots and highchairs are available for families with toddlers. Packed lunches can be arranged, and with prior notice guests can enjoy a splendid dinner cooked by Roger, a chef with 30 years experience. Tenby has four beaches providing safe family bathing, and fishing, riding and golf are all available in the vicinity.

Hotel
11 rooms for B&B; evening meals by arrangement

Credit Cards: Mastercard, Visa

Local Golf Courses: Tenby, Trefloyne, Milford Haven, Haverfordwest

THE HARP INN 141

Old Radnor, Presteigne, Powys LD8 2RH
Tel/Fax: 01544 350655

Erfyl and Heather Price are perfect hosts at the Harp Inn, a beautifully restored 15th century inn with a wealth of period character. Exposed stone walls, beamed ceilings, slate-flagged floor and log fires in inglenook fireplaces make the most delightful setting for enjoying good company, good beer and excellent home cooking using the pick of the local produce. On the first floor are five guest bedrooms, all with creaky polished floorboards, tea-making facilities, colour tv and glorious views from the hillside setting. This beautiful inn, situated behind the church in a really pretty village, is an ideal spot for a break from the urban rush and a place where guests return year after year.

Inn, food & accommodation
Five bedrooms, fine home cooking, real ales and great views

Credit Cards: Mastercard, Visa

Local Golf Courses: Kington, Leominster, Llandrindod Wells

THE ROYAL OAK 142

Gladestry, Powys HR5 3NR
Tel: 01544 370669

New owners Bob and Iris Jones have breathed fresh life into the Royal Oak, a 16th century pub in a pretty village set in lovely hilly countryside on the B4594 west of Kington. Behind the white-painted frontage the look is traditional, with log fires in the bars and a beer garden at the back. Excellent-value home-cooked food includes a good choice of grills and fresh fish dishes, with daily specials adding to the choice, and real ales and well-chosen wines accompany a meal. For visitors staying overnight four letting bedrooms provide comfortable accommodation.

Pub, Food & Accommodation
Four bedrooms; bar food

Credit Cards: None

Local Golf Courses: Kington, Builth Wells, Llandrindod Wells

THE COCK HOTEL 143

Forden, Welshpool, Powys SY21 8LX
Tel: 01938 580226

Roger and June Mills welcome visitors to the Cock Hotel, which was built towards the end of the 19th century to serve the Ludlow-Montgomery coaching route. The large building has a number of different areas for enjoying a drink or something to eat (the main dining area is non-smoking), and the menu provides a good choice of freshly prepared food to suit all appetites, from a sandwich or jacket potato to hearty mixed grills and the popular Sunday roasts. Bed & Breakfast accommodation is available in two family-size guest rooms. The pub, which is located just off the A490 south of Welshpool, has a beer garden and a function room.

Pub, Food & Accommodation
Two family bedrooms; snacks and full meals

Credit Cards: None

Local Golf Courses: Chirk, Oswestry, Llangollen, Wrexham

THE BELL COUNTRY INN · 144

Llanyre, Llandrindod Wells, Powys LD1 6DY
Tel: 01597 823959 Fax: 01597 825899
e-mail: dgj.jones@virgin.net website: thebellcountryinn.com

Family run by David and Jenny Jones and their children, The Bell is located a short drive northwest of Llandrindod Wells just off the A4081. Built in the 1890s to replace an ancient drovers' hostelry, it offers great views, the friendliest of welcomes, fine food and drink and a comfortable bed for the night. The stone building has been extended to house the Stables Restaurant, where the chef's menu includes local, traditional British and International dishes complemented by a good wine list. The nine en suite bedrooms are particularly well-equipped. The courtyard is a popular spot in summer.

Inn, Food & Accommodation

Nine comprehensively equipped bedrooms; restaurant menu
Credit Cards: Access, Mastercard, Visa

Local Golf Courses:Builth Wells, Llandrindod Wells, Kington

LLANDETTY HALL FARM · 145

Talybont-on-Usk, Nr. Brecon, Powys LD3 7YR
Tel: 01874 676415

Helen Atkins offers roomy, comfortable bedrooms in a 400-year-old farmhouse on a working sheep farm in the Brecon Beacons National Park. The rooms, all non-smoking, are a double with private bathroom, a double with en suite bathroom and a double with en suite shower room. There's a tv in the residents' lounge. Breakfast is served at 8.30 and afternoon tea greets guests on arrival; evening meals are available on request. The lovely, peaceful farmhouse enjoys a superb setting on the B4558 between Talybont and Llangynidr. The Brecon & Monmouth Canal flows through the grounds at the back, and from the front there are magnificent views over the River Usk.

Farmhouse Accommodation

Three non-smoking rooms; B&B, dinner by arrangement

Credit Cards: None

Local Golf Courses: Cradoc, Builth Wells, Monmouthshire

SELAND NEWYDD · 146

Pwllgloyw, Nr. Brecon, Powys LD3 9PY
Tel: 01874 690282
website: www.selandnewydd.co.uk

Seland Newydd is the perfect place for a relaxing break. A family run inn with that personal touch. Set in a lovely rural location, it boasts a 2 AA Rosette restaurant where the food is freshly cooked to order from locally bought produce. There are log fires in colder weather and there are three en-suite bedrooms. The Inn has its own forest walk with fishing on the River Hondou, three superb golf courses all within easy reach and of course, the breathtaking scenery of the Brecon Beacons. A truly wonderful combination.

Inn, Accommodation & Food

Three en suite bedrooms; bar and restaurant meals
Credit Cards: Access, Mastercard, Visa

Local Golf Courses:Cradoc, Builth Wells, Wernndu

THE OLD FORD INN · 147

Llanhamlach, Nr. Brecon, Powys LD3 7YB
Tel/Fax: 01874 665220 e-mail: enquiries@theoldfordinn.co.uk
website: www.theoldfordinn.co.uk

A centuries old Coaching Inn enjoying a glorious setting overlooking the Brecon Beacons, 3 miles east of Brecon on the A40. There are lovely southerly views and the location is ideal for that golfing break or holiday exploring this attractive part of the world. Cosy, beamed bars and restaurant offer excellent value and choice, with a menu resourced largely from fresh local produce. Food is served lunchtime and evenings with real ale and good wine to accompany. Upstairs there are eight comfortable en suite bedrooms which have been refurbished and include colour tv and beverage trays.

Inn, Food & Accommodation

Eight en suite rooms, restaurant and bar
Credit Cards: Access, Mastercard, Visa

Local Golf Courses: Cradoc, Builth Wells, Monmouthshire

POWYS

POWYS

THE TAI'R BULL INN | 148

Libanus, Nr. Brecon, Powys LD3 8EL
Tel: 01874 625849

An immaculate white-painted pub on the A470 west of Brecon. Steve and Jan Coop are a very welcoming couple, and their cosy front bars, with a wood-burning stove in an inglenook fireplace, is particularly warm and inviting. The choice of food served in the bar or restaurant is commendably wide, from light snacks for a quick bite to hearty, filling dishes such as steak & ale pie, 16oz steaks or Welsh lamb casserole. Bed & Breakfast accommodation is available in three double rooms and two twins, all with en suite facilities and tv. the pub enjoys superb views of the Brecon Beacons, whose highest peak rises to almost 3,000 feet.

Inn, Food & Accommodation

Five en suite bedrooms; bar and restaurant menus
Credit Cards: Access, Mastercard, Visa

Local Golf Courses: Cradoc, Builth Wells, Merthyr Tydfil

THE CEDARS | 149

Hay Road, Builth Wells, Powys LD2 3PB
Tel: 01982 553356 website: www.cedars.ltd.co.uk

A handsome family residence, built around 1880, has been converted into a very comfortable guest house with an adjoining restaurant. Vic Morris, here for 12 years, welcomes guests from near and far for a meal or an overnight stay (or both). He offers seven letting bedrooms, five of them en suite, all with tv and tea-makers. One room has three beds, making it an ideal choice for families. Welsh produce is used whenever possible on the menu, typified by gammon(with egg or pineapple), Welsh lamb chops and a Welsh seafood casserole of salmon, cod, prawns and mussels. The house stands on the A470 Hay Road overlooking the River Wye.

Guest House with Restaurant

Seven bedrooms (5 en suite); à la carte restaurant
Credit Cards: Access, Diners, Mastercard, Visa

Local Golf Courses: Builth Wells, Llandrindod Wells

THE WHITE SWAN/PENCELLI PARC | 150

Llanfrynach, Brecon, Powys LD3 7BZ
Tel: 01874 665276   website: www.the-white-swan.com

A row of old black-and-white cottages was converted 200 years ago into a pub that now also incorporates one of the best restaurants in the area. Three spacious dining areas offer waitress service and a tempting menu of modern dishes - booking is advisable. Pencelli Parc is a sister establishment ½ mile down the road and is a fine new development of stylish self-catering holiday cottages set in landscaped grounds at the top of a water meadow. The five cottages each have three bedrooms and are furnished and equipped to Wales Tourist Board 5 Star standard. They cater for up to 30 people and have trout and salmon fishing rights on the River Usk.

Pub, Restaurant & Self-Catering

Pub with à la carte restaurant; five luxurious self-catering cottages
Credit Cards: Access, Mastercard, Visa

Local Golf Courses: Builth Wells, Cradoc, Monmouthshire

CORVEN HALL | 151

Hundred House Road, Howey, Llandrindod Wells, Powys LD1 5RE
Tel: 01597 823368

New owner Wade Curzon maintains the role of Corven Hall as a comfortable retreat for Bed & Breakfast guests. Just off the A483 between Llandrindod Wells and Builth Wells, the Hall is a fine Victorian house with lovely gardens and splendid views. Accommodation consists of six spacious bedrooms, most with en suite facilities, all with tv. Rooms are divided between the main house, where one room is suitable for disabled guests, and the coach house across the courtyard. A good breakfast starts the day, and in the evening free transport can be arranged to one of the excellent local restaurants. No smoking in bedrooms or public rooms.

Country Guest House

Six bedrooms, most en suite; tv. Good breakfast
Credit Cards: Access, Mastercard, Visa

Local Golf Courses:Llandrindod Wells, Builth Wells, Kington

THE LLANERCH INN 152

Llanerch Lane, Llandrindod Wells, Powys LD1 6BG
Tel: 01597 822086 Fax: 01597 824618
e-mail: llanerchinn@ic24.net

Built in the 16th century as a staging post on a major coaching route, the Llanerch inn offers traditional standards of hospitality in comfortable, relaxed surroundings. Many original features survive, including a Jacobean staircase and an inglenook fireplace in the lounge bar. John Leach and his family provide excellent accommodation in 12 en suite bedrooms, all with central heating, tv, radio and telephone. Snacks and full meals are served in the bar or dining room. Amenities include a residents' lounge, patio, garden, play area, car park and secure storage space.

Inn, Food & Accommodation
12 en suite rooms, tv, phone; snacks and full meals

Credit Cards: All the major cards

Local Golf Courses: Llandrindod Wells, Builth Wells, Kington

THE VULCAN ARMS 153

Llanwrthwl, Llandrindod Wells, Powys LD1 6NN
Tel: 01597 811180 Fax: 01597 811152
e-mail: vulcan.arms@virgin.net

Owners Robert Sluggett and Rhian Price run a delightful roadside inn on the A470 three miles south of Rhayader. Long opening hours make it a good place to pause at any time to take acre of thirsts and appetites, starting with breakfast from 7 o'clock and offering a wide selection of bar snacks and à la carte meals. Overnight accommodation is available - with additional accommodation in log cabins planned for the future. This makes the Vulcan Arms an ideal base for golfers or for enthusiastic walkers - there are plenty of testing hills hereabouts!

Roadside Inn with Food
Inn serving food from 7am; 2 en suite rooms, log cabins planned for the future

Credit Cards: All except Amex

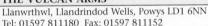
Local Golf Courses: Llandrindod Wells, Builth Wells, Cradoc

RED HOUSE FARM 154

Holly Lane, Howey, Llandrindod Wells, Powys LD1 5PP
Tel: 01597 824973 website: http://website.lineone.net/~redhousefarm

This traditional farmhouse built of stone and ship's timbers is an ideal base for golfing holidays and exploring a lovely part of the countryside. Owner Joan Adams offers spacious overnight accommodation in three bedrooms - a double en suite and twin rooms sharing a bathroom. All have tv and tea-making facilities, and guests have a pleasant lounge with a log fire. A good breakfast starts the day, and evening meals can be provided by arrangement. Salmon and trout fishing are available on a ¾ stretch of the River Ithon, a tributary of the Wye, and carp can be fished in a lake next to the farm. Great views.

Farmhouse Bed & Breakfast
3 bedrooms, one en suite; B&B, dinner by arrangement

Credit Cards: None

Local Golf Courses: Llandrindod Wells, Builth Wells, Cradoc

THE MONTPELLIER HOTEL 155

Temple Street, Llandrindod Wells, Powys LD1 5HW
Tel: 01597 822388 Fax: 01597 825600

In the centre of the elegant spa town of Llandrindod Wells, the Montpellier Hotel is a handsome redbrick building on four floors. Dating from the 1850s and recently refurbished, it offers comfortable, spacious accommodation in 11 individually styled bedrooms where period furniture harmonises with modern art works. All the rooms, from singles to the Montpellier Suite, have en suite facilities, tv, radio and telephone. Evening meals are served in the 30-cover brasserie, where the menu includes both British and Continental dishes. Food is also served in the bar areas. A health spa, with sauna and massage, is due to come on stream in 2001.

Hotel with Restaurant
11 en suite bedrooms with tv and phone; à la carte brasserie
Credit Cards: Access, Diners, Mastercard, Visa

Local Golf Courses: Llandrindod Wells, Builth Wells, Cradoc

CARDIGANSHIRE (CEREDIGION)

Farmhouse Hotel

Ten en suite rooms; B&B plus evening meal on prior notice

Credit Cards: None

PENYCASTELL FARM HOTEL 156

Llanrhystud, Ceredigion SY23 5BZ
Tel/Fax: 01974 272622   e-mail: penycastellhotel@faxvia.net
A haven of tranquillity in a glorious setting with panoramic views. Jean Vickers has created a cosy, relaxed atmosphere throughout the interior, with beams, panelling, antiques and paintings, and a log-burning stove in the lounge. A large stone barn next to the farmhouse contains a further lounge and three of the ten centrally heated en suite bedrooms, which all have tv, hairdryer, bathrobes and lots of little extras. One room has an 18th century American four-poster bed and wall paper copied from the period. Home-cooked evening meals use organic produce as much as possible, No children, no pets, no smoking.

Local Golf Courses: Aberystwyth, Borth, Penrhos

Hotel

36 en suite rooms; café-bar, restaurant

Credit Cards: Mastercard, Visa

ABERYSTWYTH PARK LODGE 157

Parc-y-Llyn, Aberystwyth, Ceredigion SY23 3TL
Tel: 01970 636333 Fax: 01970 636334
e-mail: aberparklodge.co.uk
Vince and Alison Morgans oversaw the building of this very spacious modern hotel, which opened its doors in June 2000. The low-rise complex, on a roundabout opposite Safeway, has 36 letting bedrooms, all with en suite facilities, satellite tv, telephone, modem point and tea-makers. Guests have a wide choice of eating on menus that range from sandwiches and light snacks to pasta, grills, curries and sauced main dishes. The 200-seat café-bar is open from 7pm to 10pm, the restaurant (the majority of which is non-smoking) from noon to 10pm.

Local Golf Courses: Aberystwyth, Borth, Penrhos

Hotel

36 en suite rooms; café-bar, restaurant

Credit Cards: Mastercard, Visa

ABERYSTWYTH PARK LODGE 158

Parc-y-Llyn, Aberystwyth, Ceredigion SY23 3TL
Tel: 01970 636333 Fax: 01970 636334
e-mail: aberparklodge.co.uk
Vince and Alison Morgans oversaw the building of this very spacious modern hotel, which opened its doors in June 2000. The low-rise complex, on a roundabout opposite Safeway, has 36 letting bedrooms, all with en suite facilities, satellite tv, telephone, modem point and tea-makers. Guests have a wide choice of eating on menus that range from sandwiches and light snacks to pasta, grills, curries and sauced main dishes. The 200-seat café-bar is open from 7pm to 10pm, the restaurant (the majority of which is non-smoking) from noon to 10pm.

Local Golf Courses: Aberystwyth, Borth, Penrhos

Self-Catering

4 Cottages for 2-9 people. Total bed spaces 22
Credit Cards: Mastercard, Visa, Solo, Switch, Delta

PENWERN FACH HOLIDAY COTTAGES 159

Pont Hirwaun, Cardigan, Ceredigion SA43 2RL
Tel: 01239 710694 fax: 01239 710854
e-mail: enquiries@penwernfach.co.uk www.penwernfach.co.uk
Geoff and Debbee Adamson offer self-catering accommodation of character and quality in superb cottages set in 15 acres of grounds and gardens. The cottages are conversions of the old farm buildings and whilst retaining their original charcter, they also provide all the up-to-date amenities for a self-catering holiday. All have private patios with furniture and outside lighting. There's a laundry and children's play area. Golfers have the exclusive use of a 250yd driving range, with target greens at 100, 165 and 225 yds. A special offer of one free round of golf at Cardigan Golf club with Geoff is available when a cottage is booked for 7 nights.

Local Golf Courses: Cardigan, Haverfordwest, Milford Haven

TREFEDDIAN HOTEL 160

Aberdovey, Gwynedd LL35 0SB
Tel: 01654 767213 Fax: 01654 767777

In the Cave-Brown-Cave family for 75 years, Trefeddian enjoys a peaceful, serene setting back from the A493 half a mile north of Aberdovey. The 48 en suite bedrooms are neat and attractive, the lounges spacious and inviting, the food and drink excellent. A stay here can be as relaxed or as active as you like - sitting on the sun terrace admiring the view, enjoying a drink in the bar or a game of snooker, taking a spot of exercise in the pool, on the all-weather tennis court or the hotel's own nine-hole pitch & putt course. And for walker there are miles of beautiful countryside and coastline.

Country Hotel

48 en suite rooms; restaurant, tennis, swimming pool

Credit Cards: Mastercard, Visa

Local Golf Courses: Aberdovey, Borth, Royal St David's

ST TUDWALS INN 161

High Street, Abersoch, Gwynedd LL53 7DS
Tel: 01758 712539

Ian Turner and his family are excellent hosts at St Tudwals Inn, whose varied attractions have made it one of the town's most popular meeting places. There's something of a maritime feel about the bars, where a good selection of snacks is served throughout the day, and the restaurant, whose imaginative à la carte menu relies on top-quality produce, much of it local (the seafood specials are particularly good). The inn, which was recently refurbished by Robinson's Brewery, also offers a high standard of overnight accommodation in its five en suite bedrooms. Located in the High Street, St Tudwals is close to the harbour, handy for the shops and a two-minute drive from the local golf club.

Inn, Food & Accommodation

Five en suite rooms; bar & restaurant menus

Credit Cards: All the major cards

Local Golf Courses: Abersoch, Caernarfon, Nefyn, Pwllheli

THE WHITE HOUSE HOTEL & RESTAURANT 162

Abersoch, Nr. Pwllheli, Gwynedd LL53 7AG
Tel: 01758 713427 Fax: 01758 713512
e-mail: whitehousehotel@btinternet.com

The White House is located on the A499 Pwllheli-Abersoch road, set back in spacious landscaped grounds. The setting is splendid indeed, with lovely views over the harbour to Cardigan Bay and the mountains of Snowdonia on the other side.

The White House excels in its accommodation, with 13 well-equipped en suite guest rooms, all decorated and furnished to a high standard. The rooms are centrally heated, with tv, radio, telephone and tea/coffee-making facilities. The comfortable residents' lounge is an ideal place to relax and contemplate the good things in life, and the cocktail bar is an inviting spot to meet other guests over a pre-dinner drink. The hotel has established an excellent reputation for the quality of its cuisine, and the chefs make fine use of top-class local produce on a changing menu that highlights Welsh beef and lamb, and fresh crab and lobster. In the non-smoking dining room breakfast is served from 8 to 9.30, light lunches for residents Monday to Saturday, dinner from 6.30 to

9.30. The Sunday lunch carvery is available to both residents and non-residents. Besides the normal tariff, the hotel offers all-inclusive breaks and golfing packages; it is also a popular venue for small conferences and functions, and the management can organise boat charter.

Abersoch itself caters well for lovers of outdoor pursuits, with safe swimming from long, sandy beaches, sailing, fishing, riding and a fine golf course. For walkers there are many miles of public footpaths, including the National Trust-administered coastal paths, and within a short drive are a large number of fascinating and historic sites to explore.

Hotel & Restaurant

13 en suite rooms; light lunches, full dinner menu

Credit Cards: Mastercard, Visa

Local Golf Courses: Abersoch, Caernarfon, Criccieth, Nefyn

GWYNEDD

MENAI BANK HOTEL 163

North Road, Caernarfon, Gwynedd LL55 1BD
Tel/Fax: 01286 673297 e-mail: menaibankhotel@tesconet.co.uk
website: www.menaibankhotel.co.uk

Guests soon become friends at the Menai Bank Hotel, where resident proprietors Liz and Tony Cox (he's a keen golfer) offer the warmest of welcomes and the promise of a peaceful, relaxed stay. The turn-of-the-century building, whose original features include decorated slate fireplaces and a beautiful stained-glass window, has 16 individually appointed bedrooms, all with en suite bathrooms, tv, radio-alarm clocks and hospitality trays. Liz is a great cook, and her menus include Welsh, British and Continental dishes, with fresh local produce used wherever possible. Lounge, bar, pool table, garden and patio.

Hotel & Restaurant

16 en suite bedrooms; restaurant

Credit Cards: All the major cards

Local Golf Courses: Caernarfon, Anglesey, Nefyn, St Deniel

THE THREE CROWNS INN 164

Fford-y-Fynnon, Bangor, Gwynedd LL57 1HB
Tel: 01248 351138

The oldest pub in Bangor, with a history going back to 1771, is a popular spot for a drink, for a meal or for an overnight stopover. Log fires warm the bar, where daily specials add to the choice on the menu; in the summer, the barbecue out on the patio offers an alfresco alternative. Three rooms - a single, a twin and a double - provide quiet, comfortable accommodation on the second floor, with tea/coffee-making facilities on the landing, and bath/shower room on the floor below. The inn occupies a corner site not far from the town centre.

Inn, Food & Accommodation

Three B&B rooms; home-cooked food

Credit Cards: None

Local Golf Courses: Beaumaris, Caernarfon, St Deniel, Bull Bay

THE MENAI HOTEL 165

Craig y Don Road, Bangor, Gwynedd LL57 2BG
Tel: 01248 354200 Fax: 01248 354512
e-mail: info@themenai33.freeserve.co.uk

A very cheerful white-painted hotel in Bangor Old Town on the hills above the Menai Straits. The hotel has nine well-furnished en suite bedrooms with tv, telephone and tea-making facilities; some of the rooms enjoy views over the Straits. In the bar, which has a lively modern feel, Sky tv and table football keep the young regulars happy, along with a great selection of beers and wines; snacks and bar meals are served in the café-bar, and à la carte evening meals in the dining room between 19.00 and 21.00.

Hotel

Nine en suite rooms; bar meals and evening à la carte

Credit Cards: All the major cards

Local Golf Courses: St Deiniol, Caernarfon, Anglesey, Bull Bay

CELTIC ROYAL HOTEL 166

Bangor Street, Caernarfon, Gwynedd LL55 1AY
Tel: 01286 674477 e-mail: enquiries@celtic-royal.co.uk
Fax: 01286 674139 website: www.celtic-royal.co.uk

Accommodation, restaurant, conferences, banqueting, leisure club. The Celtic Royal, built in 1841 and recently refurbished, offers all these, and its town-centre location makes it an ideal base for seeing the sights of historic Caernarfon. The hotel has 110 en suite bedrooms, all refurbished to a very high standard and all with satellite tv, telephone, hairdryer and hospitality trays. Several rooms are suitable for disabled guests. Bar snacks and full restaurant meals are served lunchtime and evening, and can guests can work up an appetite in the swimming pool or the gym, or clear their heads in the sauna or steam room.

Hotel (3 star Superior)

110 en suite rooms; restaurant, bar, gym, swimming pool

Credit Cards: All the major cards

Local Golf Courses: Caernarfon, St Deniel, Nefyn, Llandudno

YR HEN FECWS `167`

16 Lombard Street, Porthmadog, Gwynedd LL49 9AP
Tel: 01766 514625

An 18th century Welsh-stone building of great character, Yr Hen Fecws is located just off the main street of the busy town of Porthmadog. With owner-chef Helen Owen at the helm, this restaurant has established a great reputation among the people of the town and surrounding area.

Open every day in the summer and six days a week in the winter, Yr Hen Fecws - the name is Welsh for The Old Bakery - is certainly the venue of choice for lovers of good home-cooked food. In the restaurant, Helen's menus are a mouthwatering mix of traditional local dishes and flavours from all over the world; the raw materials are the best the local markets and producers can supply, and the printed menu is supplemented by tempting daily specials and a list of hard-to-resist desserts.

The surroundings are as appealing as the cooking, with warm, vibrant colours blending harmoniously with the original exposed beams, stone fireplaces and polished wooden furnishings.

The final attraction of this very special establishment is the comfortable Bed & Breakfast accommodation adjacent to the bistro. Four lovely rooms, decorated to the same high standard as the bistro, and all with en suite facilities and tv, make an ideal base for exploring a little town with a lot to offer the visitor.

Bistro with B&B

Evening menus; 4 en suite rooms

Credit Cards: Mastercard, Visa

Local Golf Courses: Criccieth, Porthmadog, Royal St David's

PLAS PENHELIG COUNTRY HOUSE HOTEL `168`

Aberdovey, Gwynedd LL35 0NA
Tel: 01654 767676 Fax: 01654 767783

Gordon and Marian Bates recently took over this superb country house hotel, which enjoys a glorious, secluded setting in landscaped gardens at the end of a wooded driveway. Comfortable armchairs, open log fires and exposed beams add up to a splendidly traditional feel in the day rooms, and the 14 en suite bedrooms offer the highest standards of decor and comfort. Home-grown produce features prominently on the top-class menu in the restaurant, and lighter snacks can be enjoyed at lunchtime in the adjacent bar or out on the terrace. Croquet, putting. No smoking in the hotel; no children under 10.

Country House Hotel

14 en suite bedrooms; top-class restaurant

Credit Cards: All the major cards

Local Golf Courses: Aberdovey, Borth, Royal St David's, Welshpool

RHINOG PARK `169`

Dyffryn Ardudwy, Gwynedd LL44 2HA
Tel: 01341 247652 e-mail: rhinogpark@countryparks.com
Fax: 01531 640280 website: www.countryparks.com

Rhinog Park enjoys a lovely quiet setting on the edge of Snowdonia National Park overlooking farmland with views of Snowdonia and the Rhinog mountains. Close to the coastal road of the A496 Barmouth-Harlech road, this park has received the David Bellamy Conservation Award and is a Wales in bloom winner. Managed by Jill and John Ensor for Country Parks Ltd, the site has cedar wood and Scandinavian-style lodges, all fitted out for a comfortable self-catering holiday. The lodges have either two or three bedrooms and all have a fully equipped kitchen, bathroom and lounge-diner. Children can romp safely in a large outdoor play area.

Self-Catering Accommodation

Lodges

Credit Cards: None

Local Golf Courses: Royal St David's, Aberdovey, Porthmadog

THE DOVEY INN · 170

Seaview Terrace, Aberdovey, Gwynedd LL35 0EF
Tel: 01654 767332 Fax: 01654 767996
e-mail: rk@doveyinn.com website: www.doveyinn.com

Situated right on the seafront, the Dovey Inn is a fine Tudor style building dating back to 1729. Ray and Jo Kearney's inn has great appeal, and behind the black-and-white facade the feel is warm and inviting. The three bars each have individual character ranging from traditional to contemporary. In these bars an exceptionally wide range of food is served, from an extensive choice of seafood and meat dishes, to generously filled sandwiches, vegetarian choices, pizzas, pasta and lite bites. A 30 seat dining room offers a large table d'hote dinner menu. For guests staying the night, there are eight en-suite rooms, two of which are two bedroom suites.

Inn, Food & Accommodation

Eight en suite rooms; extensive menus

Credit Cards: All the major cards

Local Golf Courses: Aberdovey, Borth, Harlech

GWYNFRYN FARM · 171

Llanbedr, Gwynedd LL45 2NY
Tel/Fax: 01341 241381
website: www.lokalink.co.uk/harlech/gwynfrynfarm/homepage.htm

Lesley Howie offers high-quality self-catering accommodation in five stone-built cottages, all with kitchen-diner, lounge with tv and well-appointed bedrooms sleeping from 2 to 8 guests. All are centrally heated and double-glazed, and some have private patios or garden access. There's also an en suite letting bedroom in the 16th century farmhouse. The 20-acre smallholding enjoys a fine location in a pleasant valley in beautiful Snowdonia National Park. Attractions in the vicinity include historic sites, golf, beaches, fishing and pony trekking.

Self-Catering Cottages

Five self-catering cottages on a farm; also 1 B&B room

Credit Cards: None

Local Golf Courses: Royal St Davids, Porthmadog, Criccieth

HARBOUR HOTEL · 172

Abersoch, Gwynedd LL53 7HR Tel: 01758 712406
Fax: 01758 713826 e-mail: mail@harbour-hotel.com
website: www.harbour-hotel.com

Traditional seaside Bed & Breakfast hotel with a few surprises! Accommodation comprises 14 en suite bedrooms, one with a four-poster and jacuzzi, and residents have a large lounge for relaxing, watching tv or enjoying the views. General Manager Gary Horseman has made this a popular venue, especially with the younger generation, with the opening of the night spot Wax, designed by local surfers and offering drinks, tv, pool, disco and surfing videos. There are also two bars and a wine bar, both open to non-residents.

Hotel

14 en suite rooms; wine bar, café, disco

Credit Cards: Mastercard, Visa

Local Golf Courses: Abersoch, Nefyn, Pwllheli, Porthmadog

PLAS BODEGROES · 173

Nefyn, Pwllheli, Gwynedd LL53 5TH
Tel: 01758 612363 Fax: 01758 701247
e-mail: gunna@bodegroes.co.uk website: www.bodegroes.co.uk

One of the very top places to eat and to stay in Wales, Plas Bodegroes is a handsome Georgian manor house in beautiful, secluded grounds that include an avenue of ancient beeches. The owners Chris and Gunna Chown put the main emphasis on the food, and Chris cooks in a light, modern style that is exciting and innovative. The elegant, uncluttered decor reflects Gunna's Scandinavian background, and the eight bedrooms, some with four-posters, retain the character of the house while offering all the expected modern amenities. A place of real charm and quality.

Restaurant with Rooms

Dinner Tues-Sun, lunch Sun; eight en suite rooms

Credit Cards: Mastercard, Visa

Local Golf Courses: Royal St David's, Abersoch, Nefyn, Pwllheli

MARINE HOTEL 174

Castle Street, Criccieth, Gwynedd LL52 0EA
Tel: 01766 522946 Fax: 01766 522216
e-mail: marinecriccieth@lineone.net

A friendly, traditional seaside hotel that was built as a doctor's house. Owned for the past two years by Ray Williams, the Marine has 15 letting bedrooms, all recently upgraded and most with en suite facilities. Some of the bedrooms, the bay-windowed tv lounge and the veranda enjoy sea views. Excellent home-cooked food is served in the bar-restaurant. Golfers are very welcome, and discounts are available at Criccieth, Nefyn and Pwllheli golf courses. The hotel stands opposite the 13th century castle and only 50 yards from the beach.

Hotel
Fifteen en suite rooms; bar-restaurant

Credit Cards: Mastercard, Visa

Local Golf Courses: Criccieth, Nefyn, Pwllheli, Porthmadog

THE CARISBROOKE HOTEL 175

High Street, Abersoch, Gwynedd LL53 7DY
Tel: 01758 712526 Fax; 01758 713666
e-mail: davies@abersoch-carisbrookehotel.co.uk

Golfers, sailors, anglers and walkers return year after year to enjoy the hospitality offered at this small Bed & Breakfast hotel by proprietors John and Carolyn Davies. The hotel has two twin and five double rooms plus a suite of rooms ideal for a family. Most of the rooms, including the suite, offer en suite facilities. Four of them look out to sea. On the ground floor are a comfortable lounge and a bar/dining room where a full British breakfast is served. A private car park is located behind the hotel.

Bed & Breakfast
Seven rooms and family suite for B&B

Credit Cards: Mastercard, Visa

Local Golf Courses: Abersoch, Nefyn, Pwllheli, Porthmadog

PONDS BISTRO 176

High Street, Porthmadog, Gwynedd LL49 9LR
Tel: 01766 512333 website: www.ponds-bistro.co.uk

Situated on the main street of Porthmadog, Ponds Bistro provides some of the very best cooking in the area. In a first-floor setting of beams, a slate-stone feature wall and immaculate table settings, accomplished chef David Pike produces an extensive à la carte menu served seven nights a week from 6 o'clock till late- booking is recommended for all sittings. David seeks out the best of local supplies for his dishes, which include splendid meat and fish main courses, a choice for vegetarians and unmissable sweets. The accompanying wine list is strong in New World bottles. David's wife Nia runs front of house at this really delightful bistro, which can cater for parties of up to 30.

Bistro
A la carte menu every evening

Credit Cards: Mastercard, Visa

Local Golf Courses: Royal St David's, Porthmadog, Criccieth

HAFOD WEN GUEST HOUSE 177

Harlech, Gwynedd LL46 2RA
Tel: 01766 780356
e-mail: hafodwen@enterprise.net website: www.hafodwen.co.uk

In a superb, romantic setting a mile south of Harlech on the A496, Hafod Wen enjoys tremendous views of the sea and the Llyn Peninsula, with the Snowdonia range beyond. The eight acres of grounds provide a variety of scenery and some wonderful walks, and the house has seven spacious en suite bedrooms that are full of character (just like the family-friendly owners Jan and Reg Chapman!). Superb home cooking makes the best use of local and home-grown produce, and the owners can provide luncheon baskets for guests making the most of the glorious countryside.

Guest House
Seven en suite bedrooms; four-course evening meal

Credit Cards: Mastercard, Visa

Local Golf Courses: Royal St David's, Porthmadog, Criccieth

GWYNEDD

THE PLAS RESTAURANT 178

High Street, Harlech, Gwynedd LL46 2YA
Tel: 01766 780204

The views are nothing short of sensational from this grand late-Victorian building in the middle of Harlech. The lofty position takes in the Castle and looks out across Royal St David's Golf Course to Cardigan Bay. The restaurant, which has a delightful veranda and tables set out in the garden, is open from 9am to 8pm for breakfasts, snacks and teas, and from noon for the full à la carte menu of home-cooked British fare. Neville and Adam Brown, who have owned and run the Plas for 23 years, also run three shops opposite the restaurant selling antiques, pottery, interior furnishings, crafts and novelties.

Restaurant

All-day snacks, à la carte from noon

Credit Cards: Mastercard, Visa

Local Golf Courses: Royal St David's, Porthmadog, Criccieth

AWEL MÔR HOTEL 179

29 Marine Terrace, Criccieth, Gwynedd LL52 0EL
Tel: 01766 522086 e-mail: sue.petch@virgin.net
website: www.cricciethaccommodation.co.uk/

Our friendly, licensed non-smoking hotel on the seafront at Criccieth offers tastefully decorated en-suite bedrooms which have heating, beverage trays, colour TVs, hair dryers, radios and shaver points. We have a well stocked bar and a guest lounge with open fire. Only a short walk from Criccieth town and castle and an ideal location for touring Snowdonia, the Lleyn Peninsula and visiting many places of interest.

A warm welcome awaits you from Paul and Sue Petch at the Awel Môr Hotel.

B&B and evening meals

Seafront hotel with 9 en suite rooms

Credit Cards: All major cards

Local Golf Courses: Criccieth, Harlech, Porthmadog, Nefyn, Pwllheli

THE CLIFFS INN 180

Beach Road, Morfa Nefyn, Nr. Pwllheli, Gwynedd LL53 6BY
Tel: 01758 720356 Fax: 01758 720544
e-mail: enquiries@cliffs-inn.co.uk

Glynne and Mary Roberts' white-painted inn enjoys a magnificent position 50 yards from the beach, with superb views across Caernarfon Bay to Anglesey. A hotel until 1977, it now operates as a public house that also offers overnight accommodation. Excellent snacks and main meals are served in the bar and conservatory, including filled baguettes, jacket potatoes, fresh fish and crab dishes. The accommodation comprises four well-furnished self-catering flats. All have a lounge with tv, a kitchen with fridge and a bathroom. The inn is closed Sunday evening.

Inn with Self-catering

Bar snacks and meals; 4 self-catering flats
Credit Cards: Amex, Mastercard, Visa

Local Golf Courses: Abersoch, Pwllheli, Royal St David's

YR HEN FEUDY RESTAURANT 181

Cwm Bychan Road, Llanbedr, Nr. Harlech, Gwynedd LL45 2NH
Tel/Fax: 01341 241555

A modern conversion of single-storey farm buildings has produced an eye-catching restaurant that is open from May to October (noon to 9pm). Some of the old walls and beams have been incorporated into the restaurant, and the white stone walls are set off by lovely greens and yellows for the table settings. Eloise Wilkes, here for four years after experience at such locations as Warwick Castle, offers tremendous value for money and outstanding quality on her menu, which includes home-made pizzas, fresh fish dishes - the choice changes daily - and superb griddled steaks. The restaurant is located in Llanbedr village off the A496 three miles south of Harlech.

Restaurant

Meals served 12 till 9 May-October
Credit Cards: Diners, Mastercard, Visa

Local Golf Courses: Royal St Davids, Criccieth, Porthmadog

CRANBOURNE HOTEL 182

Seaside Hotel

16 bedrooms including family rooms; bar snacks

Credit Cards: Mastercard, Visa

9 Marine Parade, Barmouth, Gwynedd LL42 1NA
Tel/Fax: 01341 280202

Janine Mander from Jersey has had a good first year at the Cranbourne Hotel, which occupies two greystone houses in a Victorian seafront terrace. Recently refurbished throughout to a high standard, the hotel has 16 comfortably appointed rooms including family rooms; all have tv and tea-making facilities and two boast the luxury of four-poster beds. A good range of beers, wines and spirits is served in the bar, along with hot and cold snacks. Parking spaces at the front. The hotel is an ideal base for a family holiday by the sea or for golfers, alone or in a party.

Local Golf Courses: Royal St Davids, Aberdovey

THE BRYN HIR ARMS 183

Inn and Bistro

Two bars, bistro-style restaurant, garden

Credit Cards: Mastercard, Visa

24 Hugh Street, Criccieth, Gwynedd LL52 0BT
Tel: 01766 522493

Eryl Roberts ran a restaurant in Blaenau Ffestiniog for several years and celebrated the new millennium by buying the Bryn Hir Arms, a handsome stone-built pub on Criccieth's main street. The pub has two convivial bars, one with prints and pictures of Criccieth down the years, the other with a pool table and wide-screen tv for the big sporting events. Bar snacks are served at lunchtime, and in the newly refurbished bistro-style restaurant local produce features prominently on the menu. There's a good selection of beers and wines, and in summer the patio garden is a very pleasant spot for enjoying a drink.

Local Golf Courses: Criccieth, Nefyn, Porthmadog, Pwllheli

CAEAU CAPEL HOTEL 184

Country House Hotel

18 en suite rooms; B&B or D,B&B

Credit Cards: Mastercard, Visa

Nefyn, Gwynedd LL53 6EB
Tel: 01758 720240

Jo and Joe Taylor welcome guests to their late 19th century house, which stands in large, attractive gardens a short stroll from the beach and scenic clifftop walks. A comfortable, peaceful stay is guaranteed in the 18 tastefully furnished en suite bedrooms, and guests on Dinner, B&B terms can look forward to a splendid five-course meal cooked by Jo and served in the dining room overlooking the grounds. The bar is a good place to meet for pre-dinner drinks, and there are two relaxing lounges and a games room with pool and darts. The hotel offers discounts at the local golf courses and special rates for golfing parties.

Local Golf Courses: Nefyn, Pwllheli, Porthmadog, Royal St David's

MYNYDD EDNYFED COUNTRY HOUSE HOTEL 185

Country House Hotel

Eight en suite bedrooms; 3-course dinners. WTB 3 stars

Credit Cards: Mastercard, Visa

Caernarfon Road, Criccieth, Gwynedd LL52 0PH
Tel: 01766 523269 Fax: 01766 522929
e-mail: mynydd-ednyfed@criccieth.net website: www.criccieth.net

Mynydd Ednyfed Country House Hotel is a handsome 400-year-old greystone house standing off the B4411 in seven acres of gardens, woods and paddocks overlooking Tremadog Bay and Criccieth Castle. Eight letting bedrooms (four-poster rooms available) are furnished and equipped to a very high standard, with en suite facilities, tv, radio, telephone and tea-makers. A fine choice of home cooking by owner Maureen Edwards is served in the restaurant or Victorian conservatory - they appear in the "Taste of Wales". The old coach house has been converted into a gymnasium and solarium, and there's an all-weather tennis court in the old walled garden. WTB 3 stars.

Local Golf Courses: Nefyn, Porthmadog, Pwllheli, Royal St David's

GWYNEDD

LASTRA FARM HOTEL   186

Rhosgoch Road, Amlwch, Anglesey LL68 9TF
Tel: 01407 830906 Fax: 01407 832522
e-mail: booking@lastra-hotel.com
website: www.lastra-hotel.com

A beautifully restored 17th century farmhouse a mile inland from Bull Bay and half a mile from the pleasant resort town of Amlwch. Over the past ten years the three partners who own the hotel -

Maurice and Ann Hutchinson and Adrian Parry - have consolidated its reputation as one of the very best places on the Isle of Anglesey in terms of both accommodation and food, and its location makes it an ideal base for exploring the natural beauty and historic sights of this lovely part of the world.

The size of the establishment allows the owners to offer personal attention at all times, and they make every effort to ensure that a stay here is as relaxed and comfortable as possible. Six tastefully furnished bedrooms in the main house all have private bathrooms, tv, clock radio-alarm, telephone and tea-makers. Three further bedrooms, equally appealing, and a private lounge are located in an adjacent Victorian lodge.

The hotel has a very pleasant bar, and memorable meals are served in the non-smoking dining room, where the talented chef makes excellent use of the best local produce from land and sea. The marine harvest includes wild salmon, lobster, oysters and trout, and local butchers supply prime meat and seasonal game. Plans for 2001/2 include the addition of an informal conservatory brasserie.

Hotel and Restaurant

Nine en suite bedrooms with tv, telephone; restaurant

Credit Cards: Mastercard, Visa

Local Golf Courses: Bull Bay, Anglesey, Holyhead, Henllys Hall

THE GAZELLE HOTEL   187

Glyn Garth, Menai Bridge, Anglesey LL59 5PD
Tel: 01248 713364 Fax: 01248 713167
website: www.gazellehotel.fsnet.co.uk

A real gem of a hotel in a picturesque waterside setting on the A545 between Menai Bridge and Beaumaris. The local climate is excellent, and it's a great delight to sit outside on the jetty enjoying a drink and the stunning views across the Menai Straits to Snowdonia. The nine large, comfortable bedrooms also enjoy the views, and guests at Mike and Lesley Coop's grand little hotel have the use of two pleasant lounges and a bar. Bar snacks are served all day, and additionally there's a fine à la carte choice of main dishes including grills and seafood.

Hotel

Nine bedrooms; bar and restaurant menus

Credit Cards: All the major cards

Local Golf Courses: HenllysHall, St Deiniol, Bull Bay, Holyhead

BULL BAY HOTEL   188

Bull Bay, Nr. Amlwch, Anglesey LL68 9SH
Tel/Fax: 01407 830223

The most northerly hotel in Wales, in a superb setting overlooking picturesque Bull Bay. Owned and run by Gary Monaghan and Peter Stainton, it's a perfect base for golfers (Bull Bay course is just moments away) and fishermen, or for anyone exploring this lovely part of the world. The ten en suite bedrooms, all with sea views, range from singles to family rooms and a four-poster room; all have tv and telephone. Guests and non-residents have a choice of dining inn the restaurant or snacking in the lounge bar or out in the garden, which runs down to the sea. Pool, darts and regular jazz and folk nights are other attractions at this fine hotel., which stands on the A5025 above the resort town of Amlwch.

Hotel

Ten en suite rooms with tv and telephone; bar and restaurant meals

Credit Cards: Mastercard, Visa

Local Golf Courses: Bull Bay, Anglesey, Henllys Hall, Holyhead

TRECASTELL HOTEL `189`

Bull Bay, Nr. Amlwch, Anglesey LL68 9SA
Tel: 01407 830651 Fax: 01407 832114
e-mail: trecastell@aol.com

Superbly situated on one of the most northerly points on the Isle of Anglesey, Trecastell Hotel is a classic 1920s seaside hotel, run with friendly efficiency by Vic and Sue and their enthusiastic staff. The guest accommodation consists of 14 en suite bedrooms - singles, doubles, twins and a family room - all with tv, radio-alarm, telephone and hospitality tray. Every room enjoys a sea view, as does the new conservatory restaurant that leads from the bar.

In the café-bar an extensive menu is available lunchtime and evening, and the bar is open all day for drinks. A full à la carte menu is served in the delightful restaurant (non-smoking), complemented by a wine list assembled from Europe and the New World. There are separate children's and vegetarian menus.

For parties, functions and special occasions the hotel has two function rooms, both overlooking the bay. Many guests return year after year to this most appealing of hotels, where golf packages with the adjacent Bull Bay course can be organised at any time of year.

Besides golf, favourite activities include walking, angling and mountain biking, and among the many attractions on the Isle are Beaumaris Castle, Parys Mountain copper mines, Penrhos Nature Reserve and Lein Railway Museum. The hotel is located on the A5025 coast road a short drive west of Amlwch.

Hotel
14 en suite rooms with tv, telephone; bar and restaurant menus
Credit Cards: All the major cards

Local Golf Courses: Bull Bay, Henllys Hall, Holyhead, Anglesey

THE KINGS ARMS `190`

Marine Square, Holyhead, Anglesey LL65 1DL
Tel: 01407 762528

Follow the town-centre signs past the station to the harbour quay to find this splendid old black-and-white pub. There's a suitably nautical theme in the spacious lounge bar, where home-cooked food is served in generous portions at kind prices. Bar snacks are available all day, with an à la carte menu and daily specials lunchtime and evening. New for 2001 are ten letting bedrooms, all with en suite facilities and tv. An ideal base for younger golf parties, run in fine style by Tommy Doyle and his family.

Pub, Food & Accommodation
Ten en suite rooms; bar snacks and à la carte
Credit Cards: All the major cards

Local Golf Courses: Bull Bay, Holyhead, Anglesey

THE ROYAL OAK `191`

High Street, Malltraeth, Bodorgan, Anglesey LL62 5AS
Tel: 01407 840015

In a village on the road that runs up from the Menai Straits to Rhosneigr, the Royal Oak is a truly delightful pub. Peter and Lynn Smith have a cheery welcome for regulars and first-timers, and behind the neat pink and green frontage, coal fires keep things cosy in the bar and lounge. The Smiths offer an excellent selection of real and cask ales, and wines by glass or bottle to accompany splendid home cooking that includes winter soups and stews, game in season, grills, basket meals and seafood specials. Overnighters can rest content in their choice of four comfortable bedrooms. Upstairs lounge with tv; pool, darts; beer garden.

Pub, Food & Accommodation
Four bedrooms; excellent home cooking
Credit Cards: None

Local Golf Courses: Anglesey, Holyhead, Caernarfon

ANGLESEY

ANGLESEY

PENRHOS COUNTRY GUEST HOUSE 192

Holyhead Road, Gwalchmai, Anglesey LL65 4PW
Tel: 01407 720508

Penrhos Country Guest House stands in delightful gardens just outside the village on the main Menai Bridge-Holyhead road. Built 200 years ago as a farmhouse, it has been converted into a most delightful Bed & Breakfast establishment, run for the last 16 years by the Hills family. The four letting bedrooms, all en suite, are notable roomy and comfortable (sleeping up to four), and all four enjoy wonderful sea views. Guests have the use of a lovely lounge with Sky tv, and days start with an excellent English breakfast featuring new-laid eggs and home-made preserves. Dinner by arrangement.

Country Guest House

Four en suite rooms; B&B, dinner by arrangement

Credit Cards: None

Local Golf Courses: Anglesey, Bull Bay, Henllys Hall, Holyhead

THE GROSVENOR HOTEL 193

106-108 Abergele Road, Colwyn Bay, Conwy LL29 7PS
Tel: 01492 530798 e-mail: thegrosvenor@freenetname.co.uk
Fax: 01432 531586 website: www.hotel-grosvenor.co.uk

Derek and Mary Toombs make sure that guests in their late-Victorian Welsh stone house have a really relaxing stay. The 18 bedrooms - the majority en suite - include many suitable for families, and baby cots, high chairs and a baby listening service are available. The Olde Worlde Bar is a good place to enjoy a drink with fellow guests, and home-cooked dishes are served on either bar snack or à la carte menus. The owners can organise tee times for golfers and pre-book fishing trips - and there are drying facilities in the hotel.

Hotel

18 rooms, most en suite; bar and à la carte menus

Credit Cards: Mastercard, Visa

Local Golf Courses: Conwy, Rhos, Abergele, Llandudno

CONWY

BERTHLWYD HALL 194

Llechwedd, Conwy, LL32 8DQ
Tel: 01492 592409 Fax: 01492 572290
e-mail: berthlwydhall@hotmail.com www.berthlwydhall.com

Berthlwyd Hall is a beautiful Victorian house of unique charm and character surrounded by unspoilt country lanes and woodland, on the edge of the Snowdonia National Park. Many of the Victorian characteristics have been preserved, such as the splendid oak panelling in the entrance hall, a wide staircase sweeping up to the galleried landing, elaborately carved fireplaces and stained glass windows. It has been tastefully planned to provide a variety of extremely comfortable en-suite bedrooms, with a discreet combination of antiques and traditional furnishings. Each room has a private bathroom or shower room, hairdryer, colour TV and hospitality tray.

Country House

En suite rooms; bar

Credit Cards: Mastercard, Visa

Local Golf Courses: Conwy, Rhos, Llandudno (Maesdu, North Wales)

ROSEDENE HOTEL 195

10 Arvon Avenue, Llandudno, Conwy LL30 2DY
Tel: 01492 876491 Fax: 01492 872150
e-mail: janet@hodgett97.freeserve.co.uk

Run for 16 years by Janet and Bill Hodgett, Rosedene Hotel is located close to the shops and the beach in a row of elegant late-19th century houses. Overnight accommodation consists of 11 bedrooms - singles, doubles and twins - with en suite facilities, tv and tea-makers. Day rooms comprise a well-appointed lounge and dining room, where a choice of evening meal (book in advance) can be served to guests and their friends. Packed lunches are available, or there are plenty of good places for lunch in town. Small front patio. Street parking.

Hotel

11 en suite rooms, B&B and dinner by arrangement

Credit Cards: None

Local Golf Courses: Llandudno (Maesdu, North Wales), Conwy, Rhos

Hotel

63 en suite rooms; restaurants, bars, health club, swimming pool

Credit Cards: All the major cards

THE RISBORO HOTEL · 196

Clement Avenue, Llandudno, Conwy LL30 2ED
Tel: 01492 876343/4 Fax: 01492 879881
e-mail: hotelrisboro@ukonline.co.uk
website: www.risboro-hotel.co.uk

The Risboro is a bright, welcoming, turn-of-the-century building on a corner site close to the shops, the beach and several golf courses (reduced green fees). All 63 bedrooms, including five family rooms, are en suite, most with both bath and shower, each with tv, telephone, hairdryer and hospitality tray. Some rooms have four-poster beds. The hotel has two bars, two sun terraces, two restaurants, a ballroom (dancing and entertainment most evenings), a Gym and Tonic health club, swimming pool and sauna.

Local Golf Courses: Llandudno (Maesdu, North Wales), Conwy, Rhos

Room only Hotel

Ten rooms, most en suite; continental breakfast

Credit Cards: Mastercard, Visa

HOTEL MESSINA · 197

Hill Terrace, Great Orme, Llandudno, Conwy LL30 2LS
Tel/Fax: 01492 875260
e-mail: catherine.murphy@talk21.com

The first venture in the hotel business for Catherine and Tom Murphy is a fine-looking room only hotel in a splendid location on the lower slopes of the Great Orme next to Happy Valley. Behind the smart white-painted facade of the 1890s building, the interior is bright, modern and spacious, and most of the ten bedrooms enjoy breathtaking views of Llandudno Bay, the Little Orme, Conwy or Snowdonia. All the rooms have tv, tea-makers and fridges, and the majority are en suite. Ramp for wheelchair access into the hotel.

Local Golf Courses: Llandudno (Maesdu, North Wales), Conwy, Rhos

Pub, Restaurant,B&B next door

Bar meals; next door B&B with eight en suite rooms

Credit Cards: Mastercard, Visa

THE QUEEN VICTORIA · 198

4 Church Walks, Llandudno, Conwy LL30 2HL
Tel: 01492 860949 Fax: 01492 878032
e-mail: tony@queenvictoriaf.s.life.co.uk

A friendly, convivial public house and restaurant close to the pier and the beach. Behind the cheerfully decorated front and patio there's a single spacious bar and an upstairs dining room with seats for 40. The menu offers a good choice of main courses at £4.50 and a three-course meal with wine for £12. Kay and Tony Evans, who have been here 15 years, recently acquired the Victoria Town House next door, a bed & breakfast hotel with eight en suite rooms - seven doubles and a family room (Tel: 01492 876144).

Local Golf Courses: Llandudno (Maesdu, North Wales), Conwy, Rhos

Hotel & Country Club

Hotel rooms, self-catering log cabins; leisure facilities, restaurant
Credit Cards: Amex, Mastercard, Visa

GRAIG PARK HOTEL & COUNTRY CLUB · 199

Allt y Graig, Dyserth, Denbighshire LL18 6DX
Tel: 01745 571022 Fax: 01745 571024

Hotel and self-catering accommodation and sports/leisure facilities in a complex set among lawns and woodland in peaceful countryside two miles from the popular holiday beaches of North Wales. Guests can choose between conventional hotel rooms - all with en suite facilities, tv and phone - and luxury log cabins with studio, one-bedroom or two-bedroom layout, lounge-dining area and fully-fitted kitchen. Residents have full use of the sports and leisure facilities (pool, spa bath, sauna, gym) and there's a lounge-bar and a restaurant whose menu offers British classics such as steak and seafood as well as Chinese and Malaysian dishes.

Local Golf Courses: Holywell, Rhuddlan, Hawarden, Old Padeswood

CONWY

DENBIGHSHIRE

DENBIGHSHIRE

FLINTSHIRE

BRIDGE END HOTEL 200

Mill Street, Llangollen, Denbighshire LL20 8RY
Tel: 01978 860634
e-mail: bridge-endhotel@btconnect.com

In the heart of town close to the river, the Bridge End Hotel is a handsome building that started life as a coaching inn. David and Jean Evans cater for all visitors, from individuals to coach parties and functions for up to 70. There are nine guest bedrooms - eight twins and a family room with three beds. Some rooms are en suite, and all have tv and tea-making facilities. In the lounge bar Robinson's ales and a small selection of wines can accompany a wide choice of dishes on bar and restaurant menus, including a good variety of main courses for vegetarians.

Hotel

Nine bedrooms, some en suite; bar and restaurant menus

Credit Cards: Mastercard, Visa

Local Golf Courses: Llangollen, Chirk, Clays Farm, Wrexham

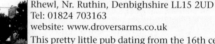

THE DROVER'S ARMS 201

Rhewl, Nr. Ruthin, Denbighshire LL15 2UD
Tel: 01824 703163
website: www.droversarms.co.uk

This pretty little pub dating from the 16th century is the heartbeat of a village on the main Denbigh-Ruthin road (A525). Charles and Sharon Gale-Hasleham welcome regulars and first-timers through the porch and into the large bar, which is divided into a lounge area, a games area with pool and darts, and a dining area where bar snacks and meals are served until 9.30. The pub is open Monday and Tuesday evenings, Lunchtime and evening Wednesday to Friday and all day Saturday and Sunday. Garden with play area.

Pub with Food

Snacks and meals served up to 9.30

Credit Cards: Mastercard, Visa

Local Golf Courses: Bryn Morfydd, Denbigh, Prestatyn, Rhuddlan

THE THREE PIGEONS INN 202

Graigfechan, Ruthin, Denbighshire LL15 2EU
Tel: 01824 703178 Fax: 01824 703812

Morton and Heather Roberts have lived in the village of Graigfechan for 26 years and recently took over this atmospheric 17th drovers inn. The long, low building has two bars, a lounge, games room and non-smoking dining room where good home-cooked food can be enjoyed. Beer is served in a jug drawn directly from the cellar, and the inn also keeps a range of country fruit wines. The beer garden and terrace enjoy beautiful views over the Vale of Clwyd. The inn offers two spacious en-suite letting rooms, both having lounge and balcony. Facilities for camping and caravan with toilets and showers are available.

Inn, Food & Accommodation

Two bedrooms, camping and caravan site; home-cooked food

Credit Cards: None

Local Golf Courses: Clays Farm, Chirk, Llangollen, Wrexham,

THE HAND HOTEL 203

Llanarmon Dyffryn Ceiriog, Ceiriog Valley, Clwyd LL20 7LD
Tel: 01691 600666 Fax: 01691 600262
e-mail: handllandcb@netscapeonline.co.uk

New proprietors Peter and Lynne Davies have completed a major refurbishment at their delightful hotel, which stands in beautiful countryside in a picturesque village at the head of the Ceiriog Valley. Darkened beams, open fireplaces and uneven walls add charm and cosiness to the 16th century farmhouse, and the 13 bedrooms all have private bath or shower room, tv, telephone, hairdryer and tea-making facilities. A self-catering cottage is also available. Excellent food is served every lunchtime and evening, à la carte in the Old Shippon restaurant, snacks and light meals in the bar. The hotel has a games room with pool, darts and tv, and an antique shop.

Hotel and Restaurant

13 en suite rooms; bar and restaurant menus

Credit Cards: All the major cards

Local Golf Courses: Chirk, Clays Farm, Oswestry, Llangollen, Wrexham

FLINTSHIRE

THE WEST ARMS HOTEL 204

Llanarmon Dyffryn Ceiriog, Ceiriog Valley, Clwyd LL20 7LD
Tel: 01691 600665 e-mail: booking@thewestarms.co.uk
Fax: 01691 600622 website: www.thewestarms.co.uk

Beams, inglenooks, slate-flagged floors and period furnishings preserve the charm and character of a bygone age at Geoff and Gill Leigh-Ford's 400-year-old country inn, which enjoys a tranquil, picturesque setting in the lovely Ceiriog Valley. The period quality extends to the 16 spacious, comfortable bedrooms, including two suites, all with private bath and shower. Light lunches can be taken in the bar or in the garden by the river, and table d'hote dinners are served in the delightful restaurant. Llanarmon DC lies on the B4500, a dozen miles from Chirk.

Hotel and Restaurant
16 en suite rooms; bar and restaurant menus

Credit Cards: Mastercard, Visa

Local Golf Courses: Llangollen, Clays Farm, Oswestry, Wrexham

THE ANTELOPE 205

Rhydymwyn, Mold, Flintshire CH7 5HE
Tel: 01352 741247 Fax: 01352 741933
e-mail: antelopeuk@aol.com

Originally a coaching inn, the Antelope is a family pub and restaurant two miles out of Mold on the A541 Denbigh road. Gwynne and Heather Williams, here since three years ago, welcome visitors for a drink, a snack, a full meal or an overnight stay. The pub has two bars (the public bar has a pool table and wide-screen tv), a dining room and non-smoking conservatory. The menus cover a good selection of snacks, bar meals and restaurant meals, and a children's menu is also available. Accommodation comprises four en suite rooms including a family room. The garden has a children's play area.

Pub, Food & Accommodation
Four en suite rooms; bar and restaurant menus
Credit Cards: Diners, Mastercard, Visa

Local Golf Courses: Old Padeswood, Padeswood & Buckley, Mold

THE SPORTSMANS ARMS 206

Burwardsley Road, Tattenhall, Cheshire CH3 9QF
Tel: 01829 770233 Fax: 01829 771886

A really charming village pub run by Mike and Julie Wardrop, daughter Natalie and son Daniel. A little flight of stone steps leads into the spacious bar, which includes a games area with pool and darts, a no-smoking section and a golf corner filled with golfing memorabilia - the Wardrops are all fanatical golfers, and Daniel plans to turn professional. From noon onwards a very tempting selection of food is served, from an excellent range of light bites to baby black puddings on a bed of cheesy leeks to piri piri chicken, salad bowls, steaks, lasagne and speciality pizzas - Italian chicken and pesto; salmon & prawns. Delicious desserts, good choice of wines.

Pub with Food
Light snacks and full menu from noon
Credit Cards: Amex, Mastercard, Visa

Local Golf Courses: Carden Park, Curzon Park, Eton & Upton

WELSH BORDERS

THE COPPER MINE 207

Nantwich Road, Broxton, Nr. Chester, Cheshire CH3 9JH
Tel: 01829 782293 Fax: 01829 782183
e-mail: coppermineinn@cs.com

Kathryn Morris runs the Copper Mine, a handsome country pub standing on the A534 Nantwich-Wrexham road. Built in brick at the beginning of the 20th century, it has a large beer garden and plenty of off-road parking. Inside are two bars and two dining areas - both the latter are non-smoking. Kathryn employs two chefs to produce an excellent variety of food, from quick snacks to three-course meals. Charcoal-grilled steaks are always among the favourites, and the Sunday lunch menu - three roasts and a wide choice from the bar - is guaranteed to bring in the crowds. Two real ales and an extensive wine list.

Pub with Food
Bar and Restaurant menus

Credit Cards: All the major cards

Local Golf Courses: Carden Park, Eaton, Upton

WELSH BORDERS

GREYHOUND HOTEL 208

High Street, Farndon, Chester, Cheshire CH3 6PU
Tel/Fax: 01829 270244
e-mail: greyhound-farndon@lineone.net

On the B5130 eight miles south of Chester, the Greyhound is an attractive redbrick building dating from the late 19th century. A family pub, run for the past five years by Marco and Sarah Paoloni, it stands at the heart of the village, and the bar is a popular local meeting place - in summer, the beer garden comes into its own. Straightforward pub food is served, where pizza and pasta are a speciality. There are real ales or wine to accompany your meal, and for guests staying overnight there are three letting bedrooms, one with en suite facilities and all with tea/coffee making facilities. Italian and German spoken.

Pub, Food & Accommodation

Three bedrooms; bar meals

Credit Cards: Mastercard, Visa

Local Golf Courses: Carden Park, Eton, Upton, Wrexham

THE ROYAL OAK 209

Clee Hill, Nr. Ludlow, Shropshire SY8 3PE
Tel: 01584 890405
e-mail: 2toes.leisure@barbox.com
website: www.2toesleisure.com

There are fine views from this pretty white-painted 17th century inn, which has a golfing fan in landlord John Harris. In the splendidly traditional bar with oak beams and log fires a good selection of real ales is served, along with an excellent choice of freshly prepared food - bar snacks or full meals in the well-appointed restaurant. The inn has extensive gardens in which John will, during 2001, inaugurate a pitch & putt course. The jazz and R&B nights are always very popular occasions.

Inn with Food

Bar and Restaurant Meals

Credit Cards: All the major cards

Local Golf Courses: Ludlow, Leominster, Church Stretton

THE BRADFORD ARMS 210

Knockin, Nr. Oswestry, Shropshire SY10 8HJ
Tel: 01691 682358

On the B4396 a couple of miles west of the A5, the Bradford Arms is a fine 100-year-old inn, its frontage very smart in black and white, with a distinctive three-faced clock built out on a gable above the pub sign. Inside is roomy and traditional, with an inviting bar and a non-smoking restaurant. Run by keen golfer Mark Batten and his wife Nicola, it offers a good selection of home-cooked dishes to cater for all appetites up to and including ravenous (for whom the mixed grill served on an 18" plate fits the bill perfectly). There's an excellent wine list and a range of ales to accompany. Golf societies are very welcome at this friendly, popular inn, which is open lunchtime and evening and all day Saturday and Sunday.

Pub with Food

Bar meals; non-smoking restaurant, beer garden

Credit Cards: Mastercard, Visa

Local Golf Courses: Llanymynech, Mile End, Oswestry, Chirk

GLEN HELEN HOLIDAY COTTAGES 211

Isfryn, Stargarreg Lane, Pant, Oswestry, Shropshire SY10 9QN
Tel/Fax: 01691 830094
e-mail: gaskill@globalnet.co.uk website: www.glenhelen.co.uk

Two cottages of character have been renovated and converted into excellent self-catering accommodation in a village five miles south of Oswestry, on the Wales-Shropshire border. Each has two bedrooms, bath or shower room, fully equipped kitchen-diner, lounge with tv and garden with paved and grassed areas and garden furniture. A clothes washer and dryer are available in the old wash house, and a well-stocked village shop is a short walk away. No smoking and no pets. A wide range of local activities includes rambling, fishing and golf.

Self-catering Accommodation

Two holiday cottages, each with two bedrooms

Credit Cards: None

Local Golf Courses: Oswestry, Mile End, Llanymynech

Bed & Breakfast

Nine rooms in six houses in the same street

Credit Cards: Mastercard, Visa

NUMBER TWENTY EIGHT | 212

28 Lower Broad Street, Ludlow, Shropshire SY8 1PQ
Tel: 01584 876996 Fax: 01584 876860 reservations: 0800 081 5000
e-mail: ross@no28.co.uk website: www.no28.co.uk

Patricia and Philip Ross offer top-quality B&B accommodation in six period houses, all in Lower Broad Street. There are 9 en suite rooms in all, individually furnished to the highest standards. Number 28 itself is early Georgian, with double brass beds in the 2 bedrooms, a sitting room and courtyard garden. Along the street are Mews Cottages (Tudor, with 2 bedrooms, a sitting room and large garden); Westwood House (late-Victorian, 2 rooms, brass beds, sitting room, garden); and Bromley Court Cottages - Tudor style, with 3 cottage suites, each with sitting room and continental breakfast bar. A traditional breakfast is served for the other properties at Number 28. No smoking in the houses.

Local Golf Courses: Ludlow, Leominster, Kington, Welshpool

Tavern and Restaurant

Two bars, à la carte restaurant
Cask Marque Award

Credit Cards: Mastercard, Visa

YE OLDE BULL RING TAVERN | 213

44 The Bull Ring, Ludlow, Shropshire SY8 1AB
Tel: 01584 872311

A landmark in the centre of Ludlow for more than 600 years, this famous old tavern has a stunning black and white half-timbered frontage complete with crooked beams and lattice-paned windows. It has been run for the past five years by Jo Haywood, who dispenses good cheer and excellent beer in the lounge and bar; darts, dominoes and quoits are played in the public bar. The 14th century comes alive in the splendid first-floor restaurant, where fine food and quality wines are served lunchtime and evening. The menu offers dishes both traditional - freshly battered cod & chips, home made steak pie, steaks - and more exotic, like grilled swordfish steaks or chicken fillets with a Mexican salsa.

Local Golf Courses: Ludlow, Leominster, Kington, Welshpool

Inn, Food & Accommodation

Nine en suite bedrooms; bar and restaurant menus
Credit Cards: Amex, Mastercard, Visa

THE CHURCH INN | 214

The Buttercross, Ludlow, Shropshire SY8 1AW
Tel: 01584 872174 e-mail: reception@thechurchinn.com
Fax: 01584 877146 website: www.thechurchinnludlow.co.uk

In the centre of town, directly behind the Buttercross, this venerable building has a history spanning seven centuries. In its time a blacksmith's, saddler's, druggist's and barber-surgeon's, it is now an outstandingly atmospheric inn providing its patrons with a choice of appetising home-cooked dishes served in the restaurant (best to book) and a selection of sandwiches, snacks and bar meals. Real ale fans will be pleased to find six varieties on tap, and wines are available by glass or bottle. Landlord Graham Willson-Lloyd also offers comfortable overnight accommodation in nine en suite bedrooms ranging from singles to family rooms.

Local Golf Courses: Ludlow, Leominster, Kington, Welshpool

Inn, Food & Accommodation

Bar and Restaurant menus; 3 bedrooms

Credit Cards: None

THE NEW HARP INN | 215

Hoarwithy, Nr. Hereford, Herefordshire HR2 6QH
Tel: 01432 840213

Three 17th century fishermen's cottages close to the River Wye have been converted into a really delightful inn offering both food and accommodation. Landlord Terry Baker plays golf for fun at the nearby Belmont Lodge course and is always pleased to welcome other players to the inn. But of course there's a welcome for everyone in the bar and restaurant, where snacks and full meals are served lunchtime and evening. When the weather is fine, it's a joy to sit out at the front in the shade of some handsome trees or in the garden at the back. Overnight accommodation is available in three letting bedrooms - a single and two twins. Hoarwithy is a pretty village with an outstanding church built in the 1870s.

Local Golf Courses: Belmont Lodge, Monmouth, Ross-on-Wye

WELSH BORDERS

BELMONT LODGE & GOLF COURSE 216

Ruckhall Lane, Belmont, Hereford HR2 9SA
Tel: 01432 352666 Fax: 01432 358090
e-mail: info@belmontlodge.co.uk
website: www.belmontlodge.co.uk

A warm welcome and friendly personal service await guests at Belmont Lodge & Golf Course, which is situated alongside the beautiful River Wye a few minutes drive from the historic Cathedral city of Hereford.

The clubhouse, bar and restaurant are located in Belmont House, which was built in 1788 by James Wyatt and extensively remodelled by Pugin in 1867. The restaurant serves a varied menu of mainly traditional dishes, and an extensive bar menu is also available.

The Lodge, situated beyond the 18th green next to Belmont House, is a modern building containing 30 purpose-built rooms - 26 twins and four double or family rooms. All have en suite bathroom, tv, radio, telephone and tea/coffee-making facilities. The golf course combines a fair test of skill with the opportunity to enjoy magnificent views, particularly from the first nine holes, which are located on higher ground. The second nine are in the valley alongside the river, which is a factor in the play of at least five holes.

Belmont offers coarse and salmon fishing on a 1½-mile stretch of the river, and other leisure facilities on site comprise an all-weather tennis court, bowling green and snooker. Golf societies are very welcome, and there's a function room with seats for up to 80 guests. Belmont is situated on Ruckhall Lane, signposted off the A465 Abergavenny road southwest of Hereford.

Hotel & Golf Course

30 en suite rooms, golf, fishing, restaurant, bar

Credit Cards: All the major cards

Local Golf Courses: Belmont

THE FOUNTAIN INN 217

Orcup Hill, Herefordshire HR2 8EP
Tel: 01981 540304

A very friendly and inviting country pub in a delightful hilltop setting off the A466 six miles south of Hereford. Angela Barnett-Barrington is a splendid host, and the lounge bar is a convivial spot for enjoying a glass of real ale. In the two restaurant areas à la carte and fixed-price menus provide a fine range of home cooking, highlighted by excellent pasta dishes, top-quality steaks and daily fish specials - all accompanied by a fine choice of wines. Golf societies are very welcome, and parties can be arranged in a private room. Bed & Breakfast nearby.

Country Pub

Full menu lunchtime and evening

Credit Cards: All the major cards

Local Golf Courses: Belmont Lodge, Burghill Valley, Ross-on-Wye

NEW PRIORY HOTEL 218

Stretton Sugwas, Nr. Hereford, Herefordshire HR4 7AR
Tel: 01432 760264 Fax: 01432 761809

Just outside Hereford's city limits, the New Priory Hotel is a handsome 19th century country house set in 3½ acres of landscaped gardens, lawns and terraces. Managed by the owner Ken Benjamin, it offers ten attractively appointed bedrooms, all with tv, telephone and lovely views over the unspoiled countryside. They range from singles with adjacent shower and toilet to doubles, twins and four-poster honeymoon rooms with en suite facilities. Guests can meet and relax in two spacious lounge bars, and the two period-style restaurants provide an intimate setting for enjoying excellent English cuisine.

Country House Hotel

Ten bedrooms; restaurants and lounge bars

Credit Cards: All the major cards

Local Golf Courses: Burghill Valley, Kington, Leominster, Herefordshire

THE HORSE & GROOM — 219

Eign Street, Hereford, Herefordshire HR4 0AP
Tel: 01432 355026 Fax: 01432 269242
website: dave@thehorseandgroom.fsnet.co.uk

Close to the city centre (follow the signs for the Cider Museum), the Horse & Groom was originally a hospital. It's now a really attractive and welcoming pub with a spotless white-painted frontage and a traditional interior complete with old oak beams. Owners Dave and Sue Morris came here from Portsmouth at the beginning of 2001. Dave was in the Navy for 25 years; he's a very keen golfer, and the pub's function room is ideal for golfing get-togethers. In the bar a good selection of home-cooked snacks and meals is served all day, along with good ales from the Wye Valley Brewery. Pool table, darts.

Pub with Food

Home-cooked food served all day. Large car park.

Credit Cards: None

Local Golf Courses: Belmont, Burghill Valley, The Herefordshire

---

THE COMET INN — 220

Madley, Herefordshire HR2 9NJ
Tel: 01981 250600
e-mail: cometinn@madley

Three cottages were combined to make this splendid inn, which stands just off the B4352 Hay-on-Wye road four miles out of Hereford. Acquired in February 2001 by Kim Powell-Aubrey and family, this friendliest of inns offers some excellent real ales and tasty bar snacks and meals served all day. There's an additional à la carte menu served throughout the week with home made main courses such as duck breast with leaf spinach and cranberry jus or rack of lamb with beans. The inn has lovely gardens with a play area for children.

Inn with Food

Bar meals and à la carte; garden

Credit Cards: All the major cards

Local Golf Courses: Belmont Lodge, Kington, Rolls of Monmouth

---

THE TALBOT HOTEL — 221

Bridge Street, Kington, Herefordshire HR5 3DJ
Tel: 01544 231744

In the town centre, easily reached from the A44, the Talbot is a fine old coaching inn dating back five centuries. Behind the corner-site frontage, its close-set stones painted white, visitors are welcomed into cosy bars and a dining area where excellent home-cooked food is served - Yorkshire puddings are a speciality. Run by Alan Morris and Andrea Wright, the Talbot also offers a good standard of accommodation in four refurbished bedrooms with tvs and tea-makers. Pool room and darts. The pub sign shows a fine white talbot - a long-extinct breed of English sporting dog.

Hotel

Four bedrooms; home-cooked food

Credit Cards: All the major cards

Local Golf Courses: Kington, Llandrindod Wells, Leominster

THE KITES NEST INN — 222

Swainshill, Nr. Hereford, Herefordshire HR4 7QA
Tel/Fax: 01981 590217

Set back from the A438 west of Hereford, the Kites Nest Inn is a popular stop for a drink, a snack or a full meal. Behind the smart 18th century frontage, the bar and restaurant areas provide a pleasant setting for enjoying first-class cooking by owners David, Kevin and Helen, with excellent wines and ales to accompany. Everything on the menu is worth trying, from omelette Arnold Bennett to lamb rogan josh, pork in a creamy peppercorn sauce or one of the daily fish specials. Behind the pub is a large garden with a petanque pitch. The pub is closed on Monday.

Pub with Food

A la carte menus; well-chosen wines

Credit Cards: None

Local Golf Courses: Burghill Valley, Herefordshire, Kington

WELSH BORDERS

THE AXE & CLEAVER   223

Much Birch, Nr. Hereford, Herefordshire HR2 8HU
Tel/Fax: 01981 540203

Tony and Brenda Waddell take great pride in their attractive black and white pub, which stands by the A49 south of Hereford. Its reputation for good food has spread far and wide, and the fine cooking is complemented by one of the area's best value wine lists as well as excellent ales and ciders. Everything on the menu is tempting, with splendid starters and delicious desserts framing main courses such as pork steak with stilton sauce, duck breast with honey and madeira or, for vegetarians, Louisiana nut roast with a mango and lime coulis. Booking is recommended. Lovely gardens enjoy views over Golden Valley towards the Black Mountains. Accommodation planned for 2001.

Inn with Food

A la carte menu; lovely gardens

Credit Cards: Mastercard, Visa

Local Golf Courses: Belmont, Rolls of Monmouth, Monmouthshire

YE OLDE SALUTATION INN   224

Market Pitch, Weobley, Herefordshire HR4 8SJ
Tel: 01544 318443 Fax: 01544 318216
e-mail: salutationinn@btinternet.com

Ye Olde Salutation Inn is a classic English country pub in the centre of one of the county's prettiest villages. The black and white timber-framed buildings date back over 500 years, and the original alehouse and cottage have been converted into a really outstanding inn and restaurant. In the kitchens of the Oak Room, talented young chefs seek out the pick of the local supplies to produce superb dishes in the modern English style; less formal meals are served in the traditional lounge-bar. The three Victorian-style bedrooms, one with a four-poster bed, are individually appointed, all with en suite facilities. No smoking in the bedrooms.

Country Inn and Restaurant

Three en suite rooms; restaurant and bar meals

Credit Cards: All the major cards

Local Golf Courses: Herefordshire, Burghill Valley, Kington

FOREST HOUSE HOTEL   225

Cinderhill, Coleford, Gloucestershire GL16 8HQ
Tel: 01594 832424

Situated in the heart of the ancient woodlands of the Forest of Dean, the Forest House Hotel is an ideal base from which to play the pleasant parkland courses of Forest Hills, The Royal forest of Dean and Ross-on-Wye as well as the demanding fairways of St. Pierre. Once an important 19th century residence, the hotel has recently been tastefully restored by the owners Geoffrey and Susan Sparkes and offers visitors eight well-appointed en suite bedrooms all with TV, tea and coffee-making facilities and telephone. Visitors can also relax in the hotel's comfortable lounge bar or walled garden and dine in the attractive dining room from an excellent choice of a la carte dishes accompanied by a selection of fine wines.

Country Hotel

8 en suite bedrooms and well-appointed restaurant
Credit Cards: Access, Mastercard, Visa

Local Golf Courses: Forest Hills, Ross-on-Wye, St. Pierre,

Alphabetic List of Golf Courses

Golfers Guide Order Form

To order any of our publications just fill in the payment details below and complete the order form *overleaf*. For orders of less than 4 copies please add £1 per book for postage and packing. Orders over 4 copies are P & P free.

Please Complete Either:

I enclose a cheque for £ [   ] made payable to Travel Publishing Ltd

Or:

Card No: [   ]

Expiry Date: [   ]

Signature: [   ]

NAME: [   ]

ADDRESS: [   ]

POSTCODE: [   ]

TEL NO: [   ]

Please either send or telephone your order to:

Travel Publishing Ltd   Tel : 0118 981 7777
7a Apollo House   Fax: 0118 982 0077
Calleva Park
Aldermaston
Berks, RG7 8TN

	PRICE	QUANTITY	VALUE

Hidden Places Regional Titles

Cambs & Lincolnshire	£7.99	....	....
Chilterns	£8.99	....	....
Cornwall	£8.99	....	....
Derbyshire	£7.99	....	....
Devon	£8.99	....	....
Dorset, Hants & Isle of Wight	£8.99	....	....
East Anglia	£8.99	....	....
Gloucestershire & Wiltshire	£7.99	....	....
Heart of England	£7.99	....	....
Hereford, Worcs & Shropshire	£7.99	....	....
Highlands & Islands	£7.99	....	....
Kent	£8.99	....	....
Lake District & Cumbria	£8.99	....	....
Lancashire & Cheshire	£8.99	....	....
Lincolnshire & Nottinghamshire	£8.99	....	....
Northumberland & Durham	£8.99	....	....
Somerset	£7.99	....	....
Sussex	£7.99	....	....
Thames Valley	£7.99	....	....
Yorkshire	£7.99	....	....

Hidden Places National Titles

England	£9.99	....	....
Ireland	£9.99	....	....
Scotland	£9.99	....	....
Wales	£9.99	....	....

Hidden Inns Titles

South	£5.99	....	....
South East	£5.99	....	....
South and Central Scotland	£5.99	....	....
Wales	£5.99	....	....
Welsh Borders	£5.99	....	....
West Country	£5.99	....	....

Golf Guides

East Anglia	£8.99	....	....
Ireland	£9.99	....	....
Wales	£8.99	....	....
West Country	£8.99	....	....

For orders of less than 4 copies please add £1 per book for
postage & packing. Orders over 4 copies P & P free.